Dirk Philips

Do not extinguish the Spirit [out]
Do not despise prophesy
Test everything and keep what is good
Avoid every evil appearance

1 Thess. 5:19-22

The Writings of Dirk Philips

1504–1568

Translated and edited by

Cornelius J. Dyck
William E. Keeney
Alvin J. Beachy

PLOUGH PUBLISHING HOUSE

Published by Plough Publishing House
Walden, New York
Robertsbridge, England
Elsmore, Australia
www.plough.com

Plough produces books, a quarterly magazine, and Plough.com to encourage people and help them put their faith into action. We believe Jesus can transform the world and that his teachings and example apply to all aspects of life. At the same time, we seek common ground with all people regardless of their creed.

Plough is the publishing house of the Bruderhof, an international community of families and singles seeking to follow Jesus together. Members of the Bruderhof are committed to a way of radical discipleship in the spirit of the Sermon on the Mount. Inspired by the first church in Jerusalem (Acts 2 and 4), they renounce private property and share everything in common in a life of nonviolence, justice, and service to neighbors near and far. To learn more about the Bruderhof's faith, history, and daily life, see Bruderhof.com. (Views expressed by Plough authors are their own and do not necessarily reflect the position of the Bruderhof.)

Copyright © 2019 by Plough Publishing House
All rights reserved.

ISBN: 978-0-874-86266-9

Hand lettering and maps by Jan Gleysteen

Library of Congress Cataloging-in-Publication Data

Names: Philips, Dirk, 1504-1568, author. | Dyck, Cornelius J., editor. | Beachy, Alvin J., editor. | Keeney, William E. (William Echard), 1922-
Title: The writings of Dirk Philips, 1504-1568 / translated and edited by Cornelius J. Dyck, William E. Keeney, Alvin J. Beachy.
Other titles: Works. English
Description: Walden, New York : Plough Publishing House, 2019. | Series: Classics of the radical Reformation; 6 | Originally published: Scottdale, Pa. : Herald Press, 1992. | Includes bibliographical references and index. | Translated from Dutch. | Summary: "The authoritative English-language resource for primary sources of the Radical Reformation. Targets a growing interest in Anabaptism among younger Christians. Features new foreword by a leading expert in the field. Valuable reference tool for pastors, professors, and other thought leaders"-- Provided by publisher.
Identifiers: LCCN 2019045742 (print) | LCCN 2019045743 (ebook) | ISBN 9780874862669 (paperback) | ISBN 9780874862676 (ebook)
Subjects: LCSH: Anabaptists--Doctrines--Early works to 1800. | Theology, Doctrinal--Early works to 1800. | Anabaptists--Netherlands--History--16th century. | Netherlands--Church history--16th century.
Classification: LCC BX4930 .P4513 2019 (print) | LCC BX4930 (ebook) | DDC 230/.43--dc23
LC record available at https://lccn.loc.gov/2019045742
LC ebook record available at https://lccn.loc.gov/2019045743

To our spouses

Wilma Regier Dyck
Willadene Hartzler Keeney
Vera Clouse Beachy

Classics of the Radical Reformation

Classics of the Radical Reformation is an English-language series of Anabaptist and Free Church documents translated and annotated under the direction of the Institute of Mennonite Studies, which is the research agency of the Anabaptist Mennonite Biblical Seminaries, and published by Plough Publishing House.

1. *The Legacy of Michael Sattler.* Trans., ed. John Howard Yoder.
2. *The Writings of Pilgram Marpeck.* Trans., ed. William Klassen and Walter Klaassen.
3. *Anabaptism in Outline: Selected Primary Sources.* Trans., ed. Walter Klaassen.
4. *The Sources of Swiss Anabaptism: The Grebel Letters and Related Documents.* Ed. Leland Harder.
5. *Balthasar Hubmaier: Theologian of Anabaptism.* Ed. H. Wayne Pipkin and John Howard Yoder.
6. *The Writings of Dirk Philips.* Ed. Cornelius J. Dyck, William E. Keeney, and Alvin J. Beachy.
7. *The Anabaptist Writings of David Joris: 1535–1543.* Ed. Gary K. Waite.
8. *The Essential Carlstadt: Fifteen Tracts by Andreas Bodenstein.* Trans., ed. E. J. Furcha.
9. *Peter Riedemann's Hutterite Confession of Faith.* Ed. John J. Friesen.
10. *Sources of South German/Austrian Anabaptism.* Ed. C. Arnold Snyder, trans. Walter Klaassen, Frank Friesen, and Werner O. Packull.
11. *Confessions of Faith in the Anabaptist Tradition: 1527–1660.* Ed. Karl Koop.
12. *Jörg Maler's Kunstbuch: Writings of the Pilgram Marpeck Circle.* Ed. John D. Rempel.
13. *Later Writings of the Swiss Anabaptists: 1529–1592.* Ed. C. Arnold Snyder.

CONTENTS

General Editor's Preface 9
Editors' Introduction 11
Dirk Philips: A Biography 19

Part A The Enchiridion (Handbook)

1. Editors' Introduction 51
2. Foreword by Dirk Philips 59
3. Confession of Our Faith (Concerning) God 62
4. Creation, Redemption, and Salvation 68
5. The Baptism of Our Lord Jesus Christ 72
6. The Supper of Our Lord Jesus Christ 112
7. The Incarnation of Our Lord Jesus Christ 134
8. Concerning the True Knowledge of Jesus Christ 152
9. An Apology or Reply 173
10. The Sending of Preachers 198
11. The Ban 238
12. The True Knowledge of God 255
13. The Tabernacle of Moses 264
14. The New Birth and the New Creature 293
15. Concerning Spiritual Restitution 316
16. The Congregation of God 350
17. Three Admonitions
    No. I 383
    No. II 398
    No. III 412
18. Register (Index) 427

Part B Other Writings

1. Answer to Sebastian Franck 445
2. The Frisian—Flemish Division
   A. Introduction 468
   B. Epistle to Four Cities 476
      a. Attachment: 1565 Agreement 484
   C. A Short but Fundamental Account 489
   D. An Appendix 522
   E. Related Letters 544

3. About the Marriage of Christians 552
4. Omitted Writing About the Ban and Avoidance 578
   Fragment 586
5. Evangelical Excommunication 591
6. A Confession About Separation 611
7. Two Additional Letters 618
8. Hymns 637

Bibliography 647
Index of Scriptures 653
Name and Place Index 681
Subject Index 689
The Editors 699
Map 702

Preface to the New Edition

Dirk Philips (1504–1568) was born at Leeuwarden, the capital of the Dutch province of Friesland (also Menno Simon's native land).[1] Dirk was the son of a Dutch priest and a concubine, which was not uncommon in those pre-Reformation times of the Roman Catholic Church.[2] Nothing is known about his childhood and education. He may have joined a Franciscan monastery in Leeuwarden, most likely as a layperson since – being an "illegal" priest's son – he would not have had permission to join any monastic order as a monk. We will never know whether he was taught in the classical languages, although some of his writings include Latin and Greek quotations. Dirk's elder brother Obbe Philips, a man of importance for early Anabaptism and Mennonitism in the Netherlands, was a barber and a surgeon – an ordinary combination of professions that suggests a lower level of intellectual education.

Around 1533 or 1534, Obbe and his younger brother Dirk manifested themselves as radical reformers during the turbulent era of the apocalyptic preaching of Melchior Hoffman, the founder of Dutch Anabaptism. After Hoffman's imprisonment in Strasbourg, his successor, Jan Matthys, resumed the enthusiastic preaching of Christ's coming to earth. This resulted in the occupation of the bishopric town of Münster, on the eastern border of the Netherlands, by some three thousand Anabaptist fanatics who were convinced that Christ would return to establish the New Jerusalem. Both Obbe and Dirk were baptized by missionaries of Matthys. Dirk was baptized by Pieter Houtsager, one of the three Münsterites who sometime later were arrested in Amsterdam as they were running down the streets with drawn swords. Later, when Obbe turned away from the Anabaptist-Mennonite movement, he stated that neither he nor Dirk had ever sympathized with violent Münsteritism. Whether this is truly the case is hard to determine. There is evidence that Obbe attended the Münsterite mass meeting at 't Zandt, in the province of Groningen, in early 1535; later he expressed his regrets over being ordained a preacher by one of Matthys's apostles. Soon after his baptism, Dirk was ordained an elder by Obbe. Dirk then lived in or near Appingedam, a flourishing town in the eastern part of the province of Groningen, where – in contrast to neighboring Friesland – persecution of the Anabaptists was hardly felt. In the aftermath of Münster, both Obbe and Dirk played a modest role in Melchiorite Anbaptism; some people referred to Obbe's following as the Obbites. However, David Joris, the Spiritualist leader of the so-called Jorists – who proclaimed himself a prophet, the third David – took the prime position in divided Dutch Anabaptism. Neither Dirk nor Obbe was present at the Bocholt meeting of 1536, which had been initiated by Joris and where the remaining leaders tried to reach consensus on how to move on in peaceful unity.

In 1537 Dirk had a dispute with the Lutheran pastor Joachim Kukenbieter at Hamburg, northern Germany. When interrogated in 1538, the captured post-Münsterite and violent leader Jan van Batenburg confirmed that Dirk was the third in line of Anabaptist leadership. Around 1539 Dirk became Menno Simons's loyal coworker, just as Menno finally came forward with his important *Foundation* book and presented himself as the new peaceful leader of the movement. Dirk was active predominantly in the northern areas of the Low Countries, Germany, and in and around Gdansk, Poland (formerly known as Danzig). Around the same time, Obbe, a man gifted with leadership skills, left the Anabaptist-Mennonite movement out of frustration over its divisiveness.

Like Menno, Dirk embraced the much-debated theory on the incarnation of Christ, which they had adopted from Hoffman. In this theological concept, Jesus's flesh had human qualities, such as the ability to bleed and to die, but its origin was in heaven. Thus, when the Word became flesh (John 1:14), it could be nourished and pass through Mary without inheriting sin – analogous to the way seed is nourished by soil without taking on its characteristics. This incarnation theory, rejected by Swiss Anabaptism, would eventually become a cornerstone of Dutch Mennonite orthodoxy. It formed the solid ground for strict Mennonite church discipline – including the ban, shunning, and (marital) avoidance – in order to keep the congregation, the Bride of Christ, pure, without spot and wrinkle, like the sinless flesh of Christ. However, time and again the Melchiorite incarnation theology caused disagreement. This became apparent in 1546 when the Mennonite elders – not only Menno and Dirk but also Adam Pastor, Gilis van Aken, and Lenaert Bouwens – held a meeting with Joris's representative and son-in-law, Nicolaas Meyndertsz van Blesdijk. The main topic was how to avoid persecution; however, the issue of Christ's incarnation caused the most trouble. Pastor, in particular, held antitrinitarian views, denying Christ's divine nature. The following year discussions about the proper features of Mennonite orthodoxy continued. It was Dirk who rejected infant baptism and who favored the ban and avoidance, including marital avoidance. At the 1547 meeting at Goch, Germany, Pastor defended his antitrinitarian position once more and was banned by Dirk. A reconciliation effort by Menno and Dirk at Lübeck, Germany, did not bring about any change, so Pastor's ban was never reversed.

Around 1554 Dirk likely moved to Emden, in northern Germany. That same year he was present at the important meeting in Wismar, Germany, where the regional elders – including Menno, Lenaert Bouwens, Gillis van Aken, Herman van Tielt, Hans Busschaert, and Hoyte Renix – tried to come to an agreement on a number of congregational matters. The *Besluyt tot Wismar* (Wismar Resolutions) included nine articles, including five articles on the ban and avoidance and single articles on issues like mixed marriages, judicial procedures, nonresistance, and the ministry. Despite the Wismar Resolutions, matters regarding church discipline – especially the ban and shunning – caused local disagreements time and again. The most notorious case was the 1557 dispute, which was caused by the refusal of Swaen Rutgers – a female member of Lenaert Bouwens's Emden congregation – to accept the measure of marital avoidance as a result of the banishment of her husband. Franeker Mennonites sided with Swaen and begged for tolerance. This resulted in a meeting of the elders at nearby Harlingen, Friesland, to settle the quarrel. Menno, then living at Bad Oldesloe in northern Germany, was invited as a middleman in order to prevent a schism. The invitation was in vain: Dirk sided with Bouwens in favor of the strict application of the ban, and they both forced Menno to take their side. This would be Menno's last visit to his homeland, and, tragically, not only was the outcome the first major division – a division that would last for centuries – but the dispute also brought about the end of Menno's leadership. A substantial number of Mennonites separated from the main body – not only from Holland and Friesland (called Naeldemans-people, Frankeraers, and later better known as Waterlanders) but also from Southern Germany and Switzerland (the so-called High-Germans), who all opposed the strict banners. Out of this division (in addition to Menno's health problems; he would pass away in 1561), not only did the leading role of Dirk rise, but so too did Bouwens's importance. Indeed, Bouwens baptized over ten thousand people in the Low Countries in the following years. Meanwhile, Dirk, then likely residing in Gdansk (1561–1567), intensified his writing of theological tracts and also published a volume of collected works, *Enchiridion or Small Handbook* (1564).

In 1561 Dirk baptized some forty people in a private home at Utrecht, the Netherlands. On that occasion Dirk was described as "an old man, not very tall, with a gray beard and white hair" (32). Then, around 1565, Dirk got involved in yet another dispute – this time about the issue of whether Bouwens should be dismissed, as some of his church members demanded. This personal matter also coincided with an ethnic and social clash in Franeker (yet again) between native Frisians and Flemish refugees from the southern Netherlands. The latter were in favor of appointing a Flemish instead of a Frisian minister, which contravened a secret agreement of four major Frisian congregations. In 1567 Dirk traveled from Gdansk to Emden to settle the matter, but he refused to come to Franeker. He sided with the Flemish minority, who at once banned the Frisians, while the Frisians, whom Lenaert had joined, consequently banned the Flemish. And so this separation of the Flemish and Frisian Mennonites became the second major division in Dutch Mennonitism, which divided the Mennonites all over the country and beyond. In both dramatic events, Dirk, though striving for the biblical ideal of the true church, played a harsh but prominent role (see texts 14, 15, and 16 in bibliography below).³

As a self-made theologian, Dirk is generally considered more skilled than Menno. When making this comparison, we must remember that Dirk had more time and opportunity to reflect on Mennonite theology. In contrast to Dirk, Menno was often forced by his opponents to defend his "heretical" views due to his position as a "leader on the run." This resulted in a substantial number of polemical writings in which Menno developed a non-scholarly, somewhat ready-made theology, which echoed the dynamics of intolerance and persecution expressed by his adversaries. In contrast, Dirk's more modest position in the background of Dutch Mennonitism allowed him to develop an intellectually more coherent theology. This may explain why Dirk's writings received more appreciation in nineteenth-century North America than Menno's works, which found a wider audience in the Low Countries.

On Dutch soil Dirk's *Enchiridion*, which included twelve tracts, found its final reprint in 1627 in a small octavo size (I–VI). In contrast, Menno's collected *Opera Omnia* appeared in 1646 and 1654 in a larger quarto-size and in 1681 in a huge folio edition (reproduced in facsimile in 1985). Quite remarkable is the French *Enchiridion* edition of 1626, printed in Amsterdam (VII), likely intended for a French-speaking audience in southern Belgium (Wallonia) and neighboring France. Since the times that the Swiss and South-German Amish and Mennonites were no longer tolerated in Europe and set sail to North America with the generous aid of their wealthy Dutch brethren, German *Enchiridion* translations were also produced (VIII–XI). An English edition appeared as late as 1910 (XII).⁴ The scholarly and annotated edition of the complete *Geschriften van Dirk Philips* by F. Pijper – published in 1914 as volume X of the monumental series *Bibliotheca Reformatoria Neerlandica* (referred to as BRN X) – forms the basis of the present English translation of *The Writings of Dirk Philips (WDP)*.⁵ Also included are two hymns of Dirk, of which "Ghy Christen Broeders te samen" (You Christian brethren all together) seems to have been quite popular.

Since the 1990s the Dutch scholar Paul Valkema Blouw, a specialist of sixteenth-century printing history, discovered where and by whom Dirk's writings had been printed in secrecy.[6] In the days of inquisition and persecution, these anonymous printers and publishers risked confiscation of their businesses, as well as capital punishment, when producing and distributing Anabaptist/Mennonite books. Previous scholars assumed that Emden was the primary location for illegal Mennonite book production. It was indeed such a center for the large and illegal Dutch Reformed book market of the sixteenth century. However, the bulk of Dutch Anabaptist and Mennonite books, including those of Menno and Dirk, came from different presses elsewhere. During his lifetime Dirk's major works had been illegally produced by Nicolaes (I) Biestkens van Diest, who owned a print shop not in Emden, as was generally assumed, but in Groessen (east of Arnhem, in the province of Gelderland) (see 5, 7, 10, and 11). Franeker, a Frisian town of key importance in the history of early Dutch Anabaptism and Mennonitism, had its own Mennonite publishing house, owned by printer Jan Hendricksz van Schoonrewoerd and his heirs. For more than fifteen years (from 1555 to 1570), this secret press produced not only works by Menno and Dirk but also Biestkens Bibles and Testaments, hymnbooks, and the first book of martyrs, *Offer des Heeren*. Hendricksz published the first complete edition of Dirk's *Enchiridion* (see its translation in this volume) and four smaller tracts (II.1d, 2, 4, and 6).

Valkema Blouw also discovered copies of formerly unknown first editions of three of Dirk's shorter works (14, 15, and 16), printed around 1566/1567 on a still unknown press, as well as the first 1567 edition of the second ban book (19a), printed by Gillis Coppens van Diest in Antwerp. Since the text renderings of these writings in this volume are based on later editions than the ones subsequently discovered by Valkema Blouw, they should be considered somewhat less accurate.

Dirk wrote about the major theological themes of the day: baptism (II.1c), the Lord's Supper (II.1d), the incarnation of Christ (II.2, 3), rebirth (II.9), ban and avoidance (II.6; 16, 19, 20), marriage (18), and church leaders (II.5). In all his writings, Dirk's biblicism is apparent. For his early writings, he most likely used the so-called

Dutch Liesvelt Bible (1526, based on Luther's German translation), whereas for his later writings he would have used the specially Mennonite Bible version, the Biestkens Bible (1560), as well as the textually differing Biestkens [New] Testament (1556).

While he hardly made any distinction between the canonical and apocryphal biblical books, Dirk's exegetics were Christocentric: Christ's coming was prefigured in the Old Testament – a view that matched Melchiorite incarnation theology. Like Menno, Dirk preached the doctrine of nonresistance, though there is not much in his writings on this subject. Against Pastor he upheld the doctrine of the Trinity. Unlike his brother Obbe, he always stressed the visible church, without spot or wrinkle. This implied a strict application of the ban and avoidance because the church of God, consisting of the elect, should be pure and holy. In his book on the church (II.11), Dirk deals with seven ordinances of the church of God: pure doctrine, scriptural use of the sacraments, washing the feet of the saints, separation (ban and avoidance), the command of love, obedience to the commands of Christ, and suffering and persecution.

Although Dirk's pen was less polemical than Menno's, he did write a tract against the Münster ideologist Bernhard Rothmann (II.10). He also attacked the Spiritualistic views of Sebastian Franck in a tract from around 1541, of which only a printed version of 1602 has survived (13). Dirk's 1556 tracts *Explanation of the Tabernacle* (II.8) and *Brief Admonition on Rebirth* (II.9) were also directed against Spiritualists such as Franck and Joris, who opposed the visible church and its outer sacraments. Around 1560 this last tract was contested by the Rhineland Spiritualist Matthijs Weyer. While tendencies of Spiritualism – so relevant for the development of early Dutch Anabaptism and Mennonitism – can also be detected in Dirk's views on baptism and the Lord's Supper,[7] on the whole his theology is marked by a certain moralism, biblicism, and legalism.

When compared to Menno, Dirk was a strict and even obstinate person and a proud elder, which can best be seen in Dirk's conflict (together with Bouwens) with Menno, resulting in the split of the Waterlanders and the High-Germans, and his subsequent disagreement with Bouwens, followed by the tragic division of the Frisians and the Flemish in 1566–1567. Despite these personal qualities, his writings continue to be used and valued by Anabaptists and Mennonites around the world – and particularly among North American Old Order Amish communities.[8] For this reason, the republication of this English translation of his writings is a welcomed development.

Piet Visser

Bibliography of Printed Editions [9]

Collected Works

I. *A Short Confession and Statement* / Een korte bekentenisse ende belydinge (Deventer: S. Steenbergen, 1564) [Dutch; Keyser 1; a pirated edition of II].

II. *Enchiridion or Small Handbook* / Enchiridion of Hant-boecxken (Franeker[?]: Mennonite Press, 1564) [Dutch; Keyser 2]. Includes twelve collected works. This 1564 edition was used for the 1914 Dutch annotated edition of Dirk's writings, which in turn has been translated into the present English edition (cf. BRN X, 55–469, and *WDP*, 51–440). The volume starts with a confessional tract (without a separate title page), which is subdivided into four sections (cf. the title of the previous pirated 1564 edition: *A Short Confession and Statement*). All subsequent tracts, 2–12 below, have separate title pages:

  1a. *A Confession of Our Faith, Including the Confession of God* / Bekentenisse onses gheloofs [BRN X, 55–64 / WDP, 57–68].

  1b. *Our Confession of Creation, Redemption, and Salvation* / Onse bekentenisse vander scheppinge, verlossinge, ende salichmakinghe des menschen [BRN X, 65–68 / WDP, 68–71].

  1c. *About the Baptism of Our Lord Jesus Christ* / Vander Doope Onses Heeren Christi [BRN X, 69-111 / WDP, 72-111]. Other editions: Middelburg: Jeronimus Wullebrechts / printed by Richard Schilders, 1589 [Keyser 18]; Middelburg: Bernaert Langhenesz, 1589 [=1597] [Keyser 19].

  1d. *Our Confession of the Supper of Our Lord Jesus Christ* / Van dat Auontmael des Heeren Iesu Christi, onse Belijdinghe [BRN X, 111–34 / WDP, 112–33]. An earlier edition, including 1a–1d: Franeker: Jan Hendricksz, 1557 [Keyser 17].

  2. *A Brief Confession of the Incarnation of Our Lord Jesus Christ* / Van der Menschwerdinghe ons Heeren Iesu Christi . . . een corte bekentenisse [BRN X, 135–53 / WDP, 134–51]. An earlier edition: Franeker: Jan Hendricksz, 1557 [Keyser 20].

  3. *A Brief Admonition of the True Knowledge of Jesus Christ* / Vande rechte kennisse Iesu Christi . . . een corte vermaninge [BRN X, 155–78 / WDP, 152–72]. An earlier edition: [?], 1564 [Keyser 20b].

  4. *An Apology, or Justification that We . . . Are Neither Rebaptizers, Nor Sect Makers* / Een Apologia, ofte verantwoordinghe, dat wy . . . gheen wederdoopers noch sectemakers zijn [BRN X, 179–203 / WDP, 173–97]. An earlier edition: Franeker: Jan Hendricksz, 1563[?] [Keyser 32].

  5. *On the Mission of Preachers or Teachers* / Van der Sendinge der Predicanten oft Leeraers [BRN X, 205–248 / WDP, 198–237]. An earlier edition: Groessen, Nicolaes Biestkens, 1559 [Keyser 24].

  6. *A Lovely Admonition [on the Ban]* / Een lieffelijcke vermaninghe [van den Ban] [BRN X, 249–65 / WDP, 238–54]. An earlier edition: Franeker, Jan Hendricksz, 1558 [Keyser 23].

7. *A Nice Admonition... about the True Knowledge of God* / Een Schoone vermaninghe... van de warachtige Kennisse Gods (Groessen: Nicolaes Biestkens, 1558) [Keyser 21] [BRN X, 267-77 / WDP, 255-63].

8. *A Very Nice... Explanation... of the Tabernacle or Tent of Moses* / Een seer schoone... verclaringhe... des Tabernakels ofte der Hutten Moysi [BRN X, 279-311 / WDP, 264-92]. An earlier edition: Emden: Steven Mierdman, 1556 [Keyser 16].

9. *A Brief Admonition on Rebirth and the New Creature* / Van der wedergeboorte en[de] nieuwe Creatuere een corte vermaninge [BRN X, 313-37 / WDP, 293-315]. An earlier edition: Emden: Steven Mierdman, 1556[?] [Keyser 22].

10. *About Spiritual Restitution* / Van de geestelijcke Restitution [BRN X, 338-76 / WDP, 316-49]. Earlier editions: Emden: Willem Gailliart[?], 1559[?] [Keyser 26]; Groessen: Nicolaes Biestkens, 1562 [Keyser 27].

11. *A Short Confession of God's Church*[10] / Vande Gemeynte Godts... Een corte Bekentenisse [BRN X, 377-414 / WDP, 350-82]. An earlier edition: Groessen: Nicolaes Biestkens, 1562 [Keyser 28].

12. *Three Sincere Admonitions or Letters* / Drie grondighe Vermaningen ofte Sendtbrieuen [BRN X, 415-59 / WDP, 383-426].

[-] *A Convenient and Profitable Index* / Een grieffelijck ende profijtelijck Register [BRN X, 460-69 / WDP, 427-40].

III Enchiridion of Handt-boecxken (Ghent: Gautier Manilius, 1578) [Dutch; Keyser 3].

IV Enchiridion of Hantboecxken (Leeuwarden: Pieter Hendricksz, 1579) [Dutch; Keyser 4].

V Enchiridion of Hantboecxken ([?], 1600) [Dutch; Keyser 5].

VI Enchiridion of Hantboexken (Haarlem: Hans Passchiers van Wesbusch, 1627) [Dutch; Keyser 6].

VII Enchiridion ou Manuël (Amsterdam: Abraham Biestkens, 1626) [French; Keyser 8].

VIII Enchiridion oder Hand-Büchlein ([?]: C. J. Conert [a pseudonym?], 1715) [German; Keyser 9].

IX Enchiridion oder Hand-Büchlein (Basel: Gebrüder Von Mechel, 1802) [German; Keyser 10].

X Enchiridion oder Hand-Büchlein (Lancaster, PA: Joseph Ehrenfried, 1811) [German; Keyser 11].

XI Enchiridion oder Hand-Büchlein (Elkhart, IN: John F. Funk & Brother, 1872) [German; Keyser 12].

XII *Enchiridion or Hand Book* (Elkhart, IN: Mennonite Publishing Co., 1910) [English; Keyser 13].

α De geschriften van Dirk Philipsz [BRN X], edited by F. Pijper (The Hague, 1914) [Dutch; Keyser 7].

β *The Writings of Dirk Philips* [WDP], translated and edited by Cornelius J. Dyck, William E. Keeney, and Alvin J. Beechy, Classics of the Radical Reformation 6 (Scottdale, PA: Herald, 1992).

Separate Titles (not in Enchiridion)

13. *A Response and Refutation to Two Letters by Sebastian Franck* / Een verantwoordinghe ende Refutation op twee Sendtbrieven Sebastiani Franck, in Van die Echt der Christenen (Haarlem: Passchier [I] van Wesbusch, 1602) [Dutch; Keyser 50b; BRN X, 473-508 / WDP, 445-67]. Other editions: Haarlem: Hans Passchiers van Wesbusch, 1634 [Keyser 51]; Rotterdam: Gerrit A. van Bueren, 1644 [Keyser 52].

*14. *A Letter... Written to the Four Cities* / Eenen Sendtbrief, aen de vier St[eden]. geschreven (Amsterdam, Nicolaes [II] Biestkens, ca. 1580) [Dutch; Keyser 33; BRN X,

xvii

511–34 / WDP, 468–88]. Other editions: [?], 1567/1568 [Keyser 34]; Haarlem: Vincent Casteleyn, 1619 [Keyser 35].

*15. *A Short but Fundamental Account about the Conflicting Acts . . . in Friesland* / Een cort, doch grondtlick verhael vanden twistigen handel . . . in Fr[iesland] (Amsterdam: Nicolaes (II) Biestkens, ca. 1580) [Dutch; Keyser 37; BRN X, 537–81 / WDP, 489–521]. Other editions: [?], 1567/1568 [Keyser 38]; Haarlem: Vincent Casteleyn, 1619 [Keyser 39].

*16. *An Appendix to Our Booklet about the Conflicting Acts in Friesland* / Een Appendix aen ons Boecxken van den twistigen handel in Vr[iesland] (Amsterdam: Nicolaes [II] Biestkens, ca. 1580) [Dutch; Keyser 40; BRN X, 585–613 / WDP, 522–43]. Other editions: [?], 1567/1568 [Keyser 41]; Haarlem: Vincent Casteleyn, 1619 [Keyser 42].

17a. *A Copy of a Letter . . . to Hoijte Reinicks, an Elder from Friesland* (7 June 1567) / Een copije van een brief . . . an Hoijte Reinicks, in Vriesland een oudste, in J. ten Doornkaat Koolman, *Dirk Philips. Vriend en medewerker van Menno Simons* (Haarlem: Tjeenk Willink, 1964), 200–205 [Keyser 36; BRN X, 689–90 (a fragment only) / WDP, 544–48].

17b. *A Letter to Jan Willems and Lubbert Gerrits* (30 June 1567) [BRN X, 690–91 and 692–93 / WDP, 548–50].

17c. *A Letter to the Congregation at Hoorn* [BRN X, 691–92 / WDP, 550].

18. *About the Marriage of Christians* / Van die Echt der Christenen (Emden: Willem Gailliart[?], 1569) [Dutch; Keyser 49; BRN X, 617–49 / WDP, 552–77]. Another edition: Haarlem: Passchier (I) van Wesbusch, 1602 [Keyser 50].

*19a. *A Posthumous Writing about the Evangelical Ban and Avoidance* [The second ban book] / Naeghelaten Schrift Van den Euangelischen Ban ende Mijdinghe; a Dutch translation by C[arel]. V[an]. M[ander], in Van die Echt der Christenen (Haarlem: Passchier [I] van Wesbusch, 1602) [Dutch; Keyser 50a; BRN X, 653–66 / WDP, 578–88]. An earlier edition: Antwerp: Gillis Coppens van Diest, 1567.[11]

19b. *A Clear and Manifest Exposition of Evangelical Excommunication* / Claire et Manifeste Remonstrance de l'Excommunication Euangelique [from the French edition of Enchiridion, VII] (Amsterdam, Abraham Biestkens, 1626), in facsimile in J. ten Doornkaat Koolman, *Dirk Philips. Vriend en medewerker van Menno Simons* (Haarlem: Tjeenk Willink, 1964), 207–223 [French; Keyser 48; WDP, 590–610]. The content of this text is quite similar to the Dutch version of 19a, although style and phrasing differ.

20. *A Confession about Separation Briefly Summarized* / Eine bekentenisse van der afsonderinghe int korthe vervatet (ca. 1549), in J. ten Doornkaat Koolman, *Dirk Philips. Vriend en medewerker van Menno Simons* (Haarlem: Tjeenk Willink, 1964), 193–99 [WDP, 611–17].

21. *A . . . Christian Epistle . . . to the Wife of I[oachim]. den. S[uyckerbacker]. Who Lay Imprisoned at Antwerp* / Een Christelijcken Sendtbrief . . . aen die Huysvrouwe van I. den S. die welcke tot Antwerpen gheuanghen lach (Leeuwarden: Pieter Hendricksz, 1579) [Dutch; Keyser 25; BRN X, 675–88 / WDP, 618–31].[12]

22. *A Letter to the Rhineland Brethren about God and the Incarnation of Christ* / [No Dutch title] (ca. 1547–1550), published by J. ten Doornkaat Koolman in *Nederlands Archief voor Kerkgeschiedenis* N.S. 43 (1959): 15–21 [WDP, 631–35].

23a. "You Christian Brethren All Together" / "Ghy Christen Broeders te samen" (hymn) [Keyser 61a; BRN X, 693–97 / WDP, 638–42].[13]

23b. "Rejoice Now and Be Glad" / "Verheucht nu en weest verblijt" (hymn) [Keyser 61b; BRN X, 697–99 / WDP, 642–46].[14]

Notes

1. The sixteenth-century Dutch spelling of Dirk Philips's name would have been *Dirck* (spelled with *ck*) *Philipsz*, the common Dutch abbreviation of *Philipszoon* (Philip's son). The common spelling *Dirk Philips* is an Anglicized and/or Germanized adaptation, which disrespects its Dutch roots. However, I am afraid that it now is too late to correct this historical neglect of the original spelling of Dirck Philipsz's name.

2. Unless stated otherwise, I generally refer to "*Dirk Philips: A Biography*," included in this volume (19–47), which the editors note in their introduction is predominantly the work of William Keeney (12). Except for some bibliographical details, this sketch of Philips's life, works, and relevance is still accurate. In addition to the bibliographical references provided in this volume, the following articles and books should also be included: Keith Ian Conant, "The Marriage Views of Hans Denck, Dirk Philips, and Menno Simons" (MA thesis, Northeast Missouri State University, 1994); Jacobus ten Doornkaat Koolman, "Een Onbekende Brief Van Dirk Philips," *Nederlands Archief voor Kerkgeschiedenis / Dutch Review of Church History* 43, no. 1 (1961): 15–21; Jacobus ten Doornkaat Koolman, *Dirk Philips: Friend and Colleague of Menno Simons, 1504–1568*, translated from Dutch by William E. Keeney and edited by C. Arnold Snyder (Kitchener, ON: Pandora; Scottdale, PA, Herald, 1998); Gerke van Hiele, "'De duivel verzaken': Onderzoek naar de doopleer van Bernhard Rothmann, Menno Simons en Dirk Philips," *Doopsgezinde Bijdragen* 19 (1993): 53–80; Marja Keyser, ed., *Dirk Philips, 1504–1568: A Catalogue of His Printed Works in the University Library of Amsterdam* (Amsterdam: University Library of Amsterdam, 1975); John D. Rempel, *The Lord's Supper in Anabaptism: A Study in the Christology of Balthasar Hubmaier, Pilgram Marpeck, and Dirk Philips* (Scottdale, PA: Herald, 1993), 165–95; Paul Valkema Blouw, "Een onbekende vertaling van Dirk Philips: Traicté de quelques poincts (1567)," *Doopsgezinde Bijdragen* 15 (1989): 149–50; Paul Valkema Blouw, "Drukkers voor Menno Simons en Dirk Philips," *Doopsgezinde Bijdragen* 17 (1991): 31–74; also in English as "Printers for Menno Simons and Dirk Philips," in Ton Croiset van Uchelen and Paul Dijstelberge, eds., *Dutch Typograhy in the Sixteenth Century: The Collected Works of Paul Valkema Blouw* (Boston: Brill, 2013), 455–94; Dirk Visser, "Interview met Alvin J. Beachy: de herwaardering van Dirk Philips," *Doopsgezinde Bijdragen* 7 (1981): 92–96; Piet Visser, "Zes onbekende martelaarsbrieven van Jeronimus Segers (†1551)," *Doopsgezinde Bijdragen* 29 (2003): 198–201; Sjouke Voolstra, "Innerlijk en uiterlijk vertoon van Christus: De verhouding tussen spiritualisme en doperdom toegelicht aan de hand van de reactie van Matthijs Weyer (1521–1560) op een traktaat over de wedergeboorte van Dirk Philips (1504–1568)," in *Van masker tot aangezicht: Opstellen over bijbelse, theologische en kerkelijke confrontaties*, edited by Karel Deurloo and Alle Hoekema (Baarn: Ten Have, 1997), 53–71; also in *Beeldenstormer uit bewogenheid: Verzamelde opstellen van Sjouke Voolstra*, edited by Anna Voolstra, Alle Hoekema, and Piet Visser (Hilversum, Verloren, 2005), 99–104; Gary K. Waite, "Philips, Dirk," in *Mennonitisches Lexikon* V, online: www.mennlex.de/doku.php?id=art:philips_dirk.

3. All in-text citations below refer to numbered references in bibliography.

4. It is noteworthy how formative the sixteenth- and seventeenth-century Dutch Mennonite theological, educational, and edifying literary output in print has been for many generations of the Swiss and South-German settlers in the New World. See, for instance, Robert Friedmann, *Mennonite Piety through the Centuries* (Scottdale, PA: Herald, 1980), esp. 105–26; David Luthy, *A History of the Printings of the Martyrs' Mirror: Dutch, German, English, 1960–2012* (La Grange, IN: Pathway, 2013).

5. See Sjouke Voolstra's review of the first edition of the present volume in *Doopsgezinde Bijdragen* 18 (1992): 145–49, esp. 145.

xix

6. See Valkema Blouw, "Drukkers voor Menno Simons en Dirk Philips" (English: "Printers for Menno Simons and Dirk Philips"); Valkema Blouw, "Een onbekende vertaling van Dirk Philips." During the 1980s and 90s, Valkema Blouw, an expert of analytical bibliography at the University of Amsterdam, identified some 85 percent of the places of production and/or the names of the printers and publishers of all clandestinely and/or anonymously printed books and tracts from the sixteenth-century Low Countries, including those of the Anabaptists and Mennonites.

7. Voolstra, "Innerlijk en uiterlijk vertoon van Christus"; Rempel, *Lord's Supper in Anabaptism*, 176–78; Aart de Groot, "Dirk Philips," in *Biografisch Lexicon voor de Geschiedenis van het Nederlandse Protestantisme*, edited by J. van den Berg et al. (Kampen: Uitgeverij Kok, 1998), 4:119–21, esp. 120.

8. As noted in Nanne van der Zijpp, "Dirk Philips (1504–1568)," *Global Anabaptist Mennonite Encyclopedia Online*; https://gameo.org/index.php?title=Dirk_Philips_(1504-1568)&oldid=145802.

9. For title identification, Keyser refers to Keyser, ed., Dirk Philips; BRN X refers to F. Pijper, ed., *De geschriften van Dirk Philipsz*, Bibliotheca Reformatoria Neerlandica X (The Hague: 1914); and WDP refers to the present volume, *Writings of Dirk Philips*. The names of places and printers of sixteenth-century editions are based on the findings of Valkema Blouw, "Printers for Menno Simons and Dirk Philips." Title numbers with an asterisk indicate methodologically inadequate text renderings in this volume since the discovery of older/first editions by Valkema Blouw.

10. Although the former editors of this English edition, Keeney, Beachy, and Dyck, made an accurate translation of the original Dutch versions, it should be noted that their rendering of the Dutch "Ghemeynte" as "Congregation" is contextually inaccurate in most cases. Dirk was incidentally referring to the local congregations, but more frequently he referred to the "general Church of God" or "the Apostolic Church of Christ." Therefore, a translation of "church" would have been more adequate than using the modern Mennonite equivalent of "congregation." See Voolstra's review of *Writings of Dirk Philips*, 147.

11. Of the original French version of this text, which had been translated by the Old-Flemish Mennonite poet and artist Carel van Mander from Haarlem in 1602, a first edition was discovered by Paul Valkema Blouw in the holdings of the Herzog August Bibliothek at Wolfenbüttel, Germany. It came from the Antwerp press of Gillis Coppens van Diest in 1567. See Valkema Blouw, "Een onbekende vertaling van Dirk Philips."

12. A handwritten version of this letter, with striking textual variations, is included in an older sixteenth-century manuscript volume of the Doopsgezinde Bibliotheek, Amsterdam University Library. See Piet Visser, "Zes onbekende martelaarsbrieven van Jeronimus Segers," 201–202.

13. Included in eight Mennonite hymnbooks, between 1556 and 1629; see Keyser 61a.

14. Included in only one 1618 edition of a Mennonite hymnbook; see Keyser 61b.

GENERAL EDITOR'S PREFACE

For many years a committee of German and North American historians known as the *Tauferaktenkommission* (TAK) has published source materials of the sixteenth-century Anabaptist movement under the title *Quellen zur Geschichte der Taufer* (QGT). Recently a similar organization has begun work in the Netherlands with Dutch source materials. It is known as the *Commissie tot de Uitgave van Documenta Anabaptistica Neerlandica* (CUDAN). These developments have been deeply rewarding to scholars and others, as the many articles and books using these documents testify.

There are, however, still relatively few sixteenth-century Anabaptist materials available in the English language, though their number is increasing. The Classics of the Radical Reformation (CRR) series was begun some years ago to meet this need. The CRR series goal is to offer, in English, scholarly and critical editions of the primary works of major Anabaptist and free church writers of the late fifteenth, sixteenth, and early seventeenth centuries. The list of these volumes appears on page five. The present volume is sixth in the series. Additional volumes are in process.

It has not been considered essential to the purposes of the CRR series to include every known document of the writers under translation. Nor has it been considered essential to pursue at length critical textual issues, except when this would contribute to a fuller understanding of the text. Those scholars interested in the details will, in any case, turn to the original language text. Where a choice had to be made between clarity and awkward literalism, the translators were encouraged to favor readability but without compromising the text.

Appreciation is due to the Institute of Mennonite Studies (IMS) and its sponsoring institution, the Associated Mennonite Biblical Seminaries (AMBS) of Elkhart, Indiana. In addition, gratitude is due to Herald Press for its continuing commitment to the work and needs of the church, as the publishing of this series testifies.

> *Cornelius J. Dyck, Editor, CRR*
> *Institute of Mennonite Studies*
> *Elkhart, Indiana*

EDITORS' INTRODUCTION

Dirk Philips ranks second only to Menno Simons in his influence on Dutch Anabaptism during the first decades of the movement. Dirk wrote less polemically than Menno. His treatises on baptism, the sending of preachers, the new birth, spiritual restitution, the congregation [church], marriage, and the ban are articulate and comprehensive. His knowledge of the Scriptures was phenomenal. It is time that his thoughts enter more fully into believers church dialogue.

Many of Dirk's writings have been long available in Dutch, German, and English editions, some also in French.[1] The 1910 English edition by Kolb has been used most in North America.[2] It was prepared from an earlier German translation, inserted King James Scripture quotations rather than translating Dirk's own Scripture quotes, and contained only three of the documents included in Part B of the present volume. No attempt was made to annotate or contextualize the documents within the framework of Dirk's life and thought. Still, it has served well for many years. In 1957, George H. Williams included Dirk's treatise on the congregation [church] in his *Spiritual and Anabaptist Writers* volume in the Library of Christian Classics series.

In 1914, Frederik Pijper, professor at the University of Leiden, published all of Dirk's writings available to him as Volume X of the BRN [Netherlands Reformation Library].[3] This volume and the entire set was prepared in the best scholarly tradition of that time. It had extensive annotations, commentary, and bibliographical references. It was based on the 1564 edition Dirk himself had prepared.

The present translation is based in equal parts on the original 1564 edition and on Pijper's 1914 one. The two copies lay at either side of the final editor's computer, supplemented by the IDC microfiche of Dirk's writings where necessary.[4] Documents B 5, 6, and 7 were translated from J. ten Doornkaat Koolman, *Dirk Philips, 1505-1568: Vriend en Medewerker van Menno Simons*.[5] Some notes and introductory materials are particularly indebted to the BRN volume as will be indicated.

The Translating and Editing Process

This translation project has been on the CRR agenda for many years. Following Alvin J. Beachy's retirement in 1978, he began a first draft translation, using both the BRN and 1564 documents. After several years, when he had sent about one-half of the manuscript to Dyck, failing health forced him to terminate his work. Following a two-year interval, he asked to be relieved of further involvement in the project. We mourned his death in 1986. He had, however, made a final contribution by suggesting several possible sources of funding for the project.

In due course William E. Keeney was able to continue the project part-time. He reviewed Alvin's work in a second draft process and completed the translation. It remained for C. J. Dyck then to prepare the final draft, checking every line, editing and retranslating as seemed best, footnoting, writing some of the introductions and, in general, preparing the volume for the press. The // page identification is correlated with the BRN text. The biography is basically the work of Keeney.

The translators-editors hope that this corporate process will have helped to achieve the goal of the CRR series, namely to prepare a readable volume still reasonably faithful to the original. Many sentences and paragraphs could easily have been made more readable by paraphrasing them, but that would have violated the integrity of the text. A certain literalness has been found acceptable, even preferable, to undue smoothness.

As translators-editors we resonate with Martin Luther (1483-1546). In commenting on Jerome's (d. 420) preparation of the Vulgate, he added that it "would have been quite as well had he called to his aid one or two learned men, for the Holy Spirit would then have more powerfully manifested itself to him, as it is written '. . . for where two or three are together. . . .' [Matt. 18:20]. Interpreters and translators should not work alone; for good and appropriate words do not always occur to one mind."[6] In translating the Waldensian catechism he wrote, "For I have found in my translating that it takes luck to make a precise rendering even when the original is perfectly clear and certain."[7] We believe the volume has benefited from our joint work.

One of the challenges of translating Dirk's writings are his long sentences and paragraphs. We have carefully modified them. The reader should also note that upper case spelling of key words now and then, like GOD, JESUS CHRIST, LORD, and others were so placed by Dirk and retained to communicate his intended emphasis. Among the many words for which several translations might be appropriate is *Heyligen*, which has been translated *saints*, though *holy ones* would also be correct. So also *wedergeboren* has been translated as *born again*, though reborn would also convey the meaning. These are given as examples of many words. Dirk always speaks of *Gemeynte/ Ghemeynte* which is *congregation*. He reserves *Kerk*, that is *church*, for Protestant and Roman Catholic institutions. He did not encourage people to go to a *church*.

Annotations have been kept to a minimum in keeping with CRR policy, but some were essential to correct understanding. They have been placed as *Endnotes* with each document. The division of the documents into Parts A and B follows Dirk's own division which treated the *Enchiridion* (Handbook) as a unitary collection.

Dirk's Use of Scripture

Dirk seems to have known Scripture exceptionally well and used it constantly, as the following pages show. Following the accepted practice of the day, however, he often quoted from memory. Because of this it became important to translate the text as he had it rather than to insert a given modern, or other, version. This procedure meant that quotation marks could be added to a given text only when we were certain that it was a fairly literal quote.

Dirk's quotation from memory also means that Scripture references translated from his own wording are, by nature, not quite the same as in a given modern Bible. However, all quotations of Scripture can be checked through the references, which are placed within the document itself—not in the margin as the 1564 and BRN X editions have them.

Although we checked these texts as we translated and edited the documents, further verification was needed. Wilma Regier Dyck undertook the task of checking every text, locating where they seemed to belong, verifying their accuracy as well as finding and placing in brackets [ ] many of the citations of the texts Dirk seemed to have had in mind.

It must be remembered that, while chapter divisions had been made, versification was just beginning in Dirk's time. Many of his references do not give a verse but rather an *a, b, c,* or *d*. These were sections within a given page and chapter to which he was referring. Often only a chapter reference is given and some have had to remain that way.

Related to this pattern was another problem. Dirk made heavy use of Scripture, in keeping with the primacy of its authority for him.

Sometimes, however, the given text does not really seem to support the argument. Where the intended text could not be definitely identified, the one listed by Dirk was left as given. The only Dirk texts changed were corrections of chapters, verses, or books, including the Apocrypha, where his intention and meaning was clear. And, as indicated, all of these are in brackets [ ].

Which Bible(s) did Dirk use? This becomes a particularly difficult question when, as indicated, he quoted from memory. Some references seem to be based on the Latin Vulgate text. He used Latin more often in his writings than Menno did. It would be surprising if Dirk, as a Frisian, would not have used the East Frisian Bible published by Bugenhagen in 1545, based on Luther's German Bible. It may also be assumed, though a detailed analysis was not made by us, that he used the famous Zurich or Christoffel Froschouer version, of which there were many editions and of which the Anabaptists were very fond.[8] It would certainly have been available to him. It is likely that he also used the Greek New Testament of Erasmus.

Editor Dyck determined that, for our purposes, the differences between the different editions of the Nicolaes Biestkens Bibles were not significant. Then as he worked with the documents, Dyck compared texts from Dirk's writings with the 1560 Biestkens edition and the 1560 Jacob van Liesveldt Bible, of which there were many editions after 1526.

It was originally assumed that Dirk, being long inclined towards the Flemish and given the early availability of the Liesveldt version, might have favored this Bible printed in Antwerp. However, this did not seem to be the case. Without making a definitive claim, these editorial comparisons have led to the conclusion that both direct and indirect quotations were generally taken from the Biestkens rather than the Liesveldt Bible. The Biestkens Bible was an improved version of the Liesveldt Bible. It was the first to provide versification. Still, as mentioned above, he also drew on other resources available to him.[9]

Acknowledgments

The translators-editors express appreciation to their spouses, to whom this book is dedicated, for their continuing moral support and encouragement. We are grateful for the financial support which came from many Beachy Amish congregations and for their patience in waiting for the finished volume. Daniel S. Bontrager, Beachy Amish minister and lay historian, was always encouraging and supportive.

The generosity of Lake S. Clemmer, John S. Keller, Gerald Hartzel, Ernest Landis, and Elvin R. Souder of Pennsylvania also did much to make the project financially possible. The work of our late mutual friend Harry E. Martens in coordinating the latter funds is not forgotten.

The members of the former CRR Editorial Council—Walter Klaassen, John S. Oyer, John H. Yoder and Jarold K. Zeman—were most helpful in the initial stages of the project, as was the Institute of Mennonite Studies and its officers, including the new CRR editor H. Wayne Pipkin. Joe Springer of the Mennonite Historical Library and other staff members are thanked for their efficient and expert help. Word processor operators Sue DeLeon and J. Kevin Miller are thanked for their competent and cheerful work with the manuscript.

Cornelius J. Dyck
William E. Keeney
Advent 1990

ENDNOTES

1. See Keyser.
2. Kolb. The last three documents of this volume are not part of Dirk's *Enchiridion*.
3. *Bibliotheca Reformatoria Neerlandica*. Geschriften uit den Tijd der Hervorming in de Nederlanden. Tiende Deel. De geschriften van Dirk Philipsz. 's-Gravenhage [The Hague]: Martinus Nijhoff, 1914. Samuel Cramer (1842-1913), professor at the Mennonite seminary in Amsterdam, worked with Pijper in the series, preparing three other Anabaptist volumes (II, V, and VII), but his illness and death prevented his working extensively on Vol. X.
4. Inter Documentation Company, AG. Zug, Switzerland has prepared microfiche copies of many Anabaptist and Mennonite source documents up to 1600.
5. Sub-title: "Friend and co-worker of Menno Simons."
6. Hazlitt, *The Table Talk of Martin Luther*, pp. 2-3. [Cf: *Weimar Ausgabe*, TR Vol. I, p. 486, No. 961].
7. *Luther's Works*. Vol. 36. *Word and Sacrament*, ed. Abdel R. Wentz, general ed. Helmut T. Lehmann (Philadelphia: Muhlenberg Press, 1959), p. 276 [WA 11, 417-418].
8. The 1536 edition was reprinted by Amos B. Hoover of Denver, Pennsylvania, in 1975. See also "Froschauer Bibles and Testaments," ME II:415-16 and S. Muller, "Het Ontstaan en het Gebruik van Bijbelvertalingen," *Jaarboekje voor de Doopsgezinde Gemeenten*, (1837), pp. 56ff.
9. For a helpful discussion of Bibles used by Menno Simons, see Poettcker, pp. 73-78.

*The Writings of Dirk Philips
1504–1568*

DIRK PHILIPS: A BIOGRAPHY

Introduction

Dirk Philips was born in 1504, probably in Leeuwarden. He was the younger son of a priest named Philips, so most properly he should be called Dirk Philipszoon, or the son of Philips.[1] His older brother was Obbe. They were both sons of a priest, thus nothing is known about their mother and not much more about their father. The practice of a priest having a concubine, or somewhat legal wife, was common enough in Friesland that the sons could inherit property from their fathers. Two of the leading humanists of the period were also sons of priests, Rudolf Agricola (1443-1485) and Desiderius Erasmus (1466-1536). Schools were set up for these boys, and they were sometimes employed making copies of the Scriptures before printing made that labor unnecessary.

Little is known about the early life of Dirk. He probably attended school, for he had a better than average education, as attested by his later writings. He no doubt knew Latin and gave some evidence of a knowledge of Greek and possibly Hebrew, though his usage of some words and phrases from each would not require extensive knowledge of the languages.[2] His brother Obbe was a barber and a surgeon, a common combination in that time. It would indicate that Obbe also had a fairly good education.

Dirk apparently was related to the Franciscans, perhaps being in the cloister Nieuw Galilea, which had recently been moved from outside the city into Leeuwarden. One of his opponents referred somewhat disparagingly to Dirk as being from that "crowd of Franciscans."[3] Otherwise we know nothing of his early life before he joined the Anabaptists.

We do know that Dirk was born and raised in a time of much change and unrest. The fifteenth century saw new developments in several areas. In the middle of the century moving type was invented and printing became increasingly common. Earlier a renewed discovery of the Greek language and philosophy resulted in changes in philosophical thinking and more critical examination of the Scriptures. Scholars went back behind the Latin Vulgate, which was the standard text in the medieval church, and began studying the original Greek and Hebrew texts.

In addition, through the Moslems in Northern Africa and Spain, then the Jews in Spain and other parts of Europe, Aristotle was rediscovered. This raised questions about the Neoplatonic philosophical forms in which most of Christian theology was cast from the early period until the medieval time. These linguistic and philosophical trends challenged some of the generally accepted theological thoughts upon which church practice was based.

The fifteenth century was also a time of geographic discovery for Western Europe. Marco Polo had made his trips to the East, including China, and had brought back new ideas and practices. Columbus had sailed West to try to find a quicker route to the East but instead opened up exploration of the Americas.

Travel and trade also brought changes in the economy. Medieval feudalism based on an economy of localism and barter was breaking down. A new mercantilism based on money and international trade was emerging. That change caused a considerable disruption in society. As usual, it was the poorer people who were suffering from inflation and a demand for money payment for goods and taxes—even as they waited for payment for their services.

Inflation was rampant. Prices for rye, a staple for the common people, increased threefold between 1510 and 1532.[4] Prices in general increased 30 percent during the period.[5] Speculation and monopolies drove prices up. Even the church contributed to the difficulties, since it owned 35-40 percent of the land in the Netherlands and had monopolies of goods in certain areas.[6]

A number of natural disasters aggravated the conditions described above. Floods raged through the Netherlands, which has always had a battle with the seas. In 1502 salt water covered most of Friesland. Another flood in 1505 was followed by a drought. A mild flood occurred in 1508, followed by a severe flood in 1509 in which many people and cattle drowned. Again in 1511 a flood took lives and destroyed hundreds of houses. Then in 1516 came the worst flood in a hundred years. In 1530 a tragic flood occurred in Zeeland and another in 1532.

All of these events led people to feel that they lived in a time of despair. They looked for solace to the church. But the church suffered corruption despite periodic movements of internal reform. The church had become subject to much political machination. Cornelius, a church historian from Münster in Germany, writes that the election of the shepherd depended less on his "piety, scholastic ability and spiritual gifts" than on his political advantage or the use which could be made of his military abilities and personal or family connections.[7]

The immorality found among some of the priests and religious was notorious. Idleness was common. Drunkenness and whoredom were also frequent enough to make some wary of priests and monks. Mention has already been made of the practice of concubinage and the acceptance of the children as legal heirs of priests.

Martin Luther (1483-1546) arose in Germany in 1517 as a reformer of the church. His teachings were known in the Netherlands, though Lutheranism never gained a wide following. A movement called the Sacramentarians arose in the 1520s, and, indeed, Dutch views of the Lord's Supper were adopted by Zwingli and later by Calvin in the Swiss reformation.[8] That is perhaps one reason why, at a later time, Calvinism was to become the predominant reformation movement in the Netherlands.

Sacramentarianism prepared the way for the opposing Anabaptist movement. In fact, some of the martyrs of the Sacramentarians were claimed by the Anabaptists, such as Weynken Claes Dochter of Monnickendam. She was arrested in November of 1527 and executed on November 20 of that year.[9] That was about three years before any movement identified as Anabaptist entered the Netherlands. When her examiners questioned her about the sacraments, she replied, "I take your Sacrament for bread and meal, where your members take it for a God, I say that it is your devil."[10]

After the invention of printing and the recovery of the Greek and Hebrew texts of the Bible, the next step was to translate the Bible into the common languages of the people. In the Netherlands alone, thirty printings of different translations appeared between 1522 and 1530, according to Kühler.[11] Twenty-four were of the New Testament wholly or in part. Four contained the Old Testament wholly or in part. Two were of the complete Bible. Blaupot ten Cate states that over one hundred editions of Dutch translations of the Old and New Testaments appeared between 1522 and 1543. Most followed Luther's translations.[12]

The availability of the Bible in the language of the people gave them a base for a new look at the teachings of the medieval church. It prepared the way for a religious revival out of which came the Reformation as a whole, and the Anabaptist movement in particular.

ANABAPTISM COMES TO THE NETHERLANDS

Melchior Hoffman was a furrier or tanner (*bontwerker*) from

Schwabisch-Hall in Germany.[13] He first became a Lutheran preacher in Livonia but was driven out by the Teutonic Knights. He went to Wittenberg to meet with Luther and others in June 1525, and then to Dorpat, apparently with Luther's endorsement. After a conflict with Lutheran preachers there, he proceeded to Sweden and began his writings based on allegorical interpretation of the Scriptures. They had a great influence on lay people.

After some controversies in Sweden, he was expelled and traveled to the Holstein area where the Danish king, Frederick I, supported him as a general evangelist. In Holstein, Hoffman moved theologically from Luther to Zwingli and possibly became aware of the issue of infant baptism. After a period of popularity, he came into conflict with the Lutherans and eventually engaged in debate with them on April 8 and 9, 1529. After this his goods were confiscated and he was banished.

Hoffman was briefly in Emden, East Friesland, with Karlstadt, Luther's former colleague. From there he traveled to Strasbourg, arriving by June 30, 1529. He soon came into contact with the Anabaptists and engaged in active rebaptizing, which he supported in his writing of "The Ordinance of God."[14]

In 1530, Hoffman returned to Emden and established an Anabaptist congregation. Among his converts was Jan Volkertszoon, or Trypmaker, who became the leader. He probably also traveled into the Netherlands. There one of his converts was Sicke Freerks, or Snyder, a tailor, whose martyrdom for rebaptism aroused Menno Simons to consider the issue of infant baptism.[15]

Upon Hoffman's return to Strasbourg in December 1531, he became increasingly enamored with prophecy and the millennium. He announced that Strasbourg was the New Jerusalem and that 144,000 prophets would proclaim the coming of the kingdom. He believed the time was ripe for the coming of the kingdom, that it would take place in Strasbourg, and that it would be done in some nonresistant fashion by God's direct intervention.

In the meantime in the Netherlands, Jan Volkertszoon was banned from Emden. He went to Amsterdam to form an Anabaptist congregation. Believing that no harm would come to him, he gave himself up to the authorities in November 1531. He also gave them the names of the other leaders of the Anabaptists. He and seven of his followers were arrested and executed on December 6, and another of the leaders was executed on May 11, 1532. When Hoffman heard of the executions, he was so horrified he declared a two-year moratorium on baptism, justifying it on the basis of Ezra 4:24, where the Jews ceased work on the temple for two years.

Hoffman had traveled to East Friesland but returned again to Strasbourg in 1533. He was arrested and imprisoned, spending the rest of his life there as far as is known but still expecting the coming of the kingdom and his deliverance.

After Jan Volkertszoon's execution and Melchior Hoffman's imprisonment, the Anabaptists in the Netherlands were at first in confusion. Jan Matthys, a baker from Haarlem, claimed a revelation by which he was to assume the leadership in Amsterdam. He proceeded to organize the followers of Hoffman. He sent twelve apostles to resume baptism and to ordain bishops (elders) in various parts of the country.

Münster was one of the destinations to which the apostles traveled. Because of the reception they received, including the support of the preacher Bernhard Rothmann who had already instituted a reform, Matthys came to assume that Münster, and not Strasbourg, would be the New Jerusalem.

Another location to which the apostles traveled was Leeuwarden in Friesland. Bartel de Boeckbinder and William Cuiper baptized Obbe Philips.[16] He and Hans Scheerder were commissioned to the office of preacher—to baptize, teach, and lead the congregation. The two of them immediately set out on a trip around Leeuwarden to carry out their task.

While Obbe and Hans were gone, another of the apostles sent by Jan Matthys, Pieter Houtsagher, appeared. Sometime between Kerstmis (Christmas) and Lichtmis (thus between December 25, 1533, and January 2, 1534), he baptized Dirk Philips, Obbe's younger brother.[17] Houtsagher came into conflict with the Sacramentarians and had a debate with them through which the Anabaptists came to the attention of the authorities. When Obbe returned to the city he had to go into hiding.

Obbe had another shock on March 22, 1534. That day the three apostles who had come to Leeuwarden, Bartel de Boeckbinder, William Cuiper, and Pieter Houtsagher, ran through the streets of Amsterdam. Waving swords and proclaiming that the day of the Lord had come, they called people to repentance. They were promptly arrested and executed shortly thereafter in Haarlem. The authorities placed their heads and the heads of others executed at the same time on posts as examples to the people. Obbe, with a traveling companion, probably Hans Scheerder, went to Haarlem to see if they could discover which of the three was among those who had baptized them and announced the great mission and promise. The heads were so disfigured by the fire and smoke that Obbe could not recognize them.[18]

The shock of the events in Leeuwarden, Amsterdam, and Haarlem probably started Obbe Philips on a different course from the followers of Jan Matthys. He continued to travel, going to Leiden where he baptized and apparently later ordained David Joris as bishop. Joris came out of the earlier Sacramentarian movement. In fact, he had a hole bored through his tongue for disrupting a procession on Ascension Day in 1528.

Obbe Philips was back in Amsterdam in the fall of 1535 where he had a critical discussion with the Anabaptist bishop in that city, Jacob van Campen.[19] They disagreed over the interpretation of Scripture. Jacob van Campen used a typological interpretation of the Old Testament, following the figure of a split hoof given by Melchior Hoffman. He contended that the Old Testament types must have both a literal and a spiritual fulfillment in the Christian era. The literal fulfillment was the justification for setting up a kingdom at Münster.

Obbe insisted instead on a spiritual application of these types. This interpretation was to be more fully developed and applied in the writings of Obbe's brother Dirk at a later time.[20] At any rate, that difference seems to have resulted in a definitive separation between Obbe, the leader of the more quietistic Anabaptists, and the more revolutionary Anabaptists who supported the occupation of Münster. It seems Obbe returned to the northern part of the country, for the next trace we have of him is in the northeastern province of Groningen.

About this time Obbe came into contact with Menno Simons, who left the Roman Catholic church in January 1536.[21] Obbe probably baptized him and later, with others, recruited him as a bishop of the Anabaptists. It seems that Menno was placed in Groningen, Dirk as bishop in Appingedam, and David Joris in Delft. Further evidence of the break with the revolutionary Anabaptists was Obbe's insistence that he and Dirk did not participate in an attack on the Old Cloister (*Oude Klooster*) near Bolsward in March 1535.

In the meantime, the revolutionary Anabaptists had taken over the city of Münster under the leadership of Jan Matthys. They were besieged by the Catholic bishop, Franz van Waldeck. Jan Matthys was killed in a foray against the bishop's army and his body placed in a basket before the city walls. He was succeeded by Jan Boekholtszoon from Leiden. Under the extreme severity of conditions brought on by the siege, Jan van Leiden introduced communism, polygamy, and harsh treatment of any dissenters. These practices brought scandal on the whole movement for many years to come.

Münster eventually fell to the forces of the bishop. The three leaders who survived were captured, put on public display, and eventually executed, their bodies hung in iron cages from the cathedral tower as an example to others who might consider similar attempts.

Some efforts were made after the fall of Münster to reconstitute the movement. For a time a remnant under Jan van Batenburg continued to use militant tactics, but eventually he was captured and executed, and the revolutionary Anabaptist movement came to an end. The more quietistic, nonresistant Anabaptist movement survived, though not without trials and difficulties of a different sort.

A TRANSFER OF LEADERSHIP

Dirk's activities and location after the fall of Münster are not well known. Aside from his functions as bishop in Appingedam, about the only clear record is a debate he had with a Joachim Kukenbieter (Nossiophagus) in Hamburg in 1537.[22] He probably was active in the general area around Emden. The problem of tracing the activities of all the Dutch Anabaptists during this period is complicated by the fact that they only used initials in their writings and apparently also took other names at times to prevent the authorities from identifying them. They also at times changed their clothing, as suggested by Kukenbieter.[23]

After his capture in 1538, Jan van Batenburg made a confession in which he placed Dirk third on his list of Anabaptist leaders. He put David Joris at the head of the list, above Obbe, who was second, and Dirk next. He apparently did not mention Menno Simons.[24]

In the latter part of the 1530s, Obbe Philips became disillusioned with his baptism and ordination as bishop and left the movement. He apparently took the name of Albrecht and became a spiritualist while feigning membership in the state church at Rostock. In 1560 he wrote a confession which is a primary source for understanding his position and why he left the movement.[25]

With the defection of Obbe from the movement and the disarray following the defeat at Münster, it was not clear if the movement would survive. The work and writing of Menno Simons was the primary factor in the survival and spread of the movement, but the work and writing of Dirk were second only to Menno's.

Dirk probably participated with Menno in the ordination of two new elders, Gillis van Aken and Adam Pastor, in about 1542. The years following were to be ones of differences with Adam Pastor and David Joris over the direction the movement should go.

The next clear trace of Dirk's activities was in a dispute with Nikolaas Meyndertsz van Blesdijk. Nikolaas was at first a follower of Menno but later became convinced that David Joris had a special revelation. This led to a disputation near Lübeck in 1546. Menno Simons, Gillis van Aken, Leenaert Bouwens, and Adam Pastor also participated in it.

The issue was over the form of baptism and the church. David Joris contended that for the sake of avoiding persecution one could let children be baptized and could participate in the services of the Roman Catholic, Lutheran, or Reformed churches while still holding contrary views. Joris assumed that the external forms were of no real consequence since only internal faith mattered. Indeed, he had already gone to Basel in 1544. There he took on a new identity and lived under a cloak of respectability within the Reformed church, while continuing to write and foster his own movement secretly.

During the course of the disputation with Nikolaas, certain other differences between the Anabaptist leaders and Adam Pastor apparently came to the surface. Adam Pastor tended to unitarian views which questioned the divinity of Jesus Christ. As a consequence, a series of debates were held with him. The first was in Emden in 1547 where Menno and Dirk attempted "to blow out the spark" as put by the author of *Successio Anabaptistica*.[26] The issues included the incarnation of Christ, the rejection of infant baptism, and the place of avoidance in marriage. Since no agreement could be reached at the time, the participants agreed not to preach openly on these issues.

A second disputation was held at Emden in 1547. In addition to those Anabaptist leaders present at Lübeck, Hendrik van Vreden, Antonius van Keulen, and Gillis van Aken were present. The question of avoidance of those under the ban was discussed. On November 12, 1556, Menno wrote a letter to the congregation at Emden. It suggests that Menno and Dirk agreed it was best to avoid the banned person, even if the banned person was your spouse. If, however, a person's conscience did not require avoidance, the person was not to be compelled by a legal code.[27]

A second issue was the question of marriage outside the faith (*buitentrouw*). Dirk refers to it in the last of his writings, "About the Marriage of Christians."[28] Published in 1569, it makes reference to a discussion of "more than twenty years ago," which Nicolai guesses was about 1547.[29] The final question was about the incarnation. Adam Pastor was apparently the main opponent of the position taken by Menno and Dirk.

A further disputation was held at Goch in Cleve in the same year. It was by then clear that Adam Pastor denied not only the divinity of Christ but the trinitarian view as well. The conclusion of the debate was the banning of Adam Pastor, with the sentence being announced by Dirk Philips. It is likely that Dirk was at that time acting as the elder or bishop in the area and thus was given responsibility on behalf of the others to pronounce the ban against Pastor.

Adam Pastor continued to preach and attract a following in the area. He no doubt prepared the way in the area for the coming of Socinianism, with its unitarian doctrine, at the end of the century. Dirk Philips wrote a poem or hymn of twenty-two stanzas against the teachings of Adam Pastor.[30] One letter, which was generally unknown until recently rediscovered by ten Doornkaat Koolman, was also written at the request of Dirk's followers to offset the teachings of Adam Pastor.[31]

The conference in Emden and Goch probably led Dirk to write his short treatise on "Confession About Separation."[32] In any event it was written in or before 1549, for Menno refers to it in 1549 in his *A Clear Account of Excommunication.* [33]

Sometime between 1547 and 1553, Menno and Dirk ordained Leenaert Bouwens as an elder, according to a report in *Successio Anabaptistica.*[34] Blaupot ten Cate gives the date as 1551.[35] Others would give a date as late as 1553, about the time Menno Simons wrote a letter to the wife of Leenaert Bouwens to console her in the face of the risks the office of bishop entailed in those times.[36] Ten Doornkaat Koolman believes that Dirk may actually have been the person who ordained Leenaert Bouwens as bishop.[37]

Adam Pastor seemed to feel he was not given an adequate hearing at the meeting in Goch in 1547 where he was banned. Upon his request another discussion was held with him at Lübeck in 1552. Participants included Menno Simons, Dirk Philips, Gillis van Aken, Heinrich Ebbink, and Leenaert Bouwens—all introduced only with initials preceded by B., which probably indicated bishop.[38] The result of the meeting was no more satisfactory than the previous ones since Adam Pastor persisted in his unitarian tendencies.

Another important meeting occurred in 1554 in Wismar, which probably indicates a relocation of Dirk from the area around Goch and Cleve to the northern part of Germany. Menno was living in Wismar at the time as he mentions in a letter to Emden in 1556.[39] Seven leaders were present, including Menno, Dirk, Leenaert Bouwens, and Gillis van Aken. The principal subject was the ban, but other topics included marriage outside the church, the bearing of arms, the use of courts, and problems related to the activities of unauthorized itinerant preachers. Out of the conference emerged a statement of nine articles, though the various reports have some discrepancies which make the exact content of the articles uncertain.[40]

A secret meeting was held in Mecklenburg in 1554. Whether or not it was the meeting where the nine articles were drafted is not certain. The occasion for the meeting was that Gillis van Aken had committed adultery with some of the newly baptized women members. He was banned about the time of the earlier meeting at Lübeck in 1552, and perhaps even at that conference. At the meeting in Mecklenburg, Gillis repented and promised to reform. The leaders restored him to his office.

DIVISIONS INSIDE THE ANABAPTIST MOVEMENT

Divisions had occurred prior to the mid-1550s, but they had largely been in movements outside of the main Dutch Anabaptist movement, such as the Münsterites, the Jorists, and Adam Pastor. In the mid-1550s divisions began which split the movement within groups that retained a similar Anabaptist orientation but differed over some issues, generally of practice rather than theology.

The first major evidence of the subsequent divisiveness occurred in 1555, a year after the conference at Wismar which had established the articles about which differences arose. Leenaert Bouwens had banned the husband of Swaen Rutgers in Emden for unknown reasons. He also insisted that Swaen Rutgers should avoid him. Yet she "would not shun her husband at the bed and table."[41] Leenaert Bouwens proceeded to pronounce the ban upon her, even though otherwise she was a pious woman.

Henrik Naeldeman and Joriaen Heyns of Franeker defended her and were joined by Jacob Jan Scheedemaker of Emden. Menno was called on and replied in a letter to three brothers at Emden on November 12, 1556.[42] He referred to a decision which he and Dirk had arrived at in 1547 and to the articles drawn up at Wismar.

Menno was invited to a conference at Harlingen to try to resolve the matter, probably early in 1557. He traveled by way of Dokkum where Nette Lipkes, a minister, joined him, and also to Leeuwarden where Apollonia Ottes joined them. They went to Franeker for the conference with Naeldeman and Heyns.

They disagreed on three major points: (1) The question of shunning in the family and marriage relationship (*echtmijding*); (2) keeping sins confessed in confidence a secret; and (3) the requirement that the three admonitions of Matthew 18 be omitted in case of heinous or criminal offense and the ban be instituted immediately. Menno conceded on a moderate interpretation of the third. It is reported that when he left the meeting Menno said, "If I also find them in the same way at Harlingen, I will jump for joy upon my crutch."[43]

Menno went on to Harlingen where a meeting was held which included Leenaert Bouwens, and Dirk Philips. Apparently Dirk was in agreement with Leenaert Bouwens and a different spirit from Franeker prevailed. Menno was overruled and the ban was pronounced against Naeldeman, Heyns, and Scheedemaker. According to a report attributed by Alenson to Apollonia Ottes, Menno was intimidated by Bouwens with the threat of the ban and further division.[44] The point of continuing contention was whether avoidance and shunning should be practiced within the family. The official decision favored the stricter position.

In despair over the continuing divisions and ruthless banning, a new and separate group known as the Waterlanders (after the low region where they were located in the province of North Holland) emerged. The Swiss and South Germans also raised questions when the report of the actions reached them. At conferences in Strasbourg in 1555 and 1557, they discussed and acted on questions of the ban, the incarnation, and other issues. As a result a delegation composed of Zylis and Lemke was sent to see Menno in April 1556. Subsequently a meeting of more than fifty bishops at Strasbourg resulted in adopting a more moderate view on the ban, but this did not include the Dutch.[45]

Menno and Dirk both published works on excommunication in 1558 in which they defended a stricter view than the South German conference had accepted. Menno's tract was entitled "Instruction on Excommunication." Dirk's is entitled "The Ban."[46]

It is ten Doornkaat Koolman's view that Dirk and Leenaert Bouwens were sent to meet with Zyles and Lemke at Cologne to try to resolve the issue between the Dutch-North Germans and the South German-Swiss.[47] Apparently the effort was not successful and Dirk and Leenaert proceeded to pronounce the ban on the South Germans and to refuse to recognize their baptism as valid. This probably occurred in 1559. Ten Doornkaat Koolman also speculates that Dirk at the same time wrote his letter to Adriaentgen, the wife of Joachim the Sugarbaker, and sent it to her with elders who attended the meeting in Cologne.[48]

Sometime in the period after 1555, Dirk probably had relocated from Emden to Fresenberg, where Menno was located. There Dirk would have had access to a printer. More of his writings began to appear in print about this time, though some of them had probably earlier circulated in handwritten form. In 1555 a trial of seven people took place in Amsterdam. Among them was a certain Otto Barentszn. from Zutphen who knew Latin. He was not baptized nor had he partaken of communion. He had received a book from the wife of Henrick Janssen. At first he thought Henrick had written the book, but then he heard that Dirk Philips was the author.[49] Thus some indication is given that some of the writings of Dirk had circulated in handwritten form by 1555.

A pamphlet exists with three treatises of Dirk Philips, written in seventeenth-century handwriting. It contains the letter to the brothers about Christ's divinity and incarnation, "Confession of Our Faith (Concerning) God," "Concerning Spiritual Restitution," and "The Congregation of God."[50]

It is likely that, after the meeting at Harlingen in the spring of 1557, Dirk traveled to North Holland where he ordained Jan Willems as elder for the congregation at Hoorn. He may have again traveled to North Holland from Cologne in 1559 and ordained Lubbert Gerrits.

Other writings of Dirk Philips can be dated from this same period. "The Tabernacle of Moses" was printed in 1556. "Confession of Our Faith" appeared in 1557. "The True Knowledge of God" appeared in 1558. In the same year the admonition about "The Ban" was completed on February 5th. "The Sending of Preachers" appeared in 1559. J. ten Doornkaat Koolman believes that "The Incarnation of Our Lord Jesus Christ" and "Concerning the True Knowledge of Jesus Christ" appeared about 1557.[51] "The New Birth and the New Creature" appeared before 1560 since it was opposed by Matthijs Wijer who died on April 25, 1560.[52]

PRUSSIA AND UTRECHT

The area around Danzig in Prussia early became a place of refuge for Anabaptists from Flanders and the Netherlands. The shipping trade to the Hanseatic cities afforded transportation to the area. The rulers were at the time fairly tolerant of diverse opinions and needed industrious workers to make use of the land. The experience of the Dutch with diking and making use of swamp land was useful for settlement and development of the Vistula Delta. Dutch settlers had traveled to the area as early as 1527 to 1530, when the Sacramentarians fled persecution. Jacob van Campen was planning to flee to the area at the time of his capture in Amsterdam in 1535.[53] Vos gives a report from a captured Anabaptist in 1550, in which he says that many of the Melchiorites fled to the area after the revolt in Amsterdam in 1535.[54] The refugees were not allowed to settle inside the city of Danzig but instead located in the "garten" or suburbs.

In the summer of 1549, Menno Simons visited the area according to a letter he addressed to them on October 7, 1549. He wrote:

> To the elect holy children of God in the land of Prussia, grace and peace. You know . . . what grievous solicitude, care, trouble, labor, and sorrow we experienced in your midst this past summer, as well as how it ended; a matter that still at times causes us to be greatly troubled at heart on your behalf, fearing lest the disturber of all peace and Christian love, that is, that ancient coiled serpent which never ceases his raging, might by means of the past transaction once more sow his seed among many, and by means of all that follows, these might fall in God's sight and come to shame and our services of some weeks expended in your behalf be lost again; a thing which even though I write this, I nevertheless hope not.[55]

Menno had apparently settled some discord and possible division among the Anabaptists in Prussia. Mannhardt believes that Dirk Philips and Hans Sikken accompanied Menno on this trip to the Danzig area.[56] It is certain that Dirk was located in Danzig, but the time of his move there is debated. Kühler places the time as early as 1550, but that seems unlikely, given the number of conferences in which Dirk participated in the 1550s.[57] He could not have traveled back and forth from Danzig to the Netherlands that frequently. Mannhardt would place it after Menno's death, which would make it as late as 1561 or later.[58] Again, that may be too late.

The evidence for Dirk's location in Schotland, a suburb of Danzig, is fairly firm. In the church records from Danzig, the following is found:

> The year 1567. Dirk Philips had been an elder here at Danzig, who in the time of division in Friesland was sent there and died there in the following year.[59]

In *The Beginning of the Divisions among the Doopsgezinden*, the author says that Dirk Philips "had also come from Danzig to Emden."[60] J. ten Doornkaat Koolman also finds confirming evidence in the fact that about this time Dirk apparently translated his writings, "Concerning Spiritual Restitution" and "The Congregation of God" from the Dutch into the Lower Saxon dialect. He also cites a report from 1627 that Dirk was in Prussia from 1561-1568.[61]

Dirk's stay in Prussia was not continuous. In 1561 he appears to have traveled to Emden to confer with Leenaert Bouwens, perhaps on the occasion of Menno's death in January of that year. He may have gone on to Friesland by way of Appingedam, where he formerly was an elder and where he met Hoyte Renix in Bolsward. From there he apparently traveled to Hoorn, then baptized Willem Janszen in Waterland.

A court record establishes that Dirk was in Utrecht in late December 1561. He baptized and served communion to the congregation of thirty to forty people gathered in the basement of a fairly well-to-do citizen, Cornelius van Voordt. According to Willems Willemsz, a participant, they gathered about four o'clock in the morning and remained until about seven o'clock in the evening when it was again dark.[62] They hoped thus to escape notice as they gathered and departed.

One report suggests Dirk spoke Brabants, though that might have been because he had been so long in northern Germany and his Dutch was affected. The source was an unlettered household worker, Beatris, who would not be very reliable as an expert on dialects. She also said that he was clothed in black and had an ordinary round hat.[63]

Another witness, Anna Heinrick Emkens described him as "an old man with a gray beard with white hair, a medium built man."[64] This is about as full a description as we have of Dirk Philips. J. ten Doornkaat Koolman guesses that Dirk waited until spring shipping started along the coast again before returning to Danzig.[65]

Dirk probably had the time and security during his stay in Prussia to revise previous writings and put them in publishable form. They appeared in "Handbook" form in 1564 as *Enchiridion* or *Handbook*.[66] It was probably printed in Emden.

THE COVENANT OF THE FOUR CITIES

About 1560 the church councils and ministers of four congregations in Friesland, Franeker, Dokkum, Leeuwarden, and Harlingen, entered into a *Verbond* or covenant. They kept it secret, so the exact details are not fully known. The four congregations agreed to cooperate on programs covered in nineteen articles. Kühler lists the three major areas of agreement.[67]

(1) If a dispute within a congregation could not be settled, the other congregations would assist. If they were unable to settle it, outside ministers would be called to help.

(2) Because of a large influx of refugees from the severe persecutions in Flanders, a financial aid program was carried out by the con gregations. They agreed to cooperate in the program and appointed two deacons to supervise the program in all four cities.

(3) Ministers should serve all four congregations. No congregation would choose its ministers separately. Ebbe Pieters was appointed to divide the preaching assignments in all four congregations and to handle the discipline problems.

In 1565 two events occurred which led to division within the congregations and to Dirk Philips' bitter disappointment over the condition in the congregations. The first involved the choosing of Jeroen Tinnegieter as minister at Franeker. He was a refugee from Flanders, which some took to be the reason why Harlingen objected to his appointment.

In the dispute that followed, a gathering of ministers, including Dirk Philips, was held at Harlingen to try to resolve the matter. In the course of the dispute, the existence of the covenant had come to light. Dirk objected to it because he considered it a human addition to the Scriptures—and Scriptures alone should be the basis for actions in the Christian congregation. Some writers have suggested that Dirk's motives were not entirely pure but arose partly from his fear that Leenaert Bouwens was gaining more authority in the congregations than he.

The second event involved Leenaert Bouwens directly. It occurred as Dirk was on his way from Harlingen back to Prussia. He stopped in Emden where Leenaert was in conflict with his congregation. The main grievances seemed to be that Leenaert was absent too often from the congregation because of trips made to Friesland. He was also accused of drinking excessively. He enjoyed the hospitality of the cordial Flemish in the area; this offended the more stolid Frisians. Leenaert's own severity in cases of the ban, such as the one involving Swaen Rutgers and his wife described earlier may have added to resentment of him.

Seven ministers, including Hoyte Renix, Ebbe Pieters, and Dirk

Philips, sat in judgment on the case. They decided to suspend Leenaert Bouwens as an elder but not ban him. Probably out of fear of banning, Leenaert accepted the judgment and moved to a place near Harlingen. There he was well received, not by the Flemish, but strangely enough by the Frisians.

Ebbe Pieters apparently dissociated himself from the judgment by at least refraining from participating in the decision. Hoyte Renix at first concurred, but later retracted his decision to suspend Leenaert, as appears in a letter he wrote later to Dirk Philips.[68]

The next step in the dispute occurred when Jeroen Tinnegieter called a hasty meeting. With only about thirty out of the three hundred members of the congregation at Franeker present, they rejected the "Covenant of the Four Cities." The majority tried in vain to have that decision reviewed and reversed. Ebbe Pieters emerged as the leader of the Frisians who objected to the decision. The dispute began to harden along cultural and personal lines.

The Flemish people in general cared little about their household appearances but did like to wear fine clothes. They were also more temperamental than the Frisians, being quick to show anger but just as quick to change. The Frisians, on the other hand, cared more about their household appearances and less about clothing. They were also more reserved and slow to anger, but more likely to persist once aroused. These cultural differences contributed to the intensity and polarization of what seemed on the surface just a churchly dispute.

Hoyte Renix attempted to mediate the dispute, but he was suspected by the Flemish of being too favorable toward the Frisians. Ebbe Pieters further heightened the antagonisms when he presented seven accusations against Jeroen Tinnegieter on May 1, 1566. Mutual recriminations and suspensions proceeded. By August 1566, the different groups had mutually banned each other.

Dirk Philips learned about these events. On September 19, 1566, he addressed an "Epistle to Four Cities." To it he added an *Appendix* on the appointment of ministers.[69] The ministers who suspended Leenaert Bouwens in 1565 had drawn up the statement at that time. It also suggests that Dirk believed Leenaert Bouwens was active in the dispute behind the scenes. The letter expresses Dirk's great concern for the congregations and is nostalgic about his regard for the fatherland. Some writers believe that two others whose names are not known, V. B. and J. H., also signed the letter, but the initials are probably an abbreviation of "Your brother in the Lord," (*Uwe broeder inden Heeren*).

The dispute occurred at a time when the Calvinist reform movement, which would eventually surpass the Anabaptists as the major reform group in the Netherlands, was gaining headway. Dirk no doubt felt that the dispute would affect the reputation of the Anabaptist movement and cause persons to defect to the Calvinists. He offered to help resolve the conflict.

Instead of accepting Dirk's offer at that time, the congregations agreed upon an arbitration committee. It was headed by two ministers from Hoorn whom Dirk had ordained earlier. They were Jan Willems and Lubbert Gerrits. They were to choose ten others to collaborate with them. Before they began the task, they required the parties to sign a *Compromis* or commitment which in effect bound them to accept the decision of the committee.

The committee held hearings, then called a meeting to effect the reconciliation. It was held at Harlingen on February 1, 1566. Both parties were required to kneel, to confess their guilt, and to ask forgiveness. The Frisians were then permitted to rise. When the Flemish also began to get up, they were told they must be lifted by the hands of the Frisians because their guilt was greater.

The Flemish were incensed by what they considered a humiliation and thought the committee had tricked them. Furiously they denounced both the *Compromis* and their confession of guilt. The situation was much worse than it had been before. Now it involved the committee, as well as the congregations in the four cities originally parties to the dispute.

The Frisians now felt compelled to call on Dirk Philips to use his office and prestige to bring about a reconciliation. Hoyte Renix wrote a letter of invitation on behalf of the Frisians on April 17, 1567.[70] The tone of the letter was ingratiating but implied that if Dirk did not decide in favor of the Frisians he would not be welcome. Nevertheless, Dirk obtained a commission from his congregation. With two companions, Hans Sikken and a Geert H[arms], he journeyed to Emden to seek a solution to the dispute.

The Frisians probably knew of Dirk's unfavorable opinion of both the covenant and the *Compromis*, since he considered them human additions to the Scripture and therefore not valid. He also considered the two ministers from Hoorn too young and inexperienced to undertake arbitrating the dispute. He suspected them of being too tolerant since they had accepted into the congregation at Hoorn, without waiting for word from Prussia, a man whom the Prussians had banned.

At Emden, Dirk and his two companions sent a request to the

parties involved to appear before him to present their cases. Jan Willems and Lubbert Gerrits sent word that their congregation would not give them permission to be gone again. Dirk responded with letters to Hoyte Renix, Jan Willems, Lubbert Gerrits. He also sent a letter to the congregation at Hoorn which was to be read in all the congregations in North Holland.

Dirk was likely modeling his approach on the tactic Paul used when he wrote to Philemon and the churches in the area about the return of Onesimus. In the letter Dirk suspended the men from their office as ministers until they had appeared before him and were cleared of any guilt. Dirk insisted that the only fair way to deal with the situation was to have the parties appear before him in each other's presence.

The Frisians eventually did send a delegation of nine persons, four from North Holland and five from Friesland, to consult with Dirk. They met with Dirk and the others at Emden, but Dirk insisted that Jan Willems and Lubbert Gerrits be heard in the presence of the Flemish before he would act. He again suspended all the ministers from their office.

In the meantime the ministers of North Holland had met and decided to send a delegation of four, including Jan Willems, Lubbert Gerrits, Hoyte Renix, and Pieter Willems Bogaert. These four met the nine who were returning from Emden. They decided that all thirteen should go to Emden to meet with Dirk.

Dirk was adamant about meeting with them only in the presence of the Flemish and so refused to see them. They in turn refused to concede the point. Kühler believes that Dirk then issued an ultimatum which in effect would ban the entire group, or at least was so interpreted by them. Whether in anticipation of the ban or in retaliation against it, the delegation from Friesland and North Holland met and on July 8, 1567, pronounced the ban upon Dirk Philips. Four days later they announced it to the congregation at Groningen.

The situation was now completely polarized. No further reconciliation was possible. This resulted in some strange alignments of groups. Leenaert Bouwens, who got into trouble with his congregation because of the cordiality he had received from the Flemish, was now allied with the Frisians. Dirk, who represented a strict application of the ban, was now aligned with the more moderate Flemish.

Dirk remained at Emden and apparently was joined by his family, which is the only indication we have that he was married and probably had children (though we know nothing about any of them). He spent his last days at Emden writing and publishing his defense of the actions in the Frisian-Flemish controversy.

Dirk also wrote a final tract "About the Marriage of Christians" in which he continued to struggle with the issue of marriage to persons outside of the Anabaptist congregations. In the preface he does express his feeling of failing strength, "In addition, we are aged [63], weak and ill in the body, and are looking to the Lord for our deliverance that we may enter into the blessed rest."[71]

The treatise was finished on March 7, 1568. Dirk Philips died shortly thereafter at a place called Het Faldern near Emden and was buried in Emden at the Gasthuys Kerck-hof.[72]

DIRK PHILIPS' CHARACTER

Dirk never wrote an autobiographical account as Menno Simons did in his "Conversion, Call, and Testimony."[73] We have to infer much of his character from his activities and his writings. Some accounts from others may also give clues to his character.

Being the younger brother of Obbe and eight years younger than Menno, Dirk probably did not exercise much leadership in the early stages of the Anabaptist movement. He probably stood in the shadow of these older colleagues. He did show a persistence and steadiness that made them value his support and cooperation. Both Obbe and Menno at points indicated their agreement with Dirk and did so in a way which pointed to the value they placed on his collaboration.[74]

In later years, particularly as Menno's health and vitality diminished and especially after his death, Dirk assumed a larger responsibility for the direction of the movement. He did not always do so with the greatest success, which is indicative of other characteristics. Still, we must remember what the late Roland H. Bainton said about his work with Martin Luther: "It is a grave problem to psychoanalyze the dead."

Dirk appears not to have been as warm and outgoing a person as Menno. He was much more a systematic thinker than a person oriented to pastoral concern for people. Only his letter to the wife of Joachim the Sugarbaker shows a warm regard for persons. Otherwise his writings show some detachment and coolness.

As a theologian, Dirk was more a systematic and clear thinker and writer than Menno Simons. His writings are well organized and do not appear as roundabout and tedious as Menno's sometimes do. They do at times become repetitious because of his frequent citing or paraphrasing of Scripture passages.

Dirk's writings show his great command of Scripture. He makes constant reference to Scripture in his writing, either by direct quotation or paraphrase. He also refers in many marginal references to supporting texts. He ranges widely in the Old and New Testaments and includes many citations from the Apocrypha of the Old Testament.

Dirk does not show the tendency to vitriolic condemnation and name-calling of opponents common among other writers of the period. His style contrasts sharply in that respect with Luther and Calvin, and even with Menno Simons. Dirk rarely makes reference to other writers. He does refer to Erasmus, Luther, and earlier classical writers on several occasions, but always to indicate that he is not taking them as a greater authority than the Scriptures.[75]

Though he is obviously refuting some of the writings and thinking of persons such as David Joris and Adam Pastor, Dirk does not refer to them directly, but deals only with their positions. Sebastian Franck is the only adversary whom Dirk directly refutes (in answer to letters of Sebastian Franck long after Franck's death).

Dirk's firmness and tenacity in the face of the opposing forces he faced throughout his adult life seems sometimes to have degenerated into brittleness and inflexibility in dealing with controversy. His pursuit of an ideal church and the demand for moral perfection on the part of others probably contributed to the splits which occurred within the church. This was particularly true from the early 1550s on and in the controversy between the Frisians and the Flemish. Conflict mediation does not seem to have been his primary gift.

Dirk's contribution to his labors and his writings were probably equal to Menno's in bringing into existence and maintaining the Anabaptist movement during the difficult years of struggle and oppression. Some of his writings are still the best expression of the positions which led to the founding and survival of the church. If anything, he has been neglected unduly because he stood in the shadow of Menno, whose writings and labors have been more fully recognized.

DIRK'S THEOLOGY[76]

Dirk's theology tended to have a double focus: one focus was on the words of Scripture and the other on the Word incarnated in Jesus Christ. Because of that double focus, he sometimes had difficulty separating the letter from the spirit of the law. However, he generally resolved any conflicts between the two with a Christocentric interpretation of the Scripture. He gave Christ preeminence in his theological thinking.

A major problem for all the reformers was how to deal with the Old Testament. As noted earlier, Hoffman tried to resolve the problem with the metaphor of the split hoof. The Old Testament was to be fulfilled literally and spiritually. Dirk agreed with Obbe in finding the Old Testament figures and symbols as types to be fulfilled spiritually in the New Testament.

Dirk found support for this view primarily in Hebrews 1 and 10. The preeminence of Jesus Christ came from Hebrews 1 where it recognizes that God spoke in diverse ways in times past through the prophets but now through Jesus Christ. It was further explained by Hebrews 10, where Jesus Christ is seen as the true reality of which the Old Testament types were only shadowy images. In Christ, Dirk believed, one can now more fully understand what the Old Testament types were intending to reveal, though inadequately in comparison with the fuller revelation offered by Christ. He shows great skill in using Old Testament and apocryphal texts, as well as typology, in supporting a given point.

The incarnation became a central concept in Dirk's theology because it was the Word become flesh. Another theological problem which arose early in the Christian church and persisted among the reformers was how Jesus could be truly a person, yet escape original sin. Hoffman resolved the problem by the concept of the "celestial flesh." The Word came down into Mary and was born out of her—but did not partake of her substance. Hoffman used the figure of heavenly dew deposited in an oyster, out of which came a pearl. The pearl did not partake of the nature of the oyster.

Dirk accepted the process though he did not use the crude metaphor from Hoffman. Jesus was conceived in Mary by the Holy Spirit. His nature was not from her, but from the Father. She nurtured him and he was born out of her but did not partake of her nature and so was free of original sin. He was, however, truly human in that he partook of the nature of Adam *before the fall*; he was created a true human being as was Adam. Thus he became the second Adam. At the same time, because his substance was from God and not from Mary, he remained truly divine in a way other human beings could not be.[77]

Because Christ was the second Adam and free from the taint of original sin, he could offer himself for the salvation of other persons. Through his sacrificial death he offered freedom from original sin.

Salvation is in a certain sense the reverse process of the incarnation. Just as Christ became human in Jesus, so human beings could partake of the divine nature in Christ (cf. Irenaeus, d. 202). If they repented and believed, the Holy Spirit could work in them a new creation. They could partake of the nature of Christ and grow in likeness to him through trust and obedience. But because they did not have their substance from God, they could never share fully in the divine nature. They were always subject to sin, even though in principle sin, hell, and death had been overcome through the second Adam, Jesus Christ.

In this conception of salvation, the Anabaptists differed from the other reformers. The other reformers saw salvation as a change in status. Through justification by faith, the person's status was changed from guilty to innocent. This "forensic change" was brought about by God's acceptance of the person. The Anabaptists saw the transformation as a real and continuing change in nature. It was not simply a change in status. For the Anabaptists justification began a dynamic process by which the believer partook of the nature of Christ and so was enabled to live increasingly like Jesus.

The work of the second Adam also resolved the problem of infant baptism. Since the Anabaptists held that the sacraments did not have a magic ability to directly produce change in the person, they had to deal with original sin in infants. Dirk resolved the problem by accepting the work of the second Adam as covering the innocence of infants. While they have original sin, which is the tendency to rebellion against God, it does not become actual sin until they reach the age where they know they rebel and consciously choose to do so. At that point original sin becomes actual sin. Jesus' death on the cross as the second Adam takes care of the innocence of children.

Dirk did not accept that sacraments worked in and of themselves. He understood them to symbolize spiritual realities which occurred in the life of the believer but were invisible. The sacraments, which he preferred to call ordinances, served two functions. They were a manifestation of the readiness of the believer to be obedient to Jesus Christ as Lord. Jesus had commanded that they be done. If the believer was obedient, the Holy Spirit was enabled to create the new nature in the believer.

The ordinances were also needed to make visible to other believers the spiritual reality which was within the believer. Through the visible witness, the believers could recognize one another and be gathered into a fellowship which was the church.

Baptism was the symbol of the death of the old nature and its cleansing by the Holy Spirit. It was the beginning of the new creature or new life in the believer. That was a once-and-for-all experience.

The Lord's Supper was the symbol of the continuing trust and obedience through which the believer grew to the fullness of the maturity of Jesus Christ. That was an ongoing process within the nurturing fellowship of the church. So it was repeated. It was symbolic of the reality that Christ was present in the believer rather than in the signs of bread and wine.

John 6 was an important passage for Dirk. It talked about the process of trusting and obeying by which the spirit of Christ grew in the believer. This was analogous to the physical process of eating and drinking by which the fleshly body grew.

The church was for Dirk the fellowship of "holy beings" (saints). It had a prehistorical beginning, was transferred into history, and would have a posthistorical fulfillment. Dirk tended not to use the term *Kerk* (church) which he applied to the established groups, such as the Roman Catholics, Lutherans, and Calvinists. They had added human traditions and practices to the words of Scripture. They could even be "Churches of Satan" though he recognized the possibility of "Churches of God" existing.

Dirk preferred to use the term *Gemeynte*, best translated as congregation or fellowship. He also referred to certain groups as sects. They were ones which held to heretical views, such groups as led by David Joris, Sebastian Franck, and Adam Pastor.

The congregation or fellowship of saints was established in prehistory in heaven. Because of rebellion, a conflict began between the "Church of Satan" and the fellowship of saints who remained faithful to God. The conflict was transferred to history in the fall of Adam and Eve and the resultant conflict between Cain and Abel. In history, wherever the faithful fellowship of saints arises, its counterpart arises in opposition to it. That explains the absolute separation which exists between the congregation or fellowship of saints and the world.

The congregation will know persecution and martyrdom as it persists in opposition to the world. The world in its disobedience uses the outward or external sword to bring conformity among the disobedient people. The church does not use the external or outward sword but only the internal sword of the spirit, which is the Word of God. The church is not to force persons against their conscience. Neither is it to root out the false prophets with the outward sword. Thus, because the true church is separated from the world, it is not to use worldly methods. In this principle was found a basis for religious liberty.

The congregation is to be made up of saints separated from the world. This concept led to the search for the pure church. The church is in a real sense the extension of the incarnation of Christ, since it is made up of believers who share his divine nature. It does not have the external sword to maintain its purity. It does have the power of the keys to the kingdom, that is the power to forgive sins and also to bind.

Out of this power comes the practice of excommunication, more commonly called banning and shunning. As believers are separated from the world into the congregation of saints, so those nonbelievers need to be returned to the world. They demonstrate by their life and words that they are not ready to be obedient and trusting in Jesus Christ.

There are three reasons to separate persons from the congregation. The original statement gives the reasons in this order: (1) To bring the person to awareness of the person's true condition so that the person may repent and be restored to the fellowship; (2) To protect the fellowship against the infection that would come from having unbelievers in the congregation; (3) To protect the congregation's reputation in the world. The latter became increasingly important after the Münster debacle. As a result, the Anabaptists were charged with being revolutionaries engaging in all kinds of abhorrent practices, such as occurred in Münster and among such groups as the Batenburgers.

As the Anabaptist movement developed, the emphasis was reversed. Protection of the church's reputation came to be placed first and redemption of the person third. That occurred in part because of the rapid growth in popularity of the Calvinist movement, which became the ascendant Protestant group in the Netherlands after 1560. The reversal of priorities led to the use of the ban for punishment rather than redemption. This shift helps explain the schisms which arose in the 1550s and later within the Anabaptist movement in the Netherlands as well as northern Germany.

Dirk had an apocalyptic view of history. Because of the absolute opposition between the church and the world, persecution and martyrdom were to be expected. Dirk was convinced that the persecution the Anabaptists experienced from the beginning was an indication that the church was living in the last and fearful time. At some point the church would be fulfilled by the intervention of God. God would establish the New Jerusalem, the kingdom of heaven. Dirk did not try to establish any timetables or schedules for this to happen. The Melchiorite and Münsterite attempts to do so had led to disasters and taught Dirk to avoid anticipating God's timetable.

Until the fulfillment of history, the believers are to expect persecution. Martyrdom then becomes a seal of faith to be accepted with thanksgiving. Only those enabled by the Holy Spirit and worthy to undergo martyrdom will be subject to it. It is not something to be sought, but when it comes can be accepted with rejoicing.

This understanding of the meaning of martyrdom gave Dirk and others the endurance to persist and remain faithful despite the daily dangers which they faced. They could live victorious lives even in the midst of such terrible times.

ENDNOTES

1. The date of birth seems to be traced back to a note of Gerard Maatschoen in a translation of Hermannus Schyn, *Uitvoeriger Verhandlung van de Geschiedenis der Mennoniten.* Vol. II, Amsterdam: 1744, p. 387, n. 4. Koolman also cites the date on an early portrait of Dirk Philips with the description of Dirk as "geboren te Leewaerden in Frieslant 1504" and indicates that the painter lived in the beginning of the 17th century according to a note in DB, 1890, p. 69f. Koolman, *Dirk Philips.*, p. 5, n. 1.

There are a variety of spellings for Dirk Philips. The abbreviation of Philipszoon to Philipsz. was common for "zoon"—son of Philips in this case—was common throughout the Netherlands during his time and later, but has become less frequent. For the various spelling forms see Keeney, "Dirk Philips' Life," MQR 32 (1958), 171, n. 1.

2. Georg Cassander, *Opera ovae Reperiri Potvervnt Omnia,* p. 671-72, says, "After the death of this Menno, Dirk Philips, a brother of Obbe, undertook [his] task with no less zeal and with an equal popular eloquence, but with greater learning and knowledge of letters, which some books written by him of late years declare."

Dirk's writings reflect his knowledge of classical languages. In the *Enchiridion* he inserts a parenthetic explanation of "the Word" as *Logos* in Greek and *Sermo* or *Verbum* in Latin, BRN X, p. 138. In another place he paraphrases 1 Tim. 1:5 in Dutch and quotes the Latin, BRN X, p. 558. He also quotes from Isa. 30:15 (cited as Isa. 18) from the Latin, BRN X, p. 593. In the same writing, he quotes Latin proverbs and a Latin poet Horace from *Arte Poetica,* BRN X, pp. 606ff. Finally, he quotes Zech. 11:17 in an abbreviated Latin, BRN X, p. 611. In addition to the Greek *Logos* referred to earlier, he also uses *Paracletus* in referring to the Holy Spirit, BRN X, p. 63. Dirk also made use of three Hebrew terms: *Schadae* and *Sebaoth* in the same paragraph, BRN X, p. 60 and *tetragrammaton* for the name of God written but not pronounced, BRN X, p. 160.

3. A letter of Joachim Kukenbieter (Nossiophagus) to "Herrn Gerdt" (Gerhard Herbordingk) reprinted in *Zeitschrift für Kirchengeschichte,* Vol. VI (1844) p. 502, with accompanying comments by Albrecht Ritschl under the title "Wiedertäufer und Franziskaner," p. 499ff.

4. Kühler, *Geschiedenis* I, p. 96.

5. Ibid., p. 48.

6. Mellink, *De Wederdopers in de Noordelijke Nederlanden, 1531-1544,* 1953, p. 6, 7.

7. Cornelius, *Geschichte des Münsterischen Aufruhrs,* Vol. 1, 1855, p. 16.

8. The view which Zwingli at least found supportive of his own symbolic interpretation of the Lord's Supper has been traced back to Wessel Gansfort of the Brethren of the Common Life, then transmitted to Zwingli through Cornelis Hoen and Hinne Rode. See, for example, Edward Waite Miller, *Wessel Gansfort (Life and Writings), principal works,* tr. Jared Waterbury Scudder. New York: G. P. Putnam's Sons, 1917, pp. 144f., 10f., 187-202. See for possible influence of Hoen on Dirk, Koolman, *Dirk Philips,* p. 78 and n. 170-171.

9. See account of her martyrdom in *Het Offer des Heeren,* BRN II, ed. by Samuel Cramer, 1904, pp. 422-429. Cf: *Martyrs Mirror,* pp. 422ff.

10. Ibid., p. 423.

11. Op. cit., p. 42.

12. Blaupot ten Cate, *Geschiedenis der Doopsgezinden in Holland, Zeeland, Utrecht en Gelderland,* 1847, p. 41.

13. For a summary of the life of Melchior Hoffman, see the article by Christian Neff in ME 2:778b-785a. For an analysis of his thought, see Kawerau, *Melchior Hoffman*; Deppermann, *Melchior Hoffman.*

14. *Spiritual and Anabaptist Writers,* edited by George H. Williams and Angel M. Mergal, Vol. XXV, The Library of Christian Classics. Philadelphia: The Westminster Press, 1957., pp. 182-203.

Dirk Philips: A Biography / 45

15. For an account of Sicke Freerks' martyrdom, see Thieleman J. van Braght, *Martyrs Mirror*, p. 441Bf. For Menno Simons' reference to him and his influence on causing him to search the issue of baptism, see CWMS p. 668. For more information on Sicke Frerichs or Freerks, see the article by K. Vos, "Sicke Freerks" in ME 4:523.
16. See the "Confession" of Obbe Philips, BRN VII, p. 129. Cf: Williams, op. cit., pp. 204-227.
17. Ibid., p. 130. See also, Mellink, op. cit. p. 243.
18. Cornelius, op. cit., p. 409f.; Mellink, op. cit., p. 196f.
19. Mellink, op. cit., p. 118f. and 245.
20. For locations where Dirk deals with the problem, see the following pages, in BRN X, pp. 96f., 109, 208f. 342, 449. For a fuller discussion of Menno and Dirk's understanding of the relationship of the Old Testament to the New Testament, see Keeney, *Dutch Anabaptist Thought*, pp. 35-39.
21. BRN VII, p. 461. This seems to be the only extant indication that Obbe Philips baptized Menno.
22. See footnote 3 above.
23. Ibid.
24. Hullu, *Bescheiden betreffende de Hervorming in Overijssel*, Vol. I (Deventer 1522-1545.), p. 252.
25. See BRN VII, pp. 89-138. Cf: Williams, op. cit., pp. 204-227.
26. V. P. [Simon Walrave?] a non-Anabaptist, BRN VII, p. 50.
27. See Koolman, op. cit., p. 35, n. 27.
28. *Van die Echt der Chritenen*. BRN X, pp. 623-649.
29. Ibid., p. 48, based on *Gerardus Nicolai's Inlasschingen [insertions] in het vertaalde werk van Bullinger: "Tegen de Wederdoopers."* BRN VII, p. 442.
30. See below pp. 638-642, also BRN X, pp. 693-697.
31. See below pp. 631-634, translated from *Nederlands Archief voor Kerkgeschiedenis*, Nieuwe Serie, Vol. XLIII, 1959, pp. 15-21, where the letter is reprinted with an introduction by Koolman.
32. *Bekentenisse van der afsonderinghe*. Koolman, pp. 193-199.
33. *Klaar bericht van der Excommunicatie*. See CWMS, p. 480; *Opera Omnia*, fol. 475B, where Menno says, "Therefore I say with our faithful brother, Dirk Philips, that we should not use the ban to the destruction of mankind as the Pharisees did their Sabbath, but to its improvement. . . ."
34. BRN VII, p. 51. The ordination probably took place prior to 1553 since Menno then wrote a letter to Leenaert Bouwen's wife to allay her fears when he was ordained as an elder. For the letter, see CWMS, pp. 1038-1040; *Opera Omnia*, fol. 455A-456B.
35. Blaupot ten Cate, *Geschiedenis der Doopsgezinden in Friesland*, Leeuwarden, p. 60; *Geschiedenis der Doopsgezinden in Groningen, Overijssel en Oost-Friesland*. Vol. I, p. 21.
36. See CWMS, pp. 1038-1040.
37. See Koolman, *Dirk Philips*, p. 53 and n. 10.
38. Ibid., p. 54.
39. CWMS, p. 1050; BRN VII, p. 448.
40. BRN VII, pp. 52-53
41. "Dese vrou wilden haren man in t' bedde ende de tafel niet myden." BRN VII, p. 54.
42. CWMS, p. 1043; BRN VII, pp. 444-447.
43. BRN VII, p. 258. Apparently Menno was a cripple as a result of an accident or illness about 1545-50 since he occasionally signed his letters as "the cripple" after that date. See CWMS, pp. 1045, 1051, 1056. See also, p. 919.
44. BRN VII, p. 258f. The report is of fairly late date and so is suspect. See Krahn, *Menno Simons (1496-1561)*, p. 92f. for discussion of the issue.
45. See Oyer, "The Strasbourg Conferences of the Anabaptists, 1554-1607,"

MQR 58 (1984), 218-229. Also Blaupot ten Cate, *Geschiedenis der Doopsgezinden in Groningen, Overijssel en Oost-Friesland,* Vol. I, Appendix III, p. 251ff., for fuller accounts and conclusion reached at these conferences. See also, Brons, *Ursprung,* pp. 93-99.

46. For Menno's see CWMS, pp. 959-998. For Dirk's see pp. 238ff. below, and *Lieffelijcke vermaninghe wt des Heeren Wordt.* BRN X, pp. 249-265.

47. Koolman, *Dirk Philips,* p. 102.

48. Ibid., p. 103. See also below, pp. 618ff.

49. See Ibid., p. 63, citing testimony given in Grosheide, *Bijdrage tot de Geschiedenis der Anabaptisten in Amsterdam,* p. 173f.

50. *Bekentenisse unses gelouwens, Vande geestelijcke Restitution,* and *Vande Gemeynte Godts.* Koolman, *Dirk Philips,* p. 64.

51. *Uitlegginghe des Tabernakels ofte der Hutten Moysi, Bekenntenisse onses gheloofs, Van de warachtige Kennisse Gods, Lieffelijcke vermaninghe . . . van den ban, Van der Sendinge der Predicanten oft Leeraers, Van der Menschwerdinghe ons Heeren Jesu Christi, Vande rechte kennisse Jseu Christi.*

52. *Van der wedergeboorte ende nieuwe Creatuere.* "Vorders soo is ook *Dirck Philipsz.* van Dantsick tot Embden gekomen." BRN VII, p. 542.

53. Mellink, op. cit., p. 395.

54. Vos, "Kleine bijdragen Over de Doopersch bewegen in Nederland tot het optreden van Menno Simons," DB, vol. 54 (1917), p. 137.

55. CWMS, p. 1030. See the article "Danzig, Free City of," in ME 2:7-8.

56. Mannhardt, *Die Danziger Mennonitengemeinde,* p. 25.

57. Kühler, op. cit., p. 310.

58. Mannhardt, op. cit., p. 42.

59. "Anno 1567. Is hier te Dantzig oudsten gewest Dirk Philipsen die in den Scheuringstijt van Vriesland gesonden en aldaar het volgende Jaar 1568 overleden." In the *Danzig Mennonite Church Record,* starting with the year 1567. The quotation is found at the end of a list of ministers who had served the church. The original is now in Bethel College Historical Library, North Newton, Kansas.

60. "Vorders soo is ook *Dirck Philipsz.* van Dantsick tot Embden gekomen." I. H. V. P. N. (Carel van Ghendt), *Het beginsel en voortganck der geschillen . . .* BRN VII, p. 542.

61. *Vande geestelijcke Restitution* and *Vande Gemeynte Godts.* Koolman, *Dirk Philips,* p. 118.

62. See reprints of abstracts from "Verhooren van verschillende getuigen en andere stukken betreffende het process voor het Hof van Utrecht van den Procureurgeneraal tegen CORNELIUS VAN VOORDT en zijn huisvrouw wegens herdooperij, 1562." Found in Cramer, "De Doopsgezinde gemeente te Utrecht van 1560 te 1562, uit onuitgegeven becheiden." DB, 1903, pp. 1-47.

63. Ibid., p. 39.

64. Ibid., pp. 22-42.

65. Koolman, *Dirk Philips,* p. 121.

66. *Enchiridion Oft Hantboecxken van de Christelijcke Leere ende Religion.* BRN X, pp. 55ff.

67. Kühler, op. cit., pp. 397-98.

68. See pp. 534 below, also BRN X, p. 602ff.

69. See pp. 524ff. below, Cf: *Sendtbrief . . . aen de vier St.* (1567), in BRN X, p. 517-34

70. See pp. 544ff. below. BRN VII, pp. 462, 543f.

71. See pp. 554 in this volume. Cf: *Van de Echt der Christenen.* BRN X, p. 627. The "we" is an editorial usage to refer to the writer.

72. BRN VII, pp. 462, 543f. The date of 1570 given by Scheffer in "Het Verbond der Vier Steden," DB, 1893, p. 75, n. 5, for the death of Dirk Philips is in error, as is Hermannus Schyn, *Uitvoeriger Verhandlung van de Geschiedenis der Mennoniten . . .,* 2

vols., tr. and annotated by Gerardus Maatschoen. p. 387, n. 4, but the latter does recognize that 1568 is a possible date of death.

73. See CWMS, pp. 668-76; *Opera Omnia*, fol. 256A-260B.

74. For Obbe's statement, see BRN VII, p. 135. For Menno, see the CWMS, pp. 761, 1050, 1060.

75. See pp. 85, 101 which follow. Cf: BRN X, p. 100.

76. For elaboration of the theology of the Dutch Anabaptists derived largely from Menno Simons and Dirk Philips' writings, see Keeney, *Dutch Anabaptist Thought*, where the topics dealt with below are discussed more extensively. It would be easy to identify Dirk's positions from the citations given.

77. For a detailed discussion of the precise theological formula which Dirk Philips always used and the grammatical and historical basis for the distinctions made to give a very careful formulation to the doctrine of the incarnation, see Keeney, *Dutch Anabaptist Thought*, pp. 80-100 and Appendix II. See also Voolstra, *Het Woord is Vlees Geworden*.

Part A

ENCHIRIDION OR HANDBOOK OF CHRISTIAN DOCTRINE AND RELIGION

Prepared in Short Summary from Holy Scripture
For All Who Love the Truth
Now Newly Corrected and Enlarged
By D. P. in the Year of Our Lord 1564
1 Thessalonians 5:19

THE ENCHIRIDION OR HANDBOOK

Editors' Introduction

Dirk did not originally set out to write an *Enchiridion* or Handbook. Instead, over the years he responded to various needs of the congregations and wrote to particular situations. After the death of Menno Simons in 1561, and with growing dissension within the movement as well as threat from outside, Dirk compiled and edited into a handbook the various pieces he had written earlier. He did not put the various writings in chronological order, but organized them according to a systematic approach to the Christian faith.

There is some disagreement as to whether Dirk published an earlier edition of the *Enchiridion* and revised it for its definitive publication in 1564. M. Schagen reports an edition of 1544 and Blaupot ten Cate cited two early publications of 1544 and 1562.[1] These reports are probably in error. It is true that Dirk says on the title page of the *Enchiridion* of 1564 that it is now newly corrected and enlarged.[2]

Apparently an unauthorized edition appeared earlier in 1564. M. Keyser lists that edition and says, "This first (unauthorized) edition of the *Enchiridion* was not printed by Willem Gailliart at Emden, but may have been produced by a press in the eastern area of the Netherlands (Steenwijk? Kampen?)."[3] Dirk was probably unhappy with this edition because it included ornamental woodcuts he felt were inappropriate. It also contained numerous printing errors and Germanisms, and the order in which the various articles were printed was arbitrary or random.[4] Ten Doornkaat Koolman found two copies of the first edition, one in the University Library at Amsterdam and another in the Zentralbibliothek at Zurich.[5]

The first section of the book was apparently first printed in 1557. It is sometimes referred to as *'t Geloofsboek* or "The Faith Book."[6] It contained "Confession of Our Faith," "Confession . . . about Creation," "About the Baptism," and "About the Supper." It is quite possible that the treatises about baptism and the Lord's Supper circulated earlier and separately in handwritten form.

J. ten Doornkaat Koolman demonstrates that Thomas von Imbroich, who was martyred at Cologne on March 5, 1558, used the confession about baptism. He wrote a statement of his beliefs to submit to the authorities. After an introduction in which he maintains that the Anabaptists were not revolutionaries and did not intend to take over the government once they were powerful enough, he writes a "Confession." This follows Dirk Philips' arguments almost word for word, with occasional summaries in Thomas' own words.[7] It seems Thomas either had a handwritten copy of the treatise about baptism or possibly could have had the newly published edition of "The Faith Book."[8]

If J. ten Doornkaat Koolman is correct in assuming that Dirk referred to a citation from Luther on Menno's "Confession of the Distressed Christians," then Dirk must have composed the treatise between 1552 and 1557.[9] The other citation is taken directly from Sebastian Franck's *Chronicle*.[10] Other Anabaptist and related writers used Franck's work as an encyclopedia and cited information from it.

If the treatise about baptism was circulated first in handwritten form, then it is likely that the additional confessions were added for the printing in 1557. The first two articles summarized very briefly the orthodox views on the trinity, perhaps in opposition to Adam Pastor and his followers. They also treated creation, deliverance, and salvation.

The next two treatises in the *Enchiridion* may have been written at least in part as a response to the conflict with Adam Pastor and his followers and their tendency to unitarian views. The two treatises were published together, probably about 1557, with the same cover and with the numbering of the signatures following in sequence.[11]

The first of the two, "The Incarnation of Our Lord Jesus Christ," is one of the most controversial topics about which Menno and Dirk wrote. They subscribed to a view held by Melchior Hoffman that accepted the most prevalent view concerning heredity held in the sixteenth century. It was, however, being challenged by a newer understanding which became the accepted view.

The older view held that the traits of the child are transmitted only through the male seed. The mother's role was completely passive. Therefore, Jesus would have received his nature entirely from the Holy Spirit's impregnating of Mary and nothing from her nature. Thus Jesus was born as the first Adam without the taint of original sin.¹² It was this theological concern which prompted Menno and Dirk's interest in the incarnation and led to their somewhat peculiar view. Their understanding was based on wrong biological suppositions but took a theological position which, while not the most common in Christian history, was not unknown in earlier writers.

"Concerning the True Knowledge of Jesus Christ" was published with the previously described treatise with one cover.¹³ Thus it would also have been published about 1557. The previous treatise dealt mainly with the issue of how God could become a human being. This treatise deals more with the humanity of Jesus.

"An Apology or Reply" is dated quite early by Pijper. He would place it as early as 1545 and finds it written against the influence of Sebastian Franck.¹⁴ J. ten Doornkaat Koolman would place it as late as 1562. This is because he finds it citing Dirk's treatise "The Congregation of God" which did not appear until 1559, and because it reflects a time of renewed persecution which had as a consequence the apostasy of many from the fellowship of the Anabaptists.¹⁵ M. Keyser places it around 1560, apparently accepting the later dating of J. ten Doornkaat Koolman.¹⁶

"The Sending of Preachers" was published in 1559.¹⁷ The issue of the ordination of pastors or ministers was a difficult one for the Anabaptists. They rejected the Roman Catholic claim that ordination is by tactical transmission of the commission given to Peter in Matthew 16:18. They also did not find the life of the ministers of the other reformed churches according with obedience to Christ. So the Anabaptists added the requirement of an ethical or practical evidence of discipleship to the test of proper calling.

Another problem arose from the self-proclaimed ministers. In response the congregations declared the requirement that the calling sensed by the minister must be confirmed by a true congregation of believers. An opposite problem was Obbe Philips, brother of Dirk. He left the movement in part because he felt his ordination and call to be an elder was not given by truly authorized agents—that is, the followers of Melchior Hoffman and Jan van Haarlem. Dirk felt the double call to the individual, confirmed by the true congregation of believers, safeguarded and confirmed his and other Anabaptists' calling and appointment to offices in the Anabaptist movement. He stressed the importance of accountability.

"The Ban" is dated February 5, 1558. It is not the first writing on this topic by Dirk. See, for example, his "Confession About Separation," pages (611-617) which was written earlier. It maintains the same fairly strict position both on the ban and the avoidance of persons who are banned.[18]

"The True Knowledge of God" was also published in 1558.[19] The main emphasis of the treatise seems to be to remember the forgiveness which God has granted and to live faithfully and purely according to God's word.

"The Tabernacle of Moses" was one of Dirk's first writings to appear in print.[20] It was published in 1556 when he first had safety and leisure to write, as well as a publisher who would print his works. J. ten Doornkaat Koolman differs from the writers who contend that this treatise was written as an apologetic against Bernhard Rothmann's *Eyne restitution* and *Van verborgenheyt der schrifft des rykes Christi*.[21] Koolman recognizes that Dirk would have known Rothmann's writings and position. However, Dirk's treatment of the difference between the holy of the tabernacle and the holy of holies, and between Jacob and Esau is not in contention with Rothmann. Rather Dirk reflects the position of Melchior Hoffman, who was a predecessor of Rothmann.[22] Some of the interpretations of images are also directed against David Joris and his followers, especially in the latter part of the treatise.[23]

"The New Birth and the New Creature" is disputed as to its date. Pijper would put it fairly early, in connection with the publication of the treatise on the tabernacle, which would place it about 1556.[24] J. ten Doornkaat Koolman would place it later, largely on the internal evidence that it deals with foot washing. He believes that the issue did not arise as early as 1556. Nevertheless, he places it no later than 1560, since it was disputed by Matthijs Wijer who died on April 25, 1560.[25]

In the treatise Dirk is contending primarily against those who would find the experience of salvation primarily an inner experience. He rejects either a sacramental forgiveness or a pietistic experience without any outward evidence of a changed life. While salvation is by grace and not by works, something new is created in the experience which must manifest itself in a transformed life.

Two other treatises were closely allied in their composition and publication. They are "Concerning Spiritual Restitution" and "The Congregation of God."[26] At least the latter must have been written after the treatise about the sending of preachers, because it seems to have a quotation from that treatise. Since that treatise was published in 1559, the treatise about the church must be later. They are both generally placed at about 1560 to 1562. The spiritual restitution treatise seems to be directed against Bernhard Rothmann's *Restitution rechter und gesunder christlicher Lehre*.[27]

"Three Admonitions" are the final selections in the *Enchiridion*.[28] They are apparently of fairly late composition. They do not appear in the first, unauthorized edition of the *Enchiridion*. They appear only as an appendix in the second edition of 1564. No separate publication of them seems to exist. J. ten Doornkaat Koolman believes that the letters were not written in the order in which they appear in the *Enchiridion*, but that numbers two and three should be reversed.[29]

Koolman believes the first of the letters was probably directed to a congregation in Friesland, for it speaks of renewed persecution and reflects the danger of influence from the teachings of David Joris and the need to exercise discipline in the congregation. The emphasis upon freedom may be in response to the teachings of David Joris and his followers. Some doubt is raised by the caution about godless preachers, though it might be possible that some members were seeking to escape notice as Anabaptists by attending services of the Roman Catholics or the increasingly popular Reformed movement.

What is placed as the third letter, ten Doornkaat Koolman thinks is the second, for it seems to be shortly after Dirk has visited the congregation and made his farewell with it. He rejoices in the steadfastness and unity within the congregation, though after his departure he had heard of the outbreak of new persecutions. Ten Doornkaat Koolman suspects the congregation might be Harlingen. (Dirk does make reference in what is given as the second letter—which ten Doornkaat Koolman believes to be the third letter—to a previous letter written to H. which most likely would be Harlingen but could also be Holland. If ten Doornkaat Koolman is correct, this would be the letter written to H.). The letter was perhaps written from Emden while Dirk was on his way to Danzig.[30] The emphasis in the letter on the covenant may be a consequence of his concern about the "Covenant of the Four Cities," which was to play such a prominent role in the coming dispute and division between the Frisians and the Flemish.

The third letter, actually the second letter in the order in the *Enchiridion*, is a very personal letter. It shows Dirk's deep concern for the congregations, probably in Friesland. According to ten Doornkaat Koolman, it was likely directed to Franeker after his return to Danzig. If so, it was later than the two other letters included in the collection. The letter shows Dirk's feelings of anxiety for the situation in the congregations as he feels both external pressures from renewed persecution and internal pressures from the conflicts and threatening divisions.

The conditions which gave rise to the three letters or admonitions may also have caused Dirk to put together his previous writings in the form of an *Enchiridion,* or *Handbook of the Christian Religion.* He felt the need for strengthening the congregations through a systematic presentation of his understanding of the Christian faith.

J. ten Doornkaat Koolman thinks Dirk may have commissioned Leenaert Bouwens to have the writings published at Emden, which resulted in the first edition but which Dirk found unsatisfactory. When Dirk came to Emden in 1565 and discovered the first edition, he proceeded to revise, expand, and issue a second edition, still carrying the date of 1564. He probably made an attempt to have all the copies of the first edition destroyed because of its unsatisfactory nature.[31]

ENDNOTES

1. Schagen, *Naamlijst*, p. 78; Blaupot ten Cate, *Geschiedenis*, I, p. 246.
2. Keyser, p. 41, where the expression "nu nieuws ge//corrigeert ende // vermeerdert // Door D. P." appears in a reproduction of the title. This is the edition used in the translation of the *Enchiridion* (Part I) in this volume, also having available the IDC microfiche copy and copies of later editions. However, because of its general reliability, and for the sake of convenience, Volume X of the BRN was used as the working text. The pagination / / included in the text to facilitate locating a given passage is based on BRN X. The editors have also used the annotations and introductions of BRN X, as prepared by Frederik Pijper, extensively.
3. Ibid., p. 37.
4. Koolman article in MQR, XXXVIII, (1964), and sample of woodcut in Keyser, p. 38, from the early (unauthorized) edition contrasted with a title page from the second (authorized) edition on p. 50.
5. Koolman, p. 63. For details of the two publications, see Keyser, pp. 37-43.
6. See Koolman, p. 65. The publication is listed in BRN X, p. 25f., n. 4.
7. Koolman, p. 74.
8. Ibid., p. 75.
9. Ibid., For Menno Simons' quotation, see CWMS, p. 514, *Opera Omnia*, p. 468A.
10. Koolman, p. 75.
11. See BRN X, p. 27. Also p. 26f., footnote 4. See also, Keyser, pp. 85-87.
12. For fuller discussion of the topic of incarnation, see Keeney, *Dutch Anabaptist Thought*, pp. 89-113 and 207-221. See also Voolstra, *Het woord is vlees geworden*.
13. See BRN X, p. 27, n. 1. A copy is found in the University Library of Amsterdam in the special collection of the Mennonite Church of Amsterdam. See also, Keyser, p. 85.
14. BRN X, p. 15. He gives the details concerning its publication in n. 4. A copy is found in the University Library of Amsterdam in the special collection of the Mennonite Church of Amsterdam.
15. *Dirk Philips*, p. 64
16. Koolman, p. 105.
17. See BRN X, p. 32. The details of publication are given in n. 5. A copy is found in the University Library of Amsterdam in he special collection of the Mennonite Church of Amsterdam. See Keyser, p. 95f.
18. See BRN X, p. 30f. Details of the publication are given on p. 30, n. 4. A copy is found in the University Library of Amsterdam in the special collection of the Mennonite Church of Amsterdam. See also, Keyser, p. 92f.
19. See BRN X, p. 32. For details of publication, see the same page, n. 3. A copy is found in the University Library of Amsterdam in the special collection of the Mennonite Church of Amsterdam. See also, Keyser, p. 88f.
20. BRN X, p. 17, n. 3. A copy is found in the University Library of Amsterdam in the special collection of the Mennonite Church of Amsterdam. See also, Keyser, p. 76f. For a discussion of Dirk's use of allegory, see also Beachy, *The Concept of Grace*. pp. 142ff.
21. See Koolman, p. 66, and n. 58.
22. Ibid., p. 68, esp. n. 76, where he says, "Obbe Philips: Hoffman has begun to exposit the Tabernacle of Moses. BRN VII, p. 123. For fragments, see Kawerau, no. 50, 55, 71; further an illustration, p. 68 and pieces from 'Der Leuchter,' p. 124f. See also Deppermann, *Melchior Hoffman*.
23. See Koolman, p. 69ff.
24. BRN X, p. 19. For details of publication, see the same, n. 2. A copy is found in the University Library of Amsterdam in the special collection of the Mennonite Church of Amsterdam.

25. Koolman, p. 64.

26. For details of publication of the treatise on spiritual restitution, BRN X, p. 10, n. 7. A copy is found in the library of the University of Amsterdam in the special collection of the Mennonite Church of Amsterdam. See also Keyser, pp. 99-103.

27. See BRN X, p. 10. Note 1 gives the location of a reprint of Rothmann's booklet in the *Neudrucke deutscher Literatur werke, Flugschriften aus der Reformationszeit.* VII, Halle a./S., 1888. The importance of Rothmann for Reformation thought has led to numerous publications about him. A critical edition of his writings has been published by Stupperich, *Die Schriften Bernhard Rothmanns*.

28. See BRN X, p. 33, n. 7. They were known to the editors and translators of BRN X only out of their printing in the second edition of the *Enchiridion* of 1564.

29. Koolman, p. 121f.

30. Ibid., p. 122.

31. Ibid., p. 124ff.

Foreword /57/

Since many persons out of good and Christian intention rightly desire to know what we believe, but many out of bitterness and some out of frivolity mock and ridicule our faith, and yet know basically nothing about what we believe, but speak about it as the blind about colors; therefore, we wish with the grace of God, according to the teaching of Peter, 1 Pet. 3:15, to give a brief and simple account of our faith, of our salvation, from whence it comes, about baptism, and the Supper of our Lord Jesus Christ, what we (according to the gift and measure of the Spirit given to us from God) believe about such issues, Rom. 12:6.

But we desire, through the mercy of God and the love of Jesus Christ, that every person who claims the Christian faith and the gospel will read this our confession impartially and measure and judge it with Holy Scripture as the only true guiding principle, remembering the words of the apostle who said, "And the Lord's servant must not be quarrelsome but fatherly to everyone, an apt teacher, endure evil patiently, correcting his opponents with gentleness. God may perhaps grant that they will repent and come to confess the truth, and escape from the snare of the devil, after being captured by him according to his will," 2 Tim. 2:24[-26].

Oh, that everyone who holds himself to be a Christian, especially one who claims to be a preacher of the divine Word, were minded to have such an apostolic spirit, such a Christlike manner, and showed such patience toward his opponents. Then Christianity should fare better than it does now.

But now criticism, blasphemy, judgment, and damnation without measure has no end. The whole world bellows and rumors against us in particular, calls us Anabaptists or rebaptizers or fanatics and heretics, and can better endure the destructive and deadly works of the flesh than our faith./58/ All this we surrender and commend to God and his judgment. People may blaspheme us as they will, but the almighty God, who knows the hearts and searches the minds, [Jer. 17:10], before whom we must also give an account of our faith and conduct, knows that we do not desire nor seek anything other than the honor of God and the salvation of our souls through the grace of

Jesus Christ, who is the Savior of all believers, Acts 4:12; 1 Tim. 2:6. And then some [persons] nevertheless say that we wish to earn our salvation through our own good works, which is as far from our faith as heaven is from earth. For we believe and confess that we are saved through the grace of Christ and have forgiveness of sins alone through his blood, Rom. 11:6.

And even if we were such people, which we by the grace of God are not, though we fail without our knowledge through human stupidity and weakness, then it would be right for every Christian to have compassion on us and pray to the Lord for us. Also to remember that Paul carried great sorrow and anguish in his heart, and had desired to be banished from Christ for his brothers and kinsmen after the flesh, who were zealous for God but with ignorance and did not believe in Jesus Christ. So also Moses had prayed so faithfully for the Israelites, yes, he would rather that God should blot his name out of the book of life than that God, according to his resolve, should punish the children of Israel so severely and entirely destroy them, Exod. 32:11 [-14]; [31-32]; Rom. 9:3.

Now we certainly believe in Jesus Christ and with all our ability place our hope in his grace, John 3:15; 1 Pet. 1:13. So we also have not made nor erected nor worshiped any golden calf, but honor the only true living God of heaven and earth and serve his Son, Jesus Christ, and know of no idol. Therefore, may every Christian always show such patience toward us as Paul showed toward the unbelieving Jews and Moses toward the idolatrous and backslidden Israelites, Exod. 32:4; 1 Thess. 1:10; Acts 17:24; 1 Cor. 8:5.

Above all that Jesus Christ is the genuine and express example of love and patience, Matt. 11:29; 1 Pet. 2:[20-21], set before all believers from God the Father, who has taught us by words and deeds that we should show love and compassion to all persons and judge no one unjustly, Matt. 5:44; Luke 6:29; Matt. 7:1. Therefore, the apostle says, "There is one lawgiver who is able to save and to condemn. Who are you that you should judge another?" James 4:12; Matt. 7:1; Rom. 14:4; [James 2:12]. "An unmerciful judgment shall be passed upon those /59/ who have shown no mercy. And mercy triumphs over judgment," James 2:13.

So we wish now, through the suffering of Jesus Christ, to have admonished and appealed to everyone that he should judge no further than he is commanded. "For it is a fearful thing to fall into the hands of the living God" [Heb. 10:31] and to interfere with his judgment.

We do not say this as our excuse but as a warning to everyone.

For we are comforted through the grace of the Lord, to suffer for the sake of the gospel all that is laid upon us by him, and hope also that he in his mercy will give us power and strength. We also do not regard what the world says and maintains about us, but we submit ourselves with all humility to the judgment of all genuine Christians, before whom we confess in a manner similar to that which Paul said and confessed in his reply before the judge, "I admit to you, that according to the way, which they call a sect, I worship the God of our fathers, believing everything that is written in the law and in the prophets," Acts 24:14.

We also say that we, according to this way which many persons consider to be a heresy, and blaspheme, desire to serve the only almighty and living God and his ever blessed Son, our Lord and Savior, Jesus Christ. [We say also] that we believe all of Moses and the prophets, Christ and his apostles, and consider as good and true the entire holy biblical Scripture, Deut. 4:35; Isa. 44:6; 1 Thess. 1:10; Rom. 9:5; Deut. 18:15; Rom. 15:4; 2 Tim. 3:16, as shall certainly be seen in the following account of our faith and our confession of the two sacramental signs of the Lord if it is read with a pure impartial and devoted heart. The almighty God grant his grace for this to all who desire it.

Amen.

Confession of Our Faith (Concerning) God

In the first place, /60/ we believe and confess that there is one God and Lord just as is basically contained in all of Scripture and expressly stated in writing, Deut. 4:35; 6:4; Isa. 44:6; [1] Cor. 8:[4]; 12:6; Eph. 4:6; 1 Tim. 2:5; Gen. 1:1; Isa. 45:21. This only God is a Creator of all creatures, a sustainer of all things, and a mighty King. [He is] a most high Lord, a God El Shaddai, that is, the almighty, and an all sufficient perfection of all goodness, a Lord and God Sabaoth, that is of the heavenly host, Isa. 6:3. He is a Lord of heaven and of earth, an eternal, true, holy, living, merciful, righteous, long-suffering, and alone good and wise God, the first and the last, who knows all past, present, and future things, Eccles. 1:6; John 17:3; 1 Tim. 1:17; Isa. 41:4; Isa. 44:6. He alone is a Redeemer and Savior in whom alone we must believe, whom alone we must fear and love, Matt. 10:28; 22:[37]; Ps. 34:9; to him alone we must pray, and serve him alone, and in whom alone we must hope and trust, Exod. 20:2; Isa. 43:11. Him alone we must hold and confess for our God and Lord; in him alone we must place our salvation and from him alone hope for recompense, Heb. 11:6. To him alone be glory and praise in eternity. Amen.

This one God and Lord is and remains an only God and Lord from eternity to eternity, and has, in accordance with his character, nature, and activity, many names in the Old Testament with which he was called. But, in the New Testament God is actually called the Father, Son, and Holy Spirit by Jesus Christ himself. With these three names, the whole divine being (insofar as it is humanly possible to comprehend it) was expressed by the Lord himself. In these three names, the Lord has also commanded the apostles to baptize the believers, Matt. 28:19. From this it is clearly to be understood that these three previously mentioned names express the only, almighty and living God in the variety of his divine being. /61/

The Father we confess as the eternal God and heavenly Father, Eph. 3:[14-]15, who is a self-sufficient being from whom everything that is has its being, 1 Cor. 8:[6]; Exod. 3:14; Jer. [3:23], a fountain of all good from whom all that is good has its source and origin, James

1:18; Mic. 5:[2]; yes, out of whom his only begotten Son, Jesus Christ, from the beginning and from eternity was divinely and inexpressibly born and proceeds from the Holy Spirit, Eph. 3:[14-]15; Isa. 44:[3]; Gen. 1:[2]; Ps. 18:10. Therefore, he is also a God and Father over all, the first and the last, the most high God, the almighty Creator, sustainer and Governor who sits upon his throne, Isa. 40:10; Deut. 32:[39-]40; Isa. 44:[14]. [He is] a reigning God over all, who lives from eternity to eternity, and his nature, character, and attributes are self sufficiency, omnipotence, immortality, immutability, eternal life, strength, power, wisdom, truth, glory, righteousness, faithfulness, love, friendliness, goodness, mercy, long-suffering, gentleness, and all virtues, James 1:5; 1 John 4:16; Ps. 103:10[-14]. Thus we confess the eternal God and Father in his divine being, in his activity, nature, character, and attributes, Eph. 4:6.

We confess the Lord Jesus Christ as the first and only begotten and own Son of the almighty Father, the living God, and believe that in this same only Jesus Christ there are two natures, a divine and a human nature, John 1:14; Col. 1:15; Rom. 8:32; Heb. 1:2[-3]. According to the divine nature he is that Word about whom John wrote, "In the beginning was the Word, and the Word was with God, and the Word was God. He was in the beginning with God. All things were made through the same and without the same was not anything made that was made" etc., John 1:1[-3]. According to the same divine nature, he is also the wisdom of God, 1 Cor. 1:29[-30], the truth and the life, John 14:6, the first born and beginning of all creatures of God, a reflection of the eternal light, a likeness of the invisible God the Father, and his being, Col. 1:15; Heb. 1:3; Rom. 8:29, an unblemished mirror of divine truth [purity], and an image of his goodness which was in the beginning with the Father in divine form, glory, and truth [purity],[1] John 17:5; Phil. 2:6.

But with his human nature, it was given him thus that the previously mentioned Word which was in the beginning with God and God was the Word, this same has become flesh, as John says, John 1:[1], 14. But how this took place is described for us in the other Gospels; namely, that the Holy Spirit came into the virgin Mary, and the power of the most high overshadowed her whereby she became pregnant and what was conceived in her was from the Holy Spirit, and what was born out of her was called a Son of the Most High, which is Jesus Christ,/62/ our Lord, Luke 1:31; Matt. 1:[18-]19. And according to this human nature, he is a servant of his Father, sent from the Father to serve us to salvation, Isa. 53:1[-2]; Phil. 2:5[-7]. He is our Apostle and High Priest, Heb. 3:1; 6:20, our Master and Prophet, Matt. 23:[10]; Deut. 18:15, our King and Messiah, our Redeemer and Savior, Col. 1:22; 2:14, our Mediator and Advocate, 1 John 2:1, our Intercessor and Reconciler, John 17:[1-26], our Peacemaker and mercy seat before God, the Father, Eph. 2:13; Exod. 25:[17-18]; Heb. 9:5, the Shepherd and Bishop of our souls, John 10:11; 1 Pet. 2:25, and whatever more the holy, biblical Scripture testifies about it.

Thus, we now confess in Jesus Christ these two natures, and on account of these two natures he also has different names. For at many places in the Scripture, in the Old as well as in the New Testament, he is called God and Lord and additional other names, which are appropriate for no one nor may they be given to anyone except God alone, Rom. 9:5; 1 John 5:1; Heb. 1:8, Ps. 45:7. Once again, according to his human nature, according to his ministry, office, and work, he is called a human being and Servant, and has many other names which actually testify to his humanity and Servanthood, his office and work, Ps. 102:24; Isa. 42:1; Phil. 2:5[-7]; John 8:28; 1 Tim. 2:5. Nevertheless, he is according to both his divinity and humanity, according to the Spirit and the flesh, one Jesus Christ, God and human in one person. And both were true in him because he is one with his Father, one divine being, undifferentiated from him in the glory, majesty, and activity John 14:9; Matt. 28:19. "Therefore, in his name every knee must bow in heaven and on earth and in hell, and every tongue must laud him, and all people must praise him and fall down before him," Phil. 2:10; Ps. 97:7; Eph. 1:20[-22]. Yes, he is worshiped by all the angels and by every creature in heaven and on earth with divine honor just as his Father is rightly honored, Heb. 1:6.

Also, it is true in him that he is human. Yes, he is our brother, like us in all things, except sin and all sinful nature, John 8:28; Heb. 2:17; 5:2. For he is entirely innocent, unblemished, pure, and holy, who has not known of any sin, neither was any deceit found in his mouth, Exod. 12:5; 2 Cor. 5:21; 1 Pet. 2:21. He is also not from the earth and earthy as we are; but he is from heaven and heavenly as is written: "Whoever comes from the earth is earthy, and speaks of the earth; but whoever is from heaven is above all. He bears witness to what he has seen and heard," John 3:[31-32]. Again, "the first man is from the earth and earthy; the second is the Lord himself from heaven," 1 Cor. 15:47. Again, "I am the living bread which came from heaven; whoever shall eat of this bread, will live in eternity; and the bread which I shall give /63/ is my flesh which I shall give for the life of the world," John 6:51.

Likewise Melchizedek, King of Salem and priest of the most high God, was described by the apostle in the epistle to the Hebrews to be without father, without mother, without race, without beginning of days and without end of life and a priest in eternity, [Heb. 7:3]. These words actually may not be taken to indicate the figurative Melchizedek but one must understand them to apply to Jesus Christ, the Son of the most high God, our only High Priest according to the order of Melchizedek, [Heb. 5:5-7]. For he is a king of righteousness and of peace who himself has neither beginning of days nor end of life. For he is the A[lpha] and the O[mega], that is the first and the last. Thus also, he has neither father nor mother, nor lineage on earth, like other human beings, but he has gone forth from God and was conceived in the virgin Mary from the Holy Spirit and was born out of her a Son of the Most High, a marvelous child, above all human nature and understanding.

Whoever will now rightly observe and understand these and similar passages of Scripture can easily recognize the difference between Jesus Christ and ourselves, not alone according to his divinity, but also according to his humanity.

We confess the Holy Spirit as the eternal and only Holy Spirit who is the one Spirit of both the Father and the Son, 1 Cor. 12:3; John 14:26; 16:7; Wisd. of Sol. 1:[7]. He is a spirit of truth and of all heavenly wisdom and of all divine understanding; a distributor of faith and all spiritual gifts, 1 Cor. 2:10; Rom. 12:3; 1 Cor. 12:4, a comforter of the conscience through whom all Christians pray to God and cry, "Abba, Father," John 15:26; Rom. 8:15. He is the Spirit through whom they rightly call Jesus Christ Lord, [1 Cor. 12:3], through whom they believe and upon their faith are baptized into one body, Matt. 28:19; 1 Cor. 12:13, through whom they are and will be sealed in the day of redemption, Eph. [1:13]. He is the Spirit through which Jesus Christ reigns directly in his congregation, by whom teachers are sent forth to preach the gospel, and bishops and shepherds are installed to nurture the congregation of God, Acts 20:28. For he is the Paraclete about whom Christ has spoken to his apostles saying, "I will pray the Father, and he will give you another Comforter, the Spirit of truth whom the world cannot receive, because they do not see him and know him not; but you know him, for he remains in you and will be in you," John 14:16[-17], "He will teach you all things and shall explain all that I have said to you," [John 14:26].

Thus the Holy Spirit teaches and reigns over the Christian congregation which is a fellowship of the saints, that is, of the believers and newborn children of God, in which fellowship /64/ is forgiving of sins (through the blood of Jesus Christ). And in the last day all people who are at rest from death will be awakened through the power of God, the righteous, to eternal life, but the wicked to eternal damnation, 1 Cor. 15:51; 1 Thess. 4:15; Matt. 24:31; John 5:28[-29]; 2 Cor. 5:10.

All this and what more is yet included and grounded in the holy biblical Scripture about God, the Father, and about his only born Son, Jesus Christ, about his Holy Spirit, and about the other previously mentioned articles of our Christian faith (which to relate here would be much too long), and in addition whatever is rightly taught and included by any God-fruitful and believing Christian out of divine truth, and what may yet be taught and included, to this we are not opposed. But we consent all together with all who so believe [this] with our whole heart.

Yes, our greatest pride and joy is the pure unwavering knowledge of God, the Father, and the Lord Jesus Christ, who through the enlightenment of the Holy Spirit in a true faith and understanding is imaged in our hearts. We are also entirely hopeful that with this our confession, so far as our common Christian faith is concerned, to satisfy every person who is of good will and understanding. Therefore, we will also not write more about it. But, because we are severely accused and blasphemed by some, as though we would justify ourselves and seek our salvation in works and signs (which are called sacraments), we want through God's grace to do our confession briefly of that which we hold ourselves to be and whereby we hope to be saved.

ENDNOTES

1. *Claerheyt* is difficult to translate when used to describe a divine attribute. Alternate readings might be transparent, lucid, holy, perfect, free from disguise or falseness.

OUR CONFESSION CONCERNING THE CREATION, REDEMPTION, AND SALVATION OF HUMANITY

We believe and confess that God, the almighty Lord and Creator of all creatures, created [all] people in his image and according to his likeness, Gen. 1:27; 2 Esd. 6:54, and for eternal life. However, they did not remain in their first creation, Gen. 2:7, but transgressed the command of the Lord and through this, together with all their descendants, came into corruption and damnation; they have all become sinners and of a sinful nature, Wisd. of Sol. 2:23[-24]; Eph. [2:1-2]; Rom. 5:12.

Therefore, we regard ourselves, by reason of our first and fleshly birth, not other than what the apostle says, "We were by nature the children of wrath even as the others," Eph. 2:3. In addition, we confess out of the law of God what poor sinners we are in ourselves, and that no good thing dwells in our flesh, Rom. 3:20; 7:7; that we were all included under the curse of the law and included in sin, Gal. 3:13, so that we with our sins had well deserved the punishment of God many times over, Deut. 27:[15-26].

But over against this we comfort ourselves with the grace of God and the Lord Jesus Christ, Eph. 2:4, and we believe the gospel, Mark 1:15, namely that God, the heavenly Father, out of his bottomless mercy, has given us his only begotten Son, Jesus Christ, as a Redeemer and Savior, John 3:16; Col. 1:20, who has fulfilled all the righteousness of God for us, Rom. 8:3, taken away all our sins, 1 John 3:5; John 1:11[-12], stilled the wrath of God, Col. 2:13, made peace between ourselves and God, Rom. 5:1, and more than conquered Satan, the world, hell, and death for us, Eph. 2:4[-7].

He is the promised seed who has trampled the head of the serpent, the seed of blessing, in which all peoples upon earth who believe in his name will be blessed, Matt. 12:[28-]29; Gen. 3:15; 12:[2]; 22:18. He is the true Messiah, our King and High Priest, John 11:25; Heb. 5:1; 9:11; [2 Cor. 5:19]; [1 Pet. 1:19], who with the one holy sac-

Creation, Redemption, and Salvation / 69

rifice of his life and blood has reconciled his people with God. He is the throne of grace established for us by God, [Exod. 25:20-22], through whom we come to God and have free access to him in the Holy Spirit, [Heb. 9:11]; [Eph. 2:4-5]. /66/ He is the horn of our salvation, Lev. 25:9, the hope of our salvation, Luke 1:[46-55], and in summary our eternal life. For to us there is given no other name under heaven whereby we must be saved than in his name alone, Acts 4:12.

But the means whereby we grasp the grace of God, which appeared to us in Christ Jesus, and receive true righteousness, holiness, and salvation, [which has] appeared to us in and through him, John 1:[1-14], is a true faith, believing with our whole heart, out of God's Word through the Holy Spirit and are entirely certain of this, that Jesus Christ with all his heavenly blessings is granted to us as our Savior and Redeemer, Mark 16:[15-18]; Rom. 3, 4, and 5; Gal. 3:5; Heb. 11, [and] that through him we have peace with God and have become children and heirs of God, Col. 1:4[-5]; Eph. 2:13; Rom. 5:1; 8:16.

[Thus] the apostle Paul says that God who has loved us from the beginning through his eternal love, has chosen and destined us to salvation, Eph. 1:[3-5], and called us in Jesus Christ. He has justified us out of grace without merit through the redemption that has taken place in him, Rom. 3:[21-]25. He has set before us the selfsame one as a mercy seat through faith in his blood, [Eph. 1:5-8], and has included all those under sin in order that he alone may be justified and in turn justify all who have faith in Jesus Christ, Rom. 3:[19-26].

However, such faith is a work of God in us whereby we are inwardly transformed and renewed, yes, become participants of the divine nature, of the Christian reality, of the Holy Spirit and of eternal life, 2 Pet. 1:4; Heb. 3:14. Therefore, faith brings with itself true divine righteousness, Rom. 5:1; 1 John 3:3, makes us spiritual and mindful of heavenly things, [1 Pet. 1:4], desirous of and prepared for every good work, 2 Tim. [2:21].

All this the apostle comprehends and expounds to the Ephesians in a few words and says, "God, who is rich in mercy, out of the great love with which he loved us, even when we were dead in our sins, has made us alive together with Christ (by grace you have been saved), and has awakened us together with him, and made us sit with him in the heavenly places in Christ Jesus, that in the coming ages he might show the overflowing riches of his grace with his friendliness to us through Jesus Christ. For by grace you have been saved through faith; and this is not your own doing, it is the gift of God, not because of works, lest anyone man should boast. For we are his workmanship, created in Christ Jesus for good works, which God has prepared, that we should walk in them," Eph. 2:4[-9]. /67/

Out of these words it is clear that faith is a work and a gift of God. But out of such faith comes love, as Paul says, the chief commandment is to love, Rom. 13:8, from pure hearts and a good conscience and from sincere faith, 1 Tim. 1:5. Good works follow out of this love as the apostle indicates with these words: "In Christ Jesus neither circumcision nor uncircumcision is of any avail, but faith which works through love," Gal. 5:6.

Therefore, those who boast of their faith without love and good works, their boast is false and their faith is idle. They are indeed the people of whom the Lord said in the Gospel, "Many will say to me in the last day, 'Lord, Lord, have we not prophesied in your name, and have we not in your name driven out devils, and have we not in your name done many works?' Then I shall confess to them, 'I have never known you; depart from me, you evil doers,'" Matt. 7:22[-23]. Paul is in accord with this and says, "To the impure and unbelieving nothing is pure, both their mind and conscience is impure. They say they confess God, but deny it with their works, since they are an abomination to God, disobedient, and incapable of all good works," Titus 1:15[-16]. In a similar manner the apostle James reproves all those who boast of their faith but do not prove their faith with works, James 2:[17]. It follows then that faith cannot be based on any work or sacrament, but on Jesus Christ alone [through] trust in his grace and merit, Rom. 3:24.

Therefore, we confess and also believe conclusively that we are saved through the grace of our Lord Jesus Christ, Eph. 2:4. But we grasp this salvation through the faith that God works in us through his Holy Spirit, [Eph. 2:8-10]. However, through this faith we confess that we love God our heavenly Father and the Lord Jesus Christ because of what he has done for the sake of our salvation, 1 John 4:16. But the love in our hearts originates out of our knowledge of the love of God and the benefits of Jesus Christ which we receive and have on account of the overflowing love of God which he has manifested toward us in Christ Jesus, Isa. 53:[4-5]; 1 John 4:19. Out of such love, which is kindled in our hearts through the Holy Spirit, we desire in our weakness to observe the commandments of our Lord Jesus Christ, John 3:16; Rom. 8:1, as he himself said to his disciples, "If you love me, then keep my commandments. [Again], whoever loves me shall keep my words, but whoever does not love me, will also not keep my words," John 14:21 [23, 24].

However, it is impossible for one to observe simultaneously the [commandments] of God and human commandments, Matt. 15:3. For God and the world are opposed to each other. /68/ Christ and Belial are not in accord, 2 Cor. 6:15. Therefore, if anyone wishes to serve God he must forsake the world, [Matt. 6:24]. If anyone wishes to follow Christ, he must despise Satan, [Luke 16:13]. For this reason Paul says that he would not be Christ's servant if he pleased people, Gal. 1:10. For the friendship of this world is enmity with God, 1 John 2:15, and whoever would be a friend of the world must become God's enemy, as the apostle James says, James 4:4. Christ also says the same in the Gospel, that is, that which "is exalted among men is an abomination before God," Luke 16:15.

That is the reason we are not inclined to observe all human institutions of the world, all false worship and ceremonies of the Roman Church which are opposed to Christ, Matt. 15:[3]; 1 Cor. 10:14. Rather, we desire in our simplicity to remain and abide, for good or ill, in the teaching and example of Jesus Christ and to allow ourselves to be guided by the first apostolic congregation insofar as the Lord gives us grace, Eph. 2:19[-20]; 1 Pet. 2:21. And since we find such an abuse of both baptism and the Supper of Jesus Christ, such disdain and transgression of the godly ordinances by the papists and others in the first place, we can neither consent to nor practice it, but confess with both signs or sacraments our Lord Jesus Christ as here follows.

The Baptism of Our Lord Jesus Christ

We believe [hold] and confess that there is a Christian baptism which must take place internally and externally, internally with the Holy Spirit and with fire, Matt. 3:11; Mark 1:8; 11:[30]; Luke 3:16, but externally with water in the name of the Father and the Son and the Holy Spirit, Matt. 28:19. /69/ The baptism of the Spirit is administered by Jesus Christ himself to the penitent and believing, just as John the Baptist said, "I baptize with water for repentance, but he who is coming after me is mightier than I, whose sandals I am not worthy to carry; he shall baptize you with the Holy Spirit and with fire," Matt. 3:11.

This Christ told his apostles, when he charged them not to depart from Jerusalem, to wait for the promise of the Father which you (he said) have heard from me, Luke 24:[49]. For John baptized with water, but you shall be baptized with the Holy Spirit not long after these days, Acts 1:4; Joel 2:28. Jesus said this because they were to receive the Holy Spirit from the Father in heaven and were to be clothed with power from on high, just as happened at Pentecost, when Christ sent them the promise of the Father, and they were all abundantly endowed with the Holy Spirit, John 20:22; Acts 1:8; 2:1; Joel 2:28. So also Cornelius, with all those who in his house heard and received the words of life, the gospel of Jesus Christ from the apostle Peter, were baptized with the Holy Spirit coming down from above, which after all no human being did but the Lord Jesus Christ himself, Acts 10:44.

But the external baptism with water is a witness to spiritual baptism, a proof of true sorrow, and a sign of faith in Jesus Christ, Acts 2:38; 8:[12]. [This baptism] is given on the command of the almighty Father, his Son Jesus Christ and his Holy Spirit, and in the name of the same only God is administered by a messenger and servant of the Lord, in the office and power of the Spirit. [It is administered] to those who have sorrow for their sins, seek improvement [in their life], believe the gospel, confess their faith /70/ and desire to be baptized upon it, Acts 2:41. [These] dedicate themselves willingly to God as a service of righteousness, yes, to servanthood of God [and] in fellowship with Jesus Christ and all the saints, Matt. 28:19; Mark 16:15-16; 11:[30]; Acts 8:[12]; 16:33.

This is clearly understood from the words with which Christ instituted baptism, for in Matthew he speaks to his disciples as follows: "Teach all people, baptize them in the name of the Father and the Son and the Holy Spirit, teaching them to maintain all that I have commanded you," Matt. 28:19. Mark establishes it also [saying], "Preach the gospel to all creatures. Whoever believes and is baptized will be saved, but whoever does not believe will be damned," Mark 16:15[-16].

In these words of the Lord, the ordinance and institution of Christian baptism and all that serves and belongs to the perfection of this divine ordinance is fully included. For Christ is the eternal wisdom of the Father, 1 Cor. 1:19; John 15:15; 16:[30], who has perfectly instituted and expressly commanded all things since he came down from heaven as the light and Savior of all people, John 1:9; 1 John 1:5; John 3:2. Therefore, it cannot be denied that the ordinance of the Lord about baptism is fully included in these few previously mentioned words, and that all who were baptized according to this Christian ordinance have received a true baptism, that is, those who have received and accepted baptism on the basis of their faith, Mark 16:[16]. For Christ has instituted and commanded with explicit words the teaching of the gospel and faith before baptism. Now this Scripture may after all not be broken and one should neither add to nor subtract from the words of God, Deut. 4:2; Gal. 1:8. Yes, the smallest letter and tittle of the gospel may neither pass away nor be changed. Therefore, this ordinance and institution of the Lord about baptism must remain unaltered, for it is the Word of God which abides in eternity, Isa. 40:8; 1 Pet. 1:25.

This is the true, unalterable ordinance and institution of the Lord with respect to baptism, just as the words of Christ above, quoted out of both Gospels, Matt. 28:19; Mark 16:15[-16], clearly bring together and testify. The teaching of the gospel before and after baptism must be pursued, so that everyone may by the teaching of the gospel come to a genuine faith through the grace of God and may be baptized on the basis of his faith, manifest his sorrow over sin, and demonstrate his faith therewith, Acts 2:38; 3:[19]. Thereafter, he must still hear God's Word at all times and diligently apply himself to maintain all the commandments of Jesus Christ. For so Christ also said to his apostles: "Teach them (namely those who believe and are baptized) /71/ to maintain all that I have commanded you," Matt. 28:19.

This ordinance and institution of the Lord about baptism is also observed regularly and with full earnestness by the apostles, without addition or subtraction, just as is indicated throughout the Acts of the Apostles and is proven thereby. For in the first place the apostle Peter replied thus to the Jews when they asked him what they should do, "Amend yourself and let every one of you be baptized in the name of the Lord for the forgiveness of sins and you shall receive the gift of the Holy Spirit," etc., Acts 2:38.

Likewise, when the eunuch had come to faith through the instruction and teaching of Philip and desired of him to be baptized, Philip said to him, "If you believe with your whole heart, this may well take place," Acts 8:36[-37][1]. And when the eunuch confessed his faith in Jesus Christ, the Son of God, Philip baptized him on the confession of his faith.

Again, when Peter preached Jesus Christ in the house of Cornelius and spoke the words of life, the Holy Spirit fell upon all who heard him. Then Peter said, "Can anyone forbid water that these not be baptized who have received the Holy Spirit just as we? And he commanded them to be baptized in the name of the Lord," Acts 10:47[-48].

Once more, Paul and Silas preached the Word of the Lord to the jailer and all who were in his house. Then the jailer allowed himself to be baptized at once and rejoiced that he with his whole household had come to believe in God, Acts 16:33.

Again, Paul found some disciples at Ephesus to whom he said, "Did you receive the Holy Spirit when you believed?" They said to him, "We have never even heard whether there is a Holy Spirit." And he answered, "Upon what were you then baptized?" They said, "On John's baptism." But Paul said, "John baptized with the baptism of repentance saying to the people that they should believe in the one who would come after him, that is Jesus, Acts 19:2[-4], that he is Christ." When they heard this they allowed themselves to be baptized in the name of the Lord Jesus, [Acts 19:5].

Again, Paul himself was struck down by the Lord on the way, and at Damascus heard and learned the command of the Lord from Ananias and was taught by him what he must do. When he again received his sight, was filled with the Holy Spirit, /72/ and became a chosen instrument or tool of God, he allowed himself to be baptized and called upon the name of the Lord, Acts 9:[4-19].

Out of all this it is now clear that the apostles first taught the people and preached the gospel, Mark 16:15. Those who repented and believed the gospel were baptized by them upon the confession of their faith. Therefore it is obvious, both according to the ordinance and institution of the Lord and the practice of the apostles, that the teaching of the gospel must take place before baptism, for out of this teaching comes repentance and faith. But genuine penitent faith must be confessed, manifested (and, so to speak) sealed with Christian baptism. But after Christian baptism a steadfast, good, and pious life must follow. This is the correct order of the Lord Jesus Christ and the practice of the apostles.

In addition [to these statements] everything concerning baptism as previously said is strongly defended and established in the sayings and writings of the apostles. In the first place Paul wrote to the Romans as follows: "Do you not know that we who have been baptized into Christ Jesus have been baptized into his death? So then we are also buried with him by baptism into death, that as Christ was awakened from the dead by the glory of his Father, so we too shall walk in a newness of life. For if we have now been planted with him in a death like his, we shall also be partakers of the resurrection. Thereby we know that our old self was crucified with him, so that the sinful body might cease and we now no longer serve sin. For he who has died is justified from sin," Rom. 6:3[-7].

With these words the apostle gives us to understand what Christian baptism means to the believer, namely, the dying of the flesh or putting to death the old Adam, the burial of sins, the putting off of the sinful body, and a resurrection to a new life, Col. 2:[11]-12. For this reason and with this instruction, since Christ has died, was buried on behalf of our sins, and was raised from the dead for our justification, Rom. 4:25, we through faith are first incorporated into him and then become partakers of his death, his righteousness, his holiness, yes, of all that is his. To this his fellowship we have been called by God out of grace and become established in and through baptism. Therefore, we must also for his sake die to sin, /73/ bury it, and live in righteousness in the Spirit so that we may be his true members.

This Paul also clearly testified to the Colossians and said, "You are perfect in him, that is in Jesus Christ, who is the head of all principalities and authority. In him you were also circumcised with the circumcision made without hands, by putting off the sinful body of the flesh, namely with the circumcision of Christ. You were buried with him through baptism, in which you were also raised with him through that faith that God worked who raised him from the dead. And he has also made you alive with him when you were dead through the sins and uncircumcision of the flesh," Col. 2:10[-13].

First of all, these words give us enough to understand that external circumcision was not a symbol of external baptism (as the perverted scribes say and the blind world thinks), but of the circumcision of Christ, which does not take place on the foreskin of the flesh but in the heart, not with hands nor with a stone, but without hands through God's Word and Spirit.

Thereafter, the apostle here explains to us what the baptism of Christ signifies, namely, a putting off of the sinful body in the flesh, burial with Christ, and resurrection through faith to a new being of the Spirit. For in Christ Jesus no external sign alone is of any value without true faith, without the new birth, and without a sincere Christlike being,[2] Gal. 5:6; 6:[15]; John 3:3. For it is through this faith primarily that a person is united with God, incorporated into Christ Jesus, and [becomes a] partaker of the Holy Spirit, Rom. 8:10. Therefore, external baptism alone is also not valid in itself if the person being baptized does not believe and is not born anew out of God through Christ Jesus, is not baptized inwardly with the Holy Spirit and with fire, has not died to sin, and does not live in righteousness, John 1:12; Matt. 3:11; Rom. 6:1[-2].

Now then, since young children neither know nor understand nor have all that baptism signifies and what belongs to it, therefore it is not appropriate for them and is also of no benefit to them, since neither faith nor the correct understanding and nature of the sacrament is there. The sign does not follow what is signified and received through this, namely, that one is baptized into Christ Jesus and into his death in order to die with him, to be buried with him, /74/ and to rise to a new life. Where this does not take place in and through baptism and thereafter does not proceed in true power, there baptism has not been truly received, although the external sign is there.

In the second place, Paul said to the Galatians: You are altogether the children of God through faith in Jesus Christ. For as many of you as were baptized, these have put on Christ, Gal. 3:26. Here one may clearly see how those who shall be truly baptized must first be God's children through faith, and how the truly baptized Christians have put on Christ. But to put on Christ is through faith to become partakers of Christ and his being, to be united with Christ and be incorporated into him, yes, to be transplanted out of the fleshly nature of Adam and transformed into the spiritual heavenly divine nature of Christ, Heb. 3:14; Rom. 11:17. And this must take place in all Christians. For humanity has become wretched, poor, and naked through Adam and is thus born out of him, Gen. 3:7. Over against this Christ Jesus is the garment of righteousness, yes, the innocent and unblemished Lamb of God with which every believing and baptized Christian is clothed,

Exod. 12:5; John 1:29; 1 Pet. 1:19.

But how this comes to pass is portrayed for us in Adam and Eve. That is, that Adam and Eve before the fall in Paradise were innocent, upright, and naked, Gen. 2:[25], and needed no garment, for they were of a good nature, without falsehood, and knew no evil. Yes, they were made after the image and likeness of God and were created for eternal life, Wisd. of Sol. 2:23. The pious nature which was imaged in them by God was the garment with which they were gloriously clothed.

But as soon as they had eaten of the tree of the knowledge of good and evil, against the command of God, they recognized their nakedness, felt shame, and made a cover of fig leaves, Gen. 3:[7]. However, they could not find cover nor hide from God but had to stand red with shame before the Lord on account of their transgression, and therefore suffer and bear his punishment. Nevertheless, he did not leave them comfortless but comforted them overall with his boundless mercy, inwardly with the promise of Christ, outwardly with bodily attire. For God had promised Christ Jesus to them as a Redeemer and conqueror of the serpent. As a true sign of this, he gave them coats of skin with which to clothe themselves as a witness that Christ Jesus, the Lamb of God, would cover and take away the sin of Adam and of the whole world, John 1:29, and that all believers should be clothed with him./75/

Therefore, now the sin of Adam and Eve may neither judge nor condemn anyone, since Christ Jesus, through his death and blood, has taken it away, Rom. 5:1, 12, (as we with God's help will further clarify). But just as sin had its origin in disobedience and began with the knowledge of good and evil in Adam and Eve, in like measure it also occurs with children. For, though they all come from a sinful Adam, yet original sin (as people call it) is not imputed to them by God to damnation, for the sake of Jesus Christ. For they are in part like Adam and Eve were before the fall, namely this, that they being simply both good and bad, understand neither good nor evil. But as soon as they come to a knowledge of good and evil and step from simple ignorance into conscious wickedness, and they sin against the Lord through their own disobedience and transgression of the divine Word and command, then it is the proper and appointed time that they first be taught, yes, with the law of God be heartily admonished to penitence so that they amend themselves, lament their sins before God, confess, and bear remorse over them, Matt. 28:19; Rom. 3:19; Mark 1:4; Acts 2:38. Thereafter, they must again be comforted with the gospel, Eph. 2:7.

But they must believe the gospel and upon the confession of their faith be baptized in the name of the Lord through the power of the Holy Spirit into the fellowship of the body of Christ, Mark 16:[16]; 1 Cor. 12:13, and so be justified through the imputation and sharing of his righteousness out of grace, so that they are born again, John 3:3, to a new life, created and renewed after the image of the heavenly Father, Eph. 4:24, that is, after Christ Jesus, to forsake the old human nature and walk in new spiritual life, Col. 3:10. This is what it means to put on Christ and to be clothed with him, Gal. 3:27.

This clothing of the believers with Christ and how it takes place is, to a certain extent, also testified to in the evangelical parable of the lost son who scandalously wasted his inheritance; then, wretched and poor he returned to his father and in all humility desired grace from him. And his father received him again with all love and joy, and for his sake let the fatted calf be slaughtered, and let him put on the very best garment, Luke 15:11[-24].

While this parable is generally directed toward Jews and Gentiles, nevertheless, since all Scripture is written for our /76/ learning, admonition, and comfort, Rom. 15:4; 2 Tim. 3:16, this parable may also be understood without distortion[3] as follows: Everyone who recognizes his misery, confesses his sins before God out of the bottom of his heart, bears genuine sorrow before God, humbles himself under his powerful hand, regards himself as unworthy of all grace and kinship, Acts 2:37; 1 Pet. 5:6; James 4:[6], yet comes to God with full faith, trusts entirely upon his boundless grace and mercy, that one God the Father accepts as his child in Christ Jesus, whom he has delivered into death for us. He also clothes every Christian with the best of clothing and makes a covenant of grace with him, and rejoices with all his heavenly host over the salvation of the sinner who was lost and has come to life again.

Now since all rightly believing and baptized Christians have put on Christ, Gal. 3:27, and to put on Christ is actually to become partakers of Christ and his being, his character and nature, his spirit, and all that is his, Heb. 3:14, this still may not take place except through faith. This faith must also actually and consciously be present, like a power and fruit, if baptism has been properly received. Out of all this it follows powerfully that baptism belongs only to those who repent and believe.

In the third place, Paul writes to the Ephesians that Christ has sanctified his congregation through the washing of water with the Word, Eph. 5:26. And to Titus he writes thus, "But when the friendliness and fellowship of God our Savior was revealed, he saved us, not on account of the works of righteousness which we have done, but according to his own mercy, through the bath of being born again and the renewal of the Holy Spirit, which he has poured out upon us abundantly through Jesus Christ our Savior, so that we by this same grace should be justified and heirs of eternal life according to our hope," Titus 3:4[-8].

These words of Paul are interpreted by some to mean the baptism of the Spirit. That may be so. Nevertheless, they may also be scripturally understood as referring to external baptism. The reason: Baptism is a waterbath because it is administered with water to believers in the name of the Lord. /77/ But since the phrase "in the Word" stands alongside of it, this shows that baptism is not a simple washing but rather is attached to the gospel and faith with the promise that whoever believes and is baptized will be saved, Mark 16:[16].

Baptism is also a bath of the new birth because, according to the ordinance and institution of the Lord, John 1:28; 3:5, it applies to the regenerate children of God, that is, to true believers in Christ. For what is the new birth other than the transforming and renewing of the person which God works in him through faith in Christ Jesus in the power of the Holy Spirit? Thus the person is created anew out of God, born of his seed, 1 Pet. 1:23, made in his image, Col. 3:10, renewed in his knowledge, becomes partaker of his divine nature, Eph. 4:24; 2 Pet. 1:4, and receives [power] from his Spirit to serve God [as] a new being of the Spirit, John 14:[17]; 16:[13], in holiness and righteousness all the days of his life, John 20:[22]; Luke [1:75]. Where this takes place and is in process as a pregnancy, there is the genuine new birth; there is the new creature in Christ Jesus, John 3:3; Gal. 6:[15].

The evangelist and apostle John testifies to this and says, "As many as accept Christ, to these he has given power to become God's children, those who believe in his name, who were not born of blood nor of the will of the flesh nor of the will of man, but of God," John 1:12[-13]. Likewise, "if you know that God is just, you acknowledge that everyone who does right is born of him," 1 John [2:29]. Again, whoever believes that Jesus is Christ, that one is born of God.

True believers in Christ, then, are the regenerated children of God. But baptism is a bath of the born again, Titus 3:5. That is, there the newborn children of God are bathed and washed, not by the power of the elements or natural water, but through the power of the blood and spirit of Christ Jesus, 1 Pet. 3:21. For this is he, as John says, "who comes with water and blood, not with water only but with water and blood. And the Spirit is witness that the Spirit is truth. For there are three who give testimony here on earth, the Spirit, the water, and the blood; and these three agree," 1 John 5:6[-8], the Spirit through which the person believes, the water with which the believer is baptized, and the blood of Christ Jesus with which the believing and baptized Christians are sprinkled in their souls and consciences, 1 Pet. 1:2, of which sprinkling of the blood of Jesus Christ the apostles clearly testify in their writings. Therefore, on the cross Christ also allowed his side to be pierced through and water and /78/ blood to flow from it, John 19:34, as a testimony of his true humanity and that he has with his blood sprinkled, washed, and cleansed his congregation (which is taken out of his side, flesh of his flesh and bone of his bone), Eph. 5:[29-]30, from all her sins, and has poured the water of the Spirit over her, of which baptism is a sacramental sign, John 4:2.

Since then believers are born again of God and baptism is a bath of this new birth, Titus 3:5, and young children have not come to this new birth so long as they still lack understanding and do not believe, baptism does not apply to them. For baptism belongs to no one and may not be given rightly to anyone except the born again children of God, that is, to believers who have been inwardly renewed after the image and likeness of God, 2 Cor. 3:[18]; Col. 3:10; Eph. 4:24, to those forsaking the old Adam so that the new person, yes, Christ lives and works in them through faith, Matt. 16:10. To such Christian baptism applies, for there baptism is a bath of regeneration and gives testimony of the new creature in Christ Jesus, Gal. 5:6.

In the fourth place, the apostle Peter says of baptism, "When one expected the divine long-suffering in the time of Noah, when the ark was prepared, in which few, that is, eight souls were kept through the water, Gen. 6:5ff., which now also saves us in baptism which is thereby signified, not as a removal of the uncleanness of the flesh, but the covenant or assurance of a clear conscience with God, through the resurrection of Jesus Christ," etc., 1 Pet. 3:[21-22].

In these words of the apostle, we observe how Christian baptism is signified and portrayed through the flood with which the whole world was punished, but Noah with his own was preserved in the ark through that same water; so also the children of Israel passed through the Sea of Reeds or the Red Sea with dry feet and so were delivered from their enemies. But Pharaoh with the Egyptians who pursued them were all drowned and perished in the same sea, Exod. 14:[28]-29. That is the way it is with all the works of God. What is life to the pious is death to the godless, just as Paul also testifies with these words: "We are the good aroma of Christ to God, both among those who are being saved and among those who are being lost, to one a fragrance of death to death, but to the other a fragrance of life to life," 2 Cor. 2:[15-16].

Now to understand the figure of the flood correctly, one must observe how Noah is a figure of Christ, the household of Noah of the believing souls, the ark of the congregation, /79/ and the flood of baptism. For just as Noah in his time was a preacher of righteousness, so also Christ Jesus is the genuine Preacher of righteousness and the true Teacher who has gone forth from God, John 8:[18]; 14:24; 16:5. Again, just as Noah at the command of God prepared the ark for the preservation of his own and the souls of others, so also Christ Jesus has built and equipped a spiritual ark, that is, his congregation. Also through his apostles as instruments and wise carpenters, 1 Cor. 3:10; 4:[1], he made and erected it for the eternal preservation and salvation of all his children and household, Eph. 2:[19], of whom he himself said, "Behold, I and my children which God has given me," Heb. [2]:13.

Again, just as no one outside of the ark of Noah could preserve his life, but all that was outside of the ark, that is, from the earth, perished through water, Gen. 6:14[ff.], so also no one may preserve his soul nor be saved except he be in the ark of Christ Jesus. For outside of Christ and his congregation is neither salvation nor eternal life, Acts 4:12. No one comes to the Father except through Christ, John 14:6. In him all is included. All grace and truth has come through him, "From his fullness we all receive grace upon grace," John 1:[16]. "Whoever believes in him and abides in him has eternal life, but he who does not believe in him is judged already, for the wrath of God rests on him," John 3:36, and, "whoever does not abide in him is already cast away as a withered branch," John 15:6.

Again, just as the flood drowned all flesh that was outside of the ark, Gen. 6:[21], and the ark was preserved through the same water, so also in baptism all fleshly lusts must drown and be killed, Rom. 6:3, but the soul is preserved to eternal salvation in the ark of Christ, through the power of his Word, Spirit, and blood, Col. 2:12. Again, just as few persons, namely, eight souls, were preserved and kept alive in the ark, 1 Pet. 3:20, so also there are few who with Noah find grace before God's eyes because they rightly believe in God, enter into the Christian congregation, and are baptized in the name of the Lord. [Through this] they have and guard the power, meaning, and mysteries of true faith and the baptism of Christ for the mortification of the flesh and the resurrection to eternal life. The Lord himself testified that there are few who find the true and narrow way, few are chosen, few believe and are saved, Matt. 7:13; [2] Esd. 7:7; Matt. 20:16.

Of this interpretation, Peter says that baptism is a contrary image of the flood which saves or preserves us, "not as a washing away of the uncleanness of the flesh but as the covenant of a good conscience with God, through the resurrection of Christ Jesus," 1 Pet. 3:21. /80/ Here the apostle says clearly that in baptism the washing or pouring with external water does not accomplish the matter but [only] the covenant of a good conscience with God through the resurrection of Christ. And this is the covenant of a good conscience with God, that God, the almighty Lord and merciful heavenly Father, according to his eternal love and boundless mercy, Eph. 2:4, is gracious to us, loves us, and binds himself to us. Also that he wants to be our God and Father, 2 Cor. 6:16, has forgiven all our sins, delivered us from eternal death and given us eternal life, chosen and accepted us as children and heirs of his kingdom through Jesus Christ, Col. 1:12[-13]; Eph. 1:5. [He also desires] that we accept such a gracious covenant, Luke 1:69, with a firm faith, surrender ourselves again to God to be obedient to him, to remain firm and steadfast by his Word, to serve him all the days of our lives, and to walk before him with a good conscience.

[It is] upon such faith and such trust in God's grace and mercy, and upon such a promise of the divine covenant that one ought to receive Christian baptism in the name of the Lord in order to walk with a good conscience in God's covenant, 1 Pet. 3:21, and to be mindful of what grace God has shown to us through Christ Jesus. It is he who died on behalf of our sins, Isa. 53:[5]; [Rom. 5:6], and on behalf of our justification was awakened from the dead, 1 Cor. 15:3[-4], leaving us an example, 1 Pet. 2:21, that we should die to sin and live for righteousness, that we be awakened from sleep and be brought from death to life, Eph. 5:14.

Since, then, the covenant of a good conscience with God through Christ Jesus, 1 Pet. 3:21, belongs to baptism and is actually valid before God, and [since] there is no good conscience without sincere faith, 1 Tim. 1:5, (for the grace of our God appeared to us in Christ Jesus and [when] accepted with genuine faith assures the conscience, bears fruit in the heart, and gives good courage), therefore it follows that everyone who is to be baptized in a Christlike way must have and maintain an upright faith, a good conscience, and all that the apostle Peter has attached to baptism if the baptism is to be correct and the words of the apostle have been satisfied, Mark 16:16; Acts 8:[12]; 1 Pet. 3:21.

So we have now briefly indicated what baptism is, how it was commanded and instituted by Christ Jesus, taught and practiced by the apostles, how it must still be practiced and received, [as well as] what it signifies to the believers, demonstrates, and reminds them of. /81/ By contrast, we now wish to write a little about how miserably this baptism is abused and despised by some. The Lord Jesus Christ help us to [do] that with his grace. Amen.

In the first place, baptism is scandalously abused by the child baptizers who ascribe this baptism (a sign and testimony of sincere penitent faith) to ignorant children lacking in understanding and abuse the same even though all Scripture about baptism uniformly testifies that baptism belongs to the mature who have heard and accepted God's Word. Yes, these have recognized God's wrath through the law, severity, and righteous judgment over sin and therefore borne remorse before the Lord; and again, have out of the gospel rightly acknowledged God the Father in his grace and mercy, Christ Jesus the only begotten Son of God in his merit through the enlightenment, and power of the Holy Spirit, John 1:14; 3:16. Baptism belongs to these who comprehend such a confession and with firm faith and trust grasp it in their heart and confess it with their mouths, Rom. 10:9, and who submit themselves to God as a holy, living, and acceptable sacrifice, Rom. 12:1. Baptism belongs to these, and these should receive it because of their faith in God, their repentance from sin, [these] who in being baptized acknowledge, witness, and testify to its meaning.

This ordinance Christ himself has made, instituted, and established, and the apostolic congregation maintained it, which no one can assume authority over or censure unless he contradict Christ himself and his apostles, Matt. 28:19; Mark 16:15[-16]; Acts 2:38; 8:[12]; 16:33; 19:5. But of child baptism the Holy Scripture testifies nothing certain. Yes, even when we read the whole [New] Testament through and through, we do not find that Jesus Christ ("in whom are hidden all the treasures of wisdom and knowledge," Col. 2:[3], who has declared the perfect will of his heavenly Father to us, John 15:15), has spoken a single explicit word about child baptism or that the apostles of the Lord ever baptized children.

Therefore, we cannot accept child baptism as a word and service of God. The reason: the holy divine Scripture teaches us everywhere that we should neither accept nor believe nor observe anything except God's Word and command alone, and that we should neither add to nor subtract from God's Word, Deut. 4:2, /82/ that God does not want to be served with human teaching and institutions, that "every plant not planted by God the heavenly Father shall be rooted up," Matt. 15:13, and that "a little leaven leavens the whole lump," etc., 1 Cor. 5:6.

This many ancient and modern teachers have well understood and, therefore, have openly written and confessed that all that which God has not commanded, that he has also forbidden. Thus [for example] all divine worship which is not established with a single express Word of God is false, no matter how much it is glossed over or disguised. Again, this is primarily what idolatry is: to undertake divine worship without God's command on the basis of our own reason. For he does not wish to be controlled by us. He wants to teach and show us how one must serve him. His Word shall be present, shall enlighten and lead us. Yes, without his Word, all is idolatry and idle lies though it shine as gloriously and beautifully as it will.

Likewise, let everyone see to it that he be certain that his divine worship has been instituted by God's Word and not founded upon well-meant, good intentions. Whoever celebrates divine worship and has no [scriptural] witness for it, he shall know that he does not serve the true God but his own adorned idol, that is his own opinion and false ideas. Thereby he serves the devil himself. This is what Martin Luther wrote in his foreword to the prophets, etc.[4]

But because we have cited this from the teachers does not mean that we should stand or build upon their opinion. Oh, no! God's Word is certain for us, sufficient, and an immovable foundation of truth. However, we have done [written] this on account of our opponents as a testimony that we are not the first who have repudiated human teaching, commandments, and ceremonies, and recognized them as idolatry.

Since then Scripture attests nothing certain about child baptism, but much more the opposite, namely, directs us toward the baptism of adults, the penitent, and the believers, Matt. 28:19; Mark 16:[16]; Acts 2:38, and since all self-made opinions, all strange teaching, all human institutions and ceremonies, all false worship and idolatry are so sternly forbidden us by God, Matt. 15:9; 1 Cor. 10:7, how can we regard child baptism as true? Who may with any modesty, reasonableness, and truth blame us because we simply abide by the Scripture, Rom. 15:4, and confess one true God and eternal Father, one Lord Jesus Christ, 1 Cor. 8:6, one Holy Spirit, /83/ one faith, and one baptism, Eph. 4:5, which by Christ himself is attached to faith and the gospel?

The antichrist, however, will not tolerate this. The Pharisees and scribes set themselves against it with might (for they have at all times scorned the counsel of God, on which account the publicans enter the kingdom of heaven before them), Luke 7:[30], and seek many excuses to prove their baptism. But since they all build on the tower of Babel, God has confused their speech so that one does not understand the other, they are far from each other, Gen. 11:4[-9], are not of one mind about child baptism and do not speak uniformly out of one mouth. For some, indeed, acknowledge that children themselves do not believe. Nevertheless, they want to have them baptized (as they say) upon the faith of the Christian church. Others, such as Luther and his followers, say openly that children themselves believe and must be baptized upon their own faith. For so he writes in a certain place: No one will be saved or justified through the faith or justification of another but through his own. Therefore, the sacraments may not be received without faith unto salvation. Therefore, for those who think that young children do not believe, for these it would be entirely better not to baptize any child than to baptize without faith, since they thus use both the sacrament and God's holy name in vain.

Again, [Luther] chides the Waldensians, who baptize their children and yet do not believe that they have their own faith and so take and use God's name in vain. Again, young children are not baptized upon the faith of the church or their fathers but their own, and that out of grace, not out of the power of baptism which would forgive sin. Again, baptism helps no one and is to be given to no one except he believes for himself; and without faith one should not baptize anyone, since it is not the sacrament but faith which justifies the sacrament.[5] Again, the child itself must believe or the fathers must lie if they say in the child's stead: I believe. Again, it would be better never more to baptize a child than thus to mock and deal dishonestly with God's Word, etc. Foolish children are more qualified to believe than rational adults! In contrast to this, some hold that the grace of God and faith are first infused into the child in baptism. Read Sebast.[ian] Fr.[anck] in his *Chronicle*.[6]

Since then, the learned ones together with all the common people are and remain so contentious about child baptism, /84/ they thereby sufficiently indicate that they neither have nor know anything certain about it, and that it has no foundation in Scripture since it takes place and is practiced in so many different ways. For all human teaching is divided in itself, is unstable and changeable, has doubts, and is full of quarrels and disputes. But the Christian and apostolic teaching is uniform, flowing out of one Spirit, and has a secure and abiding ground which is Christ Jesus, 1 Cor. 3:11.

And even though child baptism has no basis in Scripture and our opponents are not united in this matter, nevertheless, they all wish to prove child baptism with Scripture, each in his own way. For those who say that children shall be baptized on the basis of the faith of the church or of their fathers, these wish to prove this with the fact that when some persons brought a paralytic before the Lord and he saw their faith, he said to the paralytic, "My son, your sins are forgiven," Matt. 9:2. And he made him well. In a similar way, they allege how the centurion and the Canaanite woman with their faith and prayer received help and comfort from the Lord Jesus Christ for others, Matt. 8:5; Luke 7:9; Matt. 15:28.

Thereupon we answer briefly that all these aforesaid had prayed the Lord Jesus Christ for restoration to health of the others and they were heard. In the same way, we must also pray for our neighbors with fiery hearts, primarily for the salvation of their souls, just as Moses prayed to the Lord for Israel, for his brother Aaron, and for his sister Miriam. So also Paul writes to the Romans that his heart's desire is that Israel might be saved and he prays to God for them, [Rom. 10:1]. Thus James teaches us to pray for our neighbor and says, "Is anyone sick? Let him call the elders of the congregation to him, and let them pray for him, and anoint him with oil in the name of the Lord; and the prayer of faith will help the sick man, and the Lord will raise him up; and if he has committed sins, they will be forgiven him," James 5:14[-15]. John says, "If anyone sees his brother sinning a sin not unto death, let him pray, and give him life for those whose sin is not unto death," 1 John 5:16. Yes, the whole Scripture teaches everywhere that we shall pray one for another, and we have received the promise from the Lord that all that we ask of his heavenly Father in his name, that he will give to us, Matt. 7:7; John 14:13. /85/

However, we have no command nor example in the entire Scripture which instructs us that children shall be baptized upon the faith of the church and their fathers. But we do have in the Scripture another example of how one should pray for the children, namely, that believing parents brought their children to Christ and desired of him that they might be blessed through the laying on of his hands, Matt. 19:13. So we must offer our children to Christ with our prayers, with a firm faith and a confident trust that in him, as in the promised seed, they have already received the blessing to eternal life, Gen. 3:15.

Further, Scripture clearly testifies that the justified person lives his faith, Hab. 2:4, that everyone shall be judged according to his faith, Heb. 10:38, and that no one may save another with his faith, Rom. 1:17. Otherwise, the pious Lot would have, indeed, preserved his wife through his faith. But now the Lord says through Ezekiel that Noah, Daniel, and Job could not deliver either their sons or daughters but their own souls alone through their piety, Gal. 3:11; Gen. 19:26; Ezek. 14:14. The apostle Peter also says about the meaning of this that the righteous one will scarcely be saved, 1 Pet. 4:18, from which it is easily understood that the wise virgins had oil in their lamps for themselves but not for the others, Matt. 25:9.

Therefore, it is a great misunderstanding and entirely contrary to Scripture that some want to base child baptism upon the faith of the churches or the fathers and do not observe the order and meaning of the Lord Jesus Christ, Matt. 28:19; Mark 16:[16], the practice of the apostles, Acts 2:38; 8:[12]; 10:48; 16:33, and the basic understanding and content of all Scripture about baptism. All of this testifies uniformly that every one baptized shall be baptized upon the confession of his sins and his own faith in the name of the Father and the Son and the Holy Spirit, Rom. 6:3; Col. 2:12. This ordinance and meaning of the Lord Jesus Christ, the practice of the apostles, and the understanding and content of divine Scripture must remain immovable and unchanged, "for heaven and earth, (says Christ), shall pass away, but my words shall not pass away," Matt. 5:18.

Further, when some say that children themselves believe, they twist the meaning of Scripture to say whoever does not believe shall be damned, Mark 16:[16]. Again, "without faith, it is impossible to please God," Heb. 11:6. Therefore, children must believe (they say), or they will be damned and cannot be acceptable to God.

Answer: This is a great misunderstanding and through this Scripture is severely /86/ broken. The reason: In the first place, it is contrary to Scripture that one should apply these previously mentioned and other additional passages to children. For such Scripture does not speak of children but of adult understanding, who have ears to hear and a heart to understand, Matt. 11:15. Christ spoke with such persons as he himself said in the gospel, "He who has ears to hear, let him hear," Matt. 13:9.

Accordingly, it is evident that the eternal, almighty, and only wise God has so ordered it that faith should come and be received out of the hearing of the divine Word, through the power of his Spirit, just as Paul openly testified to the Romans and said, "So faith comes from what is heard, but what is heard comes through God's Word," Rom. 10:17.

Beyond this faith is (as the apostle describes to us), "a certain trust in which one hopes, a clear revelation, yes, a certain understanding of things not seen," Heb. 11:1. Since then faith is such a sure trust and hope in the grace of God through Jesus Christ, and exists always according to heavenly things, seeking what is above where Christ is seated at the right hand of his Father, Col. 3:1, how can children have such faith? Do not both Scripture and experience testify against it?

Therefore, we finally conclude from all of this that children do not believe since they understand neither good nor evil, Deut. 1:39, and have no ears to hear and therefore the Scripture does not speak to them and they cannot be taught with it, and if they are not qualified to be taught, how can they be qualified for faith? Did not the apostle say, "How shall they believe in him of whom they have not heard," Rom. 10:14? So we may rightly ask, how can children believe without understanding, without teaching, without hearing?

Yes, some say, God is almighty and can readily give faith to children. Thereupon, we reply as follows: God is after all almighty and he can, indeed, give faith to children, yes, not only faith but also understanding to comprehend faith and speech to confess it. But now God gives the children neither understanding nor speech, much less faith, which after all, cannot be comprehended without understanding nor confessed without speaking. Is God then now not almighty? This be far hence! However, though he is, indeed, omnipotent /87/ and does what he wills in heaven and on earth, nevertheless, he keeps in all his works an order that is pleasing to him.

Since then the almighty and only wise God through his eternal wisdom has decreed and regarded it as good that chldren be simple, lacking in understanding, speechless, and without knowledge of good and evil, Deut. 1:39, it is after all certainly right that people should be satisfied with this. For who wishes to dominate God, "who wishes to be his counselor," Rom. 11:34? Who can interrupt or alter his ordinances?

But now some throw before us that Jeremiah was sanctified in his mother's womb, Jer. 1:5, and that John [the Baptist] in his mother's womb rejoiced in Christ his Lord and Savior, Luke 1:[41].

Answer: This is with Jeremiah and John an exceptional and marvelous work of God and not a general rule, just as Isaac was supernaturally conceived of Sarah through faith, Gen. 17:[16-]17. That took place because he in godly works and as a figure bore the image of Jesus Christ, Rom. 4:19; Heb. 11:11. Thus it also took place with Jeremiah and John, namely, since God wanted to accomplish something exalted and marvelous with the two of them, therefore, they were also filled with the Holy Spirit from the mother's womb. But not all children are as Jeremiah and John. Yes, as little as all children, also of believing and God-fearing women, are conceived and born above the ordering of God and nature, even as it happened with Isaac, just so little children (even of believers) do not understand or manifest the power of the Spirit and their faith because God dealt so wonderfully with Jeremiah and John. [We know] that a miraculous act of God is not a general rule, even as a special divine command does not break a general and common law, of which we have examples and testimony enough in Scripture. Therefore, all children may not be compared in the gift and power of the Spirit with Jeremiah and John. Yes, Christ himself testified of John that he was more than a prophet and that /88/ "among those born of women there has arisen no one greater than John the Baptist," Matt. 11:11.

From this, it is clearly to be noted and understood that out of the marvelous action of God with Jeremiah and John it does not follow, nor may it be verified with any degree of truth or proof, that children believe when, after all, the Holy Scripture expressly testifies to the contrary, (as has been sufficiently proved and explained above), John 4:[53]; Deut. 1:39. Experience also indicates much otherwise, for through it we trace and find that there is neither faith nor the power of faith in children. Faith that is a powerful work of God, Heb. 11:1[-3]; Eph. 2:[8], and a gift of the Holy Spirit may not lie hidden, asleep, nor fruitless in people as some fantasize, but must according to its nature break out through love and works, Gal. 5:6, in a confident trust of the recompense of God and a sure grasp of heavenly things. Where this does not take place, there is no faith.

Again, if children believe, why do they not know about sin nor about the law nor about grace nor about the gospel? One must teach them the first grade level of the words of God and all the articles of the Christian faith as one does to those who do not know of God and all godly things. And how have they become so ignorant and unbelieving, if they were wise and believing in childhood? Have they then so completely forgotten all knowledge of God, his Word, and their faith?

Therefore, it is nothing but human opinion what the scribes and worldly-wise with their adherents say about the faith of children. But we keep to the Holy Scripture, which ascribes no understanding to children, Deut. 1:39, much less faith, together with experience (which so openly shows and testifies to us that no knowledge of God and his Word, no faith nor fruit of faith is to be traced or found in children), John 7:38. In this we are more certain than all human opinion, which does not count before God.

We must also observe that the grace of God /89/ and the power of the Spirit did not lie hidden or asleep in John but openly manifested themselves in him while he was yet enclosed within his mother's womb. And after his birth he became strong in spirit, Luke 1:[17], and walked before the face of the Lord in the spirit and power of Elijah, etc. Where, after all, does one trace the same in ordinary children? Therefore, they may also not be compared with John in all things.

Again, those who wish to uphold child baptism with Jeremiah and John are not in agreement among themselves and act against their own confession. They compare the children with Jeremiah and John who were sanctified in their mother's wombs and were partakers of the Holy Spirit from the mother's womb on, Jer. 1:5; Luke 1:[41], as Scripture testifies. Out of this it must, after all, follow undeniably that if children have the Holy Spirit through which they are sanctified, why then do the child baptizers presume to banish the unclean spirit out of children? They have not done thus to the holy prophets and men of God, Jeremiah, and John. And where, after all, does Holy Scripture testify of such exorcism of devils at the baptism of Jesus Christ?

Out of all this it is now easy to determine that they err who say that children themselves believe. Yes, it is a great misunderstanding that one should ascribe faith to children who are minors and lacking in understanding. It is a still greater misunderstanding that one wants to banish an unclean spirit from the children whom one regards as believing. For if children believe, then they must without doubt have the Holy Spirit, since no one can believe except through the Holy Spirit, 1 Cor. 2:12; 12:3. Thus it is not right that one wants to banish the unclean spirit out of them. But if they do not believe (just as Scripture testifies and experience teaches), Deut. 1:39; John 4:[51-53], then it is incorrect that one should regard them as believing and baptize them on the basis of such a superstition. Through this the correct ordering of the Lord is despised since Christian baptism (according to all the testimonies of the gospel and the apostolic scriptures) may not be practiced nor received without faith, Matt. 28:19; Mark 16:[16]; Acts 2:38; 8:[12]; 16:33; 19:5.

So one might then think or ask: If the children do not believe, why are they saved and pleasing to God? We answer, out of grace, through Jesus Christ, who by his death has taken away the sins of the whole world, Rom. 5:18; John 1:29; 3:17, so that adults in their penitent faith but children in [their] simplicity are pleasing to God so long as they remain therein. /90/ The Lord himself testified to this in Deuteronomy thus: "Moreover, your little ones, who you said would become a prey, and your sons, who this day have no understanding of good or evil, shall enter the promised land, and to them I will give it and they shall occupy it," Deut. 1:39. See then that what the adult Israelites could not receive on account of their unbelief and disobedience, the children, who understood neither good nor evil, received from God's grace. Thus now the children of the true Israelites, the Christian believers, receive and inherit the true promised land, that is, the kingdom of heaven out of grace through Jesus Christ in order that the promise of God (from the seed of Abraham, the children of the heavenly Sarah, who are included under the promise), Rom. 3:28; Gal. 3:29, remains fixed on the basis of grace and the election of God in the merit of Jesus Christ, not on the basis of any works or merit of human beings, Eph. 2:7.

In the second place, those who contradict us say Christ spoke in the Gospel, "Let the children come to me, for to such belongs the kingdom of heaven," Matt. 19:14. Herewith they wish to support child baptism and say that since the kingdom of heaven belongs to children, they may, therefore, certainly be baptized, etc.

Answer: That children receive the kingdom of heaven we believe without doubt, just as we have confessed above. But that this salvation of children should depend upon baptism and be bound to it, this we do not believe and cannot consent to. For Christ accepted the children and promised them the kingdom of heaven on the basis of grace and mercy, and not on account of baptism. For he neither baptized them nor commanded that they be baptized but blessed them through the laying on of his hands.

Christ also gave us to understand sufficiently why children are pleasing to God, since he set children before us as an example and in addition admonished us that we should become like them. For thus he spoke to his disciples, "Truly, I say to you, unless you turn and become like children, you will never enter the kingdom of heaven. Whoever humbles himself as this child, he is the greatest in the kingdom of heaven," Matt. [18]:3[-4].

Since Christ has now set the children as an example for us and said that we should become as children and humble ourselves, it follows from this without any contradiction; first, /91/ that children (so long as they are in [their] simplicity) are guiltless and reckoned as without sin by God; second, that if there is still something good in children (though they have, indeed, become participants of the trespass and sinful nature of Adam), namely, the simple and unassuming and humble nature in which they please God (yet all out of pure grace through Jesus Christ) so long as they remain in it. For this reason Christ also set the children as an example for us that we, in this regard, must become like them.

But now many arrogant persons dispute about the salvation of children and become fools before the Lord over such disputations, no matter how wise and intelligent they are regarded by the world. For they dispute and chatter much about the salvation of children, but where this concern is of the greatest necessity for themselves, that is, to learn true simplicity and humility from the children, as Christ admonishes us, that they do not even think of a single time.

Since then infants are saved and included in the hand and grace of God, and the kingdom of heaven belongs to them, Matt. 19:14, therefore, it is a great lack of understanding that one should baptize children so that through this they might be kept and saved, and besides this condemn children who die without baptism. This is an open diminishing and denial of the grace of God and merit of Jesus Christ. For since the sin of Adam, yes, of the whole world, is paid for and taken away through Jesus Christ, John 1:29, and sin may not be ascribed to children except what comes from Adam, how then may children be condemned on account of Adam's sin? Yes, who may condemn the children for whom Christ shed his precious blood? Who will damn the children to whom the Lord in his boundless grace has promised the kingdom of heaven, Matt. 19:14? Or who can forsake Holy Scripture, which so expressly testifies that the sins of Adam and the whole world are taken away, Rom. 5:18, the handwriting that was against us is wiped away and nailed to the cross, Col. 2:14, that grace has taken the upper hand over sin, and that life has overcome death through Jesus Christ, our Lord and Savior?

Therefore, no one may either accuse or damn young children on account of original sin except he denies the death, blood, and merit of Jesus Christ. For if children may be damned through Adam and on account of his transgression, then /92/ Jesus Christ has died in vain for them, Rom. 5:19, and the guilt of Adam that has come upon us and has not been paid for through Jesus Christ. Then grace has not become mightier than sin, and life has not overcome death through Jesus Christ. This be far hence! But the Scripture which so expressly testifies about the great and saving grace of God which he has so richly and abundantly shown humanity through Jesus Christ stands steadfast and immovable and may not be broken, Rom. 5:18; Titus 2:11; 1 Tim. 2:6. The apostles who so openly witness that all the curse of humanity and the sins of the whole world are taken away through Jesus Christ are certain and true witnesses of God, Rom. 8:3; Gal. 3:13.

So we now conclude with the apostles and with the entire Holy Scripture that original sin has been paid for and removed through Jesus Christ, to the extent that children may neither be judged nor condemned on account of Adam's transgression. But while the nature of children is inclined toward evil, Gen. [6:5]; 8:21, that does not condemn them. Yes, this is not attributed to them as sin out of grace, for so long as they are simple and without knowledge of good and evil, they are pleasing to God and acceptable to him through Jesus Christ. But what needs many words? It is a sure and undoubted word that the children as well as the adults, the children in their innocence, but the adults in faith, are saved through the grace of our Lord Jesus Christ, Acts 15:11.

Therefore, it is a great blindness and ignorance, yes, even madness, that one should regard innocent and simple children as damned whenever they are not baptized according to the popish institution and manner, for whom, after all, Christ did not die in vain. Yet this takes place as the Lord complained over the false prophets through Ezekiel, that is, that they consigned to death the souls that shall not die, and again promised life to souls that shall not live. And this they did for a handful of barley and a piece of bread, Ezek. 13:19, for the sake of shameful gain.

Yet it is here to be noted that the young children of the Israelites in the wilderness, even though they did not believe (for they understood neither good nor evil) and had no external sign (for they were uncircumcised), yet they were acceptable to God out of grace, in their simplicity, ignorance, and uncircumcison, and heirs of the promised land, Deut. 1:39. Why then should the children of Christians, although they do not believe, not be acceptable to God and heirs of his kingdom although they have /93/ not received external baptism? Is the salvation of children then bound more closely to an external sign in the New Testament than occurred in the Old Testament? Or is the mercy of the Lord shortened so that he should not be as gracious toward the infant children of Christians as he was toward the infant children of the Israelites? This be far hence! "For the law," (says John), "is given through Moses, but grace and truth is through Jesus Christ," John 1:17. It follows then that grace has now taken the upper hand and proceeds in full power, Rom. 5:15.

Therefore, God in the Old Testament has shown his grace so abundantly to the Israelites and to their children, [who were] without faith and without external signs, that is, in the time when they understood neither good nor evil, Deut. 1:39, and were uncircumcised, and received them as heirs of the promised land. How much more abundantly has God shown his grace toward Christians and their children, having chosen and accepted them as heirs of his kingdom through Jesus Christ, although they neither believe nor are externally baptized. But they are baptized, washed, and cleansed with the precious blood of our Lord Jesus Christ, Heb. 12:24; 1 Pet. 1:2, as has been sufficiently clarified above.

So we wish now to return to the previously mentioned words of the Lord: "Let the children come to me, for to such belongs the kingdom of heaven," Matt. 19:[14]; let these words remain unfalsified in their true meaning, namely, that children are saved and that the kingdom of heaven belongs to them. But nothing is said here of the baptism of children. For the parents had brought their children to Christ, not in order that they might be baptized by the Lord, but in order that they might be blessed. And Christ also did not baptize them nor command that they be baptized, but blessed them through the laying on of his hands. Therefore, child baptism may not be supported by this, since the children were not baptized but blessed by the Lord. We wish to be satisfied with that and want in all things to make no addition to the words and action of Christ and the example of Scripture, as the blind world does, so that we may neither be punished nor found to be deceitful.

In the third place, those who contradict us have yet another proof text, namely, the words which Christ spoke to Nicodemus: "Unless someone is born out of water and the Spirit, he may not enter the kingdom of God," John 3:5. On the basis of these words, they wish to conclude that children must be baptized or they may not enter into the kingdom of God. /94/ Some also say that since the Lord placed water before Spirit, therefore children may be baptized without faith.

Answer: That these words of the Lord about the new birth out of water and Spirit do not apply to children but alone to mature adults is certain and cannot be denied. The reason is this: Christ here openly spoke of the new birth, for he first said to Nicodemus, "Truly, truly, I say to you, unless one is born from above he cannot see the kingdom of God," John 3:3.

But what this new birth is, that we have said above. To explain the words which Christ spoke to Nicodemus we say once again that the new birth cannot take place without God's Word, without faith, and without the Holy Spirit. But it takes place in such a manner as the apostle Peter said, "You have been born again, not of perishable seed but of imperishable, that is, out of the living Word of God," 1 Pet. 1:23. The apostle James agrees with this and says that "God is the Father of light with whom there is no variation or changing of light and darkness. He brought us forth of his own will through the Word of truth that we should be a kind of first fruits of his creatures," James 1:17 [-18].

But baptism belongs with this new birth (which takes place from above out of God, the heavenly Father, through his eternal Word, 1 Pet. 1:25, in the power of his Holy Spirit through faith in Jesus Christ). For the true order of the Lord is that the newborn children of God, that is the believers, shall be baptized, Acts 2:38, and receive the gift of the Holy Spirit as Peter said.

Therefore the previously quoted words of the Lord about the new birth out of water and Spirit must also be understood to mean that the new birth must come first. But baptism is a bath of regeneration, Titus 3:5, and the newborn and baptized shall receive the gift of the Holy Spirit from God through Jesus Christ, to a renewal of their hearts, a transformation of their minds, and as a seal of their salvation, 2 Cor. 1:22; Eph. 4:30.

That this understanding is true and scriptural is attested to not only by the foregoing words alone, that is, Christ said how a person must be born anew from above, otherwise /95/ he cannot see the kingdom of God, John 3:5, but also by the words which followed. For after Christ had spoken of the new birth out of water and Spirit, he spoke the following: "What is born of the flesh is flesh and what is born of the Spirit is spirit, and do not marvel that I said you must be born anew. The wind blows where it wills, and you hear the sound of it, but you do not know from where it comes or where it goes; so it is with everyone who is born of the Spirit," [John 3:7-8].

With these words the Lord Christ gives us to know clearly that he speaks primarily of the new birth and of what the newborn person primarily is, that is, spirit born from the Spirit, just as the natural human being is flesh born from the flesh. And he compares the same, that is, the new birth, to the wind, that is that as the wind does not blow nor move without sound which is heard and yet is not seen, so it is also in and with the new birth of the Holy Spirit with his power, which can certainly be recognized in the newborn children of God through the Spirit, but is not seen with the intellect or human eyes. Because of this Christ also said in the Gospel, "If anyone thirst, let him come to me and drink. He who believes in me, as the Scripture has said, out of his body shall flow streams of living water," John 7:37[-38]. But this he said of the Spirit which those who believe in his name should receive. And this is, indeed, found in many; that as soon as they become believers and are born anew out of God, they then receive the gift of the Holy Spirit, and he has revealed himself in them, of which we have examples and witnesses enough in Scripture, Acts 2:38. Since now these infant children have not come to this new birth, to all that belongs to it, and may not come to it so long as they lack understanding and thus are not ready to believe, for that reason the previously quoted words of Christ may not be applied to them. So also many other passages of Scripture do not apply to them, for Scripture speaks primarily to the adult and mature, of which we have already given enough proof above, Matt. 13:9.

In the fourth place, our opponents charge that Paul wrote to the Corinthians, 1 Cor. 10:1[-4], "I do not want to withhold from you, dear brethren, that our fathers were all under the cloud," Exod. 13:21, "and all passed through the sea," Exod. 14:22[-29], "and all /96/ were baptized under Moses with the cloud and the sea. All ate the same spiritual food, and all drank the same spiritual drink," Exod. 17:6; Num. 20:10. But God was not pleased with many of them, for they were struck down in the wilderness, Num. 14:[35]. Our opponents understand this Scripture thus, that the exodus of the children of Israel out of Egypt through the sea is a figure of external baptism.

Answer: The apostle himself says that all such incidents happened to the Israelites as an example. If this then is an example or a figure of a true being that is symbolized through this, then one may not signify and understand letter upon letter (for this is against the nature of figures and against the proper sense of Scripture), but the letter must be transformed into Spirit and the figure into true being. It then follows that the exodus and the deliverance of the children of Israel out of Egypt through Moses, Exod. 3[-12], portrays for us primarily the deliverance of the human race which has taken place through Jesus Christ. For Pharaoh signifies the rulers of this world, the reign of darkness, of Satan, Eph. 2:2, who has power over the human race, and whose slaves we have been, taken captive by him according to his will, 2 Tim. 2:26. The iron furnaces and the house of servitude, Deut. 4:20, signify the captivity of the sins with which the devil has held us captive, Deut. 5:6. Egypt signifies to us the darkness in which we have all sat, Exod. 10:21, for we have all been darkened in our understanding, Eph. 4:18, and have not known God as one ought to know him, Exod. 3:[18].

Moses, who at God's command led Israel out of Egypt and was their pioneer and leader, Exod. [3:18], portrays Jesus Christ for us, the beginner and perfecter of our faith, Heb. 12:2, our pathfinder who has delivered us out of the kingdom and power of the devil. The Red Sea is a figure of the blood of Jesus Christ whereby our souls are baptized, Rom. 3:24; 6:3, and our consciences are sprinkled, freed, washed, and cleansed of all sin, Heb. 12:24; [1] Pet. 1:2. Pharaoh and his servants, [signify] our enemies and persecutors, who have reigned over us with violence; namely, the devil, sin, death, and hell, although they have been overcome, drowned, and annihilated through the blood of the cross of Jesus Christ, Heb. 2:[9]. For God has acquitted us of all sin, as the apostle says, having expunged the handwriting which was against us /97/ through the law, this he set aside, nailing it to the cross. He robbed the principalities and powers and made a public show of them, and triumphed over them in himself, Col. 2:14[-15].

The cloud signifies the gift of the Holy Spirit which was poured out abundantly over the believers from God the Father through Jesus Christ, Acts 2:38; 10:44; Titus 3:[5-6]. In a similar manner, the heavenly bread signifies the true, living, heavenly bread come down from heaven, that is, Jesus Christ, who is food for all believing souls, John 6:[33]. The spiritual drink, that is, the water that flowed out of the rock which followed Israel, [1 Cor. 10:4], through the stroke of the rod of Moses, [Exod. 17:6], signifies to us the living waters of the Holy Spirit which spring out of the spiritual rock, that is Christ Jesus through the power of the most high, and runs for the cooling and quickening of all thirsty souls, who are thereby refreshed in their faith, to eternal life, John 4:10; 7:37[-38].

This is, indeed, the proper significance of these figures, at least if one wants to let the Scripture be unbroken. For in this manner, the Spirit comes to agreement with the letter and the true being with the figure. On the other hand, if one wants to interpret this literally and upon an external symbol [alone], then one must also understand the other in the same way. But now if one must understand Egypt, Pharaoh, the iron furnace, the house of servitude, the bread of heaven, the drink and the rock, only spiritually, how does this agree with the truth that one should understand the baptism of the children of Israel under Moses, the clouds, and the sea in a literal sense only? In addition, we are not delivered primarily through external baptism, but through the precious blood of Jesus Christ, Rom. 3:[25], to whose sprinkling we have come by faith and have thus been baptized into Jesus Christ and his death, 1 Pet. 1:2; Rom. 6:3[-4], of which external baptism is a sign and witness.

And even if one were to interpret this baptism of the Israelites under Moses according to the letter, so that it would signify external baptism, we may yet not allow this interpretation and understanding to extend beyond the adult and mature, that is, the six hundred thousand who went out of Egypt and under whom only fighting men, not children, were counted, Exod. 12:37; Num. 11:21. The reason: The apostle says not only that they were all baptized under Moses with the cloud and with the sea, but that they all ate one kind of spiritual food and drank one kind of spiritual drink, /98/ but God was not well pleased with many of them, for they were struck down in the wilderness, 1 Cor. 10:3[-5]; Num. 14:27[-29]; Heb. 4:2[-3].

This can after all not be applied to young children but only to adults, for the adults who went out of Egypt had sinned, and therefore they were punished by God and could not occupy the Promised Land. But the children who came out of Egypt and were born in the wilderness did enter, Deut. 1:39. Consequently, it follows that the apostle spoke alone about the adults, just as Scripture also emphasizes that the city of Jerusalem, the whole Jewish countryside, and all the lands beyond the Jordan went out to John, Matt. 3:5; Mark 1:5. Yet this meant only the adult and the mature as is well proven by the following words, that is, that they allowed themselves to be baptized of him in the Jordan and confessed their sins, Mark 1:5; John 1:25; 3:26. Out of these words it is clear that no one was baptized with the baptism of John except those who believed and confessed their sins. Therefore, children were not numbered among them.

And that is also why John in his baptizing taught the people who were baptized by him repentance, confession of their sins, and faith in Jesus Christ. How much more appropriate it is then at baptism to teach those being baptized in such a manner and to require this of them, Matt. 3:5; Mark 1:5; Acts 19:4.

It is also important to note and remember that some disciples who were already baptized with the baptism of John knew nothing about the baptism of the Holy Spirit. These Paul baptized again or commanded that they be baptized in the name of the Lord Jesus, Acts 19:[1-6]. How much more then is it appropriate that those who were baptized under the papacy, without any knowledge or awareness of the difference between good and evil, yes, without the true knowledge of the almighty God and his only begotten Son, Jesus Christ, John 3:16, and the Holy Spirit, in ignorance, according to the papal manner, that they should not allow themselves to be satisfied with that, but receive Christian baptism orderly in the pure knowledge of the Holy Trinity and on the confession of their faith, according to the Word and command of the Lord, Matt. 28:19; Mark 16:[16]?

Further, our opponents wish to support infant baptism with reference to the fact that the apostles baptized some households. This must also be understood, as is said above, namely, that although the Scripture speaks of households, believers alone are meant by this. For of the household of Stephanas, Paul himself testifies that they were the firstfruits in Achaia and they had committed themselves to the service of the saints, 1 Cor. 16:15. Luke writes about the jailer's household in the Acts of the Apostles /99/ that Paul and Silas spoke the Word of the Lord to the jailer and to all who were in his house and that he rejoiced that he and his whole household had become believers, Acts 16:[32-]34.

Hereby one may clearly understand what households the apostles had baptized and that no children were counted among them. For they are not such first fruits, as the apostle says, that is, those who are born of God the Father through the Word of truth as a kind of first fruits of his creatures, James 1:18. They cannot adapt or give themselves to the service of the saints and cannot preach and teach the Word of God. In summary, they do not believe, as long as they are children and have no distinction between good and evil, Deut. 1:39.

In the fifth place, our opponents take as a proof text, in order to prove their infant baptism, what Paul wrote to the Corinthians, namely, "For by one Spirit we were all baptized into one body and are all refreshed with one Spirit," 1 Cor. 12:13. Hereby they argue that baptism is incorporation into the congregation of Christ and that outside of the congregation there is no salvation. Therefore, children must be baptized or they cannot obtain salvation.

Answer: That the children are not saved through external baptism but through the grace of Christ we have sufficiently proven above with the clear irrefutable testimony of Holy Scripture, and shall here through the grace of God explain this yet more broadly. But this previously quoted passage of the apostle does not apply to children but to adults and the mature. The reason: The apostle here writes primarily about the baptism of the Spirit and of the embodiment with the Christian congregation which takes place through the spirit of faith. For his words are thus: "We are all baptized by one Spirit into one body and all are refreshed by one spirit," [1 Cor. 12:13]. From these words it is easy to determine that Paul here speaks primarily of the baptism of adults which occurs through the Spirit and, therefore, [he] means only mature believers. For these are fit for such baptism and not the children. For what is the baptism of the Spirit other than that we receive the gift of the Holy Spirit from God, the heavenly Father, through Christ Jesus, Acts 2:38, through whom we truly confess God and /100/ truly believe in Jesus Christ. [This is] as the apostle testifies and says that "no one may call Jesus Christ Lord, except through the Holy Spirit," 1 Cor. 12:3, who gives to each the gift of faith and apportions all spiritual gifts according to his will, [1 Cor. 12:11]. Therefore, faith is a gift of the Holy Spirit through which all believers are gathered into one body, and thereupon they are baptized as a sign and proof of a genuine inner being and the spiritual fellowship they have with Christ and all the saints.

Since then children do not have the spirit of faith, how shall they then through that same spirit be baptized into one body with all believers? Or if one after all wants (yet incorrectly and with force) to prove the gift of the Spirit and faith in children, then they must also through that same Spirit not only be baptized with the believers into one body, but also receive the benefit of and participate in the Lord's Supper. For all those who through one Spirit have been baptized into one body and are refreshed with one Spirit, [1 Cor. 12:13], and have thus become one body and one loaf in Christ Jesus, these must also break bread with one another according to the institution of the Lord and according to the apostolic doctrine, 1 Cor. 10:16; 11:19.

Finally, the meaning is this: If the children must be baptized, they must also keep the Lord's Supper. For the apostles broke bread with the believing and baptized Christians, Acts 2:42. And since now the children are not permitted at the Lord's Supper (which is also reasonable and correct), thereby it is openly testified that one regards children as lacking understanding and not believing, just as also Scripture together with experience sufficiently teaches and emphasizes. Or if one regards children to be understanding and believing (yet against the clear words of Scripture), Deut. 1:39, then it is not right that one should keep them from the Lord's Supper. For whoever has a true faith in Christ Jesus, and is baptized through the Spirit into one body with all believers, may not be turned away from the Supper of the Lord. Yes, since they are one body and one loaf with all believers, so they must also be partakers of that loaf with the same.

Thus also Erasmus of Rotterdam wrote in his *Apology* to the bishop of Spain, that a pope, together with Augustine and other scholars, concluded that children must be made participants of the sacrament of the altar (as they say) just as commonly takes place in the papacy.[7] In opposition to this, others hold that children must only be baptized, /101/ and then be regarded as saved and, even if they are baptized, do not permit them to come to the Lord's Supper.

However, both are false and unfair, idle foolishness, and lacking wisdom. It all comes from the fact that they follow blind reason and not the express Words of God. For if baptism is appropriate for infants, the Lord's Supper is also reasonably appropriate for them. If they are not qualified for the Lord's Supper, then they are also not qualified for Christian baptism. For baptism is just as much a sacramental symbol as the Lord's Supper. Therefore, all that belongs to a sacrament of Christ, that is faith, confession, and the mystery of the sacrament, Acts 8:39, in a good conscience, 1 Pet. 3:21, with the consequent power and activity of God to full salvation, belongs also to baptism. And as little as children are injured in their salvation by the fact that they do not practice the Lord's Supper with the Christian congregation, so also it is not injurious that they remain unbaptized. Everything has its time according to which one must know how to observe it.

In the last place our opposing parties think to support child baptism with the covenant God made with Abraham and with the circumcision God gave him as a sign of the covenant, Gen. 15:18; 17:10; 21:4. They compare baptism with circumcision. Therefore, we will briefly indicate our understanding and decision concerning this matter.

God made his covenant with Abraham that he would be his God and the God of his seed, and he gave him circumcision as a sign of the covenant. But circumcision was there as a figure of the fact that the newborn children of the true Abraham, that is, of the heavenly Father, must be circumcised in the foreskins of their hearts with the living stone, Christ Jesus, Col. 2:11; 1 Cor. 10:4.

God had previously also made his covenant with Noah and gave him the rainbow as a sign of the covenant, Gen. 9:13. And Jesus Christ is also portrayed for us through the rainbow, the true sign of grace that in his heavenly being is at the right hand of God as a reconciler and intercessor for all believers with God the eternal Father, [1] John 2:2.

Such and similar signs and figures of divine grace were, indeed, for the most part given from God to the believers in the Old Testament. They all direct us primarily to Jesus Christ through /102/ whom we all receive grace from God, [John 1:16]. For he is the Lamb of God who takes away the sins of the world, John 1:29. He is the one Mediator between God and human beings, 1 Tim. 2:5. He is the Reconciler, Col. 1:20, and Peacemaker, Eph. 2:13, who with his bitter death and precious blood has earned for us peace, salvation, and eternal life, 1 Pet. 1:3.

Therefore, the figure of Abraham must be understood according to the true being of the Spirit in a twofold manner. In the first place, God the heavenly Father is signified to us through Abraham; Isaac is a figure of Jesus Christ and of all Christians; Sarah [is a figure] of the New Testament; circumcision of the flesh of the circumcision of the hearts, Rom. [4:12], which is the circumcision of Christ that takes place in the Spirit, Phil. 3:3; Col. 2:11. This is the meaning and interpretation of circumcision everywhere in Scripture as we have also explained above.

Thereafter, then one must understand this dealing of God with Abraham as follows: that God made a covenant with Abraham and his seed, that is, with all believers, has accepted them with all their children out of grace, as heirs of his eternal kingdom, [James 2:5], and surrendered Jesus Christ, his only Son, into death for us, John 3:16, as a sure sign of divine grace. For through this the love and mercy of God the Father is recognized primarily, 1 John 4:9, "that he gave his only Son into death for us so that everyone who believes in him will not be lost but have eternal life," John 3:16; 2 Cor. 1:21.

But the pledge and true seal of this grace of God and Jesus Christ is the Holy Spirit, who is poured into the hearts of believers from the heavenly Father and through Christ as a witness to the divine covenant, as a sealing of their salvation, 2 Cor. 5:5; John 14:16; 15:26; 16:7, and as a renewing of [human] thoughts and emotions, [Heb. 4:12]; Eph. 1:13; 4:30.

This grace and this covenant of God with all believing Christians is bound to no external symbol, but to Jesus Christ alone, who is the only and true sign of grace, Rom. 5:2; Heb. 5:3, and faith alone grasps this through the Holy Spirit, [Heb. 11:1], who assures our spirit that we are God's children, Rom. 8:16. Therefore, some lack understanding who hold not Christ Jesus but primarily baptism for the true sign of grace, and therefore ascribe to baptism what belongs primarily to Christ himself.

It is, indeed, true that baptism and the Supper of the Lord are signs through which the Lord sets before our eyes and images his grace, his suffering and death, and all that he has done for us are imaged and set before us, Matt. 26:[28-29]; Mark 14:22[-25]; Luke 22:[15-19]; 1 Cor. 11:[23-25]. For both baptism and the Supper are a public /103/ witness of the love of God and the benefits of our Lord Christ Jesus.

Nevertheless, Christ is and remains the true and only sign of grace, and all external signs direct us from themselves to him, admonish us from themselves to him, admonish us and remind us of him, witnessing about him, witness to him, Exod. 25:22; Rom. 3:25; Heb. 5:[5], and in the use of these signs nothing is accomplished for our salvation except that which Christ himself works in us, which we receive and accept through faith, John 1:[12]. For Christ is the one who baptizes us inwardly with the Holy Spirit and with fire, Matt. 3:11, who accepts us into his fellowship as members of his body, [1 Cor. 12:12], who sprinkles our conscience with his blood, cleansing and washing away all sin, Heb. 9:14. Christ makes us partakers with him in the Supper, feeds us with true heavenly bread, Exod. 16:5; Wisd. of Sol. 16:20, gives us his flesh to eat and his blood to drink, John 6:32[-33]. It is by his grace and work in us that we through faith in the spirit, and the power of his Word, have eternal life from his body and blood which was sacrificed for us on the cross, John 19:34.

Thus Christ fulfills in us what the sacraments signify. Therefore, whenever we utilize or receive the external signs of baptism and the Lord's Supper, we look not primarily upon the external sign but upon Jesus Christ himself, "from whose fullness we have all received, grace upon grace," as John says, John 1:16. And just as it is written there that God had given the children of Israel a saving sign in the wilderness, Num. 21:8, and those who looked upon it became well, not through what they saw with bodily eyes, but through the Lord, the Savior of all, so also no external sign will help us but alone the Lord Jesus Christ with his grace. And according to this rule one must understand all that the Scripture says about signs, though it indeed appears sometimes to sound otherwise according to the letter.

Further, baptism is not principally a comparison with circumcision so far as its practice is concerned. In the first place, God in the Old Testament expressly commanded that children must be circumcised. No teaching was required before circumcision, nor was faith required, but it took place and was used as a figure with children who had not reached understanding. But Christ Jesus did not express a single word about child baptism, and in addition instituted and required both teaching and faith before baptism, Matt. 28:19; Mark 16:[16]. No one can prove with Scripture that baptism /104/ was practiced otherwise by the apostles in the congregation of Christ.

But some say that just as God first gave circumcision to adults and after that it was applied to children, so it must also be done with baptism. To this we answer briefly as follows: Abraham received circumcision as a seal of the righteousness of his faith, and thereby God commanded him to circumcise all the males of his household, Gen. 17:10. Thus Abraham did this, and not otherwise. After that, God gave an express command about the circumcision of children. But now Christ has instituted baptism for believers, yet has said nothing about child baptism. And if child baptism were pleasing to God and necessary to the salvation of children (as the perverted world thinks and her learned ones chatter about), how was it possible that Christ Jesus (who has come from heaven to proclaim all truth to us and to give us to know everything he heard from his Father), John 16:25, did not give a single word or command in the whole New Testament about it as God had given about the circumcision of children in the Old Testament? Likewise, Paul has not hidden the whole counsel of God from us, but has made it known to us, Acts 20:27, yet he has written nothing about child baptism.

Therefore, we are certain that Christ required no baptism of children since he has not commanded it. Yes, he required no baptism before they believe and no faith before they are taught with God's Word, Matt. 28:19; Mark 16:[16]. And they may not be taught with God's Word before they have understanding, Rom. 10:14, and they have no understanding as long as they are children, as is witnessed to above and explained with Scripture.

The other reason that circumcision (with regard to practice) may not be compared to baptism is this: God appointed a time to Israel, that is, the eighth day, on which circumcision should be received; so Christ also appointed a time when baptism shall be received, that is, on confession of faith, Rom. 8:36[?]; [Acts 8:12, 36, 38]. Just as no child had to be circumcised before the eighth day, so also in the spiritual Israel, in the Christian congregation, no child shall be baptized except it must first believe and confess its faith, Mark 16:[16]. For baptism is of the Lord, based on the confession of faith, just as was circumcision on the eighth day. /105/

The third reason is that only the boys were circumcised in Israel, but the girls without circumcision and external signs, nevertheless, were God's children in his covenant as well as the boys. From this it is clearly to be understood that circumcision is nowhere a figure of baptism and has no similarity with it, otherwise boys alone would have to be baptized. But now baptism is given to girls as well as boys without distinction of persons. What similarity then has the practice of circumcision with the practice of Christian baptism? That boys only were circumcised in Israel is, according to our understanding, a figure of the spiritual children of Abraham, the Israel of God, those who are circumcised in the heart, Rom. 2:29, have a manly nature, character, and the power of faith, Eph. 4:[2-]3; [Gal. 6:15; Col. 2:11].

Likewise, though the boys were circumcised only after seven days, they were still children of God's covenant both before and after circumcision. Their salvation did not depend on fleshly circumcision but on the grace and mercy of God, who out of eternal love chose them and made a covenant with Abraham that he would be his God and [the God] of his seed, Gen. 17:3[-4].

This is also clearly to be understood from the fact that Ishmael according to the flesh was a son of Abraham and also circumcised as was Isaac, [Gen. 16:15; 17:10-11]. Nevertheless, God made his covenant with Isaac, not with Ishmael. Thus not Ishmael, but only Isaac, had an inheritance in the house of Abraham, Rom. 9:7. [Isaac] was born from free Sarah through the promise, Gen. 21:2, signifying that God, the heavenly Father, has chosen the spiritual children of Sarah, Gal. 4:23; Rom. 9:7, that is, of the New Testament, out of grace. These are the children of his promise, Gal. 3:29, and are counted as that seed, Rom. [4:12], and their salvation lies in the boundless grace and mercy of God, Eph. 1:7, in the innocent death of our Lord and Savior, Jesus Christ, Col. 1:14.

In summary, just as circumcision is practiced upon the fleshly children of Israel, so also baptism shall be practiced upon the spiritual Israelites, upon the newborn children of God, that is, upon believing Christians. Again, just as circumcision is commanded by God and appointed for the eighth day, Gen. 17:[12], so also baptism is instituted by Christ and ordained and commanded upon faith, Mark 16:[16]; Acts 8:[35-38]. Again, just as the salvation of children rested primarily in the grace of God and not in the fleshly circumcision in the Old Testament, in the same measure now in the New Testament, the salvation of children rests in the mercy, love, and goodness of the heavenly Father and in the merits /106/ of Jesus Christ, Rom. 3:24; 5:1; 11:6, not in external baptism.

Finally, just as the boys in Israel that were always uncircumcised for seven days, and in the wilderness were not circumcised, and the girls likewise, who had no such external sign were not harmed in their salvation and were not therefore excluded from the covenant and God's congregation, so also the children of Christians are neither hindered nor harmed in [their] salvation, and they were not excluded from the covenant and God's congregation even though they have not received the sign of baptism. They are already washed and baptized with the blood of Jesus Christ which saves their souls, Heb. 9:12; Heb. 12:24; Rev. 1:[5]; 1 Pet. 1:19. But the sign of baptism they shall receive at the appointed time, on the confession of their faith, according to the ordinance and institution of Jesus Christ and the practice of the apostles.

Since we have now written about the misuse of baptism, we also want to indicate a little about how some despise it as an external ceremony, though this does not surprise us or weaken us. We confess and by the grace of God most surely know that everything Christian and evangelical is regarded as ridiculous and foolish by the world. Furthermore, what is regarded as exalted by the world is an abomination and foolishness before God, as Christ himself said in the Gospel, Luke 16:15. Thus, God and the world are against each other since the wisdom of God is folly with the world. The natural person does not taste of the spirit of God, for it is folly to him, which he cannot understand since he must judge spiritually, 1 Cor. 2:14. In a similar way, the wisdom of the world is foolishness before God, as the apostle testifies, 1 Cor. 1:[20].

Therefore, it is no wonder that baptism is despised by the world, but that matters little; it is still an ordinance of God firmly grounded in the Gospel, Matt. 28:19. He who despises it despises not a human but a divine ordinance. Yes, he ridicules the name of God in which Christians are baptized, he despises Christ Jesus and his death into which believers are baptized, Rom. 6:3, he is disobedient to the Gospel since it teaches and directs us how baptism is to be received on confession of faith, Mark 16:[16].

Therefore we let the world and all mockers and despisers of divine truth go their own way, for they are blind and leaders of the blind. But we desire (through the Lord's grace) to follow Christ Jesus, /107/ for God the Father has set him before us as an example that we should be conformed to him, Rom. 8:29. Yes, he is a true light that has come into the world, [John 1:9], and "he who follows him will not walk in darkness but have the light of life," John 8:12.

Since then Jesus Christ, our forerunner, pioneer, and master of our faith, himself personally received baptism, Matt. 3:13[-16], instituted it, and connected it to the teaching of the gospel and to faith, Matt. 28:19; Mark 16:[16], we have in the only Jesus Christ the eternal God's sufficient truth and wisdom, example and witness of how necessary baptism is and how it may in no wise be despised nor regarded as insignificant.

In addition, the apostles of the Lord have also upon his command and in his name taught, extolled, and practiced baptism, as the previously quoted words and testimonies from the acts and the epistles of the apostles clearly indicate and support.

Therefore, both the institution of the Lord and the teaching and practice of the apostles are enough for us to stand firm as upon a certain and unshakeable foundation of truth against all who misuse and despise Christian baptism. We do not wish to follow these, but much more Christ Jesus and his apostles, holding baptism to be a good ordinance of the Lord which belongs to the gospel and to faith. In this we follow the example and order of Christ, the teaching and practice of the apostles, regarding everyone who believes the gospel and who must be received upon his confession of faith.

We are neither weakened, nor made to err [by the fact] that some (who, after the nature of spiders, turn good into evil, yes, honey into poison) mock us and ask what baptism benefits us, and why we suffer persecution since we ourselves confess that salvation is not bound to the external sign. Likewise, they say also that faith and love can break or alter all external ordinances and institutions of the Lord, such as baptism, the Lord's Supper, and whatever more there is. They argue that just as Moses discontinued circumcision in the wilderness, so Christians may also discontinue these practices and deal with them according to their own discretion. /108/

Although we do not take such sharpwitted objections and questions seriously and have already answered them sufficiently, we will, nevertheless, give a further response as follows: First, that just as in the Old Testament salvation rested primarily in the grace of God and not in circumcision, Rom. 3:1[-2], nevertheless, circumcision as an ordinance of God was profitable to those who observed the law, so now in the New Testament, salvation rests primarily upon the mercy and grace of God, the heavenly Father, and in the merits of Jesus Christ, Rom. 3:24; 5:1; 8:1; 11:22. However, baptism is nevertheless (as an ordinance of the Lord Jesus Christ) profitable and beneficial to all who believe the gospel and are obedient to it. "For the words of the Lord are spirit and life" John 6:[63], and a person lives by all the words that proceed out of the mouth of God, Deut. 8:3; Matt. 4:4, and the signs which Jesus Christ has attached to the word, these are not to be despised. Yes, in as much as they are given and commanded by God, they may not, therefore, be regarded as insignificant nor ridiculed without despising God, nor discontinued without peril.

Thus also the believing Abraham (whom all believers must follow and in whose footsteps of faith they must walk) through his faith did not reject external circumcision (even though it was only a sign and a small thing in itself), but received and accepted it as a seal of his faith, Gen. 17:10. In like manner, Christians should also, because of their faith, not reject baptism, but accept and receive it with wholehearted zeal and earnestness, since they have not only Abraham but Jesus Christ himself as an example, Rom. 4:11[-12].

Therefore, they boast in vain of faith and love, who in [their understanding of] obedience to the Word do not follow faithful Abraham, yes, Jesus Christ.[8] And what they do with baptism, contrary to the practice of the apostles, yes, outside of the teaching, ordinance, example, and command of Christ Jesus, is incorrect, false, and idolatrous. But those who follow Christ and receive baptism according to his Word, these cannot be deceived, because Christ is the truth and the life, John 14:[6].

Also, it is well to observe that the Lord met Moses as he journeyed toward Egypt and was in the inn and would have killed him. Then Zipporah took a sharp stone and cut /109/ her son's foreskin, etc., and the Lord left him alone, Exod. 4:24[-26]. If this is what happened to Moses, what shall happen to and come over these despisers and mockers of Jesus Christ and his ordinance?

Again, that Moses allowed circumcision to lapse in the wilderness does not prove that Christian baptism may be discontinued in the same manner. For, in principle, we are not to be guided by the figures, images, and incompleteness of the Old Testament, but by the true and perfect being and spirit of the New Testament, Heb. 7:11. We are not under the law but under the gospel, Rom. 6:14. We are not to serve according to the old nature of the letter but according to the new nature of the Spirit, Rom. 7:6. Finally, we are not disciples of Moses but of Christ. Therefore, we have also received a command from the heavenly Father that we shall hear Jesus Christ, his dear Son, and be obedient to his words and follow his example, Matt. 3:17; 17:5. Nevertheless, we do not wish herewith to despise Moses with his law, figures, and schemes, but to look upon them with spiritual eyes, yes, to have them judged and understood according to the true spirit and being of the New Testament.

In addition, baptism is not now discontinued out of necessity, just as it took place in the wilderness, but it is completely transformed into an idolatrous misuse. The baptism which Christ instituted for all the penitent believers, and which was also practiced everywhere by the apostles according to the ordering of the Lord, this same baptism has now been turned around by the antichrist into a child baptism. There is [now] so much scandalous abuse and idolatrous ceremony with this same child baptism that it may not be looked upon by any understanding, God-fearing and believing Christian as a Christian act or work. Everyone who fears God and is taught of him, may well say and lament with the prophet: Oh, how has the fine gold (of the divine Word) been darkened, Lam. 4:1, and falsified, the silver has become dross, and the wine mixed with water, Isa. 1:22; Ezek. 22:18. The planting of the heavenly Father has been pitifully trampled down, and a human planting set in its place, Matt. 15:3. The blind pharisees have destroyed the ordering of the Lord for the sake of their own order and this pleases the world well. Therefore, one blind person leads the other until they both fall into the canal /110/ [Matt. 15:14; Luke 6:39]. The almighty God protect us through Jesus Christ from these blind leaders. Amen.

Conclusion

This is our confession of the baptism of our Lord Jesus Christ according to the understanding of Scripture which God out of his grace has given us. But some out of wickedness [and] some out of lack of understanding persecute, blaspheme, and blame us because of this baptism; yes, they compare us with the Donatists, Münsterites, and other revolutionary and erring spirits, and say that we are also of such a nature. This is unjust before God, the righteous Judge, and does us much wrong. For when some hypocrites now (just as Judas Iscariot and Simon Magus and many others had done previously) receive baptism falsely and abuse the same, this hurts us deeply. Yes, we lament out of the great distress of our souls that many persons in this time cloak their wickedness with the holy and precious name of God, with the appearance of a false piety and with twisted Scripture.

However, we are not weakened in our faith through this, Rom. 1:16, for we have not built upon human persons, Ps. 116:11, but upon the foundation of the apostles and prophets of which Jesus Christ is the cornerstone, [Eph. 2:20]. Therefore, we say with the apostle, Shall the unbelief of people make the promise of God powerless, Rom. 3:3? This be far hence! It shall much rather be that God is true and all persons liars, [Rom. 3:4], as it is written, so that you are justified in your words and conquer when you are judged, Psalm 51:[4],6.

Therefore, we maintain that the ordinance of our Lord Jesus Christ about baptism is at all times correct in him and remains as a word and command of God; notwithstanding that some so deplorably abuse baptism and some despise it, whereby they heap God's wrath upon themselves and shall not escape his judgment.

However, we thank God the almighty Father through Jesus Christ, who out of his grace has given us a better understanding. For we confess one God, one eternal Father, who has created us, Eph. 4:5, one Lord and Savior, the only born Son of the living God, who has redeemed us, that is Jesus Christ, [1 Tim. 2:5], [and] one Holy Spirit, who is a true comforter and teacher, John 14:16; 15:26; 16:7. We confess one Christian congregation, one faith, one new birth, and one baptism, Eph. 4:4, which follows faith as a seal or witness of faith and as a bath of the new birth, Rom. 4:3. /111/

In summary, we hope by the grace of God that we believe and confess all that the divine Scripture teaches us to believe and confess, human weakness and imperfection at all times still excepted. And we desire to live our faith in quietness, to be obedient to government in all things not against God, Rom. 13:1; 1 Pet. 2:13, to seek and to maintain peace with all persons as much as is possibile for us, Rom. 12:18; Heb. 12:24. Finally, it is our intention and purpose to follow Jesus Christ through his grace. God, who knows the human mind and heart, Jer. 17:10, knows that we do not lie. Now we want also with God's help briefly to make our confession about the Lord's Supper.

ENDNOTES

1. Some ancient manuscripts do not contain the eunuch's confession as we find it in v. 37 of the KJV but not in the RSV.
2. *Wesen* may also be translated as conduct, nature, reality.
3. onformelijc, that is without doing violence to its meaning.
4. Luther, "On the contrary let everyone see to it that he is certain his worship and service of God has been instituted by God's Word, and not invented by his own pious notions or good intentions. Whoever engages in a form of worship to which God has not borne witness ought to know that he is serving not the true God but an idol that he has concocted for himself. That is to say, he is serving his own notions and false ideas, and thereby the devil himself; and the words of all the prophets are against him." *Luther's Works*. Eds. Theodore E. Bachmann and Helmut T. Lehmann. Philadelphia: Muhlenberg Press, 1960, Vol. 35, p.273.
5. These references are to Martin Luther's (1483-1546) 1523 "The Adoration of the Sacrament," *Luther's Works*, Vol. 36, "Word and Sacrament," II, edited by Abdel Ross Wentz and Helmut T. Lehmann. Philadelphia: Muhlenberg Press, 1959, pp. 300-301: ". . . it would be better not to baptize any children anywhere at all than to baptize them without faith . . . faith must be present . . . it is our judgment that through the faith and prayer of the church young children are cleansed of unbelief and of the devil and are endowed with faith. . . ." Luther's reference to the "Waldensians" is to the Bohemian Brethren, whom he often called by that name. See also the following note.
6. For an identification of Franck, see Dirk's treatise against his writings, pp. 445ff. In this reference to baptism and faith, several sentences are taken directly from Franck's *Chronicle* (1558 ed.), fol. Ciiiid, though Dirk seems to have had Luther's treatise before him as well.
7. Dirk here again relies on Franck's *Chronicle* (see fol. Lxxxc, 1595 ed.) in which the latter cites Erasmus' *Apologia ad Episcopum Hispaliensem*, pointing out that children participated in the Lord's Supper, receiving both bread and wine, until long after the time of Augustine (d. 430).
8. Dirk here clearly has in mind Zwingli's, Luther's and Heinrich Bullinger's (successor to Zwingli) stress on "faith and love" as the way to avoid schism, to wait until the people might be ready for changes in worship practices. The Anabaptists and other reformers saw this as false forbearance and compromise. For a fuller discussion see Yoder, *Täufertum und Reformation im Gespräch*. pp. 52, 141, 193, and Harder, *The Sources of Swiss Anabaptism*. p. 677, note 17.

THE SUPPER OF OUR LORD JESUS CHRIST— OUR CONFESSION

We ourselves do not want to accept the highly subtle and hairsplitting disputations about the Lord's Supper. They damage much more than they promote the memory of the death of Christ [as well as] the love and unity on which account the Supper was, after all, instituted by the Lord. But [we want] with simple and plain words to witness to our understanding and belief about it, so far as the Lord grants us grace. /111/

In the first place, we hold that one must believe all that is written about the Lord's Supper. The Lord Jesus Christ out of great love ordained it primarily as a memorial of his death for the believers, as an admonition, promotion, and establishment of Christian love and unity. In such a manner he took the break into his hands; after giving thanks he broke it and gave it to his disciples to eat and said, "This is my body which shall be given for you," Matt. 26:[26]. After this, he also gave the cup to his disciples that they should all drink out of it and said, "This cup is the New Testament in my blood, which is poured out for you for the forgiveness of sins," Matt. 26:[28]; Mark 14:[23-24]; Luke 22:[17], "this do to my memory," 1 Cor. 11:[24].

This institution and ordinance of our Lord Jesus Christ shall be maintained by all Christians as follows: Bread and wine shall be set forth in a Christian assembly and the death of the Lord proclaimed by a servant of the Word and be taken thoroughly to heart by every Christian and on account of the same thanksgiving to God shall take place. After this, the bread shall be broken and received and eaten by every Christian, /112/ and the wine shall be drunk with a true faith and to the memory that Christ Jesus gave his body for us and poured out his blood for us. This one must firmly believe and not doubt about it. For we hold that before all things and above all things one must believe and this same belief must conform to every word of God. Where this does not take place, there human understanding reigns and faith must perish, John 7:16[-17].

Thus, the Holy Scripture now teaches us to believe and take to heart about the Lord's Supper four principal parts or points:

In the first place, Christ broke the bread and gave it to his apostles and said, "Take, and eat; this is my body that is broken for you," etc., Matt. 26:26; 1 Cor. 11:[24].

In the second place, Paul said to the Corinthians, "The cup of thanksgiving which we say thanks for, is it not the fellowship of the blood of Christ? The bread which we break, is it not the fellowship of the body of Christ?," 1 Cor. 10:16.

In the third place, the bread and wine in the Supper are a memorial sign of the death and blood of Christ. For he himself said, "As often as you do this, do it to my remembrance of me." Again Paul said, "As many times as you eat from this bread and drink from this cup, thus you proclaim the Lord's death until he comes," Luke 22:19; 1 Cor. 11:[26].

In the fourth place, the Lord thus said of the cup, "This cup is the New Testament in my blood," Luke 22:20. Matthew and Mark thus add, "This is my blood of the new covenant which is poured out for many for the forgiveness of sins," 1 Cor. 11:[25]; Matt. 26:[28]; Mark 14:24.

All this we believe and confess about the Supper of the Lord without any doubt. However, whenever we search all these previously quoted words of Scripture and consider well how to understand them, and shall not take from them more than the right sense and understanding which is applicable everywhere, and [consider] that in addition no Scripture is opposed to faith; then we discover nothing other than that the Lord Jesus Christ out of great overflowing love has given his body and poured out his blood for us. And as a memorial he has thus instituted the Supper with bread and wine and left it for us so that we should remember with thanksgiving by the bread his body given for us and by the wine his blood which was poured out for us. /113/

Therefore, the words of Christ in the Supper, "This is my body" and "This is my blood," must be spiritually understood. For how might it otherwise exist that in the Supper the bread and the wine at the same time are the body and blood of Christ, the fellowship of his body and blood, and a memorial of his suffering and death, and the New Testament in his blood, and all Scriptures be given sufficient weight? Thus, we want now to examine all these Scriptures in an orderly manner and explain them thoroughly through the grace of the Lord.

In the first place, the Lord Jesus Christ instituted his Supper with bread and wine, and this agrees well with the fact that he himself is the living bread which came down from heaven with which souls are spiritually nourished through faith to eternal life, John 6:33. He is also the true vine planted by his Father the true vinedresser, John 15:1, and his Word the pure wine with which believing souls have their thirst quenched and rejoice in the Holy Spirit, Isa. 55:1. Now as often as Christians eat from the bread and drink from the wine they are admonished of this and renewed.

Thereafter, Christ thus broke the bread after giving thanks, gave it to his apostles and said, "Take and eat, this is my body which is broken for you." Because of these words, much is disputed and discussed both among the learned and unlearned. Many hold firmly that Christ is bodily in the bread. With this we are not in agreement, and we understand the previously mentioned words of Christ not literally but spiritually. The reasons that motivate us thereto, yes, even compel us, are many, some of which we want to present and indicate here.

The first one is because in the Scripture eating is so often used as believing and drinking as trusting. But the food and drink that is eaten and drunk is the bread of heaven, the Word of God, the waters of the Holy Spirit, yes, the flesh and blood of Christ. This is clear from the sixth chapter of John, where the Lord said: "I am the bread of life; he who comes to me shall not hunger, and whoever believes in me shall nevermore thirst," John 6:[35]. And again [saying], "I am the living bread which came down from heaven; whoever eats of this bread, that one will live in eternity; and the bread is my flesh which I shall give for the life of the world," John 6:51. And again, "My flesh is a true food, and /114/ my blood is the true drink. Whoever eats my flesh and drinks my blood abides in me, and I in him," etc., John 6:[55-56]. Out of all this it follows incontrovertibly that whoever has eaten the flesh of Christ and drunk his blood, that one believes Jesus Christ, the Son of the living God, who was crucified and died for us.

Thus sometimes eating is called believing in the Scriptures. For Christ is the true bread of heaven that is eaten, John 6:51, and the bread of heaven is God's Word, and the Word has become flesh, John 1:14, and the flesh of Christ was sacrificed and given for us, John 6:33. Therefore, whoever believes in the crucified Jesus Christ, his soul will be nourished with the bread of heaven, with the Word of God, yes, with the flesh and blood of Christ.

These three, that is, the bread of heaven, the Word of God, the flesh and blood of Christ, are all alike called a food of life, and Christ himself speaks in the gospel without distinction of the one from the other. For in the first place, he speaks much about the bread of heaven and calls it a bread of life. After this he speaks in the same manner and way about his flesh and blood and calls his flesh a true food and his blood a true drink.

However, at last (when some of his disciples took his words in a fleshly manner and therefore could neither believe nor tolerate them), he explained all the words which he had spoken about the bread of heaven, about eating his flesh and drinking his blood, and in conclusion thus said, "The flesh is of no avail, the Spirit makes alive; the words spoken to you are spirit and life," John 6:63. As if he would say, "All that I have spoken about the bread of heaven, similarly about eating my flesh and drinking my blood, that is spoken, intended, and to be understood from my words; for they are spirit and life and a nourishment of believing souls."

Therefore, whoever believes in the Lord Jesus Christ, the Son of the living God, who was crucified and died for us, and believes and trusts in him, Matt. [27:43]), that one receives Jesus Christ, the Word of the Father, John 1:1, and is fed with the heavenly manna, Exod. 16:15. Yes, he eats the flesh and drinks the blood of Christ Jesus, Num. 20:11, but spiritually with the mouth of the soul, not fleshly with the mouth of the body. For spiritual food (such as the flesh and blood of Christ) must be received spiritually. /115/

Out of this it may now be gauged clearly that Christ in the Supper spoke his words about eating his body and drinking his blood figuratively and meant them spiritually. For what he here once taught in John and portrayed for his disciples with many words about the spiritual eating of his flesh and drinking of his blood, and in addition demolished and disciplined the carnal understanding about eating of his natural flesh and drinking of his natural blood (which some through their misunderstanding had wrongly taken from his words), the same he did not alter in the Supper (for his Word is unchangeable), neither may it be broken, Matt. 24:35; Ps. 119:89; Isa. 46:[11], (for his Word may not be abrogated), for his Word is eternal, 1 Pet. 1:25; he has established and confirmed the same.

Therefore, it must remain without all doubt and contradiction just as Christ has spoken and concluded in John. That is, that the bread which he gives us to eat, which is also his flesh given for the life of the world—that is primarily the true and living bread come down from heaven; that is God's Word which we receive and accept through faith that our souls be fed therewith, quickened and strengthened with this to eternal life.

The second reason is that Christ himself explained his words in the Supper, for he said, "Take and eat, this is my body which shall be given or broken for you," Matt. 26:[26-28]; Mark 14:22; Luke 22:19. The last words explain the first; for this is after all certain and true, in addition, also incontrovertible, that it was not the bread but the true body of Christ that sat with the apostles at the table and gave them bread and wine and spoke the words, "This is my body," etc. This same body and no other is given and broken for us and sacrificed on the cross. How can we then believe otherwise than what Christ himself said? That is, that his body, yes, his natural body conceived of the Holy Spirit and born out from the virgin Mary, Matt. 1:20; Luke 1:31, is delivered into death for us? But the apostles ate the bread and drank the wine; therewith they were assured with all believers of the redemption Christ has won for us with his body and blood.

The third reason is that Judas also ate of the bread and drank of the wine, but nevertheless he did not receive the flesh and blood of Christ. /116/ For all that God gives us in the use of the sacraments, that faith receives, and God works in his elect alone through his spirit what the sacraments signify externally. Therefore, it is impossible without faith to become partakers of Christ and his gifts. It is even more impossible that the unbelieving and evil ones (in whom Satan dwells) may receive the pure unblemished and holy flesh and the precious blood of Jesus Christ. But a hungering and thirsting soul (after righteousness) is fed with it and refreshed (as with a spiritual food and with a spiritual drink), yes, is established and maintained through this in the fellowship of Christ Jesus just as he himself said, "Whoever eats me shall live because of my will." Again, "whoever eats from my flesh and drinks my blood abides in me and I in him," John 6:56.

From this it follows incontrovertibly that the unbelieving and evil ones have no part in the flesh and blood of Christ, so little as they are and abide in Christ, and Christ in them. Though they may eat the bread with Judas, they did not through this partake of the body and blood of Christ, but much more become guilty because of it. This is what Paul writes to the Corinthians: "Whoever therefore, eats unworthily from the bread and drinks the cup of the Lord, that one is guilty of the body and blood of the Lord," 1 Cor. 11:[27]. For to be guilty of the body and blood of the Lord and to partake of the body and blood of Christ is not the same thing; they are far separated from each other. For through faith one becomes spiritually partaker of Christ and his gifts, yes, of his flesh and blood. But through the abuse of the Supper one becomes guilty of the body and blood of the Lord and drinks judgment upon himself, [1 Cor. 11:29], etc.

We have an example of this in Judas, for even though he ate the bread and drank the wine with the apostles, nevertheless, the bread was for him no fellowship of the body of Christ, and the cup no fellowship of his blood (as it was for the other apostles). For he was and remained before, in, and after the Supper in the fellowship of Satan. But all those who eat Christ are in his fellowship (just as he himself testified with the previously spoken words), and they may not be in the fellowship of Satan. Therefore, Paul says, "You may not drink the cup of the Lord and the cup of demons at the same time. You may not partake of the table of the Lord and the table of demons at the same time," 1 Cor. 10:21. If the cup of the Lord may now not be drunk, with the demon's cup nor the bread of the Lord eaten with the sacrifice of devils, /117/ how much less may the cup of the Lord and the bread, yes, the flesh and blood of Christ Jesus, be eaten and drunk by the evil ones in whom Satan dwells?

But just as the apostate Christians through their apostasy from God and his Word, through their willful sin and despising of the truth and the Holy Spirit, themselves crucify the Son of God and tread him under foot, Heb. 6:[6]; 10:26, so also the hypocrites become guilty of the body and blood of the Lord through the abuse of the Supper. However, Christ is not now bodily crucified in his human person, for he died once for our sins, Rom. 6:10, and death shall have no more dominion over him but he sits personally at the right hand of his Father in his heavenly being, Eph. 1:20. And neither, indeed, is he bodily crucified by evil persons, as the apostle says, for they are companions and followers of the bloodthirsty Pharisees and Jews who killed and crucified Christ Jesus.

Thus in like manner, Christ is not eaten bodily by evil and false Christians. Nevertheless, they thus become guilty of the body and blood of the Lord (through the abuse of the Supper) for they eat the Lord's bread without spirit, without faith, without love to Christ and the brothers, without discerning the body of Christ. Yes, they have evil in mind against the Lord and their neighbors just as one can observe by their works. Therefore, it is impossible that they through the bread of the Lord should receive Jesus Christ.

But just as it took place with the betrayer Judas, that is, that after the morsel of bread, John 13:27, (which Christ had given him), Satan thus entered him (though he was already in him previously), so also it happens with these. For Christ has no part with Satan, 2 Cor. 6:15, nor with all the children of unbelief in whom Satan is and works. All these have neither fellowship with Christ nor Christ with them. Yes, where Christ comes, there Satan must flee as the evangelical parable clearly indicates to us, Matt. 12:29.

The fourth reason is so that the Scripture often speaks in a figurative manner, and literally calls many things other than what may be understood according to the Spirit and the true being. Just as the Scripture calls Christ the door to the sheepfold, John 10:7, a true vine, John 15:1, a rock, 1 Cor. 10:4, and additional other names which one must all understand and interpret spiritually.

Also, it is a common manner of speaking in Scripture that it gives the sign the name of that which it signifies.

So also [as] Christ in the Supper calls the bread his body and the cup his blood, he does not mean that his natural body /118/ and blood is essentially in the bread and the cup, but that both the bread and wine indicate and signify to us that Christ has given his body for us and shed his blood for us; and that we in the Spirit out of the power and fruit of his one holy sacrifice, Heb. 9:12, namely, his flesh once sacrificed for us, and his blood once shed for our sins, Heb. 10:10, have eternal life through true faith.

Therefore, when he gave the bread and the cup to his disciples and said to them, "Take and eat, this is my body, drink all thereof, this is my blood of the New Testament," he attached there "that is given for you," or "is shed for you," whereby he gave [us] to know that we by the bread and wine of the Supper shall remember and be assured of our redemption and reconciliation with God the Father through the sacrifice of the body and blood of Christ. Thereby, we also become renewed and admonished of the spiritual fellowship we have with Christ Jesus; that is, that he through faith with his spirit is in us and we in him. Yes, he is our head and we are his members, Eph. 5:[30]; 1 Cor. 10:16; Eph. 4:15, flesh of his flesh and bone of his bone, and, therefore [we] are also partakers of all that he has won through his sacrifice and shed blood which is peace with God, forgiveness of sins, righteousness, salvation, and eternal life.

And we are very much astonished that persons are so lacking understanding and want to include Christ bodily under the elements of bread and wine and bind him to these because in the Supper he called the bread his body, and do not notice that he, indeed, spoke expressly and much more about eating his flesh and drinking his blood in John than he did in the Supper. Nevertheless, he thus meant a spiritual eating, that is, believing, although he spoke literally and figuratively about it, which they also admit and confess.

And yet at the same time, they want in opposition to this to understand the words of the Supper completely fleshly—to eat Christ bodily in the bread and receive and drink his natural blood in the wine. [If this] were correct, Christ would be divided and opposed to himself, though he is the only truth, John 14:6, and all his words eternal which shall not pass away as he himself said, Matt. 24:35.

The fifth reason is because the Scripture so clearly and richly testifies, and we believe and confess, that Jesus Christ has a fully human person, Heb. 2:14; 5:2, just as we have (with the exception of sin and all sinful nature); and with the same /119/ he is now not on earth but in heaven at the right hand of God, Ps. 110:1; Heb. 1:13, and remains there until the last day in which he shall personally appear from heaven with the glory of his Father, Heb. 9:24, and with his angels to judge the living and the dead, Matt. 16:27.

This is an article of our Christian faith. This is the Word of the Lord which he has spoken to his disciples, saying, "The poor you shall always have with you, but you will not always have me with you," Matt. 26:[11]; Mark 8:38; Luke 9:26. Again, "I went out from God and came into the world; again, I am leaving the world and going to the Father," John 16:28. Again, Luke the evangelist writes in the Acts of the Apostles that Christ in the presence of his disciples was visibly taken up and a cloud took him up before their eyes. And while they were gazing into heaven as he went, look, two men stood there by them in white clothes and also said, "You men from Galilee, why do you stand looking into heaven? This Jesus, who was taken up from you into heaven, will come in the same way as you saw him go into heaven," Acts 1:9[-11]. Peter and Paul also both testify similarly that Christ sits at the right hand of the omnipotent God, and that eternally, 1 Pet. 3:22; Col. 3:1 until his enemies are laid at his feet for a footstool, Heb. 1:13, but at another time he shall appear without sin to those who wait upon him for salvation, Heb. 10:[12-14].

Here it is not valid that some present that since Christ is bodily in all creatures, he is, therefore, also in the bread and wine of the Supper. But this is open and unashamed lying and a falsification of the Scripture against the clear testimony of Christ and his apostles. It is true that Christ with his divine power is in all things, since all things exist and are upheld through him, Heb. 1:3; Col. [1:17]. However, bodily and with his human person he is thus not everywhere, nor in all creatures, nor in all places, as the angel certainly confessed when he said to the women standing by the grave of the Lord, "Do not be afraid, I know that you seek the crucified Jesus; he is not here; he has risen, as he has said. Come here, examine the place where the Lord lay," Matt. 28:5[-6], etc.

And why is it necessary to write much about it? Christ himself says everywhere in the gospel that he has gone to the Father and is no more in the world, which must after all be understood about his human person and not about his spiritual being and divine power. /120/

These and additional other reasons motivate, yes, compel us that we cannot believe that Jesus Christ, the only begotten Son of the living God, one with his Father, is bodily in the bread and cup of the Supper. However, we believe that he in divine purity and in human form is personally and actually at the right hand of God his heavenly Father, but with his Spirit he is in and with his disciples, the true Christians, to the end of the world as he himself said, Matt. 28:20.

And herewith is now in part explained why we do not believe that Jesus Christ is bodily in the bread and the cup of the Supper, but those who teach such [things] we reject as perverted interpreters of the Holy Scripture. Besides this, we have (according to our thinking) sufficiently safeguarded with Scripture that rightly to believe in Jesus Christ is to eat his flesh and drink his blood, but spiritually rather than fleshly, John 6:53, just as Christ also had a secret food about which his disciples did not know for he spoke to his disciples, "I have a food which you do not know," John 4:32.

What wonder is it then that the blind world neither knows nor understands about the true food of the believers? "My food is that I do the will of the one who has sent me," John 4:34. Thus he has also commanded us to labor for such food, for he said in the Gospel, "Work for food which does not perish, but which endures to eternal life, which the Son of Man will give," John 6:27.

Now just as it was the food of Christ to do the will of his heavenly Father, so it is also the food which God and the Son of Man, Jesus Christ, gives to us that we do the will of God and work his works; that is, that we believe in Jesus Christ whom he has sent, John 6:29, accepting, and keeping his words. For this is God's work, will, and command, as one may read in John.

However, the world is now so blinded and perverted that it, indeed, does not once think to labor for such food or to desire it from Christ, but allows itself to think, that if she only out of habit eats and drinks the bread and wine of the altar, its own sacraments (as it calls them) even though with false thoughts and superstitious opinions, as if it has then bodily received Christ. Therewith, everything is accomplished. Oh, no, those who think thus shall find themselves deceived as they shall appear before the judgment seat of Christ and give account of their faith. For neither bread nor wine nor water bring Christ into our hearts, nor washes us from sin, nor makes us saved; but Christ alone does this if we accept him /121/ with a true faith, hear him, and follow after him and thus do God's will.

As a further consideration, Paul calls the bread the fellowship of the body of Christ, 1 Cor. 10:16, and the cup the fellowship of his blood. To understand this thoroughly, what the fellowship of Christ with believers and of the believers with Christ is, one may observe that as Christ accepts the believers, he unites himself with them, so that he is the head and the believers are his body, Eph. 5:23, he pours his eternal life into them, gives them his Spirit, and grants them all his good and makes them partakers of it.

This is the spiritual fellowship of Christ and the believers which they have with each other. It has its beginning out of the grace of God through faith, Rom. 8:1; that is, all those who are chosen out of grace from God in the sanctification of the Spirit and in the belief of the truth, 2 Thess. 2:13, so that they believe in Jesus Christ, these are in his fellowship; that is, they are his and partakers of all of his heavenly goods and gifts.

Thereafter, the fellowship of Christ and the believers is renewed and confirmed through baptism and the Lord's Supper. For all believers are baptized through one Spirit into one body, 1 Cor. 12:13, although they were all one body with Christ through faith, just as Paul was already chosen of Christ before baptism and filled with the Holy Spirit, Acts 9:15. In the same manner, Cornelius, and others who in his house listened to the words of the apostle, had already received the Holy Spirit before they were baptized, Acts 10:44. Nevertheless they were baptized through one Spirit into the fellowship of the body of Christ, that is, they were established and admonished in it and were thus also gathered into the external fellowship.

This fellowship and incorporation with Christ is also established and renewed through the Supper; that is thus, that Christians in true unity of the Spirit and of faith, break the bread and drink the wine, whereby is signified to them and [they] are admonished of the fellowship of Christ and partake of all his merits, all his righteousness and holiness, yes, all that which is his that they all with each other have enjoyed all that to eternal salvation. For this fellowship consists in this, that all the goods of Christ are shared and become common to each individual Christian.

Therefore, Paul says, "This cup of blessing which we bless, /122/

is it not the fellowship of the blood of Christ? The bread which we break, is it not the fellowship of the body of Christ? For we many are one body, and one bread, since we all partake of the one bread," 1 Cor. 10:16[-17].

This meaning he clarifies further with one example of the Israelite people and says, "Behold Israel of the flesh, what sacrifices they eat and are they not in the fellowship of the altar?" 1 Cor. 10:18. Just as now the children of Aaron in the fellowship of the altar, that is, of the sacrifices of the altar, were participants in it. Thus it is also with the children of the spiritual Aaron, Jesus Christ, the only true High Priest, they are in the fellowship of his altar. For they are, on account of the new birth from his race and, therefore, they benefit in the Spirit through faith of the pure sacrifice of Christ which he through the Holy Spirit has offered on the altar of the cross, Heb. 9:13; 10:5.

Thereupon they break the bread and drink out of the cup as a witness that they are in the fellowship of the body of Christ. They have come into this fellowship out of God's grace and election through faith, and they are established therein through true baptism. In this fellowship they are also preserved and established through the Supper of the Lord, through which fellowship they are also partakers of all that Christ has and is his, just as the children of Aaron in the fellowship of the altar were also partakers of all that Aaron their father had given and administered for them.

So also through the bread and through the wine of the Supper, the unity and the agreeableness and fellowship of believers is portrayed and testified. However, in order to signify this fellowship, the Lord has taken and ordained such symbols in the Supper which over all merge back and forth and with their forms arouse and motivate to such fellowship. For just as the bread is made of many grains, poured together and ground, and the many grains become one loaf in which each individual grain loses its body and form, and similarly with the grapes with the changing of their form become a common wine and drink's body, so also all Christians must be united with Christ and with each other.

In the first place [they are united] with Christ, whom they receive through faith and are nourished with him. But there is now none greater, more firm, and can no more be separated one from the other /123/ than the unification of the food with the one who is fed by it. The food goes into and is transformed into the nature and becomes one being with the one who is fed. So also true Christians are through faith in Jesus Christ completely united with him, incorporated in him, yes, transposed and changed into his nature and character. Therefore, Christ also accepts them more firmly so that whoever harms them harms Christ himself, and again whoever does them good does it to Christ himself, Matt. 25:45; Acts 9:5, as he himself said, "What you have done to one of the least of my brothers, that you have done to me," [Matt. 25:40].

However, through this fellowship and love of Christ, Christians must thus again be enkindled in love, so that they regard all Christian need to be common, take their form and need upon themselves, and so become united through the true love which bears the burden one for the other and so fulfills the law of Christ, Gal. 6:[2].

Oh, that is a great sacrament and a great mystery, says Paul, that Christ and his congregation are one flesh and bone, Eph. 5:30. That is also a marvelous and blessed union that all Christians are one body and bread in Christ Jesus. They are one bread from the good seed which the heavenly Father has sown in the field of this world, Matt. [13]:3. Baked through the fire of love, they are one body of many members of Christ; baptized through one Spirit into one body, 1 Cor. 12:13; and must, according to the example of the natural body, be of one heart and soul and serve each other, be helpful and comforting, just as the members of the natural body do.

In the third place, the bread and the wine in the Supper are thus a memorial sign of the bitter suffering, the innocent death, and shed blood of Jesus Christ; that is, that we thereby remember that Christ Jesus out of great love gave his body and shed his blood for us. This the gracious, merciful Lord has made into a memorial and has given food to those who fear him, Ps. 111:[5]. He has instituted a Supper for the believers with bread and wine in order that they should thereby remember his suffering and death.

However, since the bread and the wine of the Supper are a memorial sign of the suffering and death of Christ, therefore, they have the names of that which is thereby remembered, namely, the body and blood of Christ, just as the figurative Paschal Lamb of God was called the Passover of God, in order that thereby the Passover should be remembered, Exod. 12:[27]. For because the Israelites should remember and not forget the benefits and miracles which had happened in Egypt, that the angel of the Lord had slain all the firstborn of Egypt in one night, and passed over their houses (because the doorposts were painted with the blood of the Paschal Lamb which was a sign of grace.) Therefore, God gave them a command that they should eat the Paschal Lamb yearly, and the same was named the

Passover and was a memorial of the Passover.

So also Christ has done for us. He has delivered us out of Egypt and out of the power of Satan. Therefore, he is a true Paschal Lamb, slaughtered on the cross, 1 Cor. 5:[7], and roasted through the fire of love, and through the sprinkling of his blood, 1 Pet. 1:19, we are cleansed and washed of our sins and guarded before the slaying angel, before the punishment of God which shall come upon Egypt, that is, upon the blind world. And so that we shall not forget this but remember it at all times, [he] has thus instituted the Supper with bread and wine and left it for us, that in the breaking of the bread we should remember with thankfulness his body given and broken for us, and in the cup his blood shed on our behalf.

And this memorial of the suffering of Christ is very necessary for us and teaches us to fear God and to hate sins, since we out of the suffering of Christ observe and see the strong wrath and unchanging zeal of God over sin and sinners in that he also struck so severely his well-beloved, only begotten Son on account of the sins of his people, as it stands written in the prophet Isaiah, Isa. 53:6. It must have been an unspeakable and unbearable zeal that he should have acted against such a great and immeasurably high person, namely, God's only Son and the wisdom of the Father himself. And, still, the Father did not free the sinners for him, except as he first did such a heavy repentance for them out of the righteousness of God can be known. And we have also to remember thereby that Jesus Christ had to taste such a bitter death on account of our sins. That it why it all took place. /125/

Whenever now a person thinks about this rightly, he is thus frightened and humbled. His heart becomes broken and his emotions battered, and he trembles before the Lord his God, before his severe judgment and earnest wrath over sin and thinks of how very much God hates sin and that it is a reason of the bitter suffering and innocent death of Jesus Christ, Isa. 53:7[-8]; 1 Pet. 2:24. Therefore, he guards himself from sin through the grace of the Lord so far as this is possible for him and thanks Christ for his love and faithfulness which he has manifested toward the human race. And the correct use of the Supper serves this objective, in order to admonish us of this, to place it before our eyes at all times, and to bring it into remembrance so that we may concern ourselves heartily therewith, which is very necessary in order to come to our self-knowledge, to the true humility, to the pure fear of God, to the true remembrance of the suffering of Christ, and to the hatred of sin.

In the fourth place, Christ also says of the cup of the Supper thus,

"This is the cup of the New Testament in my blood," Matt. 26:[28], or "This cup is the New Testament in my blood," Mark 14:[24]; Luke 22:[17]; 1 Cor. 11:[25]. However, what the New Testament is the prophet Jeremiah and the apostle Paul testify and say, "Behold the days are coming (says the Lord), that I will complete with the house of Israel and the house of Judah, not according to the testament which I made with their fathers on the days I took their hand to bring them out of the land of Egypt, for they have not remained in my testament, and I have no longer regarded them, spoke the Lord. But this is my testament which I will make with the house of Israel after those days, spoke the Lord: I will put my law within their minds and I will write it in their hearts, and I will be to them a God, and they shall be to me a people. And no one shall teach his neighbor nor his brother, saying, 'Confess the Lord,' for they shall all know me, from the least of them to the greatest, for I will be gracious to their unrighteousness, and I will remember their sin no more, Jer. 31:31[-34]; Heb. 8:8[-12].

Out of these words may be easily understood what the New Testament is, namely, the Word of the Almighty God and Father, proclaimed through Jesus Christ, John 7:16, and written in the believers' hearts through the Holy Spirit, [2] Cor. [3:3]; 1 John 1:1[-2], and the grace of God which has appeared through Jesus Christ for a teaching and enlightenment of troubled hearts, for the forgiveness of sins, for eternal salvation and the comfort of souls and consciences. For God the eternal and merciful Father, a giver of all good gifts and distributor of all heavenly goods, has made a new and gracious testament, wherein he shows his love /126/ overflowingly to us in that he has given us his only begotten Son, Rom. 8:32, and with him all things through which we have received grace, forgiveness of sins, knowledge of God, and all good gifts, John 1:16; Rom. 3:[24]; 5:1.

This New Testament (a word of the saving grace, witness of divine love, a comfort of the consciences, and eternal salvation of souls) Jesus Christ, as the true and only mediator of the New Testament, Heb. 12:[24], has received from God his Father. He has proclaimed the same to his chosen apostles and all God-fearing persons and with his Holy Spirit written it in their hearts. And, therefore, this is basically called a testament, even as is the testament of the outer and inner will of a dying person, who allows his will to be written in order that he might give his friends to know his will and desire, and gives his decision how after his death the right heirs should divide his estate. Thus Jesus Christ has also done. Before his death he called the apostles, his dear friends, to himself, revealed his Word to them, and gave them to know his will, and commanded them after his death to preach his gospel (that is, the joyful message of the grace of God, the merits of Christ, namely, that he with his suffering and shedding of blood has made sin and eternal damnation into nothing and has overcome death and the devil, Col. 2:13, and over against this has earned salvation and eternal life for us, Rom. 5:1, to all creatures, Matt. 28:19; Mark 16:15, and has given as a possession to all who believe all his goods, that is, all his glory, righteousness, and salvation with which he has endowed us and made us partakers of eternal life.

And since a testament without the death is not firm and the Old Testament is not established without blood, therefore, Christ has also established the New Testament with his innocent death and precious blood. And the New Testament has a much more costly sealing and establishment than the old had, which Moses was sprinkled with the blood of calves, Exod. 24:8, and thus established. But Christ Jesus, the true Moses and ruler of our faith, who has led us out of Egypt through the sea and has received from God his Father a law of the Spirit and a commandment of life, the same he has delivered to the true Israel and imprinted in their hearts. He has established and empowered his testament with his own precious blood, Heb. 9:13. /127/

And as a witness and memory of this before his death he has thus instituted for the apostles and all believers a Supper with bread and wine, and named the bread his body and the cup the New Testament in his blood as a true sign and memorial symbol that he has redeemed us with his body and established his testament with his blood.

He then rose from the dead on the third day and appeared to the apostles, Matt. 28:6[-7]; Mark 16:6[-7]; 1 Cor. 15:4[-5], and has established them as servants of the New Testament with his Holy Spirit and commanded them to preach the gospel to all creatures and to baptize the penitent and believing in the name of the Father and the Son and the Holy Spirit and to teach them to maintain all that he had commanded, Matt. 28:19; Mark 16:15.

Finally, he ascended to heaven and has seated himself at the right hand of God his heavenly almighty Father in the heavenly being, Mark 16:19; Acts 1:9; Col. 3:1; [1] Pet. 3:22. And he sits there personally and eternally, yet in such a manner that he is on earth with and in his own with his spirit, as long as the world exists, Matt. 28:20. And he expects that all his enemies shall be subject to him and he shall come from heaven on the last day to judge the living and the dead.

Out of all this it is now clearly to be observed that Christ Jesus is not bodily in the bread and cup of the Supper. For a testament maker is not personally in his testament, but he is there with his power whereby the testament is powerful and mighty. So also Christ is in his testament with his divine power, and with his Spirit he comforts and quickens everywhere the hearts of the believers who remain in his testament, his teaching and grace, and hold his Supper to his memory according to the Scripture. In this Supper they through faith in the crucified Son of God, Jesus Christ, and through the memory of his death are comforted, admonished, and assured in the consciences that they are God's children, brothers and sisters of Jesus Christ, incorporated into him, united with him, justified, holy and saved through him, Rom. 5:1; 1 Cor. 12:13; Gal. 3:28. They also have right and power with all believers to utilize (with whom they are one body in Jesus Christ) all that Christ Jesus has ordained and instituted.

So we hold that Christ Jesus is now bodily in heaven and yet has a spiritual being upon earth. But this spiritual being of Christ we understand thus, that he through the Holy Spirit /128/ has his work and being in all his members. This he himself testified with these words, "Whoever accepts you, accepts me," Matt. 10:40; Luke 9:48, "for it is not you who speak, but the Spirit of your Father who speaks through you," [Matt. 10:20]; John 9:48. Therefore, Paul says, "I dare not speak anything except what Christ has worked in me, Rom. 15:18. Again, "Whoever does not have the Spirit of Christ, that one is not his," Rom. 8:9. And "Do you not know that your bodies are a temple of the Holy Spirit," 1 Cor. [6:19]. Again, "No one can call Jesus a Lord except through the Holy Spirit," 1 Cor. 12:3. And John says, "By this we know that we are in Christ and he in us because he has given us from his own Spirit," 1 John 4:13.

Christ spoke about this spiritual being in the Supper to his disciples [when he said] that it were better for the believers that he depart from them than if he had remained bodily and personally with them, and he said thus, "I tell you the truth: it is better that I go away, for if I do not go away, then the comforter does not come to you; but if I go away, I want to send him to you," John 16:7. Again, "I will pray to the Father, and he will send you another comforter, that is the Spirit of truth," [John 14:16], "who proceeds out of the Father, the same he will bear witness to me," [John 15:26], glorify me, John 15:8; 14:26, reprove the world, John [16:8], "and admonish and lead you into all truth for he will take what is mine and declare it to you and he will remain with you eternally, [John 16:15].

In this manner Christ is with his own to the end of the world. But that he should be bodily in the bread and wine of the Supper, there to be eaten and received by the wicked as well as the pious (as the blind corrupt world thinks), this is against the spirit, intention, and meaning of the entire Holy Scripture. [It is also] against the Christian faith, and against the evidence of experience, and in addition against the characteristics of the natural body of Jesus Christ, as has been sufficiently explained above.

When now the belief about the Supper of the Lord is basically grounded and built upon God's Word, then it is also necessary to consider well the correct practice of the Supper and take it to heart. For what the Lord has instituted and commanded us to maintain, the same must be rightly practiced as well as rightly understood, believed, and confessed. But to the correct use of the Supper belong the following points:

In the first place, there must be a Christian congregation which gathers itself in the name of the Lord, declares the death of Jesus Christ /129/ with a true faith, and with the confession which Jesus Christ gave to the apostles and all believers to eat the bread and drink the wine, so also he has given the same his body and blood to an eternal salvation.

Hereby an admonition and heartfelt remembrance about the suffering and death of the Lord, about conforming to his suffering and death, about the unity of spirit and faith, Phil. 3:10, and about the love of God and one's neighbor, which belong primarily to the Supper serves [us] well.

In the second place, we maintain that this Supper shall not be held except only with the friends of God, the true Christians, who have accepted the gospel and through it have improved themselves, and upon the confession of their faith are correctly baptized in the name of the Father, the Son, and the Holy Spirit, Matt. 28:19, [those who] are truly concerned in their faith to walk as Christians, and earnestly reflect upon conformity to Christ, his suffering and death, his burial and resurrection. In summary, [those] who are one body with Christ and all the saints—these and no others are according to the evidence of the gospel to be renewed, admonished, and established with this Supper in the fellowship of Christ and all the saints.

In the third place, the Supper shall be harmoniously kept with all believers (as many as are together), not with one person alone as commonly takes place. For so the Lord has ordained and wants also to have it held, according to which all Christians must know how to conduct themselves. For if it is not right to disdain or change the established will of a person, Gal. [3]:15, then it is after all much more unreasonable to despise the testament of Jesus Christ and to break his ordinance.

So also the minister shall hold the Supper with the congregation and the bread shall be broken. For the Lord did so and the apostles maintained the same. Therefore, Paul wrote to the Corinthians, "The bread which we break," etc., 1 Cor. 10:16, and Luke writes, "They remained steadfastly in the apostles' teaching and in the fellowship and in the breaking of bread and in the prayers . . . and they were with one another in the temple daily and broke bread here and there in the houses," Acts 2:[42], 46. Again, the disciples came together in order to break bread. Therefore, the bread in the Supper must be broken, and in addition both parts of the Supper, that is, the bread and the cup, be given and distributed and be received by every Christian. And each person shall not eat his own particular bread, /130/ as it regrettably takes place in the world. For whoever does such a thing shows thereby that he holds his own supper and not the Supper of the Lord.

In the fourth place, Paul admonishes us that a man must first test himself before he eats the bread of the Supper and drinks from the cup, 1 Cor. 11:[28]. For whoever does not have a true faith in Jesus Christ, whoever is not incorporated into Christ, whoever does not want to die and live with Christ, whoever does not have an upright love to Christ and his neighbor, whoever is not one body with Christ and all the saints, that one may never more rightly use the Supper (which is after all a symbol of divine and brotherly love and unity) nor rightly distinguish the body of the Lord.

In the body of Christ two things are primarily to be noted, the head and the members. The head, which is Christ, must be noted, how we have all received grace and live through it, Eph. 1:[22-]23, and that we must adhere to the head alone, and must also take an example of love therefrom, reflecting on how faithfully the Lord Jesus Christ has served us. Thereafter we must notice the members of the body with whom we are one and reflect upon how Christ has served and still serves us with his gifts, so that we also serve our members with our gifts which we have received from God, be they spiritual or bodily, to the improvement and upbuilding of the body of Christ, and that all in love. This then is called rightly distinguishing the body of Christ.

It is also by this test that we, indeed, need to observe how the Israelites have eaten the figurative paschal lamb, namely, that in the first place the paschal lamb had to be unblemished and roasted on the fire, Exod. 12:5, [8]. And this signified the pure Paschal Lamb, Jesus Christ, 1 Cor. 5:[7], who through the eternal and fiery love was roasted for us on the rod of the cross, whom we eat spiritually through faith, and through the sprinkling of his blood are guarded and kept from the punishment of God which shall come over Egypt, [Exod. 12:7], that is, over the blind world.

In the second place, the Israelites were not permitted to have any leaven in their houses as they held the Passover, and the Passover Lamb had to be eaten with unleavened bread. This Paul also interpreted for us to the Corinthians thus: "Sweep out the old dough so that you may be a new dough, just as you are unleavened. For we have a Paschal Lamb killed for us, that is Christ. /131/ Let us, therefore, hold passover, not with the old leaven, also not in the leaven of malice and cunning, but with the sweet bread of sincerity and truth," 1 Cor. 5:[7-8].

In the third place, the Israelites thus had to eat the paschal lamb with bitter herbs, Exod. 12:[8]. Thereby is signified that our paschal lamb, Jesus Christ, seeks and desires a sorrowful soul, Ps. 51:[17], who suffers with him and is troubled, Matt. 5:4, who remembers his martyrdom and death with heartfelt reflections and is filled with divine sorrow, 2 Cor. 7:11.

In the fourth place, the Israelites thus had to have their loins girded, have a staff in hand, and had to eat in haste while standing, [Exod. 12:11]. And this signifies to us that we must keep our passover thus that we must gird up the loins of our minds, Luke 12:35; Eph. 6:14; 1 Pet. 1:13, and we must have the staff of the divine Word and comfort in hand, and say with David, that we will not fear even though we walk in the shadow of death, for the Lord is with us and his rod and staff comfort us, Ps. 23:4. Also we must keep the passover with desiring hearts that are hungering and desirous after Christ, out Passover Lamb and long to come out of Egypt into the promised land, that is, out of this evil world into the eternal Kingdom of God.

In the fifth place, no stranger or one who was uncircumcised was permitted to eat from the figurative Paschal Lamb. Much less may anyone keep passover with Christ, except he be circumcised in the heart, and is reckoned and found in the fellowship of the covenant, a companion of Christ and all the believers.

Finally, the children of Israel had to eat the paschal lamb in its entirety, and what was left over they had to burn with fire, [Exod. 12:10]. This signifies to us that we must not eat Christ, our Paschal Lamb, piecemeal but entirely. That is, we must hear and keep all his words, his entire teaching, and not do as some do who accept one word and reject the other. But all that has come out of the mouth of God and Christ, all this we must believe, and therein we must remain steadfast to the end. For man lives by all the words which proceed out of the mouth of God, Deut. 8:3; Matt. 4:4.

Again, whoever remains steadfast in Christ and his teaching, that one shall be saved, Matt. 10:22; 24:13. And since there are many things in the Scripture which are hard to understand, therefore, it is necessary at all times to pray to our heavenly Father in the name of Jesus Christ for the gift of the Holy Spirit, that our hearts may be kindled by the burning of the consuming fire to the love of God, /132/ and through the shining of the eternal light may be enlightened to know him for our salvation. Amen.

If all this is rightly reflected upon in connection with the Lord's Supper, then it is very good. For although it is, of course, primarily a figure of the fact that we eat Christ Jesus, our Paschal Lamb, through faith, 1 Cor. 5:7, and keep passover in the new being of the Spirit, holding this is spiritual eating and keeping of passover in the Supper before us admonishes and renews us. We must, therefore, reflect upon this, that the sign must be used according to the example and signification of the true being.

Whenever Christians now worthily practice the Supper with pure hearts and with a true faith, they are (through Jesus Christ who according to his promise is in the midst of such a gathering, Matt. 18:20) quickened in their souls, admonished in their consciences, and assured of the grace of God, of the fellowship of Jesus Christ and all the saints. Yes, [they are assured] that they are united with God through Jesus Christ, righteous and innocent members of his body, Rom. 3:24; 5; 8:1, temples of the Holy Spirit, 1 Cor. 3:16, and that Christ is their Brother, Bishop, Mediator, Intercessor and Reconciler, 1 John 2:1; Heb. 2:17; 5:1. And with his merit he desires to justify them and redeem all their frailties with his eternal sacrifice and steadfast prayer, and through the Holy Spirit reign and lead them into eternal glory, [Heb. 9:11-12].

[Christians] are also united with each other as members of one body, Rom. 12:4; 1 Cor. 10:17; 12:12, as one bread out of many grains, and one wine out of many grapes. They are, therefore, partakers of all that Christ has wrought in his own person and in all believers, and still works. They also have the right and power with all the saints to enjoy all the divine things which Christ has instituted for us to the sanctification of his name and the promotion of faith and love.

This rejoices and comforts the heart of a Christian, so that it is kindled and aflame with love toward both God and neighbor. It springs up and breaks forth into thanksgiving, lauds, and praises the Lord for his grace and welfare, [and] speaks with the prophet, "Praise the Lord my soul, and all that is within me, praise his holy name! Praise the Lord my soul, and forget not what good he has done for me," Ps. 103:1[-2], etc. /133/

This is our confession about the Supper of the Lord Jesus Christ. But that some slander this our confession and regard it as fanaticism (because we believe and confess that Jesus Christ is bodily in heaven at the right hand of God, Mark 16:[19]; John 6:62; Acts 1:9; Heb. 1:13, but is and works with his Spirit in all believers and is spiritually eaten and received because they believe him and accept and keep his Word), in this we must have patience. We may not after all believe contrary to Scripture, but measure our faith with the Scripture. For faith comes out of the Word of God and must conform to the same, Rom. 10:17.

Since then the Scripture so richly testifies that Jesus Christ is bodily and personally in heaven, and spiritually on earth (as we have sufficiently proven with Scripture above), therefore, we believe this with our whole hearts. And since we thus believe in addition the words of Christ, "This is my body," etc., and all that is written of the Supper of the Lord as has been touched upon and explained above, confess them as correct, and hold them as genuine, therefore, we take out of all these Scriptures a single understanding which is over all conformed to the truth and not contrary to any Scripture.

But such an understanding we cannot have nor come upon, except we understand the words of Christ, "This is my body," etc, spiritually, believe and confess that Christ is received by a hungry soul, yes, his flesh and blood is spiritually eaten and drunk through faith, John 6:54. So all Scriptures are in agreement therewith and remain unbroken. However, if we understand the previously quoted words of Christ literally and carnally, then we are smitten in the consciences with many Scriptures, yes, convinced and overcome, as if we did not believe [that] all the words of God do enough.

Therefore we thus hold about the Supper of the Lord as we have here acknowledged, and that out of Christian simplicity, according to the right sense of the Spirit, according to the meaning and content of the Scripture, and according to our deepest comprehension and understanding out of God's Word. In summary, according to the measure of the gift and of the Spirit and faith received from God, we can neither better nor more certainly confess nor discern about it.

May the almighty God, Father of all mercy and grace, who has from the beginning provided and chosen believers for salvation, enlighten all earnest and well-intentioned hearts with the light of his Holy Spirit and /134/ gather the scattered sheep in the unity of true faith under the one good Shepherd and Bishop of all believing souls, that is, under Christ Jesus, [to] whom be praise and honor in eternity. Amen.

Soli Deo Gloria [To God Alone Be Glory.]

THE INCARNATION OF OUR LORD JESUS CHRIST, THE ONLY BEGOTTEN SON OF HIS ETERNAL AND ALMIGHTY FATHER

A Brief Confession

By Dirk Philips

"The Word became flesh," John 1:14

"That which was from the beginning, which we have heard, which we have seen with our eyes, which we have looked upon and touched with our hands, concerning the word of life—the life was made manifest." 1 John 1:1[-2]

"Great indeed, we confess, is the mystery of our religion: He was manifested in the flesh, vindicated in the Spirit, seen by angels, preached among the nations, believed on in the world, taken up in glory." 1 Tim. 3:16

FOREWORD

/137/ Since we are severely blasphemed and mocked by many people on account of our faith, yes, some lie about us and say that we do not believe in Jesus Christ, because we cannot accept the old leaven of the Pharisees with which they compose and make such strange glosses upon the Scriptures concerning the incarnation of Christ. And we are by some mistakenly accused of not believing in Jesus Christ who after all is our only hope before God the Father. Therefore, we wish (through the grace of the Lord) briefly to indicate our faith concerning Christ Jesus, the only begotten Son of the living God, our Lord and Savior, Col. 1:27; 1 Tim. 1:1; 1 Thess. 1:3, in order that everyone may see, read, and hear what we maintain about Christ Jesus, about his divinity and humanity; namely, that we are neither heretics nor Jews (even though the world reviles us as heretics and Jews) but Christians alone and confess all that Scripture teaches and witnesses concerning Christ Jesus. For this is our hope and our joy before God the Lord, that we firmly believe in Christ Jesus, trust and hope entirely upon him, John 3:16; Eph. 2:7, are baptized in his name upon the confession of our faith, Matt. 28:19; Mark 16:[16], and have become and desire to remain (out of grace) his disciples. But the eternal God and Father of all mercies, who has elected us to salvation from the beginning and taught us the pure knowledge of his Only begotten Son, Jesus Christ, through the enlightenment of his Holy Spirit, 2 Thess. 2:13; 2 Pet. 1:2, and impressed it into our hearts, to him be praise and glory in eternity, 2 Tim. 4:[18], for his unspeakable grace and blessing. Amen.

CONCERNING CHRIST JESUS THE ONLY BEGOTTEN SON OF THE LIVING GOD AND HIS INCARNATION— OUR CONFESSION

/138/ We believe and confess that Jesus Christ is our Lord and Redeemer, Matt. 16:16, the first-born and only begotten Son of the eternal and almighty Father and the living God, John 1:14; [5:18]; Heb. 1:2, a reflection of his glory and an express image of his nature, unspeakably begotten of the Father before the beginning of the world, divine from eternity and one nature with the Father so that they are one God and Lord, 1 John 4:9, and together eternally have identical power, might, love, glory, work, and wills, Heb. 1:3; Mic. 5:[4]; Isa. 53:11; Col. 1:15; John 5:19; 8:14; 9:4; 10:17; 13:3; 14:7; 15:1; 17:3.

But because the Son is named the Word (in Greek *Logos*, in Latin *Sermo* or *verbum*) it is not to be understood that every word which God speaks is God's Son. Oh, no! For the Son is not a spoken but an essential Word of which all the spoken words of God (which are the Holy Scripture) give witness, 1 John 1:1; John 1:1; 2 Pet. 1:20[-21]. But that the Son of God is called the Word has this reason (according to many learned ones) and this meaning (so far as we can grasp the content of Scripture) that the Son has gone forth out of the mouth of the Most High, an image of the fatherly disposition; gone forth (we say) as an essential word and as a natural Son of God who is one substance, identical in character and nature with the Father, Ecclus. 24:1[-4]; Heb. 1:3. Yes, the one into whom the Father has infused his essential nature and express image, John 10:25; 13:3; 2 Cor. 4:4; Col. 1:15, wherefore also the apostle says that God had spoken to us in former times through the prophets but afterwards through the Son, Heb. 1:1[-12], yes, through the personal Word. Also that the Son is not a spoken but a speaking Word, and through this Word, that is, through the Son's powerful Word, all things exist, and have their being, [Col. 1:17]. Therefore, the apostle John says that the Son is the Word of life of whom the apostles proclaimed to us all that they had seen and heard, 1 John 1:1. /139/

This same Word, namely, the Son of God, was from God out of grace and love promised and pledged as a Savior to Adam and his descendants. Therefore, he also became a human being, Phil. 2:5[-6]; for since he is a Savior of mankind and a mediator between God and humanity, [1] Tim. 2:5, he had to be truly God and man. According to his divinity, he was able to help us eternally and completely reconcile us to the Father, Heb. 10:14, and accomplish his will, John 10:17; yes, the will of the Father is also the will of Christ, John 17:20[-21]. But according to his humanity, he was able to offer himself for us as a pure, holy, and well-pleasing offering and fragrant sacrifice to the Father, Eph. 5:2, for the forgiveness and cleansing of our sins, Eph. 1:7; 2:4 [-5]; Rev. 1:[5-]6, because he died innocently in our behalf, and human nature in him was unblemished and without sin, [1] Pet. 1:18 [-19]; Isa. 53:8[-9]; 1 Pet. 3:18.

Therefore, we believe and confess that Jesus Christ, our Redeemer, Savior, and Mediator, is truly God and man, Gal. 1:4. He is truly God from eternity and was begotten of the Father before the beginning of the world. But he became truly man in the last times, 1 Tim. 2:5; Mic. 5:[2-3]. However, how his incarnation took place the evangelists and apostles write for us with clear and express words. Matthew says that the angel spoke to Joseph, "Do not fear to take Mary your wife, for that which is conceived in her is of the Holy Spirit," Matt. 1:20. Luke writes that the angel spoke to Mary, "The Holy Spirit will come upon you, and the power of the most high will overshadow you; therefore, the child to be born (out of you) will be called holy, the Son of God," Luke [1:35]. And John says, "In the beginning was the Word, and the Word was with God, and the Word was God. All things were made through it," John 1:1[-3], and this same Word became flesh, and is the only begotten Son of God, full of all grace and truth, John 1:14. And John also says, "That which was from the beginning, which we have heard, which we have seen with our eyes, which we have looked upon and touched with our hands, concerning the word of life—the life was made manifest, and we saw it, and testify to it, and proclaim to you the eternal life which was with the Father and has appeared to us," 1 John 1:1[-2].

In all of these words we see and note clearly that Jesus Christ the only begotten Son of the living God, 1 John 4:9, did not become man from a human seed (which after all is unclean), Job 4:17, /140/ but from[1] the eternal and unchangeable seed of God the heavenly Father, 1 Pet. 1:23; 1 John 3:9, in Mary through the power and activity of the Holy Spirit.

John confirms this and says, "He who is of the earth belongs to the earth, and of the earth he speaks; but he who comes from heaven (namely Jesus Christ) is above all," John 3:31. Paul in his letter to the Corinthians agrees with this and says, "The first Adam is from the earth and earthy, the second Adam is the Lord himself from heaven," 1 Cor. 15:[47]. These words are a clarification of the previously quoted words of John in which there is a clear distinction between Christ and Adam; namely, that Adam is from the earth, but Christ to the contrary is from heaven.

However, if the body of Christ was made in Mary (as the world thinks and speaks of so foolishly), then there would be no difference between the body of Christ and the body of Adam. The reason: Just as Christ was conceived in Mary through the Holy Spirit, so also Adam was made by God and had no other Father than God, Matt. 1:20; Luke 1:31; Gen. 1:27. What distinction would there be between the body of Christ and the body of Adam, if the body of Christ as well as that of Adam were made of the earth? And the body of Christ must be made of the earth if he is of a human seed, for all persons are, because of the body, dust and earth, Gen. 2:7. Thereafter, it is yet further to be reflected upon that Adam was made by God out of pure earth. But after the earth was soiled through sin and all men were cast under the curse and corrupted in their nature, Rom. 3:10; Gal. 3:10, how should the body of Christ remain pure if it were of a human seed, which is, after all, impure, Job 14:4? This be far hence. However, God the heavenly Father prepared a body for his only begotten Son, Heb. 10:5, but not of impure human seed; rather of his imperishable seed with which he made Mary fruitful and impregnated her through the power of his Holy Spirit as the previously quoted sayings of the evangelists and apostles clearly indicate, Matt. 1:20; Luke 2:31.

Therefore, Christ testifies everywhere that he came down from above, from heaven, John 3:31; 8:23; 15:22; 16:5; 17:5. But particularly in John, he speaks of his origin as follows: "I am the living bread which came down from heaven in order that anyone who eats of this bread will never die; and the bread which I shall give to you is my flesh, which I shall give for the life of the world," John 6:51. /141/

If Christ is now the bread of heaven and the bread of heaven is the flesh of Christ, then it is impossible that Christ's flesh is made of the seed of Mary, since neither Mary's seed nor any earthly creature, of all things, is or may be called the living bread which came from heaven.

Again: Christ speaks much in John of eating his flesh and drinking his blood, John 6:50. So we must now look at and reflect how the flesh shall and must be eaten and his blood drunk; namely, through the fact that we with pure hearts and with true faith receive and guard God's Word. Wherefore then do we eat the flesh of Christ and drink his blood? Because the Word of God has become flesh, John 1:14, and also because the Word of God and the flesh of Christ are one, as Christ himself testified with these words, "I am the living bread which came down from heaven. The bread which I shall give you is my flesh, which I shall give for the life of the world," John 6:51. And this living bread (which is Christ and his flesh) this is without doubt and contradiction the Word of God. Therefore, if anyone believes the words of God and guards them, he receives Christ, the Word of life, and the bread of heaven. Yes, he eats the flesh and drinks the blood of Christ, John 6:53. On this account Christ called his flesh a true food and his blood a true drink since the Word of God is after all verily the food of souls, [John 6:55]. But since the Word became flesh, John 1:14, and therefore the Word and the flesh of Christ are one, therefore, the flesh of Christ is also true food and his blood true drink.

Finally, Christ Jesus is that living bread which descended as a dove from heaven. And what was a bread of angels has also become a bread of humanity, Ps. 78:25; Wis. of Sol. 16:20. But the bread which is he himself and which he gives to humanity to eat, that is to the believers, is his flesh which he has given for the life of the world, John 6:51.

Further, it is here to be observed and reflected upon that humanity, once it had fallen, could in no way be helped except by the one by and through whom it had been created. Therefore, the eternal and omnipotent God (who created the first Adam and all creatures), Gen.

1:[20-27], according to his fathomless grace and mercy, promised his eternal Word and only begotten Son /142/ (through whom humanity and all things were created), John 1:3; Heb. 1:2, to fallen and corrupted humanity and allowed the same, in the fullness of time and grace, Gal. 4:4, to become a man; in order through the same Son through whom he had created humanity, he might again help, redeem, and eternally reconcile humanity with himself, John 3:16; 2 Cor. 5:15 [-19]. Therefore, John says so expressly, that Word through whom all things were created, that Word has become flesh and lived among us [an indirect reference to John 1:1; 1:3; 1:14]. And Paul says, "God did not spare his own Son but gave him for us," Rom. 8:[32]. Again, God has sent his own Son in the place of sinful flesh. Again, "God was manifested in the flesh, vindicated in the Spirit, seen by angels, preached among the nations, believed on in the world, taken up into glory," 1 Tim. 3:[16]. Again, "everyone should be minded as Christ Jesus also was, who, though he was in the form of God, did not count it as robbery, but emptied himself, taking the form of a servant being born in the likeness of other people. And being found in human form, he humbled himself and became obedient unto death, even death on a cross," Phil. 2:5[-8].

Out of all of these words, a Christian understands well that God's eternal Word, John 1:1, God's only begotten and firstborn Son, John 3:16, yes, God himself became a human being, Rom. 8:[32], and took off his divine form and left his divine glory and put on a human and servant-like form. In summary, he who was God became man and he who became man was God and man, and he who was God and man, he died as man and he who died as man rose from the dead as God, John 1:14; Rom. 9:5; [1 John 4:2]; 1 John 5:1; John 20:[17].

All this, the figure of Melchizedek, Gen. 14:18, of whom the apostle writes to the Hebrews, foretells and confirms as follows: "This Melchizedek was a king of Salem, a priest of the most high God, who went to meet Abraham returning from the slaughter of the kings and blessed him; and to him Abraham gave a tenth part of everything. He is first, by translation of his name, king of righteousness, and then he is also king of Salem, that is, king of peace. He is without father or mother or genealogy, and has neither beginning of days nor end of life, but resembling the Son of God, he continues a priest forever," Heb. 7:1 [-3].

This text testifies clearly of the eternal divinity and of the humanity of Jesus Christ the Son of God. For the apostle /143/ says of the person of Melchizedek that he had neither beginning of days nor end of life, and thereby the Son of God is compared with his person which is eternal. For so it is also written of the person of the Son of God. His origin is from the beginning and from eternity, Mic. 5:[2]. Again: He is the mighty God, the eternal Father, Isa. 9:[6]. He is God whose throne is from eternity to eternity, Ps. 45:[6]; Heb. 1:8. He had glory with God before the world was, John 17:5. "He is before all things and all things exist in him," [Col. 1:17]. He is the Word that was in the beginning with God, John 1:1. "In him was life," [John 1:4]. He is the first and the last, the living one who was dead and lives from eternity to eternity, Rev. 1:17.

These and similar passages of Scripture actually speak of the divinity of the eternal Son. For the humanity, office, and priesthood of God's Son are not from eternity, but the person of the Son of God is without beginning, was always God, God's Word, God's wisdom, truly God himself and essentially in divine form, glorified as God, Ecclus. 1:1; 24:[3-4]; John 1:1; 17:5; 1 John 5:20; Heb. 7:3.

However, that the apostle says of Melchizedek that he was without father, without mother, without genealogy, this he himself explains at another place; namely, that Melchizedek's generation was not named and this happened because he was an image and figure of the Son of God, the genuine priest, Heb. 7:[16].

For one knows very well that Melchizedek always had father and mother, along with the rest of humanity since the entire Scripture does not mention that God has created a single person without father and mother, except Adam and Eve, Gen. 1:27. But the Spirit was silent about the generation of Melchizedek in order that he might correctly be compared with the Son of God as one among those who truly was on earth, loved, served, and offered himself just as a human being, and yet was not from the earth, but from heaven, born as the Son of man, yet the life and Savior of all humanity, Gal. 1:4; Eph. 5:2; Titus 2:14; John 3:31; 1 Cor. 15:45.

Finally then, this is the meaning of the apostle—that the genuine Melchizedek, Jesus Christ, is God and man, God's Son and the Son of man, and God's Son from eternity to eternity, Isa. 9:[6]; Gal. 4:6; Col. 1:13; 1 John 1:1, Heb. 7:3. But he became a human being and a Son of man in the last times, yet also in such a manner that he had neither father nor mother nor genealogy among men and yet he did have. For Mary called Joseph his father, Luke 2:[48], and she herself was his mother. According to the flesh he was born out of the genealogy of Judah, Heb. 7:14; Matt. 1:3; Mic. 5:[2].

However, he also had neither father nor mother nor /144/ genealogy among men as though he had become a man from human seed for he is the second Adam, the Lord himself from heaven, 1 Cor. [15]:45. The same Lord from heaven is truly God and man, Rom. 9:5, God's Son and the Son of man, one Jesus Christ, our High Priest in eternity according to the order of Melchizedek, Heb. 2:17; 5:1; 8:1, our eternal King and Prince of Peace, Isa. 9:[6], who rules in the house of David with the scepter of the divine Word, Luke [1:69]; Ps. 45:[6]; Heb. 1:8, and makes the believing consciences peaceful with his grace and assures them of the grace of God and their eternal salvation, [Rom. 8:31-35]. Yes, he makes all his Christians kings and priests to God his heavenly Father, 1 Pet. 2:9; Rev. 1:6. To him be glory and praise in eternity! Amen.

But that the Scripture calls Christ a seed of the woman, Gen. 3:15, does not irritate us and this we wish with God's grace to show, namely, as follows: In the first place the Scripture speaks in a figurative manner at many places, and names many things according to the letter, other than what they are according to the true reality of the Spirit as may be understood. Therefore, Christ also has many names in Scripture which according to their eternal reality are in no sense applicable to him. For he is named a rock, 1 Cor. 10:4, and a vine, John 15:1, not because he essentially and naturally is a rock and a vine, but because of the significance he is so named. In like measure he is also named the seed of a woman, Gen. 3:15, and a seed of Abraham, Gen. 22:[17-]18, not because he essentially and naturally is of the fleshly seed of the woman and Abraham, but because he was promised Adam and Eve and Abraham as a future Savior who should be born out of them according to the flesh, Gal. 3:8. But if it were really true that Christ was of a natural human seed, then humanity would be helped of God through its own seed, that is, through itself. But this be far hence, for God has helped fallen and corrupted humanity, not through fallen and corrupted human seed, but he willed and had to help it through his eternal Word and Son so that he was the Redeemer of humanity as well as its Creator, Ecclus. 1:4; John 1:1.

In addition, all Christians know well that Eve is a figure of the Christian congregation which God the eternal Father has made the bride of the second Adam, Christ Jesus, Eph. 5:22[-23]. For she is flesh of his flesh and bone of his bone, and her children are all believing Christians who are born out of the imperishable seed of God, 1 Pet. 1:23, /145/ and have a constant enmity with the seed of the serpent; that is, with all children of the devil (who are the seed of the serpent), John 8:44; Gen. 3:15], and are assailed by the same with all craftiness; nevertheless, at all times they triumph and overcome through Christ Jesus, as Paul says, "Thanks be to God, who always helps us keep the field in Christ Jesus," 2 Cor. 2:[16], and yet another, "Thanks be to God, who has given us victory through our Lord Jesus Christ," [1] Cor. 15:57.

In the second place, the promise of God to Abraham that in his seed "all nations of the earth should bless themselves," Gen. 22:18, took place. Thereupon God gave him his natural son, Isaac, who bore the image of the promised seed, of the true Isaac, Jesus Christ, Gal. 3:8. Since then Isaac is a natural son of Abraham and a figure of Jesus Christ, and flesh may not signify flesh nor be so understood, therefore, also Christ may not be a spiritual seed of Abraham but is a natural seed of the spiritual Abraham, his heavenly Father who was promised the patriarch Abraham from God out of grace, Gen. 17:8; 22:18; Rom. 4:3; Gal. 3:8.

After that Paul explains the figure of Abraham, Sarah, and Isaac so that Abraham is a figure of God the Father, Sarah of the New Testament, and Isaac of Christ, Gal. 4:22[-26]. Yes, that not only Christ but all Christians are Abraham's seed and, like Isaac, children of the promise, for Paul also says, "Not all who are descended from Israel belong to Israel, and not all are children of Abraham because they are his descendants; but 'through Isaac shall your descendants be named.' For this is what the promise said, 'About this time I will come and Sarah shall have a son,' " Rom. 9:6[-9].

In these words we see clearly that true Christians alone are Abraham's children because of the fact that they believe in Jesus Christ in whom Abraham also believed, John 8:39; Gal. 3:[6-]7; Rom. 4:16. But those who are Abraham's children and believe in Jesus Christ, these are also born out of God, 1 John 5:1, and those who are born out of God, these are also children of God, the genuine (or true) Abraham, and the eternal heavenly Father of whom the patriarch Abraham was a figure. But those who do not believe in Jesus Christ are neither God's nor Abraham's children; even though they are already born of Abraham according to the flesh, they are nevertheless not included under the promise nor counted as Abraham's seed, Rom. 9:6; Gal. 3:8[-9]. Fleshly birth counts so little before God, Rom. 9:6, and the true relative of Abraham /146/ depends entirely upon the imperishable seed of God, 1 Pet. 1:23, out of which the new birth takes place, 1 John 3:1; 5:1. Therefore, what the Scripture says about Abraham and his seed has more a spiritual than a carnal sense and must on this account be looked upon more with spiritual than with carnal eyes.

In the third place, all these previously quoted sayings and witnesses of the incarnation of Jesus Christ must be selected out of Scripture. That is that the Holy Spirit came down into Mary and what was conceived in her came from the Holy Spirit, Matt. 1:25, and that holy [child] that was born out of her was the Son of the Most High, Luke 1:[35], and that Christ, the Word of life, of whom the apostles have proclaimed all that they saw, heard, looked upon, and touched with their hands, 1 John 1:1, became flesh, John 1:14; and that Christ is the second Adam, the Lord himself from heaven, 1 Cor. 15:45, and that he is the living bread which came down from heaven and that the living bread is his flesh which he has given for the life of the world, John 6:51. All these passages and testimonies of Scripture (we say) which all alike so clearly testify from whence and through which the incarnation of Jesus Christ took place, must be broken and suffer violence if one regards Jesus Christ as the natural seed of the woman and Abraham.

Therefore, we simply remain with the previously touched upon passages and testimonies of Scripture, believe and confess that Jesus Christ was conceived of the Holy Spirit, Matt. 1:[20]; 25, born out of the virgin Mary, the holy Son of the Most High, Luke 1:31, the Word of life, John 1:[4]; 1 John 1:1, the second Adam, the Lord himself from heaven, [1 Cor. 15:45-47], the living bread which came down from heaven, which living bread he called his flesh that he has given for the life of the world, John 6:51. All this we believe without all doubt, without all additions and subtractions, as the Word of God which shall and may neither be added to nor taken away, Deut. 4:2; 12:32; Prov. 30:6.

Further, just as Christ was called the seed of the woman and of Abraham, Acts 3:[25], so in like manner he is also called the fruit of the loins of David, as God had promised him that he would be born of his seed according to the flesh. For the natural son of David and the /147/ bodily fruit of his loins of which the text of Scripture testifies according to the letter was actually Solomon who sat upon the throne of his father, David, 1 Kings [2:12], who bore the image of Jesus Christ, the peaceful Solomon and eternal king who rules over the Israel of God, Isa. 9:[6-7]; 11:1; Luke 1:[69-73]; Gal. [3:28-29]. However, Christ is not a natural son of the patriarch David, but of the living God; therefore, he himself said to the Pharisees, "What do you think of the Christ? Whose son is he?" They said to him, "The son of David." He said to them, "How is it then that David, inspired by the Spirit, calls him Lord, saying, 'The Lord said to my Lord, sit at my right hand, till I put your enemies under your feet,' Ps. 110:1? If David thus calls him Lord, how is he then his Son" Matt. 22:40[-45]? With which words Christ clearly testifies that he is not a natural son of David, otherwise he could not be and be called David's Lord, since the son is not lord of the father but the father is lord of the son. However, Christ is David's God and Lord; therefore, he is not his natural Son as one conceived of his seed and become man, but born out of his seed according to the flesh and out of the genealogy of Judah, out of which genealogy David had descended, Rom. 1:3; 9:[6]; Heb. 7:14. And no one who is understanding of Scripture should be astonished that Scripture calls Christ the seed of the woman and Abraham and the fruit of the loins of David and the body of Mary. For since the Scripture calls Christ sin, who knew of no sin, on account of the fact that he was sacrificed for our sins, Rom. 8:3; 2 Cor. 5:21, what wonder is it that the same Scripture calls Christ the seed of the woman and Abraham, a fruit of the loins of David and the body of Mary on account of the reasons previously touched upon, even though he neither actually is nor may be considered as such by any Christian.

Yet some persons still cast before us the fact that the apostle says to the Hebrews that they all come from one origin, both he who sanctifies and those who are sanctified, on account of which he is not ashamed to call them brethren, Heb. 2:11, and says, "I will proclaim your name to my brethren, in the midst of the congregation I will praise you," [Heb. 2:12]. And again, "Since the children share in flesh and blood, he himself likewise partook of the same nature," [Heb. 2:14]. To this we reply briefly as follows:

That the apostle neither said nor meant that Jesus Christ became man from our flesh and blood is sufficiently clear from all that we have said above about the /148/ incarnation of Jesus Christ and indicated out of Holy Scripture. For that is neither right nor reasonable (as some learned ones also say) that many sayings of Scripture should give way to one saying and on account of one saying the others should be broken, twisted and changed. But one saying shall give way to many sayings and be understood and interpreted according to many witnesses, yet all things with discretion, truth, and righteousness.

According to this it is certain and undeniable that the previously mentioned words of the apostle must also be so understood that both Christ who sanctifies and Christians who are sanctified are not from one Adam but from one God the heavenly Father, from whom Christ is born from eternity, Mic. 5:[2]; Col. 1:15, of whom all Christians are born through Jesus Christ in the Holy Spirit as Paul says, "You are all together children of God through faith in Jesus Christ," Gal. 3:26. And

Peter says, "You have been born anew, not of perishable seed, but of imperishable, through the Word of the living God," 1 Pet. 1:23. Again: Everyone who believes that Jesus is Christ is born out of God, 1 John 5:1; therefore, all Christians are brothers and sisters of Jesus Christ, Rom. 8:29, not on account of the fleshly, but of the spiritual birth, as Christ himself has indicated in the Gospel, Matt. 12:48[-50].

Since then these brothers and sisters, yes, children of Christ, have flesh and blood, Christ has also become participant of the same in like measure, that is, that he has become a human being as his brothers and sisters and children are, Heb. 2:14. But that he should have become man from our flesh and blood, that the apostle did not say, and it is also not his understanding, and that may not be supported on the basis of his words with any truth. For Christ is the unblemished Lamb of God, without sin, John. 1:36; 1 Pet. 1:19; Rev. 5:6, but his brothers, sisters, and children are, according to the flesh, of a sinful nature. Yes, what dwells in their flesh Paul testifies quite clearly to the Romans where he says, "I know that nothing good dwells within me, that is, in my flesh," Rom. 7:18. Therefore, the holy flesh of Christ, yes, that which is true food and makes alive, John 6:55, has not originally come from our flesh and blood, but he, Christ, is given to us from God the heavenly Father out of grace as a gift and true sign of his eternal love and fathomless mercy; born to us, Isa. 7:14, and become a human being as we are, but how, through what, and wherefrom enough has been said and explained above.

In order to understand this yet more thoroughly, everyone should observe the similarity /149/ and fellowship of God and Christ with all believers; that is, that all believers are participants of the divine nature, yes, and are called gods and children of the Most High, 2 Pet. 1:4; Acts 17:28; Ps. 82:6, and are in the world as Christ was in the world, and shall become like him at his coming, John 10:34; 1:12. Whenever now human beings become participants in the divine nature, yes, conformed to Christ on earth and in heaven, Rom. 8:14; Gal. 4:6; 1 John 3:1, they yet do not become identical in nature and person itself to what God and Christ are. Oh, no! The creature will never become the Creator and the flesh will never become the eternal Spirit itself which God is, John 4:24, for this is impossible. But the believers become gods and children of the most high through the new birth, participation, and fellowship of the divine nature, John 3:3, of the piety, glory, and purity of eternal life, and they will be purified as God, shine as God shines, and live as God lives eternally, John 6:[47]; 14:3. And even as God is Spirit, so they will also become spirits and spiritual, those who according to the external body and nature are or were flesh, and will be taken up into glory as God is in glory, 1 Cor. 15:20; Ecclus. 10:13. But human beings are and remain creatures and God is creator and ruler. Nevertheless, they are one and God is all and in all, John 17:21; 1 Cor. 15:28.

Just as the believers are now elevated through Christ and transposed into God, participants of the divine nature, 2 Pet. 1:4, and become like Christ in glory, so Christ has also humbled himself for the sake of his brothers, Phil. 2:5[-8]. That is, since his brothers have flesh and blood, so he has become participant of the same in like measure, Heb. 2:14, and in the humility of human nature has become like them in weakness, temptation, and mortality (sin excepted), Heb. 5:2. He has appeared in the form of sinful flesh, Rom. 8:3, and upon him as the strong duke (or leader) has fallen the weakness of all his brothers, Isa. 53:9; 1 Pet. 2:24. Nevertheless, he is that Word which has become flesh, John 1:14, the other Adam, that is, the other human being, the Lord himself from heaven, 1 Cor. 15:47, John 3:16.

Finally, Christ is similar to his brothers, and his brothers are, again similar to him. That is, Christ is God and God's Son, 1 John 4:9. His brothers are, by the grace of God through Jesus Christ, gods and children of the Most High, Ps. 82:6; John 10:34; 1 John 3:1; Heb. 2:14. And since they /150/ have flesh and blood, Christ himself has become participant of the same in like measure, 1 John [4:2]; Rom. 8:3. Nevertheless, there is a difference between Christ and his brothers. In the first place, because Christ is naturally God and God's Son, Eph. 1:3, his brothers have become gods and children of God (through Jesus Christ) out of the grace of God through election, adoption, and impartation of the divine nature and gifts, 2 Thess. 2:13. In the second place, because Christ the eternal Word became flesh, John 1:14, was conceived of the Holy Spirit in the virgin Mary, Matt. 1:20; Luke [1:35], and was born out of her, therefore, his flesh is also pure, spotless, and holy, and has not seen corruption, Acts 2:31; but is the living bread which gives life to the world, John 6:51. But his brothers come, according to the flesh, from the earth and return again to the earth, Gen. 3:19, even though they shall be clothed in the future with an immortal and glorified body through the power of God, 1 Cor. 15:43; 2 Cor. 5:1; Phil. 3:[21], and shall also be conformed to Christ, they are by nature evil and sinful. Nevertheless, this will not be reckoned to them as sin out of grace through Jesus Christ so long as they are in him and abide in him, Rom. 4:5; 8:1; Ps. 32:1.

This then is now the common question: If Christ has not received his flesh and blood from Mary, how could he then suffer and die? Thereupon this is our question in return: If the flesh of Christ is from the earth and earthy, yes, from Adam and his seed, which after all is of a sinful nature and subject to corruption, Rom. 5:12, how then has God's Word become flesh, John 1:14; 1 John. 1:1? How then could Christ make eternal satisfaction and pay for our sins, John 1:14; 3:16? Therefore, Scripture also says everywhere how God has delivered his own and only begotten Son, through whom the world and all things in it were created, into death for us, Heb. 1:[2]. If anyone would then say, "Did God then die?" we answer that neither the Father nor the Holy Spirit but the Son took on human form, John 1:14; 3:16, and he has taken off his divine form and has taken the form of a servant, Phil. 2:6[-7], and has died according to the flesh, but has been made alive according to the Spirit, as Peter says, 1 Pet. 3:18.

Therefore, Paul says to the bishops of the congregations, "Take heed to yourselves and to all the flock, in which the Holy Spirit has made you guardians, to feed the congregation of the Lord which he obtained with his own blood," Acts 20:28. At these words of the apostle, we are well pleased and we wish neither to add to them nor to subtract from them, Deut. 4:2; 12:32; Prov. 30:6, in order that we may neither be punished nor found to be deceitful. We also are not ashamed to confess openly with Paul that God has appeared in the flesh and has shed his blood for us, Acts 20:28; 1 Tim. 3:[16]. But if /151/ anyone wishes to dispute the matter, he does not dispute with us but with the apostle, yes, with the entire Scripture. In addition to that, also with many bishops and teachers who decided unitedly against Nestorius, the bishop of Constantinople, that God's Word suffered in the flesh and was crucified in the flesh.[2]

Again, we say that Christ's flesh makes alive and that Christ himself named his flesh the food of life, John 6:55[-57]. Now it is certain and true that the Spirit makes alive, and God's Word is Spirit and life, John 6:63, and alone nourishes the soul. Since then the flesh of Christ makes alive and is a food for souls, therefore, the flesh of Christ must also be the Spirit and the Word of God. Therefore, Christ also calls his flesh the living bread, John 6:51, which is God's Word, and therefore John says, "The Word became flesh," John 1:14.

So this is, therefore, finally our faith and heartfelt confession before God the Lord, before his angels, before all true Christians, and before everyone, that Jesus Christ is the natural, only begotten, firstborn Son of the living God, John 1:14; 3:16; Rom. 8:32; Heb. 1, truly God and God's Son, a true man and the Son of man—God and God's

Son from eternity with God and in God (from whom he is begotten) unto eternity, Mic. 5:[2]. But he became a human being in the last time according to the promise of the Father through his own willing submission, obedience, his diminishing of himself, the laying aside of his divine form, and the taking on of a human-like and servant-like form, out of overflowing love.

For this reason he is also the only true Mediator between God and humans, 1 Tim. 2:5. For he stands right in the middle, that is, he is not alone God and God's Son, but he is also a man and the Son of man. He is like the Father according to his divinity, John 10:30, but he is like to us according to his humanity with the exception of sin and all sinful and earthly nature of our flesh. For he is the other Adam, the Lord himself from heaven, 1 Cor. 15:47. His flesh he has delivered over into death for us and commended his spirit into the hand of his Father, [Luke 23:4]. Yes, that the sun was darkened at the death of Christ, Matt. 27:[45]; Mark 15:33, and yet did not vanish, appears to signify, and may not inappropriately be taken to point to the fact, (since God is after all portrayed in Scripture as the sun and is called the sun), Ps. 84:11, that the glory of God, Jesus Christ, Wis. of Sol. 5:6[-7], died according to the flesh, even as he lives according to the Spirit, 1 Pet. 3:18, as he himself said, "I am alive, and was dead; and behold I am alive from eternity to eternity," Rev. 1:18. /152/

Three hours the sun was darkened contrary to her nature, yet did not disappear. Three days and nights Jonah was in the whale and remained alive contrary to nature, John 1:17. Jesus Christ was also dead for three days according to the flesh, contrary to his divine nature, 1 Cor. 15:4. He rose from the dead on the third day and was made alive according to the Spirit, contrary to his human nature. Again that noble grain of wheat, Jesus Christ, fell into the earth and has through his suffering and death brought forth much saving fruit, John 12:24; Titus 3:4[-5]. Also the trustworthy and only Good Shepherd, Jesus Christ, out of the command of his heavenly Father has of himself given his life and taken it to himself, John 10:[16-17]. Also that innocent Lamb of God, Jesus Christ, who takes away the sins of the world, Isa. 53:10; John [1:36], was offered on the cross as a sweet-smelling savour to his heavenly Father, Eph. 5:2, but for our eternal salvation, for he himself willed it.

This is in brief form our confession concerning the incarnation of Jesus Christ, the Son of God. In addition we also say that he who does not confess the eternal divinity and the true humanity of Jesus Christ is an antichrist, 1 John [4:2-5], for he does not believe in the testimony which God has testified about his Son. And we say further with Paul, "From now on we know no one according to the flesh. Even though we knew Christ according to the flesh, we now know him thus no longer. Therefore, if any one is in Christ Jesus, that person is a new creature; the old is gone, look, everything has become new," 2 Cor. 5:16[-17].

Therefore, it is not enough that we confess that Jesus Christ is the Son of the living God, conceived in Mary through the Holy Spirit, and born out of her as a true human being, etc. But we must also receive him as the eternal Word, John 1:1; 1 John 1:1, and the imperishable seed of God the heavenly Father, 1 Pet. 1:23; 1 John 3:9, through the Holy Spirit, prove him and through this be preserved. If not, then all our boasting of knowledge and faith will not help. For the devil well knows and confesses that Jesus Christ is God's Son, James 2:19. But as little as such learning and knowledge helps the devil, so little shall the oral confession of faith help us without the living, discernible, and actual power of God, of which all pious Christians are participants. Therefore, Christ also says he "who believes in me" has eternal life, John 3:16; 11:25. Why? Because he has received a divine power, yes, a quickening power of eternal life—creating life in his heart which so thoroughly penetrates, purifies, and renews, /153/ and finally drives, leads, and transposes to the origin from which it has sprung, namely, eternal divine life itself.

So now if anyone who thus believes in Jesus Christ has received such a living power of God and who feels this throughout himself, he is a true believing Christian and confesses Christ according to the Spirit, for he is one Spirit with him, John 3:18; 1 Cor. 6:17. He also actually understands what the flesh of Christ is; for he himself is flesh of the flesh of Christ and bone of his bone, Eph. 5:30. In addition, he has in the Spirit and true faith eaten the flesh of Christ and drunk his blood, John 6:54, through which he has become united in one common nature with Christ. This knowledge of God and of Christ is eternal life, John 17:3.

But whatever anyone says about Jesus Christ without such an inner power of God, without such an enlightenment of the Holy Spirit, and without such fellowship and impartation of the divine seed of the character and nature of Jesus Christ, this is idle chatter and like the speech of a blind person who (according to the common proverb) disputes and discusses about color which he has neither seen nor can see. For this reason we wish to have everyone who claims to be a Christian to be faithfully admonished that he thus learn to know Jesus

Christ, believe in him, and receive him in order that Jesus Christ in the last day may confess him before God his Father and before the elect angels for his brother, sister, and mother and receive him into his eternal kingdom, Matt. 12:50.[3]

Amen.

ENDNOTES

1. Or "of."

2. A central problem for the early Ecumenical Councils, Cyril of the Alexandrian school and opponent of the Antiochian school which Nestorius favored, at Ephesus 431 stressed that in Christ existed "from two natures, one." Where Nestorius stressed the importance of the human (as well as the divine) nature of Christ, Cyril had little actual humanity in the divine Christ.

3. With Menno Simons and others, Dirk defended the "heavenly flesh" Christology—that Christ did not receive his body from Mary but from God. Consequently he and the others were frequently, but wrongly, accused of Docetism, that is, of not really believing in the incarnation. The most recent definitive study of this issue is by Voolstra, *Het Woord is Vlees Geworden.* Pp. 209ff. include both an English and German summary. But see also Keeney, *Dutch Anabaptist Thought.* pp. 207-221. *Idem,* "The Incarnation, A Central Theological Concept," in Dyck, *A Legacy of Faith.* pp. 55-68. Also ME 3:18-20.

CONCERNING THE TRUE KNOWLEDGE OF JESUS CHRIST

The Only Begotten Son of the Almighty and Living God, Our Lord and Savior—and of the Immovable and Unchangeable Ground of His Saving Teaching. A Brief Admonition

"I then did not claim to know anything among you than Jesus Christ alone, and him crucified." 1 Cor. 2:2

Foreword

To all brothers and sisters whom God from the beginning chose for salvation, Rom. 8:29, but has now enlightened through the Holy Spirit, 2 Thess. 2:13, and called into the fellowship of his Son through the gospel, I wish grace, peace, and mercy from God our heavenly Father, 1 Cor. 1:[3], and from Jesus Christ who gave himself for our sins in order that he might deliver us from the present evil world, according to the will of God his Father, to whom be praise from eternity to eternity. Amen. Gal. 1:4[-5].

Concerning the True Knowledge of Jesus Christ, the Only Begotten Son of God, and His Saving Teaching—A Brief Admonition

/157/ Dear brothers and sisters in Jesus Christ and joint heirs in the grace of God and in the fellowship of the gospel, Phil. 1:5: since these are now the perilous times of which Christ and the apostles have prophesied, that is, that many false Christians arise and lead many astray, Matt. 24:4; 1 Tim. 4:1; 2 Tim. 3:1; 2 Pet. 2:1; Jude 1:4, therefore I am compelled, out of the duty of Christian love, to write a little through the grace of the Lord about the true knowledge of Jesus Christ and the immovable ground of his saving doctrine, even though

I indeed have the confidence that you as children of the New Testament have been taught of God himself through the anointing that you have received from him.

Nevertheless, since the members of a body (as the apostle says) do not have the same function, and since they serve each other, each member according to its nature, gift and function, and that all to the improvement and safeguarding of the body, Rom. 12:4; 1 Cor. 12:12; Eph. 4:16; therefore I desire, my beloved brothers and sisters, my members in Jesus Christ, to serve with my small gift to present Jesus Christ and his Word correctly, to show and to portray it.

I see and hear that there are many who undertake to belittle Christ Jesus. The one denies his true divinity, the other does not confess his incarnation correctly. The third corrupts his blessed teaching so that the only begotten Son of God, Jesus Christ, is blasphemed in many ways (just as the Holy Spirit had previously said Christ should be to the unbelievers, a stone of stumbling, a rock of offence, Isa. 28:16; 1 Pet. 2:6[-8], a sign that shall be spoken against), Luke 2:34. So the love of my lord and master, Jesus Christ, constrains me that I (as much as is in me, his poor and unworthy servant) do my confession, /158/ first of his true divinity, then of his holy humanity, and third, of his saving teaching. For my heart's joy is to praise and glorify Christ against all blasphemers and despisers of Christ and his Word. Those who are wise in their own eyes and consider themselves discerning, yet with all of their wisdom are fools before God, Jer. 10:8, in which wisdom the Pharisees, the scribes, the disputers of this world and the seekers after high incomprehensible things have at all times become and still become fools, Baruch 3:[20-21], just as it is written: "I will destroy the wisdom of the wise, and the cleverness of the clever I will thwart. Where is the wise man? Where is the scribe? Where is the debater of this age? Has not God made foolish the wisdom of this world?" 1 Cor. 1:18[-20], Isa. 29:14.

Therefore, I beseech, all my brothers and sisters, through the mercy of God and the love of the Spirit, that you do not wish to be wise in your own eyes nor discerning in your own eyes, but that you maintain, confess, and attest Jesus Christ alone as the wisdom of God, that all grace has come into existence through him and that all salvation has come through him, and that no other name is given under heaven whereby we must be saved than the name of our Lord Jesus Christ, Acts 4:[12].

But to this salvation no one can come except he first correctly confess Jesus Christ. And this is the correct knowledge of Jesus

Christ, that we confess both his genuine divinity and his pure unblemished humanity. For of his genuine divinity Isaiah also witnesses, "For to us a child was born, and a Son was given, and the kingdom will be laid upon his shoulders and with his name will be called 'Wonderful Counselor, Mighty God, Eternal Father, Prince of Peace.' He will make no end to the increase of the kingdom and peace, and will sit upon the throne of David in his kingdom, to prepare and establish it with fairness and justice to eternity," Isa. 9:[6-7]; Luke 1:[32-33].

Isaiah also says, "Behold, your God, behold the almighty Lord shall come, and shall rule his people with his arm and he shall like a shepherd feed his flock," etc., [Isa. 40:10-11]. This Shepherd, promised of God the heavenly Father to the people of Israel, is Jesus Christ, the true David, King of Israel, Prince and Shepherd, who has come to seek the lost sheep of the house of Israel, Matt. 10:6. Therefore, he also witnesses of himself that /159/ he is a Good Shepherd and gave his life for his sheep, John 10:11. And Peter says, "For you were once as straying sheep, but now you have returned to the shepherd and bishop of your souls," 1 Pet. 2:25.

Further, Isaiah prophesies about the new and heavenly Jerusalem (which is the Christian church) and says, "He who made you shall be your husband, his name is the Lord of hosts, and your Redeemer shall be the Holy One of Israel, the God of the whole earth," Isa. 54:5. This prophecy testifies to us sufficiently of the genuine divinity and glory of Jesus Christ. For if one already wished to say and advocate that God the Father himself is Lord and husband of his congregations, we also confess and affirm that it is then not in the least so incontrovertible that Jesus Christ is actually in the New Testament the Lord and bridegroom of Jerusalem, as he himself testified with these words: "How can the wedding guests mourn as long as the bridegroom is with them? But the time will come, when the bridegroom is taken away from them, and then they will fast," Matt. 9:15. And John the Baptist confessed that he was the bridegroom's friend, but Christ was the bridegroom, and said, "He who has the bride is bridegroom, but the friend of the bridegroom stands and listens to him, the same, my joy is now fulfilled. He must increase, but I must decrease," John 3:29[-30]. Paul says to the Corinthians, "I betrothed you to Christ to present you as a pure bride to her one husband," 2 Cor. 11:[2]. And John said in Revelation, "I saw the Holy City, the new Jerusalem, coming down out of heaven from God, prepared as a bride adorned for her husband, and I heard a great voice from the throne saying, 'Behold, the tabernacle of God is with the people. He will dwell with them, and they shall be his people, and God himself will be with them and be their God,' " Rev. 21:2[-3]. And thereafter an angel came to him and said, "Come, I will show you the wife, the bride of the Lamb. . . . And in the Spirit he carried me away to a great, high mountain and showed me the Holy City Jerusalem coming down out of heaven from God, having the glory of God," [Rev. 21:9-11].

From these words it is clear that Christ Jesus the Lamb of God is also the bridegroom and husband of the new Jerusalem. Therefore he is also the Redeemer who loved his bride and has given himself for her, as Paul said, "that he sanctifies her, having cleansed her by the washing of water in the word, that he might present a glorious church, without spot or wrinkle or any such thing, that she might be holy and without blemish," Eph. 5:[26-]27. /160/

This harmonizes with what the prophet David said, "Hear, oh daughter, consider, and incline your ear, forget your people and your father's house, and the king will desire your beauty since he is your lord, and you shall worship him," Ps. 45:[10-]11. This King is Christ Jesus who has a name written upon his robe and on his thigh, "a king of all kings and a Lord of all lords," Rev. 19:16. Therefore, also the bride, that is, the Christian congregation, shall honor and worship him.

In addition, Jeremiah prophesied also of Christ and said, "Behold, the days are coming, says the Lord, when I will raise up the righteous plant of David, and he shall reign and execute wisely. In his days Judah will be helped, and Israel will dwell securely. And this is the name by which he will be called: 'The Lord our righteousness,' " Jer. 23:5[-6]; 33:15. This name "Lord," just as the prophet here names him, is among the Jews the unutterable name which they call *tetragram*, a name which holy biblical Scripture gives to no one, except the true God and Lord.

Again, where Daniel points toward Christ and his kingdom, he speaks of the stone which is hewn without hands out of the great mountain and itself becomes a great mountain that fulfills all, Dan. 2:[34-35]. This is a basic prophecy and an incontrovertible testimony of the true divinity of our Lord Jesus Christ. For that the stone was hewn out of the mountain without hands signifies to us the marvelous, incomprehensible, and unexpressible birth of the Son of God, Jesus Christ, out of God his heavenly Father, which took place before the beginning of all creatures, Prov. 8:22; Isa. 53:[2]; Acts 8:32. Therefore, also all creatures cannot grasp the same nor give expression to it, Col. 1:15[-16]. It is enough that we know this without all doubt and firmly believe that Jesus Christ is the Son of the living God from the beginning and from the days of eternity. His going forth and his origin is from God, Mic. 5:[2], as the Scripture richly testifies in many places, wherewith his true divinity is sufficiently manifested, witnessed to, and also established. For this is an undoubted word, yes, the witness of Jesus Christ himself, that like is born of its likeness, John 3:6, and therefore the Father and his only begotten Son, Jesus Christ, are one divine being just as the great mountain and the stone that is hewn out without hands are one substance. /161/

Creaturely likenesses are all too weak to actually portray the divine nature, for the imperfection of the creature cannot entirely express the perfection of the Creator. Again, that the stone which was hewn out of the great mountain without hands and itself became a great mountain that fulfilled all, this Daniel himself interprets as follows: that the God of heaven shall bring his Christ to have all power on earth and in heaven, Matt. 28:18, which honor and might and glory God the Father gives to no one except his only begotten Son, who was born of him and gone forth and is one with him, so that what the Father has, the same the Son also has, and what the Son has, the same the Father also has, Luke 10:22; John 16:15. Also Christ himself testifies to the same in many places in his gospel.

Yes, the time would become too short for me if I should repeat and interpret all the passages and testimonies to Jesus Christ from the Old Testament about his true divinity and of his eternal kingdom, about his divine honor and glory, and in addition all the shadows and figures of Melchizedek, Gen. 14:[18], of Isaac, Gen. 22:[2], of Joseph and Simeon [Gen. 42:18-25], of Moses and Aaron and of their rods that bloomed in one night and bore almonds, [Num. 17:8], of the heavenly bread, Exod. 16:16, of the rock from which water had flowed, Num. 20:10, Ps. 78:15, of the serpent which Moses erected in the wilderness as a saving sign, Num. 21:9, Wisd. of Sol. 16:6, of David and Solomon, of the holy of holies both in the tabernacle of Moses and in the temple of Solomon, Exod. 36; [1 Kings 6:19-20], of the golden altar [1 Kings 6:22], of the manifold offerings, [Lev. 1-3], of the mercy seat, [Heb. 9:5], and other additional figures which all point us toward Jesus Christ.

Therefore, I confer this to the Christian reader that he might himself search the Scriptures thereupon (as Christ also spoke to the Jews that they should search the Scriptures for they witnessed to him), John 5:39, and to pray to God for wisdom which he shall give to him, James 1:5. Nevertheless, I will yet briefly indicate several passag-

Concerning the True Knowledge of Jesus Christ / 157

es from the New Testament with which to establish the true divinity of our Lord Jesus Christ.

In the first place, Christ Jesus is the firstborn, the only begotten, and own Son of the almighty and living God, which alone is enough to indicate his true divinity, as is said above, Ps. 2:7; Heb. 1:5. For since the Son is born of the Father in a natural, yet indescribable manner (just as beams from the sun and the reflection from fire goes forth naturally), Wisd. of Sol. 7:25, therefore, he is also in all things like his Father, so that he himself said to Philip, "He who sees me also sees my Father," John 14:[9]. Therefore Scripture also names him /162/ an image of the invisible God, a beam of eternal light, a mirror of divine purity, a gleam of the honor of God, an express image of his nature, Wisd. of Sol. 7:25[-26]; 2 Cor. 4:4; Col. 1:15; Heb. 1:3. From this it may be easily understood how fully the Father is portrayed in his Son and how completely the Son expresses the Father. Therefore, Christ also says that "no one knows the Son except the Father, and no one knows the Father except the Son and those to whom the Son chooses to reveal him," Matt. 11:27. So entirely one are the Father and the Son and they also alone know each other, just as they are the same divine nature, have one will together eternally, do all things together, and have all things together in common, John 5:20; 16:14; 17:22.

John testifies to this in the beginning of his Gospel where he writes of the true divinity of Jesus Christ as follows: "In the beginning was the Word. It was in the beginning with God, etc. And the Word became flesh and we have seen his glory, glory as of the only begotten from the Father who is full of grace and truth," John 1:1[-2, 14]. This is an incontrovertible witness of the eternal deity of Jesus Christ, the only begotten Son of the Father, because he was the Word in the beginning with God and God himself was the Word, etc. This Christ also confirmed himself when he said to the Jews, "Truly, truly, I say to you, before Abraham was born, I am," John 8:58. And in his prayer he said, "Father, glorify me in yourself with the glory which I had with you before the world was made," John 17:5. And in the Revelation of John, Christ testifies and speaks of himself in the same manner as God speaks of himself through Isaiah: "I am the first and the last," Rev. 1:17; Isa. 41:4; 44:6; [48]:12.

Again, John also testifies strongly in his epistle to the true deity of Jesus Christ in that he calls Christ the Word of life and also eternal life and says, "That which was from the beginning, which we have heard, which we have seen with our eyes, which we have looked upon and touched with our hands, concerning the Word of life—and that life was made manifest, and we saw it, and testify to it, and proclaim to you the eternal life which was with the Father and was made manifest to us," 1 John 1:1[-2].

"Again, we know that the Son of God has come and has given us understanding, to confess him who is true; and we are in him who is true, in his Son Jesus Christ. This is the true God and eternal life," 1 John 5:20. This agrees with what Paul said to the Romans concerning his brothers and friends who were of Israel according to the flesh /163/ and to whom "belong the sonship, the glory, the covenant, and the law, the worship of God, and the promises; which also the patriarchs are, out of whom Christ is according to the flesh, who is God over all blessed in eternity. Amen," Rom. 9:4[-5].

But this saying is incomprehensible to reason and must be grasped by faith alone, that Jesus Christ who is out of the patriarchs according to the flesh is himself God over all blessed in eternity. Therefore Paul said, "Great indeed is the mystery of our religion: that is, he was manifested in the flesh, vindicated in the Spirit, seen by angels, preached among the nations, believed on in the world, taken up into glory," 1 Tim. 3:[16].

This mystery the apostle Thomas could at first not confess, but when he was enlightened by God through the Holy Spirit and taught correctly through experience and had also become truly believing, he said to Christ, "My Lord and my God," John 20:28, which confession Thomas did not speak to the Father but to Christ and therefore must be understood not as spoken of the Father but of Christ.

Again, Paul writes to the Colossians that all things are created through Jesus Christ (as is also written in the first chapter of John), that which is in heaven and upon earth, "visible and invisible, whether thrones or dominions or principalities or authorities—all things were created through him and in him. He is before all things, and all things exist in him," Col. 1:16[-17]. In addition, in him "lie hidden all the treasures of the wisdom and knowledge of God, yes, the fullness of God dwelt in him bodily," Col. 2:[3]; [1:19]. Therefore, the apostle testifies so clearly to the Hebrews that the Son upholds all things with "his word of power," Heb. 1:3. "And again, when he brings the firstborn into the world, he says, 'Let all God's angels worship him,' " Heb. 1:6. However, what kind of worship this is Christ himself explains in John and says that the Father "judges no one, but has given all judgment to the Son, that all may honor the Son, even as they honor the Father. He who does not honor the Son does not honor the Father who sent him," John 5:22[-23].

Concerning the True Knowledge of Jesus Christ / 159

Again, the apostle writes also in the same chapter of the difference between the Son of God and the angels and says that God makes his angels spirits and his servants flames of fire but to the Son he said "Your throne, O God, is for ever and ever, the righteous scepter is a scepter of your kingdom. You have loved righteousness and hated lawlessness; therefore God, your God, has anointed you with the oil of gladness /164/ beyond your comrades. And, you, Lord, founded the earth in the beginning, and the heavens are the work of your hands; they will perish, but you remain," etc., Heb. 1:[8-10]; Ps. 45:[6-]7.

There are yet many more passages and testimonies in the New Testament which ascribe and attribute to Jesus Christ all divine honor, power, might, omnipotence, glory, and identity, but it is not necessary to repeat all of these here. Out of all the previously mentioned ones it is sufficiently clear who Jesus Christ is and what he is. The prophets and apostles also express and bear him witness that he is the "mighty God, the everlasting Father," Isa. 9:[6], the omnipotent Lord, Isa. 40:25, the Lord of hosts, the Holy One of Israel, Isa. 54:5, the righteous branch of David, Jer. 23:5, the Lord our righteousness, Jer. 33:15, the only begotten Son of the most high and living God, Matt. 16:16, through whom all grace and truth have come into existence, John 6:69; 1:17, in whom are hidden all the treasures of the wisdom and knowledge of God, Col. 2:[3], the Word of God in whom the whole fullness of God dwells bodily, Col. 2:9, yes, the same is the wisdom of God, the Word of God, 1 Cor. 1:[21]; Rev. 19:[13], the truth and eternal life, Col. 2:3; Prov. 8:22; John 1:1, God whose throne shall endure for ever and for ever, Ps. 45:[6]. He is the Creator of heaven and earth for all that is was created through him, and without him nothing that is was created, Heb. 1:[10]; John 1:3; Col. 1:16. All things exist in him, [Col. 1:17], and he does all that he sees the Father doing, Heb. 1:2; John 5:[36]. Therefore, he also has divine honor with the Father and sits with him upon his throne at the right hand, and shall be worshipped by all the angels of God, and all believers on earth must honor, fear and love him, just as they love the Father, and believe in him just as they believe in the Father, Rev. 3:[20-]21; Heb. 1:6; Phil. 2:9[-11]; 1 Pet. 3:22; John 14:1.

All this and whatever more the holy biblical Scripture teaches and witnesses concerning the true divinity of our Lord Jesus Christ, we must believe before all things and without any doubt, otherwise we cannot be saved. For this is God's command, says John, that we believe in the name of his Son, Jesus Christ, 1 John 3:23. "He who believes in the Son is not condemned; he who does not believe is condemned already, because he does not believe in the name of the only Son of God," John 3:18. And again, "he who believes in the Son has eternal life; he who does not believe in the Son shall not see life, but the wrath of God rests upon him," John 3:36. Again, "he who believes in the Son of God has the testimony in himself. He who does not believe God has made him a liar,/165/ because he has not believed in the testimony that God has borne to his Son. And this is the testimony, that God gave us eternal life, and this life is in his Son. He who has the Son of God has life; he who has not the Son of God has not life," [1 John 5:10-12].

Therefore, we must believe in the Son of God or we cannot receive salvation. Now no one believes correctly in the Son of God except he first confess him as Lord and God. For this is always certain—that we must believe in the true God alone, "for no one can come to God nor yet believe in him except he then believe that God exists and that he rewards those who seek him," Heb. 11:6. Since we must believe in the Son even as we believe in God (as Christ himself taught his disciples saying, "Believe in God, believe also in me"), John 14:1; therefore the Son must be true God with the Father and in the Father. The Father is also in the Son so that the two are one; yes, one undivided, incomprehensible, unsearchable, inexpressible, and living God and divinity in eternal unity, power, and activity of the one and eternal true Holy Spirit. So much then concerning the true divinity of our Lord and Savior Jesus Christ, as the first part of knowing him is briefly stated.

In the second place, we must certainly confess the incarnation of our Lord Jesus Christ; namely that he through the power of the most high and through the Holy Spirit became human in the virgin Mary, was born out of her, Matt. 1:20; Luke [1:35]; Heb. 5:2, and was entirely outside of the bite of the serpent, Gen. 3:1, that is, stood outside of sin, and is not contaminated with the poisoned root of the sinful flesh in order that he might tread upon the serpent's head and make us, who were enemies of God and children of wrath, children of God and heirs of eternal life, Rom. 5:10; Eph. 2:[16]. Therefore, he could not become a man from the first Adam who was poisoned and made naked by the serpent, but that Word which in the beginning was with God and was God, [John 1:1], that has become flesh, John 1:14, in order that Jesus Christ, though he has indeed appeared in the form of sinful flesh, Rom. 8:3; Heb. 5:2, was yet free from all sin and sinful nature, had a pure body prepared for him, Heb. 10:5, by God the heavenly Father through the Holy Spirit. And thus he was an unblemished

Paschal Lamb, Exod. 12:3; 1 Cor. 5:[7], and took our sins away and we are sprinkled with his blood, 1 Pet. 1:19, /166/ and through his death we have been liberated out of Egypt and from Pharaoh's power, that is, set free from this blind and evil world, Gal. 1:4, and might be made free and delivered from Satan's prison. Also therefore he became our brother, that we might be conformed to his image and might become of his character and nature, Rom. 8:29; 2 Pet. 1:4.

Therefore the only begotten Son of the living God, he who before the beginning of the world was glorified with God, John 17:5, has now become a mortal man, he who was rich for our sake became poor, 2 Cor. 8:9, he who was in divine form has appeared in human and servant-like form, Phil. 2:[7]. The wisdom who before all creatures was born out of God, Prov. 8:22, has allowed himself to be seen on earth and has lived among humans, John 1:[14]. The Word which in the beginning was with God and was God—that Word has become flesh, says John, and lived among us, "and we have beheld his glory, glory as of the only Son from the Father," [John 1:14]. That holy thing which Mary conceived and wherewith she was impregnated in her body—that has come into her through the Holy Spirit and through the overshadowing of the divine power, and the same one that is born out of her is called the Son of the Most High, Luke 1:31, [35].

The true bread of life has been given us of the Father and has come down from heaven; which bread is Jesus Christ, yes, his flesh which he has given for the life of the world, John 6:51. He is the other Adam who was broken through death and has brought us life again. He is not from the earth (of which the first Adam was made) but he has gone forth from God and come down from above. He is the Lord himself from heaven, [1] Cor. 15:[21-22]; [15:47]; John 3:31; 8:23; 10:36; 16:5; 17:5. He is the first and the last and the living one. He was dead and is alive for ever and ever, Rev. 1:17.

In summary, God is revealed in the flesh, 1 Tim. 3:[16], and has allowed himself to be seen on earth, Baruch 3:[37], the Lord God Sabaoth has come from his holy place in order to redeem Zion and has had his dwelling with her, Zech. 2:10.

Thereafter it is necessary for all Christians to reflect and to weigh the reason on account of which the wisdom of God and the Word of God, and the Son of the Most High has so humbled himself that he became a human being, namely, in the first place, to take away our sins, 1 John 3:5. For since Adam had forsaken God's Word and contrary to the command of the Lord had eaten from the tree of the knowledge of good and evil, he died the death, according to the Word which God had spoken to him, "in the day you eat of the tree of the knowledge of good and evil you shall die the death," /167/ Gen. 2:16; 3:[3]; and with him all those who come from him to the end of the world, Rom. 5:15; 1 Cor. 15:21[-22]. For they have all come from a dead Adam. Therefore, they also are all cast under death.

Should this sin now be paid, this death taken away, the righteousness of God be satisfied, and life be brought again to a dead humanity, then the son of the Most High had to appear and become human, Luke 1:31; Rom. 8:3, take our sins upon himself and die for us, Isa. 53:8, and through his death and blood triumph against the devil, sin, death, and hell, 1 Pet. 2:24; 3:18; yes, reconcile us forever with God his Father through the one sacrifice of his body, Heb. 10:10. Therefore, John says that the Son of God appeared in order that he might take away our sins and sin is not from him, 1 John 3:5. And Paul says, for "Christ redeemed us from the curse of the law, having become a curse for us," Gal. 3:13. And yet another reference, what was impossible for the law (because it was weakened through the flesh), that God did, "sending his own son in the likeness of sinful flesh, he condemned sin in the flesh," Rom. 8:3, through sin. That is, as the apostle himself declares with other words, namely, that God made the one who knew no sin (which is Jesus Christ his only begotten Son) to be sin for us; that is, has been made to be a sacrifice for sin in order that we in him might become the righteousness which avails before God, 2 Cor. 5:21.

For the sake of this righteousness, that is, in order that we might be justified, Christ has delivered himself to death and has become the most despised person among all humanity, just as the prophet says, "he shall have no form or comeliness if we should look at him, and no beauty that we should desire him. He shall be the worst and most despised, a man acquainted with suffering and sickness. We shall consider him so unworthy and rejected that we shall hide our faces from him, though he alone really takes our sickness away and carries our sorrows. Yet thus we consider him, though he was beaten and punished by God, and weakened. But he was wounded for our transgressions and beaten for our iniquities. Upon him lies the penalty of our punishment, and with his stripes we are healed," Isa. 53:[2-]5; 1 Pet. 2:24.

Therefore, Christ in the time of his suffering might well say as David had prophesied of him, "I am a worm, and no man; scorned by men, and despised by the people. All who see me mock at me, they make mouths at me, they wag their heads," Ps. 22:[6-7]. And again, "dogs are round about me; a company of evildoers encircle me; they have pierced my hands and feet /168/—I can count all my bones—they stare and gloat over me; they divide my garments among them, and for my raiment they cast lots," Ps. 22:[16-18]; Matt. 27:35; Mark 15:24.

Thereby the righteousness of God is now fully revealed in that he has so severely beaten and humbled his only begotten Son on account of the sins of his people. For how very much God hates sin is revealed out of this—that he because of the disobedience and transgression of one man (through whom then we have all become sinners), Rom. 5:[12], did not allow himself to be reconciled (for his righteousness endures forever) before he allowed his beloved only begotten Son to be so miserably handled by the godless and the heathen, Matt. 27; John 19. His pure and holy body he also allowed to be wounded, and allowed his head to be crowned with a crown of thorns and finally, he allowed him to suffer the bitter and most shameful death for us on the cross.

Oh, what has the only begotten Son of God, Jesus Christ, our Lord and faithful Savior, suffered for us all, John 3:16! He who is the eternal wisdom and truth of God, he who cannot lie nor fail, him they have reproached as a liar and deceiver of the people, John 7:12. He who is the righteousness and holiness of all believers and the innocent Lamb of God who knows of no sin, yes, who takes the sins of the world away, 1 Cor. 1:[30]; John 1:29, him they have numbered among the transgressors, Matt. 27:[38]. He who is the peace of all Christians and the reconciliation of all that is in heaven and upon earth, 2 Cor. 5:19; Eph. 1:10; Col. 1:20, him they have accused and deplored as a revolutionary sectmaker. He who was the appearance of eternal light, an unblemished mirror of divine purity, Wisd. of Sol. 7:26, and the image of the invisible God, [2] Cor. 4:4; Col. 1:15, in whose face the angels in heaven rejoice and in whose purity all believers on earth are reflected, Heb. 1:3; 1 Pet. 1:12; 2 Cor. 3:18; before him they have hidden their faces and cried before Pilate, "Away, away, crucify him," Matt. 27:22!

He who is the Lord of the whole world they have rejected and refused to accept as their King. He who clothes all true believing and baptized Christians with the garment of righteousness and with the mantle of salvation, Gal. 3:27, him they stripped and afterward nailed naked to the cross and divided his clothes among themselves and cast lots over his robe, Ps. 22:[18]; [Matt. 27:35]. He who gives the water of life free to all thirsty souls, John 4:10; 7:38; Rev. 22:1, him they have in his thirst given vinegar to drink, Ps. 69:[21]; John 19:29. And he who is the pioneer of life, him they killed, Heb. 12:2.

And this, nevertheless, the heavenly Father, the almighty God, laid upon his only begotten Son, Jesus Chirst, because of our sins. And yet this, alas, /169/ is so little reflected upon by the whole world. There are indeed many people today who boast of the merits of Jesus Christ, his death and blood, but few are found who with true zeal reflect upon the suffering of the Lord and take it to heart so that through this they become better, die to sin and live to righteousness.

On the other hand, God sent his only begotten Son into the world that we should live through him, 1 John 4:9. With this God has shown his fatherly kindness and overflowing love toward us, Eph. 2:6, not because of anyone's good works (for we had all sinned), Titus 3:5; Ps. 116:11, but because God who is true in his words wished to keep his promise which he had made with Adam, Abraham, Isaac, Jacob, David, and the other patriarchs, Rom. 3:4; Gen. 17:19; 22:16[-17]. The richness of his grace, he wished to pour out upon us and save us according to his mercy, Eph. 2:6, as it is written: "God so loved the world that he gave his only Son," John 3:16. And Paul to the Romans, "If God is with us, who will be against us? He who did not spare his own Son but gave him for us all, will he not also give us all things with him?" Rom. 8:31[-32]

Therein has now appeared the love of God as John says, that he has sent his only begotten Son into the world that we should live through him, 1 John 4:9. "In this is love, not that we loved God but that he loved us and sent his Son to be the reconciliation for our sins," [1 John 4:10]. And this God did for us while we were yet his enemies, as Paul testifies that Christ, "while we were still weak, died for us ungodly [people]," Rom. 5:6. And again, "God shows his love for us in that Christ died for us while we were still sinners, [Rom. 5:8].

Therefore, we may well say with the prophet that God "does not deal with us according to our sins, nor punish us according to our unrighteousness," Ps. 103:10. For we must all confess with Paul that we previously had our walk among the children of unbelief and "lived in the passions of our flesh, following the will of body and mind, and so we were by nature the children of wrath, like the others. But God (says the apostle), who is rich in mercy, out of the great love with which he loved us, /170/ even when we were dead in our sins, made us alive together with Christ, for by grace you have been saved, and awakened us with him, and made us sit with him in the heavenly places in Christ Jesus, that in the coming ages he might show the overflowing richness of his grace in kindness toward us in Christ Jesus. For by grace you have been saved through faith; and that is not your own doing, it is the gift of God—not because of works, in order that no one should boast," Eph. 2:3[-9].

As we now rightly reflect upon this fathomless grace and mercy of God the Father which has appeared to us in Christ Jesus, through which the love of God is kindled in our hearts, how should we not have love in return for such a gracious and merciful Father who has loved us so heartily? Therefore John says, "We love God because he loved us first," 1 John 4:10. And "thereby we confess that we love God, that is, that we keep his commandments," 1 John 5:3, just as Christ himself said to his disciples, "If you love me, then keep my commandments," John 14:15. "Whoever has my commandments and keeps them loves me," [John 14:21]. Again, whoever loves me shall keep my words, but, "whoever does not love me does not keep my words," [John 14:24]. Similarly, we know through this that we love God if we love his children, that is, all true Christians. For no one can love God, except he also love all those who are born out of God, as John testifies, 1 John 4:21.

Out of all this previous discussion it is now clear which is the true knowledge of Jesus Christ, our Lord and Savior, both according to his true divinity and humanity. [Also] that we must consider both the righteousness and the love of God revealed to us in Christ Jesus, and must remember that the righteousness because of sin on account of which such a glorious person, that is, the only begotten Son of the living God, had to be so severely rebuked and punished, Isa. 53. But the love of God toward us is, that he, the heavenly Father, has given his only begotten Son for us "that whoever believes in him should not be lost, but have eternal life," John 3:16.

This is now the true knowledge of Jesus Christ which is also eternal life, just as Christ himself said, "This is eternal life (oh, Father), that they confess you as the only true God, and Jesus Christ whom you have sent," John 17:3. But this confession is not an historical knowledge of Christ, as many imagine, but a living and powerful work of God in people through whom they are transformed, born anew out of God, enlightened and gifted with the Holy Spirit, John 1:13; 1 John 5:1; Gal. 3:5, so that they are minded /171/ like Christ Jesus whose brother and companion they are become out of grace through faith and the new birth, 1 John 2:3.

Therefore not all know Christ who confess him with the mouth but through this we know, says John, that we have confessed Christ, "if we keep his commandments. Whoever says 'I know him' but disobeys his commandments is a liar and the truth is not in him; but whoever keeps his word, in him truly love for God is perfected. Whoever says he abides in him ought to walk in the same way in which he walked," [1 John 2:3-6]. Out of these words, it can easily be measured [seen] who truly confesses Christ or not.

So now Christ Jesus is the only begotten Son of the living God, truly God and [truly] human, and this one God has been given to us as Lord and Master and has witnessed from heaven that "he is his beloved Son, in whom he is well pleased; him we must hear," Matt. 17:5; 3:17; 2 Pet. 1:17. Thus the Holy Spirit also witnessed concerning Jesus Christ, 2 Pet. 1:21, in part, that through the apostles and prophets he has spoken all that stands written in Scripture about Christ Jesus, and in part in that he came and remained upon Christ Jesus in the bodily and visible form of a dove, Matt. 3:16; Luke 3:[22]; John 1:14; 1:32, signifying to us that the fullness of the Spirit is essentially in Christ Jesus.

The Father loves the Son, says John, and gives him his Spirit not according to measure, John 3:34[-35], but it pleased him that all fullness is and dwells in the Son; yes, that in him all the fullness of God was essentially to live in him," Col. 1:19; 2:9, and that eternal life should be in him, 1 John 5:11; and that we all [should] receive out of his fullness grace upon grace, John 1:16, and that we receive eternal life through him, from him, and in him, according to the words which Christ himself spoke to Martha, "I am the resurrection and the life; he who believes in me shall live even though he die, and whoever lives and believes in me shall not die in eternity," John 11:[25].

Since then life is in the Son of God, 1 John 5:11, and he upholds all things with the word of his power, Heb. 1:3, and all things exist in him, [John 1:3], therefore, human beings are also in him and in his word as long as they remain therein with true faith and obedience, as Christ himself testified saying, "Truly, truly, I say to you, whoever hears my word and believes him who sent me, has eternal life and does not come into judgment, but has passed from death to life," John 5:24. And again Christ says, /172/ "Truly, truly, I say to you, if any one keeps my Word, they will never see death," John 8:51, for the words of Christ "are spirit and life," John 6:63.

The gospel, says Paul, is the power of God which saves every one who believes, Rom. 1:16; 1 Cor. 1:[18]. The teaching of Jesus Christ is the Word of the heavenly Father, John 7:16; 8:28; 14:10. The teaching of the Son and the witness of the Holy Spirit exceeds all the teaching of the prophets, and therein is contained all that is necessary for and furthers salvation. The will of the heavenly Father may nowhere be so clearly known as in the words of Jesus Christ through whom the Father has spoken to us in these last times, Heb. 1:2, fully proclaimed and expressed his will to us, so that what is contrary to the words of Christ or not in conformity with them is not God's Word nor will. "For no other foundation can any one lay than that which is laid, which is Christ Jesus," [1] Cor. 3:11. And no other gospel may, therefore, be preached, except the one left to us by Christ and the preaching of the apostles.

Paul writes to the Galatians, "If we, or an angel from heaven, should preach to you contrary to that which we have preached to you, let them be accursed." As we have said before, so now I say again, "If any one is preaching to you contrary to that which you received, let them be accursed," Gal. 1:8[-9]. These words every Christian may well consider, namely, that even an angel from heaven is accursed who teaches other than Paul and the other apostles have taught.

Therefore, no teaching is now valid which is not in agreement with the teaching of Jesus Christ and his apostles. And humans do not live by other human words brought forth out of human will, but alone by the words of God proclaimed to us through Christ Jesus and his apostles, Deut. 8:3; Matt. 4:4. Here is the bread of heaven, John 6:51. Here is the water of life, [John 4:13-14]. Does any one hunger after righteousness? Here he finds the bread of life and whoever eats of it will become strong and well in Christ; he will become satisfied in his soul so that he shall not hunger after the leaven of the Pharisees and Sadducees.

[Therefore], does anyone thirst after salvation? Here he shall find the most pure fountain and whoever drinks out of this fountain, in him shall come to be a fountain of living water which springs up to eternal life, John 4:14; 7:38, so that he shall nevermore thirst after the impure water of human teaching. Is anyone desirous after heavenly wisdom let them come to Christ and learn of him, for he is gentle and lowly in heart, and in him his soul will find rest, Matt. 11:28. Then he shall be taught of God and then he shall receive true wisdom.

/173/Christ Jesus is such a master and his Word is of such nature and power that whoever receives and keeps it with a believing heart shall find in the simplicity of the teaching of Christ the unspeakable counsel of heavenly wisdom. They shall, in the words of the cross that in the first glimpse appears simplistic and despised, 1 Cor. 1:[18], see and observe much that far surpasses all human cleverness, no matter how high and wonderful it may appear.

Therefore, Paul says to the Corinthians, "I did not act among you as though I knew anything else than alone Christ Jesus, and him crucified," 1 Cor. 2:2. Every Christian must do the same and have all his desire in the gospel, concern himself therewith day and night, Ps. 1:2, and express himself therein. Then he shall taste the sweetness therein so that he with David shall say, "Oh Lord, how sweet is your word to my taste, sweeter than honey to my mouth!" Ps. 119:103.

If it is now a fact that the prophet has tasted such sweetness in the law (as he also says in many other places) that the ordinances of the Lord are more precious than gold, and much fine gold, and sweeter also than honey and the honeycomb, Ps. 19:[9-10], it is always right that a Christian tastes and finds such sweetness in the gospel of Jesus Christ, (wherein God reveals to us all grace and love, all friendliness and goodness). And if it was possible for the figurative bread of heaven to give everyone all desire, and everyone according to his taste could make of it what he would according to everyone's choice, as it stands written in the book of wisdom, Wisd. of Sol. [16]:20[-21], much more is it possible for the true bread of heaven to give to all hungry souls who are hungry and thirsty after righteousness every desire and taste of the divine sweetness.

But this sweetness and power of the true heavenly bread no one can taste except he who hungers and thirsts after righteousness and says with David, "As a hart longs for fresh water, so thirsts my soul for you, oh God. My soul thirsts for the living God," Ps. 42:1[-2]. And again, "oh, God, you are my God, I will seek for you early, my soul thirsts for you, my flesh longs for you in a dry and weary land where there is no water," Ps. 63:1.

Whoever is now thirsty for the living God, hungry for the bread of heaven, and desirous for the water of life, they shall /174/ without doubt be well satisfied, as Christ said, "Blessed are those who hunger and thirst for righteousness, for they shall be satisfied," Matt. 5:6. And Christ further says, "I am the bread of life; whoever comes to me shall not hunger, and whoever believes in me shall never thirst," John 6:35. And in the Revelation of John is written of those "who have come out of great tribulation; they have washed their robes and made them white in the blood of the Lamb. Therefore they are before the throne of God, and serve him day and night in the temple, they shall hunger no more, neither thirst any more; the sun shall not strike them, nor any scorching heat. For the Lamb in the midst of the throne will rule them, and will guide them to springs of living water, and God will wipe away every tear from their eyes," Rev. 7:14-17.

These are now those who believe in Jesus Christ, who live by every word that goes out of the mouth of God, [Matt. 4:4], and are nourished with the bread of heaven, these shall here not lack the food of life and shall hereafter be eternally satisfied, as God shall be all in all, [1 Cor. 15:28].

Contrary to this, those who have now tasted the sweetness of the divine Word and the power of the coming world, and have received the Holy Spirit, and again turn away therefrom and sin willfully, according to the known and accepted truth, despise Christ and his Word out of pride—these may not, according to the word of the apostle, be renewed through repentance. For they have themselves crucified the Son of God and made mockery with it, Heb. 6:5[-6]. Yes, they trample the Son of God with their feet and regard the blood of the testament through which they are sanctified as impure, and outrage the Spirit of grace, Heb. 10:29. Therefore also no sacrifice is left for their sins, but a strong and fearful fire is prepared for them which shall consume the adversary, that is, those who set themselves against Christ and his Word, [Heb. 10:27-28], "for our God is a consuming fire," [Heb. 12:29].

Therefore, my brotherly admonition, my friendly request, and my faithful counsel, which I give all my beloved brothers and sisters out of heartfelt love, is that you indeed exercise care over your treasures. Insofar as you have received understanding from God, insofar as Christ has come into your hearts, 2 Cor. 4:6, as much of God as has been given you through his Spirit, insofar as you have tasted of the bread of heaven and drunk of the water of life out of the fountain of salvation, that you faithfully guard the same; /175/ progress therein, increase, and through this grow up and become strong in your inner being, [Eph. 3:16]. [All this] in order that you may walk with joy on the way of the Lord, toward the promised land, toward that heavenly Jerusalem, and nevermore allow yourselves to lust after the flesh of Egypt, [Exod. 16:3], nor after the leaven of the Pharisees, Matt. 16:6, nor after the impure water of human wisdom, Jer. 2:[13]; Ezek. 34:18, but that all your desire and hunger be after the true bread of heaven, and all your thirst be after the water of life.

Oh, what a precious table is this that God has prepared for us in the dry and barren wilderness of this world! The fleshly Israel God had indeed given the figurative bread of heaven to eat, Exod. 16:16; Wisd. of Sol. [16]:20, and he gave them natural water to drink out of the rock, Num. 20:10; Ps. 78:15; 1 Cor. 10:4, (which without doubt was a great miracle of God). But God, the heavenly Father, has given us to eat of the true living bread that has come down from heaven, John 6:54, in order to feed all hungry souls. To us he has given to drink of the water of life that springs out of the living rock, Christ Jesus, for a cooling and quickening of all thirsty souls, John 6:35.

Therefore, Christ said to the Jews, "Moses did not give you bread from heaven, but my Father gave you the true bread from heaven. For this bread is the bread of God which gives life to the world," John 6:32[-33]. And Paul says, "Our fathers have all eaten the same spiritual food, and have all drunk the same spiritual drink, but with many of them God was not pleased, for they were destroyed in the wilderness, 1 Cor. 10:3[-5]. And Christ Jesus said that whoever eats of him as from the true bread of life shall live in eternity, John 6:54, and that whoever drinks of the water that he shall give him shall nevermore thirst, but it shall become in him a fountain of living water which springs into eternal life, [John 4:14]. And Christ says further, "If anyone thirst, let him come to me and drink. Whoever believes in me, as Scripture says, 'Out of his body shall flow rivers of living water,'" John 7:37[-38].

This the Spirit of God had previously testified through Isaiah and said, "Oh, you thirsty ones, come to the waters; and you who have no money, come and buy wine and milk without money and without price," Isa. 55:1. Here we hear that the thirsty are invited to come, but to whom shall they come other than to Jesus Christ? For he strengthens all who are weary and heavy laden, [Matt. 11:28], and to those who come to him he gives the water of life freely as a refreshing of their souls. To those he bestows the pure wine of his divine Word without money toward a liberation of their consciences /176/ and feeds them with the unadulterated milk in order that through it they may grow up, 1 Pet. 2:2. Yes, and what is more, he gives them his flesh to eat as food for their souls just as he himself testified in John and said, "Truly, truly, I say to you, unless you eat the flesh of the Son of man and drink his blood, you have no life in you; he who eats of my flesh and drinks of my blood has eternal life, and I will raise him up at the last day. For my flesh is food indeed, and my blood is drink indeed. Whoever eats of my flesh and drinks of my blood abides in me and I in him. Even as the living Father sent me, and I live because of the Father, so he who eats of me will live because of me," John 6:[53-57].

How and in what manner Christ is eaten by us, namely not through the external natural bread, but through the true living bread which has come down from heaven, not in a fleshly but in a spiritual manner, to eat of his flesh and drink of his blood, he himself has sufficiently indicated in John. For after he had spoken much about how we must eat of his flesh and drink of his blood, he said in conclusion, "This is the bread which came down from heaven, not such as your fathers ate and died; whoever eats of this bread will live for ever," [John 6:58]. And again, "it is the spirit that gives life, the flesh is of no help; the words that I speak are spirit and life," [John 6:63]. And therefore he said, "I am the living bread which came down from heaven; whoever eats of this bread will live forever; and the bread which I shall give for the life of the world is my flesh," John 6:[51].

Herewith Christ explained his words which he had spoken about eating his flesh and drinking his blood, namely, that they are not to be understood carnally but spiritually, and that his flesh which he has given us to eat is actually the true living bread of heaven. Whoever now receives this bread of Christ Jesus and eats it, that is whoever receives and keeps the words of Christ, and believes firmly in Jesus Christ the crucified one, Rom. 3:25, that he has given his flesh for us and shed his blood for the forgiveness of our sins, Gal. 1:4; Eph. 2:13; Col. 1:20, eats spiritually of the flesh of Christ and drinks spiritually of his blood. And through the power of the spiritual food of the flesh and blood of Christ as the true bread of heaven, [that person] is nourished and strengthened to eternal life. /177/

Therefore, every Christian may well say with the prophet, "Praise the Lord, my soul, and forget not all his benefits," Ps. 103:2. And again, "how shall I repay the Lord for all the good he gives to me?," [Ps. 116:12]. But whoever despises these benefits of God, disdains Christ Jesus, transgresses his doctrine, and does not remain or wish to remain therein, he shall not escape the judgment of God, as it stands written: "For if the message declared by angels was valid and every transgression or disobedience received its just retribution, how shall we escape if we do not respect such a salvation? It was declared first by the Lord, and it came to us through those who heard him, while God also bore witness with signs and wonders and various miracles and by giving the Holy Spirit according to his own will," Heb. 2:2[-4]. And in another place he wrote as follows: "See that you do not refuse him who is speaking with you. For if they did not escape but refused him when he spoke on earth, much less shall we escape if we reject him who warns from heaven," Heb. 12:25.

This Moses had certainly seen in the Spirit; namely that one should now hear Christ Jesus alone and that the punishment of God shall come upon all despisers and transgressors of the saving teaching of Jesus Christ. Therefore, he spoke to Israel as follows: "The Lord your God will raise up for you a prophet like me from among you from your brethren—him you shall heed in everything he shall say to you. . . . And it shall happen that whose soul will not hear this prophet shall be rooted out," Deut. 18:15, [19].

This prophet is Jesus Christ as both Peter and Stephen testify, [Acts 3:22; 7:37]. Whoever now hears this prophet Jesus Christ, the Son of the most high God, believes in him and keeps his Word, shall be saved. But whoever despises him and does not accept his Word, [already] has one that judges them. "The Word that I have spoken," said Christ, "will judge them on the last day," John 12:48.

Therefore, beloved brothers and sisters, and fellow heirs of faith, I appeal to you through the mercy of God, Rom. 12:1, that you hold fast to Christ and also know and confess him just as the holy biblical Scripture teaches, John 8:31; 15:4, and I have done a little admonition out of love. Remain steadfast in his teaching, keep his commandments in true faith, and follow after his footsteps, 1 Pet. 2:21. Serve /178/ him with your whole heart, love him with your whole soul in order that at his appearing we may receive the crown of eternal glory. The grace of the Lord Jesus Christ be with you all. Amen. Titus 2:13; 2 Tim. 4:8.

D. P.

AN APOLOGY OR REPLY

Introduction

The possible dating of this writing, approximately 1560-1562, has been discussed on page 53. As indicated there, F. Pijper believes this treatise to have been directed primarily at the spiritualizing influence of Sebastian Franck among the Dutch Anabaptists. (See pp. 445ff. for Dirk's reply to him.) Franck was a friend of the Anabaptists but also a threat. He did not consider them to be the "true church" as they claimed, nor did he believe that they had a valid ministry. He also thought it unnecessary for them to suffer as they did, counseling instead an inner faith while conforming externally to the established church. The references to true Christian freedom likely referred to the place of rules and regulations in both the Roman Catholic and Reformed traditions, while the references to idols, useless ceremonies, and the dominance of tradition over Scripture would have referred primarily to the former.

Another reason for the "Apology," however, may have been internal pressures. Violence by small, radical, fringe Anabaptist groups in the wake of Münster was waning, but divisions among the peaceful Anabaptists were just beginning. The influence of David Joris was still felt. Dirk's brother Obbe had recently left the movement, disillusioned. Socinianism was becoming a continuing issue. We sense that Dirk felt the vision needed to be clarified. Thus we note a strong emphasis on separation from the world, unbelievers, and false worship. It is clear that Dirk sees Anabaptism in continuity with the apostolic church, not simply spiritually or potentially, but actually in essence and form. It was this vision which contributed to his rigorous emphasis on the ban. Note his treatise on the church (congregation).

This was also a time of increasing persecution as we know from the edicts issued against the Anabaptists and from the work of the Inquisition in the Netherlands. The Spanish occupation was a constant burden to all of the Dutch people, but for the Anabaptists there was also the continuing harrassment of the Reformed until long after Dirk's death. We note his comments about false peace.

We also note Dirk's use of the "Apocrypha," in this instance the books of the Wisdom of Solomon, Ecclesiasticus, or the Wisdom of Jesus the Son of Sirach, Bel and the Dragon, 1 and 2 Maccabees and Tobit. Not used here, but popular with the Anabaptists, was also Esdras. *Apocrypha* means secret or hidden, but early came to mean books that were not included in the Hebrew or Christian canon, usually taken to be thirteen in number. They were, however, included in the Latin Vulgate prepared by Jerome in the fourth century. With the increased emphasis on Scripture in the Reformation, Luther put these books between the Testaments with the notation that they were not equal to Scripture, but useful and good for reading. The *Biestkens Bible* of 1560, which many Anabaptists used, likely including Dirk, contains the Apocrypha. It is the first Dutch edition where the text is divided into verses. While Dirk may have agreed with Luther's judgment, he does not seem to distinguish between the authority of the canonical and the non-canonical books. It is likely that Dirk also used the *1545 East Frisian Luther Bible* prepared by Bugenhagen.

The Text

An Apology or Reply that we (who are scolded as Anabaptists by the world with great injustice) are no rebaptizers nor sectmakers, but that we are one with the true congregation of God which has been from the beginning. In addition, an instruction of the difference between true and false worship, and why a Christian must flee from false worship and must separate himself from the fellowship of those who serve idols. As a ministry to all lovers of the truth brought together out of Holy Scripture through the grace of the Lord.

By D. P.

"Since we have one spirit of faith, therefore we speak, etc."
2 Cor. 4:13.

"Flee before the service of idols," 1 Cor. 10:14.

I say that what the heathen sacrifice, that they sacrifice to the devils, and not to God. Now I do not want that you shall be in the fellowship of devils. You must not drink alike of the Lord's chalice and the devil's chalice. You must not partake alike of the Lord's table and the devil's table, 1 Cor. 10:20[-21].

"Therefore depart from the midst of them, and be separate from them, and touch nothing unclean, etc." 2 Cor. 6:17.

"The eternal love of God our heavenly Father, the peace of our Lord Jesus Christ, and the fellowship of the Holy Spirit be with all lovers of the truth." 2 Cor. 13:[14]. Amen.

/181/ Beloved brothers and friends in the Lord. Since we are severely taunted by the world, heavily blamed by the learned and misguided, and abominably persecuted by the tyrants as those who are a rebaptizing sect, and they have unjustly and without cause separated us from them—therefore, we are moved and compelled to reply a little and to explain and relate out of God's Word the reason for our separation, (that is, why we have separated ourselves from the world, from her false worship, and from her unfruitful works of darkness, Eph. 5:[7-9]). But we want to indicate clearly beforehand, that no one shall so interpret and understand our reply as though we want to extol and praise ourselves. For we know well that to extol and praise oneself is but foolishness. Because the world slanders us so severely, the learned write against us, and the tyrants so rant and rage against us, they compel us to write this brief and simple reply, just as the false laborers who always despised and belittled the person of Paul, the apostle (who was, after all poor, in spirit and humble of heart), drove him to where he had to defend and praise himself, 2 Cor. 11:13.

It is from these reasons that we too speak against the braggarts and boasting spirits, who with great exaggeration and lies, according to the nature and activity of Satan, severely despise, slander, and revile us, /182/ but present themselves with boasting and praising as God's people and as the true congregation, though they indeed with their false teaching, with their scandalous idolatry, with the many ceremonies and pomposity of their churches, with their reckless lives and godless walk demonstrate the opposite, as everyone who fears God can well observe and see.

Therefore, we so desire, according to our small gift, to prove to all lovers of the truth that we are no rebaptizers nor sectmakers, but that we are one with the true Christian, apostolic, and catholic church; and that we, out of highly necessary and weighty reasons, with every right, separate ourselves from all false religion and the fellowship of the servants of idols. And we are, indeed, certain and assured through the sealing of the Holy Spirit in our consciences that we are right, Eph. 1:13. And such shall also every submissive, understanding, God-fearing reader well understand out of this our poor defense, if he at least reads it correctly and takes it to heart. To that end may the almighty God grant his grace.

Amen.

In the first place, so far as the common word of reproach (wederdooper) [rebaptizer, Anabaptist] wherewith we are reproached is concerned, we have made our reply in our confession about baptism and about the Supper of our Lord Jesus Christ, and have proven powerfully with Scripture that child baptism was neither instituted by Christ nor taught or practiced by the apostles, but that true Christian baptism applies to the penitent and believing. Therefore, it is not necessary to repeat that here. For if anyone now desires to know our reply, they may read that earlier mentioned confession. There they shall find enough about why we have denied and rejected the idolatrous child baptism, which is administered to us in the kingdom of antichrist in the temple of idols from the priests of Baal in the time of our ignorance when we understood neither good nor evil, with terrifying exorcism of devils, with many idolatrous ceremonies, as not from God, 2 Thess. 2:3; 1 John 2:18; 2 Cor. 6:16; Bel and the Dragon 1:9; Deut. 1:39.

Now in the kingdom of Christ, in the temple of the living God, from the messengers of the Lord in the time of God's grace, through his Word /183/ that is preached to us we have heard, have become converted, penitent, and believing. We have allowed ourselves to be baptized in the name of the almighty God the Father, and the Son and of the Holy Spirit, according to the example and command of our Lord and Savior Jesus Christ, according to the teaching and practice of the apostles, Matt. 18:19; 3:15; 28:19; Mark 16:[16]. Therewith we have introduced no rebaptizing but we show and practice with it the true and only Christian baptism, which is valid before God, which takes place in spirit and in truth, which is practiced according to Scripture, and is received upon the confession of faith, and whose praise is not from people but from God, Acts 2:41; 8:36[-38]; 10:47; 16:[33]; 18:8; 22:16.

So if on this account people now call us rebaptizers and slander us, this takes place, after all, with injustice and violence. Yet this is the way it has gone with all pious people since the beginning of the world, that they have been accused and reproached with lying words. Therefore, they also prayed to the Lord that he would deliver their soul from the lying mouth and from false tongues, Ps. 120:2; that he would guard them from evil people and protect them from perverse people who plan evil things in their hearts and daily stir up strife, and sharpen their tongues as a serpent and the poison of adders is under their lips, Ps. 140:[2-3], which tongue desires to do harm and cuts with lies as with a razor. These would rather speak evil than good and rather falsehood than truth; these would gladly speak all that serves to destroy with false tongues. Nevertheless, they [meaning the pious] have always comforted themselves that an evil mouth shall have no good fortune on earth and that the Lord shall rightly execute the cause of the afflicted and the poor, Ps. 140:[12].

We are also comforted and rejoice with a firm trust and a living hope in the grace of God and of the Lord Jesus Christ and want to await with patience the time which shall comfort us, namely, when the righteous one shall stand with great joyfulness against those who have oppressed him and destroyed his work, Ecclus. 1:29[-30]. And then from great anxiety of the spirit they [their opponents] shall sigh and say, "This was he whom aforetime we held in derision and made a parable of reproach: We fools accounted his life for madness, and his end a scandal: how is he now numbered among the children of God? And how is his inheritance among the saints? Therefore we went astray from the true way, and the light of righteousness has not shined for us and the sun of understanding has not risen for us. We have walked the idle, wrong and harmful detours, but /184/ the way of the Lord we have not known. What did our arrogance profit us, our richness, our ostentatiousness? Those things have all passed away as a shadow," Wisd. of Sol. 5:[3-9].

Whenever this shall take place and this Scripture will be fulfilled and the righteous judgment of God shall come upon the world, then the world shall comprehend that we are no rebaptizers and that we have not been rightly baptized more than once upon the confession of our own faith, according to the institution of our Lord Jesus Christ and according to the example of the teaching which we have received from the apostles, Matt. 28:19; Mark 16:16; Acts 2:41; 8:36 [-38]; 10:47; 16:[33]; 18:8; 22:16.

In the second place, we have written in our treatise about the congregation of God whereby one should know it and differentiate it from all sects, which ordinances it must maintain and thus demonstrate that it is the congregation of the Lord. But now let everyone note well therein among which people such are already found, namely, a true confession of the one and eternal God, the Father, Son, and

Holy Spirit, Matt. 3:16; 28:19, true differentiation of the teaching of the law and the gospel which bears fruit, a true new birth, John 3:3, true servants of the Holy Word, 1 Tim. 3, true scriptural use of the sacraments of Jesus Christ, true foot washing of the saints, John 13:4[-5], true evangelical separation, Matt. 18:17; 1 Cor. 5:[9-13], and in sum, all ordinances and signs of the congregations of God.

One reads Holy Scripture and observes therein the signs by which the congregation is purified and set before our eyes, measure ourselves according to this true plumb line, and test ourselves with this touchstone, 2 Cor. 10:13. Then it shall be seen and discovered whether we or our opponents are closer to the truth. Yes, if we then, or they, shall be held as the Christian congregation. If the kingdom of God were to exist in high sounding words, in false idle boasting, and not in power and truth, in righteousness, peace, and joy in the Holy Spirit, 1 Cor. 4:20, then the false prophets and false Christians would always have won the game.

But now the Lord looks upon the heart and faith and does not regard outward appearance nor the artificial being, 1 Sam. 16:7. Therefore, he acknowledges as his disciples those who do the will of his heavenly Father, Matt. 7:21, and the same he has elected and separated out of the world as he himself said, "If you were of the world, so should the world love its own; but because you are not of the world, and I chose you out of the world, therefore the world hates you," John 15:19. And in his prayer /185/ he spoke to his Father about his disciples as follows: "I have given them your word; and the world hates them because they are not of the world, even as I am not of the world," John 17:14. Therefore, Paul says that Christ has given himself for us so that he should deliver us from this present evil world, according to the will of his Father, Gal. 1:4.

These and similar words, which are abundant in the Scripture, testify clearly to us that true Christians and disciples of the Lord are not one with the world, but are delivered, chosen, and separated from it. And, therefore, they may have no fellowship with her false worship and evil works, 2 Cor. 6:14; 1 Cor. 10:14; Eph. 5:11. For God himself has commanded and prescribed for his people a true worship, and he also wants the same to be observed, as he indeed also testifies through Moses and the prophets, for Moses spoke thus to the children of Israel, "And now, Israel, listen to the statutes and the rules which I teach you, that you shall do them; that you may live, and go in and take possession of the land which the Lord, the God of your fathers, gives you. You shall not add anything nor subtract anything to what I command, that you keep the commandments of the Lord your God, which I command you," Deut. 4:1. And another passage: "Everything that I command you, that you shall keep; you shall not add to it or take from it," Deut. 12:32.

Likewise, the first commandment of God sounds as follows: "I am the Lord your God, who led you out of Egypt. You shall have no other gods besides me," etc., Exod. 20:2[-3]. Again, you shall worship the Lord your God and serve him alone, Deut. 6:13; Matt. 4:10. Again, God commanded his people Israel that everyone should cast away the abominations which were before them and not contaminate themselves with alien gods. Yes, not to touch anything unclean, but to separate themselves and go out of the midst of the godless, Josh. 24:[23]; Ezek. 20:7; Gen. 19:15; Num. 16:26. Again, God said to Israel, "Do not walk in the statutes of your elders, nor observe their rules, nor defile yourselves with their idols. I am the Lord your God; you shall walk in my statutes, and keep my rules," Ezek. 20:18[-19]. [See also Isa. 52:11 and 2 Cor. 6:17.]

Out of these words it is evident that all that God has not commanded and has not instituted with an express word of Scripture, that he does not want to have done, and therewith he also does not want to be served. He will not have his Word set back nor have it feigned according to people's good pleasure, just as one may indeed clearly observe in the behavior of Saul. For he was disobedient to the words of God and feared his people and spared the king and the most beautiful animals in /186/ Amalek, which he should have banished with the sharpness of the sword, 1 Sam. 15:[9], and would have sacrificed them to God. But the Lord had no pleasure therein, for Samuel spoke as follows to King Saul, "Do you think that the Lord has as great pleasure in sacrifices and burnt offerings as in [your] obeying the voice of the Lord? Look, obedience is better than sacrifice, and to listen [better] than the fat of rams. For disobedience is as the sin of divination [witchcraft], and stubbornness is as blasphemy and idolatry," 1 Sam. 15:22[-23].

Therefore true worship is this—that one serves God according to his Word, honors and worships, fears and loves, ceases from sin and does no more wrong, Deut. 4:2; 12:32; 6:2; Ecclus. 4:1, has God's Word before ones eyes, Ecclus. 33:10,[1] comforts widows and orphans and keeps himself unspotted from the world, James 1:27; 1 Sam. 15:13. Contrary to this, all sacrifice and work is done out of one's own opinion, a false worship and idolatry. Thereby it confesses that God has not commanded such, but that it is instituted and kept out of devotion and the good intentions of the people, or for other reasons, instead of the divine worship and command, just as the Pharisees did to whom Christ spoke, "Why do you transgress God's commandment, for the sake of your tradition? God has commanded, 'you shall honor father and mother,' and 'whoever curses father and mother shall surely die.' But you teach: whoever says to father or mother, 'If I sacrifice it, it is more useful to you,' and it is done. Thereby it happens that no one any longer honors their father or mother, and thus make void God's commandment for the sake of your traditions, Matt. 15:3-6. And this the Pharisees did as though they had therewith wanted to render God a service, though it was nevertheless nothing other than hypocrisy. Therefore, Christ also spoke to them, "You hypocrites! Well did Isaiah prophesy of you, and has spoken, 'This people draws near to me with their mouth and honors me with their lips, but their heart is far from me; in vain do they worship me, since they teach doctrines which are nothing other than commands of people,' " Matt. 15:7; Isa. 29:13.

So it is also with all ceremonies, commandments, and teachings of the new Pharisees, yes, with all that people undertake out of their own opinions and understanding, according to the manner of the Pharisees, a liability instituted as a substitute for divine worship and command. Even though this is elaborated with a glittering appearance (as though one wished to serve God thereby), it is yet regarded as incorrect and hypocrisy before God, and he does not want to be served with it. Therefore all Christians must shun and avoid such. The reasons are these which follow:

The first is that the commandments of men are instituted and observed for this reason, /187/as though one through them pleased God, washed sins away and fulfilled righteousness, which is a diminishing of the grace of our Lord Jesus Christ. For this is an undoubted word and an unchangeable basis of truth, that we are not saved through any commandments or ceremonies of human beings, but through the grace of Jesus Christ and through faith in his name, Acts 4:10; 15:11; Eph. 1:7; 2:4[-5]. And now it is clear and well known to all God-fearing persons that the world seeks righteousness and salvation through human commandments, institutions, and teaching, just as the Galatians sought righteousness through circumcision and the law. Therefore, Paul also severely reprimanded the Galatians and wrote to them that they did not understand and were bewitched and did not believe the truth, that they had lost Christ and were fallen from grace since they wanted to be justified by the law, Gal. 5:4. How much more then has the world fallen from grace and lost Christ, since it seeks righteousness through human commandments and teachings? And if Paul overthrew circumcision and the figurative law, notwithstanding that both were given and commanded by God, because they were fulfilled in Christ and that the Galatians would also be justified through them, how much more then must the commandments, ceremonies, and teachings of humans, through which the world thinks that it can be saved, be overthrown, Matt. 15:3; 23:3?

The second reason is because the ceremonies and institutions of humans neither serve nor further the upbuilding of the neighbor, since all the works of Christians must be directed toward them, but they are offensive, particularly to the weak. Therefore, if anyone maintains human commandments and ceremonies with the world, they sadden and offend the congregation of God therewith, create an evil appearance, and gives others a bad example which is a serious sin, Matt. 18:6; Rom. 14:13; 1 Thess. 5:22; Wisd. of Sol. 4:6. For it stands written that bad examples lead astray and corrupt the good for others, and that evil desires pervert innocent hearts. Whoever now with their bad example leads another astray and corrupts the good for them sins seriously against the Lord and the neighbor, just as Christ himself testified with these words: "Woe to the one by whom the aggravation comes. It would be better for him if a millstone were hanged on his neck and he be drowned in the sea where it is deepest, than that he should offend one of the least of these who believe in me," Matt. 18:6; Mark 9:[42]; Luke 17:[2].

This they should rightly observe and take to heart, /188/ those who so little regard the offense to the congregation of God and do not reflect upon how seriously they sin, nor upon how severely God will punish them. Therefore Paul had rather nevermore eat meat so that he should not offend his brother, Rom. 14:15; 1 Cor. 8:11. The reason, he himself says, is that whoever sins against his brother and hurts his sick conscience sins against Christ. So then if Paul wanted rather to give up his Christian freedom to eat all kinds of food than to offend a single brother therewith, where will those then stay who make themselves a freedom which God has not given and who with this same false freedom offend the congregation of God, John 8:33?

The third reason is because through the keeping of human commandments and ceremonies, false worship is established, the world is strengthened therein, and takes it as a reason of boasting against the Christians. For this is the nature of all idolaters, that they want to have their idolatry praised and honored by everyone and compel people to do it, just as Nebuchadnezzar wished to compel the three young men, Shadrach, Meshach, and Abednego, that they should honor his image and worship his God, Dan. 3:14. Antiochus did similarly and compelled the Jews to his idolatry and many cooperated. But those who remained steadfast in the faith and would not turn away from the law of God were punished horribly and put to death just as the books of the Maccabees testify, 1 Macc. 1:[50-]53; 2:15; 2 Macc. 6:1; 1 Macc. 1:60; 2 Macc. 7.

This is the working and driving of the devil in the children of unbelief to establish and preserve his kingdom, Eph. 2:2. For with his fearsome tyranny, he frightens many that they do not believe the truth, nor are obedient to it, and makes many to fall away from it. And then whenever unbelievers and idolaters see that others who pride themselves of the gospel and faith and reproached their idolatry and for a long time avoided it, now fall into it again, whether it happens out of free will or compulsion, then they are strengthened in their false worship and allow themselves to think that they are correct and boast of their substitute as the true worship, to the disdain of all pious Christians.

But whenever they see that Christians separate from them, /189/ then it is peculiar to them, just as Peter said, that you do not run with them in that past wrong track and ungodly being, they slander, 1 Pet. 4:4, yes, they blaspheme, as it stands written in the book of Wisdom,

> "Let us lie in wait for the righteous one,
> For he creates much displeasure for us,
> And is contrary to our business,
> And upbraids us that we sin against the law,
> and labels our being as sin.
> He professes to have knowledge of God,
> And names himself God's child,
> He reproaches all that we have in our heart.
> He does not tolerate us,
> For his life is not as our life,
> And his being is an entirely different being,
> He holds us as useless,
> And avoids our life as he would an unclean thing,
> And proposes that the righteous
> Shall have it good at last,
> And boasts that God is his father, etc.
> Wisd. of Sol. 2:12-16.

So [live] that the world may not think that Christians are of one mind with them, but may know that they hold opposite and contrary [views]. Therefore they may not have any fellowship with their godless being and their unfruitful works of darkness, Eph. 5:11, but they must discipline themselves much more, in order that they may separate themselves from them, and thus give witness that these [worldly ones] are evil, John 7:7.

The fourth reason is that human commandments and ceremonies obscure the truth and freedom of the gospel of Jesus Christ; that one allows God's Word to lapse and burdens the consciences which are freed through Jesus Christ through faith, with useless and unnecessary things, Col. 2:16. But they are not bound to any human commandments, to the elements of the world, but to Christ alone, to serve him in obedience, holiness, and righteousness, Luke 1:69. For Jesus Christ is Lord over conscience, therefore they must be free from all alien service which is not a service of Christ.

Also one must exercise care that with the works one does not break what one has built with words. For therefore Jesus Sirach says, "If one builds, and [then] breaks the same again, what profit does he have from his toil?" Ecclus. [34:23].

Paul also reprimanded Peter about this because he separated from the believing Gentiles out of fear of the brethren who had come from Jerusalem, Gal. 2:11[-12], and broke with that which he had previously built when he confessed the truth of the gospel and testified to Christian freedom by which /190/ he made himself one with the Gentiles and took food with them. This, according to the law, he was not free [to do], and thereafter he conducted himself against them and separated himself from the Gentiles to please the Jews. Thus he broke the freedom of the gospel through his separation from the Gentiles which he previously had built through his fellowship with them. And thereby he again erected the law which he had previously broken away from. Because of this he was blameworthy for he did not remain of one speech and manner in these matters, and did not walk according to the truth of the gospel, and led others astray with his hypocrisy.

How much more then, are those blameworthy, who confess God's Word, reject human commandments and ceremonies and teaching, and regard them as incorrect, and then forsake God's Word, despise the sacraments of the Lord, and in order to please the world and take away the offense of the cross of Christ, Gal. 5:11, maintain and practice human traditions, thereby offending many and misleading some through their hypocrisy? Wherewith are they going to excuse themselves? Peter, after all, separated himself from the Gentiles according to the law and behaved in a Jewish manner to please the brothers who came from James. Yet he was censured by Paul because he had not behaved according to the evangelical truth and Christian freedom, with [the result that he became] a stumbling block to the believing Gentiles. But these behaved neither according to the law or the gospel. For they maintain human commandments and ceremonies, which both the gospel and the law censure, discard, and forbid, yes, curse and which are an abomination before God, Isa. 29:13; Matt. 15:9; Gal. 1:10. And they do the same to please people, though they may yet not please people as long as they desire to be servants of Jesus Christ. Therefore, they are wrong and judged before God and his congregation.

The fifth reason is because Christians are in fellowship with Jesus Christ and all the saints and break the bread of the Lord's Supper there and drink the cup as a witness that they are one body and bread with each other in Jesus Christ, Matt. 26:[26]; Mark 14:22; Luke 22:19; 1 Cor. 10:16; 11:23[-24]. Therefore they must also shun all false worship and the fellowship of idols and the servants of idols and the places where one serves idols and not appear there /191/ just as Paul's words clearly indicate, which are as follows: My beloved, flee before the service of idols. I speak as with sensible persons; judge for yourselves what I say. The cup of thanksgiving for which we give thanks, is it not the fellowship of the blood of Christ? The bread which we break, is it not the fellowship of the body of Christ? Because we many are one body, and one loaf, we all partake of one loaf. Behold the Israelites, according to the flesh, who eat the sacrifice, are they not in the fellowship of the altar? What then shall I now say? Shall I say that the idol is anything? Or that an idolatrous sacrifice is anything? No, but I say that what Gentiles sacrifice, they offer to demons and not to God. Now I do not want that you shall be in the demons' fellowship. For you may not drink the cup of the Lord and likewise the cup of demons. Thus you may not partake of the table of the Lord and likewise the table of demons. Or do we want to provoke the Lord? Are we stronger than he is? I have all power but not all things are profitable, etc., 1 Cor. 10:14[-23].

In these words we observe how Christians must flee from the service of idols because they are in the fellowship of Jesus Christ, and one body with all believers and saints, which they testify to and confirm with the Lord's Supper, just as the priests and children of Aaron who served the altar in the fleshly Israel and lived therefrom were in the fellowship of the altar. That is, they were partakers of all that God had attributed and given to the altar, Aaron and his children.

So it is also with those who with the servants of idols eat from their bread and drink from their cup. These are one body with them and are also in the fellowship of the servants of idols, yes, and of the devils themselves. For the unbelieving, idolatrous, and godless are one with the princes of this world whom they serve, and with the Babylonian harlot to whom they cling, and are also one body with her and they carry on many spiritual harlotries, that is, idolatry with her, Rev. 17:1. So now anyone who mingles with such and eats idolatrous sacrifice, that is, supports her false worship, he is in the same fellowship and must await the same punishment with her, Rev. 18:4. Yes, he shall share from the plagues that shall come over Babylon, and shall be cast with the dragon into the fiery lake which burns with fire and sulphur (which is the second death), Rev. 21:8, so long as he does not improve himself and does no sincere repentance. /192/

The sixth reason is that Christians are a temple of the living God, as it stands written: "Do you not know that you are God's temple and that God's spirit lives in you? If any one violates God's temple, God will violate him. For God's temple is holy, which you are," 2 Cor. 6:16; 1 Cor. 3:16; 6:19. Likewise, Christ has served in his own house as a Son which house we are "if we otherwise remain faithful and hold fast the pride of our hope to the end?," Heb. 3:6.

Since then true Christians are a temple and a house of God, Christ, and the Holy Spirit; therefore they must thus separate themselves from the temple of the idols where one runs to the golden calves of Jeroboam, 1 Kings 12:28, where one serves Baal, where one worships the Dragon and Bel, [and] honors Moabism, 1 Kings 18:26; Bel and Dragon 1:3. Yes, there such a multitude of idolatry takes place that it is a shame to speak about it and all too long to relate. Therefore a Christian must also shun such idol houses, purify himself and separate from them, just as Paul says, "Do not put on a strange yoke with unbelievers. For what partnership has righteousness with unrighteousness? Or what fellowship has light with darkness? What accord has Christ with Belial? Or what part has the believer with the unbeliever? What comparison has the temple of God with idols? For we are the temple of the living God; as God spoke, 'I will live and walk in them, and I will be their God, and they shall be my people. Therefore come out from the midst of them, and separate yourself from them, spoke the Lord, and touch nothing unclean; then I will accept you and be your father, and you shall be my sons and daughters,' spoke the almighty Lord," 2 Cor. 6:14[-18]; Rom. 14:[3-]4.

We also have a clear pattern and example in the pious Israelites who did not want to go to the golden calves of Jeroboam but forsook their homes, separated from idolatrous Israel, and lived in the cities of Judah and Benjamin, so that they might honor and worship the Lord their God in his temple at Jerusalem according to his command given through Moses [2 Chron. 11:13-16].

This the pious Tobias also did when he was among the captive Israelites in Assyria, he yet did not forsake the way of truth. But when the others all went to the golden calves which Jeroboam the king of Israel had made, /193/ he alone fled from their association and went to Jerusalem into the temple of the Lord, and there he worshiped the God of Israel and faithfully brought his first fruits and tithes, and even though all the others ate the food of the Gentiles, yet he guarded himself that he not defile himself with the same food, Tob. 1:5-6.

Similarly the prophets, the children of the prophets, and many God-fearing people in Israel (whenever they already lived among the godless and the servants of idols, in the time that Baal and other idols of the heathen were honored in Israel) bowed neither their knees nor their hearts nor their bodies before any idol, but they honored and worshiped the God of Israel, the Lord of heaven and earth, Dan. 3:16; 6:10, and they hid themselves before tyrants and kings, 1 Kings 18:13, yes, God guarded them marvelously by his grace, just as he himself spoke to Elijah saying, "I have left me seven thousand in Israel, who have not bowed their knees before Baal," 1 Kings 19:18; Rom. 11:4.

Again, the brave and God-fearing Mattathias did not act against the law of God because of the command of King Antiochus, but as many of the people of Israel were apostate from the law and sacrificed to idols, he spoke to the messenger of the king with a loud voice, "Even if all who are in the house of the king are obedient to the king, to depart from the faith and institutions of their fathers, yet will I and my sons and my brothers remain in the law of our fathers. God forbids us that we should forsake his institutions and accept the institutions of the king. We will not turn aside neither to the right nor the left hand, 1 Macc. 2:19[-22].

Again, the old Eleazar, how immovable did he remain by the law of God? How faithfully he shunned all hypocrisy and evil appearance, openly confessed and said, "I would rather die before you. For it is not fitting to my old age that I should waver, that through this many of the young should think that Eleazar, the ninety-year-old man, had now at last gone over unto an alien faith and practice; and so they, by reason of my wavering, and for the sake of this brief perishable life, should be deceived and act disgracefully in my old age. For even if I now might escape the pain and punishment of men, yet I may not escape the force of the almighty, either living or dead. Therefore, I will die manfully and do what is fitting to him in my old age, /194/ and therewith leave behind an example of bravery and manliness to the young. Thus I die with a willingly inclined spirit and will die manfully and honorably for the holy law," 2 Macc. 6:18[-28].

In like manner the seven brothers with the mother all suffered with great patience and steadfastness of faith all the abominable tyranny of the king and did not act against the law of God, but they all died willingly for it and had their comfort in the future resurrection and glory which was promised and prepared for them by God, 2 Macc. 7.

See how steadfastly all these together remained to the law of God and in no wise wanted nor might waver. Thereby they left us an example that we should follow in their footsteps. For all that is written, is written, (says the apostle) as our admonition so that we through patience and encouragement of the Scriptures, should have hope in God, Rom. 15:4.

In addition, [the need for] these previously explained separations, is shown to us through the two abominable beasts which are written of in the Revelation of John, of whom the first "opened its mouth to utter blasphemies against God, blaspheming his name and his dwelling, that is, those who dwell in it, and the animal is allowed to fight with the saints in order to conquer them. And authority was given it over every tribe, language, and tongue, and all who dwell on the earth will worship it, every one whose name has not been written in the living book of the Lamb that was slain from the beginning of world," Rev. 13:6[-9].

And that other beast "climbed up out of the earth, and had two horns like the lamb and it spoke like the dragon. It exercises all the authority of the first beast in its presence, and makes the earth and its inhabitants worship the first beast, and those who would not worship the image of the beast shall be killed. Also it causes all, both small and great, both rich and poor, both free and slave, to be marked on their hand or the forehead, so that no one can buy or sell unless he has the mark, or the name of the beast. Here is the wisdom, etc." [Rev. 13:11-18].

Whoever now is wise and intelligent and God-fearing, let him reflect and take to heart what this signifies and fear before it: listen and take to heart what the angel has spoken with a loud voice, namely, that "if any one worships the beast and its image, and takes his mark on his forehead or on his hand, he also shall drink from the wine of God's wrath that is mixed /195/ with pure drink in the cup of his anger, and he shall be tormented with fire and brimstone before the holy angels and before the lamb. And the smoke of their pain shall climb up to eternity; and they have no rest, day or night, these worshipers of the beast and its image, and if anyone has taken the mark of its name. Here is the yieldedness of the saints, those who keep the commandments of God and the faith in Jesus," etc., Rev. 14:9[-12]. Do take note.

Likewise, it is also well to observe here that the Holy Spirit in the Scripture testifies how that [when] the ugly abomination is set up in the place of the saints and then it is time to flee therefrom, Dan. 9:27; Matt. 24:15[-16]; how that the antichrist shall exalt himself and has already exalted himself for many hundreds of years above all that is called God or the worship of God and represents himself as God, and has his activities through the power of the devil in those who are lost, 2 Thess. 2:4. Yes, how the great harlot from Babylon sits "on a scarlet beast which was full of blasphemous names, and it had seven heads and ten horns. The wife was clothed with purple and scarlet, and bedecked with gold and jewels and pearls, and has in her hand a golden cup full of abominations and the impurities of her harlotry; and on her forehead was written a name, the secrecy of 'Babylon the great, mother of harlots and of all earth's abominations.' And she has made all the heathen drunk with the wine of her harlotry, and she herself is drunk from the blood of the saints and the witness of Jesus," Rev. 17:[3-6].

And she speaks in her heart:

"I sit and I am a queen,
and I shall be no widow, and shall
bear no sorrow nor see mourning,
Therefore her plagues shall come in a single day,
death, mourning, and hunger
and she shall be burned with fire;
for mighty is God the Lord who shall judge her," Rev. 18:7[-8].

Therefore all Christians are also admonished through a voice from heaven which speaks thus:

"Depart from Babylon, my people,
So that you do not partake of her sins,
and do not receive of her plagues.
For her sins reach unto heaven,
and God thinks on her iniquity," Rev. 18:4[-5].

Out of all this [it] now follows conclusively and incontrovertibly that true Christians must serve God the Lord according to his Word alone and may not conform themselves to the world, Rom. 12:2, nor maintain her false worship nor carry out an evil appearance (just as Paul says, "Abstain from every evil appearance"), 1 Thess. 5:22, as though they were truly one with the world to have her friendship (which is yet at enmity with God), James 4:4, in order not to bear the cross of Christ (in which all believers pride themselves), Gal. 6:[15], /196/ and keep this temporal life, which is yet impossible to do without harm and loss of eternal life, just as Christ himself said, "Who will keep his life shall lose it, but whoever loses his life for my sake, shall find it," John 12:25.

Here it will not avail that some propose that one may indeed have outward fellowship with false worship if one does not believe in it with the heart nor consent to it. Thereupon we reply that such a proposal is none other than deceit as Jesus Sirach says: "Guile is not wisdom, and godless whims are not cleverness. But it is wickedness and idolatry, and foolishness without wisdom," Ecclus. 19:[22-23]. Therefore let no one deceive themselves with such words. "For with the heart we believe to righteousness, and with the mouth occurs the confession for salvation," Rom. 10:10. The bodies of Christians are temples of the living God and his Holy Spirit, "and their members are the members of Christ," 1 Cor. 3:16; 2 Cor. 6:16. Just as the apostle Paul now says, one may not take the members of Christ and make them the members of a prostitute according to the flesh, 1 Cor. 6:15. Thus one may also not make the members of Christ, according to the Spirit, into members of the Babylonian harlot and the temple of God into a temple of idols, 2 Cor. 6:17.

Therefore all that the Scripture teaches about separation, that is, that one must separate and keep himself from all false worship, from the temple of the idols, from all evil work and appearance, this is thus to be understood that one must do this inwardly with the heart and demonstrate it outwardly with works, Eph. [1:11-13]; 1 Thess. 5:[21]-22. That is, the light that is not hidden under a bushel, but must be put on a lamp stand that it then enlightens others, Matt. 5:15. The city that lies on a high hill may remain hidden, but will be seen by everyone, Matt. 5:14. This is the glory with which Christians glorify the Lord with their body and spirit which both belong to God, 1 Cor. 6:[20]. This is the confession that one must confess Christ before people, and must not be ashamed to acknowledge him and his gospel before this perverse unbelieving nature and races, Matt. 10:32; Mark 8:38; Luke 9:26.

Those then who teach and propose how Christians have freedom to mingle hypocritically with the world and to carry on an evil appearance, these lie and deceive themselves and others who listen to them and the truth is not in them, 1 Thess. 5:[22]. But this is the glorious freedom of the children of God, that we poor, miserable, corrupted humans are through the power of the blood of Christ /197/ delivered from the devil, sin, death, and hell, Rom. 3:[21-24]; 5:6; 1 Pet. 1:2, and are free before the face of God, that the slavery of sin has been removed from us, Rom. 6:17, that we through faith in the Son of God are freed before the judgment, before the accusation and guilt of sins, before the power of Satan, before the future wrath of God, and have passed from death into eternal life made free through the truth, Heb. 2:14; 1 Thess. 1:10; John 5:24. In summary, all our enemies are overcome through the glorious victory of Christ and our faith is the overcoming of the world, Rom. 6:8; 8:2; John 8:32; 16:33.

In addition, all that has been figurative and burdensome to the conscience in the law, bound up with manifold external ceremonies on stated days, times, and places, all this the truth and spirit of Christ has loosed and unbound, and all the saints are freed from them through faith, so that we are now not under the law but under grace, Col. 2:14; 1 John 5:4; Col. 2:16; Heb. 8:5; 10:1, Rom. 6:14. For Christ is the end and the fulfillment of the law for us and through his grace we believe and hope to be saved, Rom. 10:4; Acts 15:11.

Nonetheless, if we are already freed through Jesus Christ, we have again become the servants of the Lord and of righteousness, in order in all humility and obedience, after the example of Jesus Christ, to serve God our heavenly Father, to the praise of his holy name, and to remain steadfast in the teaching of his Son to the end, Rom. 6:18. For he himself said that heaven and earth shall pass away, but his words shall not pass away, Matt. 5:18; 24:35. He is an eternal king and his kingdom is an eternal kingdom, Isa. 9:6[-7]; Dan. 7:14. He shall sit upon the throne of David and reign in the house of Jacob in eternity, Luke [1:69].

Wherefore, what he and his faithful servants and messengers have taught and testified to through the power of his Spirit, this must be kept rigidly unaltered and uncorrupted to the end of the world, by everyone who prides himself of the name of the gospel and faith in Christ, Matt. 28:20. The freedom which Christ and his servants taught and practiced, the same all true Christians may rightly accept and practice themselves in the fear of God to the glorification of the splendor of Jesus Christ and to the building of his congregation. But

[let] everyone beware that he does not reach further nor act [differently] than the example he has in Christ Jesus and his faithful followers and the Scripture teaches us. Then he remains undeceived.

So also some suggest that one may indeed associate with the world out of love and for the sake of peace. This is right /198/ there under the cleverness of the crooked serpent and deceptive lying, Gen. 3:1. For what true love is John indeed teaches us with these words: "God is love, and he who remains in love remains in God, and God in him," 1 John 4:16. Again, "love is from God, and he who loves is born out of God. He who does not have love does not know God," 1 John 4:7[-8]. Again, "this is the love of God, that we keep his commandments. And his commandments are not heavy," 1 John 5:3. And Paul says that "the main summary of the commandments is love out of a pure heart and a good conscience and sincere faith which some have missed and are turned around to useless chatter and fables, desiring to be masters, and do not understand what they are saying or what they assert," 1 Tim. 1:5[-7].

Out of these words one may recognize genuine love and distinguish it from the appearance of false love. For where God and the new birth are not, where the commandments of the Lord are not maintained, but much more despised and willfully transgressed, where there is not a pure heart, a good conscience, and a sincere faith, there also love is not. And God is and dwells with those who have a humble spirit, who fear his Word and keep the same, Isa. 57:[15]; 66:2. And the new birth is there where one does right, there where one leads a holy life, 1 John 2:29; 1 Pet. 1:15. And a pure heart and a good conscience and a sincere faith all come out of the Word of God, 1 Tim. 1:5; Rom. 10:17. For that cleanses the heart, assures the conscience, and out of that comes faith through the activity of the Holy Spirit, John 15:26; Heb. 11. Therefore, faith looks upon God and his Holy Word alone, despises every pressure on account of the Lord and his Word and has regard for no creature who wishes to hinder such. Yes, faith compels one to this, that he loves God above all creatures, also above his own life, Matt. 22:[37]; 16:24[-26].

This is well noted and found in faithful Abraham, in the severe temptation with which God tempted him when he spoke to him, "Take your only son Isaac, whom you love, and offer him to me as a burnt offering at the place which I shall show you." And Abraham did as follows: He rose up early in the morning, split wood for the burnt offering, he journeyed there with his son, and they went together. Abraham carried the knife and Isaac the wood for the burnt offering, and as they neared the place of the burnt offering, Gen. 22:[2-6], then "Isaac spoke to his father Abraham, 'My father!' And he replied, 'Here am I, my son.' And Isaac spoke, 'Here is the wood and the fire; where is the lamb for a burnt offering?' And Abraham /199/ replied, 'God will provide for a burnt offering, my son,' " [Gen. 22:7-8]. And when they came to the place of which God had told him, Abraham through his faith and out of the fear and love of his God, built an altar there, laid the wood upon it, and bound Isaac thereon and seized the knife in order to slay Isaac his son as a burnt offering to the Lord, [Gen. 22:9-10]. Then the angel called from heaven and gave witness that he feared God, since he had not spared nor preserved his only son on his account.[2]

Such nature and power of faith and of the love of God is also observed and found in the Levites who spared neither father nor mother, nor the brothers nor the neighbor but punished the worshipers of idols and the golden calf, according to the command of God and had not looked upon the human love, Deut. 33:9 and [Exod. 32:26-28]. Also Phinehas because of [his] zeal for God, set brotherly love aside when he thrust [his spear] through both the Israelite and the Midianite and thereby stayed the plague over Israel. Thereby Phinehas also received an eternal priesthood, Num. 25:[5-9].

This took place in figures according to the letter of the Old Testament, yet as a witness to a true faith and honest love of God and is written for our teaching and admonition, Rom. 15:4, that we should love God above all creatures, just as Christ also taught us in the gospel that one must for his sake, forsake all things, that is, father, mother, brothers, sisters, wife and children, in addition to his own life, take his cross upon him and follow after him, Matt. 10:[36]. And whoever loves anything more than him, that one is not worthy of him, namely, Christ and his gospel, Matt. 16:24; Mark 8:34[-35]; Luke 9:23[-24]; 14:27; 17:33; John 12:25. For this is the first and the highest commandment, both in the Old and the New Testaments, that one must love God the Lord from the whole heart, from the whole soul, out of all powers, and out of all ability, Deut. 6:5. And this love is confessed by the keeping of God's commandments, just as Christ himself said, "He who loves me keeps my commandments, but he who does not love me does not keep my commandments," Matt. 22:36,[37]; John 14:21.

Therefore the apostle says love does not rejoice at unrighteousness, but rejoices with the truth, 1 Cor. 13:6. Therefore love does not act hypocritically and does not deal deceitfully. Love does not transgress the teaching and rule of Christ. It shuns all false worship, all idolatry, ceremonies, and institutions of humans which are contrary to God. /200/ It does not seek the friendship of this world; it does not desire to please people. It knows well that all which is regarded as high among people is an abomination before God. It does not adorn the flesh; it does not seek what is temporal and perishable. It does not fear the cross of Jesus Christ but it rejoices in the same, Gal. 6:16.

In summary, love demonstrates her genuine and near divine nature through the power of the Holy Spirit, both toward God and the neighbor, 1 Pet. 1:22; toward God with obedience to the truth and with diligent keeping of the commandments of God, John 14:15, and toward the neighbor therewith, that it seeks primarily his salvation and desires it with fervent prayers to God, with good instructions, discipline and admonition; and thereafter shows constant comfort, friendship, and mercy in all bodily need, in every sadness, sickness, and temptation, 1 John 3:16; James 1:27; 2:15. In this, one has a good model and example in Jesus Christ, in Moses and Paul, and in all the saints of God, Deut. 2; Rom. 9.

But since some have missed this love and all that belongs to it, and still miss it, therefore they have given themselves to an idle, beautiful chatter about love whereby they boast and write much and propose that out of love one may indeed turn away from God's Word, transgress God's command, and make themselves conform externally, that is, hypocritically to the world in her idolatrous and godless being, Rom. 12:2; which is after all, idle falsehood and lies, and openly contrary to God and his Word, and contrary to the true nature of Christian love which does not consist of words nor in appearance but in the truth and power of God, which energizes them to keep the commandments of God and faithfully serve the neighbor, 1 John 3:16; James 2:15; 1 John 5:2. Where that does not take place there is no love but a false boasting about love, puffed up knowledge which does not improve and before God is foolishness and all misunderstanding and error in divine matters.

Thus it is also with those who boast much about peace and wish to make a cloak out of it for all hypocrisy, idolatry, and unrighteousness. Therefore it is also necessary to know, to observe, and to remember what the true peace of God and Christ is, and how Christians must keep peace with each other, and how far they should seek peace with all people, Eph. 4:1[-3]; Rom. 12:17[-18]. And this is the peace of God, that we have peace with God the Father through Jesus Christ, the true peacemaker and reconciler between God and everything, whether it be in heaven or on earth, Eph. 1:10. For the apostle Paul spoke thus to the Romans, "Now since we have become justified through faith, thus we have /201/ peace with God through our Lord Jesus Christ, through whom we also have access in faith to this grace in which we stand, and we pride ourselves in our hope of the future glory, which God shall give," Rom. 5:1[-2]. And to the Ephesians, "You who are in Christ Jesus, and in earlier times were far off are now brought near through the blood of Christ. For he is our peace, who has made us both one," Eph. 2:[13-14]. And to the Colossians, "It has been the pleasure of his Father that in Christ Jesus all fullness should dwell, and that through him everything will be reconciled to himself, whether it be on earth or in heaven, making peace by the blood of his cross through himself," Col. 1:19,[20].

And this is the true peace of Jesus Christ which he gave to his disciples as he said, "Peace I give you; my peace I leave to you; not as the world gives do I give to you," John 14:27. Therefore the peace of Christ is not the peace of this world, but the peace of the conscience which God gives through the grace, redemption, and reconciliation of Jesus Christ, [in whom we] have peace and joy in the Holy Spirit. The world does not know but hates and slanders it, Rom. 14:17. Thus the peace of Jesus Christ is enmity with the world and again the peace of the world is enmity with Christ. So he also testified where he said, "You should not think that I have come to send peace but a sword. For I have come to arouse a man against his father, and a daughter against her mother, and a daughter-in-law against her mother-in-law; and people's enemies will be those of their own household," Matt. 10:34 [-36]. Such discord Christ instigates through his gospel. Therefore Paul says, "If I were still pleasing people, I should not be Christ's servant," Gal. 1:10.

Out of this it is clearly to be understood how completely wayward and perverted those are who want to interpret this peace of Jesus Christ so that one through hypocrisy and fellowship with evil works seeks to keep peace with the world, which is far from all true Christians. For these allow themselves to be well content that they have peace with God through Jesus Christ, Rom. 5:1, and are well comforted that they, for the sake of righteousness, have hostility and discord with the world, Rom. 5:10. For since they are reconciled with the almighty God and Father through the blood of his Son and are called with all believers into one body, therefore they thus seek and have peace with one another just as Christ commanded them, saying, "Have salt in yourselves, and peace among you," Mark 9:50. And Paul wrote to the Ephesians, "Be eager to maintain the unity of the Spirit in the bond of peace," Eph. 4:3. /202/ Again, to the Colossians: "the peace of God take the upper hand in your hearts, to which you were called in one body. And be thankful," Col. 3:15. Again, to the Philippians: "the peace of God, which passes all understanding, keep your hearts and minds in Christ Jesus," Phil. 4:7.

So Christians are obligated to keep peace with all people, as much as in them is, just as the apostle says, "If possible, keep peace with everyone," Rom. 12:18. Again, "strive for peace with all people," Heb. 12:14. But this is not to be understood that one shall seek peace with the world (which after all lies entirely in evil), 1 John 5:19, in [seemingly] divine actions through any hypocrisy or appearance of evil. For both Peter and John witness to the contrary before the Pharisees and scribes, that one must obey God rather than people, Acts 4:19.

See, here we have briefly in our simplicity given an account and related the reasons why we have separated ourselves from the world and from her false worship. Even if we are now blasphemed by the false prophets on account of this separation and are persecuted by the tyrants, we must entrust ourselves to the Lord our God and rejoice. For we know, after all, and are certain through the grace of God and the sealing of the Holy Spirit in our hearts, 2 Cor. 1:22; Eph. 4:30, that we have not separated nor do separate ourselves from the true Christian apostolic church or congregation which has been since the beginning, Eph. 4:4. For we believe in the eternal, almighty and only God, Creator of heaven and earth, who made his covenant with Adam, Noah, Abraham, Isaac, Jacob, and all God-fearing persons, Gen. 3:15; 9:[9]; 22:15[-17]; 28:13, and in his only begotten Son, Jesus Christ, promised and given to them as a Messiah, Redeemer, and Savior, Isa. 9:[6]; Matt. 1:21, in whom we also believe and hope to be saved through faith in his name, Acts 15:11; Gal. 3:9; Eph. 2:4[-6]. We also desire in our weakness to serve our Lord Jesus Christ, to remain steadfast in his doctrine and to accept no false teaching in all eternity, 2 John 10.

And we thank almighty God our heavenly Father, who has called us out of grace to the fellowship of Jesus Christ and the saints, that "we are no strangers but members of the household of God and citizens of the holy place, built upon the foundation of the apostles and prophets, of which Jesus Christ himself is the cornerstone," Eph. 2:19-20. Yes, that we have "come to Mount Zion and to the city of the living God, to the heavenly Jerusalem, and to /203/ the multitude of many thousand angels, and to the congregation of the firstborn who are enrolled in heaven, to the spirits of the completely righteous, to God the judge over all, and to Jesus, the mediator of the new covenant, and to the sprinkled blood that speaks better there than the blood of Abel," Heb. 12:22[-24].

This is the fellowship of God and the saints to which we have come through the reconciliation, election, and calling of God, in which we also desire to remain and to serve God therein in obedience and truth and keep his ordinances. Therewith we do not separate ourselves from the true congregation of God with which we are[3] [of course] one. But we separate ourselves from all sects, from all false worship, from all teachings, ceremonies, and commandments of humans which are contrary to God's Word, and from all evil appearance, so that we do not desire to pretend to please the world. And this we do not do out of our own natural intention, nor out of stubbornness, nor wrath, nor out of any other carnal reasons, but we do it out of faith through the compelling love of our God, in the fear of the Lord, because of the previously mentioned reasons, about which we shall not come to shame. For we know that it is thus God's command and will and are certain that every plant which God the heavenly Father has not planted shall be rooted up, Matt. 15:13.

But may God the Father of all mercy, 2 Cor. 1:3, who has freed us from the power of Satan and transferred us to the kingdom of his beloved Son Jesus Christ, Col. 1:13, keep us therein and gather many thousands in addition, that they may be saved, and place us all with each other in one spirit of faith, unblamable before his face and keep us for his heavenly kingdom through the power of his Holy Spirit, Heb. 13:[21]. To the same one and eternal God be praise, honor, and gratitude in eternity.
Amen.

D. P.

ENDNOTES

1. This reference from Ecclesiasticus or Sirach does not seem to fit the context of Dirk's comments. It may be that 42:15 of this book is more nearly what he had in mind. See also the earlier note in this treatise about the Apocrypha. It may be that he had Ecclesiastes in mind, which places great emphasis on integrity and justice.

2. In the absence of clear evidence to the contrary, we may assume that Dirk wrote the Abraham-Isaac story simply on the basis of his own reading of the Genesis 22 account. However, the flow of words and ideas raises the question of whether he may have been familiar with Martin Luther's account, told dramatically in the latter's "Lectures on Genesis," which he gave at Wittenberg in 1539-1540. Jaroslav Pelikan, ed., Walter A. Hansen, assoc. ed., *Luther's Works*. St. Louis: Concordia Publishing House, 1964., Vol. 4, pp. 91ff.; cf : *D. Martin Luthers Werke. Kritische Gesamtausgabe*, Weimar, 1883—, Vol. XL111, pp. 201ff. For a compact translation of the story, see Bainton, pp. 11-12.

3. "... met welcke wy doch eens zijn. . .," p. 203. The *doch* might be translated as obviously, of course, surely, in any case, etc. This becomes an important point in Dirk's view of Anabaptism as standing in direct continuity with the true church of Christ through the ages.

THE SENDING OF PREACHERS OR TEACHERS

That is, who are the true teachers who are sent by God and rightly chosen and called by the Christian congregation: Whereby these are recognized and what fruits they bear. Similarly, how one may know the false teachers and how one may shun them and not hear them. A small instruction out of Holy Scripture with an explanation of some contradictions and blasphemies introduced by the disgruntled blasphemers, and spoken in a mocking manner, against the true ministers[1] of the gospel. /205/

By D. P.

"He whom God has sent speaks God's words," John 3:34.

I, Dirk Philips, out of grace a fellow member of the faith and of the Christian congregations,[2] wish all God-fearing lovers of the truth genuine spiritual wisdom and a pure understanding of the divine Word from our heavenly Father, and of Christ Jesus his only begotten Son, our Lord and Savior, through the enlightenment of the Holy Spirit. Amen.

The Text

/207/ Beloved in the Lord, all you who fear God and love the truth; since some at this time create much controversy and discord concerning the sending [of ministers], and in addition all ministers, be they whoever they are, boast of the gospel and allow themselves to think that they are sent of God, and that also without any doubt, now is the time of which Christ and the apostles have prophesied, namely that many false prophets and false Christians should come and lead many astray, Matt. 24:11; 1 Tim. 4:1; 2 Tim. 3:1; 2 Pet. 2:1; Jude 4; therefore I was compelled, out of brotherly love, to prepare a brief instruction about the sending of true ministers in order that you may know how to distinguish true prophets, teachers, and Christians from false ones. For this is the nature, character, and skill of Satan, that he transforms himself into an angel of light, 2 Cor. 11:14. Therewith he hides his guile and hypocrisy, disguises and conceals his ministers, and sets them before the world in a beautiful appearance of piety.

For what has a more beautiful appearance than Satan in all hypocritical and unspiritual work as saints who seek righteousness through their own works and efforts, and present themselves so splendidly with words and appearance, with many ceremonies and churchly pomp? Who is more presumptuous and audacious with words of high praise than the false, deceptive, and lying prophets; those who run but are not sent from the Lord, those who prophesy but not through the Spirit of the Lord? Who pride themselves more of the gospel and Christendom, of true theology and knowledge of Holy Scripture than [do] the highly praised wise [ones] of the world, the perverse scribes who allow themselves to think, since they have studied in advanced schools (and, therefore, according to the common proverb, the more learned the more perverted they have become), so they alone are teachers and masters of Scripture and yet themselves have neither received nor taught the divine words of the first school primer? For they have not yet been in the school /208/ of Christ and they have not had the true master teacher, namely, the Holy Spirit, yes, have neither seen nor known [him]. But they speak about the Scripture which they do not understand, and even when they already do understand something, they yet do not wish to act in accord with it, John 14:26; 15:26; 16:7.

These are the genuine false Christians and false prophets of whom the Lord warns us and of their fine image, saying, "Beware of false prophets, who come to you in sheep's clothing but inwardly are ravenous wolves. You will know them by their fruits," Matt. 7:15[-16]. And at another [place] Christ says, "Not every one who says to me, 'Lord, Lord,' shall enter the kingdom of heaven, but he who does the will of my Father who is in heaven" [Matt. 7:21]. And after this follows: "On that day many will say to me, 'Lord, Lord, did we not prophesy in your name, and cast out demons in your name, and do many mighty works in your name?' And then I will declare to them, 'I never knew you; depart from me, all you who do evil,' " [Matt. 7:22-23].

Out of these words of Christ it is clear that those are the false Christians and false prophets who boast much about Christ, prattle beautifully about the gospel, and portray themselves in a splendid manner and, in addition, live according to the flesh and have the nature of a wolf in order to destroy the sheep of Christ in every way they can.

Christ has truly warned us about these, although there are few who heed this warning. The people are generally so minded as Ahab the king of Israel was minded, namely, they love lies and hate the truth and cannot endure it that a Micaiah should come and tell them the truth, 1 Kings 22:[8]. Therefore, they cannot understand the truth. "For the foolish, (says Jesus Ben Sirach), shall not find wisdom, and the godless shall not get to see her. She is far from the proud and hypocrites shall not know her," Ecclus. 15:[7-8]. Therefore Paul also says, "If our gospel is veiled, it is veiled only in those who are being lost, in whom the god of this world has blinded the minds of the unbelievers, so that the light of the gospel of the glory of Christ, who is the exact image of God, does not shine on them," 2 Cor. 4:3[-4].

It is on account of this that false prophets have always had such great respect and attention, but the good prophets, regarded as those who lead astray, are shamed and persecuted. And that is the way it still goes. For Satan can so deceive the world /209/ that it accepts appearance for reality, darkness for light, and lies for the truth; yes, completely rejects Christ because his being is an offense to the world as the Lord says through Isaiah: "Behold, my servant shall deal wisely. [He] shall be exalted and lifted up, and shall be very high. And many shall be agitated on his account because his appearance is so marred, beyond human resemblance, and his form beyond that of human beings," Isa. [52:13-14]. And Simon spoke to Mary concerning Christ: "He is set for the fall and rising of many in Israel, and for a sign that shall be spoken against," Luke 2:34. And Peter said that Christ Jesus is the cornerstone of God laid in Zion, which is precious to the believers, but to the unbelievers he is the stone which the workmen have rejected and has become the head of the corner, "a stone that will make people stumble, a rock of irritation for they stumble because they do not believe the Word on which they were founded," 1 Pet. 2:[8].

Therefore spiritual judgment, keen insight, and clear eyes are necessary [for] all believers, particularly in these our times, whereby they may see Christ rightly, rightly recognize his ministers and distinguish them from the ministers of Satan. These reasons move me, through the Lord's grace, to show all God-fearing persons out of the biblical Scriptures, which teachers are sent of God and whereby and through what [they are recognized]. [I do this] in order that all pious Christians may be strengthened a little in their faith, comforted and refreshed in their hearts, and that all blasphemous mouths who speak blasphemously against the true messengers of God, against the faithful ministers of Christ in order to hide their [own] hypocritical nature, may be stopped. The eternal and omniscient God grant us grace thereto. Amen, 1 Tim. 1:17.

In the first place there are two kinds of calling or sending (whereby God calls anyone to an office) included in Scripture. The first is from God alone. Thus, Moses was called by God alone, Exod. 3:10; Num. 12:6[-8]. Thus also Aaron was chosen by God alone, Heb. 5:[4]. Thus also the prophets were called by God alone and spoke, being driven by the Holy Spirit, 2 Pet. 1:21. Thus also the apostles were called by Christ Jesus alone, chosen, and sent out to preach the gospel to all creatures [Mark 16:15; Rom. 8:19-22; Gen. 9:8-17].[3]

These were sent out by God without mediation from any persons in order to prophesy and to teach, and [were] driven through his Spirit. /210/ But because of the [fact] that Satan also sends out his ministers and at times drives [them] powerfully, yet under the appearance that they are sent by God and driven by his Spirit, 2 Cor. 11:[13-14], therefore the Lord has left us a sure test whereby one may recognize both good and false prophets and [it] is this:

In the first place, if the prophet prophesies something and it does not take place, then he is false. For thus says the Lord: "Whenever a prophet presumes to speak in my name [that] which I have not commanded him to speak, or who speaks in the name of other gods, that same prophet shall die. But you say in your heart, 'How can I know the word which the Lord has not spoken?' When a prophet speaks in the name of the Lord, if the word does not come to pass, that is a word which the Lord has not spoken. The prophet has spoken it presumptuously, therefore you need not fear him," Deut. 18:[20-22].

These are the clear words of the Lord wherewith all prophesies must be measured and judged. Therefore the prophet Jeremiah spoke thus to Hananiah (who prophesied falsely about the release of Judah from Babylon): "The prophets who preceded you and me from ancient times, who prophesied in many lands and kingdoms against war, famine, and pestilence or prophesied peace, will be tested whether God truly sent them whenever that comes to pass which the prophet said," Jer. 28:8[-9].

In the second place, even though a prophet gives a sign or miracle, and it takes place as the prophet said, and the prophet in addition teaches that one should serve other gods, then the prophet is false. For thus says the Lord, "If a prophet arises among you, or a dreamer, and gives you a sign or a miracle, and the sign or miracle which he tells you comes to pass, and if he says, 'Let us go after other gods,' which you have not known, 'and let us serve them,' you shall not listen to the words of that prophet or to that dreamer; for the Lord your God is testing you, to know whether you love him with all your heart and all your soul," Deut. 13:1[-3].

In these words it is to be observed that although a prophet gives a sign or a miracle and it comes as the prophet said, this is not enough to establish his sending /211/ that it is from God, if his teaching is not unblamable, fruitful, and wholesome. To this Paul also says, "Should it be that an angel from heaven proclaim another gospel than we have received, let him be accursed," Gal. 1:8[-9].

The other calling is from God and from his congregations. Thus Paul and Barnabas were first called by the Lord and thereafter by the congregations through the co-witness of the Holy Spirit, and were confirmed in the divine call as the work of the apostles indicates, namely, that the Holy Spirit said to the congregations, "Set apart for me Barnabas and Saul for the work to which I have called them. Then after fasting and praying they laid their hands on them and let them go," Acts 13:2[-3]. Thus Paul and Barnabas also ordained bishops or elders in all congregations (through united voice) with fasting and prayers, Acts 14:23. Again, Paul writes to Timothy, "Do not neglect the gift you have, which was given you through prophecy when the elders laid their hands upon you," 1 Tim. 4:14. Similarly he commands Titus [to do] the same in the cities of Crete, to appoint elders over all as he [Paul] had ordained him, Titus 1:5. Thus also the congregation at Jerusalem set seven deacons before the apostles, and they prayed and laid their hands on them, Acts 6:6.

From these [examples] it is clear that the apostles and elders with the congregations, through the power of Jesus Christ and the testimony of the Holy Spirit, called, chose, and ordained teachers and ministers. Therefore no one may assume such an office by himself, except he is called of God (like the prophets and apostles) or by the congregations of God with the laying on of hands (as Timothy and Titus and others in addition, were ordained by the apostles and elders, with the voluntary consent of the congregations) and thus others also were called and chosen. For thus says the apostle, "And how shall they preach unless they are sent," Rom. 10:15. And another passage, "No one takes this honor upon himself, except he is called by God, just as Aaron was," Heb. 5:[4]. Therefore, also the Lord so severely punished Dathan, Korah, and Abiram, and their followers because they wished to take up the priesthood without God's election, Num. 16. [See especially 16:28-35.] Thus the Lord rejects all prophets who run of themselves and are not sent by him, who speak in his name /212/ but are nevertheless not driven by his Spirit, Jer. 23:21.

Therefore, everyone may well see to it that he does not run by himself before he is called by the Lord or by his congregation according to these previously described methods. But now no one will be sent by the Lord nor correctly chosen by the congregation, except through the Holy Spirit who must touch his heart, make him fiery with love, in order thus to voluntarily feed, lead, and send out the congregation of God, John 21:15; 1 Pet. 5:2, as it is written of Paul and Barnabas, "they went out sent by the Holy Spirit," Acts 13:4, and Paul said to the elders of the churches, "Take heed to yourselves and to all the flock, in which the Holy Spirit has made you guardians, to feed the congregation of the Lord which he obtained with his blood," Acts 20:28.

But because the true teachers must be driven, sent out, and set over the congregation of God by the Holy Spirit, it is clear how these must be prepared. For it is certain and undeniable that the Holy Spirit sends out no drunkards, nor adulterers, nor misers, nor servants of idols, nor hypocrites, who dissemble for the sake of the belly, and make merchandise with God's Word. For it is written: "The holy spirit who teaches rightly flees deceit, and avoids the reckless," Wisd. of Sol. 1:5. Therefore, Christ also says that the world cannot receive the Holy Spirit for she does not see nor know him, John 14:17. But those who do not have the Spirit of Christ do not belong to him, Rom. 8:9. But how can those who do not belong to Christ have an office in his congregations and serve correctly, 1 Cor. 12:8? The apostle says that no one may call "Christ Jesus Lord except by the Holy Spirit," [1 Cor. 12:3], much less then can he preach Christ Jesus correctly except through the Holy Spirit.

Out of this it follows forcefully that the ministers of Christ, the teachers and bishops in his congregations, must have the Holy Spirit through whom they first and before all things must be well instructed in God's Word. The common people will err and walk in darkness if the teachers themselves are unwise. The reason? Christ calls teachers a light of the world and salt of the earth, Matt. 5:[13-]14. How shall the world see correctly whenever those to whom it belongs to be a light of the world are themselves darkness? Again, how shall the world correctly understand and know the Holy Scriptures and the power /213/ of God, when those who should be the salt of the earth have lost the power of the divine Word and themselves do not know what it behooves a good Christian to know? Again, how should the world not err when those who properly and with truth should be the city (built upon a high mountain) and show all erring ones the right way are themselves those who lead astray? Therefore, I say again, that the teachers themselves must before all things be well instructed and taught in God's Word. As it is written: "For the lips of a priest should guard knowledge, that one may seek the law from his mouth, for he is the messenger of the Lord of hosts," Mal. 2:7. And Paul says that "a bishop must hold firm to the sure Word, so that he may be able to give instruction in saving doctrine and to admonish those who contradict it," Titus 1:9.

In addition, the teachers of God's Word must teach correctly and without falsification, as the evangelist says, "He whom God has sent utters the words of God," John 3:34. And Paul says, "I will not dare to speak of anything except what Christ has worked through me," Rom. 15:18. And again, "we are not like some who falsify God's Word but we speak in Christ out of sincerity and out of God, and before God," 2 Cor. 2:[17]; 4:2. Likewise, "we are messengers in Christ's place, God admonishes through us. We beseech you on behalf of Christ, be reconciled to God," 2 Cor. 5:20. Again "our admonition does not spring from error or uncleanness, nor is it made with guile; but just as we have been approved by God to be entrusted with the gospel, to preach it, so we speak, not as though we would please people, but to please God who tests our hearts," 1 Thess. 2:3[-4]. The apostle Peter says, "If there is anyone who speaks, he shall speak as God's Word," 1 Pet. 4:11. Therefore, the Lord also said through Jeremiah, "Let the prophet who has a dream tell the dream, but let him to whom my Word is revealed proclaim it faithfully. For what does chaff have in common with wheat? says the Lord. Is not my Word like fire, says the Lord, and like a hammer which breaks the rock in pieces," Jer. 23:28 [-29]?

Out of these and similar words of Holy Scripture, the true teachers may certainly be easily recognized, particularly as far as true doctrine is concerned, namely, if they teach God's Word correctly, if they seek therewith the glory of God and the salvation of persons, if they are spiritually minded, if they have renounced all earthly and /214/ temporal things, if they know no one according to the flesh, 2 Cor. 5:16, if they love God above all and do his work without deception and hypocrisy. For such leaders the Lord desires to have as Moses also said, "Who says to his father and mother, 'I do not see you'; and to his brother, 'I do not know him,' and to his neighbor, 'I do not recognize him,' he has kept your Word and preserved your covenant. He shall teach Jacob your ordinances, and your law to Israel," Deut. 33:9[-10].

Therefore Christ also chose and sent out such apostles to preach who had first forsaken all things, Matt. 10:[5], and had followed after him, and remained with him in his temptations, Matt. 4:19; 19:27; Luke 5:11; 18:28; 22:28. These the Father gave him out of the world and to these he first revealed the Father's name, as he himself said, "I have revealed your name to the people whom you have given me out of the world; they were yours, and you gave them to me, and they have kept your Word," John 17:6. These Christ also chose himself and separated from the world, just as he said, "You did not choose me, but I chose you and appointed you that you should go and bear fruit and that your fruit should remain," John 15:16. These Christ also commended to his Father and prayed for them saying, "I am praying for them; I am not praying for the world but for those whom you have given me, for they are yours; all mine are yours, and yours are mine, and I am glorified in them. . . . Holy Father, keep them in your name which you have given me, that they may be one even as we are one," John 17:9[-11]. "I have given them your Word; and the world has hated them because they are not of the world, even as I am not of the world," [John 17:14]. These [disciples] taught by God, chosen and separated from the world, Christ sent out and said to them, "Even as the Father has sent me, so I send you," John 20:21. But how Christ was sent from the Father, and how he forsook all things and gave up all his glory and became a faithful messenger of his Father [who] did not do his own will nor speak his own Word nor seek his own honor, but spoke and did as the Father commanded him, the Scriptures, both the Old and New Testament, testify so abundantly that we do not think it necessary to repeat such here, Isa. 53:1[ff.]; Jer. 23:5[-6]; Ezek. 34:15[-16]; John 1:1; 3:[13]; 5:19; 6:32; 7:16; 8:28; 10:14[-15]; 12:49.

Just as Christ now sent from the Father was entirely faithful in his office, so also all his servants must be faithful according to the example of their Lord and Master, Heb. 3:5[-6], disregard all earthly things, deny the world, pursue heavenly things, and not seek their own glory but the /215/ glory of Christ who sent them. Of such an interpretation Christ said, "He who speaks on his own authority seeks his own glory; but he who seeks the glory of him who sent him is true, and in him there is no unrighteousness," John 7:18. Therefore, those are without doubt sent of God who teach God's Word correctly and with their whole heart seek the praise and glory of God, as Paul did. "For we," he says, "never used either words of flattery, as you know, or a cloak for greed, as God is witness; nor did we seek glory from people, whether from you or from others, though we might have made demands as apostles of Christ. But we were gentle among you, like a nurse taking care of her children. Thus our heart was filled with joy for you to share with you not only the gospel of God but also our own lives, because we had come to love you," 1 Thess. 2:5[-8].

In these words one may clearly see how the apostle Paul was minded, and what he actually sought, namely, the glory of God and the salvation of souls. But thus the hypocrites and false prophets do not do, but they seek their own honor, they incline toward money and goods, they preach for a wage, they serve their belly and are enemies of the cross of Christ, Rom. 16:[18]; Phil. 3:18. Therefore, they also can [neither] do nor teach anything good as it is written, a godless [person] cannot teach correctly for it does not come from God. For to the correct teaching belongs wisdom, then God grants his grace thereto, Ecclus. 15:14[?].

Since then a godless person cannot teach correctly, and he who is actually godless is he who transgresses and does not abide in the doctrine of Christ as John says, 2 John 1:9, it follows therefrom without contradiction, that no one can teach God's Word correctly unless he himself remains in Christ and his doctrine. But no one can understand Christ's doctrine, much less abide in it, except through the Holy Spirit. And no one has the Holy Spirit except one who is no longer carnally but spiritually minded, as Paul says, "But you are not in the flesh, you are in the Spirit, if the Spirit of God really dwells in you. Any one who does not have the Spirit of Christ does not belong to him. But if Christ is in you, although your bodies are dead because of sin, your spirits are alive because of righteousness," Rom. 8:9[-10]. Therefore, he who has not died to sin and does not /216/ live in righteousness does not have the Spirit of God. But he who does not have the Spirit of the Lord does not understand the Word of the Lord and does not experience what is spiritual. How should he then be able to teach God's Word correctly or correctly distribute the gifts of the Spirit, 1 Cor. 2:14? Therefore everyone may well see to it that he does not accept the office of teacher before he himself has been taught by God and enlightened with the Holy Spirit through whom he may speak God's Word correctly.

Further, so Scripture testifies, a true teacher must bear or bring forth fruit. For wherever God's Word is implanted in the human heart and spoken in the power of the Spirit, there it must, according to its nature, be active and fruitful. To that end the true teachers are chosen and ordained of Christ that they may go forth and bear fruit and that their fruit may abide, John 15:16. But the fruit which all true teachers through God's Word and spirit must bring forth is [of] two kinds.

The first is that whenever God's Word is spoken through the Holy Spirit it bears fruit and is not barren just as the evangelical parable of the sower and his seed testifies, in which parable Christ gave us to understand that his Word is not without fruit, Matt. 13:3[-9]; Luke 8:[5-7]; [Mark 4:3-9]. For while most of the seed fell upon bad earth and brought [forth] no fruit (which then is not the fault of the good seed but of the bad earth), nevertheless another part fell upon good earth and brought forth much fruit. Therewith the Lord teaches us two things. The first, that there are at all times few Christians upon the earth although many have the name Christian and boast themselves of the gospel as then he also said to Matthew in the seventh chapter, "The gate is wide and the way is easy, that leads to condemnation, and many walk on it. But the gate that leads to eternal life is small and the way is narrow, and there are few who find it," Matt. 7:13[-14].

The second [is that] Christ gives us to understand, that even though the largest part remains evil, his Word is nevertheless not without fruit. There is yet perchance a good acre into which the seed of the divine Word is cast, sprouts, and brings [forth] fruit. This [is] what God has also said through Isaiah. "Just as the rain and snow fall from heaven, and do not return but water the earth, making it fruitful and [bring forth] growth, giving seed to the sower and bread to eat, so shall the Word that goes out of my mouth not /217/ return to me empty, but accomplish that which pleases me, and shall prosper in that for which I send it," Isa. 55:10[-11].

But because the Word of God is now the seed that is planted by God in the hearts of human beings and desires and must have good soil, therefore it is necessary that the field of the heart be properly cultivated through the grace of the Lord, [that] all weeds be plucked up or uprooted, so then the field will be made receptive of the divine seed and bring forth fruit, as James says, "Put away all uncleanness and all wickedness and receive with meekness the Word which has been planted in you, which is able to save your souls," James 1:21.

To that end, namely, in order to cultivate and prepare the field of the heart, the law of God serves [well]. Therefore, true preachers must also first and before all things proclaim and preach repentance to the people (even as Christ and the apostles did) and teach them out of the law God's wrath and severe judgment upon sin, Matt. 3:8; Acts 24:25; but out of the gospel rightly to know God the Father in his eternal love and fathomless mercy, Christ Jesus in his grace and merits, through the cooperation of the Holy Spirit in order that the hearts, smitten and broken through the law, may again be comforted and strengthened through the gospel. For this is the nature, character, and power of the divine Word, that where it is spoken orderly and through the motivating of the Spirit flinty hearts are smitten, Jer. [23:29], the cold made fervent, and the sorrowful are comforted thereby.

This is also the true teacher's office and work, according to the command of Christ, first to preach the law, thereafter the gospel. But false teachers preach to the people, also to the unrepentant, nothing but grace, proclaiming peace to them, and as Ezekiel says, "They lay cushions under the arms of the people and pillows under their heads and shoulders," Ezek. 13:18. With this they strengthen the hands of evil persons in order that no one may be converted from their wickedness and unrighteousness as can be seen and found daily. But because they do not convert anyone, therefore they are also not sent from God and also do not have God's Word. For thus says the Lord, "I did not send the prophets, yet they ran; I have not spoken with them, yet they prophesied. But if they had remained in my council, and had heard my words, /218/ then they would have turned my people from their evil ways, and from the evil of their doings, Jer. 23:21[-22].

These words testify to us clearly that those who have God's Word correctly teach and speak it; these are they who convert the people from their reckless living and evil ways. Again, those who do not do this also do not have God's Word. They may well have the letter of Scripture, but the living, powerful, and fervent Word of God that pierces and cuts through hearts and souls as a two-edged sword, Heb. 4:12, that they do not have. They may speak many words, but because the Lord has not cleansed their lips with fire, (as the lips of the prophet Isaiah), Isa. 6:7, and has not given his Word into their mouths, (just as into the mouth of Jeremiah) that they [may] pluck up and break down, destroy, build up, and plant, Jer. 1:9; therefore they are not sent from the Lord and they also accomplish nothing, as is seen and felt much in the present day [from those] who want to be evangelical preachers but have not yet discontinued the human idolatrous ceremonies and institutions and again accepted true worship and ordinances. But so much some may well do, that they with Jehu hate the harlotry and sorcery of Jezebel and have a zeal against the priests and prophets of Baal. Nevertheless, they themselves walk in the sins of Jeroboam and allow the golden calves (which were erected in the place of divine worship by the godless king) to stand and remain a judgment upon themselves but a stumbling block and destruction to others, 2 Kings 9:22; 10:[28-29]. Thus one blind person leads another until they both finally fall into the canal, Matt. 15:14.

The second fruit of a true teacher is that he himself leads an unblamable life which is conformed to the gospel. "For the kingdom of God does not consist in words but in power," 1 Cor. 4:20. The wisdom which the teacher [needs] to open his mouth in the congregation, Ecclus. 15:10, does not enter an evil soul, nor a body enslaved to sin, Wisd. of Sol. 1:4. Therefore James also says, "Whoever is wise and understanding among you, let him show [this] with his good life and works in the meekness of wisdom," James 3:13. Thus Paul also did as he himself said, "I pommel my body and subdue it, in order that while I preach to others, I myself will not be rejected," 1 Cor. 9:27. And nothing is accomplished and leads to no end that anyone praise and chatter at length about himself, but let him who wishes to boast (says the apostle) /219/ "boast of the Lord," 1 Cor. 1:[31]; 2 Cor. [10:17]; Jer. 9:23-24. For he is not praised who praises himself but whom the Lord praises. But the Lord praises the righteous who praise and honor him as he himself said, "Those who honor me I will honor, but those who despise me shall be lightly esteemed," 1 Sam. 2:30.

But what the true honor of God is, Christ testified with these words: "By this my Father is glorified, that you bear much fruit, and that you become my disciples," John 15:8. But which are the fruits of the Spirit Paul told the Galatians, namely, love, joy, meekness, goodness, faith, moderation, Gal. 5:22[-23]. Again, who are the true disciples of Christ he himself said, namely, those who continue in his Word, these will know the truth and the truth shall make them free, John 8:32. But no one abides in Christ and his teaching except those who walk as he walked, 1 John 2:[6]. But whoever does not walk thus, does not remain in Christ, yes, that one has neither seen nor known Christ as John clearly testified in his epistle, 1 John 3:6.

Therefore, true Christians and primarily the teachers must themselves as disciples of Christ lead a Christlike life and faithfully follow Christ. But if they do not do this, then Christ has not sent them. For he said that we would recognize false prophets by their fruits even though they come in sheep's clothing, Matt. 7:15[-16]. He taught us this through parables saying, "Can one gather grapes from thorns, or figs from thistles? So, every good tree bears good fruit, but the bad tree bears evil fruit. A good tree cannot bear evil fruit, nor can a bad tree bear good fruit. Every tree that does not bear good fruit is cut down and thrown into the fire. Therefore, you will know them by their fruits" [Matt. 7:16-20].

In these words Christ compares every good Christian, but in particular an honest teacher (for he speaks primarily of the teachers) with a good tree and a false teacher with a bad tree. Just as now a good tree brings good fruit and therewith shows its good nature and serves humanity in its necessity and feeds the body, so also a good teacher bears good fruit; therewith he shows his Christian nature and that he has been sent of God. But the others, that is, the goodhearted listeners and lovers of the truth, he thus serves to their salvation, /220/ just as Paul said to Timothy, "Take heed to yourself and to your teaching; remain in it, for by so doing you will save both yourself and your hearers," 1 Tim. 4:16.

Again, just as a bad tree can bring no good fruit, and just as one can pick no grapes from thorns and no figs from thistles, so also a false prophet cannot teach nor do right. The false prophet can indeed boast himself of the gospel, but that he should accurately teach or speak the teaching of the gospel and bear the fruits of the Spirit, that he does not do; his leaves are and remain leaves, that is, a useless noise beautiful in appearance all that he teaches, and hypocrisy all that he does.

If then now through the particular grace of God, the gospel (which has sharp eyes and looks not upon the sheep's clothing but upon the inward nature, and does not inquire about the leaves but about the fruits of the tree) has come to the [light] of day and been revealed to us, and has given to us [the ability] to know the tree by its fruits out of God's Word; therefore [let] everyone pay attention to that and guard himself before the false prophets that he be not deceived by them.

Likewise, how a teacher should be qualified Paul describes very beautifully for us to both Timothy and Titus. There one has a true description, yes, an express example of an evangelical teacher. And Peter says, "So I exhort the elders among you, as a fellow elder and a witness of the suffering that is in Christ, and also as a partaker in the glory that is to be revealed. Feed the flock of Christ that is in your charge, care for them, not by constraint but willingly, not for shameful gain but with a compassionate spirit, not as those who domineer over the inheritance but being examples to the flock. So shall you (when the chief Shepherd reveals himself) receive the imperishable crown of glory," 1 Pet. 5:1[-4].

Here Peter gives all elders, leaders, and teachers a good lesson, that is, how they should be qualified, and says among other words, that they shall feed the flock of God out of a willing mind and not for the sake of shameful gain. For he knew well that the Lord Christ had asked him three times, saying, "Peter, do you love me? Then feed my sheep," John 21:15[-18]. Thus also all true ministers of the Word of Christ must teach God's Word /221/ unfalsified out of true love without desiring shameful gain. For this is called feeding in the Scripture.

But how many now at this present time accept the office of teacher who do not reflect upon this teaching of Peter, but it takes place even according to the words of the prophet, namely, "its priests teach for reward, its prophets prophesy for money; in addition they want to be seen as though they rely upon the Lord and say, 'The Lord is among us, no evil can come upon us.' Therefore because of you Zion shall be plowed as a field; and Jerusalem shall become a heap of stones, and the mountain of the temple a wooded height," Mic. 3:11 [-12]. The same prophet also says in another place [that] the false prophets "declare war against him who puts nothing into their mouths," Mic. 3:5.

God complains similarly through Ezekiel over the false prophets who proclaimed death to souls who should not die and affirmed life to souls who should not live; that is, they condemn the innocent and pious and justify the godless, and they do this for a handful of barley and a piece of bread, Ezek. 13:[18-]19. And this still happens daily and proceeds in full power. Yes, Balaam, the son Beor, who loved the wages of unrighteousness, he still has many followers and companions, Num. 22:5. And even though the Lord had opened the mouth of the ass to punish such Balaamites, they are yet so stubborn and blinded that they cannot discontinue [their] greediness, Num. [22:21-35]; 23; 24; 2 Pet. 2:15. And then above that they still wish to be regarded as though they were true servants of Christ, and take the liberty which Christ has given to the true ministers of the gospel, (namely, that they may live off of the gospel and have seemly necessities), as a cloak for greed, 1 Cor. 9:14.

But this is a shameful thing that one under the guise of the gospel (which after all teaches scorn of all temporal things) seeks money and goods, Matt. 10:37[-38]. This is also an abomination before God, that someone who undertakes to teach God's Word does not himself live according to it. To all such the Lord says, "What right have you to proclaim my statutes, or take my covenant in your mouth? For you hate discipline and cast my words behind you. If you see a thief you run with him, and you keep company with adulterers," Ps. 50:16[-18].

And Paul says, "You presume to be a guide to the blind, a light to those who are in darkness, an instructor of the unwise, a teacher of the simple, you have the form to know something, and what is right in the law. /222/ Now you teach others but do not teach yourself? You preach against stealing but you steal? You say that one must not commit adultery, but you do commit adultery? You abhor idols but you rob God of his own? You boast about the law but you dishonor God by transgressing the law? 'The name of God is blasphemed among the Gentiles because of you,' " Rom. 2:19[-24].

Oh, that many (who accept their teaching position and yet are so selfish, haughty, unrighteous, idolatrous, and lead such godless lives) would earnestly observe and consider well what great complaint is in all Scripture over the false prophets and shepherds with the implication that the corruption of the people has most of its origin from them. For it behooves the shepherds to feed the sheep, just as Christ commanded Peter and Peter commanded the elders, John 21:[17]; 1 Pet. 5:[2]. But how is this to take place when the shepherds trample the precious pasture of the divine Word with their feet and then give the sheep to eat the same which they have trampled with their feet, Ezek. 34:18[-19]? It behooves the shepherds also to dip the water of divine teaching out of the fountain of salvation and give the sheep to drink; but how lamentable is it when the shepherds become Philistines and stop up the spring of living water by throwing in earth. Yes, when they are wolves who do not save the flock [but] feed themselves and scatter and strangle the sheep, Acts 20:29[-30]?

Again, whenever they are such, as the prophet Hosea says, "The bands of priests are just like robbers who murder on the streets and lie in wait for the people on the way to Shechem. For they complete all villainy," Hos. 6:[9]. And as Isaiah says, "Your watchmen are all blind and have no knowledge; they are all mute dogs who cannot punish, they are lazy, sleepy, lying down, and snoring, loving to slumber. They are unashamed dogs who have a mighty appetite, they never have enough. Similarly the shepherds also have no understanding; they each look to their own way, each to his own gain in his own place. 'Come,' they say, 'let us get wine, let us drink ourselves full and do tomorrow just like today, yes, and much more.' " Isa. 56:10[-12].

Oh, God, why have the false prophets, priests, and shepherds always been so many in the world and the pious ones so few? Against so many hundred prophets and priests of Baal, it is scarcely possible to find one Elijah, 1 Kings 18:22. Among so many lying prophets of Ahab, it is scarcely possible to get one Micaiah, 1 Kings 22:5[-23].

Thus also sometimes the sins of the people deserve that God allows an hypocrite and idolator to rule in the place of a shepherd. /223/ For since the people are so minded that they hold good teaching in contempt, as Paul says, and have such weak ears that they desire more to hear what is pleasing than fruitful teaching, therefore they choose such teachers for themselves, after whom their ears itch, 2 Tim. 4:3. And it then happens just as the Lord said through the prophet, "It is horrible and dangerous in the land: the prophets teach lies and the priests rule in their office, and my people like to have it that way, but what will you do when the end comes?" Jer. 5:[30-31].

Therefore Christ also said to his disciples, "Woe to you, when all speak well of you, for thus they did to the false prophets who have been before you," Luke 6:26. Contrary to this you are blessed "when people revile you and persecute you and utter all kinds of evil against you falsely on my account. Rejoice and be glad, for your reward is great in heaven, for so they did to the good prophets, etc." [Matt. 5:11-12].

Therefore it is certain that the true teachers must be tested with the cross. And this comes because they desire, speak, and do other than the world; therefore the world hates them as is written in the book of Wisdom: "Let us lie in wait for the righteous one, because he is of no good to us, and is contrary to our works, and blames us that we sin against the law, and calls our being out to sin. He claims that he knows God and boasts of being a child of God, punishing us for what we have in our heart. He is grievous for us to look at, for his life is unlike others, and his being is a very different being. He holds us to be unfit, and avoids our doings as defiled, and claims that the justified shall be rewarded at the last, and boasts that God is his father," Wisd. of Sol. [2:12-16].

Thus Christ was treated and opposed as he himself says, "The world hates me because I testify of it that its works are evil," [John 7:7]. This he also promised all his disciples and said, "I send you out as sheep in the midst of wolves; so be as careful as serpents and as innocent as doves," Matt. 10:16. Continuing, he said, "You will be hated by all people for my name's sake," [Matt. 10:22], but "if the world hates you, know that it has hated me before it hated you. If you were of the world, the world would love its own; but because you are not of the world, and I chose you out of the world, therefore the world hates you. /224/ Remember the word that I said to you, 'A servant is not greater than his master.' If they persecuted me, they will also persecute you; if they kept my word, they will keep yours also. But all this they will do to you for my name's sake, because they do not know him who sent me," John 15:18[-21].

In summary, how all good prophets and true teachers have been persecuted from the beginning, and shall be persecuted to the end of the world, yes, as even the most high prophet and master, Jesus Christ, the Son of the living God had to suffer and thus enter into his glory, Luke 24:[26], the Scripture, both the Old and New Testaments, testifies so openly and abundantly that it is unnecessary to discuss and write more about it.

Therefore then they are not ministers of Christ who are so great and highly regarded by the world, who are seated on high and who persecute others purposely. For that is far from Jesus Christ and from his gentle divine spirit, Matt. 13:28. It is also far from all Christians who have the mind and spirit of Christ. It is not Christlike but tyrannical to persecute, to expel, to strangle the people because of faith and religion. Those who do this are certainly a remnant of the pharisaical race to whom Stephen said, "You stiff-necked people, uncircumcised in heart and ears, you always resist the Holy Spirit. As your fathers did, so do you. Which of the prophets did not your fathers persecute? And they killed those who announced beforehand the coming of the righteous one, whose betrayers and murderers you have now become, you who received the law as delivered by angels and did not keep it," Acts 7:51[-53].

Oh, how many pride themselves now at the present time that they have received the gospel out of the grace of God and yet do so little, yes, nothing according to it! They want to be great masters in the Scripture [and] be called evangelical preachers, but Christ Jesus and him crucified they know not, 1 Cor. 2:2. For Christ himself was poor and also chose poor disciples who had to deny themselves for the sake of the Lord, who forsook all things for the sake of the gospel, Matt. 8:[20]; Luke 9:58; Matt. 4:18[-19]; 19:27; 1 Cor. 8:9, who were a spectacle to the world and the refuse of the world, and the offscouring thrown out by all people, 1 Cor. 4:9[-13]. But these are rich and powerful, therefore also, according to the word of the prophet, their pride or /225/ haughtiness must be a costly thing and their cruelty must be called well done, Ps. 73:6.

Christ said to his disciples, "You are not to let yourself be called rabbi, for one is your Master, Christ. The greatest among you shall be your servant. He who exalts himself shall be humbled, and whoever humbles himself will be exalted," Matt. 23:[8-11]. But these allow themselves because of the gospel and their ministerial office to be called masters, licentiates, doctors, yes, worthy fathers and lords in Christ. How splendidly does that accord with these previously mentioned words of Christ? Yet these are of no avail to them, they pay no attention to them but puff up their person, as the prophet says, "They do only what they think; [they] speak evil of the devout, blaspheme the truth, and what they say must be spoken from heaven; what they propose and institute must prevail upon earth," Ps. 73:7[-9]; for they think and also say, "Our tongue shall take the upper hand. We have the authority to speak. Who is he who can master us," Ps. 12:[4]?[4]

But what shall follow and happen to them after such presumption and pride, let them be aware of. The Scriptures testify clearly that Jezebel, while she indeed ruled for a period of time, feasted her prophets lavishly, and kept them in great splendor, yet finally had to be brought to shame together with all her followers, Rev. 2:20. And although the harlot of Babylon has made the heathen drunk with the wine of harlotry, [Rev. 18:3], and has become proud and says in her heart, " 'I sit, and am a queen. I shall be no widow, mourning I shall never see,' so nevertheless, her plagues shall come in a single day," Rev. 18:7[-8].

Thus we have now briefly indicated which teachers are sent of God, that is, those who are thus qualified, just as the Scripture testifies, speak God's Word rightly, and are conformed to the image of Christ and his saints. And what they yet lack, they seek with [their] whole zeal at the fountain of all grace, Jesus Christ. Whoever is such an one is without doubt sent of God.

Again, those who are otherwise minded, speak and do other than what is seen in this previously described and presented mirror of the prophets of Christ and his apostles, these are also not sent from God. They can also teach nothing good nor speak God's Word correctly, for that must be spoken through the Holy Spirit, as Christ said to his disciples, "For it is not you who speak, but it is the spirit of your Father speaking through you," Matt. 10:20. And Peter said, "No prophecy ever came out of the will of humans, /226/ but the holy people of God, moved by the Holy Spirit, have spoken," 2 Pet. 1:21. Therefore all that the spiritless people say, that has no power and bears no fruit. Yes, and if it were possible that they could speak with the tongues of angels, yet it is nothing more than a sounding brass or a tinkling bell, 1 Cor. 13:1.

We also urge and admonish every individual, be he teacher or listener, that he heed it well. The teacher may well see whose servant he is, of which spirit he is motivated, whether Christ is and works in him, whether he portrays the living Word of God in open testimony of the

Holy Scripture to the people, images it, bears fruit with it, and himself walks according to it. The listener may well take heed to himself that he not believe every spirit, but that he at all times recognize the teacher by his teaching and fruits, 1 John 4:1. And the teaching must test and measure right according to the plumb line of the divine Word.

Similarly, observe, test, and prove fruit not alone according to their external and splendid appearance, but according to the Spirit and true reality. And whichever teacher he recognizes and finds false, him he himself watches and hears him not, but turns from him, just as God commanded through Jeremiah and Christ through the gospel, namely, that one should not hear the words of the false prophets, that one should beware of them, Jer. 23:16; Matt. 7:15, that his sheep hear his voice, and follow him and the stranger they do not follow after but flee from him for the reason that the voice of the stranger is unknown to them. Yes, all those who did not enter into the sheepfold through Christ Jesus, as through the true door, but have climbed in through another way, these are thieves and murderers who come nowhere except to steal and to kill and to destroy, John 10:4[-5]; [8-10]. Therefore the sheep of Christ fear for themselves before such thieves, murderers, and destroyers.

But that some suggest that Scripture does not forbid the external hearing of the false prophets, but the internal hearing only, this is craftiness and philosophy, yes, an open falsification of the divine truth. For this is certain and undoubtedly true, that two kinds of hearing are included in Scripture, one the internal hearing which is faith, that which comes through the external hearing of the divine Word through the cooperation and enlightenment of the Holy Spirit, as may clearly be seen in the following words of Paul: "How shall they call upon him in whom they do not believe? And how shall they believe in him of whom they have never heard? How are they to hear without a preacher? And how shall they preach when they are not sent? /227/ As it is written, 'How lovely are the feet of those who proclaim peace and preach good news!' But they are not all obedient to the gospel, for Isaiah says, 'Lord, who believes our preaching?' So faith comes from hearing, but the hearing is through the Word of God. But I say to you, have they not heard? Indeed their voice has now gone out to all the lands, and their words to all the world," Rom. 10:14[-18]; Isa. 52:7; 53:[1]; Ps. 19:4.

Here the apostle speaks expressly about the external hearing through which the preaching of the gospel by the apostles' voices and their words were heard by all creatures under heaven, Mark 16:15; Col. 1:6, through which many have also come to faith, yet all out of grace through the internal working of God and his Holy Spirit, as God now through the external hearing of his Word creates faith in his elect, as through a mediator. Thus Satan also creates unbelief in his children through the external hearing of his false doctrine. Therefore Holy Scripture also admonishes us to hear God's Word and that is to be understood that we shall hear God's Word with external ears and believe thereon with the heart, John 5:24; 8:51; 10:27. This then is called to hear God's Word aright.

In like measure the Scripture forbids us to hear false teachers, Jer. 23:16; Ps. 1:1; John 10:[5]; and this is the meaning, that we should not run to the false teachers in the house of idols where they stand upon the stool of pestilence and falsify God's Word, nor hear their words nor believe them, 2 Cor. 6:[14-15]. This the Scripture calls not hearing false teachers, to shun the strange ones and to flee from them, John 10:5. On this opinion the apostle John also says that false teachers are of the world; "and what they say is of the world, and the world listens to them. But true teachers are from God. Whoever knows God listens to them, but whoever is not of God does not listen to them. By this one knows the spirit of truth and the spirit of error," 1 John 4:5[-6]. This is what we have now said in brief of the sending of teachers.

But there are many who contradict [us] here. In the first place, some say that no one may teach and restore the fallen worship again, except they be called of the Lord through a living voice from heaven. Just as Elijah (they say) did not punish the priests of Baal nor restore the fallen worship in Israel before he had received a command from the Lord and was sent to Ahab, 1 Kings 18. Again, just as Joshua did not again begin circumcision /228/ (which was not practiced for a period in the wilderness), before the time that the Lord commanded him, Josh. 5:2.

Answer

God does not now, at the present time, speak with us through an external voice from heaven, nor through visions and dreams as happened in the Old Testament, but he speaks with us through his Son, Jesus Christ, Heb. 1:1[-2], and Christ speaks with us through his Word. And the Word of Christ is Spirit and life, John 6:63. Whenever Christ now grants and impresses his living Word in someone's heart, and thereby calls, that person is without any doubt called of the Lord through his Word. But whereby one shall know that anyone is thus called of God through the living Word and through the Spirit of Christ, we have said above, namely, that he speaks God's Word truly, bears fruit, and seeks the honor of Christ and the salvation of souls with wholehearted zeal, Isa. 55:10[-11]; John 3:34.

Further, so we have maintained above, that the apostles and elders, with the congregations of God, called and ordained deacons and teachers through the power of Christ, Acts 6:1[-6]; 13:1[-2]. What now the Christians of their time did correctly, that is not forbidden or discontinued for the Christians of this time, but the Christians must conduct themselves according to the practice and procedure of the first churches. The reason: "For no other foundation can any one lay than that which is laid, which is Jesus Christ," 1 Cor. 3:11. Therefore, just as the fallen temple of the Lord in Jerusalem was built again on the first foundation and all worship therein was resumed and practiced according to the law, so also now must the fallen house of God, namely the Christian congregation, be built up again on the first foundation of the apostles and prophets, (of which Christ Jesus is the cornerstone) 1 Tim. 3:[1-12]; Heb. 3:5[-6]; Eph. 2:19[-20]; and all things therein must be conducted and carried out according to the ordinance of Christ and his apostles.

Since then the apostles and elders with the congregation of God chose leaders and ministers through Christ and placed and established them in their office, therefore the Christians of this time must also, according to the example of the apostolic congregations, choose and ordain teachers. And necessity also demands this, for it is certain and incontrovertible, that a Christian congregation may not be built, established, and gathered without correct doctrine, faith, and baptism. /229/

In addition, without the Lord's Supper, admonition, discipline, excommunication, or separation, it cannot stand. For where God's Word is not taught correctly and the gospel of Christ is not preached, how then shall people believe? As the apostle says, "And how are they to believe in him of whom they have not heard," Rom. 10:[14]? But where faith out of the hearing of the Word of God through the cooperation of the Holy Spirit is not rightly grasped in the heart, how can baptism be practiced orderly and received, since baptism upon faith was commanded and instituted by the Lord himself and practiced by the apostles, Matt. 28:19; Mark 16:[16]; Acts 2:41; 8:[38-39]; 10:47 [-48]? But where the baptism of Christ is not practiced properly, how shall one then be baptized into Christ Jesus, into his death and [added] to the fellowship of his body through the Holy Spirit, Rom. 6:3; Col. 2:12; 1 Cor. 12:13? How then shall the dying away of the flesh, the burial of sins, and the resurrection into a new life be rightly considered and carried out [Rom. 6:6-11]?

Where the Lord's Supper is not rightly observed, how can his Word and command (that one by and with the breaking of bread should proclaim his death and preserve his memory) be adequately done there, Matt. 26:25; Mark 14:22; Luke 22:19; 1 Cor. 10:16; 11:22? How can the fellowship of Christ, yes, his body and blood, be indeed taken to heart there, brotherly love and unity be truly signified and established? Again, where admonition does not proceed in full power, there the love to both God and neighbor usually grows cold. And where discipline is not correctly practiced, there the one entangles himself in sin with the other. Therefore the Lord says, "You shall not hate your neighbor in your heart, but punish him, that you may not be guilty because of him," Lev. 19:17. Again, where excommunication and the ban are not correctly observed with the gospel, there the one corrupts the other, as Paul says, "Do you not know that a little leaven ferments the whole lump of dough," 1 Cor. 5:[6]?

And if the congregation of God without all these previously mentioned items (and whatsoever more the Lord has ordained for the upbuilding and sustaining of his congregation), can neither stand nor be maintained, therefore there must also be ministers of the Word in the congregation. For it is not everyone's thing to teach God's Word and to distribute the sacraments of Christ. But it is with these things as Paul says, "Similarly, as in one body we have many members, and all the members do not have the same function, so we, though many, are one body in Christ, but among each other the one is the member of the other and they have many kinds of gifts /230/ according to the grace that is given to us," Rom. 12:4[-6]. Again, "there are many kinds of gifts, but there is one Spirit; and there are many kinds of service, but there is one Lord; and there are many kinds of powers, but there is one God who works all things in everyone. But in each individual the manifestation of the Spirit is given for the common good," 1 Cor. 12:4[-7].

In addition the apostle says, "Grace is given to each one among us according to the measure of Christ's gift, and he has established some as apostles, some as prophets, some as evangelists, some as pastors and teachers, that the saints should all be joined together for common service, for improving the body of Christ, until we all extend our hand to the other in one faith and knowledge of the Son of God, to become a mature person who is there in the measure of the fullness of Christ," Eph. 4:7, [11-13]. And Peter says, "Serve one another, each with the gift he has received, as good stewards of God's varied grace: if someone speaks, that he speaks God's Word; if someone renders service, that he renders it out of the strength which God gives in order that in everything God may be praised through Jesus Christ. To him be honor and dominion from eternity to eternity. Amen," 1 Pet. 4:10[-11].

Out of all these words it is easily understood in the first place, how God places his ministers in his congregations and distributes many kinds of gifts. In the second place, how necessary ministers are in the congregation and what their work and service is. In the third place, that the congregation (since it is one with Christ) has the power to choose teachers and ministers according to the Scripture. But which is the congregation of Christ, which has received such power from Christ (not only to choose teachers and leaders, but, what is more, to bind and to loose, to forgive sins and to retain them), Scripture testifies clearly at many places, namely, that it is a gathering of believers, that is, of living saints and born-again persons who believe the Word of God entirely, teach the same correctly, bear fruit with it, practice the sacraments of Christ fittingly, correctly maintain the ban, walk in love, and conduct and carry out all things according to the gospel, Matt. 16:19; 18:18; John 20:23; 8:30.

Yes, the congregation of Christ is the fellowship of the saints, who through the providence of God the Father, through the grace of Jesus Christ, and in the sanctification of the Spirit and belief of the truth, was gathered through the preaching of the gospel, and through one Spirit baptized into one body, unified, and joined together, 1 Pet. 1:2; 2 Thess. 2:13; 1 Cor. 12:13a; Eph. 4:4; /231/ so that it is the body of Christ, his bride, taken out of his side, made from his flesh and bone, washed in his blood, cleansed through the water bath in his Word, and sanctified through his Spirit, Eph. 5:30; Col. 1:14; Eph. 5:26.

For therefore he also allowed his side to be opened and pierced through on the cross and allowed blood and water to flow or run from it so that he might gain, purify, and save his congregation, John 19:34; Eph. 5:25[-26]. Therefore it is also his pure bride, his most beloved friend, the Holy City, the New Jerusalem, come here out of heaven from God, and illumined with the glory of God and of the Lamb, etc., Rev. 19:7[-8]; 21:2.

This congregation has the power through Christ Jesus (from whom it has received everything) to choose leaders and ministers. And if anyone should ask, "Where is this congregation?" we answer, "Where God's Word is correctly taught, believed, and kept, for they are Christ's disciples who have his word, believe, and keep it," John 8:30; 17:6; Matt. 18:20; Luke 24:14[-15]. Where now such disciples are gathered in his name, there he is in the midst of them. But if Christ is among them, then they are always a congregation of Christ. If they are a congregation of Christ, then they must also have the same power which Christ gave the congregation. But the power which Christ has given his congregation (namely, not only to choose teachers and ministers of the Word, but also to bind and to loose, to forgive sins and to retain them), has been adequately related and explained above, Matt. 16:[19]; 18:18; John 20:23.

Therefore we conclude that, since God's Word has now come to the [light of] day, there must, therefore, also be a congregation of God; for God's Word is not without fruit, Isa. 55:10[-11]. If then someone says that there is no congregation of God, he must also say that there are no believers upon the earth, yes, that God's Word is nowhere upon earth; for where God's Word is, there is also a congregation of God, be it small or large. But the congregation of God is not only invisible, as some permit themselves to think and imagine an invisible Christian people, but also visible. For believers recognize each other and join with their kind, (as also all animals do according to Ecclesiasticus), Ecclus. 13:[15-16], and love each other since they are the children of one heavenly Father, born out of one God, brought forth out of one seed, partakers of one divine nature, and endowed with one Holy Spirit, John 1:13; 1 John 5:1; 1 Pet. 1:23.

Out of this comes /232/ the difference between brotherly and common love, 2 Pet. 1:7. And this is the reason the apostles wrote all their letters to the Christians, to their brothers and companions of faith and not to the world. This would not have taken place if they had not known the Christians and had not known the difference between Christians and the world.

Yes, the Christian congregation is also in part manifest to the world, just as Abraham was manifest to the world through his faith, righteousness, and glorious deed according to God's Word, and left to us as an example in Scripture to teach and admonish that we should follow in his footsteps with sincere trust and fruitfulness of works which God commands us, Gen. 15:6; 22; Rom. 4:3; Gal. 3:6; James 2:23. Yes, Christ Jesus our Lord and Master, Matt. 23:[8], our Pioneer and Ruler, Heb. 12:2, revealed himself to the world through words and works and thus also commanded his disciples and said, "Let your light shine before people, that they see your good works and praise your Father in heaven," Matt. 5:16.

To this Paul also admonished the believers that they should walk such good lives through which they would become manifest to unbelievers, and says, "Do all things without grumbling or questioning so that you may be irreproachable, innocent, and children of God blameless in the midst of a crooked and perverse generation, among whom you shall shine as lights in the world, that you will remain with the Word of life," Phil. 2:14[-16]. And Peter says that the godless and blasphemers indeed recognize Christians whenever they do not run with them as earlier in their licentious, unseemly, and godless ways, 1 Pet. 4:4.

Herewith it is adequately shown that the congregation of God is not alone invisible, but also visible and in part revealed to the world. But it is not in a particular location or place like the figurative Jerusalem was nowhere on earth except in the Jewish land alone. But the heavenly Jerusalem is everywhere, wherever the Word of God is rightly taught, believed, and kept, Gal. 4:26; Rev. 21:2; Matt. 28:[18], and the sacraments of Christ are used correctly according to the Word. For the Lord has added his sacraments to the gospel, attached them to it, and commanded not only that his gospel should be preached but also that his sacraments should be practiced and maintained, Mark 16:[16]; Matt. 26:[26-28]; Mark 14:22; Luke 22:19; 1 Cor. 11:[23-25].

Thus has the Lord ordained and thus it shall also remain to the end. "Heaven and earth," says Christ, "will pass away but my words will not pass away," Matt. 24:35. Therefore we still say that where /233/ God's Word is correctly taught, believed, and kept, and the sacraments are properly practiced, there is the heavenly Jerusalem, there dwells God the almighty Lord and the Lamb, Rev. 21:2; Heb. 12:22, just as Christ himself testified and said, "Whoever loves me shall keep my word, and my Father will love him and we will come to him and make our home with him," John 14:[23]. And in another place God says, "I will live in them, and walk among them, and I will be their God, and they shall be my people," Lev. 26:[11]; Ezek. 37:27; 2 Cor. 6:16, says the almighty Lord.

In the second place, some say that the teachers now should confirm their sending with signs and miracles like the apostles did.[5]

Thereupon we answer that to require signs and not permit oneself to be satisfied with the words is a sign of unbelief as Christ testified with these words: "Whenever you do not see signs and wonders you do not believe," John 4:48. Therefore we may indeed say that they do not have the true faith who demand and desire signs beyond the Word of Christ. But where they have such faith as the centurion had who said to Christ, "Oh, Lord, do not trouble yourself, for I am not worthy to have you come under my roof; therefore I also did not consider myself worthy to come to you. But speak a word and my servant will be healed," Luke 7:6[-8]. Had they such faith (we say), they should always believe the words of Christ and now demand no signs but allow themselves to be satisfied with the fact that Christ in the beginning and thereafter the apostles have adequately confirmed the teaching of the gospel with signs and miracles.

And should it be that they already saw signs and wonders, they would perhaps mistakenly do as the Pharisees; namely, they might attribute the works of God to the devil or seek another reason in order to blaspheme the works of God. But now that they see no signs they speak with the Pharisees, "We would like to see a sign." But what did Christ answer to the Pharisees? "This evil and adulterous nature seeks a sign but no sign shall be given to it except alone the sign of the prophet Jonah," Matt. 12:38[-39]. What did Abraham reply to the rich man (who desired that he would send Lazarus to his father's house that he testify to his brothers in order that they would not come to the place where he was)? "They have Moses and the prophets; let them hear those." But he said, "No, father /234/ Abraham; but if some one goes to them from the dead, they will repent." He said to him, "If they do not hear Moses and the prophets, neither would they believe if someone should rise from the dead," Luke 16:27[-31]. And Paul says, "The Jews demand signs and the Greeks seek wisdom, but we preach the crucified Christ, a stumbling block to the Jews and folly to the Greeks, but to those who are called, both Jews and Greeks, we preach Christ a divine power and wisdom," 1 Cor. 1:[22-24].

Out of these and similar words of Holy Scripture we may clearly observe what kind of people these are who require signs and do not allow themselves to be satisfied with the Word and how one must believe God's Word more than signs and miracles and how those cannot be helped who will not hear Moses and the prophets. But if these are not to be helped, how then shall those be helped who will not hear Christ and his apostles? But if they wish to hear, why do they then demand signs?

It is true that the miracles and signs of wonder are witnesses of the gospel and the divine Word and that they confirm and strengthen the same. The miracles also move the people toward faith but with the understanding that not the teaching which is already accepted and established must be therewith confirmed, but every new doctrine, that it is from God. Therefore these signs are not necessary now at the present time just as they were necessary at the time of Christ and his apostles. [The] reason: Since Christ is the end of the law and a mediator of the New Testament, therefore his teaching had to be confirmed with strong signs and wonderful works, just as the Old Testament was confirmed with signs and miracles, Rom. 10:4; Heb. 7:11; Gal. 3:20; Heb. 12:24. But now that the teaching of Christ has once been established, and no other teaching is taught or may be taught, yes, cursed is the one who preaches another gospel than that which Christ and his apostles have preached to us, Gal. 1:9.

Thus the signs are not a necessity. For the law was after all not established more than once with signs and with the blood of calves and goats, Exod. 19:16; 24:6; Heb. 9:13. And as it was for a period of time obscured and hidden and was again found and came to the light of day, even so, it was not confirmed by signs a second time, 2 Kings 22:8. So also the pious Josiah, as he heard the book of the law read /235/ desired no sign but indeed allowed himself to be satisfied with the words and carried out all things according to it, and also kept the Passover. The same no king in Israel had done before him [2 Kings 23:21-23].

Because the gospel has now been confirmed with such glorious miracles (the like of which had never taken place) [and] in addition was empowered with the innocent death and precious blood of the spotless Lamb, Jesus Christ, Heb. 9:13[-14], and was for a long time obscured, but now through the grace of God [has] again come to light, so all devout Christians must allow themselves to be satisfied therewith. So that whoever requires a sign beyond this must hear "an evil and adulterous nature seeks for a sign," etc. Matt. 12:39.

Thus we must again also administer and maintain all the ordinances of God according to the gospel. For to that [end] God reveals his Word to us that we through this should learn to know his will, turn ourselves to God, abstain from sin, believe rightly, live a Christlike life, and maintain all his commandments, as Christ says to his apostles, "Teach them to observe all that I have commanded you," Matt. 28:20. But even as we accept and must accept the teaching of the gospel without signs if we would be saved, James 1:21, in the same manner we must also accept the teachers who proclaim the teaching to us without signs and recognize [them as] good. The work always praises the master, and blameless teaching and walk [praises] a Christian teacher. Nevertheless, even though a teacher is blameless in all things, the hypocritical and pharisaical nature will yet not believe the gospel.

False teachers can also sometimes indeed perform signs. One knows well how the Egyptian magicians withstood Moses and what they did through their magic, Exod. 7:11[-12]; 2 Tim. 3:8. And Christ says that many false prophets and false Christians shall arise [and] do great signs and wonders so that (if it were possible), even the elect should be led astray, Matt. 24:11. And Paul says, "The coming of the antichrist will happen according to the activity of Satan with all kinds of deceitful signs and wonders among those who will be lost," 2 Thess. 2:9[-10]. Therefore then, a Christian may not look upon the signs alone, but much more upon God's Word which is always certain and true, John 17:8.

And if one still requires signs, then one must demand them not only of the teachers but also of all believers. For Christ says, "Truly, truly, I say to you, whoever believes in me will do the works that I do, and will do greater works, because I go to the Father," John 14:12. And at another /236/ place Christ says, "The signs which will accompany those who believe are these: in my name they will cast out demons; they will speak with new tongues; they will drive out serpents, and if they drink any deadly thing, it will not hurt them; they will lay their hands on the sick, and it will become better with them," Mark 16:17[-18]. But now we do not see that anyone does such outward signs. Who will therefore say that there is no one who believes?

This be far hence! Does Paul not say after all, that they are not all workers of miracles, 1 Cor. 12:29. Therefore, just as external signs do not follow faith at the present time, and there is without the slightest doubt faith to be found in some persons, therefore also external signs do not follow the sending of God. Nevertheless, some without doubt are still sent out from God in order to preach his Word whom one shall not attempt to recognize by the signs (for these are many times false and deceptive), but by their sound teaching and fruits (which will not be found with all false prophets and false Christians).

Paul also describes to us expressly how a bishop shall be qualified, but he does not say that he must also perform signs, 1 Tim. 3:1[-7]; Titus 1:5[-9]. One reads nowhere in Scripture that Timothy, Titus, and others in addition, who were full of the Holy Spirit did signs. Therefore someone can indeed be a bishop and yet not do any sign. But a bishop's office or service is to preach the gospel and thus to feed the flock of Christ, 1 Cor. 1:1[?]; [Acts 20:28; 1 Pet. 5:2-4]. But preaching the gospel is more than to distribute the sacramental signs, yet the one was established and commanded with the other of the Lord Christ Jesus, as was said above, Matt. 28:[20]; Mark 16:15.

Out of all this it now finally follows that a teacher may indeed be sent of God, teach God's Word, and serve the congregation of Christ, yet nevertheless do no signs. Therefore they err who look upon signs and watch for them to come. But [let] them beware that they do not accept and receive Satan (who is very cunning and hides all his wickedness under the guise of hypocrisy) as Christ, 2 Cor. 11:[14-15], and that it not happen to them as with the Jews, to whom Christ said, "I have come in my Father's name, and you did not accept me; but if another comes in his own name, him you will receive," John 5:43. /237/

In the third place, some say, that a teacher who is sent of God should not teach secretly but should proclaim the Word of God openly before everyone.

Answer

Thus it also happened to Christ. For his brothers (says the evangelist) said to him, " 'Leave here and go to Judea, that your disciples may see the works you are doing. For no man works in secret if he seeks to be known openly. If you do these things, show yourself to the world.' For even his brothers did not believe in him," John 7:3[-5]. Thus the unbelieving and evil world also says now at the present time [together] with the apostate and false brothers, that teachers, if they are from God, should make themselves manifest to the world. But what did Christ answer his brothers (who did not believe in him and therefore wanted that he should reveal himself to the world?): "My time has not yet come, but your time is always ready. The world cannot hate you, but it hates me because I testify about it that its works are evil," John 7:6[-7]. Thus all disciples of Christ must now do also, maintain their silence, accommodate themselves to the time (yet in such a way that they do not act against God's Word) and not regard what the perverted and godless say, Rom. 12:[12]; Eph. 5:16. For the world has always blasphemed the works of God and cannot look upon them with good eyes. It must all be evil, however good that is which the good Lord Christ Jesus does.

Therefore he also says in the Gospel, "To whom shall I compare

The Sending of Preachers / 227

this generation? It is like children sitting in the market places and calling to their playmates, 'We piped to you, and you did not want to dance; we lamented, and you did not want to cry.' John came neither eating nor drinking, and they say, 'He has a demon'; the Son of man came eating and drinking, and they say, 'See what a glutton and drunkard this person is, a companion of tax collectors and sinners!' Yet wisdom must let itself be justified by her children," Matt. 11:16 [-17]; Luke 7:31[-32].

From this one may recognize the evil, hypocritical nature which always seeks a reason to oppose Christ and finds none. Here one may clearly see that the perverted and malicious [persons] who hate the gospel, and it does not help whether it is sweet (as Christ makes it) or sour (as John makes it). But they pervert it into evil every time they [have opportunity to] abuse the gospel. The apostle Paul had to be regarded by the Jews as an agitator and by Festus as mad, Acts 21:38; 26:24. Thus the world has always been perverted like it still is and deals in a perverted /238/ manner with the Christians. For if they reveal themselves and come forth boldly and proclaim God's Word, the world can yet not, above all other things endure such, and abuses them as enthusiasts [and] agitators; yes, persecutes them with sword, water, and fire. But if they keep themselves secret and live their faith in quietness, then the world blasphemes them nonetheless and calls them rabble spirits, corner-preachers, and does not know how to blaspheme them disdainfully enough.

Is this not a perverse nature which castigates Christians whenever they keep themselves hidden and remain quiet, and whenever they are open they cannot endure a single Christian? So there is here now no other counsel to be found than that the Christians, if they are exposed, will be persecuted by the world, and if they are hidden they will be blasphemed and disdained by the world. This is also the prediction of the Lord, as all Christians and God-fearing [persons] well know, Matt. 5:10; 10:16[-17]; 24:9; John 15:18. Therefore then, they do not regard what the world and the false brothers say. Nevertheless we thus wish, through the grace of the Lord, to serve all goodhearted [persons], but give to our ministers a more reasonable answer [and] broader information thereon, and speak thus.

In the first place, we have indicated above, with many clear testimonies of Scripture, whereby a true teacher shall be known and differentiated from a false teacher. Whoever now is such an one, just as the Scripture portrays a true teacher, and remains always conformed to Christ his Lord and master, yes, out of true fervent love of God and the neighbor is driven to his ministerial office, he is without doubt sent of God whether he teaches secretly or openly, 1 Cor. 10:[33]; Phil. 3:17.

The opponent then says, yes, [but] Christ and his apostles taught openly.

Answer

Christ was promised to the Jews and sent to the lost sheep of the house of Israel, Matt. 10:6; 15:24. To them he proclaimed his Father's Word and performed such works among them as no one else had done in order that they should believe in him, and if not, that they then had no excuse. In addition, Christ could slip away in the midst of his enemies, Luke 4:30. Yes, he caused them to fall to earth through his powerful Word and no one could lay a hand on him before his hour was come, John 18:6. Nevertheless he still hid himself and did not trust the people, for he knew well (as John says) what was in the people, John 2:24[-25].

/239/ The apostles were chosen by Christ and sent out to preach the gospel to all creatures, and to be witnesses of Christ to the end of the world, Matt. 28:[17-20]; Mark 16:15; John 15:27; Acts 1:22. Therefore God also worked marvelously with them. But God does not work thus with all teachers, for they are not all like the great apostles, and God also does not want to accomplish through all teachers what he accomplished through the apostles. Therefore he also did not lay upon all teachers what he laid upon the apostles. The apostles were commanded of the Lord to preach the gospel to all creatures which they also did through God's grace, Matt. 28:[18-20]; Mark 16:15; Col. 1:6. The teachers who now follow them must then preach not only to so-called Christians, but also to Jews and Turks and all heathen. But now Paul says to the teachers and bishops of the congregations that they should take heed to themselves and to the congregation over which the Holy Spirit had set them, Acts 20:28.

The apostles spoke at Pentecost with tongues of fire and everyone understood them, Acts 2:[3-]4. This had not happened before that time nor since. Thus God also miraculously released the apostles from prison, Acts 5:18; Acts 12:7; 16:25[-26]. Thus if anyone now wants to say that the teachers should preach openly as Christ and his apostles did, he [should] still consider that Christ was able to free himself out of the hands of his enemies as he willed and that God worked and dealt so marvelously with his apostles. The one must always be observed with the other so that one does not with indiscretion lay upon every teacher [to do] what Christ and his apostles did. But just as God apportions to every individual the measure of the Spirit and faith, and has given him his particular service, he himself will know [what] to observe, and also [what] should be observed by the congregations, 1 Cor. 12:[4-11].

Yes, says the opponent then, God's hand is not shortened. He is still able to help his own as he helped the apostles.

Answer

That we know and indeed believe. The disciples at Damascus also knew and believed that God is almighty, but nevertheless they helped Paul over the wall /240/ at night and thus he escaped out of the hands of the authorities of Damascus, Acts 9:25. The Christians at Ephesus also knew and indeed believed that God is almighty and could certainly protect Paul from all his enemies. Nevertheless they would not permit Paul to go among the people and give them a reply, Acts 19:30. But now some wish to expel the teachers into the midst of their enemies, even when it has been shown before their eyes how extremely blood-thirsty the world is and with abominable tyrannies persecutes the teachers unto death. But what kind of a spirit, disposition, and love these people have may be seen and understood [when compared with] the example of these disciples at Damascus and at Ephesus.

Elijah also well knew that God is almighty. He also trusted his Lord and God that he could protect him well. Nevertheless, he feared [for] himself before Jezebel and fled into the wilderness, 1 Kings 19:3. But Jezebel could cherish no more evil purpose against Elijah than the world now has against all Christians, and in particular against the true teachers and preachers of the gospel.

Above all this, Jesus Christ our Lord left the land of Judea when he heard that Herod had thrown John into prison, Matt. 14:13. If then Elijah hid himself from Jezebel [and] Christ from Herod, why should not a true teacher also do the same?

The opponent then says [that] Elijah revealed himself before Ahab and Jezebel and the whole people of Israel, 1 Kings 18:1; [18:17; 18:30; 19:1-2], and Christ did not always remain outside of the land of Judea.

Answer

That Elijah revealed himself was the will of the Lord, therefore he was also driven thereto by the Spirit of the Lord. When God also wills that the teachers should come into the open and not fear for themselves before murderous Jezebel, then the Lord will indeed work and drive [them] thereto through his Spirit.

The opponent then says, yes, since the teachers of this present time are not driven through the Spirit of the Lord to reveal themselves to the world, therefore they should remain silent and not take it upon themselves to teach, to distribute the sacramental signs of Christ, and thus to gather a congregation of God.

Answer

/241/ If after all the apostles out of fear of the Jews came together secretly, held their gathering [behind] locked doors, taught, baptized, and broke bread in houses, and that not by day only but also by night, why may and should it not now also take place in this way, John 20:19; Acts 1:13; 2:46; 20:7? Or will one accuse and censure the apostles because of this? Or is it now sin and censurable what in that time was good and useful?

The opponent then says thus: Christ after all said in the gospel, "Whoever does evil hates the light, and does not come to the light, so that his deeds will not be punished. But whoever does the truth comes to the light, that their works may be revealed, for they have been done in God," John 3:20[-21].

Thereupon we answer that these words are not against us. They are spoken by Christ to mean that evildoers hate the light of the divine Word in order that they may not be disciplined nor shamed thereby. Therefore the apostle says to the Thessalonians, "You are all children of light and of the day; we are not of the night or of darkness. So then let us not sleep, as the others do. Those who sleep, sleep at night, and those who get drunk are drunk at night," 1 Thess. 5:5[-7]. Again, [he wrote] to the Romans, "The night is gone, the day has come. Let us then cast off the works of darkness and put on the weapons of light; let us conduct ourselves honorably as in the day . . . ," Rom. 13:12[-13].

Therefore the previously mentioned words of Christ are not to be understood that one may not teach God's Word secretly (for the contrary there is proof enough in the Scriptures), but that unbelievers and evildoers hate the true light, that is the Word of God, and flee from [it] because God's Word disciplines and judges. Yes, (as the apostle says), "it is sharper than any two-edged sword, piercing to the division of body and soul, also through nerves and marrow, and is a judge of the thoughts and intentions of the heart. And no creature is invisible before him. . . ," Heb. 4:12[-13].

Since then God's Word thus pierces, disciplines, and judges, evildoers hate the light of the divine Word so that they may neither be disciplined nor judged by it. For the godless hate discipline, Prov. 9:8 and seek corners /242/ to slip into in order to hide themselves. They love darkness and are not eager to be seen, since what they indeed do secretly is a shame to say, as the apostle writes to the Ephesians, Eph. 5:12.

Likewise, let us observe with understanding what this signifies and what our Lord willed to give us to know therewith when he sent Elijah in the time of drought to Zarephath to a widow and there preserved him before Ahab and Jezebel, and fed, nourished, and kept him and the widow through a little oil and meal, 1 Kings 17:9. The Lord could well have fed and kept Elijah even had he not sent him to the widow. He could also have comforted the widow even if Elijah had not come to her. But it now pleased the Lord that Elijah with the widow and the widow with Elijah, would be kept (as is said) through a little oil and meal. But what this signifies we will give to all God-fearing persons to consider. According to our understanding these figures (as also all other figures), happened and [were] written for our learning, "so that by patience and the encouragement of the Scriptures, we might have hope," Rom. 15:4; namely, that God does not forsake his own, but helps them in every need and gathers them to each other that they may live their faith in quietness and solitude, guarded before Ahab and Jezebel, fed and nourished by God through his Word and Spirit. For the Lord does not forsake his saints but in evil times they are kept, Ps. 33:19; and in the time of drought they shall have enough.

The rich must suffer want and hunger, but those who fear the Lord have no lack, Ps. 34:[9-10]. But what [does] Christ say? "I tell you, there were many widows in Israel in the days of Elijah, when heaven was shut up three years and six months, when there came a great famine over all the land; and Elijah was sent to none of them but only to Zarephath, in the land of Sidon to a woman who was a widow,"

Luke 4:25 [-26]. Thus it still goes. For Ahab and Jezebel reign now also at this time and have brought Baal into Israel; therewith they make Israel to sin against the Lord. Therefore the Lord is also angry over Israel and has sent them a time of famine (that is) hunger and want of his Word upon earth, [Amos 8:11], as Israel in the time of Elijah had want of bodily bread. And just as Elijah was sent alone to the widow in Zarephath, so also few are now found who are pleasing to the Lord, so that they receive the comforting and quickening of their souls /243/ from God through his Word and Spirit with the cooperation of the servants and ministers of Jesus Christ.

But that Elijah had to keep himself hidden [and] also was not sent by the Lord to many, but alone to the widow in Zarephath, that was not his fault but that of the others. That the teachers must now also hide at this time and not be sent to the world by the Lord—the fault is not the Lord's (for he desires that all persons should be saved), also not of the sincere ministers (for they are of good will and inclined to serve everyone and to proclaim God's Word) but the wicked will not hear nor endure them, Ezek. 18:23; 1 Tim. 2:4; 2 Pet. 3:9.

Finally, since Jezebel is so hateful against all servants of God, it is better to serve God in secret than to bow the knees openly before Baal; better to teach God's Word secretly among those who have a desire for the truth and bear fruit according to it than to keep completely silent about it. It is better to teach the mystery of the kingdom of God and explain it secretly, where it is accepted and understood, as Christ and the apostles did, Matt. 13:11, than to hear that the harmful throne openly serves evil with the law,[6] Ps. 94:20. It is also better to practice the sacraments secretly with the God-fearing and true believing [persons] according to God's Word than to openly misuse them with unbelieving and false Christians, or to despise them and abandon them entirely as the erring and prideful spirits do who think and say unashamedly, "They are rich and have prospered, and need nothing; not knowing that they are wretched, pitiable, poor, blind, and naked," Rev. 3:17.

Further, as Scripture clearly indicates, one may not speak about God's Word wherever and whenever one wills, but alone when and where God wills. But the Lord wills that his Word shall be spoken where it bears fruit. Again, where it does not bear fruit, there it shall not be spoken. Therefore Eccleciasticus says, "Where there is no hearing, there one shall not speak in vain," Ecclus. 32:[4]. And Christ said to his apostles, "Do not give dogs what is holy; and do not throw your pearls before swine, lest they trample them under foot and tear

The Sending of Preachers / 233

you to pieces," Matt. 7:6. These words give us adequate /244/ recognition that God's Word (which is the holy thing and the pearl) shall not be preached to the persecutors of truth (which are the dogs who gnash their teeth together over the righteous), Ps. 37:12, and the unclean who are drowned in the desires of the flesh (which are the swine).

Moreover, it is well to observe here that the Holy Spirit forbade Paul to speak in Asia but sent him to Macedonia to preach the gospel there, Acts 16:6[-9]. Therefore the same apostle said, "Speak what is profitable, for improvement where it is needed, that it may be profitable to hear. And do not grieve the Holy Spirit of God, in which you were sealed for the day of redemption," Eph. 4:29[-30].

Yes, Christ himself did not want to give the Pharisees an answer to their question and also did not want to answer all the questions of Herod with a single word, [Luke 23:9]. In addition, Christ often spoke to the people in parables, Matt. 13:10; Mark 4:10, but the mystery of the gospel he explained secretly to his disciples to whom he said, "To you it has been given to understand the secrets of the kingdom of God, but to the others it has not been given," Matt. 13:11; [Mark 4:11], as it stands written, "he made known his ways to Moses, his intentions to the people of Israel," Ps. 103:7. And further, "he declares his word to Jacob, his manners and rules to Israel," Ps. 147:19. And Paul says that God's Word, that is, the mystery which was hidden from the foundation of the world, and from former times, is now revealed to the saints. "To them God chose to make known how great among the Gentiles are the riches of the glory of this mystery, which is Christ among you, the hope of glory," Col. 1:[27].

Therefore Christ also says, "I thank you, Father, Lord of heaven and earth that you have hidden these things (the gospel) from the wise and understanding and revealed them to those without understanding and the simple ones; yes, Father, thus it has been pleasing to you," Matt. 11:25[-26]; Luke 10:21. And Christ further says, "Whoever has my commandments and keeps them, that is the one who loves me; and whoever loves me will be loved by my Father, and I will love him and reveal myself to him." Judas (not Iscariot) said to him, "Lord, how is it that you will reveal yourself to us, and not to the world," John 14:21[-22]?

Out of all these words it is easily observed that God himself hid his Word from the world, that Christ spoke to the people in obscure parables, the Holy Spirit forbade Paul to speak God's Word in Asia, and God revealed his Word to his saints and not to the world. How then may the ministers of the Word be blamed with any reasonableness /245/ that they act according to this example in these dangerous times, to conceal the mystery of the gospel from this evil world, and in quietness secretly to reveal and speak what is profitable to the goodhearted who are receptive to hear them,[7] in order that they not grieve the Holy Spirit, Eph. 4:[30]?

In summary, how a teacher shall primarily be tested and recognized by his teaching and fruits is adequately explained above. But whether to teach openly or secretly is beside the point. For to teach openly is good and right according to the opportunity of the time; to teach secretly is not forbidden according to the opportunity of the time. Public teaching, if it is false, does not therefore become good because it is publicly taught. That which is false must be and remain false even if it were taught publicly a thousand times and were it wonderfully decorated with beautiful sounding words. Again, to teach secretly does not therefore become false because it was taught secretly. For what is right, that must remain right (says the prophet) and this shall please all devout hearts, Ps. 94:15. And God's Word is and remains the truth whether it be taught secretly or publicly. And if it were [so] that the true teachers might teach publicly, they should yet proclaim to us nothing other than this same Word of God that is revealed and taught us through the grace of the Lord.

Therefore here is not to be twisted, here no looking around after another gospel, since after all, both angels and people must be cursed who preach us another gospel than that which we have received from Christ and his apostles, Gal. 1:8[-9]. So let us now, according to the word of the prophet, give God the honor, and observe the light before it becomes dark and our feet stumble on the dark mountains, Jer. 13:16.

We also see before [our] eyes how perilous the times now are, much more than at the time of the apostles. Then the apostles and Christians could flee from one city to another, Matt. 10:23, but now all lords and princes, cities and lands have made a covenant against us.[8] Then the heathen government was so reasonable and proper that they did not wish to oppose strongly the faith and affairs of the Christian religion, Acts 17:9; 18:14[-15]; 23:22. But now almost everyone wants to be a lord over the conscience [of others] and a judge of faith (which after all belongs to Christ alone). Now the papal caesardom with all who are included therein, /246/ persecutes our faith as abominably as Antiochus persecuted the God-fearing Jews.

[In] particular the remnant of the pharisaic race, the perverted scribes, the presumptuous wise and arrogant of the world shout and rage against us, those who are of the seed of Cain and not of Abel, Isa. 5:21; Gen. 4:8. Therefore they persecute and kill the righteous, 1 John 3:[12]. And even though they are many times warned and instructed by God's Word, both orally and in writing, yet they remain stuck in their blindness, wickedness, and abominable tyranny. How then could it go otherwise with these despisers and persecutors of the divine Word, than it went with the rebellious, unbelieving, and malicious Jews; that is, that the kingdom of God would not come to them or again would be taken from them because they, after all, did not want to bring [forth] its fruits, Matt. 21:43?

And how much more is there to say? The world has no inclination to hear God's Word, therefore it is also not worthy to hear it. It despises righteousness, therefore it has also fled far from it. It persecutes Christ and has no desire whatever for that which [is] his; thus Christ also does not desire it. It will not cease from evil; therefore it also will not be disciplined by God's Word. It hates the truth, as Ahab did; therefore a lying spirit misleads them in the mouth[s] of all the prophets of Baal, 1 Kings 22:[22]. It will not endure true teachers; therefore the Lord sends it false prophets in heaps who speak to it what it gladly hears. And stated in the briefest form it happens even as Isaiah laments, namely, "that they are a rebellious people; lying, faithless children who will not hear the law of the Lord; who say to the seers, 'you should not see'; and to the prophets, 'Do not tell us what is right but what is pleasing to us; show us illusions, leave the way, turn aside from the path, let the Holy One of Israel cease among us,' " Isa. 30:9[-11].

Since then the world wants to have such prophets, the Lord thus sends her such teachers as she desires. But they must all come to shame as the Lord says through Ezekiel, "If the prophet be misled and speak a word, I, the Lord myself have misled that prophet, and I will stretch out my hand against him, and will root him out of my people Israel. And they shall both bear their misdeeds, the misdeeds of the inquirer shall be the same as the misdeeds of the prophet, etc. Ezek. 14:9[-10]. /247/ Jeremiah also lamented over Jerusalem that it was so miserably led astray by the false prophets and was brought into captivity, and says, "Oh, daughter of Jerusalem, wherewith shall I comfort you? Whom shall I liken to you, daughter of Zion, with which to comfort you? For your injury is great. Who can heal you? Your prophets have preached idle and foolish visions and have not revealed their misdeeds. Therewith they could have avoided your captivity, but they have preached idle sermons, so that they have preached you out of the land," Lam. 2:13[-14].

Thus the false prophets deceived Jerusalem, brought it to Babylon, and [they] themselves also came there. Yes, some received abominable punishments for their deceptive prophecies, Jer. 28:16. Thus it shall also go with the world and her false prophets as long as they do not amend themselves. But the Lord wants to convert them that they may honestly repent and turn to the living God and may come from darkness to the true light that they may be saved.

See, dear brothers, we have written a little through the grace of the Lord, out of brotherly love, about the sending of the evangelical teachers. Our friendly desire is that you will accept this for the best and test it well with the touchstone of Holy Scripture. We certainly might write much more about the matter, but we hope that we have done enough for the understanding and good-hearted. The perverted and malicious are not to be helped, even though an angel from heaven were to preach the truth to them. But the almighty God, a Father of all mercies and a God of all grace, 2 Cor. 1:3; 1 Pet. 5:10, who enlightens, strengthens, and confirms all true teachers and ministers of his Holy Word, whom he has set over his congregation through Christ Jesus with his Spirit, [grant] that they may remain steadfast in the evangelical teaching and show themselves irreproachable workers, who rightly divide the Word of truth, 2 Tim. 2:15, so that at the revelation of Jesus Christ they may receive from him the unfading crown, 1 Pet. 5:4.

And you, dear brothers in the Lord, "you who were straying like sheep, but are now converted to the shepherd and guardian of your souls," to Christ Jesus, 1 Pet. 2:25, remain steadfast in his teaching, hear his voice alone, follow in his footsteps, and be at peace with your leaders and teachers who rightly teach you God's Word, John 10:27; 1 Thess. 5:12[-13]. [Do this] so that the God of peace /248/ may be among you and that the Lord Jesus Christ may recognize you as his sheep on the last day and set you on his right hand and say to you, "Come here, you blessed of my Father, possess the kingdom of your Father that was prepared for you from the beginning of the world," Matt. 25:34. To that end the eternal God help us all through Christ Jesus.

Amen.

D. P.

ENDNOTES

1. *Dienaers*, literally servants but used generally, in this context, to refer to ministers. So also *Leeraers*, literally teachers, means ministers but will be translated as teachers to avoid redundancy since Dirk often uses both terms in conjunction.

2. *Ghemeynte* is often translated *church*, but *congregation(s)* is the more accurate translation. By "church" most Anabaptists tended to think of the Roman Catholic and Protestant institutions. Cf: the well-known church and sect typology of Troeltsch (1865-1923), *The Social Teaching of The Christian Churches*, pp. 694ff. and related literature.

3. The "gospel of all creatures" is referred to frequently in early Anabaptism, particularly in the baptismal theology of Hans Hut (d. 1527). Drawing on both medieval mysticism and on natural theology it held that true knowledge of God can be had through all of his creation, Rom. 1:20, and is preached to every creature, Col. 1:23. Creation itself prepares the way for the gospel of Christ, particularly through suffering. Thus Hut writes, "In the gospel [of] all creation is nothing else signified and preached than alone Christ the crucified, but not only Christ the head, but the whole Christ with all [his] members, this Christ preach and teach all creatures. . . . Here is not [to be] understood that the gospel is [to be] preached to dogs and cats, cows and calves, foliage and grass, but as Paul says, the gospel that is preached to you in all creatures." Müller, *Glaubenszeugnisse*, p. 16. That is, the gospel is not preached *to* but *in* or *of* [through] all creation. To make this point, Hut changed the Mark 16:15 text from the dative to genitive case. For a translated excerpt of Hut's "Of the Mystery of Baptism," see Rupp, *Patterns of Reformation*, pp. 379ff. See also Packull, *Mysticism*, and Williams, *The Radical Reformation*. In Genesis 9:8-17, we note that the covenant was not only made with Noah and his descendents but also with "every living creature."

4. The quotations from Psalm 73 and 12 are translations of the Dirk text but do not correspond with the Dutch text of the Biestkens Bible of 1563. They do, however, correspond with the German text of Luther's translation. This raises the possibility that Dirk sometimes worked with a German Bible whose text he simply translated into Dutch.

5. Dirck V. Coornhert and others argued that for a ministry to be valid the minister must be either called/sent by a legitimate congregation or be able to perform miracles. They did not accept the Anabaptist congregation(s) as legitimate and, since Anabaptist ministers could not perform miracles, their ministry was not of God.

6. Dirk's meaning here is not clear. The reference may be to Ps. 94:20 where the RSV reads, "Can wicked rulers be allied with thee, who frame mischief by statute?"

7. The identity of these "good-hearted" people, a phrase frequently used by Dirk, is not clear. He may, in fact, be referring to Anabaptists, but it is also possible that he had friends of Anabaptists in mind, people who largely agreed with them and often helped them, but did not join them for fear of persecution; hence the "in quietness secretly to reveal . . ." words. The attitude toward these "friends" [true-hearted] was to become an issue in the Amish division of 1693-97. See "Half-Anabaptists" in ME II:634 and related literature.

8. The article "Mandates" in ME 3:446-53 lists 221 decrees against the Anabaptists from 1525-1761. The listing is not exhaustive. The imperial mandate issued by Emperor Charles V on January 4, 1528, was reaffirmed at the second Diet of Speyer in 1529 and extended to the entire area then known as the Holy Roman Empire. A specific edict was issued against Menno Simons by Charles V on August 31, 1544, followed by others in the Lowlands and Rhine Valley area. Dirk's assessment of persecution in the early church is too optimistic.

The Ban

A loving admonition out of the Lord's Word in which is taught and narrated, in a discerning and orderly way, how and in what manner the Christian congregation shall deal with those who have given themselves to the fellowship of the saints and then still fall and are found in public and mortal works of the flesh. /249/

By D. P.

"We command you, dear brethren, in the name of our Lord Jesus Christ, that you withdraw from every brother who walks disorderly," 2 Thess. 3:6.

"If any one lets himself be called a brother and nevertheless is an adulterer, or greedy, or a servant of idols, or a reviler, or a drunkard, or robber—you should not eat with them," 1 Cor. 5:[11].

The Text

/250/ The grace of God, our heavenly Father, and the peace of our Lord Jesus Christ increase in you through the power and activity of the Holy Spirit. Amen.

Beloved brothers and friends in the Lord: I thank almighty God, since I hear about your faith, about your love for the Lord Jesus Christ and of his saints, about your patience and steadfastness in all the persecutions which you suffer, as an assurance of your salvation, and as a proof and testimony of the righteous judgment of God, who shall punish your persecutors insofar as they do not amend themselves and do not seriously repent. 2 Thess. 1:4.[1] But he shall strengthen and refresh you when the Lord Jesus Christ shall reveal him with the angels of his might and with flames of fire in order to do vengeance upon all who have not confessed God and who were not obedient to the gospel of our Lord Jesus Christ. They shall suffer pain, that is, an eternal exclusion from the face of the Lord when he shall come in order to be glorified in his saints. He shall appear marvelously in all believers who now through the power of their faith forsake and overcome the world, who now for the sake of the gospel despise all perishable and temporal things, and seek that which is above where Christ is sitting at the right hand of the Father, 2 Cor. 4:18; Col. 3:1, who now for the sake of righteousness are so miserably persecuted and put to death by the tyrants and bloodthirsty people [2 Thess. 1:5-8].

For this is now the time when the heathen come into the inheritance of the Lord, defile the temple of God, Ps. 79:1, and give the bodies of the servants of Jesus Christ as food to the birds under heaven, roast the flesh of the saints at stakes, /251/and present it to the wild beasts of the field as bait and game, so that they shed innocent blood as water round about Jerusalem and no one need bury the dead. And this all comes about because the great whore of Babylon is so thirsty after the blood of the saints and witnesses of Jesus, and cannot be satiated therefrom before she is completely drunk, that the number of the servants of God (who must be killed for the sake of his Word) is fulfilled, Rev. 17:6; 18:24; 6:11.

And then the most high God shall judge and punish the great Babylonian whore because she is a mother of all abominations on earth, Rev. 17:5, and because the blood of all the righteous was found in her and because she has so deceived the world with her beautiful appearance (since she is so arrayed in silk and purple and gilded with gold and has the golden cup full of all kinds of abominations in her hand and gives out of this to all her lovers and beaus), that the kings of the earth commit fornication with her and she makes all the heathen drunk with the wine of whoredom and enchantment, Rev. 17:4; 18:24; 18:[9]; [17:2]; [18:3]. Therefore, God shall punish her and her plagues shall come unforeseen and all those who cling to her and do not separate from her shall not remain unpunished.

Oh, Lord, how dreadful shall it then be for all those who now so stoutly blaspheme the Lord, take the truth captive, serve the Babylonian whore so faithfully, protect her, and because of her bring down the true Christians with fire, water, and sword, Isa. 59:[14-]15. Again, how joyful shall the servants of the Lord be, who have not received nor accepted the mark of the beast but are sealed with the seal of the living God on their forehead.[2] Of these it is written in the Revelation of John, namely, that John saw a great number of the servants of God who were sealed by the angels on their forehead with the seal of the living God, from all the tribes of the children of Israel Rev. 7:3[-8].

And after this he saw a great multitude which no one could

count, from every nation, peoples, and tongues, standing before the throne and before the Lamb clothed in white robes, and with palm branches in their hands, and crying out with a loud voice, "Blessed is he who sits upon the throne, our God and the Lamb!" And all the angels stood round the throne and round the elders and the four creatures and they fell on their faces before the throne and worshiped God, saying, "Amen! Praise and honor and wisdom and thanksgiving and glory and power and might be to our God for ever and ever! Amen."

"Then one of the elders answered and spoke to me, /252/ 'Who are these, clothed with white robes, and from where have they come?' and I spoke to him, 'Sir, you know.' And he spoke to me, 'These are they who have come out of great tribulation and have washed their robes and made them white in the blood of the Lamb. Therefore they are before the throne of God, and serve him day and night in his temple; and he who sits upon the throne will dwell above them. And they shall neither hunger nor thirst, the sun shall not fall upon them, or any scorching heat. For the Lamb in the midst of the throne will pasture them, and lead them to the fountain of living water; and God will wash all tears from their eyes,'" [Rev. 7:9-17].

My heartily beloved brothers and friends, you who have now become a derision and a byword of the whole world because of the truth, and are hated and persecuted unto death by the abominable beast (that has opened his mouth to blaspheme the almighty God, and his tabernacle, and those who live in it), Rev. 13:5, comfort yourselves with these and similar glorious and beautiful promises of God. Await with patience the glory which shall be revealed at the future coming and appearing of our Lord and Savior Jesus Christ, Matt. 16:25; Titus 2:13, who gave himself for us so that he should deliver us from this present evil world according to the will of his Father, Gal. 1:4, and make us children of God and heirs of eternal life, John 1:12, if we otherwise suffer with him here, Rom. 8:17, remain steadfast in his teaching, John 8:31, and follow in his footsteps with a firm faith, 1 Pet. 2:21.

And praised be God, the heavenly Father, the God of all grace, 2 Cor. 1:[3], who has provided for and chosen you and has called you through the gospel in the sanctification of the Spirit, and in the belief of the truth, to a glorious possession of our Lord Jesus Christ and as members of his congregations, Eph. 1:3[-4]; 2 Thess. 2:13; 1 Pet. 5:10. Therefore be at all times peaceful with the Christian congregation and remember that our God is a God of peace in all his congregations, Rom. 12:4; 1 Cor. 12:12, and that Christ Jesus has given and left us his peace, 1 Cor. 1:[10]; 14:33; John 14:27; Eph. 4:3, and that the apostle so earnestly admonished us to peace and said, "The peace of God, which goes beyond all understanding, keep your hearts and minds in Christ Jesus," Phil. 4:7. Again, "the peace of God take the upper hand in your hearts, to which you were called in one body. And be thankful," Col. 3:15.

Through such and similar Scriptures let yourselves be admonished and learn from the Holy Spirit that you seek true Christian peace /253/ as much as is possible for you, and see well to it that no discord or sectarianism be found among you; that one be not a Cephist, a second a Paulist, a third an Apollist, and a fourth a Christist, 1 Cor. 1:12, but that you be one heart and soul with each other in Christ Jesus, Acts 4:32. Be on your guard before the frivolous and famous spirits who parade themselves with high sounding words and despise others. Therewith they attract the ignorant of whom there are also a number who blaspheme the congregation of the Lord and compare the ministers of Christ, who rightly and properly separate public sinners and carnal persons from the congregation with the Word of the Lord, to the foolish shepherds of whom the prophet says that they do not seek the lost, do not bind up the crippled, do not heal what is wounded, yes, eat that which is fed and fattened, Ezek. 34:[3-]4; Zech. 11:10.

Oh God, how your Holy Word is yet always contradicted, and those who confess it and have it before their eyes, and do according to it, they must therefore suffer and be despised. Those who risk life and limb, goods and blood, and pawn these, are daily delivered up to death, Ps. 44:[22]; Rom. 8:36; 2 Cor. 4:11, and do it without regard [in order] to win many souls to Christ Jesus, these must still hear that they do not seek the lost. These who desire neither silver nor gold, and feed the sheep neither for the sake of the milk or the wool, but out of a willing spirit, those who so earnestly apply bandage and salve with the true ointment of God's Word and the comforting of the Holy Spirit, 1 Pet. 5:2; James 5:14; Rev. 3:18, these must be slandered as those who eat the fat and best, just as though they devoured the sheep like the false prophets do.

Yes, what is more, these themselves who have so dealt with such blasphemers and slanderers out of brotherly love and out of the desire of God-fearing persons, [and] also upon their own solicitation, have so instructed and convinced them with Scripture, that they thanked them for their good instruction, these now are slandered by the same persons, not alone with words, but also in writings. Their words are twisted, perverted, and falsely interpreted. Oh merciful, eternal God and Father, have mercy upon such blindness if it is your holy will and forgive these their sins and slanders who do not know what they do. This I pray and desire out of the depth of my soul.

But to you, beloved brothers and companions of our Christian faith, I want to teach you out of Holy Scripture, how God's ordaining from the beginning was /254/ to punish the evil, and to separate public transgressors and despisers of the divine Word from the congregation, and how great the need is for this separation, what a true penitence is which avails before God, and before his congregation, and may stand according to Scripture.

In the first place, Holy Scripture testifies everywhere, that God is righteous and therefore loves righteousness and hates unrighteousness, Ps. 7:12; 9:5; 45:7, that he is gracious and merciful toward the penitent and pious, but severe and wrathful toward the evil [ones], yes, that he visits the iniquity of the fathers upon the children until the third and fourth generation of those who hate him, and shows mercy to many thousands of those who love him and keep his commandments, Exod. 20:6; 34:[6-]7; Num. 14:18; Deut. 7:[7-10]. Therefore John says "that God is light and in him is no darkness. If we say that we have fellowship with him and walk in darkness, then we lie and do not do the truth; but if we walk in the light, just as he is in the light, we then have fellowship with one another, and the blood of his Son makes us clean from all sins," 1 John 1:5[-7]. And again, "by this we note that we have known Christ Jesus if we keep his commandments. He who says, 'I know him' but does not keep his commandments, that one is a liar, and no truth is in such people; but whoever keeps his word, in such the love of God is truly perfected. By this we confess that we are in him: he who says he abides in him that one shall walk in the same way as he walked," 1 John 2:3[-6]. Again, "whoever sins does wrong and sin is wrong. You know that Jesus Christ has appeared to take away sin, and there is no sin in him. No one who abides in him sins; whoever sins has neither seen him nor known him. Little children, let no one deceive you. He who does right is righteous, just as he is righteous. He who commits sin is of the devil; for the devil sinned from the beginning. The reason the Son of God appeared was to destroy the works of the devil. Whoever is born of God commits no sin; for God's seed abides in him, and he cannot sin because he is born of God. By this is revealed who are the children of God and who the children of the devil: whoever does not do right is not of God, nor he who does not love his brother," etc., 1 John 3:4[-10].

In order to understand these sayings of the apostle correctly, it is necessary to know which darknesses and sins separate us from God. John means the open works of the flesh /255/ which God's Word judges and punishes with death. These are such darknesses and sins, and not those of weakness and mistakes which still cling to all persons. Otherwise the apostle would contradict himself where he confesses and says, "If we say we have no sin, we mislead ourselves, and the truth is not in us. But if we confess our sins, he is faithful and just, that he will forgive our sins and cleanse us from all unrighteousness. If we say we have not sinned, we make him a liar, and his word is not in us," 1 John 1:8[-10].

Therefore, all these previously mentioned words of the apostle must be understood differently, namely, that all those who are carnally minded do works of the flesh and thus sin against God. These have no fellowship with him. These do not know Jesus Christ and they are not from God but from the devil, Rom. 8:5; Gal. 5:19; Eph. 5:5, 1 John 1:6; 3:4. Therefore, the apostle Paul also says that to be carnally minded is death, Rom. 8:6, and enmity with God, James 4:4, and those who walk according to the flesh shall die the death, for the wages of sin is death, Rom. 6:23.

But if anyone through human weakness makes a mistake and is overtaken with a fault, then this sin is not reckoned to him but it is forgiven and covered through the righteousness of our Lord Jesus Christ, Gal. 6:3; Ps. 32:1; Rom. 4:7[-8]; 8:1, as it stands written that Christ is the reconciliation for our sins, 1 John 2:2; 4:10, and blessed is the man whose unrighteousness is forgiven and his sin is covered, and blessed is the man to whom God does not impute his sins, Ps. 32:1. For there is "no condemnation in those who are in Christ Jesus, Rom. 8:1, . . . who walk not according to the flesh but according to the Spirit," [Rom. 8:4].

In the second place, God has testified and confirmed that in his law he has instituted sacrifices for the sins of ignorance and error, Lev. 11; 12; 13; Num. 15, but willful sinners and evildoers, such as murderers, adulterers, servants of idols, God blasphemers, magicians, and similar transgressors, he has commanded to be punished with death, and thus to root them out of Israel, Deut. 13. And there was regarded neither prince nor judge, neither man nor woman, nor a whole city, but all those who did evil before the eyes of the Lord, the God of Israel, or transgressed his covenant and served other gods, or committed other serious sins, these had to die, and Israel had to be cleansed of such evil persons, Lev. 20; Deut. 17:[1-]7].

In addition, God the Lord has set before us many and manifold beautiful figures about the purification of Israel, Lev. 11; 12; 13; 14. For they must not eat any unclean food nor touch anything unclean. /256/ The people had to be pure, similarly the houses and no one must contaminate the camp of Israel, for the Lord walked in the midst of their camp, Deut. 23. Therefore their camp had to be pure and holy, that nothing scandalous be seen therein, and that the Lord did not turn away from Israel, and that they not die in their uncleanness, Lev. 15:31, just as God spoke to Moses and Aaron, namely, that they should warn the children of Israel of their uncleanness so that they did not die in their impurity whenever they made the dwelling of the Lord which was in their midst unclean. To Israel God spoke, "Sanctify yourselves therefore, and be holy; for I your God am holy. Keep my statutes, and do them. I am the Lord who sanctifies you," Lev. 20:7[-8].

Therefore, also Miriam, the sister of Moses, when she was stricken by the Lord with leprosy (because she had murmured against Moses), Num. 12, was separated from the community of Israel. And it also did not help that Moses himself cried to the Lord for her and spoke, "Heal her, Oh, God." For the Lord responded to him thus: "If her father had spit in her face, should she not be shamed seven days? Let her be shut up outside the camp seven days, and after that she may be brought in again," [Num. 12:13-14]. Thus Miriam was excluded outside the camp seven days. And the people did not journey farther until Miriam was taken up again, etc.

And through this is portrayed for us how holy and pure the congregation of the Lord must now be, just as Peter also admonishes us and says, "Gird up the loins of your minds, be sober, set your hope fully upon the grace that will be offered to you through the revelation of Jesus Christ. As obedient children, do not follow the earlier passions of your ignorance, but since he who has called you is holy, be also holy yourselves in all your conduct. For it is written, 'You shall be holy, for I am holy,' " 1 Pet. 1:13[-15]; Lev. 20:7.

Likewise the apostle admonishes us [through his letter] to the Hebrews, that we should much more take heed of the Word which we hear, so that we not be destroyed, Heb. 2:1. "For if the message spoken by angels was valid and every transgression and disobedience has received its just wage, how shall we escape if we despise such a salvation? After it was preached at first by the Lord, it has come upon us by those who heard it. God has also given witness to it by signs and wonders and many kinds of powers, and with the distribution of the Holy

Spirit according to his will," [Heb. 2:2-4]. And again, "look out that you do not /257/ refuse him who speaks there. For if they did not escape when they refused him who warned them when he spoke on earth, much less shall we, if we refuse him who speaks from heaven," Heb. 12:25.

These words give us to understand sufficiently that the transgressors and despisers of godly teaching and the saving grace of our Lord Jesus Christ shall much less escape the punishment of God than those escaped who sinned against the law of Moses. Now, therefore, for that reason also evil and carnal people may not be tolerated in the congregation of the Lord, just as the apostles expressly testify. For Paul writes thus to the Corinthians, "Do you not know that the unrighteous shall not inherit the kingdom of God? Do not be misled, neither the immoral, nor servants of idols, nor adulterers, nor effeminates, nor homosexuals, nor thieves, nor the greedy, nor drunkards, nor slanderers, shall inherit the kingdom of God," 1 Cor. 6:9[-10]. Again, "the works of the flesh are plain: such as adultery, whoring, impurity, passion, idolatry, sorcery, enmity, strife, jealousy, anger, dissention, party spirit, murder, drunkenness, carousing, and the like, about which I told you before and say again, that those who do such things shall not inherit the kingdom of God," Gal. 5:19[-21]. Again, "that you shall know that no immoral, or impure, or greedy person who is a servant of idols, has any inheritance in the kingdom of Christ and of God," Eph. 5:5. Again, "the wicked shall not remain standing in the judgment, nor sinners in the congregation of the righteous," Ps. 1:[5]. Therefore, the Holy Spirit also says in the Revelation that outside of the heavenly Jerusalem, that is, outside the congregation of God "are the dogs and sorcerers and fornicators and murderers and servants of idols, and those who love and practice falsehood," Rev. 22:15.

Since now both the Old and the New Testament place these previously mentioned and similar transgressors outside the congregation of God, just as those who do not belong to God as long as they live in such sin and have done no sincere repentance therefrom, they may, therefore, also not be reckoned with the congregation of God. They must be separated from her and endure the deserved punishment until the time of their improvement and reconciliation with God and with his congregation, just as Paul punished the fornicator at /258/ Corinth so severely, and separated him from the congregation through the power of Christ, so that his flesh might thereby be chastised, but his spirit be kept in the day of the Lord Jesus, 1 Cor. 5:3[-5].

Thereby he teaches expressly that the believers shall have nothing to do with those who allow themselves to be called brothers and are fornicators, or greedy, or servants of idols, or blasphemers, or drunkards, or robbers. With such the Christians shall also not eat or have fellowship, 1 Cor. 5:[9-]10; 2 Thess. 3:6. For they must separate them and afterward shun them and this because of three principal reasons. The first is so that the congregation not become participant of the estranged ones' sins, 2 John 1:11, and that a little leaven not ferment the whole lump, 1 Cor. 5:[6]; Gal. 5:9. The second reason is so that those who have sinned be shamed and disciplined in their flesh, and that their spirit be saved in the day of the Lord Jesus, 1 Cor. 5:[5]. The third reason is so that the congregation of God not be blasphemed because of evil and bear no guilt before the Lord on account of them, 2 Thess. 3:14; Ezek. 36:20; Rom. 2:24; Josh. 7:20[-26]; 1 John 1:3; Deut. 13:[6-10]; 17:7; 19:19.

Out of all this it follows now that one must separate the evil and public sinners from the congregation of the Lord. For if their fellowship is not with God, they are banned and rooted out of the literal Israel. If they do not know Jesus Christ, they have no part in the kingdom of God and Christ. If they shall not inherit or possess it, and if Christians shall have nothing to do with them, how can they remain in the congregation of God, be called 'holy brothers' and greeted with the peace of Jesus Christ and the holy kiss, 2 John 1:7; Eph. 5:5; Gal. 5:21; 1 Cor. 5:10[-11]; 2 Thess. 3:6; Heb. 3:1? Yes, how shall they be the pure bride of the Lamb, Rev. 21:2, and the members of the body of Christ, Rom. 12:4; 1 Cor. 12:27; Eph. 4:4? Or do we not know that Christians are the members of Christ, and their body the temple of the Holy Spirit? Or shall now the fornicators, adulterers, or servers of idols and other evildoers be reckoned as members of Christ and the temple of God, 1 Cor. 3:16; 6:19; 2 Cor. 6:16?

This be far hence! For Jesus Christ does not have such unclean members, and the temple of the Holy Spirit is holy, 1 Cor. 6:19. Yes, Jesus Christ has his congregation, who is now his bride, his body, flesh of his flesh, and bone of his bone, Eph. 5:30. She who formerly lay naked and deformed in her blood; who was not rubbed with salt and uncircumcised in her navel Ezek. 16:4; Hos. [2:3-4], he has accepted her out of grace and has chosen her as his bride through his eternal love. He has cleansed her through the water bath of the word, Eph. 5:26; Titus 3:5, /259/ and has washed her from all her sins with his precious blood, 1 Pet. 1:19; Rev. 1:[5]. He has rubbed her with the salt of divine wisdom, Matt. 5:13, and circumcised her with his powerful word, Col. 2:11. He has anointed her with the oil of gladness, [Ps. 45:7]; [1] John

2:[20-]27, and placed upon her the crown of honor, [1 Pet. 5:4], and clothed her with the beautiful silk of righteousness, Rev. 19:8, and with the cloak of salvation so that she might be justified through his grace, Titus 3:7, and be unblamable and without guilt before God the Father, Eph. 5:26; Col. 1:22. Therefore, it is also a great ingratitude and an abominable sin if this bride forsakes the Lord Jesus Christ, the loving Bridegroom, and carries on harlotry against him, that is, loves the world, lives according to the flesh, serves idols or commits other sins which the Lord abhors.

Then some now say that whenever a whoremonger or adulterer has committed these or similar sins accuses himself, has remorse, and promises amendment, then his sin is forgiven him by God already and he should not be separated. To this I reply in brief thus—that the kingdom of God does not consist in words but in power, just as the apostle says, 1 Cor. 4:20. Therefore, true penitence does not consist of words alone but has three characteristics and signs whereby it is recognized. The first is that one heartily lament before God the Lord, Ps. 32:5, bears remorse over his sins, and is at all times troubled with it, as the prophet says, "My misdeed is ever before me," Ps. 51:[3]. The second is that out of a broken heart and a smitten conscience one confesses his sins before God, asks for forgiveness, Ps. 32:[3-]5], trusts firmly upon the grace of God through Jesus Christ, and says with the prophet "Be gracious to me, Oh, God, according to your goodness; according to your great mercy blot out my sins, Ps. 51:1. Wash me thoroughly from my misdeeds, and cleanse me thoroughly from my sin! For I confess my sins and do not hide my misdeeds." The third is that one should cease from sin and do righteousness as the prophet says, "For to depart from wickedness is a true worship which pleases the Lord; and to cease from doing unrighteousness is the true sin offering," Ecclus. 35:[3]; Ezek. 18:27; 33:[14, 15, 16].

Therefore, now no penitence avails before God when one does not bring forth the fruits of repentance, just as John also indeed confessed when he said, "The ax is now laid to the root of the tree; every tree therefore that does not bear good fruit is cut down and thrown into the fire," Matt. 3:10.

But when Christ says in the Gospel, "If your brother sins against you, discipline him between you and him alone," Matt. 18:15, that is not said nor to be understood about public works of the flesh but of the secret misdeeds wherewith one brother /260/ offends the other. As Peter also asked of the Lord and spoke, "Lord, how often shall I forgive my brother? Is seven times enough? Christ answered him, 'I tell you, not seven times, but seventy times seven, and as often as he asks you for forgiveness,' " [Matt. 18:21-22]. Now there is no one who is taught of God who is so unreasonable that he does not understand what sins Christ here meant, that is, such failures and violations as often happen through human weakness and are not reckoned under the works of the flesh which bring death with them.

Likewise, that Christ did not condemn the adulteress to death, that happened and has this explanation that the adulteress was not in the congregation of Christ but in the synagogue of the Jews, and the Pharisees would not have judged her according to the gospel, but according to the law, John 8:11. Now Christ had not come in order to condemn and kill people according to the law, but to convert and save them through the gospel and through faith in his name, Matt. 9:13. Therefore, Christ did not institute such a ban so that one through this should kill the transgressors of his Word but that one should separate them from the congregation for their improvement and restoration.

Yes, some still say how the prophet David, the apostle Peter and others, had indeed sinned and just as well remained in the congregation of God and were not separated therefrom.

Answer

Ecclesiasticus certainly says correctly that "a godless man does not let himself be disciplined but knows how to help himself with the example of other people in his intention," Ecclus. [32:17]. Thus the drunkards help themselves with Noah and Lot, the adulterers and whoremongers with David, which is no sign of their repentance and piety, but much more of godlessness and perverseness.

But as one understands the examples of Scripture, as Paul says, namely that "what things were prescribed for us, were written for our instruction so that we through patience and comfort of the Scriptures might have hope to God," Rom. 15:4, thus one understands them correctly.

Therefore, we may take out of these previously mentioned examples of Scripture no freedom nor opportunity to sin or support others in their sin. But we shall learn therefrom that God is gracious and merciful, longsuffering and of great goodness, and takes away the misdeeds and /261/ transgressions and forgives the guilt of all those who amend themselves from their hearts and make sincere repentance, Num. 14:18; Ps. 103:3.

So now if anyone sins with David and Peter and does such repentance as they have done and manifests his penitence before God with these fruits, to such a one God shall no doubt be gracious and the congregation should also indeed deal with him in love and according to Christian discretion. But that one should wish to compare ordinary public sinners and carnal persons with David and Peter or not separate them from the congregation of God, that is openly against the Scripture and the ordaining of the Lord, against the power and effect of the evangelical ban, as has been sufficiently stated above, 1 Cor. 5:[11]; 2 Thess. 3:6.

Also a truly penitent person will certainly be content that the deserved punishment be laid upon him from the Lord and from his congregation, just as David was so patient when the Lord punished him on account of his sin and Shimei cursed him when Absalom his son persecuted him and sought after his life. Then David confessed that it was God's just punishment which had come upon him and placed himself in all submissiveness before God, whether to come again into his kingdom or not to return, just as it pleased God, 2 Sam. 16:7[-12]. Should then one who has sinned before God and desires to do penitence not be content with the fact that the congregation of the Lord, on account of his sin, punishes him a little according to the Word of the Lord, and chastises his flesh so that his soul be neither corrupted nor lost, [1 Cor. 5:4-5]? Moses says openly that God forgives the guilt but does not let it go entirely unpunished, Num. 14:18. The ban is a punishment of sins, laid upon the sinner from God, therefore he must also endure it and accept it for his improvement.

Finally, this is the meaning, if anyone commits fornication, adultery, and similar sins, he will be, through this sin, separated from God, as the prophet says, that the sin of the person makes a difference between God and him, Isa. 59:2, and as witness of this he is put away from the congregation of God, 1 Cor. 5:[1-5]. Again, if anyone does true repentance, he is again taken up by God in grace, this as a proof and sign, so he is received again by the congregation with joy, 2 Cor. 2:8; 7:[9-11]. This is a sure rule of the divine Word about which no one can be deceived.

Therefore, my beloved brothers and friends in the Lord, my companions in the faith, in the kingdom, in the persecution, and in the patience of Jesus Christ, Rev. 1:9, remember after all, that you were delivered from spiritual Egypt by the strength of God, through his powerful hand and outstretched arm /262/ and that he led you through the Red Sea, Exod. 14:[13-31], where you were baptized into Jesus Christ and his death, Rom. 6:3, that you have received the gift of the

Holy Spirit, Acts 16:31[-33], where all your enemies were drowned and brought to naught through the glorious victory of Jesus Christ, who through the blood of his cross has triumphed over the prince of the world and the rulers of darkness, Eph. 2:13; Col. 2:15. Remember, I say, what grace the merciful God has shown herein, Col. 2:6, and how you have accepted the Lord Jesus Christ, when you bowed your knees before the most high God and were marked with the sign of the Lord, Ezek. 9:4, and sealed with the seal of the living God on your forehead, Rev. 7:3, how then no persecution has been able to frighten or hinder you. The strong mandates and placards of the tyrants you have not regarded. The devil you have forsaken with all his works, the antichrist you have renounced with his idolatrous being and false worship, the world and all that is in it you have overcome through your faith, 1 John 5:4. Flesh and blood you have crucified, with its lusts and desires, Gal. 5:24, your bodies you have offered to God as a living sacrifice, Rom. 12:1, you have surrendered to fire, water, and sword for the sake of the witness of Jesus Christ. You have made a promise to the Lord with denial of your self to serve him in holiness and righteousness all the days of your life, Matt 16:24. You have committed yourself to the Holy Spirit to be obedient to him and to allow yourselves to be ruled by him.

As this took place, how strong was your faith at the time that even the gates of hell were not able to prevail against it, Matt. 16:18. How fervent you then were in the Spirit, how your hearts burned in the love of God, how your conscience was then comforted with an eternal comfort of the grace of God, and what joy there was then with God, our heavenly Father, and with his angels in heaven, Matt. 18:[12-]14; Luke 15:7, and with the believers on earth over your amendment, when you were converted from unrighteousness to the living God, 1 Thess. 1:9[-10], when you had forsaken the Babylonian harlot and had come to your Father. He has taken you up in grace, yes, into the fellowship of his Son, Jesus Christ, 1 Cor. 1:[9], has slain the fatted calf, clothed you with the very best garment, placed the ring on your finger, and caused him to rejoice with the heavenly host, that you who were dead had again come to life, and that you /263/ who were lost had now again been found, Luke 15:[22-]23. For the true Shepherd, Jesus Christ, who came from heaven to seek the lost sheep, Ezek. 34:23; John 10:11, has sought and found us poor lost sheep in the wilderness, yes, has taken us upon his shoulders when he carried our sins with his body on the wood of the cross, Isa. 53:[4-6]; 1 Pet. 2:[24], and has brought us to the fold of Israel, that is, to the congregation of God.

So this is now my friendly desire and brotherly admonition to you, that you, after all, observe your calling and direct your walk according to the gospel in the fear of the Lord and nevertheless do not hear the false prophets of whom the apostle Peter writes thus: "These are waterless springs and clouds driven about by a storm, for them the nether gloom has been reserved in eternity. For they speak strong words which they do not follow, they entice through uncleanness to licentious passions of the flesh men who have barely escaped from those who live in error. They promise them freedom, although they themselves are slaves of corruption, for whatever overcomes a person, to that he is enslaved. For if, after they have escaped the defilements of the world through the knowledge of our Lord and Savior Jesus Christ, they are again entangled in them and overpowered, then the last state has become worse for them than the first. It would have been better for them never to have known the way of righteousness than after knowing it to turn back from the holy commandment delivered to them. It has happened to them according to the true proverb, the dog eats again what he has vomited, and the sow wallows in the mud again after she is washed," 2 Pet. 2:17[-22].

These apostolic teachings and witnesses of the Holy Spirit, however, take to heart and watch for these sins, yes, watch for these sins as Sirach teaches and says, "My child, have you sinned? Sin no more and pray that your former sins be forgiven. Flee before the sin as before a serpent, for if you draw too close, it will bite you; its teeth are like the teeth of a lion and kill the people. Every sin is as a sharp sword and wounds so that no one can heal it," [Ecclus. 21:1-3]. The apostle admonishes us similarly that no one shall be found among us who has an evil, unbelieving heart that turns away from the living God, but that we shall admonish /264/ one another among ourselves so long as it is called today so that no one be hardened through the deceitfulness of sin, for we have become participants in Christ insofar as we maintain the beginning of his being [in us] firm to the end, Heb. 3:12[-14].

Dear brothers, since we (regretfully) in our blindness and ignorance have in fact sinned much, and acted perversely toward our God so that we might well say with the prophet, "Oh, Lord, remember not the sins of our youth, nor our ignorance, but remember us according to your great mercy, for your goodness' sake," Ps. 25:7. And God has now bestowed grace to us in Christ Jesus, whom we have accepted and have received the beginning of his being, Col. 2:6; Heb. 3:14, so let us then be found fruitful in him. For he says in the Gospel, "Every branch on me that bears no fruit, my father shall cut off, and every branch that does bear fruit he cleanses so that it bears more fruit," John 15:2. And again, "whoever does not abide in me, he is cast away as a vine branch which withers; and people gather them and throw them into the fire and must burn them," [John 15:6]. Therefore it is terrifying that one does not remain in Christ Jesus, that is, that one transgresses as his teaching and does not remain therein, as John says, whoever transgresses and does not remain in the teaching of Christ has no God, 2 John 9, but whoever remains in it has both the Father and the Son, 1 John 2:24.

Therefore let us remain firm and unmovable in Christ Jesus and his teaching and not look back with Lot's wife toward Sodom, Gen. 19:26; Luke 17:32, nor become lustful after the flesh pots of Egypt, Exod. 16:[3]. And if these others do such and with the rebellious Israelites get a loathing toward the bread of heaven [Num. 11:6] and with the disciples at Capernaum who were offended at the words of the Lord, John 6:52; John 6:60[-61], (which are, after all, spirit and life), [John 6:63] and considered the sayings of Christ too hard, John 6:60, (which are, however, full of divine sweetness and spiritual quickening), Ps. 19:[10]; 119:103, and therefore turned away from him, [John 6:66], then let us nevertheless say with Peter, "Lord, where shall we go? You have the words of eternal life, and we have believed, and have confessed, that you are Christ, the Son of the living God," [John 6:68-69].

This agrees with what Jeremiah says, "Lord, all who forsake you shall be put to shame; those who turned away from you shall be written in the earth, for they have forsaken the Lord, the fountain of living water," Jer. 17:13. Therefore Solomon also says that, "A person /265/ who wanders from the way of understanding will rest in the assembly of the dead," [Prov. 21:16], that is, where the antichrist reigns, where Satan dwells, 2 Thess. 2:[9-11], and the second death has supremacy, Rev. [20:6].

But God, a Father of all mercy, 2 Cor. 1:3, who made you alive from the dead, Eph. 2:[1], and has begun the good work of faith in you, he must also bring the same to completion in you, Phil. 1:6, and make you fruitful in all righteousness and place you blameless before his face, [Col. 1:22], guard you from all evil, and preserve you for his heavenly kingdom. Amen.

To the same omnipotent, eternal, and only God I commend you for all time. The love of God the Father, the peace of our Lord Jesus Christ, and the comforting of the Holy Spirit be with you all in eternity, 2 Cor. 13:[14]. Amen.

Written out of brotherly love to the service of the God-fearing.

> D. P. Y.[our] B.[rother]
> In the Lord
> Anno 1558, The Fifth of February

ENDNOTES

1. The judgment Dirk refers to is a biblical theme. It appears frequently in Anabaptist writings, including Dirk, Menno Simons and, especially, the *Martyrs Mirror*. Was it an implicit vengeance motif for them? We are willing to suffer now, but God will "get you" in the end—unless you repent. They did *not* say "unless you become an Anabaptist."

2. With this and later parallel references [pp. 250, 297, 377, 381, 424], Dirk draws upon deep eschatalogical and medieval roots. Biblically, Ezekiel 9, Revelation 7 and 14 speak of the sign of the Greek *thau*, or *tav*, the last letter in the Hebrew alphabet, as the mark T on the forehead as a sign of the elect of God on the last day. Dirk could have been familiar with this from his use of the Vulgate or Zurich bibles, or from secret writings of the South German Anabaptist Hans Hut (d. 1527). Hut, perhaps the foremost Anabaptist missionary, was given to "baptizing" (sealing) the elect by making the T, or the sign of the cross, on the forehead of believers with a moist finger in the name of the Father, Son and Holy Spirit. This was opposed to the sign of the antichrist according to Revelation 13:16-17. Numerous early church fathers used the *thau* as a sign of the cross, as did a variety of medieval groups. It was believed that it had appeared on the forehead of St. Francis of Assisi and was his personal (and therefore the Franciscan) seal.

Karel Vos made an early brief reference to this in his "Het Teeken Thau," in DB (1917), 156-159. More recently Gottfried Seebass wrote on this in his 1972 Erlangen dissertation, *Muntzer's Erbe. Werk, Leben und Theologie des Hans Hut*, of which an excerpt appeared in Hans-Jurgen Goertz, *Umstrittenes Taufertum, 1525-1975*, Gottingen: Vandenhoeck & Ruprecht, 1975, pp. 138-164. A helpful summary of key issues and literature may be found in Werner O. Packull, "The Sign of Thau: The Changing Conception of the Seal of God's Elect in Early Anabaptist Thought," MQR, October, 1987, pp. 363-374.

THE TRUE KNOWLEDGE OF GOD

*A Beautiful Admonition and /267/
Brief Instruction About the True Knowledge of God.
by D. P.*

"He who hears my word," Christ says, "and believes him who sent me, has eternal life." John 5:24

"This is eternal life, that they confess you to be the only true God, and Jesus Christ whom you have sent." John 17:3

The Greeting

/268/ To the beloved and faithful brothers and sisters, who have received the same faith with us, 2 Pet. 1:1, we wish much grace, peace, and mercy from God, our heavenly Father, and from Jesus Christ, our only Lord, Redeemer, and Savior, who gave himself for us to redeem us from the present evil world, according to the will of his Father, to whom be praise eternally. Amen. Gal. 1:4[f.].

The Text

/269/ I thank the Lord, the most high God of heaven and earth, and it makes me happy out of the innermost part of my soul, according to what I hear about your faith in God, about your knowledge of Christ Jesus and of the Holy Spirit, and about your love of all believers, Col. 1:3[-4]; 2 Thess. 1:3. And I pray God, the eternal Father, through Jesus Christ, that he will keep you in true faith, a fervent spirit, and pure love until the end, 2 Thess. 1:11. I pray that you also may increase and mature therein daily, so that you might be unpunished in the day of the Lord, Col. 1:22, filled with all the fruits of righteousness, which come through Jesus Christ, to the honor and glory of God.

I admonish you through the love of the Spirit, that you thank God at all times for his immeasurable mercy, which he has demonstrated to you so richly. Remember that you earlier sat in Egypt (that is, in darkness, Eph. 5:8), being the servants of sin, kept captive by the devil according to his will, and how wonderfully God delivered you from it. Take to heart that you were so deeply in debt and could not repay it, and God so graciously gave you everything and canceled the charges. Remember that you, along with the prodigal son, Luke 15:[11ff.], were for a long time alienated from your heavenly Father. You pursued so much spiritual whoredom (that is, idolatry) with the Babylonian whore, and God in his great goodness and long-suffering so graciously accepted you. He made his eternal covenant with you, gave you Christ Jesus, and has rejoiced with all the angels in heaven over your conversion.

Therefore take heed to yourself, that you have not received God's grace in vain, 2 Cor. 6:1. But remember that you are called thereto by God, out of darkness into his wonderful light, that you might walk as the children of light, Eph. 5:8. You therefore were forgiven many sins, Eph. 5:1[ff.], so that you might no longer sin, John 8:11. You have been received in grace by God, /270/ the heavenly Father, so that you may serve him all the days of your life in holiness and righteousness, 1 Pet. 2:24. For God has chosen, called, and accepted you in Christ Jesus, Luke 1:69. And this is clearly portrayed in the gospel for you by many whom Christ healed, and whom he told to go forth in peace and no longer sin, so that nothing worse would happen to them.

For this reason I have undertaken to admonish you briefly, and to hold before you by God's grace the principle articles of our salvation. These are: the true knowledge of God, true faith, upright unmerited love, and the living hope. For where there is no knowledge of God, Wisd. of Sol. 15:3, there is great ignorance, and evil has the upper hand. Where there is no faith, one cannot please God, Heb. 11:6. Whoever does not have love remains in death, 1 John 2:[11]; 3:14. And where there is no living hope in God and in eternal salvation, there is a fainthearted mind and a troubled conscience, 1 John 3:20.

First, one must rightly know God the Father, and his Son Jesus Christ, and the Holy Spirit, John [17]:3. Three things are primarily included in the knowledge of God the Father: that one rightly confess his eternal, almighty power and wisdom (by which he created everything); his eternal divine righteousness, by which he has so severely punished sins, both of the angels and mankind, 2 Pet. 2:[4-6]; and his immeasurable fatherly mercy, by which he has given Jesus Christ as a Redeemer and Savior, John 3:16.

The knowledge of the almighty power and wisdom of God teaches us that we should trust in God alone, seek, pray for, and desire help, protection, Ps. 33:16[-20], salvation, and all good gifts from him alone, and not from any creature, neither in heaven nor on earth, Ps. 111:[2 ff.]. No one can help us except almighty God alone. He said to Abraham, "I am the God Shaddai," Gen. 17:1, that is, the fulfiller and the sufficient fullness of all good. He has said to Israel, "I am your Lord and Savior, the Holy One in Israel, the righteous God and Savior, and there is no other God than I."

The knowledge of the righteousness of God teaches us to fear God, to repent sincerely, Ps. 7:12; Matt. 3:[2], to cease sinning, to shrink from God's anger /271/ and judgment, and to seek after righteousness, so that we may not fall into the hands of the living God. For that reason God has demonstrated his justice openly to the angels in heaven who sinned, 2 Pet. 2:4[ff.], to Adam and Eve in paradise, Gen. 3, to the cities of Sodom and Gomorrah, Gen. 19:24, and to many others. He did this to reveal a public example of his eternal justice, and so we might learn from it to fear him as a righteous God and judge, yes, as a sternly jealous God, and as a consuming fire, and to keep that before our eyes.

The knowledge of the mercy of God teaches us to love God as he has loved us and gave his only born Son even unto death so that we might live eternally through him, John 3:16; 1 John 4:10. "For God has had so much love for the world," John says, "that he gave his only born Son, that he who believes in him should not be lost, but have eternal life," John 3:16. Likewise, therein has the love of God appeared, that he has given his only born Son for us, that we might live through him. In sum, God's love for us is revealed from heaven, in that he has presented such a costly treasure to us, his most beloved only Son, yes, he has given all his heavenly goods to his own.

In the knowledge of Jesus Christ, three things especially are to be confessed and remembered; his true divinity, according to which he was born from God, Micah 5:[2], from the beginning and is one from eternity with the Father, John 1:1; John 10:30; 14:9; 17:21; his pure, unstained humanity, which has come from the Word through the working of the Holy Spirit, Matt. 1:20; Luke 2:7, and not from any persons' flesh and blood; and his grace, wisdom, righteousness, holiness, deliverance, and salvation, Jer. 23:6.

The knowledge of the true divinity of Jesus Christ teaches us that we must keep him for our only Redeemer and Savior, John 17:25, and believe in him as our Lord and God, 1 Cor. 1:[24]; John 20:28. We do this to be saved through him, for that is the will of the heavenly Father, 1 Tim. 2:[f.], that those who see the Son and believe in him shall have eternal life, John 14:1; 3:16; 6:46. But he who despises him and does not believe in him shall not see life. The wrath of God shall remain upon him, John 3:[36]; 1 John 5:10. Now no one can believe in the Son of God, Jesus Christ, unless he rightly confesses his true divinity. For one must not believe /272/ in anyone except God alone. Outside of that, there is no salvation, Heb. 11:6. (I speak about adults and those who understand.) Therefore the knowledge of the true divinity of our Lord Jesus Christ is necessary above all else for salvation.

The knowledge of the holy humanity of Jesus Christ teaches us to remember and understand the overflowing richness of God's grace, that he has sent his own firstborn and only begotten Son, his eternal almighty Word, in the form of sinful flesh, Eph. 2:6,[7]; John 1:14; 3:16; Rom. 8:3. He has delivered him for us to the most shameful death of the cross, Rom. 8:32. He has also guaranteed to us that we have free access to God the Father through him, Eph. 2:[18], in the Holy Spirit. He could do this because he became our brother, Phil. 2:5[ff.]; Heb. 2:[11]; 5:2; Ps. 32, 23(?) like us in every way, except for sin; because he is our true High Priest, Reconciler, and Mediator by God, 1 Tim. 2:5; Heb. 5:1; 8:1; to come to our help and have compassion with our human weakness, Heb. 2:14; 5:2. We must have such a mediator who was both God and human, in order that in his true divinity he may help us completely. He can also have patience with our failures, since he is a person, tempted in all things, yet without sin, which he has not known.

The knowledge of the grace of our Lord Jesus Christ teaches us that we shall not be saved through our works, neither through any other means than through the merit of Jesus Christ alone, Eph. 2:4. For he is our righteousness, holiness, and eternal life, 1 Cor. 1:[30]. He is our redeemer, 1 Tim. 2:5, Advocate, 1 John 2:1, Reconciler, Savior, and throne of grace, through faith in his blood, Rom. 3:25. His suffering is our joy; his cross is our triumph, Col. 2:14; and boasting, his death is our life; his resurrection from the dead is our rising to eternal glory, 1 Cor. 15:21; his ascension is our way to the Father; his union with us is our union with God, John 17:21; and makes us partakers in the divine nature and immortality, 2 Pet. 1:4.

Likewise, in the knowledge of the Holy Spirit, three things are to be noted: First, his true divine being, according to which he proceeds

The True Knowledge of God / 259

from the Father through the Son, John 16:13. Second, his working in all believers, for he comforts, strengthens, and seals us to the day of deliverance, Eph. 4:30. He teaches them to fear God, to believe in God, to call upon God and pray, Rom. 8:26; Wisd. of Sol. 9:17[f.] and in summary, he distributes to them all the good divine gifts, 1 Cor. 12:4, according to his will. /273/ Third, his punishment for the sins of the world, that is over the unbelief, false righteousness, and that unjust judgment that the world exercises over the children of God and over all divine affairs, John 16:8.

The knowledge of the Holy Spirit's divinity teaches us that we should believe his teaching and witness, because he is God who alone is real and cannot fail, Ps. 116:11; Rom. 3:4. Therefore everything that the Holy Spirit has declared and spoken through the prophets and apostles, 2 Pet. [1]:21, yes, through Jesus Christ himself, that is the eternal and trustworthy truth, and the testimony of God.

The knowledge of the power and work of the Holy Spirit in all believers teaches us always to pray to God, the heavenly Father, Matt. 7:7, through Jesus Christ for the Holy Spirit, so that he will lead us into all truth, John 14:26; 15:26; 16:7; make us partakers of all of his divine gifts; comfort, strengthen, and keep us in the sanctifying teachings of Jesus Christ, in the true faith, until our end; and help us to come into that eternal kingdom of our heavenly Father.

The knowledge of the punishment of the Holy Spirit teaches us to recognize the unbelief of the world, its false righteousness, and its unjust judgment. For the Holy Spirit punishes the world through the children of God, through the witness of Jesus Christ because of its unbelief, since they do not believe in Jesus Christ, but reject his Word, his teaching, and his covenant, and accept, believe, and follow human doctrines.

Likewise, the Holy Spirit punishes the world for false righteousness since they seek, along with the Jews, to establish their own righteousness, Rom. 10:3, through such works and ceremonies which people have invented, thought up, and instituted. For that reason they do not want to submit themselves to the righteousness which comes from faith in Jesus Christ and counts before God.

Likewise, the Holy Spirit punishes the world for that judgment by which it values and justifies the godless, but accuses and condemns the pious, since they call the good, evil and the evil, good; hold the light for darkness and the darkness for light Isa. 5:20. Thus neither Christ with his friendliness and fellowship, nor John with his strictness and seclusion, Matt. 11:16[ff.] can do enough. But they always slander and revile the pious unjustly, judge and kill them as heretics, thinking that thereby they do God a service. All such persons are punished by the work of the Holy Spirit, that is through the pious Christians in whom he performs his works.

Therefore we must confess the Father, Son, and Holy Spirit rightly, /274/ Matt 3:16; 28:19; 1 John 5:6[ff.], since they are the truly living God, besides which no other God exists in heaven or upon earth. This God has created us, he has redeemed us, he has taught and illuminated us, he is our protector, Ps. 18:1, Helper in need, Savior, and everything, and we must believe in him. What true faith is the apostle to the Hebrews describes for us, namely, that faith is a certain trust, which is to hope, Heb. 11:1, and direct one to the things not seen, that is, faith trusts the invisible God, Heb. 11:27, and hopes on his grace, and strives toward eternal, invisible things. For faith has three characteristics whereby it may be known and truly distinguished from all unbelief.

The first is that one believes nothing other than God's Word, for that faith comes from hearing the divine words, Rom. 10:17, and not from any human doctrine, since faith looks only upon God. It holds him truthful in all his words and promises, and holds all persons capable of lying, Ps. 116:11; Rom. 3:4. Therefore faith is not judged according to any person's word, no matter if it appears as wonderful as possible, but it accords with God's Word only.

The second is that faith believes all of God's words, and excepts none. For all of God's words are as active as fire, [Jer. 23:29], and they are a shield for everyone who trusts in them, [Ps. 119:114]. God has earnestly commanded that persons should add nothing to his words, nor subtract anything from them, but only act according to his word and command, Deut. 4:2; 12:32. And Christ says in the gospel: One shall live by every word that proceeds from the mouth of God, Deut. 8:3; Matt. 4:4. Therefore one must believe every word of God, and not only some of them when they please us, and reject others.

The third characteristic of true faith is that it seeks God alone and eternal salvation, Col. 3:1. It searches for the invisible heavenly things, putting behind it everything that is temporal and perishable, knows no one according to the flesh, 2 Cor. 5:[5], does not taste human things but divine things, and does not look at any person's work and righteousness but at Jesus Christ alone.

Abraham, the father of all believers, had such faith, for he believed God above nature in the conception and sacrifice of Isaac, Rom. 4:[16f.]; Gal. 3:6. He also believed every word of God, Gen.

15:5[f.]; 17:1[f.], 22[f.], not seeing, although it was difficult for his flesh, as one can certainly observe in the matter of the circumcision, and that he so willingly offered his son Isaac to the Lord. He also did not look at things according to temporal matters, but left his father's house, Heb. 11:8[-10], (according to God's command), and looked for another city which has its foundation /275/ in heaven, whose Builder and Creator is God, as the apostle says. By this it is evident that those who have true faith reject all human doctrines and opinions, hold his Word alone for truth. They also acknowledge God's words as true and obey them, and seek the eternal heavenly things with full zeal. Again, to put any human doctrine above or equal with God's Word, to reject any words of God, to seek any temporal thing more than God's kingdom and his righteousness, Matt. 6:33; 22:[37], those who do so are unbelievers even if they speak so beautifully of the Scripture and faith. It is but an idle chattering which merits nothing. From this faith springs love, which is the highest and first command, both in the law and the gospel, that is, that we should love God with all our heart, all our soul, with all our strength and with all our abilities, Deut. 6:5. The other is the same, that we should love our neighbors just as ourselves. On these two commandments hang all the law and the prophets, as Christ says.

But now the love of God must take precedence, so that one must leave everything, every creature, everything that is visible, yes father, mother, brothers, and sisters, wife, and children, Deut. 33:9; Matt. 10:37, and our own life, Luke 14:26, for God's will, as the Scripture plainly indicates in great clarity with words and examples. For God (who is a jealous and affectionate God, Exod. 20:5; Deut. 5:9) also wants love and affection from us, since he has commended his love to us, as Paul says, that Christ Jesus, his only born Son, has died for us godless ones, Rom. 5:6, he has shared his Holy Spirit with us, prepared his eternal kingdom for us, called us to a knowledge of his words, Rom. 1:[8]; 1 Cor. 1:2, and, in sum, has done every good thing for us. Therefore we must love him in turn above all that is in heaven and on earth. And we must show this love with eager keeping of all his commands, John 14:21; 15:10; 1 John 5:2, as Christ himself has taught us with clear words. Otherwise, there is no love, but a false boasting of love.

Thereafter, we must love the brethren, and the Scripture. Christ and his apostles have taught us so abundantly about this brotherly love, John 13:34; 15:12; Rom. 12:9[f.]; Col. 3:14; 1 Pet. 4:8; 2 Pet. 1:7, so we do not need to write more about it. But this love is not only found in supplying the bodily needs of our poor brothers, but one remembers the brothers and sisters in every prayer, prays to the Lord for them, cares for their souls, and if one sees anyone falling from the way of truth, we should instruct him with God's Word and with a gentle spirit, so that we may uphold his soul and win it from destruction, Gal. 6:[2ff.]; James 1:21; 1 John 5:16. /276/

Where this love is, everything is good. Yes, God is there, who himself is love, 1 John 4:8; there Christ dwells; there the Holy Spirit lives; there is the lovely gathering of the brothers and sisters who are one in heart and soul, Acts 2:44; 4:32. There flows healing from the head of Christ, the holy oil of gladness, upon all the members. There the dew of his divine grace falls on Mount Zion and makes them fruitful in all righteousness and holiness, for those are well-liked by God. There God bestows his heavenly benediction and gives eternal life. There is the heartfelt joy, not of the flesh, but of the spirit. There is that beautiful Jerusalem that comes from above, Gal. 4:26; Rev. 21:2, that will be built as a city and holds one another fast to each other. There the tribes of Israel gather to praise God. There the Holy Spirit makes the consciences and hearts of the believers at rest and peaceful in genuine Christian love and unity. There also is the living hope through which one hopes to be saved by the grace of Jesus Christ, yes, that one is aware and certain of his salvation, that one feels the witness of the Holy Spirit in the heart. There one is assured of being a child of God, Rom. 8:16, of the brotherhood of Jesus Christ, and the fellowship of the Holy Spirit, 2 Cor. 13:[14].

There the person becomes so free, so well comforted, and so happy of heart that he is rich in the midst of poverty, is happy in oppression, persecution, prison, yes, in the middle of death. And he says with Paul, I know whom I have believed, 2 Tim. 1:12, and that one becomes my refuge, that is, the crown of righteousness that he has entrusted and given to me, well kept against that day, 2 Tim. 4:8. That agrees with what the prophet says: The Lord is my light and my salvation, of whom shall I be afraid; the Lord is the strength of my life, before whom shall I shudder, Ps. 27:1. Likewise, God is our refuge and strength, a help in great need which has afflicted us. Therefore we do not fear, although the world were to come to an end, and the mountain was sinking into the middle of the sea. Although the sea were raging, and flowed into a heap, and the mountains quaked before the same tempest, the city of God shall still remain standing firm and delightful with its fountains. There are the holy dwellings of the most high. God is within them, therefore they shall certainly remain, God helps them, Ps. 46:[1-5], and the prophet says further: Oh Lord, whenever I but have you, then I do not ask for heaven and earth, /277/ even though my body and soul were languishing. So are you, oh God, even the comfort of my heart and my portion, Ps. 73:25[-26].

Such is the liberty brought about by a living hope in God, and the certain assurance of the grace of Jesus Christ, and the victory seal of eternal salvation by the Holy Spirit, Rom. 8:16; 2 Cor. 1:21[f.]; Eph. 4:3. Through this the heart becomes so happy that people everywhere are comforted, and have a desire to come to the Lord, and to possess in true being everything that he now expects by faith according to hope, and sees but recognizes through a mirror and dark word, 1 Cor. 13:12.

Therefore my beloved and cherished friends in the Lord and elect of God in Jesus Christ, be attentive to the true knowledge of God, remain firm in the faith, love God and the brotherhood of Jesus Christ, and hope in his grace. So shall you nevermore come to shame. Watch out for all false teaching, Matt. 7:15, for all idolatry, 1 Cor. 10:[14], for every appearance of evil, 1 Thess. 5:22. Do not let yourself be terrified by tyrants and persecutors. Do not fear mortal human beings, Luke 12:4, but fear the almighty living God who has created you, has given body and soul, and has called you to his eternal, unperishable kingdom. Think about the great joy and glory that shall be revealed to you in the future, Rom. 8:17, and in the appearing of our Lord Jesus Christ, 1 Pet. 1:3. Take as example the patience of all the holy people of God, who have been from the beginning of the world, James 5:10, and have suffered and followed their faith, Heb. 12:1. But the God of all grace, and the Father of all mercy who through Jesus Christ has chosen you to eternal glory, may he strengthen, empower, and establish you in his eternal truth, 1 Pet. 5:10, complete you in the faith and in every good work, and keep you for his heavenly kingdom, Heb. 12:28, that you may inherit it with all the saints and occupy it eternally. Amen.

THE TABERNACLE OF MOSES

A very beautiful and truthful explanation and interpretation of the tabernacle or tent of Moses wherein many beautiful and necessary figures of the Old Testament are lifted out and harmonized with the spirit of the New Testament, to the service and profit of all lovers of the truth who seek and desire to understand the spirit of the letter. /279/

By D. P.

The Lord said to Moses, "See that you make everything according to the pattern which was shown to you on the mountain," Heb. 8:5.

The Greeting /280/

Grace, peace, and true knowledge of the divine Word be increased with all true Christians and lovers of the eternal truth from God the heavenly Father, and Jesus Christ, our Lord and Savior, through the power of the Holy Spirit. Amen.

/281/ It is, in part, wellknown to all brothers and companions of our Christian faith that for some period of time a strange and curious, yes, an alien teaching of the tabernacle of Moses and the disputed passages (just as it sounds and appears according to the letter) of the Holy Scripture has been introduced and taught by some persons. From this (according to our understanding and also according to our research) no improvement of life, nor of love, nor of faith has come, but many more sects, great errors, and harmful annoyances have taken their origin, both in and outside of the Christian congregation. Through this we were caused, according to the grace of God given to us, to write against such misleading teaching, not to seek our praise and glory, (for he who seeks his own glory is not a messenger of God, nor a witness to the truth, John 7:18), but alone to the praise of God and to seek for Christian unity. For our Lord and Savior, Jesus Christ,

The Tabernacle of Moses / 265

is a Lord of peace and love and unity in all his congregations. And he has proclaimed to us and left behind a saving teaching out of the mouth of the most high God, his heavenly Father, which teaching is a secure way, an eternal truth, and everlasting life, John 14:6. And if so be that we all alike with our whole hearts believe in this teaching, remain therein, and earnestly observe it, then we shall not come to shame in eternity. Yes, then shall the Holy Spirit, who is poured out upon us from the Father, abide with us, dwell within us and bring love, peace, and unity among us. And he shall not leave us as long as we abide in Christ and keep his teaching, John 14:16. For that is the office and work of the Holy Spirit to declare Christ Jesus and proclaim his teachings to humanity. Therefore he also has desire for those who walk in and act according to the divine peace in true unity of the faith and saving teachings of Jesus Christ.

But those who quarrel with Christ and with his congregation /282/ and bring in a sect or a strange teaching contrary to the gospel of Jesus Christ, from such the Holy Spirit departs and has no fellowship with them, Wisd. of Sol. 1:4[-5]. Therefore, all their undertakings shall have no progress; all their teaching is powerless and fruitless, and they shall also not remain standing before the judgment of God, Ps. 1:[5-]6. Therefore, all our desire and seeking is toward God that he would give us his grace that we may abide with Jesus Christ, his beloved Son, our Lord, keep his teaching and follow in his footsteps. He is our Shepherd and we are the sheep of his pasture, [Ps. 23:1-2]; Isa. 40:11; Ezek. 34. He is our Lord and Master, and we are his servants and disciples in order to serve him with all obedience and keep his commandments, Matt. 10:[12-14]; John 10:[26-27]; Matt. 23:[8-10]; [John 13:13].

Now that we are all the sheep of Christ Jesus, the one good Shepherd, we must all walk in the one way and follow the one Shepherd, John 10:4. If we are all servants and disciples of the one Lord and Master, Jesus Christ, then we must hear his teaching only and keep only his commandments, John 14:21; 15:10. For both his Word and commandments are spirit and life, and eternal truth and power of God to salvation to everyone who believes thereon and directs his walk according to them, 1 John 5:3; Rom. 1:16; 1 Cor. 1:16[-17].

Therefore, we must believe the teaching of Jesus Christ entirely, earnestly keep his commandments, and in addition neither introduce nor accept anything new, so that true peace may be and remain among us. For to that we are called, and therefore Christ has reconciled us with his precious blood to God the Father, Rom. 5:1; Eph.

2:13, so that we should have peace with God and with each other in truth and righteousness. Again, therefore, we are baptized through one Spirit, into one body, 1 Cor. 12:13. Yes, therefore Christ is our head, and his Holy Spirit is our life so that we should all alike hold firmly to Christ, Eph. 4:16, become conformed to him, Rom. 8:29, and proceed in the one Holy Spirit, speak through him alone, and be driven of him to all true peace, to all perfect love and unity. But now at this time, many seek wisdom with the Greeks and do not allow themselves to be satisfied with the gospel, while nevertheless in Jesus Christ lie hidden all the treasures of the wisdom and knowledge of God, Col. 2:[3]. Wherefore Paul also prided himself that he wished to know nothing other than Jesus Christ and him crucified, 1 Cor. 2:2.

We pray and desire also from everyone who boasts to have faith in Christ that he, with Paul and with all true Christians, will thus hold to Christ and his teaching, /283/ that he would shun all strange teaching which is against the gospel, although it appears ever so beautiful, and pursue peace, Rom. 12:18, not seeking his own honor, that he may say with the prophet, "Not to us, not to us, oh, Lord, but to your name give honor," Ps. 115:1.

Also, we would beseech and admonish all brothers, through the mercy of God and the love of Jesus Christ, Rom. 12:1, that you read these, our writings, with simple and unbiased eyes and with impartial heart,and measure them with the plumb line of the divine Word. For we desire nothing other than to uphold the praise of God, Rom. 15:9, that the truth may take the upper hand and all eyes may see the glory of God: the eternal, almighty, merciful, and only wise God, 1 Tim. 1:17, give us and all our brothers wisdom and understanding, in order to distinguish righteousness from unrighteousness, light from darkness, and truth from falsehood, so that we may be safeguarded from all errors and may be preserved in the saving teaching of Christ.

The eternal, almighty, and only wise God, 1 Tim. 1:17, had made Moses, his servant, a tabernacle or tent according to the model that he had seen, Exod. 25:8[-9], and this tent was divided into three parts, that is, into the courtyard, into the holy place, and into the holy of holies. And this was a figurative action of God with Israel, and it took place as an illustration of future things. For the law has the shadow of the coming good things but not the reality of these good things themselves, just as the apostle said to the Hebrews, Heb. 10:1. Similarly [the apostle writes] to the Corinthians that many things happened to the Israelites in figures but were written for our learning, 1 Cor. 10:[1]. Thus it is also without doubt that the tabernacle of Moses, built according to God's command, is a figure and image of the true reality which is signified through it. For it was not built in vain by Moses according to God's command, but the Lord therewith wished to give us to know something in particular. Yes, the truth of the New Testament is therewith established. And this is then a firm and immovable ground, whenever the shadows and sayings of the law come together and are in agreement with the truth of the gospel. Therefore, Christ also says in the gospel that every scribe who has been taught for the kingdom of heaven is like the father of a household who brings out of his treasure both old and new, Matt. 13:52.

But now the figures of the Old Testament must be well /284/ observed and understood, not according to human tradition, 2 Pet. 1:20, but just as they came forth from God through the Holy Spirit, were spoken and given, thus they must also be revealed, taught, and interpreted to Christians through the same Spirit. Therefore, we also do not think to write something new or strange about the tabernacle of Moses, but the apostolic interpretation is the foundation upon which we build. Also we interpret some things a little more broadly than the apostle did. Nevertheless, there is one foundation. But the present necessity and the misunderstanding of some brethren move and cause us to clarify these things more broadly. Even then, the apostle is our master teacher in these matters, and his interpretation we wish actually to follow just as it came out of the Holy Spirit, and thereby we wish simply to remain.

In the first place then, we wish to note the words of the apostle to the Hebrews, with which he has revealed and written the correct understanding of the tabernacle.

As it was then ordained, so the priests did the service of God in the first tabernacle, Heb. 9:6. But into the second tabernacle, the high priest went alone once a year, not without blood which he offered for himself and for the people in their ignorance. Thereby the Holy Spirit indicated that the way to the holy place had not yet been revealed, so long as the first tabernacle still remained standing, as a parable of the time which was then present, in which gifts and sacrifices were offered, which could not make the consciences of those who offered them perfect. For it was no more than food and drink, and manifold washings, and justifications of the flesh, which at that time were instituted for improvement.

These words give us a clear understanding of the tabernacle, therefore they must also be well observed. In the first place then, the apostle thus speaks of two tabernacles, that is, of the holy place and the holy of holies. Of the courtyard he says nothing in particular, except that it was an entrance to the tabernacle. He names the first tabernacle a parable of the time which was then present, in order to indicate to us with the two tabernacles two times; (that is, the time of the law and the time of the gospel.) For just as the tabernacle of Moses was built at God's command, one tabernacle and one holy place, /285/ even though it was divided into two parts, and each had its own wash basins, sacrifices or offerings, and its own glory, thus also the law and gospel are one Word and one truth of God. Nevertheless, they are also divided, namely, the law has the shadow of the coming good things, but the gospel has the being of these things themselves, Heb. 10:1. The law has many figures and ceremonies, Col. 2:16; which are all fulfilled in Christ, but the gospel has the clear steadfast truth which abides in eternity. The law is the letter which kills, but the gospel is the Spirit which makes alive, 2 Cor. 3:7[-8]; John 6:63.

Therefore the gospel and the law are divided so far as the figures, shadows, and letter of the law are concerned or involved, which are all removed through the gospel. But it is because of this that one observes the spirit of the law, (for the law is also spiritual, as Paul says), Rom. 7:14. So we discover that the meaning, content, and actual understanding of the law accords with the gospel in every way and corresponds with it, yes, is one truth. For just as there is not more than one God, so also there is not more than one truth: for God himself is the truth. But the letter (in which the truth is hidden), will indeed come to an end. Thus that literal command of the Lord about the circumcision of the flesh has come to an end. Nevertheless, that command of the spiritual circumcision of the heart thus remains, Rom. 2:29; Col. 2:11. Yes, thus have all the figures of the law (which are too long to relate here) come to an end so far as the letter is concerned. Nevertheless, the genuine and essential significance of these same figures remains and harmonizes with the gospel.

Thus the apostle correctly and with all insight compares and indicates that the tabernacle of the Lord (which was divided into two parts and was nevertheless one tabernacle) with the law and the gospel of the two Testaments are one in spirit and truth and belong to each other. Therefore Paul also said that the believing Israelites and we have one spirit of faith, 2 Cor. 4:13. Also thus have the apostles, yes, the Lord Jesus Christ himself, frequently and many times, established the truth of the gospel with the sayings and testimonies of the law and the prophets, thereby letting us know that the truth of the gospel is included in the law and the prophets.

In the second place, the apostle says that the priests went into the first tabernacle, for they had to sacrifice to the Lord daily /286/ which indicates the imperfection of the law, Heb. 9:6, as the apostle says in the same letter that the law has not brought us to perfection, but it is an introduction to a better hope through which we draw near to God, Heb. 7:18. But into the holy of holies, says the apostle, the high priest went alone once a year and offered there a sacrifice. This signifies to us that Jesus Christ has made a sacrifice (wherewith we are reconciled to God), and that sacrifice shall not happen any more, for it endures eternally and is sufficient for the sins of the entire world. And that is prefigured through the fact that the high priest yearly offered a single sacrifice in the holy of holies and that no one of the priests, of the Levites, or of the whole people of Israel might go into the holy of holies in order to offer the yearly sacrifice and reconcile the Lord, other than the high priest alone, who was ordained of God thereto, Exod. [30]:10, Heb. 9:7. Thus no one was able to reconcile us to God, than Jesus Christ alone, the true high priest, anointed by God the Father with the Holy Spirit and ordained according to the order of Melchizedek, Ps. 110:4; Heb. 5:9[-10]; 7:[17]; 9:[7].

In the third place, so says the apostle, the priests went daily into the holy place and there sacrificed to the Lord, but the high priest went into the holy of holies once a year, but not without blood, which he offered for himself and for the people in their ignorance. Therewith the Holy Spirit signified that the way to the holy place was not yet revealed so long as the first tabernacle still stood. This signified to us not only the one sacrifice of Christ, which is spoken of above, but also that as long as the law of Moses was in its power and ran in its true course, then the gospel of grace in Christ Jesus was indeed promised, but had not yet appeared or been revealed in glory.

But when this was revealed, then the law of Moses, according to the letter, had to cease and come to an end in Christ. Yes, as Jesus Christ, the true High Priest came, he went into the holy of holies and offered there his own flesh and blood as a sweet smelling offering to God the Father for the sin of the whole world, with which sacrifice he has opened a new and living way to the holy of holies (that is, to the hiddenness and fellowship of the divine and heavenly goods, yes, to heaven itself) for all those who believed in him, Eph. 5:2; Heb. 7:26; [9]:14; Rom. 5:10; 8:3; 2 Cor. 5:21. For just as he through his death /287/ destroyed death, and through sin (that is, through his sacrifice for sin) condemned sin, thus he has through that veil, that is, through his flesh, taken away the veil before the holy of holies. And this is clearly to be observed through the fact that the veil before the holy of holies was rent in the death of Christ Jesus, Matt. 27:[51]; Mark 15:38; Luke 23:44[-45]. This is a sure sign that through the Lord Jesus Christ the veil that hung before the face of Moses (because the children of Israel could not bear the glory of his face) is removed and his death is the portal and entrance into eternal life, to the kingdom of heaven, and that the most costly and most glorious gifts of God are given and revealed to us, and that we have free access to God, who now speaks to us from the throne of grace, that is, through Jesus Christ, who has reconciled us with God through his flesh and blood, which he has sacrificed in the holy of holies as the only true and most holy sacrifice. And all who believe in Christ have come to faith in his name in the Holy Spirit, 1 Pet. 1:18[-19]; Heb. 10:19; 12:22[-24].

In this manner we understand by the priests and the Levites and by that holy place in which they served, that they served Moses and his law in the time of the Old Testament. But by the high priest and the holy of holies, where he entered once a year and offered a sacrifice for his and the people's sins, we understand Jesus Christ, our High Priest, his gospel, his death and sacrifice, and the time of grace which from God has fully appeared to all people in Jesus Christ as an eternal comfort and salvation of all penitent or converted and believing souls, Titus 2:11; 3:4[-5].

Again, there was also placed between the tent of witness and the altar a hand basin, and there was water to wash, for Aaron and his sons washed their hands and their feet in it, Exod. 30:17[-18]. For they had to wash themselves as they were to go into the tent of witness or to come to the altar; thus the Lord had commanded them. This signifies to us that all those who wished to go into the house of the Lord, in order to serve God and to make a sacrifice or offering to the Lord, these had to cleanse themselves of all filthiness of spirit and the flesh, and lift up holy hands to God, and wash off with the waters of the Holy Spirit the evil lusts and desires which strive against the soul. For whoever desires to serve and sacrifice to God must do so with a clean heart and a good conscience, and with an unfeigned faith, yes, in the Spirit and in truth. Otherwise it is an uncleanness and an abomination before the Lord. Therefore it is written, "Guard your /288/ foot when you go to the house of God, draw near to hear, for that is better than to offer the sacrifice of fools, for they are offered in sin," Eccles. 5:1. Again, the sacrifice of the godless is an abomination to the Lord, Prov. 15:[8]. Again, to the impure all things are impure, and a godless person can neither speak nor do anything good, Prov. 21:27.

Furthermore, it must be remembered that in the holy place was the golden candelabra or lampstand with its seven branches and with its seven lights or candles, which burned at all times before the Lord and were never extinguished. This candelabra is a clear figure of Jesus Christ. The pure gold of the candelabra represents (according to our understanding) the most holy both of the divinity and humanity of Jesus Christ. The seven branches of the candelabra signify the seven spirits which rest upon Christ of whom the prophet Isaiah said, "There shall come forth a branch from the stump of Jesse, and a branch shall grow out of his roots. On him shall the Spirit of the Lord descend, the spirit of truth and understanding, the spirit of counsel and might, the spirit of knowledge and the fear of the Lord. And his delight shall be with the fear of the Lord," Isa. 11:1[-3]. Thus the seven spirits rested upon Christ and are prefigured and signified through the seven branches of the candelabra. The seven burning lights of the candelabra indicate the seven powers of the seven spirits of Christ, and also the clarity of his divine Word, Ps. 19:9; 119:105; that there is an eternal and true light, as the prophet says. And the fact that this candelabra (being a figure of Christ), nevertheless stood in the holy place, indicates to us that in the law, shadows, promises, and prophecies about Christ are included.

Also thus the golden table was in the first tabernacle, and upon the table the shewbreads were always before the Lord, and no one might eat thereof except the priests alone, and the children of Aaron, Exod. 25:[30]; Matt. 12:4; Ps. 23:5. This table with the shewbreads signifies the Holy Scripture and the Word of God which is a bread of life and a food for souls, John 6:53. And that no one might eat of the shewbreads except the priests alone and the children of Aaron. This signifies to us that God's Word is applicable to none except the true Christians who have all been made kings and priests of Christ, Rev. 1:6, and are given to him as children by God, just as he himself says, "Behold, I, and my children whom the Lord has given me," Heb. 2:13.

These children of the spiritual Aaron, Jesus Christ, have God's Word as food and the Holy Scripture as a table prepared from the Lord, just as the prophet says, "Oh Lord, /289/ you have prepared me a table against all my enemies," Ps. 23:5. But those who are not of the race and seed of Christ, these have no part at this table nor at the shewbreads. Wherefore Christ also spoke to his disciples, "To you it has been given to know the secrets of the kingdom of God, but to them it has not been given," Matt. [13:11].

Further, thus the golden altar was in the first tabernacle, whereupon the high priest burned the costly incense to the Lord as a sweet smelling savor. This indicates to us that Jesus Christ, the true high priest, has offered his precious flesh and blood for us to God the Father as a sweet-smelling savor, Heb. 5:1; 6:20; 8:1, through the fire of his love, and that we out of grace have become a kingdom of priests according to the image of Jesus Christ, Acts 20:28, in order to bring God the Father spiritual and living sacrifices which are acceptable to him through Jesus Christ, Heb. 9:12; Rom. 12:1; Eph. 5:2; 1 Pet. 2:5.

All these figures were in the first tabernacle for the sake of the things previously written about, that is, on account of the fact that the law points toward Christ with images, promises and prophecies and is an introduction to a better hope, Heb. 7:18.

But in the holy of holies was the ark of acadia wood and it was overlaid with all the finest gold, Exod. 25:10, and it was a figure of the Christian congregation, just as was also the ark of Noah, Gen. 8:16; 1 Pet. 3:20. In this ark were the tablets wherein God had written the Ten Commandments with his finger, Jer. 31:33; and this signified to us that God has given his law into the hearts of Christians, and has written his commandments therein with his Holy Spirit as in fleshly tablets, 2 Cor. 3:3; Heb. 8:10. Furthermore, the heavenly bread was in the ark, a figure of Christ Jesus, the true heavenly bread, John 6:51; and the eternal word of the Father, through which our souls must live, John 1:1; 1 John 1:1. That figurative heavenly bread was in a golden vessel which gives us to understand that the hearts of believers, upon which God's Word shall rest, must be clean, pure, and bright.

Also the rod of Aaron was in the ark, which was the only one that bloomed among the twelve rods of the twelve tribes of Israel, Num. 17:1[-8]; even though it was indeed at first dry, Heb. 9:4; which admonishes and signifies to us that Jesus Christ was elected of God as High Priest above all his brothers, Ps. 45:[7-]8; Heb. 1:9, and that through him the curse of the law is taken away and changed into a blessing, Gal. 3:13. [So] that whereas we who were completely terrified and made fearful before the law, have now received the comforting and saving gospel, Rom. 3:[21-26].

The mercy seat, which was made of the very finest gold, also stood on the ark, Exod. 25:17, and is a figure of Christ Jesus, Rom. 3:25, who is given to us of God the Father as a mercy seat, /290/ Heb. 5:[1-6]; and placed by God as head of the congregation, just as the mercy seat stood on top of the ark, Eph. 1:22; 4:15; Col. 1:18. And above the mercy seat between the two cherubims was the place out of which God through Moses gave his commands to the Israelites, and this signifies to us that God has spoken through Jesus Christ and has given his commandments to all Christians through him, and that the evangelical teaching in origin came out of the invisible God through Jesus Christ, Heb. 1:2; John 5:30; 7:16; 8:28; 12:49; 14:10.

In addition, two cherubims were made of the very finest gold and covered the mercy seat with their wings, their faces looking one toward the other, [Exod. 25:20], which signifies to us the two Testaments which agree with each other and point us unitedly toward Christ, who is included in both Testaments, the end of the Old and the beginning of the New Testament, Rom. 10:4.

Thus whoever will note these figures and their significance may clearly understand and acknowledge that the two tabernacles, that is, the holy place and the holy of holies portray and signify the two times, the time of the law and of the gospel, Heb. 9:1. Yes, the apostle has expressly (as was said above) indicated the first tabernacle and the sacrifices which were offered therein and were imperfect (because they could justify no one nor make them perfect) at the time of the law. But the high priest and the sacrifice that was offered by him once a year in the holy of holies, he has pointed toward Jesus Christ and toward his one sacrifice. Out of this it follows incontrovertibly that Jesus Christ offered his sacrifice in the holy of holies. Wherefore the holy of holies also signifies without any doubt the time of grace and of the New Testament.

But now some persons have not observed these figures, and they have not been satisfied with the apostolic exposition of the tabernacle, but they have found and considered a strange exposition that is, that they make a distinction between Christians out of the tabernacle. Some they place in the courtyard, some into the holy place, and some into the holy of holies. In addition, they have considered two names, that is, those whom they place into the courtyard and in the holy place. These they call Esau's children, but those whom they place into the holy of holies, these they call Jacob's children. Esau's children they call warriors, carnal and firstborn children of God. Jacob's children they call conquerors, spiritual, and born again children of God.

But this interpretation of the tabernacle is in every way /291/ contrary to the biblical Scripture and is not conformed to the gospel. For in the first place, Esau is no figure of the Christians, but of the Jews or Israelites. But Jacob was a figure of the Christians. For as Rebecca had conceived of Isaac, and the children struggled with each other in her body, and she was troubled because of it, then God the Lord spoke to her, saying, "Two kinds of people are in your womb, and two peoples shall be divided out of your body; the one people shall conquer the other people, the larger shall serve the smaller," Gen. 25:[23]. These words must be well observed, namely, that God spoke about two peoples, and that the peoples should be divided, and that one people should conquer the other, and finally that the larger should serve the smaller.

In the first place, God spoke of two peoples; therefore then, this is not said about Christians only. The reason: Christians are not two peoples but one holy people, one chosen race, one royal priesthood, one congregation of the one God, one Lord, one Holy Spirit, one Christian faith, one baptism, having a single promise and a single hope of salvation, Exod. 19:6; Gal. 3:28; 1 Pet. 2:9; Eph. 4:4.

Since then such unity is among true Christians, yes, since they are one body in Christ Jesus, Rom. 12:4; 1 Cor. 12:27; Eph. 1:[22-]23; therefore they may not be divided among themselves nor be two different peoples. But the two peoples of whom the Lord spoke to Rebecca; these are the Edomites and Israelites who came from Esau and Jacob or Israel, who had a great and powerful enmity with each other. Therefore it does not agree with the truth if one should call some Christians Esau's children and some Jacob's children.

In the second place, thus God said to Rebecca, that two peoples should be separated out of her body. That is said according to the letter about Esau and Jacob. For the Edomites were enemies and persecutors of the Israelites, just as the prophet complained before the Lord and cried over Sodom saying, "Remember, oh, Lord, the children of Edom in the day of Jerusalem, how they said, 'Raze it, raze it! Down to its foundations!' " Ps. 137:7. For this reason God also threatened Edom through Obadiah and said, "You shall be destroyed through murder on all the hills of Esau on account of the violence and injustice which you have done to your brother Jacob," Obad. 1:9[-10].

Since then the situation between Israel and Edom stood thus, how may any Christian be compared with Esau? /292/ For the Christians are after all never any two peoples, who hate and persecute one another, as Esau hated and persecuted Jacob. But they are called of God in peace, yes, they are baptized and joined together through one spirit into one body. And thus whoever is not one in heart, soul and spirit with the body of Christ, that one is no Christian, 1 Cor. 12:13; 7:14. And above all this Christ has thus made of two peoples, that is, of Jews and Gentiles, one people with his death and precious blood, Eph. 2:12[-14]. He has gathered all his sheep into one sheepfold, John 10:16. Out of which then, the unity of Christians is easily understood, and also, that no Christian, therefore, may be held to be an Edomite or Esau's son, Ezek. 35:15.

In the third place, so said God the Lord to Rebecca, that one people should conquer the other. That has happened, both according to the letter and according to the spirit. For to speak according to the letter, the children of Jacob have overcome the children of Esau and reigned over them, just as one reads in the book of Kings and Chronicles. But according to the spirit, the children of Jacob, that is, the true Christians, have gone beyond the children of Esau, that is, the Jews. The royal scepter has been taken from the Jews, the temple is destroyed, the priesthood, together with the altar and the sacrifices, is completely lost, Hos. 3:4. In addition, because of their unbelief and disobedience, the kingdom of God has been taken from the Jews and given to the Gentiles, who through their faith in Jesus Christ have overcome all the righteousness of the Jews (which they have sought through works of the law), 2 Esd. 1:24; Matt. 21:43; Acts 13:46. For the conquest of Christians against all their enemies is a pure faith in Jesus Christ and the righteousness which avails before God, and does not come out of works of the law but out of faith in Jesus Christ, 1 John 5:4; Rom. 3:21. And those who have such a faith are the true children of Abraham who are blessed in the true Isaac in the promised seed, (that is, in Christ Jesus), Rom. 9:6[-7]; Gal. 3:16.

These are the spiritual Israel, who have over them a king, Jesus Christ, and his name is, "Wonderful, Counselor, mighty God, eternal Father, Prince of Peace," whom God his Father has given the throne of David, Luke [1:32], and he shall reign in the house of Jacob until in eternity, Ps. 45:[6-]7; Heb. 1:8, and the scepter of his kingdom is an eternal scepter without end, Isa. 9:[6-7]. Thus the Christians have overcome the Jews through their faith in Jesus Christ, who is a king in eternity, and the scepter of his kingdom is an eternal scepter, which will not be taken away, as the Jewish scepter has been taken away, Gen. 49:10. /293/

In the fourth place, thus God said to Rebecca, "The greater shall serve the smaller," Gen. 25:[23]. This has taken place according to the letter with Jacob and Esau, but according to the spirit with the Jews and Christians. For according to the letter and figure Esau, was the greatest and the firstborn, but Jacob was the youngest. Nevertheless, Esau was made a servant of his brother Jacob by Isaac, their father, Gen. 27:37[-40]. Thus it has also happened with Jews and Christians. For God the heavenly Father had at first chosen the Jews or the children of Israel as his people above all races of the earth, Rom. 11:2;

Exod. 13:1[-2]; and loved them as a firstborn son, just as Isaac had loved Esau, and had decorated them in costly and glorious attire (just as Esau had costly garments), and had betrothed them and revealed his word to them, Bar. 4:[36-]37.

But now they have observed the external works of the law and the letter of the prophets and have thought to receive the promised blessing of God through their own righteousness, not confessing that Jesus Christ is the true seed of which God spoke to the patriarch Abraham, "In your seed shall all the races of the earth be blessed," Gen. 22:18. This seed is Christ, as Paul said to the Galatians, Gal. 3:16.

This Jesus Christ the Jews have, through their carnal understanding of Scripture, rejected and sought to establish their own righteousness, Rom. 10:3. Thus they were not obedient to the true divine righteousness, but they have with all their running and chasing after the righteousness of the law not been able to receive the true blessing, just as Esau with all his hunting and catching of the game might not receive the first blessing of his father. But Jacob received it and came into the place of Esau, that is, the Gentiles through their faith in Jesus Christ are accepted and have become the true children and heirs of God. Hereof God said through the prophet, "I will call that my people that was not my people, and my beloved who was not my beloved, and it shall happen that in the places where it was said, 'You are not my people,' there they shall be called the children of the living God, Hos. 2:[23].

Paul says to the Romans, "What will we now say, then? This we will say, that the Gentiles who have not existed according to righteousness, nevertheless received it. (I speak about the righteousness which comes out of faith); but that Israel existed according to the righteousness of the law and could not succeed in it. Why? Because they did not seek righteousness out of faith, but out of the works of the law, etc." Rom. 9:30[-32]. /294/

These words testify clearly of the rejection of the Jews on account of their unbelief and of the election of the Gentiles through their faith in Jesus Christ, in whom they have received the blessing of God, the heavenly Father. For just as Isaac, whenever he smelled the smell of the precious and lovely scent of the clothes which Jacob had on, blessed him, Gen. 27:27[-29], thus as soon as God the heavenly Father, smelled the sweet odor of the sacrifice of Jesus Christ (with whom the Gentiles, who by their faith and true baptism accepted him, are clothed, robed, and become reconciled), thus God has blessed them, yes made them his children and heirs of his kingdom, Gal. 3:9.

Out of all these words it is clear that Esau was a figure of the Jews, but Jacob a figure of the Christians. In order to acknowledge this still more clearly, we want briefly to indicate three other figures who have a common meaning and significance with the figures of Jacob and Esau.

The first is the figure of Hagar and Sarah, together with their two sons, Ishmael and Isaac, of whom Ishmael was the firstborn son of Abraham and Isaac was born after him, Gen. 21:[1-21]. Even though Ishmael was born of the servant girl and Isaac of the free woman, nevertheless, the eldest had to serve the youngest, for Ishmael was with his mother, Hagar, cast out of the house of Abraham, and Isaac with his mother, Sarah, remained therein and became the true heir.

These figures the apostle Paul interprets to us thus—that the two wives of Abraham, with their two sons, are the two Testaments; Hagar with her son Ishmael, is the Old Testament and the Jews, Sarah with her son Isaac, however, is the New Testament and the Christians, Gal. 4:24[-30]. Just as Hagar was now overcome from Sarah, and on her account thrust out of the house of Abraham, and just as Ishmael, even though he was a son of Abraham, nevertheless had to yield to Isaac as the rightful heir; thus the figurative Jewish law had to cease in Jesus Christ. As the Christian congregation came, then the Jewish synagogue had to become the smallest and the least, just as it occurred with the servant girl and her mistress, yes, thus also the synagogue must yield and be entirely done away.

The second figure is that of Perez and Zerah, the two sons of Judah. When they were about to be born, Zerah came forth first and the midwife bound a red silk thread on his hand. Thereafter he drew his hand back, /295/ and Perez came first out of his mother's body after all. Therefore, he was also called Perez because he parted the middle wall between himself and his brother. Afterward Zerah was born and had a scarlet thread on his hand which the midwife had tied there, Gen. 38:27[-30]. Zerah who showed himself first, but was born last, prefigured the Jews who, after being the first became the last, as Christ testifies in the gospel, saying that the first should become the last and the last the first, Matt. 19:30; Luke 13:[30]. With these words Christ really meant the Jews and the Gentiles, for the Jews were the first, yes, they were a chosen people of God. Therefore, Christ also spoke to his apostles, at the time of the first mission, "Go nowhere on the streets of the Gentiles, nor on the towns of the Samaritans, but go rather to the lost sheep of the house of Israel," Matt. 10:5[-6]. Thus the Jews were the first, and the grace of God was first offered to them, but they have rejected Christ; therefore, they have become the last, Acts 13:46.

Also, it is to be noted that Zerah at his birth had a red thread bound to his hand, and this signifies to us that the Jews were given a law which punishes and kills, for according to the law (which punished many sins with death) thus much blood was shed, [2 Cor. 3:7-9]. This severity of the law, through which much blood was shed, is prefigured for us through the scarlet thread which Zerah had on the hand. But the Christians are signified through Perez, because for his sake the middle wall between himself and his brother was parted. Therefore, also his name was called Perez. Thus on account of the Christians the middle wall, which was between Jews and Gentiles, was taken away through Jesus Christ, who has made of two people one people, Eph. 2:13[-16]. And just as Perez in birth, after being the last became the first, because he parted the middle wall that was between the two (for so long as it was not broken he could not become the first); in like manner as the Gentiles accepted Christ and believed in him, they were born out of God and of the Christian church which is the mother of all Christians; and as Christ through his death had removed all that separated them from God, thus they through the death of Christ and through their faith in his name from being the last have become the first.

The third figure is that of Manasseh and Ephraim, the two sons of Joseph, whom as Joseph brought them before his father Jacob, on his account that they might be blessed by him, thus he placed Manasseh, the eldest, on the right hand of Jacob and Ephraim on his left hand. /296/ But Jacob laid his hands crosswise over each other, the right hand upon the head of the youngest and the left hand upon the head of the eldest. As Joseph saw this he was not well pleased and wanted to remove the right hand of his father from the head of Ephraim and lay it upon the head of Manasseh, and spoke to his father, it does not belong thus, for this one (that is Manasseh) is the first-born; lay your right hand upon his head. But Jacob answered and spoke, my son, I know well that this one (Manasseh) shall increase in people, but his younger brother shall be greater than he, Gen. 48:13[-20].

This has taken place, both according to the letter and according to the spirit. For according to the letter, Ephraim has indeed exceeded Manasseh and gone beyond him. Since the ark of the covenant was at Shiloh, and the worship of God, and Israel must appear there according to the law, and the rule in the time of the judges was largely under Ephraim. But Shiloh was destroyed on account of their sins, and Ephraim was rejected, and the tribe of Judah was chosen of the Lord and the temple was built in Jerusalem. Thus it has also happened with the Jews and Gentiles who have become believers in Christ, just as has been sufficiently explained above.

Thus in this manner these four figures now completely agree, that is, Ishmael and Isaac, Esau and Jacob, Perez and Zerah, Manasseh and Ephraim; and thus whoever correctly observes and understands the one, he understands them all. But we have related all of these, so that the figure from Esau and Jacob may be more easily understood.

Since then, we have exposited the figure of Esau and Jacob, according to the small gift which is given us of God; so we will further write a little more about it, in that some (we know not out of which Scriptures or reasons) have divided the Christians into warriors and conquerors, into carnal and firstborn children of God, and into spiritual and born-again children of God.

In the first place, they divide the Christians into warriors and conquerors. But we say that all pious Christians through God's grace are conquerors and warriors. The warfare of the Christians is manifold; for they have to strive against their own flesh, against sin, and against Satan with his ministers. Of this strife against the flesh, Paul says to the Galatians, "The flesh always desires against the Spirit, and the Spirit against the flesh; for these strive against each other, so that you do not do what you want," Gal. 5:17.

The Christians also have thus to fight against besetting /297/ sins, against the world, against Satan, and his ministers, Heb. 12:1. Of this warfare Paul writes to the Ephesians, as everyone may read, Eph. 6:[10-20]. Paul also had such warfare, for he said that a thorn of the flesh was given him as a messenger of Satan, who beat him with fists so that he should not exalt himself on account of the greater revelations which were shown him by God. And when he prayed to the Lord three times that Satan might go away from him, the Lord answered him, "Be content with my grace, for my power becomes stronger through weakness, [2 Cor. 12:7-9].

In these words of the apostle, we observe how God allows his saints to be tempted by Satan for the reason that they should learn to know their human weakness, humble themselves under the mighty hand of God, and rely upon the Lord's grace, [1 Pet. 5:6]. And they then will be strengthened by the Lord with his grace, and all the temptations of Satan will not harm them. Yes, Jesus Christ, our Lord and Savior, blessed in eternity, has himself striven with Satan and overcome him. For when he was baptized of John the Baptist, he was led of the Spirit into the wilderness in order to be tempted of Satan; Satan came to him and tested him with three temptations. But the Lord Jesus Christ overcame all the temptations and cunning of Satan with the sword of the Spirit, Matt. 4:1[-10].

This took place for the instruction and admonition of all pious Christians, so that they might know how they must allow themselves to be baptized with Christ, how they must be driven of the Spirit into the wilderness, and how they must fight with him against Satan and overcome him. Of this victory John also says, "I have written to you, young men, because you are strong, and have overcome the evil one," 1 John 2:[14].

Again, all that is born out of God overcomes the world, and our faith is the victory that has overcome the world, etc., 1 John 5:4. And in Revelation it stands written how the true Christians have overcome the dragon and his angels through the blood of the Lamb and through the word of their testimony, Rev. 12:[9-11].

Therefore, every Christian has to understand well that one may not divide Christians into warriors and conquerors; judging if some Christians fight all the time and never overcome, and that some have become completely victorious, and need not fight any more. But the issues do not resolve themselves thus, for fighting and overcoming both belong together. It is all in vain to have striven if one does not overcome, /298/ and no one may overcome unless he strives piously. In summary, every Christian has his temptations (for human life on earth is a struggle) and out of the temptation comes the struggle, but he who fights manfully and correctly, he overcomes, and, who overcomes receives the crown and shall possess and inherit everything with Christ, Rev. 2:7, 11, 17; 3:12, 21.

Further, as we have said above, some still marvelously divide Christians into spiritual and carnal children of God. The carnal ones they name the firstborn children of God, but the spiritual ones they name the born-again children of God. Hereupon we say in the first place that we do not find nor read in the Scriptures about the carnal children of God. For Christ himself says that God is a Spirit, and that all that is born out of the Spirit, that is a spirit, John 4:24; John 3:6. But now it is manifest that all Christians are born out of God (who is a Spirit), therefore they are also spiritual; yes, are partakers of the divine nature just as the apostle Peter says that to us the precious and great promises of God are given so that we through them should become companions of the divine nature so far as we flee from the corruption that is in the world through passionate desire, 2 Pet. 1:4.

Thus the Christians are now one spirit with God, out of whom they are born. But now some have an objection here, namely, that Paul wrote to the Corinthians (who were also Christians), "I have not been able to speak to you as spiritual but as of the flesh, as with children in Christ Jesus. I fed you with milk and not strong food for you were not yet able to bear it; and even yet you are not able [to receive it], for you are still of the flesh. For while there is jealousy, quarreling, and divisions among you, are you not of the flesh, and behaving according to the human way?," 1 Cor. 3:1 [-3].

Out of these words of Paul, some persons wish to assert that the weak and young Christians are the carnal children of God and should be so called. But we say that one may not thus understand the words of the apostle. For the reason Paul called the Corinthians carnal happened on this account; they were quarrelsome and partisan and also in part carnally-minded, as James says, "From where does quarreling and warfare come among you? Is it not out of the lusts that fight in your members?," James 4:1.

Now since the passionate desire of the flesh and ignorance were still found among the Corinthians, and also in part had the upper hand over the Spirit, therefore the apostle called them /299/ carnal. Nevertheless, they were also spiritual according to the new birth, after they had through faith received the gift of the Holy Spirit, according to the previously quoted words of the Lord: "What is born out of the Spirit, that is spirit," John 3:6. Again, "he who is united to the Lord becomes one spirit with him," 1 Cor. 6:17. Again, you are spiritual, that is, if the spirit of Christ dwells in you. Again, "whoever does not have the spirit of Christ does not belong to him," Rom. 8:9. Out of all this it is easily understood that all Christians are spiritual even though they may indeed still be tempted by the flesh, yes, indeed may become overrun and surprised with human frailties and mistakes.

Further, some thus (as is narrated above) distinguish between the firstborn and the born-again children of God. They call the firstborn children of God those who are weak and young in the faith, but those who are strong and manly in the faith, these they call the born-again children of God. But we contradict these. The reason is this: the entire Holy Scripture speaks of one new birth out of God which takes place out of the imperishable seed of God, through the power of the Holy Spirit together with true faith in Jesus Christ, 1 Pet. 1:23. For whoever believes that Jesus is the Christ, he is born out of God, as John says, 1 John 5:1. This new birth is also called born again in the Scripture because the human being is born the first time according to the flesh of Adam, and according to the Spirit is born again out of God. It also comes from this that the Scripture speaks about both the outer and the inner person, Col. 3:5. The outward the Scripture calls the fleshly, earthly, and perishable, which is of a corrupt and sinful character and nature, but the inner the Scripture calls the hidden person which is in the heart, which is created after God in righteousness, holiness, and truth, and therefore spiritual, heavenly, and imperishable; yes, has become participant of the divine character and nature, 1 Pet. 3:4; Eph. 4:24; 2 Pet. 1:4.

Thus Christians are born once out of God or born again; thereafter they grow in righteousness until they become mature persons in the faith and in the knowledge of Jesus Christ, the Son of God, Eph. 4:13[-15]. Just as a natural child, after its fleshly birth, grows up and increases through food and drink and through God's blessing and through the course of nature, thus also Christians are once born out of God; thereafter they grow up through the food of life and through that unadulterated milk, that is, through God's Word, just as Peter said, "Put away all malice and all guile, insincerity, envy, and all slander. Be like newborn babes, long for the sensible unadulterated milk, /300/ that by it you may grow up," 1 Pet. 2:1[-3].

Thus the children of God now grow and they become stronger and more mature in the faith and more perfect in the knowledge of God and his Son, Jesus Christ, but they are not born out of God more than once. Beyond this young and weak Christians may not be called firstborn children of God. For if it is so that we regard and observe the letter of the law, then the firstborn in the family in the Old Testament was the greatest. But if we observe the Spirit of the New Testament, then the apostles were the firstborn children of God, in part because they were first chosen of Christ to the faith and called to the office of preaching and came to the fellowship of the gospel. And also in part because they were the first, that is, they have had the most glorious and greatest gifts of the Holy Spirit, as Paul says, "We who have the first fruits of the Spirit," Rom. 8:23. And James says, God who is the Father of lights, "he has borne us by the word of truth that we should be the first fruits of his creatures," James 1:[18].

Again, in Revelation it is written about the hundred forty-four thousand who were bought from among the people as the first fruits unto God and to the Lamb, and these first fruits are pure virgins or maidens, in whose mouth no deceit was found and who are without blemish before the throne of God, Rev. 14:[2-5]. Out of all these it is evident that one should not call the young and weak Christians firstborn children of God, but the name belongs rather to the strong and perfect than to the sick and imperfect.

Also, some persons have proposed that the apostles did not sin any more after Pentecost; yes, that they were not able to sin, and that all who with the apostles have received the Spirit of the day of Pentecost (as they say) have come to the victory and are born again out of God, so that they cannot sin any more. To this we reply that the Scripture includes all humanity under sin and knows no one (except Christ Jesus alone) as entirely free from sin. For thus says Ecclesiastes, "There is no righteous person [on earth] who does good and does not sin," Eccles. 7:[20]. Again, Solomon says, "there is no person who does not sin," 1 Kings [8]:46. And David said, "Lord, enter not into judgment with your servant; for no one living is righteous before you," Ps. 143:2. /301/

But now some persons believe that these Scriptures witness only about young and weak Christians who are yet neophytes in the faith and have not yet received the strong spirit of faith and the knowledge of Jesus Christ. But against all such interpretations the high prophet of God, David, testifies and says, "O Lord, I have revealed my sin before you, and I did not hide my unrighteousness before you; I have said that 'I will confess against myself, my unrighteousness to the Lord'; and you have forgiven the evilness of my sins," Ps. 32:5. Therefore all the saints should pray to you at the appropriate time. David was a man of God, with greater wisdom, yes, endowed with a prophetic spirit from God. Just the same, he sinned, confessed his sins before the Lord, and prayed for the forgiveness of his sins or guilt, and also testified that all the saints must do the same. This Christ has also established in the gospel. For he taught his disciples a prayer in which they all the time, as often as they spoke it, had to confess their guilt before God the Father and ask him for forgiveness, Matt. 6:12. And this Christ did in order to teach all his disciples humility and to remove all false self-righteousness out of their hearts, "for God opposes the proud but gives grace to the humble," 1 Pet. 5:5. Yes, a humble spirit and a broken heart that sorrows on account of its sin and is diminished, seeks grace and mercy with God, doubts himself or despairs, and trusts wholly in God's fathomless mercifulness, such a heart is a pleasing and acceptable sacrifice and a sweet smelling savor before the Lord, Ps. 34:19; 51:[17]; Isa. 57:[15].

Therefore, all the saints have humbled themselves before the Lord and confessed themselves as sinners, for the Spirit of God, which is a spirit of wisdom and humility, has taught and granted them such a disposition. Through the Spirit the prophet thus called to the Lord and spoke, "If you, O Lord, should mark the misdeeds of sins, who could stand before you?" Ps. 130:3. Through the same Spirit, the apostles testified (also after Pentecost) as James says, "We altogether sin much," James 3:2. Again, Paul testified with clear words of the offenses of Peter (also after Pentecost) and said that he did not walk aright, according to the truth of the gospel, and also that Barnabas was led astray through his hypocrisy, wherefore he also openly disciplined Peter, Gal. 2:14. Again, John says, "If we say we have no sin, we deceive ourselves, and the truth is not in us. But if we confess our sins, God is faithful and just, and forgives us our sins and cleanses us from all evil. But if we say /302/ we have not sinned, we make him a liar, and his Word is not in us," 1 John 1:8[-10].

Out of these words of the apostle it is easily understood what evil comes out of falsehood and self-righteousness; namely, that when a person will not confess himself as a sinner, he misleads at first himself (according to the words of the apostle), for he regards himself more pious than he is and does not regard the divine grace. In the second place, no truth is in him, for he lied before the face of God, when he said he had no sins. In the third place, he thus makes God a liar; for the eternal and true God has testified, through the mouth of his saints, that all people are sinners just as the previously cited words of Scripture openly testify.

Thus the Scripture now includes all people (except Jesus Christ alone) under sin, Gal. 3:22; Rom. 3:9. Again the Scripture says that whoever is born out of God does not sin, for the seed of God remains in him and restrains him so that he cannot sin because he is born out of God, 1 John 3:9. Therefore one must know that a Christian has two natures in him; a carnal and sinful nature, which he has inherited from Adam; and a spiritual and divine nature, which is infused and imparted to him from God through Jesus Christ. For the Lord Jesus Christ himself said, "That which is born of the flesh is flesh, and that which is born of the Spirit is spirit," John 3:6.

Since then both of these births now occur in all Christians, namely while they are in part born out of the flesh and in part out of the Spirit. Therefore they must have both a carnal and a spiritual nature. According to the outward person, they are thus carnally minded, but according to the inner person, they are spiritually minded. Through the carnal nature they fall and sin, but through the divine nature they have a desire toward righteousness and wish to fulfill the will of God. The carnal nature must be overcome by the Spirit of God; nevertheless, flesh and blood retains its nature as long as it lives. Therefore, although someone has become participant of the spiritual and divine nature, he nevertheless remains frail and sinful, for he remains a human being; he is flesh and blood, and therein dwells nothing good, just as Paul says. For it has become corrupted, sinful, and desirous of evil through the disobedience of the first human being, so that no person who lives is entirely innocent /303/ before the Lord, and that is on account of his evil nature and the carnal lusts which tempt and cling to him, Rom. 7:18. Because of these reasons the justified person is still accused by the Scripture.

Again, after the justified person has been born out of God, and thus has become participant of the divine nature, 2 Pet. 1:4, yes, after he is a member of Jesus Christ and one spirit with the Lord, and Christ dwells in his heart through faith, Rom. 12:4[-5]; 1 Cor. 12:27; Eph. 1:23; 4:4; 1 Cor. 6:17, and the Holy Spirit has been given to him by God as a guarantee of salvation, 2 Cor. 1:22, therefore he may no longer be thus accused. For who will accuse him who is one with God, Rom. 8:33, who has God as a merciful Father, who has Jesus Christ as an Advocate, Intercessor, and High Priest, and is assured with the Holy Spirit for the day of deliverance, 1 John 2:1; Heb. 5:1[-10]; 6:20; Eph. 4:30? Therefore Paul said, "There is therefore now no condemnation for those who are in Christ Jesus, who walk not according to the flesh, but according to the Spirit," Rom. 8:[1-2]. Again, "who shall bring any charge against God's elect? It is God who justifies; who is to condemn? It is Christ who died, yes, much more, who was raised up, who is also at the right hand of God, and who prays for us," [Rom. 8:33-34.]

Thus one must now know that every individual Christian has sin and must confess himself as a sinner, so that he humbles himself under the mighty hand of God and prays to the Lord for his grace; and thus the Scripture remains true and unbroken, which accuses and disciplines all persons as sinners. But sin is not reckoned to the account of the Christian, but is already forgiven him through the innocent death of Jesus Christ, and covered with his eternal love whereby he has offered himself for us as an eternal reconciliation for our sins, and has taken our burden upon himself, paid our debt with his bitter suffering, and given us out of grace all that he has. Thus he is one with us and we with him; through which we are well pleasing to God, yes, are reckoned as God's saints, Rom. 4:7. Therefore David also says, "Blessed are they whose unrighteousness is forgiven, and their sins are covered. Blessed is the person to whom the Lord imputes no sin," Ps. 32:1[-2].

Enough has now been disclosed about these things to those of a good heart and goodwill and understanding. We must further interpret some passages of Scripture (which appear to sound contradictory to each other according to the letter) and for the Christian clarify them with the grace of God as an illustration of how one must deal with the Scriptures and not handle them with unwashed hands, as some do.

Christ says in the gospel, "He who comes to me shall /304/ not hunger, and he who believes in me shall not thirst in eternity," John 6:35. In Ecclesiasticus Jesus [son of] Sirach says of the wisdom of God, "Whoever eats me shall yet be more hungry after me; and whoever drinks me shall yet be more thirsty after me," Ecclus. 24:[21]. To understand these passages of Scripture correctly, one must note that Christ actually spoke of the satisfaction and refreshing which all Christians have at all times through God's Word and through the Holy Spirit, and shall have in perfection in eternity. For now that Christ is in them, and the Holy Spirit abides in them, they have at all times the bread of life for the hunger of the soul, and for their thirst the waters of the Holy Spirit; for Christ is the true bread of heaven, John 6:51, and whoever eats of this bread, that is, whoever believes and keeps the words of Christ, that one's soul shall suffer no hunger in eternity nor lack of the bread of life.

Christ also gives the waters of life as an eternal refreshing and quickening of the soul, just as he spoke to the Samaritan woman, "Whoever drinks of this water will thirst again, but whoever drinks of the water that I shall give him will never thirst in eternity; but the water that I shall give him will become in him a fountain of living water welling up to eternal life," John 4:13[-14]. And Christ said yet again, "Whoever believes in me, as the Scripture has said, 'Out of his body shall flow rivers of living water,'" John 7:38. This he said of the Holy Spirit (as John said), whom those who believe in him shall receive.

Now since then all true Christians have received the words of Christ (which are the food of life) and the Spirit (which is the water of life) and has included them in themselves, they can no longer suffer any hunger or thirst, so long as the words and the spirit of Christ (which is the water of life) remain in them. But the true, genuine, and perfect satisfaction and quenching they shall not receive until they are delivered out of all tribulation and have come to the perfect heavenly being, and God is all and in all, as Paul says, 1 Cor. 15:28. And in Revelation it is written about those who were clothed with white garments, "These are they who have come out of great tribulation, and have washed their robes and made them white in the blood of the Lamb. Therefore they are before the throne of God, and serve him day and night in his temple; and he who sits upon the throne will dwell above them. They shall hunger no more, neither thirst any more; the sun shall not strike them, nor any scorching heat. /305/ For the Lamb in the midst of the throne will pasture them, and he will lead them to springs of living water; and God will wipe away all tears from their eyes," Rev. 7:[14-17].

Out of these words it is clear and evident that the true satisfaction and quenching of the Christians shall come when their great tribulation has come to an end and they have come to the eternal tabernacle. Christ speaks about this satisfaction. But Ecclesiasticus speaks of a hunger and thirst which still remain in a Christian when he has already eaten the Word of God and drunk the water of life, Ecclus. 24:[21]. The reason? A Christian who is of a true character has at all times desire to hear God's Word, that the gifts of the Holy Spirit may be increased in him, that he may add to the knowledge of God and become more righteous, more pure, and more holy. Of such hunger and thirst, Christ spoke also in Matthew, "Blessed are those who hunger and thirst for righteousness, for they shall be satisfied," Matt. 5:6. In keeping with all such meanings, Christ also said, "He who is of God hears the Word of God," John 8:47. Again, in the Apocalypse the Spirit says, "So whoever is righteous, that one becomes still more righteous, and whoever is holy, he becomes still holier," Rev. 22:11.

In this way a Christian hungers at all times after God's Word, and thirsts after righteousness, for he has great sweetness and joy therein, just as David says, "The testimonies of the Lord are right, they are more precious than gold and precious jewels; they are sweeter also than honey and drippings of the honeycomb," Ps. 19:[8], 10. Again, the same prophet says, "Oh Lord, how sweet are your words to my mouth, yea, sweeter than honey to my throat!" Ps. 119:103.

In this way now the previously quoted words of Jesus Christ and those of Jesus [son of] Sirach or Ecclesiasticus agree, in this manner, in that Christ spoke about an eternal satisfaction which belongs alone to the future world and shall happen there. But Ecclesiasticus speaks about the hunger and the thirst which Christians have after righteousness here in this life. Now we want, with God's help, still to clarify some other passages of Scripture which some persons interpret very curiously and uniquely, and these are thus stretched or pressed into a strange meaning.

The patriarch Jacob said, "I have seen God face to face," Gen.

32:[30]. The apostle said, "No one has ever seen God," John 1:18. In the first place, it is here to be remembered that God the Lord did not himself personally appear to the patriarch Jacob, but it was an angel of the Lord whom he saw, with whom he strove, and of whom he said, "I have seen the Lord, face-to-face." And it is common in the Scripture that the angels, since they are messengers and servants of God, thus stand /306/ in the place of God and speak in his place, and that because of their works and offices which they carry out. Thus the angel of the Lord spoke to Moses by the bush, "I am the God of your fathers the God of Abraham, the God of Isaac, and the God of Jacob," Exod. 3:6. These words are not personally the words of the LORD himself, but the angel, spoken in the person of the LORD. For thus Stephen said that the angel appeared to Moses at the thorn bush and spoke with him on Mount Sinai, and that the law was given through the angels' ministry, Acts 7:30[-32]. Paul also testifies the same, Gal. 3:19. And nevertheless, the Scripture says that the Lord came down from heaven in a fire upon Mount Sinai, Exod. 19:18, and gave the law and spoke thus: "I am the Lord your God, who brought you out of the land of Egypt, out of the house of bondage from Pharaoh," Exod. 20:[2]. Thus the Lord did not personally come down from heaven, but an angel in the place of the Lord and has on behalf of the Lord delivered the law to Moses.

Thus it was also an angel whom the patriarchal father Jacob saw. For Moses had also seen the Lord face-to-face and spoken with him; nevertheless, he said to the Lord, "Let me see your glory." But the Lord spoke to him and answered: "You cannot see my face; for no person shall see me and live." And the Lord said further, "Behold, there is a place by me where you shall stand upon the rock; whenever my glory passes by I will place you in a cleft or split of the rock, and I will hold my hand over you until I have passed by; and when I will take away my hand, thus you shall see my back; but my face shall not be seen," Exod. 33:[18-23]. Because of these reasons John also says that no one has ever seen God, [John 1:18]. And Paul says that God is the "King of all the kings and Lord of all the lords, who alone has immortality and dwells in a light, where no one may approach, which no one has seen, nor may see," 1 Tim. 6:[15-16].

Thus the words of the patriarch Jacob and of the apostle John now agree, since the one says that he has seen the Lord, that is the angel of the Lord face-to-face, but the other speaks about the eternal invisible God whose brightness and glory may not be seen with any fleshly eyes. And just as it is with previously mentioned passages of

Scripture according to the letter, so it is also according to the Spirit; namely, just as God here in previous times allowed a reflection of his invisible glory to shine upon humanity through his angels, thus he has now in these last times /307/ revealed his invisible being and his divine nature through Jesus Christ. For Christ is the reflection of the fatherly glory and an express image of his being, 2 Cor. 4:4; Col. 1:15; Heb. 1:3. Wherefore he also spoke to Philip, "He who has seen me has seen the Father also," John 14:9. Thus the invisible God was recognized and seen through Jesus Christ, his exact image.

Nevertheless, the Christians are hindered and halted through the weakness of their flesh so that they cannot come to a perfect knowledge of the invisible God and his glory, Isa. 64:[4]. "For no eye has seen, nor ear heard, and in no human heart has come the things which God has prepared for those who love him," 1 Cor. 2:9[-10]. And in the Book of Wisdom it is written, "For what human shall know the counsel of God? Or who shall conceive what the Lord wills? For all the thoughts of humans are difficult, and our knowledge and prudence are uncertain. For the deathly and mortal body weights down the soul, and the earthly dwelling draws the understanding from many thoughts under it to earthly matters," Wisd. of Sol. 9:[13-16].

If with the greatest difficulty we can know the things that happen upon earth, and with great labor find the things we have before us, who then shall penetrate to that which happens in heaven, etc.? Wherefore the apostle also says, "Oh, what a depth of the riches, the wisdom, and the knowledge of God! How unsearchable are his judgments, and how inscrutable are his ways!" Rom. 11:33. Therefore the same apostle also says, "Our knowledge is partial and our prophecy is also nothing more than partial; but when that which is perfect comes, the partial will cease. Now we see through a mirror into a dark word, but then we shall see face-to-face," 1 Cor. 13:9[-10, 12]. Out of these words it is clear enough to understand that we shall see and recognize God with greater clarity than we do now at the present time, just as John also says, that we shall become like Christ in his splendor, for we shall see him as he is, 1 John 3:2. Therefore they err completely, those who want to cite the previously quoted words of the patriarch Jacob, and therewith prove how a person in this life should be able to come to a perfect knowledge of God. And this they want to support with several Scriptures, namely, with the words of the prophet Isaiah, "They shall all be taught by God," Isa. 54:13.

Again, "this is my testament which I will make with them, says the Lord: I will give my law in their minds, and write it in their hearts;

/308/ and I will be their God, and they shall be my people. No one shall teach his neighbor nor his brother, and say, 'Acknowledge the Lord,' for they shall all recognize me, from the smallest of them to the greatest, etc.," Jer. 31:[33-34]; Heb. 10:16. They also bring up the fact that in the Revelation of John it is written, that the city, the heavenly Jerusalem, needed no sun nor moon, that they shine there, for the glory of God illumines her and the Lamb is her light, Rev. 21:23.

This Scripture they interpret thus: that a Christian in this present time can come so far that he has no need of instruction nor admonition, but God's Word is written in his heart, and he is inwardly taught by the Spirit, without the external word. But we say that Christians must hear God's Word at all times, be taught and admonished by it, as long as they live. For God's Word remains in eternity, Isa. 40:8; 1 Pet. 1:25, to all believers as a power of God unto eternal salvation, 1 Cor. 1:18, but to all unbelievers a judgment and testimony: for heaven and earth, says Christ, shall pass away, but my words shall not pass away, Matt. 5:18; 24:35." And David said, "O Lord, you have founded your justice in eternity," Ps. 119:89.

We say further that a Christian at all times has enough to learn in God's Word. For the apostle says we must grow and increase in the knowledge of God, Eph. 4:15; [2 Pet. 3:18]. Again, "if any one imagines that he is something or that he knows something, he does not yet know as he ought to know," 1 Cor. 8:2, and deceives himself.

Therefore, we must now not thus understand the previously mentioned words or Scriptures, yes, turn and twist them as some do. For Christ himself interprets the first passage ("They shall all be taught by the Lord"), Isa. 54:[13], [as applicable] to all Christian believers. For they must all be taught of God, otherwise how should they come to Christ, just as Christ spoke to the Jews, "Every one who has heard and learned from the Father comes to me," John 6:45. And hereupon Christ related the passage out of the prophet that they must all be taught of God. For no one may believe in Jesus Christ through his own understanding nor through his natural comprehension, but he must be taught of God.

The other previously mentioned passage, namely, that God said, "This is my testament that I shall make with the house of Israel," etc., Jer. 31:33, some interpret very amazingly in this manner, as if the teaching of the gospel shall cease already in this present time or world. But we understand these prophetic passages thus: that God has written his law with his finger in the hearts of all pious Christians, that is, with his Spirit. Yes, just as God did when he gave the law through

Moses, he thus wrote the commandments with his /309/ finger in tablets of stone, Exod. 31:18, so he has also written the gospel which he has given us through Jesus Christ into the hearts of all believing Christians with his Holy Spirit. About this Paul said to the Corinthians, "You are a letter of Christ prepared through our ministry thereto, which is written, not with ink, but with the Spirit of the living God, not on tablets of stone, but on fleshly tablets of the hearts," 2 Cor. 3:[2-]3.

Thus God shall now at this time not first give his law into the hearts of Christians, but has with his Spirit already written therein, when he taught them to know Jesus Christ. Also, God is no more mindful of the previous sins and ignorance of the Christians for the sake of Jesus Christ, who has suffered the bitter death for them and has shed his precious blood for them. Again, there is no one among the Christians (to whom this Scripture actually speaks) who does not confess God the Father, the Son, and the Holy Spirit as the only true and living God, so that no one in this matter has need to teach his neighbor that he should confess the Lord. Nevertheless, the Christians who have confessed the Lord already must teach and admonish one another to a good walk which is conformed to the gospel, just as the apostles taught the people not only the knowledge of God and Jesus Christ out of God's Word, through the power of the Holy Spirit, but they also admonished and aroused the same to love, good works, and steadfastness in the faith. Therefore, the foregoing words of the prophets are not to be understood as though the teaching of the gospel should cease in this present time among the Christians. But God's Word shall remain and be taught among Christians until the time of the appearing and future coming of our Lord Jesus Christ, just as the entire Scripture sufficiently testifies, Matt. 24:35; 1 Pet. 1:25.

The third passage out of the Revelation related above, about the glorious city of Jerusalem, Rev. 21:23, speaks, according to the correct understanding, about the new heavenly Jerusalem and about the splendor which shall yet be revealed. For the sun, the moon, and the stars shall after all never pass away so long as this world stands, but in the second coming of Christ they shall pass away and melt from the heat. For all things must then be renewed, 2 Pet. 3:10; we await new heavens and a new earth, says Peter, wherein God himself shall be the light and with his inexpressible splendor illumine all things, and the righteous shall shine as the sun, and as a beam or reflection of heaven, and as the stars eternally, Matt. 13:43. /310/

In this way, one must indeed observe the Scripture, and where it witnesses of future things, then this must not be interpreted as pertaining to this present time, for many are deceived thereby. Yes, after they have wanted to signify several passages from Isaiah and the Revelation as pertaining to this time and the present congregation, which after all speak of the future splendor and glory of the heavenly Jerusalem (even though this begins here in the Spirit), they have thus come so far in their misunderstanding that they wish to go beyond the apostles in wisdom. The Lord protect us from all such misunderstanding of Scripture and give us genuine spiritual wisdom and a humble heart, to his praise and our salvation. Amen.

Conclusion

Thus we have now revealed our understanding of the tent or tabernacle of Moses, and also as much as was given us of God, and was necessary to write about the matter, in part clarified and harmonized figures and passages of the Scripture which appear to speak against each other according to the letter. And we hope we have arrived at the simple truth, and not written more than is demonstrable with the evangelical and apostolic Scripture through the grace of God. And we gladly say that every one who prides himself of the gospel should remain immovably with the saving teaching of Jesus Christ and his apostles. For God's Word is sure and true, but human understanding is deceptive. Therefore some have also erred greatly, or missed, because they did not remain with the apostolic exposition of the tabernacle.

Also, we beseech all brothers, through the mercy of God, that they accept these our writings with good will, as these are written for our teaching and admonition. For we seek not our own honor, but we hold ourselves to be poor and unworthy servants of Jesus Christ and brothers of all Christian believers, with whom we desire to maintain fellowship and unity in the Holy Spirit in eternity. What we have written against the strange teaching and exposition of the tabernacle of Moses, that has taken place in order to put to rest all misconceptions or lack of understanding, and to seek and bring peace /311/ among the brothers, so far as it is possible for us, but God who alone is wise, 1 Tim. 1:17, and reveals his wisdom to the simple and humble, Matt. 11:25. May he teach, strengthen, and comfort us with his Holy Spirit, so that we may remain steadfast to the truth of the gospel to the end.

Amen.

D. P.

THE NEW BIRTH AND THE NEW CREATURE

*Concerning the New Birth and the New Creature:
A Brief Admonition and Instruction Out of Holy
Scripture
By D. P.*

With regard to the matter that unless someone be born anew,
he may not see the kingdom of God. John 3:3

"The old is passed, behold, all has become new. Therefore it is
that if anyone is in Christ Jesus, that one is a new creature."
2 Cor. 5:17 /313/

The Greeting

The eternal, almighty, and merciful God grant you his grace through Jesus Christ his only begotten Son, our Lord and Savior; and he will strengthen, empower, and renew you in the inward person through his Holy Spirit, to the praise of his name and to your salvation, 1 Pet. 5:10; Eph. 3:14[-16]; Titus 3:4[-5]. Amen. /314/

Concerning the new birth and the new creature: a brief admonition

/315/ Dear brothers and sisters in the Lord: there are many persons at this time who pride themselves of the new birth; they chatter much about the new creature and always come forth with the saying of Paul, as if in Christ Jesus "neither circumcision counts for anything, nor uncircumcision, or foreskin but only a new creation," Gal. 6:15. But the true new birth and character [nature] of the new creature is found in few people. But the cunning and deceptive Satan, who can transform himself into an angel of light, 2 Cor. 11:[14], exhibits himself with great power in his ministers, who parade a beautiful appearance and speak with high-sounding and proud words of divine and spiritual things (nevertheless all in hypocrisy), and glory much about the new birth, about the new creature, and about the genuine internal being. Through this they have a splendid appearance in the eyes of some, for they charm and blind their eyes with fancy or adorned words and with a beautiful appearance of false piety.

Therefore, I was compelled out of Christian love to warn you of all such false Christians and messengers of Satan, and through God's grace to write to you a little about the new birth and the new creature, and then to show how not everyone who boasts of the new birth and chatters much about the new creature is therefore a new person who is born out of God. But whoever has become a partaker of the divine character, the being of Jesus Christ and the power and character of the Holy Spirit, conforms himself to the image of Jesus Christ in all submission, obedience, and righteousness serves God, in summary is a right-believing Christian; that one is a new person and a new creature in Christ Jesus, 2 Pet. 1:4; Heb. 3:14; 1 John 4:13; Rom. 8:[24]. Therefore, it is necessary to consider how the new birth takes place, from whence it comes, through what it happens, how powerful it is, and what fruit it brings forth. /316/

In the first place, one must observe that God created the first person in his image and likeness, as the Holy Scripture shows in many places; namely, that God in the beginning created human beings for eternal life, as an upright, immortal, and divine being, yes, in the image and likeness of his only born Son, Jesus Christ, Gen. 1:26; 5:1; Wisd. of Sol. 2:23; Ecclus. 17:[3]; James 3:9. For he is the image of eternal light, the image of the glory of God, an image of his being, a mirror of divine glory and image of the invisible God, Wisd. of Sol. 7:26; 2 Cor. 4:4; Col. 1:15; Heb. 1:3. Therefore, as Philip desired of Christ that he might see the Father, Christ answered him and said, "Have I been with you so long, and yet you do not know me? Philip, he who sees me, he also sees my Father," John 14:9.

Thus Christ Jesus is the image of God after which Adam was created by God. But the person did not remain in his first creation and transgressed God's command and through this came into death and corruption, Gen. 3:6. But God, who is rich in mercy, according to his great mercy has shown himself merciful toward the fallen and corrupted person, and made him a comforting promise that from the seed of the woman, from his only begotten Son Christ Jesus, should come the future Redeemer and Savior of the human race. He should release from the devil and all tyrannical powers all those who believe

The New Birth and the New Creature / 295

in him, Col. 1:13; John 3:14[-15]; 11:25.

Through this promise, yes, through this gracious gospel of Christ Jesus, the person was again comforted, yes, renewed, after the image of God and born again to eternal life. For God in the beginning actually wanted to have and still wants at the present time, to have all such persons who are conformed to him. Therefore, God in the beginning created the person in his image and likeness just as is written: "God has created the person to eternal life, that he should be just as he (that is, God) is," Wisd. of Sol. 2:23.

Since the person was created by God the Father after his image and likeness, that is, after the image and likeness of Christ, and after his fall was by grace again restored through the obedience and righteousness of the Son of God, Rom. 5:18, therefore also every person must (as he comes to maturity and is able to distinguish good from evil) be born again through the enlightenment, activity, and illumination of the Holy Spirit to a new divine being. Yes, be born again to the fellowship and likeness of Jesus Christ, and be glorified in this same image /317/ from one glory to another (nevertheless all from the Spirit of the Lord), 2 Cor. 3:18, and thus again be created anew after the image of God and to his likeness through Jesus Christ in the Holy Spirit.

Therefore, Christ said to Nicodemus, "Truly, truly, I say to you, unless one is born anew, he may not see the kingdom of God," John 3:3. And once again, "truly, truly, I say to you, unless one is born of water and the Spirit, he may not enter the kingdom of God," [John 3:5]. These words of Christ every person may indeed take to heart, since he so openly and completely denied the kingdom of heaven to all those who are not born anew; that is, those who do not lay aside the old person with his works and again put on the new person who is created after God in true righteousness and truth, and has also been renewed to the knowledge and likeness of him who created him, Eph. 4:22[-24]; Col. 3:10.

But how this new birth and renewal takes place, that the apostle Peter testifies to with these words: "You have been born again, not of perishable seed but of imperishable, that is, through the Word of the living God," 1 Pet. 1:23. James is in accord with this and says, "Every good and every perfect gift comes down from above, from the Father of lights with whom there is no variation or changing of light and darkness. Of his own will, he brought us forth through the Word of truth so that we should be the first fruits of his creatures," James 1:17[-18]. And Paul writes to Titus that God has saved us through the washing of regeneration and renewal of the Holy Spirit which he has poured out richly upon us through Christ Jesus, so that we should be justified through his grace and according to this hope become heirs of eternal life, Titus 3:5[-7].

In these previously written words, we hear that the new birth of persons occurs through the word of truth and his renewal through the Holy Spirit in such a manner that all those who out of the hearing of the gospel through the cooperation of the Holy Spirit believe in Christ Jesus, the only begotten Son of the living God, our Lord and Savior; these are born out of God, enlightened and taught by the Holy Spirit, and are God's children, just as Paul confessed with these words, "You are altogether God's children through faith in Christ Jesus," Gal. 3:26.

And John says, "As many as have received Christ, /318/ he has given power to become children of God; those who believe in his name who were born, not of blood nor of the will of the flesh nor of the will of a man, but out of God," John 1:12[-13]. And John also says, "Every one who believes that Jesus is the Christ is born out of God," 1 John 5:1. And still another passage, "all that is born out of God overcomes the world; and our faith is the victory that overcomes the world. Who is it that overcomes the world except he who believes that Jesus is God's Son?" [1 John 5:4-5].

Out of all this, it is clear that the new birth is actually the work of God in the person through which he is born anew out of God through faith in Jesus Christ in the Holy Spirit. For the heavenly Father generates or bears the new creature, but the Word of the heavenly Father is the seed out of which the new creature is born and the Holy Spirit renews, sanctifies, and keeps the new creature in a divine nature, James 1:18; 1 Pet. 1:23; 1 John 3:9; Titus 3:5. Therefore, such a new birth is also a powerful and fruitful work of God which comes from the almighty and most high God through Jesus Christ in the Holy Spirit.

Of this power and fruit of the new birth the apostle James says that the believers in Christ are born out of God the Father of lights through his Word as first fruits of his creatures, James 1:17. But what that word signifies is prefigured or portrayed for us clearly enough through the figure of the first fruits of the Old Testament which were sanctified to the Lord. For just as in Israel the first fruits were sanctified to the Lord and offered to him, thus also the apostles were the first who were called of Christ Jesus to faith and to the apostolic office. Wherefore they also without any doubt have had the greatest and most glorious gifts of the Holy Spirit, just as Paul wrote to the Romans that "not only the creatures, but also we," (says he) "who have the firstfruits of the Spirit, groan by ourselves and long for adoption as sons, awaiting the deliverance of our bodies," Rom. 8:23.[1]

Thereafter also all Christians are a separate people of God, chosen out of all peoples, bought with the precious blood of the Lamb, Jesus Christ, and sanctified through the Holy Spirit, to God as a sweet smelling savor and well-pleasing sacrifice, Eph. 1:4; Titus 2:14; 1 Pet. 1:[18-]19; 1 Cor. 6:[11]. And therefore they are also called the firstlings of the creatures /319/ of God, just as John testifies in Revelation with these words: "I saw a Lamb stand on Mount Zion, and with him a hundred and forty-four thousand who had the name of his Father written on their foreheads. And I heard a voice from heaven like the sound of many waters and like the sound of great thunder; and the voice I heard was like the sound of harpers playing on their harps, and they sing a new song before the throne and before the four animals and before the Lamb. And no one could learn that song except the hundred and forty-four thousand who were bought from the earth. It is these who have not defiled themselves with women, for they are virgins or maidens and follow the Lamb wherever he goes; these were bought from humankind as first fruits for God and the Lamb, and in their mouth no lie was found, for they are faultless before God's throne," Rev. 14:1[-5].

Out of all these words it is clear which are the firstlings of the creatures of God, namely, those who stand on Mount Zion with Christ Jesus the Lamb of God, that is, who are in his congregation, signed in their foreheads with the name of the heavenly Father, whom they confess in true faith, whose name they bear, whom they praise without ceasing, and sing a new song. For they speak with new tongues and have a new spirit, [2] Esd. 2:42; Heb. 12:22[-24]; Rev. 7:9[-10]. They are also virgins or maidens, a pure bride of the Lamb, let down from heaven and aglow with the glory of God. They are chosen from God in Christ Jesus out of all people as an only and holy people. In summary, they are faultless before the throne of God and that out of pure grace through the merit of our Lord Jesus Christ, 1 Pet. 1:2; 2:9; Rev. 5:9.

Therefore, also the new birth through which such firstlings are born out of God is a powerful and active work of God and makes the person a new creature in Christ Jesus. Because of these reasons such a new birth may not be attributed to innocent and uncomprehending children, even though some do this, Deut. 1:39; John 4:11[?]. To these persons one may speak with all modesty as the Lord spoke to the Sadducees: "You stray and are wrong, and do not understand the Scriptures, nor the power of God," Matt. 22:29. For those who attribute to minor, uncomprehending, and speechless children the new birth, faith, and baptism, those must not after all know what the new birth is, what faith is, and what baptism is and signifies. Yes, one may with all right and reason certainly say of them /320/ what is written in the Book of Wisdom, that is, they are more uncomprehending and wretched than a child, Wisd. of Sol. 15:14. For they must after all be completely uncomprehending who insist that children who do not yet understand either good or evil should have faith, seeing that faith is the genuine knowledge of God the Father and his only begotten Son, Jesus Christ, taught them by the Holy Spirit and imprinted upon them, Deut. 1:39; John 4:11[?]; 17:3. And that comes out of the hearing of the divine Word just as the apostle says that faith comes out of hearing but hearing is through God's Word, Rom. 10:17. Yes, faith (says the apostle) "is a certain trust about that which is hoped, a clear revelation, yea, a certain comprehension of things not seen," Heb. 11:1. That is, faith is a living hope and a certain trust upon God's grace, and it directs one toward invisible, eternal, and heavenly things.

Since then children are without understanding and therefore also may not be taught with God's Word (for the Scripture speaks to those who have ears to hear and a heart to understand), so I ask with the apostle, "How shall they believe in him of whom they have not heard?" Rom. 10:14. But if they do not believe, how are they then without faith born again of God's Word? Eph. 1:19; 2:4[-7]. In view of the fact that genuine faith in Christ Jesus is actually the work of God in the person through which he is transformed and born anew out of God, Col. 2:12, so that he will be brought to his own knowledge, learn to know his sin and unrighteousness, to confess it freely before God, therefore bears penitence and remorse, prays for grace, and relies upon the grace of God, Phil. 1:6; 2:13; John 1:12; 1 John 5:1; Ps. 32:5. In addition, he will love God as the uppermost and highest good, henceforth watch with a firm and trusting resolve through the grace of the Lord for the evil and do the good, Matt. 3:5[-6]; Mark 1:5; Acts 2:37[-39]; 10:30[-33]; 16:30[-31]; 20:[18-]21. Therewith he is grateful to God, does sincere works of improvement, shows love toward God and his neighbors, and brings forth the fruits of the Spirit.

Unlearned children do not have this faith, just as everyone who is taught of God well knows, seeing that the Scripture so clearly testifies and daily wisdom so openly shows that children have no faith. Never-

The New Birth and the New Creature / 299

theless, they are saved out of grace through Jesus Christ and please God in their simplicity and innocent being, Deut. 1:39; John 4:11[?], just as the mature and understanding please God through their faith, Rom. 5:1. /321/ Therefore both Christ and Paul have also set children as an example and model, not that we should be children in understanding but [innocent] in evil, and be mature in understanding, Matt. 18:1; 1 Cor. 14:20. Thus we should be aware of children at all times, observe their simplicity and humility, in order that we may conduct ourselves accordingly and conform to it.

But the new birth which takes place out of God the heavenly Father through Jesus Christ, as a transformation and renewal of persons through the Holy Spirit applies to those who understand; these must be born again from above, these must be born again out of water and Spirit; these must be born again out of the imperishable seed, that is, through the Word of the living God, John 3:5; 1 Pet. 1:23. These must be washed through the bath of the new birth in the Word and be transformed through the renewal of the Holy Spirit, James 1:18; Eph. 5:26. These must put off the old Adam and be renewed in the Spirit of tranquility, and put on the new person, yes, the Lord Jesus Christ, Titus 3:5; Eph. 4:22[-24]; Col. 3:[9-]10, which all together says this much: that when a person has come to understanding and to the knowledge of good and evil, then he must hear God's Word, amend himself, believe the gospel, be baptized upon the knowledge of his faith in the name of the Lord, receive the gift of the Holy Spirit, and be renewed in his mind, according to the image of God, that is, according to Christ Jesus, who is the expression and image of the invisible God, Matt. 3:8; Mark 1:4; Luke 3:3; Matt. 28:19; Mark 16:15[-16]; Acts 2:38; Col. 1:15. But he is an example to all Christians and a beginning of the creatures of God, through which all new creatures, that is, all true believing Christians who are born out of God the heavenly Father in the Holy Spirit, in order that they should be conformed to the exact image of his only begotten Son, Jesus Christ, so that he might be the firstborn among many brothers, Rev. 3:[14]; Rom. 8:29.

Therefore, we must observe and reflect upon the whole life and practice of Christ, how obedient he was to his Father, how faithfully he did his Father's will, and spoke his Word, yes, that he perfectly fulfilled all righteousness of both the Old and the New Testaments, Phil. 2:5[-7]; Heb. 5:2. He was circumcised according to the law and dedicated in the temple, Luke 2:21. Yes, there is not one letter of the law which he has not kept according to the intention and will of his Father, just as he himself said, "You shall not think that I have come to break the law and the prophets; I have come not to break them, but I am come to fulfill them. /322/ For truly, I say to you, as long as heaven and earth do not pass away, so shall the smallest dot not pass from the law until all is accomplished," Matt. 5:[17].

In addition, Christ is also the true mediator of the New Testament, has pioneered the way for us which we must walk, namely, that he came to John, allowed himself to be baptized by John and said, "Let it now happen at this time; for thus it is fitting for us to fulfill all righteousness," Matt. 3:15. But, if it became Christ that he was baptized with the baptism of John, how much more appropriate or becoming to us then that we be baptized with the baptism of Christ? But this is the baptism of Christ, that we be baptized inwardly with the Holy Spirit and with fire, Matt. 3:[11], but outwardly by a true messenger of Christ upon the knowledge of our own faith, in the name of the Father, the Son, and the Holy Spirit, John [1]:33; Matt. 28:19; Mark 16:15[-16]. Therefore, they err and falter or miss the true middle way, both those who emphasize inward baptism alone and despise the outward sign, and those who see only the external sign, forgetting the symbolic or the true inward being, Heb. 11:6. For just as without faith, without the new birth, without the Holy Spirit, and without that sincere Christian being, nothing avails before God, thus the external signs (which are called sacraments) such as baptism and the Lord's Supper, and whatever more the ordinance of the Lord is, must be fully practiced and not be neglected nor belittled. For the eternal wisdom, Christ Jesus, has not spoken one word in vain, Deut. 8:3, and persons live by every word that has come out of his mouth, Matt. 4:4. The only begotten Son of the most high did not do other than what his Father commanded, John 3:11; 7:16; 8:28; 12:49; 14:10[-11]. Yes, all that Christ Jesus taught and commanded is without any doubt the perfect will and counsel of God, namely, that of the eternal and only wise God (who is the wonderful Counselor, Isa. 9:[6]), through Jesus Christ and revealed to us through his Holy Spirit.

Therefore, we also may neither begin nor follow other than what Christ Jesus taught us and has done as our example. For he is the beginning and the end of all things, Rev. 1:8; 22:[13]. He is the pioneer of our faith, Heb. 12:2, upon whom we must look. He is a true light come into the world so that we should follow him, John 1:4; 8:12; 9:5; 12:46. He is the only way to the Father, John 14:6. He is the true door to the sheep. Whoever enters through him comes to the true sheepfold and finds the pasture of eternal life, John 10:7[-9]. But whoever does not enter through him but climbs /323/ in otherwise, that person is a thief and a murderer as Christ himself said, [John 10:10]. Those who do not enter through Christ, but climb in as thieves and murderers through another place, who wish to be saved through another way and means than through Christ Jesus alone, or who wish to serve God in another manner than they have received from the command, teaching, and example of Christ Jesus and his apostles, [these have no hope]. For outside of Christ Jesus there is neither wisdom, nor righteousness, nor holiness, nor salvation, nor truth, nor life. Therefore, John says thus: "That whoever has the Son, that one has life; but whoever does not have the Son, that one does not have life, and the wrath of God remains upon him," John 3:36. Likewise, whoever thus transgresses this and does not remain in the teaching of Jesus Christ, he has no God. But whoever remains therein has both the Father and the Son, 2 John 9.

This I have briefly related about Christ Jesus, in part, my brothers and sisters, as a comfort and assurance that it is the genuine grace of God wherein you stand and is the true way upon which you walk so long as you follow Christ. [I have also written] in part, my brothers and sisters, to warn you of the frivolous spirits which are arising at this time and pride themselves much about the new creature and are yet at bottom truly hypocritical, puffed-up persons, strong despisers of the words and commands of Christ, who have forsaken the true way and follow after the way of apostate Israel. They serve Baal to please the whoring Jezebel and act as hypocrites or run with the world for the sake of their belly. For the baptism, which Christ Jesus himself instituted, and which the apostles so earnestly practiced, which in addition is so highly praised in the Scriptures, they do not regard, Matt. 28:19; Mark 16:15[-16]. The Supper of the Lord which is a memorial of his suffering and death, yes, a spiritual fellowship of his body and blood, is not significant to them, Matt. 26:[26]; [1] Cor. 10:16. Foot washing, which the Lord Jesus Christ himself did and commanded his disciples earnestly to do and to follow his example, that is almost considered foolishness by them, John 13:4[-10]. The evangelical ban, without which the congregation of God cannot stand, is to them a mockery and curse, Matt. 18:15[-17]; 1 Cor. 5; 2 Thess. 3:6. And what more shall I say? They disdain all the saving teaching and ordinances of the Lord Jesus Christ; and they are so wise, so understanding, and so spiritual in their own eyes, and consider themselves so full of the true inner being that they think, and also unashamedly say, that they need not observe the external ceremonies /324/ (as they call the institution and ordinance of the Lord).

They err and discard such things, for their wickedness has blinded them so that they do not recognize God's secret wisdom (which is to the godless a hidden treasure), Wisd. of Sol. 2:21-22; Ecclus. 1:[30]. And they do not see that they are already attacked by the devil, deceived, yes, completely arrogant and in addition are drowned in unbelief and in great ingratitude toward God; that they are satiated with and tired of the gospel. They have gotten itching ears and are listening to hear something new or different. They can already (as they allow themselves to think) also be judges and masters over Christ Jesus and over the Holy Spirit, for they despise his teaching and pride themselves that they do not need to observe his institutions [ordinances].

Oh! to what have these poor miserable people come, that they want to place themselves above God the Lord? What will they do? Where will they abide when the Lord visits them?

They now indeed allow themselves to think that they are the wise virgins or maidens, who have enough oil in their lamps, but when the bridegroom shall come they shall stand as the foolish virgins or maidens who had no oil, and therefore they also shall not be able to enter with the bridegroom to his wedding, Matt. 25:1[-13]. They now regard it as clever (just as is the nature of lazy and roguish servants), that they bury their lord's money in the earth. But when the lord shall come and demand a reckoning from them, they shall hear a severe sentence and shall be punished with a horrible punishment because they have hidden their lord's money and not deposited it for interest nor made investments with it, Matt. 25:14[-30.] They are just as the congregation at Laodicea which spoke, "I am rich, and I have prospered, and I need nothing; and did not know that she was wretched, pitiable, poor, blind, and naked," Rev. 3:17. Therefore she was counseled of the Lord that she should buy gold from him that had been refined through fire so that she might become rich, and that she should put on white garments so that the shame of her nakedness would not be revealed and she should anoint her eyes with salve so that she might see, Rev. 3:[18].

These words they should wholeheartedly take to heart with all justice, reasonableness, and earnestness, who are now so rich of spirit that they think and say, "We need nothing," and do not recognize their wretchedness and misery. Now they should yet hear the counsel of the Lord /325/ and buy of him that pure gold refined through the fire of his divine Word and the noble and precious pearl of evangelical truth so that they might become rich in faith, Matt. 13:45. Now they should discard the old Adam and overcome the world and all that is in her through their faith, so that the Lord might clothe them with white garments, so that they will not come to shame before him at his coming, Col. 3:9; 1 John 5:4. Now they should correctly anoint their eyes with eye salve, Rev. 3:18, so that they might see and observe that God's kingdom does not consist in words but in power and deed, 1 Cor. 4:20. And, therefore, all boasting or high-sounding words and all nice chatter about the new creature and about the inner being is not valid before the Lord whenever one still remains and walks in the old being of the flesh. The Jews also boasted against Christ that they were Abraham's seed and had one Father, namely God, John 8:33, [41]. But what did Christ answer them? If you were Abraham's children, then you should do the works of Abraham, and if God were your Father, you would love me for I have proceeded from God, [John 8:39, 42].

Thus it is also useless, yes, an abomination before God, that these despisers of Christ and his Word boast about the inner being and the new birth since they do not want to do what Christ himself taught, commanded, and did. Therefore their boasting is completely idle and false. For if they were new creatures in Christ Jesus they would keep the beginning of his being firm to the end, Heb. 3:14. But the being of Christ is the divine nature and the upright new being (which is righteousness, holiness, truth, faith, love, friendliness, and all good virtues) which the Holy Spirit initiates within us. But the beginning of the Christlike being in us is that we make genuine improvement of life, bring forth true works and fruits of repentance, Matt. 3:[8], believe the gospel and be baptized upon the knowledge of our faith in the name of the Father, the Son, and the Holy Spirit, Matt. 28:19; Mark 16:[16]. For thus Christ himself began to teach and said, "Amend yourself and believe the gospel for the kingdom of God draws near, Matt. 4:17; Mark 1:15. In the same manner also, he commanded his disciples at his final departure and said to them, "All authority in heaven and on earth has been given to me. Go therefore and teach all peoples, and baptize them in the name of the Father and of the Son and of the Holy Spirit, and teach them to maintain all that I have commanded you," Matt. 28:[18-20].

But since they do not do this nor want to do it, therefore /326/ all that they propose and build up about the new birth, the new creature, and the inner being is nothing more than idle chatter. For were they born out of God, they should also not disdain the bath of rebirth, Titus 3:5. Were they also inwardly baptized by Christ Jesus with the Holy

Spirit and with fire, they would not refuse to receive the external baptism after the example, pattern, and command of Christ, Matt. 3:11.

Paul the apostle was also especially chosen of God and filled with the Holy Spirit. Nevertheless Ananias said to him, "Paul, why do you delay? Rise up and let yourself be baptized in the name of the Lord and wash away your sins [Acts 22:16]. "Likewise, as Peter preached Christ in the house of Cornelius, the Holy Spirit fell upon all who heard the word. And as Peter saw this he spoke, 'May anyone also forbid water that they may be baptized who have received the Holy Spirit as well as we?' And he commanded to baptize them in the name of the Lord," Acts 10:[47-48].

Out of these and similar examples and witnesses of Scripture, we may clearly observe how the Holy Spirit (who initiates the new Christlike being in the person) did not hinder or prevent the water of baptism, but they were driven and commanded to do it. For that is actually the office of the Holy Spirit that he leads the believers into all truth and obedience, and glorifies Christ, as Christ himself said that the Holy Spirit shall glorify him, for he shall "take it from his own and declare it to us," John 16:14[-15].

But this glorification of Christ through the Holy Spirit actually happens in his disciples who accept and keep his words in true faith, as he himself said, "I am glorified in them," John 17:10 (that is, in my disciples). But Christ was glorified in his disciples even as the Father was glorified in him, and the Father was glorified in Christ in these ways, that he has revealed his Father's name to his disciples, has spoken his Father's Word, done his will, and completed his work, as he himself said, "I glorified you (oh, Father) on earth and have completed the work which you gave me to do that I should do," John 17:4. Thus all disciples of Christ must keep his teaching, do his will, and complete his work, so that Christ will be glorified in them. That is the beginning and the end /327/ of the teaching of Jesus Christ (just as is also said above) that we make sincere improvement of life, believe the gospel, be baptized upon our faith in the name of the Holy Trinity, that is, in the name of the Father, and of the Son, and of the Holy Spirit, and earnestly maintain through the grace of the Lord all that Christ commanded us, Matt. 28:19[-20].

Therefore, whoever refuses to follow Christ Jesus, or is disobedient to his Word, or goes about the ordinances and truth of Christ in some other manner than he himself practiced and taught, the same does not fear God, since he is unbelieving and contrary to his Word, Ecclus. 2:18. He shall therefore not escape the judgment of God, for he who despises Christ and does not accept his Word, that one shall be judged by the Word which he has spoken in the last day, John 12:48.

But some great talkers and loose despisers here make an objection or contradiction and say how that in Jesus Christ neither circumcision nor uncircumcision avail anything but the new creature alone, Gal. 6:[15], just as Paul said. Thereupon I answer first that the apostle did not write these words with the intention therewith to nullify or undo any words or ordinances of the Lord. This be far hence! But therewith he wanted to give us to know that now in the New Testament the external circumcision is no longer valid, and that between circumcision and uncircumcision, that is, between Jews and Gentiles, there is no distinction with God, just as the apostle Peter testified when he saw that the gift of the Holy Spirit was also poured out from God upon the Gentiles, and spoke, "Now I perceive in truth that God does not regard persons, but in every nation whoever fears him and does what is right is acceptable to him," Acts 10:34.

These words of Peter have one sense or meaning with the previously quoted words of Paul, namely, that whether they are Jews or Gentiles, circumcised or uncircumcised, the important thing is that they fear God, believe in Christ Jesus, and do right. Thus they are God's children, well pleasing to him, and heirs of his kingdom, according to the promise which God made to Abraham saying, "In your seed" (which is Christ) "shall all the heathen be blessed," Gen. 22:18; Gal. 3:16.

In the second place, it is incorrect and a false interpretation of the previously quoted words of Paul, that one should liken any ordinance and institution of the Lord with carnal circumcision and uncircumcision. The reason: carnal circumcision was a figure of spiritual circumcision, Eph. 2:[11]. And /328/ uncircumcision signified the uncircumcised and unbelieving Gentiles who lived in heathendom. Therefore both circumcision and uncircumcision are and had to be transformed into a spiritual circumcision of the heart, which takes place without hands through the Word of God with the putting off of the sinful body in the flesh. But what our Lord Christ Jesus taught and commanded in the New Testament, that is and remains the eternal unchangeable truth. Therefore Christ himself said that heaven and earth shall pass away but his words should not pass away, Matt. 24:35.

In the third place, Paul explained his words thus (namely, that in Christ Jesus neither circumcision nor uncircumcision avail anything but the new creature) sufficiently himself when he said, "And those who walk according to this rule" (that is according to the rule, measure, and ordinance of Christ), "peace be upon them and upon the Israel of God," Gal. 6:[16]. And in the preceding chapter he says, "In Christ Jesus neither circumcision nor uncircumcision is of any avail, but faith working through love," Gal. 5:6. And to those from Corinth he said, "Circumcision is nothing and uncircumcision is nothing, but keeping the commandments of God," 1 Cor. 7:19. But does the keeping of God's commandments avail with him? In Christ Jesus does faith that works through love avail? And does the peace of God come upon those who walk according to the rule of Christ? Where then shall those abide who do not regard God's commandments and the institutions of the Lord Jesus Christ? Yes, who do even as the Pharisees did, to whom Christ said, "Why do you nullify the commandments of God for the sake of your own traditions?" Matt. 15:3.

Thus these loose despisers also transgress and scorn all saving teaching and ordering of the Lord Jesus Christ and help to strengthen the institutions and ceremonies of people with which God, however, wants neither to be served nor honored, even as he himself said through Isaiah, Isa. 29:13[-14], and Christ in the gospel related and confirmed the same, Matt. 15:8. And such they do out of hypocrisy to please the world. Therefore, they are enemies of the cross of Christ and love the honor of people rather than the honor of God. In addition, they ridicule us; yes, regard us as a mockery and a despicable byword because we correctly observe, believe, and recognize baptism, the Lord's Supper, and other institutions of the Lord, and therefore suffer persecution. /329/

Well then, the one abuses us, the other persecutes us, but for no other reason (God be thanked) than because of our faith and the truth of Jesus Christ. But we commend our affairs to God, the righteous Judge, and will gladly be mocked for Christ's sake by those who are so wise in their own eyes and so clever in themselves that they with the Pharisees despise the counsel of God. We allow every one to be wise and clever according to his own mind, will, and opinion and to exalt himself, Rom. 12:[16]. But we desire to make ourselves equal with the humble so that what was spoken through the prophet may not come upon us: "Woe to those who are wise in their own eyes, and regard themselves as understanding," Isa. 5:21. Likewise, "do you see a man who regards himself as wise? There is more hope for a fool than for him," Prov. 26:12. Again, "every one who exalts himself will be humbled," Luke 18:14. Therefore we desire to humble ourselves under the mighty hand of God, to walk humbly and correctly, well knowing that therein we cannot be deceived. For it is written, "he who walks in integrity and piously walks securely," Prov. 10:9. Therefore the prophet prays thus to the Lord and says, "May integrity and uprightness preserve me, for I wait for you," Ps. 25:21. Thus we desire also of the Lord that he keep us in genuine humility, integrity, and piety, correctly and uprightly, and protect us from our own wisdom and cleverness. Yes, give us such a mind that we will here eagerly become fools for Christ's sake, according to the word of Paul. "If anyone among you thinks that he is wise, let him become a fool that he may become wise. For the wisdom of this world is folly with God," 1 Cor. 3:18[-19].

We would also rather suffer persecution for righteousness' sake and be saved than that we should feign to be with the world and be condemned, Ecclus. 1:[30]. For we know that the hypocrites have no part in the kingdom of God and of Christ. Since we know that the commandments and ceremonies of people are an abomination before the Lord God, though they appear so beautiful (for what is exalted among people is an abomination in the sight of God, Luke 16:15, as Christ said.) Therefore we do not wish to fellowship with the world. We also do not regard her commands and ceremonies, and we are in no manner inclined to observe or to help to strengthen them. But what our Lord and Savior Christ Jesus, the Son of the living God, commanded and established through his innocent death and precious blood, that we desire through his grace to maintain. Yes, to live and /330/ to die thereby. If because of this, one therefore scolds, blasphemes, and persecutes us, we are well comforted in God our Savior and helper in necessity.

But while we desire to devote ourselves as poor unworthy servants, to do God's will through his grace, nevertheless, no one shall thus imagine or think nor repeat about us that we set or seek our salvation anywhere other than in the grace of God and the merits of Christ alone. For we firmly believe and openly confess that we are saved through the grace of our Lord Jesus Christ, as the apostle Peter confessed before the church at Jerusalem, Acts 15:11. Therefore we also, according to the teaching of this same apostle, set our hope with our whole hearts upon the grace of God which has appeared to us in Christ Jesus, 1 Pet. 1:13, which grace was also called a saving grace by Paul because it brings with it and accomplishes for us eternal salvation through Jesus Christ, Titus 2:11.

We confess and also know well how the Holy Scripture includes all persons under sin. Solomon says in his prayer to God that there "is no person who does not sin," 1 Kings 8:46. In Job it is written, "May mortal man be judged guiltless before God? May anyone be acknowledged and spoken of clean and pure on account of his works? Behold he has found unfaithfulness among his servants, and among his angels is stubborn disobedience, etc.," Job 4:17[-18].

And in addition he says, "What is man that he can be considered clean? Or what does he have who is born of a woman, that he might be held as guiltless? Behold, he has found unfaithfulness among his holy ones, yea, the heavens are not clean in his eyes; how much less than the rejected and base people, a man who drinks mischief like water," Job 15:14[-16]! And the prophet David said, "Hear my prayer, O Lord; hear my crying for the sake of your will! Listen to me for the sake of your righteousness! Enter not into judgment with your servant, for no person living is righteous before you," Ps. 143:1[-2].

Therefore we confess ourselves as poor sinners and unworthy servants of the Lord and mourn with the prophet that our sins have gone over our heads and have become as a heavy burden upon us; yes, they are more in number than the hairs of our heads. And were it not that the grace of God had taken the upper hand over our sins, and still takes daily through Jesus Christ, then all would be lost with us. But as is written in the Book of Wisdom, that when the children of Israel /331/ had sinned and therefore were plagued of the Lord with poisonous snakes, then they had a saving sign that was given them out of the grace of God, namely, the serpent that Moses according to the command of the Lord had erected among them. And those who turned toward that same sign became well, not through that which they gazed upon, but through the Lord, the Savior of all persons, Wisd. of Sol. 16:5[-7]; Num. 21:8[-9]; John 3:14[-15].

Thus we also confess that we of ourselves are poor sinners, born according to the sinful flesh of Adam who was bitten and poisoned by the serpent, Rom. 5:12, and all those who are descended from him, these have become partakers of his sinful nature. Against this poison of the serpent and sinful nature of the flesh, our merciful heavenly Father has given a true saving sign, namely, his only begotten and beloved Son, Jesus Christ, who has been raised up from the earth and exalted so that whoever looks upon him with true faith does not die but lives eternally, John 3:14[-15]; 12:32. And just as no herb or plaster could heal the Israelites when they were bitten by the serpent, nor may also heal them, but the Lord's Word which heals all things and which they also have believed has healed and made them well, Wisd. of Sol. 16:12; so also Jesus Christ alone heals and makes us well, and there is no other means to salvation. Yes, to us there is no other name given under heaven whereby we must be saved, Acts 4:12.

But if Christ Jesus shall make us well and save us, we must believe him and be obedient. For he who does not believe, he shall be condemned, Mark 16:16; yes, he is now already judged, John 3:18. "For disobedience is a sin of divination, and stubbornness is just like the blasphemy of idolatry," 1 Sam. 15:23. Had the matter been so that Noah did not believe the Word of God and had not built the ark according to the command of the Lord, then he would have had to pass away in the water with the whole world, Gen. 7 and 8. Had the Israelites in the wilderness not wanted to look upon the saving sign which God gave them out of grace, then they would no doubt, not have become well, Num. [21:8-9]. Had the leprous, excluded Naaman of Syria not bathed himself seven times in the Jordan, according to the prophet's word, he should nevermore have become cleansed of his leprosy, since he had despised the Lord's Word, which he had to believe and be obedient to if we were otherwise to be cleansed, 2 Kings 5:10[-14]. Had the blind man not wanted to go to the pool of Siloam and wash himself, he would certainly have remained blind, John 9:7 [-8]. And of similar examples the Scripture is full.

But now all these did not become well through any external thing /332/ but through God's Word which they believed. Therefore the Lord also said that "a person shall not live by bread alone, but by every word that proceeds from the mouth of God," Matt. 4:4; Deut. 8:3; Wisd. of Sol. 16:26. But this life of persons living by God's Word comes out of faith just as is written: "The righteous shall live out of his faith," Hab. 2:4; Rom. 1:17; Gal. 3:11; Heb. 10:38. This accords also with the Scripture which says, "That it is not the fruit which heals or feeds people, but the Lord's Word preserves those who believe in him," Wisd. of Sol. 16:26.

Of this power of the divine Word, Christ also says in the gospel, "Blessed are those who hear the Word of God and keep it," Luke 11:28. Likewise, "truly, truly, I say to you, if anyone keeps my Word, he will never see death in eternity," John 8:51. Again, he spoke to his disciples, "You are clean on account of the Word which I have spoken to you," John 15:3. And Paul says, "The gospel is a power of God that saves everyone who believes in it," Rom. 1:16. And James says, "Put away all impurity and evil and receive God's Word with gentleness, and let it be implanted in you, which can save your souls," James 1:21.

In summary, God's Word preserves the people, those who trust upon the Lord, Wisd. of Sol. 16:26. God's Word is spirit and life and makes alive, John 6:63; 15:3, only to those who believe thereon. God's

Word purifies the souls of those who are obedient to his Word, 1 Pet. 1:[21-]22. Yes, God's Word is a power of God and saves, 1 Cor. 1:[18], those who hear and keep it, James 1:21. But whoever despises the Word despises God himself; he rejects Christ Jesus and resists the Holy Spirit who has witnessed to the Word, Luke [8:21].

Now, so that I might come again to my proposition and first proposal about the new birth and the new creature, I say thus in conclusion: the born-again children of God and new creatures in Christ Jesus are those who are born again out of God the heavenly Father through Christ Jesus and are renewed and sanctified through the Holy Spirit, who have become participants of the divine nature, of the being of Jesus Christ, and of the character of the Holy Spirit, John 1:12; 1 Pet. 1:23; 2 Pet. 1:4; Heb. 3:14. They are those who have died to sin and still daily die more and more, and experience righteousness; those who never boast in themselves but only in the cross of the Lord Jesus Christ, through whom the world is crucified to them and they to the world, Gal. 6:[14]; /333/ those who in true faith walk according to the rule of Christ and follow in his footsteps, 1 Pet. [2]:21; who know no one according to the flesh, 2 Cor. 5:16; those who do not have an appetite for what is human but for what is divine, Matt. 16:23. In summary, these are righteous and do righteousness just as God out of whom they are born is righteous; these are minded like Christ Jesus and are motivated by the Holy Spirit, 1 John 2:29; Phil. 2:5; Rom. 8:14. Where this takes place, there one sees the kingdom of God, John 3:3; there one comes into the kingdom of heaven; there is a new creature in Christ Jesus, Gal. 6:[15].

Such new creatures have all been the saints of God from the beginning, such as Abel, Seth, Noah, etc., who through their faith out of a free heart voluntarily have sacrificed to God and have conducted themselves uprightly, who have kept themselves in all submissiveness and obedience toward God, Gen. 4:4; 6:9.

Such new persons also were Abraham, Isaac, and Jacob who, by their faith, according to the command and will of God gladly left their fatherland, Gen. 12:1. They have trekked out of it and lived in huts or tents, Heb. 11:9, and they were well satisfied, recognizing that they were strangers and guests on earth and they desired a better country, namely, a heavenly one, and they looked for a city which has a foundation whose builder or maker and Creator is God, [Heb. 11:10]. "Therefore God is not ashamed to be called their God," as the apostle says, "for he has prepared for them a city," [Heb. 11:16].

The great prophet Moses was also similarly minded. Thus, when he was grown up, he no more wanted to be called a son of Pharaoh's daughter and chose rather to suffer ill treatment with the people of God than to enjoy the temporal pleasures of sin. And he considered the disdain of Christ for greater riches than all the treasures of Egypt, for he looked upon the reward, Heb. 11:24[-26].

Paul was also found to be of the same nature, who for the sake of Christ regarded all that he had won in Judaism as loss. "For," spoke he, "I count everything as loss against the abundant knowledge of Christ Jesus my Lord. For his sake I have counted all things for loss, and hold them as garbage, so that I may gain Christ and be found in him, not having a righteousness of my own, based on law, but that which comes through faith in Christ, that is, the righteousness from God that is accounted to faith," Phil. 3:7[-9].

In these pious and holy men of God and all /334/ pious believers who existed before us, we may find the nature of the new birth and the power of faith and openly see how they knew and served God in the spirit, feared and trusted him, loved him above all things, despised the perishable things, and sought the heavenly things. They delighted in the Lord and his grace, well knowing that the Lord is their part, and the most high is and shall be their reward, Wisd. of Sol. 5:16, which the prophet indeed also confessed when he spoke, "Oh, Lord, whenever I have you, I ask neither for heaven nor earth, although it were also that immediately my body and soul languished, do you remain nevertheless my heart's refuge and my part," Ps. 73:25. These are the words of a newborn man; these are the fruits of the new creature; and we shall take an example therefrom, which we must pursue through God's grace, and also be thus intended and are comforted in the Lord if it is indeed the case that we are born out of God and are new creatures in Christ Jesus and want to boast of this.

And above all this as I have said or explained above, and say yet again, that Jesus Christ the only begotten Son of God, a reflection of his honor and an exact image of his being, is ordained of the Father as an example to all Christians so that they should be conformed to him. For the divine being, according to which we must submit ourselves, is shown or revealed to us completely in him, Heb. 1:3; Rom. 8:29. Therefore, all those who want to boast of the new birth, these same persons must have the character and nature of Christ and hold the beginning of his being firm to the end, Phil. 2:5; Heb. 3:14.

These are now the newborn children of God, born again to eternal life and renewed after the image of God and sanctified through the Holy Spirit. For God the heavenly Father is holy, therefore he also wants to have holy children, Isa. 6:3; Rev. 4:8. Jesus Christ, the Son of the most high, is holy. Therefore he also wants to have holy brothers and sisters, Matt. 12:49. The Holy Spirit is holy, therefore he also wants his temple, wherein he shall dwell, to be holy, 1 Cor. 3:16; 6:19. Therefore Paul says thus: "Praised be the God and Father of our Lord Jesus Christ, who has blessed us through Jesus Christ with all kinds of spiritual blessing in the heavenly goods, even as he chose us through the same before the foundation of the world was laid, that we should be holy and blameless before him in love. He has ordained us to be his children through Jesus Christ, according to the pleasure of his will, to the praise of his glorious grace /335/ through which he has made us accepted in the beloved," Eph. 1:3[-6].

In these words we hear how holy and blameless the children of God must be. Therefore, the Lord also said to his disciples, "You shall be holy; for I the Lord am holy," Lev. 19:2; 1 Pet. 1:16. And Christ said to his disciples, "You should be perfect, as your Father is perfect," Matt. 5:48. And John says, "Everyone who is born out of God does not sin," for that seed (out of which he was born and thus has become a partaker of the character and nature of the holy seed, according to the Word of Christ namely, what is born out of the Spirit is Spirit) "abides in him, and he cannot sin because he is born of God," 1 John 3:9; John 3:6. And yet another passage: "We know that whoever is born of God, that one does not sin, but he keeps him, and the evil one shall not touch him," 1 John 5:18.

Nevertheless, this must be understood with all discretion, for Christians should be holy just as God is holy, and perfect, just as the Father in heaven is perfect. This one may not understand as though Christians could become, or also be, as holy in this time just as God is, but that they should strive after holiness with complete earnestness, just as Paul the apostle did. For he said that he had striven after this with his whole zeal to acknowledge Christ Jesus and the power of his resurrection and the fellowship of his suffering that he might be conformed to his death if he might attain to the resurrection of the dead, Phil. 3:10[-11]. "Not that I have already obtained it," (said he) "or am now perfect; but I press after it, if I may grasp the same wherein I am grasped by Christ Jesus. Brethren, I do not consider myself that I have made it my own; but one thing I say, forgetting what is past, and stretching to what is present, I press on toward the goal set ahead, for the prize held up from the calling of God from above in Christ Jesus," [Phil. 3:12-14]. Thus also all Christians must do, to seek with Paul to learn to know Christ, to understand him, and to become like him.

They must also confess with the apostle and know that they have not yet attained it, and are also not yet perfect.

Likewise, John says, that everyone born of God does not commit sin, nor can sin, 1 John 3:9. This must not be understood as though the Christians have entirely no sin, /336/ for the same John also writes, "If we say we have no sin, we deceive ourselves, and the truth is not in us. But if we confess our sins, he is faithful and righteous, that he forgives our sins and cleanses us from all evil. If we say we have not sinned, we make him a liar, and his Word is not in us," 1 John 1:8[-10].

Therefore all Christians are still sinners before the Lord and must confess their sins and must pray God for forgiveness of sins, just as David said, I acknowledge my sins and do not hide my iniquity. I said, "I will confess my transgressions to the Lord; then you did forgive the misdeeds of my sin," Ps. 32:5. Therefore shall all the heathen pray to you at the right time. Therefore Christ taught all of us to pray in this way: "Father, forgive us our guilt, just as we forgive our debtors," Matt. 6:12. But now since the Christians are in Christ and Christ is in them, no sins are attributed to them from the Lord, just as David said, "Blessed are they whose transgressions are forgiven, and those whose sins are covered. Blessed is the person to whom the Lord does not add iniquity," Ps. 32:1[-2].

But this salvation comes upon all those who believe in Christ Jesus, who through him have forgiveness of sins, who are washed in his blood, and all their sins and shortcomings are covered with his righteousness, Rom. 3:22; 5:1; Eph. 2:[4-]7; Rev. 1:[5-]6, for Christ is made from God to wisdom, righteousness, sanctification, and redemption for us, just as Paul wrote to the Corinthians and the Colossians, 1 Cor. 1:[30]: "You who in past times were estranged and hostile through the mind in evil deeds, he has now reconciled you with the body of his flesh by death, so that he should present you holy and blameless, without guilt before him, if otherwise you continue in the faith, grounded, firm, and unmoving on the hope of the gospel which you have heard," Col. 1:21[-23].

In summary, Christ has sanctified himself for his own, so that they should also be sanctified in the truth, John 17:19. That is, he has sacrificed an offering for sins which is of eternal worth and with one sacrifice he has made it perfect unto eternity for those who will be sanctified. Therefore no one may accuse or condemn them, just as Paul says, "If God is with us, who will be against us? He who did not spare his own Son but gave him up for us all, how should he not give us all things with him? Who will accuse the elect of God? God is here, who justifies; who will condemn? Christ is here, who has died, yes, /337/ much more, who was also awakened, who also is at the right hand of God, and prays for us," Rom. 8:31[-34]?

Behold, dear brothers and sisters, my companions in the grace of God and of the Lord Jesus Christ and in the fellowship of the Holy Spirit, Phil. 1:5, I have written a little about the new birth and the new creature according to the small gift which is given me of the Lord, and warned you of the false spirits and despisers of Jesus Christ and his Word, and kindly desire, therefore, that you accept this my little work in good will and will watch yourselves with complete earnestness before these deceptive laborers and earnestly consider it, that you might become true new creatures in Christ Jesus, Rom. 8:29; Eph. 1:4; 2 Thess. 2:13; James 1:18; Titus 3:[4-7]. But the one who has chosen you from the beginning, and has now given you birth through the Word of truth, and renewed and sanctified you through his Holy Spirit, and all that according to his fathomless grace and mercy, to the same eternal and almighty God, our Lord and Savior, be praise, glory, and honor in eternity, Rom. 16:26[-27]; 1 Tim. 6:16; Rev. 5:[13]-14.

Amen.

ENDNOTES

1. See page 237, note 3 concerning the "Gospel of All Creatures."

CONCERNING SPIRITUAL RESTITUTION

/339/ That is, how all that happened from the beginning is spiritually fulfilled, recapitulated, and restored in Christ Jesus—a Christian and scriptural reflection, to the service of all lovers of the truth, compiled from the Holy Scriptures.

By D.P.

"Everything written about me in the law of Moses and the prophets and the psalms must be fulfilled," Luke 24:44.

"Christ must occupy heaven until the time that everything is fulfilled that God has spoken through the mouth of his holy prophets who have been from the beginning." Acts 3:21 /340/

The old has passed away, and all things have become new.
2 Cor. 5:17

Foreword

/341/ In view of the fact that divine Scripture reports or witnesses much about the restitution or restoration [of] all things which have happened in Christ Jesus from the beginning of the world, just as Peter said that Christ must occupy heaven until the time of restitution of all things which God has spoken through the mouth of his prophets who have been from the beginning, Acts 3:21; many fanaticisms have come out of this, so that everyone interprets this restitution according to their own opinion strangely and have understood it carnally, and many still do so.

Therefore, I have undertaken through the grace of God to relate briefly all that has taken place from the beginning and how all is spiritually restored in Christ and his kingdom so that the simple may receive a little instruction through this and not allow themselves to be deceived by the false prophets, who embellish and veil their deceptive doctrine with the old being of the letter as shadows and figures. For all that they cannot defend with the New Testament, that they wish to prove with the Old Testament and the letter of the prophets. Out of this many sects have come; out of this manifold false worship is established. Yes, primarily out of this fountain has flowed the idolatrous ceremonies and pomp of the anti-Christian churches and the lamentable errors of the revolutionary sects, who in our time, under the appearance of the holy gospel [and] of the faith of the Christian religion, have done much harm and stirred up many aggravations.

Therefore, just as we have, through the help of the Lord, clarified a little the tabernacle of Moses and the figurative things that were in it, and brought them to a spiritual sense, so we desire also through the assistance of the Spirit of Christ to explain the previously mentioned restitution, or at least to give our simple understanding /342/ thereof for the reflection of all Christians, and thus give the honest and simple a little instruction on how to understand Scripture correctly and to consider all things well, not according to the flesh but according to the Spirit, John 6:15. For the kingdom of God is after all not of this world, but inwardly among all genuine Christians, John 18:36; Luke 17:21. And to be carnally minded is death, but to be spiritually minded, that is life and peace, Rom. 8:6. And the flesh is not useful, but it is the Spirit which makes alive, and the words of Christ are spirit and life, John 6:63. The eternal, almighty and only wise God, give us a sincere and scriptural understanding in all things through Jesus Christ, to his praise, to the joy and quickening of our consciences, and to the upbuilding of his congregations. Amen.

Christ Jesus is the spirit and truth of all figures which have gone before, the end and the fulfillment of the figurative law, but the beginning of the true being and eternal perfection, John 6:63; John 14:6; Rom. 10:4. For in Jesus Christ (the apostle says) is a trustworthy being, Eph. 4:21, in him are hidden all the treasures of the wisdom and knowledge of God, Col. 2:2. Yes, in him dwells the whole fullness of the deity bodily, and all shadows and figures come to an end in him, [Col. 1:19]. He is the bright morning star, the sun of righteousness which illumines all [things], Rev. 22:16; Wisd. of Sol. 5:[5]. The brightness of the face of Moses (which ceased there and signified the law) is no brightness contrasted to the brightness of Jesus Christ and his gospel, 2 Cor. 3:7. That veil before the face of Moses, which still hangs before the eyes of the Jews and lies upon their hearts so that they cannot understand Moses and the prophets, was taken away in Jesus Christ, as Paul says, 2 Cor. 5:17.

Therefore, all things are transformed in Christ, are clarified and made new through him; that is, out of the letter into the spirit, out of flesh into a true being, out of the old into the new, out of the figures into the abiding clear truth, and out of the perishable brought into the eternal and heavenly. And it is very necessary to know this in order that one seek only in Christ Jesus, all truth, righteousness, holiness, salvation; yes, the divine wisdom, gifts, virtues, strengths and activity, and not outside of him, 1 Cor. 1:21; Jer. 23:5; Eph. 1:8[-9]; Col. 2:3. And that all be shamed who in these last perilous times have so presumptuously and indiscreetly, out of great haughtiness, /343/ proclaimed that they should occupy the kingdom and rightly restore all things. That no one shall do in eternity but the Lord Jesus Christ who himself is the perfection of wisdom, truth, and righteousness; who has a name above all names that may be named in this and the future world, Phil. 2:9; he who is the head of all principalities and powers, [Eph. 3:8-10]. In summary, he is the one through whom all things are created and upheld, who works in all things with God and outside of whom nothing divine is done.

In the first place the creation of heaven and earth is restored in Christ Jesus. For God has made new heavens, namely, the believers in whom God dwells, and especially the apostles and true teachers in whom the Son of righteousness, Jesus Christ, shines over all and illuminates, Wisd. of Sol. 5:6; yes, makes fruitful in all kinds of fruits of the Spirit the new earth, that is, the hearts of the Christians. There the seed of the divine Word is sown, Matt. 13:8, through the grace of God and through the power of the Holy Spirit.

This is clearly seen in the words of the prophet who spoke thus: "The heavens are telling the glory of God, and the firmament proclaims the work of his hands. One day tells it to the next, and one night tells it to the other. There is no language nor speech where their voice is not heard; their voice goes out through all the lands and their words to the end of the world. In them he has set a tent for the sun, which comes forth like a bridegroom leaving his chamber, and rises up as a hero to run the course with joy. Its rising is from the end of the heavens, and its circuit runs again to the same end, and there is nothing hid from its heat," Ps. 19:1[-6].

This is a prophecy of the gospel that went out through the apostles and is preached in the whole world, as Paul testifies, [Rom. 10:18]. Therefore these heavens, which declare the glory of God and in which the sun has a tabernacle or dwelling and shines over everything, are the apostles and all true teachers and Christians who proclaim God's Word and in whom God has his dwelling Eph. 3:5; 1 Cor. 3:16; 2 Cor. 6:16. /344/

Here is also the new moon and it illuminates these new heavens, namely, that firm word of prophecy that shines there in a dark corner, 2 Pet. 1:19. Here are also the new stars, the righteous ones, who instruct others to salvation, who shine as the brightness of the heavens and as the stars eternally, Dan. 12:[3]; here through the brightness of the divine Word and hereafter through the glory of Christ in the heavenly being, 1 Cor. 15:41; Phil. 3:20.

Therefore the congregation of God is also described as a pregnant or fruitful woman who is clothed with the glory of Christ and his Word, who may be compared with and represented by the sun and has the moon under her feet, Rev. 12:[1-2]. For the congregation stands founded upon the firm prophetic word, 2 Pet. 1:19, that Moses and the prophets have witnessed to about Christ Jesus through the Holy Spirit; and she has upon her head a golden crown of twelve stars which signifies the clean, pure, unfalsified, and true teaching of the holy apostles with which the congregation of God is adorned, Rev. 12:10. And she was also pregnant or made fruitful from the seed of God, with the Word of the heavenly Father wherewith she has been seeded. She also delivered this with great anxiety and distress and is therefore so severely persecuted by the dragon, [Rev. 12:4].

Thus the creation of the heavens and the earth is spiritually restored in Christ until the time that the perfect transformation out of the perishable into that eternal imperishable and glorified takes place, and all believers shall inherit and possess the new heavens and the new earth (which God will create and we await and in which righteousness shall dwell), 2 Pet. 3:13.

In Christ Jesus the creation of people is also renewed. For after Adam had sinned and the image of God in him, according to which he had been created, was destroyed, Gen. 3:6, there had to be a renewal of humanity; yes, a new creation occurred and that through Jesus Christ, through whom God works all things. But the image of God is that spiritual being of the invisible God, his eternal wisdom, power, righteousness, and eternal life which is Jesus Christ the essential image of his heavenly Father, the reflection of his glory, and an unblemished mirror of his divine glory, /345/ which was seen by Abraham, not with carnal eyes but in the spirit; and thus must all believers see and confess him, Wisd. of Sol. 7:26; 2 Cor. 4:4; Col. 1:15; Heb. 1:3.

The first persons, Adam and Eve, were created and made as a likeness of the divine image, Gen. 1:27; 5:1; Wisd. of Sol. 2:23. They were endowed with superior intelligence and knowledge of God and of all creatures and, in addition thereto, also with greater righteousness and holiness, with which they loved God, and were provided with a blessed and immortal life in paradise toward eternal life in heaven, Ecclus. 17:3; James 3:9.

But since humankind did not remain in the first creation but lost the image of God through disobedience, therefore they must be newly created by God through Jesus Christ, Gen. 3:15; Rom. 5:18; 1 Cor. 15:21. Therefore the Son of God was promised to Adam and has appeared to all people in order that he might destroy the works of the devil and again renew the lost image of God in human beings, [1 Cor. 15:25-26]; 1 John 3:5; that is that he takes away the sins of the world, John 1:29, swallows up death, 1 Cor. 15:54, and gains eternal life for humanity by his resurrection and victory, Heb. 2:14; Rom. 3:23[-24]; 8:3[-4]; and by his Word and Spirit should make new persons here in this life, John 3:3; Gal. 6:[15]; Phil. 3:21; and hereafter, at his glorious appearing in the resurrection, prepare perfect persons who shall be glorified and shine as the sun in the kingdom of their Father, conformed to the nature of angels and partakers of the divine nature, Matt. 13:43; 22:30. And thus there is a new creation, a new birth of humanity, appearing through Jesus Christ.

After that then, in Jesus Christ, marriage was also renewed and again made right, which had not remained with the first order of God in paradise with one man and one woman with equal personalities, that is, both created after the image of God and were joined together by God, Gen. 2:21[-22]. But in the first world, marriage was misused by the children of God through the corrupt nature and evil desire of the flesh, Gen. 6:1[-2]. And this happened in part on account of the figures (just as it happened with Abraham and several others), Gal. 4:[25] and in part on account of the stiffneckedness of the people of Israel, [marriage] has fallen to a corrupt and strange manner and practice through the /346/ permission of God and Moses his servant, Matt. 19:4. Then Christ comes and points us again to the first order of God which was from the beginning in the pleasure ground or paradise and says: Have you not read that God, who created in the beginning, created one husband and one wife? "Therefore a man leaves his father and his mother and adheres [clings] to his wife, and they two shall be one flesh," Gen. 2:24; Eph. 5:31; what therefore God has joined together, no one shall separate, Matt. 19:6.

So marriage is therefore now restored by Christ to its original and correct divine order, namely, that it is God's joining together of two persons, that is of one man and one woman in one flesh, Gen. 2:[24]; Matt. 19:4. And they both must be persons who are created of God according to his image, John 3:3; Eph. 4:23[-24]; Col. 3:[10], that is, they must be born anew out of God, conformed to Christ Jesus, and be renewed in the inner being through the Holy Spirit; they must come together in paradise, that is in the congregation of God, and God must unite them, Rev. 2:7. This is a true marriage before God in which he himself cooperates, and this occurs according to his will and in his name. This [is] what Paul calls to marry in the Lord, 1 Cor. 7:39. And in this manner, Christ has again restored marriage, and all that is done outside of this and contrary to it is wrong before God, although one may adorn and thus also decorate the matter as beautifully as one can and will.

Here in addition the figurative marriage between Adam and Eve is spiritually restored in Christ Jesus, Rom. 5:18. For he is the second and new Adam, 1 Cor. 15:45, and his bride, taken out of his side, flesh of his flesh and bone of his bone, Eph. 5:30, is the spiritual Eve; a mother of all believing Christians and from this has come and originated a new world, a new race, new born-again children of God out of his imperishable seed, that is, new born through his living and powerful Word and brought forth from his bride, 1 Pet. 1:23; 1 John 5:1; James 1:18.

But just as among the children of the first Adam, the fall came through enviousness, wickedness, and frivolity; namely that the murderous Cain strangled the righteous Abel, Gen. 4:8, evil took the upper hand and all flesh corrupted its way before the Lord. The children of God saw the daughters of men that they were beautiful /347/ of form, and they have taken in marriage those whom they themselves wanted, Gen. 6:1[-2]. Thus it has also gone with the children of the second and spiritual Adam. For the righteous children of God were strangled by Cain's seed, that is, by the ungodly and apostate.

The beautiful forms of the daughters of men, the evil lust of the flesh, the externally glorious appearance of the idolatrous congregations of the great harlot of Babylon, and the false prophets of Jezebel, have deceived the children of God and led them to idolatry, Rev. 17:1[-4]; 2:20. And thus the world is again placed wholly and entirely into evil under the power of the antichrist, [1] John 5:19, and all things are laid waste through the child of perdition, 2 Thess. 2:3. Nevertheless, there has yet remained a sprout of the righteous children of

God who have found grace before his eyes to enter with Noah into the ark and to keep their souls eternally, Gen. 8:16; 1 Pet. 3:20.

For in Christ Jesus is also again repeated the action of Noah with the ark, the flood, and the saving of a few souls. For Jesus Christ is the true spiritual Noah, the preacher of righteousness, and the members of his household are the children of God, the true Christians, 1 Pet. 3:[20]; Matt. 12:49. He has proclaimed to the corrupt world the future wrath of God and threatened the unrepentant and unbelievers with the sentence of damnation, Matt. 3:2; 4:17; 11:20, 23. He has thereby also built an ark, that is the holy Christian church,[1] for the preparation and protection of all believing souls; and all those who willfully despise God's Word, disdain the proffered grace of Jesus Christ, who have closed their eyes to the light of the gospel, and thus have remained outside of the ark, these are destroyed through the punishment of the Lord, John 5:38; 8:24.

Yes, upon these shall come wrath and disfavor from heaven on the day when God shall judge the world through Jesus Christ, Rom. 2:8. But as many as have accepted Christ with a true faith and have entered into his spiritual ark, these shall be preserved in it to eternal life and the covenant of God will be renewed and established with them through the rainbow which signifies Jesus Christ, the truly gracious sign in heaven at the right hand of the almighty Father, John 1:12; 3:36; 6:47; 8:31; 11:26; 14:21; Gen. 9:13; Eph. 1:3. And they shall be blessed of God with heavenly benedictions in order to grow spiritually, 1 Pet. 3:9, and to increase, winning many children through the gospel of Jesus Christ, just as the apostles did, and converted many thousands to God through the preaching of the divine Word and the activity of the Holy Spirit, Heb. 1:3; Gal. 3:26; 4:6; Acts 2:41; 4:[33]; 8:[12]; 10:44; 16:5.

Out of these an accursed seed has again sprouted through the /348/ mocker Ham, Gen. 9:[22-]25, previously portrayed, namely the false brethren, Dan. 11:24, the antichrist (a wicked seed remaining from Canaan), who at the time of the apostles departed from the congregation of God, despising, belittling and mocking Jesus Christ and having greatly troubled the pious, Rom. 16:17-18; [1 John 2:18-19]; 3 John 9; for where the children of God are there Satan mingles among them, Job 1:6. Therefore Paul says that there must be divisions among the Christians so that they which are tested may become manifest, 1 Cor. 11:18[-19]. Thus it has been from the beginning in the times of Adam, Noah, Lot, in the Israel of the flesh, in the congregation of the apostles and everywhere, [Titus 1:10-13, 16].

In Christ Jesus afterwards, the action of God with Abraham, Isaac, Jacob, and with the whole of Israel is again brought to pass in the Spirit and true being. For the spiritual Abraham is God the heavenly Father himself with his two wives which are the two testaments, between which the first one was barren for a long time, until the time of the promise, Gal. 4:24[-26]. Between these the bondmaiden, Hagar, that is the literal, figurative, serviceable synagogue, produces her seed and race, namely, the Jewish people and Levitical priesthood with its imperfect ceremonies and sacrifices which can justify no one nor make them perfect, Heb. 8:7; 10:9. After that the free child Isaac, Jesus Christ, was born above the natural course, God's Word became flesh, the only begotten Son of the Father came into the world, a beginning of all new creatures of God, a first born among all his brothers, who are brought forth from the free Sarah, from that heavenly Jerusalem, and in Isaac are reckoned as the seed of the promise, John 1:14; 1 John 1:1; Rev. 3:14; Gal. 4:26[-27]; Rom. 9:8. Ishmael quarreled with Isaac, derided him, and was therefore cast out and might not become an heir. That is, the Jews have rejected, mocked, and persecuted Christ and his own and would not accept. Therefore, the kingdom of heaven is also taken from them and given to the Gentiles, and they may not receive any inheritance so long as they remain in unbelief, Matt. 22:8; Rom. 11:25.

But between Abraham and Isaac comes the King and priest of the most high God, Melchizedek, a beautiful figure of Jesus Christ and of his eternal kingdom and priesthood, Gen. 14:18; Ps. 110:4. For Melchizedek was described by the apostle as a king of righteousness and of peace, a priest of the most high God who was greater than Abraham or Levi, for he /349/ blessed Abraham and Levi has given him tithes. Yes, because he bore the image of Christ, he is described as without father, without mother, without race, without beginning of days or end of life, and is compared to the Son of God, Heb. 7:1[-3].

All this one finds also in Christ Jesus, for he is the King of eternal righteousness and all divine peace, Ps. 45:[6-7]; 1 Cor. 1:2; Eph. 2:[14]; Heb. 1:8; 2:9. Yes, he is the peace and righteousness itself of all believers who is greater than Abraham for he is already before Abraham was, John 8:58. He took away the Levitical priesthood, and has himself become our only High Priest installed with a high and costly oath and sits at the right hand of God in heaven, Ps. 110:4; Heb. 1:3; Eph. 1:20; Heb. 10:12. He also has no father nor mother nor race upon earth, for [he] has proceeded from God his heavenly Father, John 8:42; 16:27; [17:8, 25], conceived in Mary of the Holy Spirit through the surrounding shining of the divine power, Matt. 1:20, became a human being, and was born out of her a Son of the most high, the first and the last, the first born of every creature, yes, eternal life itself, Luke 2:21; Rev. 1:8; Col. 1:15; John 14:6.

Likewise, the [action of God] with Sodom, with the angels, and with Lot and his wife, Gen. 19, is also repeated here. For the spiritual Sodom whereby the Lord was crucified is the evil world, full of all haughtiness, all abominations and inhuman uncleanliness, Rev. 11:8; 16:8[-9]. Out of this Sodom will be led and guided by the angels of God all those who with Lot fear God, who are pleasing to him, and who are ordained to eternal life. But the world shall pass away with her evil lusts, desires, and works, just as Sodom and Gomorrah have passed away, 1 John 2:17; 2 Esd. 2:36; 2 Pet. 2:6. And the unbelievers, who with Lot's wife looked back and therefore are not fit for God's kingdom, those remain standing, those will be blinded and hardened by God, Acts 28:27; [Rom. 1:28], and in their perverse mind delivered over so that they shall not escape the punishment of God. Therefore Christ says in the gospel, "Remember Lot's wife," Luke 17:32.

And after that is also fulfilled in Christ Jesus the figurative sacrifice of Isaac who carried the wood and the fire to the top of the mountain where his father sacrificed him upon the altar and, nevertheless, he did not die, but a wether or ram was killed and sacrificed in his place, Gen. 22:10. And this signifies to us that Jesus Christ was also obedient to his heavenly Father unto death, Phil. 2:8; Isa. 53:7, and that he carried the wood of the cross /350/ upon his body through the fervent love which he had toward us and was sacrificed for us upon the altar of the cross, 1 Pet. 2:21; 3:18. Nevertheless, he was not killed according to the Spirit, but died according to the flesh, Heb. 1:3. And just as Abraham received Isaac from the altar as one who had come to life from the dead as an example of the resurrection, thus Jesus Christ, after he had offered himself to God for us as a fragrant offering, Eph. 5:2, arose from the dead, 1 Cor. 15:4, as the established and confirmed heir of all the possessions of his heavenly Father Abraham together with his everlasting seed, that is, with all true Christians.

Likewise, in Christ the figure of Isaac and Rebecca was spiritually renewed and restored in such a form that just as Abraham made his servant swear and took an oath from him that he should take no other wife for his son Isaac than one from his race. This the servant did, and he brought the willing Rebecca to her bridegroom and lord. Gen. 24:[1-61]. Thus it also happened with the spiritual wooing of the bride of Christ through John the Baptist, through the apostles, and through many other faithful servants of the Lord, John 3:29. For these trustworthy servants of the most high God are sent out for this reason, bound with a solemn oath, that they should seek and bring to Christ Jesus, the true Isaac, the rightful heir of all his heavenly Father's possessions, a willing Rebecca (who through faith and the new birth became a member of his race, his character and nature, Acts 17:28; Eph. 5:30; [1] Pet. 2:9). Namely, the congregation which he has loved and gloriously adorned with spiritual gifts and with whom he has brought forth the children of the kingdom, born again out of God's Word and who therefore have become his brothers and companions out of grace through adoption into [a childlike relationship] with God, Gal. 3:28; 4:7; [1] Pet. 1:23; Rom. 8:17; Eph. 1:11[-12]; Heb. 2:12[-13].

Again, the springs of living water which had been dug by the servants of his father, Abraham, those which the Philistines had filled up with earth out of envy, [Gen. 26:15], Isaac had his servants reopen and cleanse, [Gen. 26:18]. Therefore the herdsmen of Gerar quarreled with the servants of Isaac, [Gen. 26:20]. Thus God the heavenly Father gave us the springs of living water, /351/ that is, his pure divine Word through his faithful messengers, the good prophets. But the false prophets have clogged these with impure human teachings and earthly wisdom and falsified the pure Word of God. The prophets also complain severely about this; namely, that the false prophets have trampled with their feet the good pasture with which the sheep should have been fed and with their feet have made unclean the pure water which the sheep should have drunk. Thus the sheep have eaten and drunk that which was trampled and made impure with their feet. That is, instead of the pure divine Word, they have heard and accepted an impure and human teaching from the false prophets and have thus been led astray, Ezek. 34:2[-3].

But Christ Jesus, the true Isaac has reopened the clogged up fountains of the Holy Scripture and brought the darkened Word of God again to the light of day. He has allowed the pure clear gospel to be preached everywhere through his servants and apostles, John 1:5; 5:26; 8:12; 10:9; 14:10; 15:5; 16:28; 17:8; Matt. 28:19; Mark 16:15; Rom. 10:15. But the uncircumcised Philistines, the scribes and the Pharisees, the uncircumcised at heart, the antichrists, and the false teachers, Acts 7:51, set themselves against it and quarrel with the servants of Isaac, the ministers of Jesus Christ, on account of the fountains of living waters which they regard and reckon as their own. For they alone wish to be interpreters of the Scripture and say boldly, "Our tongue shall take the upper hand. To us alone belongs the right to speak who is our master." Ps. [13:4]; 73:11. Therefore, there is and remains strife between the servants of Jesus Christ and the false teachers who are the true Philistines, enemies of the gospel and the spiritual Israel.

Thereafter, the patriarch Jacob is also repeated in Christ with many beautiful figures which are explained in part in the booklet about the tabernacle of Moses, for there I have written much about Esau and Jacob. But I will narrate that here in brief. Jacob was sent by his father, Isaac, to Laban, the brother of his mother, Rebecca, Gen. 28:2. Upon the way, as the sun was going down, the Lord showed himself to him at Bethel. Thus he fell into a deep sleep and saw in the dream a ladder reaching to heaven, and God stood at the top and said, "I am the Lord, the God of Abraham, your father, and the God of Isaac; the land on which you lie I will give to you and your seed; and your seed shall be like the dust of the earth, and you shall spread abroad to the west and to the east and to the north and to the south; and by you and your seed shall all the families of the earth be blessed. /352/

"Behold, I am with you and will keep you wherever you travel, and will bring you back to this land; and I will not leave you until I have done that of which I have spoken to you." And when he awoke from his sleep, he said, "Without doubt the Lord is in this place; and I did not know it." And he was afraid, and said, "How holy is this place! This is none other than the house of God, and this is the gate of heaven," Gen. 28:13[-17].

This ladder signifies Jesus Christ who is the only way to the Father and into the kingdom of heaven. Through him the believers come to God, John 14:6. Here also the promise of the gospel is portrayed through the angels on the ladder, for the angels also preached the gospel from heaven, Luke 2:9[-10]. Here is the renewal of the divine covenant through Jesus Christ, who is that promised seed in whom are blessed all those who walk in the footsteps of the faith of Abraham, not alone the Jews, but also the Gentiles who believe in Jesus Christ, Gen. 22:18; Gal. 3:9; Rom. 4:12. Here the Lord is certainly in the midst of his congregation, here is the house of God and the door to heaven, Matt. 17:4; 28:20; 1 Tim. 3:14[-15].

Here is given through Jesus Christ the new and comforting promise of that glorious spiritual kingdom and inheritance of the blessed rest in the true promised land of Canaan, Heb. 4:9; John 14:2, that is, the eternal and imperishable kingdom with God in heaven, where the Lord Jesus Christ has gone in order to prepare a place for us, John 16:22; 17:24, a tabernacle not of this building, but another, which is not made with hands, yes, whose builder and creator is God, 2 Cor. 5:1; Heb. 11:10. And the Lord Jesus Christ shall come again and take us to him that we may be where he is and see his glory and also become participant of the same in eternity, John 12:46; 14:2; 16:5; 17:24.

From Jacob were born the twelve patriarchs from whom came the twelve tribes of Israel. These twelve patriarchs represent to us the twelve apostles who were born again out of the Spirit, Luke 24:47; Acts 1:13, and endowed with power from above. These are the spiritual fathers who through the gospel and through faith in Jesus Christ, have brought forth the Israel of God, 1 Cor. 3:5; Gal. 2:8; 4:19; 6:13. Such believing Christians are the true spiritual Israelites and the seed of Abraham, Rom. 4:12, and those whom they have won to Christ through God's Word, these are the fathers as the apostles themselves testify; /353/ for they call themselves the fathers and believers, the children, 2 Cor. 3:6; Eph. 3:7; 1 John 2:1, and all this is from God who is named the true Father over all that is in heaven and on earth, as Paul says, [Eph. 3:14-16].

Furthermore, the figure of Joseph is then spiritually fulfilled in Christ Jesus. For just as Joseph was sent out to his brothers by his father Jacob, and they out of great jealousy sold him, Gen. 37:28, and he thus came into Egypt and because of his piety and innocence was thrown into prison, and by God's providence because of his wisdom was again delivered out of it, placed before King Pharaoh, and after the interpretation of the dreams, installed and exalted to be a lord over the whole of Egypt, [Gen. 39; 41:1-45].

So also it happened to Christ according to the Spirit. He was sent by God his heavenly Father into this world to his brothers, that is to the Jews (out of whom he was born according to the flesh), John 1:11; Rom. 9:5. But they have not wanted to accept him nor permit him to be their Lord, Matt. 21:39; Luke 23. Yes, they hated, persecuted, betrayed, sold, hanged, crucified, and killed him, Acts 3:15. Nevertheless, thus he, the Lord Jesus Christ, is exalted through the right hand of God above all principalities, powers, thrones, and dominions, [Acts 2:33; 5:31], and above every name which may be named in this and the future world, Phil. 2:9; Eph. 1:[20-]21. To him is given all power in heaven and on earth to distribute spiritual gifts, Matt. 28:18; Col. 1:16, and he has received from his heavenly Father all judgment over the living and the dead, John 5:26[-27], so that they should all honor the Son just as they honor the Father, fall down before him and worship him, for he sits at the right hand of God the almighty Father in the heavenly being, one Lord over all with his Father and the Holy Spirit.

Here is also to be observed the renewal of the divine covenant with Abraham, Isaac, and Jacob; made through Jesus Christ who is that promised seed in whom are and will be blessed all those who walk in the footsteps of the faith of Abraham, Gen. 22:18; Gal. 3:16. This applies not alone to Jews, but also to the Gentiles who believe in Jesus Christ, to those who are also circumcised, not in the foreskin of the flesh, but of the hearts, namely, with the circumcision of Christ which takes place in the Spirit without hands, through putting off this sinful body, through the dying of the /354/ old person, the burial of sins, and the resurrection to a new life, Rom. 2:14; 4:12; 8:2; Col. 2:11; Rom. 6:4.

[To] these is also given through Jesus Christ the new and comforting promise of that glorious spiritual kingdom and inheritance, Heb. 3:18; 4:9, of the blessed rest in the land of Canaan; of the eternal imperishable kingdom with God in heaven, where Christ Jesus has gone to prepare the place for us, John 14:3; 17:24, a tabernacle not of this carpentry but another, not made with human hands but whose builder and creator is God, 2 Cor. 5:1; Heb. 11:10. And he shall come again and take us to himself that we may be where he is and see his glory and become participants of the same in eternity, John 17:24.

In addition we also find here the spiritual Egypt, that land of darkness, just as it was earlier according to the flesh, Rev. 11:8. For [just as] the people of God, the children of Israel in Egypt were plagued by Pharaoh and his servants, Exod. 3:7, and God miraculously delivered them from it through Moses by means of many signs and miraculous deeds; yes, through his powerful hand and outstretched arm brought them through the sea and led them through the wilderness by day through the cloud and by night through the pillar of fire, fed them with the bread of heaven and gave them water to drink from the rock, 1 Cor. 10:4, and finally brought the survivors into the promised land. So we too were plagued by the imprisonment of sins, of unrighteousness, and of death under the hellish Pharaoh Satan, [2 Thess. 2:9],[2] but we have been delivered through Jesus Christ, the true Moses, baptized into his death with the cloud and with the sea, Eph. 2:13; Col. 2:12; Rom. 5:9; 6:3, that is, with his precious blood (with which our consciences are sprinkled and our sins are washed away) and with the Holy Spirit which is poured out upon us from God through Christ Jesus, 1 John 5:[6-]8; 1 Pet. 1:19; Heb. 12:1. But Pharaoh with all his servants, riders, and wagons, our enemies and persecutors, that is, the devil, hell, sin, and death are all overcome through the blood of the cross of Christ and by our faith in his name, [1 John 5:4-5]; 1 Cor. 15:[24-27]; Col. 2:10. And thus we have come into the wilderness on the way toward that promised land in heaven.

Here also is told again in Jesus Christ the figure of the Paschal Lamb. That is, just as the children of Israel had to eat the Passover lamb which they had roasted by the fire, Exod. 12:[8], and [had] to sprinkle the doorposts and lintels /355/ of their houses so that the slaying angel of the Lord as he saw the blood of the Passover lamb might pass by and not slay these as he had slain all the first born of Egypt, Exod. 12:7; thus also Jesus Christ our Passover Lamb was roasted for us on the wood of the cross through his fervent love and this Paschal Lamb we must eat spiritually through faith, 1 Cor. 5:[7]; and we must be sprinkled in our consciences with his blood, 1 Pet. 1:[19]; [Heb. 10:22], before the future wrath of God which shall come upon the blind world, Heb. 12:[25]. Whoever desires to know more about this subject, let him read our confession of the Lord's Supper.

Likewise in Jesus Christ is also fulfilled the figure of that heavenly bread with which God fed Israel in the wilderness, Exod. 16:[4-]5, that which is also called the bread of angels in the Scriptures, Ps. 78:24. For Jesus Christ is that true and living bread come from heaven, a bread of God which gives life to the world, John 6:[51], a food for all hungry souls; yes, that eternal life through which the angels in heaven and the believers on earth live and are sustained, John 14:6; Col. 1:17; Heb. 1:[5-8].

In the same manner, the figure of Christ is repeated from the rock which followed Israel and gave water when Moses struck upon it with the rod that was in his hand, Num. 20:11; 1 Cor. 10:4. For Jesus Christ is the precious cornerstone of God laid in Zion, 1 Pet. 2:6, the living stone upon which the congregation is built, Matt. 16:18, out of which flowed through the power of God (which is signified by the rod of Moses), the living waters of the Holy Spirit for the refreshing of all thirsty souls, John 4:11; 7:38.

In Christ is also fulfilled the figure of the angel of the Lord which went before Israel and led her by day through the column of fire and by day through the cloud, Exod. 13:21; Ps. 78:14; 105:39. For Jesus Christ is our guide who shows us the way in the darkness of this world with his divine Word, and with the refreshing of his Holy Spirit protects, comforts, and quickens us before the heat of tribulation, so that we are not burned. And he teaches us at all times what we should do and let undone, Ps. 118:14; John 1:4; 8:12; 12:46; 14:6. Therefore we may not presume to understand nor begin to undertake anything unless we have Jesus Christ before us who leads us with his teaching, example, and Spirit. Thus, wherever anything proceeds otherwise, there one strays into darkness. There one misses the right way /356/ in the wilderness of this world and there one cannot come upon the right way.

Here the bitter waters of Marah, that is, the waters of sadness, fear and persecution, are sweetened by the wood of life that is there in the midst of God's paradise, that is, through Jesus Christ and his comforting gospel, Exod. 15:25; Rev. 2:7. For he is with all his disciples at all times in all the perils with which they meet and his Word is their comfort, Matt. 28:20, and sweetness, Ps. [119:103]; [19:10]. Here now begins the spiritual battle against Amalek and against all other surrounding enemies of Israel. That is, here one must fight and conquer with the armor of God and with the weapons of the Spirit against the princes of the world, against the spirits of evil, against Satan through the uplifting of the hands of Jesus Christ, Eph. 6:11; 2:2, Acts 15:11, which do not become weary (as the hands of Moses became heavy, [Exod. 17:12]), whereby the weakness and inadequate authority of the law may be well understood, Heb. 8:6; 9:9[-10]; 10:1. Namely, through the eternal sacrifice and holy perfect prayer of Christ who sits there at the right hand of the almighty Father and prays for us, Rom. 8:34; Col. 3:1. Yes, he has conquered all our enemies for us and our faith in his name is the victory that overcomes the world, just as John testified, John 16:33; 1 John 5:4.

But many err and sin against the Lord. Therefore, they are struck down in the wilderness (even as it happened with the figurative Israel as an example for us) that is, that many who have once been enlightened, have come to the knowledge of the truth, and have been delivered from Egypt again fall away from the living God. This takes place in many different ways; for some are overcome by a lust after the flesh [pots] of Egypt and satiated and dissatisfied with the heavenly bread, Exod. 16:[3]; Ps. 78:[18]. That is, they became carnally minded, desirous of false human teaching after which their ears itch, [2 Tim. 4:3]. They despise God's Word, that living heavenly bread, Jesus Christ. Therefore they must be punished by God and perish.

But some, who worship the molten calf and want to have a visible God, forsake Moses who tarries on the mountain, Exod. [32]:1. That is, they turn away from the living God, 1 Cor. 10:7, and from the Lord Jesus Christ who ascended to heaven and delays his return as they imagine, [Acts 1:9-11]. Therefore they fall upon a strange worship and choose for themselves idols /357/ which are visible, Rom. 1:23. Thus they play and leap around the golden calf. For whoever loves or honors any creature above the Creator, or instead of God, or whoever regards any human doctrine as equal to or above God's Word, or whoever sets his righteousness or seeks his salvation in any false worship which God himself has not instituted with one express word, without doubt worships the golden calf and is reckoned before the Lord as a servant of idols. However gloriously he may embellish or adorn his idolatry with the appearance of holiness, calling it true worship, it is, nevertheless, before God nothing other than idolatry, Deut. 5:[7]; 12:[2-]4. For God alone will be God and Lord and be confessed as such. He will also not be served according to our opinions but according to his Word alone, Isa. 28:9; Matt. 15:2.

But some commit adultery with the daughters of Moab, Num. 25:2; 1 Cor. 10:8. That is, they allow themselves to be seduced by false prophets and idolatrous congregations so that they receive a spirit of harlotry and fall into a carnal, godless life and worldly ways. With Zimri they do not care that the congregation mourns and is sorrowful before the Lord because of such sins and abominations, but they willfully continue in their evil, [Num. 25:6-9]. Therefore they are also punished by the Lord and put out of the congregation of God so that the whole of Israel may not be plagued on their account.

The new Balaamites also already existed in the time of the apostles and shortly afterward, 1 John 2:18; 2 Pet. 2:16; Jude 11, and they are still on hand to the present day. These false teachers who love the wages of unrighteousness and therefore cannot see the angel of the Lord standing in the way with the flaming sword and they neither let themselves be turned about nor reprimanded by the ass whose mouth God has opened, Num. 22:22[-28]. That is, they do not accept the discipline of the Lord from the simple and humble, through whom God speaks and works, but they continue on and would gladly malign Israel. But God will not hear them and blesses his people all the more so that their enemies must also marvel at the glorious dwellings of Jacob and over the camp of Israel.

Some also rise up with Dathan, Abiram, and Korah against Moses and Aaron and are therefore swallowed up alive /358/ by the earth, Num. 16:31[-32]. That is, they make disputes in the congregation of God, petulant despisers, mockers, and transgressors of the God-serving teaching of Jesus Christ. They are the cause of division and sects. They grasp after an office that has not been commanded to them and are therefore judged dreadfully by the Lord. Yes, they come out of eternal life into eternal death, out of the kingdom of God into hell, unless they amend themselves, which, however, they sometimes can scarcely come to; "for a heretical person," says the apostle, "is perverted and sinful as he has judged himself," Titus 3:[10-]11. Yes, "many crucify the Son of God themselves and ridicule him," Heb. 6:[6]. They regard the blood of the covenant impure, through which they were sanctified, and they "outrage the spirit of grace," Heb. 10:[29], which now, alas, may be observed in some.

Some who murmur against the Lord are impatient in the temptation that has happened to them, 1 Cor. 10:10; Num. 20:3, when by right they should praise the Lord for them; therefore, they are destroyed by the destroyer. But some who tempt Christ and are therefore bitten by the serpent and poisoned with deadly sins, from which they must die the death; that is, unless they do genuine repentance and look once again upon the sign of grace which is Jesus Christ with the eyes of faith, John 3:14. For the figurative metal serpent is spiritually fulfilled in Christ Jesus; for as the metal serpent in the wilderness had the form but not the poison, but was rather a saving sign so that all who gazed upon it became well through the Lord who is the Savior of all, Wisd. of Sol. 16:6[-7], thus also Jesus Christ was sent from God in the form of sinful flesh; nevertheless, he did not know sin, Rom. 8:3, but he was the spotless and innocent Lamb of God who takes away the sins of the world, John 1:29; 1 John 2:2. He is the true saving sign of all grace and of eternal life and was therefore on the cross lifted up from the earth so that whoever believes in him might be healed from the bite of the hellish serpent, John 3:15, and may live eternally in God.

Likewise, here [one] should consider how twelve men were sent by Moses to spy out the land, and all of these became timid and were frightened before the strong people of the land, before the children of Anak and before the high walls of the cities, with the exception of Joshua and Caleb, who remained bold in the Lord and comforted the congregation of Israel, Num. 13:17[-30]. Therefore the others said that one should stone them. And the Lord was furious with the congregation and said that not one /359/ of those who had blasphemed him and were unbelieving of his Word and disobedient should enter the good land save Joshua and Caleb who remained steadfast in the faith, [Num. 14:26-30].

Through these spies the teachers and leaders of the congregation are actually portrayed of whom, alas, many have fallen away and do not trust God, but they are afraid before men and also make others

Concerning Spiritual Restitution / 333

fainthearted. The fruitful ministers of God oppose this and comfort the congregation with God's Word, and they must therefore often suffer many things from their own brothers. Nevertheless, the Lord knows how to deliver his own out of temptation, but [also] how to punish the apostate, the disobedient, and the unbelievers, just as he has certainly shown us an example in the children of Israel. Therefore, the apostle says, "And with whom was he provoked for forty years? Was it not with those who sinned, whose bodies died in the wilderness? But to whom did he yet swear that they should not come to his rest, except those who were unbelieving? And we see that they were unable to enter because of unbelief," Heb. 3:17[-19]; 4:5; 8:9; 10:1.

So let us now fear that in order to enter into his rest we do not abandon the promise and let not any of us be found who remains outside. For it is proclaimed to us as to them. But the word of the preaching did not help them when faith was not added by those who heard it. But we who believe it enter into his rest, Heb. 4:1[-4].

Again, the whole of God's dealings with Moses about the tabernacle, its preparation, equipment, and adornment was already figurative of the time of the law which was then present, and of the future time of grace and truth which has appeared in Jesus Christ, just as one may read in the letter to the Hebrews, Heb. 7; 8, and in our booklet about the tabernacle of Moses.

Here it is also well to observe that both Moses and Aaron died in the wilderness and were not able to take possession of the promised land because they had displeased the Lord, but Joshua had to lead the people in and divide the land, Deut. 34:5; Num. 20:28; Deut. 34:9.

This indicates to us that both the law and the Levitical priesthood with all their ceremonies cease and come to an end in Jesus Christ, Heb. 8:6; 10:1. And none of these could bring anyone to perfection, nor take sins away nor grant righteousness, nor save except the spiritual Joshua, Jesus Christ, the Prince of our faith and the perfecter of our salvation, Heb. 12:2, who brings /360/ us into the true promised land, into that eternal kingdom of God; here in the Spirit and in the power of the new birth and the abundance of spiritual riches, and hereafter into the eternal glory of heaven and the possession of all imperishable things when we shall have become like Christ and see him face-to-face in the perfection of the future being, Rev. 2:[10-]11; 3:4[-5]; 1 John 3:2; 1 Cor. 15:49[-50].

Hereafter there remains yet to be considered how the promised land and rest is to be won; namely, that one must go through the Jordan where the great waters stand high and are frightening to behold. These signify to us that we must enter the kingdom of God through much distress and suffering, as well as through the temporal death, Heb. 4:9; Acts 14:[16]. For the righteous must suffer much here and be put to death daily which greatly terrifies human nature, Ps. 44:[22]; Rom. 8:36. But for that the priests stand in the midst of the Jordan with the ark of God. They comfort us with the sanctuary, Josh. 3:17, that is with the Lord's Word, for that is our comfort and the strength of our life in the midst of death until we come out of this world, Ps. 23:[4]; 73:1, and cross over into the heavenly country, into the blessed rest where we shall rest with God from all our labors, work, and cares in eternity, Matt. 7:11; Rev. 14:4.

Thus we come first out of Egypt through the sea into the wilderness, as when one was first converted from darkness to light and delivered from the kingdom of Satan, freed from sin, hell, and death, and were placed upon the right way that leads to eternal life, Col. 1:13; Heb. 2:15; Matt. 7:14. Thereafter one passes through the Jordan into the promised land as we leave this world and come into the blessed rest, Heb. 4:9; Rev. 14:[13]. But that Joshua at the command of God circumcised with stone knives the young Israelites who were born in the wilderness and uncircumcised, Josh. 5:3, because they had to be circumcised before they could enter and possess the land; this signifies to us that all true Israelites must be circumcised in the heart with the circumcision of Christ, through the laying aside of the sinful body in the flesh before they may enter into the kingdom of the heavenly Father.

Further there follows now the figurative reign of the judges who many times delivered Israel from the Philistines and from the hands of other enemies; established peace in the land and judged the people, Judg. 6:14; 7:21[-22]; [7]:24[-25]. All of this is spiritually repeated in Christ Jesus for he is the glorious warrior and conqueror who delivers his people from all their enemies, has made peace in their consciences /361/, and is now the righteous judge in his congregation with his Word and Spirit, John 16:33; Heb. 12:2; Rom. 5:11; Eph. 2:15; Heb. 2:[8-10], and at the last day he shall hold judgment over the living and the dead, Acts 17:31; [10:42]; [Rom. 2:16]; [14:10]; 1 Tim. 6:14; 1 Pet. 4:5; Num. 12.

Likewise, in Christ is also restored the figure of Samson who was a Nazarene of God and a judge in Israel. He took as a wife a daughter of the Philistines which his father and mother did not understand, nor did they know that it was from the Lord, [Judg. 14:3]. It was Samson who strangled the young lion, [Judg. 14:6], slew a thousand Philistines with the jawbone of an ass, Judg. 15:14[-15]; he who laid the gates of the city of Gaza upon his shoulders and carried them to Mount Hebron, [Judg. 16:3]. He also fell in love with other foreign and heathen women and because of them lost his strength and fell into the hands of his enemies. They put out his eyes and made sport with him until his hair had grown long again and he received his strength again. And when the lords of the Philistines had come together to bring to their idol Dagon a great sacrifice, and to rejoice that Samson their enemy was captured and had to perform before them, then he grasped hold of the two columns on which the house was set, the one on his right hand, the other on his left, and he bent the two mightily, so that the house fell down and he in his death killed more [Philistines] than during his life, [Judg. 16:23-31].

This is spiritually fulfilled in Christ, for he is the true Nazarene, the holy Son of the most high, Matt. [1:21]; Luke 2:[29-33], and judge over the Israel of God. He took unto himself the heathen and chose a congregation out of them, and gathered it through the preaching of the gospel which he betrothed to himself by faith. This the Jews did not understand, that it was foreseen and ordained of the Lord, Rom. 11:25; Acts 10:44[-45]; 15:14; Gal. 2:8; 1 Pet. 5:8[-9]; Heb. 2:8, Hos. 2:[19-20]. He overcame the young lion, the adversary of Christians, that is Satan, out of which conquest has come all the sweetness of divine grace, all comfort and refreshing of the soul. With the jawbone of an ass, that is, with his unlearned apostles who were regarded as asses by the world, he overcame the uncircumcised of heart, 1 Cor. 1:26-28]; 3:19, the worldly wise and the scribes, the enemies of the gospel. Out of the poor Word of the cross, God gives to all true worshippers the living water of the Holy Spirit through faith, in order to refresh thirsty souls therewith, Acts 7:54; John 4:11; 7:38.

He has destroyed the gates of hell and taken captivity captive. With his body he bore the sins of the world /362/ upon the wood of the cross, John 1:29; Eph. 4:8; 1 John 2:2. He put off his divine form, his eternal glory he has laid aside. He himself went outside through love which he has had for us Gentiles, (who walked in all kinds of idolatry), Phil. 2:5[-8], and thus, according to the providence of his heavenly Father, and for the sake of our salvation, fell into the hands of his enemies, the lords of the Philistines, Annas and Caiphas, with the Pharisees and Jews, and the assembly of the Gentiles, who took him prisoner, blinded, ridiculed, and abused him, and they rejoiced at his suffering, 1 Pet. 2:[24]; 4:1; Matt. 26:56; Mark 14:46; Luke 22:52.

Nevertheless, the Lord Jesus Christ, the faithful Savior, avenged himself on his enemies. Through his suffering and death he overcame them all, Heb. 2:8. He has taken away the devil's power and vanquished death, and restored and accomplished life and our eternal salvation. Yes, he has become the death of death and the conquest of hell, Hos. 13:14; 1 Cor. 15:54; [Heb. 2:8-9]. But the Jews, who did not wish that the Lord Jesus Christ should rule over them, he has punished. He has destroyed their city and scattered them among the Gentiles, and they must still bear the guilt and vengeance of the innocent and righteous blood which they have shed, Matt. 22:5; 23:34.

Thereafter comes the figurative kingdom of David, the son of Jesse, 1 Sam. 16:[11-13], who was the least among his brothers and a shepherd of the sheep of his father, who was taken from the flocks and anointed king over Israel by the prophet Samuel. He killed the lion and the bear and rescued the lost sheep. He killed the giant, great Goliath, a hero of the Philistines, an enemy, a mocker, and a blasphemer of Israel, with his own sword. Wherefore great joy came to Israel because her greatest enemy was slain, 1 Sam. 17:[50-51]. Therefore they praised God with harps, trombones, and Psalms, 1 Sam. 18:[6-]7. Thereafter Saul out of ill will and jealousy persecuted David so that for a long time he had to journey throughout [the land] and hide himself here and there. Nevertheless, at the last he became a powerful king over the whole of Israel.

This is altogether repeated spiritually in Christ Jesus. For he is the true root of Jesse, Isa. 11:1; Rev. 22:16, the sprout of David, the branch of righteousness, Jer. 23:5, the least in appearance among humanity, the only true Shepherd of the sheep of his heavenly Father, who has redeemed the lost sheep of the human race out of the mouth of the lion and the claws of the bear, John 10:11; 1 Pet. 2:24. He was anointed by God with the oil of gladness /363/ above all his fellows, Ps. [45:7]; Heb. 1:8; Col. 2:[13-]14; Heb. 2:8. He has conquered the giant Goliath, that is Satan, with his death and blood of the cross. Therefore the Israel of God rejoices that the greatest enemy of the Christians, the hellish Satan, the adversary of the children of God, has been conquered through our spiritual David, Jesus Christ; who with his divine righteousness has abolished sin, and with his eternal life has slain death, and with his saving grace has taken condemnation away, 1 Pet. 5:4; 2 Cor. 5:19. That is a joyfully rich gospel, full of all comfort, with which the Holy Spirit comforts all penitent, saddened, and troubled hearts, John 1:14; 14:6. For this one thanks God. One sings and prays in one's heart unto the Lord with great joy of the spirit, Eph.

5:20; Col. 3:16.

Again, Christ was also persecuted by the godless and unbelieving Jews, by the perverse Pharisees and scribes and often had to depart from Judea and hide himself in the wilderness, and thus he escaped their hands, Luke 4:29[-30]; John 8:59; 10:31. Nevertheless, he has occupied his kingdom and was installed and established as a powerful King and Lord upon Mount Zion by God his Father. And God has given him the throne of David, and he shall reign in the house of Jacob in eternity, and his kingdom shall have no end, Rom. 3:24[-25]; 7:4; Ps. 2:6; Luke 2:28[-32].

And he has stepped forward as the peaceful Solomon, our peace and hope before God the Father. And has, through his apostles, who were clothed with power from on high on the day of Pentecost, built the temple in Jerusalem, that is, the Christian congregation, and has adorned her with manifold spiritual gifts, as this is clearly manifested in the apostolic congregation, as the Scripture in great clarity indicates. That is that the promise of Solomon was applied to Christ by the apostle, Acts 2:[4]; 4:31. For that God had promised David that the fruit of his loins should sit upon his throne, this was fulfilled according to the letter when Solomon became king over Israel in his father's place, just as one may clearly observe out of Scripture and as Solomon himself testifies, Acts 2:30; Ps. 132:11[-12]; 1 Kings 8:20. But according to the Spirit it is to be understood [to point toward] the true Solomon, Jesus Christ, who has a throne which abides throughout eternity, and he is King over his congregation, [that is] over the whole spiritual Israel, Ps. 45:7; Heb. 1:8.

Likewise, that the figurative temple of Solomon in Jerusalem was dedicated signifies to us that the congregation of the Lord was sanctified by God through Jesus Christ with the Holy Spirit, and /364/ is therefore a holy temple, a house of the living God, a pillar and foundation of the truth, 1 Cor. 3:17; 2 Cor. 6:16; 1 Tim. 3:[15]. In this temple God desires to be worshiped in Spirit and in truth, John 4:23. Here God wants sacrifices to be offered, Heb. 3:1; 5:[3-]4; 8:1[-2]; 10:[1-10]. Here are the true priests and Levites, the children and descendants of the spiritual Aaron our only High Priest, Jesus Christ, John 3:36. Here is the sanctuary of our God, the ark of the covenant, that pure and holy Word of the gospel, with all the gracious promises of God of the forgiveness of sins, of reconciliation with God, and of eternal life through Jesus Christ, Rom. 3:[23-]24; 5:6; 8:11; 10:11. Here is the blessed mystery of the sacramental signs of baptism and the Lord's Supper which were left by Christ to all believers, Matt. 26:[26];

28:19; Mark 14:24; 16:15[-16]; Luke 22:19; 24:25[-26]; 1 Cor. 10:16; 11:23[-26].

We must come to this temple to keep the Feast of the Passover, the Feast of Pentecost, and the Feast of Tabernacles spiritually unto the Lord. We keep the Feast of [the] Passover as we preach Jesus Christ our Paschal Lamb, sacrificed for us, believe in him, and cast out the old leaven of malice and wickedness and become a new dough. Thus in a spiritual manner we eat the Paschal Lamb with the unleavened bread of purity and truth, John 6:35; 1 Cor. 5:6[-7], remembering our severe bondage in Egypt under Satan who is a ruler of darkness, Eph. 2:2, and that we have been rescued out of this by the mighty hand of God and sprinkled in our consciences with the costly blood of the unblemished Paschal Lamb, Jesus Christ, 1 Pet. 1:2; Heb. 10:19. Thus we are guarded from the future punishment that shall come over the blind world, 1 Thess. 1:10.

The Feast of Pentecost we keep as we come before God and confess that we were in bondage in Egypt under the hellish Pharaoh, and that God has marvelously delivered us out of this bondage as a firstfruit of his creatures, James 1:[18]; Rev. 14:4[-5], and has accepted and elected us as heirs of his eternal kingdom in heaven, Eph. 1:7. And he has richly endowed and blessed us with heavenly goods for which we praise and thank God and offer him the fruits of righteousness, the thanksgiving of the lips of those who confess his name, Gal. 3:5; Heb. 13:15. And it is very necessary that we rightly acknowledge and consider well our ignorance, our blindness, and the burden of sins with which we were so heavily burdened, and by way of contrast the riches of God's grace which are poured out upon us through Jesus Christ so that we praise God /365/ and thank him for his unspeakable gifts which we have received from his goodness, Eph. 2:[7]; 4:[9-14]; 5:14[-16]; Rom. 1:8; 11:33.

The Feast of Tabernacles we keep as we confess to the Lord that we are pilgrims in this world and have no abiding place here. But we journey toward that promised land and have a longing for it that we might come to the blessed rest, to that heavenly Jerusalem, to the city of the living God where Jesus Christ has prepared a place for us, 1 Pet. 1:[4]; 2:11[-12]; Heb. 13:14; 4:9; 12:22; John 14:2. There we have a tabernacle which is not made by hands but which is eternal and heavenly, 2 Cor. 5:1. With this we shall be clothed as this our earthly house is broken; that is, as we have laid off this perishable and mortal flesh, and shall be clothed with an imperishable, immortal, and glorious body, 1 Cor. 15:49[-50].

In Christ Jesus the glory of the kingdom of Solomon is also spiritually restored, in great riches, in superabundance of gold and silver, in good peace, in his great wisdom, and in many other gifts, so that the servants who stood before him were praised as blessed and heard the speeches of wisdom out of his mouth, 1 Kings 1:[34-40]; [2:45]; [3:12-13]. All this is spiritually renewed in Christ Jesus, for through him are poured out upon us the riches of divine grace which we have through him in the pure or clean Word of God which can be compared with gold or silver, Eph. 2:[1-]2; Ps. 12:[6]; Isa. 1:16; Jer. 4:14; Eph. 2:13. Through him we have peace with God in our consciences. He has become our wisdom, righteousness, our holiness and salvation, and blessed are his servants who serve him, stand before him, and hear and keep his Word, 1 Cor 1:[30]; Luke 11:28.

Here are also the twelve officers or rulers in the royal court of Christ, namely the twelve apostles of the Lord who have the right and the authority over all lands in the Spirit, and who care for the household of the king, Matt. 22:2[-3], that is the Christian congregation, with the food of the divine Word and distribute the food [to the] souls at the right time. This took place as they preached the gospel to all creatures, baptized the penitent and believers, broke the bread of the Lord with the baptized, and fed the hungry souls with the Word of Christ, Matt. 28:19[-20]; Mark 16:[15-]16; Acts 2:38; 4:33. As spiritual conquerors they have destroyed with the weapons of righteousness every power, /366/ 2 Cor. 10:4; Eph. 6:13, have taken captive all haughtiness and understanding, and have destroyed all enmity and every opposition with the two-edged sword of the Spirit, Heb. 4:12. With the sharp arrows of God's wrath and terror, they have pierced through the hearts of the penitent, and with the chains of the righteous judgment of God have bound to eternal destruction and punishment the disobedient, the contrary, and the obstinate. And thus they have occupied the spiritual leadership, yes, have served the royal and priestly office in the peace and power of the Spirit over the Israel of God to the end of the world, [2] Pet. 2:9.

Such princes, priests, and ministers the peaceful Jesus Christ has had in his government. There were also at that time many Israelite men, warriors and house fathers, that is, the glorious company of pastors, shepherds, and leaders who are [today] fellow-helpers and builders of the holy temple, 1 Tim. 3:8. The cities and market towns in the land of the kingdom are the spiritual assemblies. The good land and earth that bears all kinds of good fruit and overflows with honey and milk is the renewed people which bring forth all kinds of sweetness in the Spirit, Ps. 1:3; Jer. 17:[7-]8. The good trees on the land are the teachers of righteousness adorned with many kinds of gifts, [Ezek. 47:12]; Dan. 12:13; Matt. 13:8. There was great comfort and joy in Zion, not of the flesh but of the Holy Spirit. There harps were played, and trumpets sounded with joy before the Lord in the spirit and in the hearts of all true Israelites, Rom. 14:17; Eph. 5:[17-20]; Col. 3:16. There one prepared and adorned oneself to honor and please the king, Jesus Christ, with silk and purple and spiritual virtues and gifts in the power of faith.

There they were anointed with the oil of gladness, ate the heavenly manna, and drank the best wine in the sanctuary for a strengthening and eternal quickening of the hearts, Ps. 45:[7-]8; Heb. 1:9; John 6:35; Isa. 55:1. There were also the daughters of Pharoah and the daughters of other foreign lands, yes, the multitude of queens and women who have come to the royal throne and chamber in Zion; which signifies the multitudes of the congregation of Jesus Christ who were brought to him out of all Gentiles and peoples by the apostles and were united with him, 1 Kings 3:1; 2 Cor. 11:4[-7].

Here in Christ and his congregation, the Song of Solomon about the king and his bride is spiritually repeated, Song of Sol. 1; 2. Here the Bridegroom, Christ, kissed his bride /367/ with the holy kiss of peace and is joyful because of her beauty and because of the costly fragrance of her ointments; that is, because of her inward gifts, virtues, and the anointment of the Holy Spirit with which she is adorned and anointed, 1 John 2:27; Ps. 45:12.

Here it now proceeds spiritually in full power so that the Bridegroom says to the bride: my beautiful friend, come and see; the winter is past, the rain is gone and has passed by; the flowers have come forth in the land; spring has come forth; the turtledoves let themselves be heard in our land; the fig tree has received buds; the vines have blossomed and given forth a lovely fragrance, Song of Sol. 2:[10-13]. That is, the time of the law has run its course, the wrath of God is stilled, the punishment of the Lord is taken away, the joyful time of grace has come. The comforting gospel has been heard, the sweet fruits of righteousness blossom, Rom. 6:11; 11:25[-27]. The land has become fruitful in faith and the knowledge of God, the plants of the Lord sprout forth, Isa. 6:13. The branches on the vine of Jesus Christ get buds and give [forth] the sweet fragrance of life through the power of Christ that is in them, John 15:2. This indeed happened in the time of the first apostolic churches and still happens daily at the present time among all believers.

Here also are in a spiritual manner the sixty strong [men] out of the heroes of Israel round about the bed of Solomon, each with a sword on his hip because of the fear in the night; that is, round about the camp of Christ and his bride where they rest with each other in all sweetness, friendliness, and love of the Spirit, Song of Sol. 3:7[-8]. These are the ministers of the Word, the preachers of the gospel out of the strength in the faith, those who are elected in Israel, Acts 2:14 [-21]. These are those who watch over the flock of Christ and are armed with the sword of the Spirit, Heb. 4:12, against the crafty attacks of Satan, Eph. 6:13[-17], and against the pestilence that stalks in the darkness, against the arrows that fly in the night, Ps. 91:5[-6], and are shot from the spirit of darkness, etc. In summary, the whole of the highly esteemed Song of Solomon is spiritually repeated in Christ with his congregation.

Thus one sees here the eternal, spiritual, and heavenly kingdom of Christ in the power of God and the H.[oly] Spirit, in which the true Solomon, the Prince and King of peace, Jesus Christ, rules with all power in heaven and on earth and sits upon the throne of his glory at the right hand of God, Ps. [45:6]; Matt. 28:18; Col. 3:1, and reigns upon Mt. Zion, that is, in his congregation with the unconquerable scepter of his divine Word, Acts 2:33; Ps. 2:6; Eph. 1:22; Jer. 23:5, with which he crushes and strikes to pieces the hearts of the Gentiles /368/ but judges and punishes the unbelievers. And in this great and glorious kingdom the righteous and believers triumph, Wisd. of Sol. 3:1. They have rest in the genuine peace of Jesus Christ and the joy of the Holy Spirit as conquerors fulfilled through faith with all kinds of heavenly goods and riches, Rom. 14:17; 1 John 5:4.

After this [it happened] just as the falling away from the kingdom of Solomon happened through Jeroboam, and he forsook the true worship in Jerusalem and erected for himself a false worship, set up the two calves, one at Bethel and the other at Dan, 1 Kings 12:[28-30]. He made priests and Levites from among the least of the people. [He] filled their hands, made an altar, and sacrificed upon it, [1 Kings 12:32-33]. Thus he led Israel astray and caused her to sin until they were led out of the land by the king of the Assyrians, 2 Kings 17:[5-]7.

In like manner the spiritual falling away from the kingdom of Christ has also taken place in the demolishing of the teaching and faith through the antichrist who has forsaken the true worship in the temple at Jerusalem and set up for himself a false worship, 1 Tim. 4:1; 2 Thess. 2:3. For all that Christ has taught and commanded, that he [the antichrist] has imitated in appearance in a hypocritical manner, with his priests, altars, sacrifices, and church services; and with great pomposity he has abominably distorted the sacraments of Jesus Christ. This he always adorns with twisted Scriptures, just as though it were true worship and as though the almighty God in heaven will be served therewith. But when it is carefully examined, it is nothing other than an abominable idolatry and blasphemy of God, for it is always openly opposed to the gospel of Christ as also what Jeroboam did in his own discretion was against the law of Moses, Tobit 1:[5-]6. For that reason the God-fearing may also not go to his calves nor pray to them, but they must, with all pious Israelites, avoid the adorned, false worship of the spiritual Jeroboam, that is of the antichrist, and journey to the heavenly Jerusalem, to the congregation of the Lord in order there to worship and honor the Most High according to his command, 2 Cor. 6:14[-16].

Likewise, just as in carnal and apostate Israel there were set up, in addition to the golden calves of Jeroboam and his false worship, all kinds of idolatries with Baal and other idols of the heathen, which also were certainly in part punished and cast down /369/ by some of the prophets and kings, nevertheless both calves remained standing until the captivity of Israel, 2 Kings 17:22[-23]. Thus also, under the reign of the antichrist, many kinds of abominable idolatries and sects were introduced in the course of time. They were resisted and broken off by some but the two golden calves of Jeroboam, the shameful abuse of Christian baptism, and the destruction of the Holy Supper of Jesus Christ remain standing. For salvation is actually bound up with these and righteousness made to depend upon them with great disregard for the grace and precious blood of Jesus Christ, Rom. 3:20; Gal. 2:16; Eph. 1:7; Col. 1:[13-]14.

Again, just as Israel became apostate through Jeroboam, thus Judah later also became apostate. That is, in the first apostasy there were still many pious Christians who remained with God and his Word. For in the time of the apostles, apostasy was already present when many antichrists and apostates were already abroad, 2 Thess. 2:3; 1 Tim. 4:1; 1 John 2:18. But many still steadfastly adhered to the house of David and to the temple in Jerusalem, that is, to the kingdom of Christ and his true worship. But with the passing of time, these also came under the apostasy so that all their descendants were led astray and also set up many kinds of idolatries until they finally came into captivity in Babylon under the antichrist. Nevertheless, just as in the time of apostasy in Israel and Judah there were some good prophets, God-fruitful priests, Israelites and Jews who had nothing to do with the false wor-

Concerning Spiritual Restitution / 343

ship, so there are also without any doubt, in this time of spiritual apostasy, still some remaining who have not followed the antichrist just as may indeed be clearly understood from the book of Revelation, Rev. 14:1; 15:2; 19:9; 20:4; 21:7.

Thus it is that the glorious kingdom of the spiritual Solomon, the beautiful congregation of Jesus Christ, which was on earth at the time of the apostles and afterwards, has been so lamentably disturbed, devastated, and the holy city given over to the heathen, to the antichrist and his power to be represented by him, just as it happened earlier with Israel and Judah according to the letter. That is, that after the building of the temple, and after the long-lasting sovereignty of kings, after many sins, apostasies, and abominations which came in with time, God gave his people into the hands of the king at Assyria and the king at Babylon, and the holy city and the temple were destroyed and devastated. /370/

The destruction of the holy city and the temple happened through the antichrist and through the harlot from Babylon who has perverted all the divine ordinances, who is adorned with purple, silk, scarlet, and gold, who has the golden cup full of all abominations in her hand, who was drunk from the blood of the saints and the witnesses of Jesus Christ, who made all the Gentiles drunk with the wine of her harlotry and sorcery, Rev. 17:3. Her merchants have become rich and mighty from the power of her wantonness, her wares, and idle things. The kings and princes of the earth have committed fornication with her and still do to this present day. In summary, she is a mother of all abominations upon earth, and all who love their souls and desire to be saved, these must forsake this whore and separate out of Babylon just as the Scripture says: my people, depart from Babylon, flee out of the land of the Chaldeans, Jer. [50:8], 51:6, depart from the midst of her, so that you do not become partakers of her sins and do not receive any of her plagues, 2 Cor. 6:17; Rev. 18:4, for her sins have climbed as high as heaven, and God has remembered her willfulness, Rev. 18:5.

Now here it is necessary to observe how Israel was twice captive, twice delivered, and twice came into the kingdom and the glory; also that the temple was built twice upon the same foundation and form. About the first captivity in Egypt and the deliverance, about the kingdoms of David and Solomon and their glory, and about the first building of the temple, [enough] has been said above. But now we have come into the second deliverance out of Babylon; now we have come to the building of the second temple and the city of Jerusalem. For now God delivers his people wonderfully every day out of the spiritual captivity of Babylon; now he redeems his chosen from all the abominations of the Babylonian whore with faithful admonitions through the Holy Scriptures and through his messengers that they should separate out of Babylon, not touch anything unclean, Rev. 18:5; Jer. 51:6; 2 Cor. 6:17, and again journey with joy to Jerusalem to rebuild the fallen temple, and the ruined city, that is, the congregation of Christ, just as one may now (God be praised) see in great clarity.

And it is well to reflect here that the Jews and the children of Israel who had taken heathen wives contrary to God's law, these had to leave them again and be separated from them so that they might be cleansed from the abominations of the heathen, which signifies and teaches us two things, 1 Esd. [9:10-13]; [Ezra 10:2, 3, 11]. In the first place, that all true Christians everywhere must withdraw themselves /371/ from all Babylonian idolatry and fellowship, and purify themselves from all contamination of the spirit and the flesh so that they may be a holy people of the Lord, fitting to serve God, 2 Cor. 6:17; Rev. 18:4; Lev. 19:2; 1 Pet. 2:9. This cannot happen unless one first forsakes all the abominations of the heathen and Babylon. In the second place, marriages between the people of God and heathen wives, entered into contrary to the law of God, could not exist before God. And they were again broken by Ezra and this took place because such marriage was unclean before the Lord, 1 Esd. [8:93-94]; [Ezra] 10:11. Yes, [such marriages] among God's children in the first world were sharply punished by him, [Gen. 6:3-4]; Gen. 7:23, and thereafter was so strictly forbidden through Moses, Deut. 7:2[-3]. Now, seeing that such impure marriages and intermingling of the children of God with unbelievers in the time of imperfection under the law could not be tolerated, how should it exist before God and his congregation in this time of the perfect Christian being according to the gospel? This each one may reflect upon and consider from the heart.

Further, the temple of the Lord and the city of the living God are now again rebuilt, and just as it happened externally in the building of the second figurative temple and Jerusalem, thus it also proceeds now in the spirit. For when the temple was built in the first form and upon the first foundation, then the opponents of Judah and Benjamin wanted to build with Zerubbabel and the others, [Ezra] 4:2. But Zerubbabel and the other elders in Israel answered thus: It is not fitting for us to build the house of our God with you; but we alone will build to the Lord, the God of Israel, just as Cyrus the king has commanded, [Ezra 4:3]. Likewise, the Gentiles mocked Nehemiah and his brothers about the building of the city and also wanted to prevent this with force and overthrow the walls of the city, Neh. 4:2-5. In opposition to this, Nehemiah with all the other Jews arose and worked all the same on the walls of the city, some of them held watch, some worked and had the sword at the side, and all were prepared for battle, [Ezra 4:16-18].

This now takes place continuously in the spirit, for now the temple of the Lord, the congregation of God, is being built upon the first foundation, upon the basis of the prophets and apostles of which Christ is the cornerstone, 1 Cor. 3:[10-]11; Eph. 2:19[-20]. Now the living stones which lie scattered about here and there are gathered together again and fitted into the house of the Lord, 1 Pet. 2:[4-5]. Now one has /372/ true ministers of the Holy Word, true preachers of the gospel of Jesus Christ, Matt. 3:[3]. Now all divine ordinances and apostolic teachings with a basic restoring and renewing of a true penitence, faith in God, the true knowledge of Jesus Christ and of the Holy Spirit, Christian baptism, the true Lord's Supper, the godly life, brotherly love and trust among all the saints, the evangelical separation or the ban, and all institutions of God are restored and accomplished through the power of the Spirit, Heb. 6:3; John 17:17; 1 John 2:1; Matt. 26:[26-27]; Mark 14:22[-24]; [Luke 22:17-19]; Mark 16:15[-16]; Matt. 18:18. Now one sings to the Lord in the heart out of great joy of the Spirit, Eph. [5]:19; Col. 3:16.

Now the Lord is offered the living, holy, and acceptable sacrifice which is the reasonable worship wherewith the God of heaven is served, 1 Pet. 2:5; Rom. 12:1. Now one brings to the Lord earnest prayers as a sweet savor and the lifting up of holy hands as an evening sacrifice, 1 Tim. 2:8; Ps. 134. And it is thus that the temple of the Lord, the house of the living God now stands on the first foundation, in the original form, shape, and glory, Heb. 11:10.

The opponents of Judah and Benjamin who wanted to build on the house of the Lord with Zerubbabel are those who falsely pride themselves of the gospel and present themselves in a hypocritical manner, just as if they also wanted to serve God but their heart is doubled, and they are not the true carpenters and co-workers of Israel; therefore, the pious Christians do not want to build with them. For no one is fitted for such a work except he be a Jew or an Israelite of the race of Abraham, Isaac, and Jacob; that is he must become a new-born person, newborn out of the heavenly Father through Jesus Christ in the Holy Spirit, 2 Cor. 3:[15-17]; 1 Pet. 1:23.

The heathen also now come and mock the elders about the restoration of the holy city, Jerusalem, [Neh. 4:2]. They regard them as much too small for this task and they speak scornfully and blaspheme very much. For to the aristocrats of this world, the learned, and the perverted, it is entirely ridiculous that such a poor, rejected people should undertake to rebuild fallen Jerusalem, Acts 17:18, the Christian congregation, and repair her walls. They do not remember that Christ built his congregation through the simple unlearned apostles and brought her to such glory. /373/ They also do not note that Christ in the gospel said, "I thank you, Father, Lord of heaven and earth, that you have hidden the secrets of the gospel from the wise and understanding but have revealed them to the little ones and the simple; yes, Father, for thus it has pleased you," Matt. 11:25[-26].

Again, Paul to the Corinthians: "The wisdom of this world is foolishness before God," 1 Cor. 1:[25]. And God has testified to this through Isaiah with these words: "I will destroy the wisdom of the wise, and the wisdom of the wise I will reject," Isa. [29:14]. "Where is the wise man? Where is the scribe? Where is the disputer of this world? Has not God made foolish the wisdom of this world?" 1 Cor. 1:[20]. And in another place, "behold, you scoffers, wonder and perish, for I work a deed in your days, says the Lord, which you will not believe, if one tells it to you," Acts 13:41.

And as these mockers of Israel then see that their mocking is ignored and that the work of the Lord, the restoration of the holy city nevertheless goes forward, then they become furious, they make a covenant with each other against the Lord and his congregation, and want to resist this so that Jerusalem will not be rebuilt again, Neh. 4:8. The tyrants with their strong mandates and placards, with water, fire, and sword, these learned ones with their philosophy, guile, and sharp-wittedness to twist the Scriptures with writing and preaching and with inciting the civil authority that one should drive away, strangle, and kill the builders of the city of Jerusalem so that the work of the Lord might be hindered.

But in opposition to this, the people of the Lord arm themselves, not with carnal weapons such as (alas) has happened to some through misunderstanding,[3] but with the armor of God, with the weapons of righteousness in the right hand and the left, with the helmet of salvation, with the shield of faith with which they can quench all the fiery darts of Satan, 2 Cor. 6:8; Eph. 6:11[-17], and with the powerful two-edged Word of God, Heb. 4:12, and with Christian patience with which they possess their souls and thus overcome all their foes [Heb. 12:1; Rom. 12:12]. /374/ And [thus] they build the walls of Jerusalem,

Heb. 12:22, with such battle armor and such an undaunted or manly heart, and comfort themselves because the God of heaven is their helper in need and the hand of Christ is with them. The heathen (who nevertheless have no part in the house of the Lord or in the city of Jerusalem) cannot with all their might prevent that both the city and the temple should be rebuilt; for the Lord is with his people and helps his servants faithfully. Amen.

Likewise, the second figurative temple and the rebuilt city of Jerusalem remained standing until the first coming of Christ. Meanwhile, the Jews suffered many temptations and persecutions and were so miserably plagued and killed by Antiochus and other tyrants because they did not want to forsake the law of God nor honor and worship the idols of the heathen, 1 Macc. 6:24[-26]; many have also thus fallen away and hypocritically served the godless tyrants and lords in order to please them. And these same [Jews] frequently have become the archenemies, betrayers, and persecutors of the God-fruitful Jews, just as one may read everywhere in the books of the Maccabees, 1 Macc. 7:5[-7], and in many [other] beautifully [written] histories.

Thus the second spiritual temple and the holy city of Jerusalem remain standing until the second coming and restoration of our Lord Jesus Christ. For the people of God under heaven are given an eternal kingdom and the kingdom of Christ has no end, Dan. 7:27; Luke 2:29[-32]. But this notwithstanding, all those who wish to live godly lives in Christ Jesus must suffer persecution, 2 Tim. 3:12[-13]. Christians are robbed, their houses are burned, they are ridiculed by the heathen, they are despised and held to be unwise, their lives are regarded as madness, Ps. 44:22; Wisd. of Sol. 5:3. The bodies of the servants of God are given to birds of heaven as food and the flesh of the saints to the beasts of the field. Innocent blood is poured out as water, and there is no one to bury the dead. In summary, Antiochus is completely mad and insane beyond measure against the pious who believe the gospel and wish to live in accordance with it. But those who honor and advocate his Maozim,[4] the unknown idol, the new falsely devised worship, these he makes magnificant and rewards them richly as one may daily see and observe, Dan. [11:38]. /375/

Out of all this it is now clear how all things are restored and are to be renewed spiritually in Christ Jesus in the time of his rule until his return and appearance as the apostle Peter said, Acts 3:20; 1 Pet. 1:5. Therefore, we may expect no other restitution[5] or restoration of all things than spiritually in Christ Jesus who is the Alpha and the

O[mega], the beginning of all creation, Rev. 1:3; 1:8; and the perfection or completion of all the works of God, here and now in the Spirit and hereafter in that perfect being as renewed and restored, shall be changed and glorified in eternity as a final reward, 1 Cor. 13:10. [So also shall the] sovereignty of all believers and saints [be restored], at the place where God the Father and the Lord Jesus Christ, with the Holy Spirit and all the angels, shall be through all times and in eternity, John 14:2; 17:24; 1 Thess. 4:[17].

And all that the prophets have prophesied and spoken of the rebuilding of the tabernacle of David, of the kingdom of Christ and his glory, of the wrath of God over Babylon, of the building of the temple and the city of Jerusalem. In summary, the whole restitution must be understood according to this rule and changed out of the letter into the Spirit, Acts 9:15; Jer. 50:2. And therewith the basis of our most holy and Christian faith is made very firm, as we openly see and understand that all that we believe and confess was first portrayed from God to us in many beautiful figures and thereafter through the eternal truth itself, that is, it is clarified, witnessed to, and confirmed through Jesus Christ, John 1:4; 14:6.

But the eternal almighty God, who has provided and worked all things from the beginning, first in the figures, thereafter in accordance with the true being, keep us in his truth through his eternal Word, through his only begotten Son, Jesus Christ, John 1:1; Col. 1:14; Heb. 1:5. Through his mercy may he renew us in the inner being, [Eph. 3:16], and keep us in an upright life until our end, so that we may stand before the judgment seat of Jesus Christ with joy, when he shall come with the angels in his power, with the four flaming ones, to impose the vengeance upon all those who have not known God and have not been obedient to the gospel; and "to be glorified in his saints and to appear marvelously in all the believers," 2 Thess. 1:8[-10]; John 12:26; 17:24; Phil. 3:11, in the resurrection and the revelation /376/ of the heavenly glory, with which they shall be clothed, through the power of Christ so that they may occupy and possess with him the eternal, imperishable glory in the complete being in eternity, Matt. 13:[16-49].

AMEN

Glory Be to the Only Wise God

(Soli Sapienti Deo Gloria)

ENDNOTES

1. Dirk here uses *kerke* (church) instead of his usual *Gemeynte*, that is, congregation. Was he, perhaps unconsciously, thinking back to his Roman Catholic days and the there prevalent image of the church as an ark "outside of which there is no salvation" (Cyprian)?

2. The original text cites Heb. 4:13, 15, which are not in harmony with the text. Dirk may have had 2 Thess. 2:9 in mind.

3. The reference appears to be to the Münster revolt of 1534-35 and perhaps to other violence associated with early Anabaptism. We note that Dirk is not judgmental, but neither does he approve violence.

4. *Maozim* was a Babylonian god for over a thousand years from the time of Hammurabi in the eighteenth century B.C., hence an idol to Christians, but much earlier also to devout Hebrews. See Daniel 11:38-39 in the Vulgate and Douay versions used by Roman Catholics. The Babylonian name was Marduk (Maruduk) and was the same god referred to as *Bel* (lord) in the apocryphal book *Bel and the Dragon*. Some modern scholars translate Maozim as power or strongholds.

5. Here Dirk likely has Bernhard Rothmann's *Restitution* of 1534 in mind. As primary theologian of Munsterite Anabaptism, Rothmann became co-responsible for the events and violence of Munster 1534-1535. Against Munster's attempt to establish the kingdom of God through an earthly restitution, Dirk argues for spiritual renewal, a renewal which will also be visible on earth but in the church or congregation.

THE CONGREGATION OF GOD

How it has been from the beginning, by what it is recognized and distinguished from all sects. A short confession. /377/

By D. P.

Do you not know that the temple of God is holy, which you are. 1 Cor. 3:16

Great and wonderful things are spoken of you, Oh, city of God. Psalm [87:3]

You are the temple of the living God. 2 Cor. 6:16

/378/ I write this to you so that you may know how you ought to walk in the house of God, which is the congregation of the living God, a pillar and foundation of the truth. 1 Tim. 3:14

Christ is set over all things from God his Father, a head of his church (that is, his congregations and the assembly) which is his body and the fullness of the one who fulfills all in all. Eph. 1:22

If anyone destroys God's temple (that is, the congregation), that one God will destroy. 1 Cor. 3:17

The Text

/379/ To the Christian reader I, D. P., by grace a fellow companion of faith in Jesus Christ and a member of the Christian congregation, wish much wisdom, understanding, peace, and mercy from God our heavenly Father and from Jesus Christ, the only born Son of God, in the love and truth blessed in eternity. Amen. 2 John 3

Since I, according to my small gift, have told about a brief spiritual restitution, wrote my opinion about it, and therewith have given the goodhearted reader a little indication to reflect on the matter more broadly according to the measure of the spirit and faith received, and the reader could also examine how in Christ Jesus all things are made new, 2 Cor. 5:17, set right; yes, [that] he started the true being, Col. 2:9, gathered the congregation of God, set it up, and brought it to great glory; therefore, I must now also write a little about the congregation of God, how it was from the beginning, whereby it is built and has come together from all people, whereby it is recognized and distinguished from all the sects, what ordinances of God it has, how the pastors must be qualified, how one must behave there, and how beautiful and wonderful it is.

Since all people are invited to the congregation of God, and everyone says here is Christ, Matt. 24:23, this is the temple of the Lord, Jer. 7:4, and every sect wants to be the congregation of Christ and called that, so all lovers of the truth need to know which is the true Christian church or congregation. They need to know how they can be joined to the same congregation, to the extent that they hope or intend to be saved. For those who scorn the offered grace of God in this time, do not repent, Matt. 3:2; 22:7; 23:12; Mark 1:4; Luke 3:[3], do not believe the gospel, nor are obedient, despising the ordinances of God, /380/ and do not want to be joined to the fellowship of the body of Jesus Christ, these shall hardly escape the judgment of God, 1 Cor. 12:3. For Christ himself says that no one comes to the Father except through him, John 14:[6]. And whoever remains in him brings forth much fruit, but whoever does not remain in him is like a dry branch, John 15:6. Whoever does not believe in him is now already judged, etc., John 3:36; 10:38; 1 John 5:10. Therefore everyone must run to Christ, to Mount Zion, and to the house of the living God, to hear the law of the Lord and the gospel, so that he may be planted in Christ and his soul may be kept to eternal salvation. Amen.

About the Congregation of God

The congregation of God was first begun by God in heaven with the angels, who were created by God as spirits and flaming fire, Ps. 104:4; Heb. 1:7, that they should stand before the throne of God, praising and serving God. They should also be ministers and fellow servants of the believers, Rev. 22:9. For although they are such noble and high creatures of God, nevertheless they are at the same time serving spirits, just as the apostle said, [Heb. 1:14], sent out from God to serve those who are the ones who shall inherit the salvation of God.

For they guard the children of God. They encamp around the camp of the God-fearing, Ps. 34:[7]. They go before Israel, Exod. 14:19. They led Lot out of Sodom, Gen. 19:16; Ps. [20:6]. In sum, they minister to the saints and the chosen people of God. They keep them in all their ways and see evermore the face of the Father in heaven, Matt. 18:10. And thus the congregation of God was first begun with the angels in heaven.

Afterward the congregation of God was also begun in paradise with Adam and Eve, Gen. 2:7. They were created after the image of God, Gen. 9:6, and were made in his likeness, Gen. 5:[1], upright, good, and pure creatures of God, incorruptible and immortal, Wisd. of Sol. 2:23. They had an upright, pious nature and divine character, /381/ a true knowledge, fear, and love of God existed [Ecclus. 16:25]; [James 3:2; 3:17], as long as they remained in the first creation and ordering of God and had borne that image of God.

Therefore the congregation of God is a congregation of saints, namely, the angels in heaven and believing born-again people on earth who are renewed according to the image of God. They are joined together through Jesus Christ, Eph. 3:6; Col. 1:[17], just as Paul in his letters certainly declared, principally to the Hebrews, 12:22 [-24], where he also wrote, "You have come to Mount Zion, to the city of the living God, the heavenly Jerusalem, to the multitude of many thousand angels, to the congregation of the firstborn who are enrolled in heaven, to God who is judge of all, and to the spirits of complete righteousness, to the mediator of the New Testament, Jesus, and to the sprinkled blood that speaks better than the blood of Abel."

From these words one may clearly understand that the crowd of many thousand angels, the congregation of the firstborn, who are recorded in heaven, and the spirits of the completely righteous, with all the believers who have come in addition, these all with one another are the congregation of God. God reigns over it there as the righteous judge, Heb. 12:23, and Christ is the head of it, Eph. 1:22, and the Holy Spirit dwells there, 1 Cor. 3:16; 6:19.

But the first apostasy from God in his congregation occurred among the angels in heaven who had sinned, and were untrue to their Creator, Job 4:[16-21]. Therefore they were cast out of heaven, bound with the chains of darkness, that they could no more do anything except what God permitted them to do, Luke 9:[1]. Although they are evil spirits and angels who now reign in the air, fight against the Christians, seeking their destruction, Matt. 4:[1]; 1 Pet. 5:8; James 4:7, working in the children of unbelief, Eph. 2:2, and [do have power] in the world. But they are kept until the day of judgment, to eternal pain and damnation, yes, to that hellish fire that shall never be put out, Matt. 25:30; 2 Pet. 2:4.

The second falling away from God in the congregation happened in paradise through Adam and Eve who were led astray through the cunning of the snake, /382/ destroyed through the corrupting sin, Gen. 3:6, and thus have lost the image of God, the pure, created, natural holiness, and highly excellent reason, full of all wisdom and knowledge of God and all creatures, Rom. 5:12; 1 Cor. 15:21. This image, which was zealous in love and obedience to God, was lost. Yes, they passed out of righteousness into unrighteousness, out of immortal being into corruption and damnation, out of eternal life into eternal death.

The first restoration of the corrupted persons, the renewal of the divine image in them, and the new upbuilding of the fallen church of God occurred through the promise of that future seed of the women, which would trample the head of the snake, Gen. 3:15. This seed is principally Jesus Christ, and was therefore called the woman's seed, because he was promised from God to Adam and Eve, and was born according to the flesh out of a woman, Matt. 1:25; Luke 2:7. For, although Mary as a pure maiden [virgin] received him from the Holy Spirit and brought him forth, she is nevertheless called a wife in the Scripture, Luke 2:5; Gal. 4:4. In this manner Christ is also called her seed and the fruit of her body. And this Jesus Christ is the true trampler and conqueror, John [17:4], of the old crooked snake, who with his death has released the human race from all the tyrannical violence of Satan, sin, and eternal death, Rom. 5:1; Col. 1:20; Heb. 2:[14].

This was the first preaching of the gospel of Jesus Christ, the only Deliverer and Savior of the world, John 3:36; 1 Tim. 2:[5], through whom Adam and Eve were again established and have again received that lost image of God. For they were created anew from GOD, born anew out of him, after which they have accepted with a genuine faith the gracious promise of the gospel through the power and enlightenment of the Holy Spirit.

From this Adam and his wife, Eve, have come two brothers, Abel and Cain, Gen. 4:1, the one upright and the other godless. Abel was a child of GOD and a member of the Christian church; but Cain was a child of the devil and captured in his fellowship, 1 John 3:12. The pious and righteous one was hated by the evil and murderous Cain, and was murdered out of the envy of his evil heart. And this is a clear symbol and witness that from that time on two kinds of people, two kinds of children, two kinds of congregations /383/ have existed on earth, Matt. 23:34[-35]. They are, namely, God's people and the devil's people; God's children and the devil's children, John 8:44; God's congregation and the synagogue or assembly of Satan, Rev. 2:9; and that God's children must suffer persecution from the devil's children, 1 John 3:1. Christ's congregation must be oppressed, hunted, and killed by the anti-Christian assembly. Of this God has also given clear knowledge that he has set enmity between the snake's seed and the woman's seed, and that the snake's seed shall lie low or bite the seed of the woman in the heel.

For although Christ Jesus is the true promised seed of the woman, Gen. 3:15, as was said above (and I speak once again of a promised seed, but not of a natural seed, for otherwise the snake's seed must also be a natural being), and though he is the only conqueror of the devil, John 16:33; Col. 1:20; Heb. 2:15, so also with every believer is a seed of the spiritual Eve, just as the unbeliever is a seed of the old crooked snake, and we mean all that in a spiritual sense. And between the children of the above named Eve and the snake an eternal enmity is placed by God, Gen. 3:15, so that the devil's children always hate, envy, and persecute God's children. Conversely, God's children conquer the snake and its seed, the world and all that is in it, through the blood of the lamb, Rev. 7:14; 12:[11], through their faith in Jesus Christ, 1 John 5:4, through the confession and witness of truth, and through their steadfastness in God's Word, even to death.

Furthermore, God has given Adam and Eve another son in place of Abel, the God-fearing Seth, Gen. 4:25, and from him other pious sons have descended to Noah. He found grace before the Lord in the time when God punished by the flood the children of men along with God's children who had mixed with them and also slipped into error, and all flesh that had corrupted his way were taken away and exterminated, except for Noah and those with him in the ark, Gen. [7:23]. But what this figure signifies we have declared in our confession about baptism and above in the *Spiritual Restitution.*

God made his covenant with Noah and his two sons, Shem and Japheth, or renewed it, and they were his congregation in that time, Gen. 9:8. But Ham, the third son of Noah, who also was in the ark and went out with the others, was a mocker of his father and therefore cursed by Noah. /384/ He took the place of Cain as the new origin of Satan's congregation on earth, the father of Canaan and its seeds. They were the evil children who have always plagued and mocked the children of God, and fought against God, Dan. 11:33.

The true line of Abraham, a father of all believers, came forth from Shem, with whom God renewed his covenant, Gen. 15:2; 17:1[f.]; 22:[16ff.], established him, and made the promise to him that he and his will be seed of God (and therewith all believers with their children are included in God's covenant), and that in his seed (which is Christ Jesus, the spiritual Isaac, that promised seed of blessing, going forth from God, his father, coming forth, and promised to the patriarch Abraham, Gal. [3:29]; Ecclus. 24:[12]; Gen. 17:1[ff.]) should be a blessing to all the generations on earth, and that Abraham should be a father of all believers, not only of those who were born and circumcised by him according to the flesh, but also of the heathen who were in the foreskin [thus uncircumcised], Rom. 4:12, and nevertheless walked in the footsteps of Abraham and still so walk. For these were reckoned as of that seed, just as the apostle testified, Rom. 9:7.

Thereafter, that covenant of God with all its gracious promises has descended from Abraham on Isaac and Jacob, on the twelve patriarchs, then on Moses and Aaron, on David, and all the God-fearers who were with him and after him, and who have served God in true faith. With these the congregation of God has been, that citizenship of Israel, Eph. 2:11[f.], the temple of the Lord, that covenant and holiness of the Most High. Here wisdom had her dwelling in Jacob, and her heritage in Israel, Ecclus. 24:12, until the time of Christ. Many other devout and God-fearing people among the Jews at Jerusalem and Judea are also included, such as Zacharias and Elizabeth, Joseph and Mary, the old Simeon, and Anna, the widow, etc.

In addition, still others among the heathen were God-fearing, such as Melchizedek, the King of Salem, a priest of the Most High, Gen. 14:18; Gen. 19:2[?]; also Heb. 7:1, whose generations were concealed by the spirit; Abimelech, the king of Gerar, Gen. 20:[2]; Rom. 2:14[-16]; Job an Idumean, Job 1:1, his friends, and many others. Therefore Paul says that the Gentiles who have not had the law but nevertheless do by nature the work of the law, /385/ they are thus a law to themselves, by which they show that although they do not have the law, what the law works is written on their hearts, while their conscience bears witness to them and also their thoughts among each other which accuse and absolve them on that day in which God shall judge the secrets of the heart by Jesus Christ, according to the content of my gospel.

Again, if a man who is uncircumcised is right before the law, do you not think that his foreskin will be regarded as circumcision? Then those who are thus by nature in the foreskin and keep the law will condemn you who have the letter and circumcision but break the law. For that one is not a real Jew who is a Jew outwardly, and that is no true circumcision which occurs externally in the flesh. But he is a Jew who is hidden inwardly, and the circumcision of the heart is a circumcision which takes place in the spirit and not in the letter. His praise is not from persons but from God, Rom. 2:26[-29].

Moreover, the promise of God to Abraham occurred that all peoples shall be blessed in his seed, and he shall be a father of all peoples and the heathen, Gen. 15:5; 22:[17-]18. And therefore God changed his name, that he should no more be called Abram but Abraham, Gen. 17:5. Just so also many prophecies report everywhere in Moses, in the Psalms, Ps. [96:3,10?], and in the Prophets, 2 Sam. 22:44, about the heathen, how they should be called through Jesus Christ to the flock of Israel, and many should believe in God and be obedient to his gospel, Rom. 11:25.

Therefore one may reckon not only the Jews and Israelites for the congregation of God, but all who truly confessed, feared, and honored God, have lived according to his will out of the law of nature, enscribed by God in their hearts. All those out of the heathen who become believers in Jesus Christ, Rom. [3:21-]26, who are in the foreskin of their flesh [thus uncircumcised] and in their heathendom are reckoned as a spiritual seed of Abraham and the promise. And thus it follows from this that they have been God's and Christ's, Gal. 3:16. /386/

Thus the congregation of God has existed from the beginning in Christ, through whom all things are renewed, yes, joined in one body, everything that is in heaven and on earth, Col. 1:19f., and from which God's congregation is built more gloriously and also is expanded. For then the figures have come to an end, but the true being has come forth, Rom. 10:4; Col. 2:9; the grace and truth have arisen through Jesus Christ, John 1:14[ff]. Then the lost sheep from the house of Israel were sought, Matt. 10:6, and were led by Christ into the true sheepfold. Then the heathen from all lands had come to Mount Zion to learn God's law and to hear the gospel of Jesus Christ, Isa. 2:3, and to walk in the way of the Lord. Then the prophecy was fulfilled that the abandoned shall be comforted, the scorning and despising of the unfruitfulness forgotten, Isa. 54:1; Gal. 4:27, for he who has created her has become her husband. His name is Lord Sabaoth, the Deliverer and Savior of Israel, the Lord and God of the whole world; then Jerusalem is raised up and become sparkling for her light has come, and the glory of the Lord has enlightened her, and his shining has shined over her, so that the heathen have walked in her light and the people in the glory that has risen upon her, Isa. [60:1f].

Then the believers through the knowledge of Jesus Christ are given the most precious promise by God, 1 Pet. 1:5. Through the same one shall they partake of the divine nature, if they flee the perishable desires of this world. In summary, then the true knowledge of God and Christ has come forth as a bright morning star, Rev. 22:16; then has grace poured forth as a living stream of water out of God's paradise, Rev. 22:1; then the Holy Spirit was poured out richly from God over his sons and daughters, Joel 2:28; Acts 2:17; then is that new testament of the Lord completed with the house of Israel and Judah, according to his promise through Jeremiah the prophet. Yes, then the congregation is extended and the kingdom of God multiplied over the whole world, Matt. 28:19; Mark 16:15; Col. 1:28, through the true messenger of the Lord, and is filled and endowed with all kinds of precious promises and ordinances, and has thus become a wonderful house of the living God.

But how this has happened and how this erection of the congregation of Jesus Christ has occurred, the Scripture shows us with great clarity, namely, through the right teaching of the divine Word, Rom. 10:18, and through the faith that comes out of hearing the divine Word, added to by the illumination of the Holy Spirit. For no one may enter into the kingdom of God, into that heavenly Jerusalem, that is into the /387/ congregation of Jesus Christ, except that he be improved in heart, Matt. 3:8; Gal. 4:7, repents truly, and believes the gospel.

Yes, just as God began his congregation on earth in paradise, Gen. 2:8, with pure and holy persons who were created according to his image and were made in his likeness, so also he still wants to have such persons in his congregation who are created after Jesus Christ and are renewed by the Holy Spirit, Heb. 2:3[f]; 5:12. For although the promised salvation was earned by the Savior Jesus Christ, Titus 2:13, and although that lost life was bought back through the blood of the unique sacrifice and has been offered to all people in the gospel, Heb. 8:2[ff]; Heb. [10:19ff.], nevertheless, not every person enjoys the same eternal salvation and eternal life. Only those who are born anew here in this life, 1 Pet. 1:23, through the Word of Jesus Christ, James 1:18; John 3:3; 8:32, who lets them seek and find with the light of the divine Word, and who follow the voice of their Shepherd, who are enlightened with the true knowledge of God and his will, and accept the righteousness of Christ with a true faith, John 12:46[ff.].

This Christ testified to Nicodemus, and said thus: "Truly, truly, I say to you, unless someone is born from above, he cannot see the kingdom of God" John 3:3. Here the kingdom of God would be absolutely denied by the Lord himself to all those who are not born anew out of God and not newly created from him in their internal being according to his image. Therefore, they who desire to come into that kingdom of God must also be born anew (I speak of those who [have reached] understanding), of those who desire to enter the kingdom of God.

This new birth does not occur externally, but in the understanding, reason, and heart of the person. It is in that understanding and reason likewise that the person learns to know the eternal, true, and gracious God in Christ Jesus, who is indeed the eternal image of the Father, 2 Cor. 4:4; Col. 1:15; Heb. 1:3, and that appearance of the divine being. Likewise, the person has love in the heart for the same almighty and living God, fearing, honoring, and believing in him, resting himself in his promise, all of which cannot happen without the power of the Holy Spirit which must penetrate the heart with the divine power which gives faith, fear, with love, hope, and all good virtues of God, 1 Cor. 13:[13]. /388/

We are also not born anew out of flesh and blood, nor out of any perishable things, but just as Peter, 1 Pet. 1:23, and James, James 1:18, testify, to wit, out of the Word of the living God, just as we have written in our booklet about the new birth and new creature, and just as anyone who desires it may read there. But that Word of God is of two kinds, that is to say, the law and the gospel.

The law is that commanded Word of God given through Moses on Mount Sinai, with such terrible voice, with such a storm, thunder, and lightning, Exod. 19:16-20:1; Heb. 12:[18ff.], that the children of Israel could not bear it, but they said to Moses, speak with the Lord, and do not let the Lord speak with us, so that we do not die. Yes, Moses himself was afraid and terrified, which indicated the severity of the law. For it points us to sin and condemnation, Rom. 4:15, since it requires of all people perfect righteousness of the internal person, Deut. 6:4, Matt. [22:37], the entire nature created holy and of high understanding, full of the true knowledge of God, and in addition, a holy, pure heart which is zealous in the love of God.

Thereafter the law condemned the internal impurity of nature, that is to say, the damage and loss of the created wisdom and knowledge of God and the inherent righteousness and holiness of heart, Ps. 51:12; Eph. 2:1. Again, it condemned the bad desire and inclination against God's law, Rom. 3:20, 7:7. So whoever reads the law with a veiled outlook, 2 Cor. 3:16, that one must tremble and become humble before God's wrath, just as with Israel. Yes, as Moses himself is depicted for us, Exod. 20:19; Heb. 12:19[ff.].

And that is why the law was given from God, not that it should bring persons to perfect righteousness, salvation, and eternal life (for out of the works of the law no flesh may be justified), Rom. 3:20; Gal. 2:[16], but that they through the revelation of sin should learn to fear God, know themselves, humble themselves under the powerful hand of God, 1 Pet. 5:6, and also be prepared to accept Jesus Christ, the only Savior, with a repentant heart, 1 Tim. 2:[5f.], and to seek and hope for salvation through his grace and merit alone, Eph. 2:13; Acts 14:14 [?]; Acts 15:8[-11]. /389/

Since the law now teaches the knowledge of sin, Rom. 7:7, and the fear of the Lord comes out of such knowledge, that beginning of all wisdom, Eccles. 1:16[f.], without which no one can be justified, and out of the fear of the Lord comes a broken, defeated, and humbled heart, Ps. 51:[17], which is well-pleasing to God, therefore the law serves partly for the new birth. Since no one can be born or made alive, and no one can believe the gospel unless he first genuinely repents, just as the Lord Jesus Christ himself testifies, for he taught the people repentance first, Matt. 3:2, and after that faith, and he has also thus commanded his apostles so to do, Luke 24:46[f.].

But that gospel is the word of grace, the joyful message of Christ Jesus, the only born Son of God, the only Redeemer and Savior, who has given himself for us, so that he would redeem us from the power of Satan, sin, and eternal death, 1 Tim. 2:3[f.]; Titus 2:13; Gal. 1:4; Heb. 2:15. He would make us children and heirs of our heavenly Father, Rom. 8:14; Eph. 1:5, a royal priesthood, a holy people, a chosen race, and belonging to God in the Spirit, 1 Pet. 2:9. Therefore he also said in the gospel, "Come here to me all who are loaded down, I will strengthen you, learn from me, for I am humble and gentle of heart. Take my yoke upon you, for my burden is light, and my yoke is sweet," Matt. 11:28[-30]. Or again, "truly, truly, I say to you, whoever hears my word, and keeps it is saved. That one will not come to judgment, but he passes over from death into eternal life," John 5:24. Or again, "I am the resurrection and the life; whoever believes, even though he dies, so shall he still live, and whoever lives there and believes in me, that one will not die in eternity," John 11:25[f.]. Or again, "God has so loved the world that he gave his only born Son, so that whoever believes in him will not be lost but will have eternal life. For God has not sent his Son to judge the world, but that the world would be saved through him; so whoever believes in him will not be judged," etc., John 3:[16f.].

That is the true gospel, the pure teaching of our God, full of grace and mercy, full of comfort, salvation, and eternal life, which was given to us from God, out of grace, without our merit and works of the law, for the will of the only and precious Savior Jesus Christ, who submitted himself /390/ under the law for us and has become for all the believers the fulfillment of the law for eternal salvation, provided we accept it with a true faith.

In this teaching Jesus Christ was given us from the heavenly Father with all spiritual gifts, with all his wisdom, righteousness, holiness, truth, and eternal life, Isa. 9:[7]; Jer. 23:6; 1 Cor. 1:[30]. Yes, with all that is God's and Christ's, just as it is written, if God is for us, who can be against us? Who also has not spared his only Son, but gave him to death for us; how is it possible, that he would not give all things to us with him, etc., Rom. 8:32. And once again, it is all yours, and you are Christ's, and Christ is God's, 1 Cor. 3:[22-]23. And Christ said in his prayer to the Father that he has given the words to his disciples which he received from the Father, in addition to the glory which was given to him from the Father, that they be one, Christ in them, and the Father in Christ, that they be perfected and confess to the world that the Father has loved them as Christ has loved them and the Father loved Christ, John 17:22[ff.].

All those who now out of the teaching of the law learn to fear God, confess sin, truly repent, Matt. 3:8; Mark 1:4; Luke 3:8, depart from their sinful life and godless being, and believe the gospel with a repentant heart, accept Jesus Christ as their Savior, these are born anew out of God through his eternal Word, 1 Pet. 1:23; James 1:18. Thus, in the power of his Holy Spirit, they are being renewed along with it and also sealed unto the day of deliverance, Eph. 4:30, and have free access to God, and to the throne of grace, Heb. 5:3; Rom. [5:2], in the faith of Jesus Christ. Here the law is now silent where it formerly condemned. Here are stilled the thunderbolt, the earthquake, the storm, and that terrible appearance, Exod. 19:16, of Mount Sinai. Here shines a brighter light of the gospel and the sun of righteousness in the believer's heart, John 12:46; Wisd. of Sol. 5:6. Here is a whole new person; a new heart, reason, and conscience; a child of God; and an heir of the heavenly kingdom, bound with God, born anew out of God, John 3:[3-8], strengthened with his power, and prepared for eternal life.

And that is the spiritual rebirth out of God's Word, 1 Pet. 1:23; James 1:18, in which we are granted or receive that lost image /391/ of the knowledge of God, his will, and that image of divine righteousness whereby we can find acceptance before God through Christ, John 3:15. And that is God's will, and the true ordering of the Lord, that we should thus be born anew out of that Word of God, and grow daily in the knowledge of God, Eph. 4:15, in faith, in love, and proceed in all obedience to the divine Word, to the praise of the Lord, and to our salvation.

For this rebirth the pure knowledge of the only God is also needed, which is the Father, the Son, and the Holy Spirit, Matt. 28:19; 1 John 5:8; Exod. 3:6. The Father is the flowing fountain of all good, a being of all things, a Creator of all creatures, the eternal, invisible God, who lives there in a light (says the apostle 1 Tim. 6:16). No one may come there, which also no one has seen, neither Moses on Mount Sinai, Exod. 20:2, nor John the Baptist at the Jordan, Matt. 3:16, nor the apostles on Mount Tabor, Matt. 17:5, nor Paul in the third heaven, 2 Cor. 12:2.

Only with devout and fruitful thoughts of God have believers seen him and confessed in Christ Jesus who is that image of the invisible God, 2 Cor. 4:4; Col. 1:15. The appearance of his glory is a mirror of his divine image, Heb. 1:3; Wisd. of Sol. 7:26. The only born from the Father, the Word through which all things were made, John 1:3, and in which is life, and that life is the light of all peoples, and that light is come into the world and shines in the darkness, but the darkness has not comprehended it. That Word has become flesh, received in the maiden Mary, Matt. 1:18, from the Holy Spirit, and born out of her as a Son of the most high, Luke 2:7. But the world has not confessed the great hiddenness that God has revealed in the flesh, 1 Tim. 1:15, that wisdom has appeared upon earth, Bar. 3:[37f.], and that the Word of life has become a human being, and nevertheless has remained that Word of life, 1 John 1:2. For since he should be the mediator between God and people, and thus make the reconciliation between us and the Father, Eph. 2:13; Col. 1:20, so must he be both God and a human being, in one person.

Again, since he should take away the sins of the world, John 1:29, making as nothing all unrighteousness with his righteousness, 1 John 2:1; Jer. 23:6, and swallowing up death, Heb. 2:15, so he must himself be righteousness, eternal life, John 14:6, and salvation, 1 Cor. 1:[30]. Again, while he should give his flesh for the life of the world, so must his flesh make alive. For this reason Christ himself called his flesh that bread of life which has come from heaven, John 6:33, and therefore it is not from the earth, nor from any mortal person's flesh and blood. /392/

In this high work of redemption, where God has redeemed that lost human race, that image of divine majesty, wisdom, righteousness, mercy, and friendliness is shown to us and placed before our eyes, that is, therein that God sent his only born Son, who was in godly form, in the form of sinful flesh, Phil. 2:6, submitted to the law, made to be sin, and was subjected to the curse, Gal. 4:4; Rom. 8:3; 2 Cor. 5:21; Gal. 3:13. And he who was immortal, yes, who ruled all things with his powerful Word, he has become weak and mortal, nevertheless he has risen again from death, Rom. 4:25, and has conquered all his enemies through his divine power, Heb. 1:3; 1 Cor. 15:25.

That is not the world's wisdom, nor of the angels in heaven, but it is God's wisdom hidden in secrecy, 1 Cor. 2:6[f.], which was preached by the apostles, not with words of human cleverness, but with such words as the Holy Spirit had taught them. That is also a severe, exalted, and valiant, yes, eternal righteousness of God, that he has punished so severely and made his own beloved Son to pay for our sins (which could be paid or taken away through no other means), Isa. 53:[8]; 1 Pet. 2:24; Gal. 1:4. And that is also no human love and mercy, but it is God's eternal love, God's bottomless grace and mercy that Jesus Christ has died for us while we were sinners, godless, and God's enemies, Rom. 5:8.

This is the God-saving secrecy which is great and wonderful, 1 Tim. 3:[16], about which Paul writes, which cannot be comprehended nor understood other than through the Holy Spirit, John 14:17, who searches all things, even the depth of God, 1 Cor. 2:10[ff.]. And since the world may not receive the Holy Spirit (just as Christ himself said, for it sees him not and does not know him), therefore it also does not understand the secrecy of this power of God. They do not know Jesus Christ truly, do not believe in him, just as the Scriptures testify, but some deny his true divinity, some contradict his holy, unspotted humanity, and some reject his God-saving teachings, etc., John 7:27; 1 John 2:22.

The Holy Spirit is the third name, Matt. 28:19, person, power, and working in the Godhead, a divine being with the Father and the Son, 1 John 5:8. For he proceeds from the Father, through /393/ the Son, and also has worked with them in the creation and is a spirit of truth, John 16:13, a comforter of consciences, a distributor of all spiritual gifts, which are poured out and infused into the heart of the believers from God the Father through Jesus Christ, through which they are enlightened, renewed, and sanctified, 1 Cor. 12:11; Titus 3:6; 1 Cor. 6:11, as a possession of God, Eph. 1:14, as new creatures in Christ, 2 Cor. 5:[17], Gal. 6:[15], and kept to eternal life, without which no one knows God, nor believes in Christ Jesus. But all good gifts come from the eternal Father, through Jesus Christ, and are imparted to us from the Holy Spirit, 1 Cor. 12:4; James 1:17; Matt. 7:11.

Thus, the Father, Son, and Holy Spirit is the only true living God and Lord, outside of whom no other god exists, neither in heaven nor upon earth, the first and the last, Rev. 22:13, the only eternal, wise, and righteous God, Deliverer and Savior, Isa. 40:28; 42:5; Rev. 1:17. And this knowledge of God must be at the new birth, in a good conscience, with a true faith out of God's Word, John 3:36, comprehended through the enlightenment of the Holy Spirit, about which we have written more extensively in other places. And from such born-again persons and new creatures, Christ Jesus has gathered his congregation, and he has instituted some ordinances, and given some commandments, which they must maintain and thereby be recognized as his congregation.

The first ordinance is that the congregation must have, above all else, the pure, unfalsified teaching of the divine Word, and with it true ministers who are called by ordination and chosen both by the Lord and from the congregation of the Lord, Matt. 28:19. But what that pure, clear Word of God is and how the same is twofold, that is, law and gospel, we have explained above. Just how the calling, election, and ordaining of the true ministers occurs, the Scripture teaches us quite clearly, Matt. 10:1, with the calling of prophets of God, with the commissioning of apostles from Christ Jesus, John 20:21, and with the ordination of elders from the Holy Spirit, Acts 13:2, and from the Christian congregation through unanimous vote, over the flock of God /394/ to feed and care for it, 1 Tim. 3:2; Titus 1:[5f.]; Acts 20:28. And we have certainly explained that in our book about the "Sending of Preachers," and say briefly again that the true ministers of the divine Word are clearly to be known by the saving teaching of Jesus Christ, by their God-fearing walk, and by the fruits which they produce, and in addition also by the persecution which they suffer on behalf of truth and righteousness.

For whoever thus speaks God's Word, that one is sent from God, John 3:34, and who does right, that one is born out of God, 1 John 2:29, and who converts persons from unrighteousness to the living God, that one remains in the council of God and proclaims the Lord's

Word to the people, Jer. 23:4. And so whoever is persecuted because he teaches and witnesses to the truth, he operates according to the Scripture, Matt. 5:11; 10:23; 12:[14]; 21:46; John 15:18, even as all good prophets and apostles, yes, the Lord himself did.

Again, how the ministers of God are ordained and must be sent, that is certainly to be learned and noticed out of the figures of Aaron and his children of the Old Testament. For as these should be ordained as priests of the Lord, so Moses had first to wash their bodies with pure water, sacrificed for them, and with the blood of the full sacrifice stroked the right ear, the thumb of the right hand, and the big toe of the right foot. And he put the linen garments on them, and girded them, and put a turban on their heads. And he took the anointing oil and the blood of the altar and sprinkled that on Aaron and his clothing, on his sons and their clothing, and thus dedicated Aaron and his clothing, his sons and their clothing, Exod. 29:20[f.]. But Aaron put on the silk robe and girded himself with the body garment, put on that ephod or breast piece, and in it the urim and thumim, that is light and truth, and set the hat upon his head, and before that the golden blade of the holy crown on his forehead, etc.

This thus appeared in the figure with Aaron and his children, as an indication of a true being of the teachers in the congregation of God, especially concerning the children of Aaron. For Aaron is really a figure of Jesus Christ, our only high priest, Heb. 2:17; 5:7; 8:1; 10:11. Nevertheless seeing that Christ sent his ministers, John 20:21, just as the Father had sent him, so it follows from this, that the ministers of Jesus Christ and his Holy Word must conform to his image, Rom. 8:29. Therefore these figures of Aaron and his /395/ children certainly may be understood rightly according to the spirit, that as ministers of Christ who preach his Word and proclaim his gospel, they must be washed with the pure water of the Holy Spirit, Heb. 10:22, and be sprinkled with the precious blood of the unblemished lamb Jesus Christ, John 1:29; 1 Pet. 1:[19], who has offered himself for us, first on the right ear, so that for them the ear of understanding might be opened to hear what God speaks with them. Second, on the thumb of the right hand, so that they may raise up clean and holy hands to God, Heb. 12:12; 1 Tim. 2:8. Third, on the big toe of the right foot, so that they may walk uprightly before the Lord in the way of righteousness.

They must put on the holy garments, that is, they must be clothed with Christ Jesus, Rom. 13:14; Gal. 3:27; Eph. 5:5; Rev. 19:8, to be girded with the belt of love and truth, Eph. 6:11, and decorated with the silk of righteousness. The shield with urim and thumim, with the twelve noble stones must be attached to them, that is, they must have the treasure of the divine Word in their heart, for they are the ministers of the Lord over the spiritual Israel, Gal. 6:8, to teach Jacob God's law and Israel his truth, Deut. 33:10. The hat with the golden blade of the holy crown is on their head, that is they rightly separate the Old and the New Testaments, Matt. 13:52, between the letter and the Spirit, and with a pure understanding of the divine secrets, Eph. 6:19; 2 Tim. 4:8.

They also have a living hope of salvation and the crown of righteousness is reserved for them in that day, 2 Tim. 4:8. They enter into God's sanctuary and offer the living sacrifice for the congregation of the Lord, Rom. 12:1; 1 Pet. 2:5, and their prayers sound and will be heard by the Most High, so that he remembers his congregation. The anointing oil is poured over them, for they have received the anointing of the one who is holy, 1 John 2:27, and they are thereby sanctified.

Christ has chosen and sent forth such ministers to proclaim his Word, to preach repentance and forgiveness of sins to all those who believe the gospel and are obedient, Luke 24:46[ff.]; John 20:23. But faith must be true, that is, of such nature and power that it is recognized that one believes all of God's Words, Deut. 4:2; 12:32, rejects all human teachings, with the whole heart sets his hope on the grace of Jesus Christ, 1 Pet. 1:3, despises all earthly things, denying himself, seeking after heavenly things with his entire zeal, Heb. 11:10; Col. 3:2; Phil. 3:20; 2 Cor. 4:18, hating sin out of pure fear of the Lord, Heb. 1:9, having the love of righteousness, thus producing the fruits of the Holy Spirit. Where that happens, there is a true faith. But where that does not happen, /396/ there is but an idle and false boasting of faith, Ps. 44:8; Gal. 6:[4].

The second ordinance which Christ has instituted in his congregation is a true scriptural use of the sacraments of Jesus Christ, namely, baptism and the Lord's Supper. For the repentant, believing, and born-again children of God must be baptized, Matt. 3:16; 28:19; Mark 1:9; 16:[16]; Acts 2:38; 8:[12f.]; 10:48; 16:15; 18:8; 22:16, and the same applies also for the Lord's Supper. For Christ has given and left us these two signs, adhering to the gospel in order to admonish, put before our eyes, and establish the unspeakable grace of God and his covenant, and us with it, as with visible signs. As first with baptism, wherein he himself baptized internally, and accepted the sinners in grace, forgave all their sins, cleansed them with his blood, granting them all his righteousness and fulfilling the law and sanctified them with his spirit, Matt. 3:11; John 3:5; Rev. 1:[5]; 1 Cor. 3:23. Second, in the Lord's Supper, Matt. 26:23; Mark 14:22; Luke 22:19, which testifies to the truth of the divine promise and redemption through JESUS CHRIST, namely, that all believing hearts, who are burdened because of their sins, run to the throne of grace, Christ Jesus, believe, and confess that the Son of God has died for us and has poured out his blood, Rom. 3:25; 4:25; 8:3, those have the forgiveness of sins, redemption, deliverance from the law, Gal. 3:13; Eph. 1:7, eternal righteousness, and salvation out of grace through Jesus Christ, without the merit of works, Rom. 11:6.

Both of these signs have been left us from the Lord that they should admonish us to a godly blessed walk, to dying to the flesh, burying of sins, arising to new life, Rom. 16:18; Col. 3:5; to thanksgiving for the great deeds which are given us from God, Matt. 26:[26ff.]; Mark 14:23; Luke 22:20; as a remembrance of the bitter suffering and death of Christ; to renewing and establishing of brotherly love, unity, and fellowship, 1 Cor. 10:17; [11]:25. Again, that they will distinguish the congregation of GOD from all sects, which do not have the true scriptural use of the sacramental signs of the LORD Jesus Christ, although they give that appearance. In true hypocrisy many boast of that, and commit and engage in shameful idolatry thereby. They do not use the sacraments of Jesus Christ according to his Word, nor according to his command and example, neither according to the teaching and practice of the apostles, but according to the world's institution and the notions of human beings.

Here, in addition, they thus remain in that old sinful life unrepentantly, /397/ full of all of the unrighteousness, greediness, impurity, pride, jealousy, backbiting, and all kinds of evil, which is a certain witness that they do not have the pure Word of God, and the true faith, with the right use of baptism and the supper of Jesus Christ according to the Scripture, Heb. 6:3. Thus whenever that gospel will be witnessed to with such high oaths to God, established with that precious blood of Jesus, sealed with the Holy Spirit, is truly taught and believed, and therein the sacraments of the Lord are received orderly in the faith, with heartfelt devotion and consideration of the secrets that are hidden under them, just as ought to happen, Gen. 15:18; 17:7; 22:17; John 3:16; 5:43, there the Spirit of God enters the heart which daily renews that lost image of God. He gives the knowledge of the Father and his image in Christ. He multiplies faith, hope, love, patience, and all of God's virtues, Acts 2:47; Titus 3:5; Eph. 4:23; Rom. 3:24; John 15:10.

The Congregation of God / 367

Again, he comforts the consciences, he cleanses the hearts, and makes them fruitful in the knowledge of God and Christ, and endows them with all kinds of spiritual wisdom and understanding of heavenly things, Col. 1:9. He also gives a bold spirit to appeal to God and to call the exalted majesty of God Abba, loving Father, Rom. 8:15; Gal. 4:5[ff.]. He teaches genuine humility, gentleness, patience, friendliness, and imparts the peace of God into the conscience, Gal. 5:22. Here the adversary, the devil, must give way, James 4:7. Here the flesh will be crucified with its lusts and desires, 1 John 5:4. Here the world lies trodden under foot through the power of faith in Jesus Christ, Gal. 6:16. And thus where such does not happen nor will be learned, there is neither God, nor Christ, nor Holy Spirit, nor gospel, nor faith, nor genuine baptism, nor the Supper of the Lord, in sum, no congregation of God.

The third ordinance is the foot washing of the saints, John 13:5[ff.], which Jesus Christ commanded his disciples, and that for two reasons. The first is to give us the knowledge that he himself must cleanse us in the internal person, and we must let the sin which clings so closely, Heb. 12:1, the soiling of the flesh and spirit, be washed away by him, that we may become cleaner day by day, just as it is written. So whoever is clean becomes even cleaner; who is holy becomes even holier; and who is just becomes even more just, Rev. 22:11. And that is necessary, yes, must happen, so that we will be saved.

Therefore Christ said to Peter, "Unless I wash you, you shall have no part in me." /398/ Then Peter answered, "Lord, not only the feet, but also the hands and head." There upon Christ answered, "Whoever is thus washed needs nothing more than that one wash his feet and he is entirely clean." Thereby he certainly made known that the foot washing (where Christ joins us in washing) is very necessary, and what that signifies, since those whom he does not wash shall have no part with him. And that those who are washed by him do not need more than that their feet shall be washed, and they are entirely clean. For it is Christ who must wash us from our sins with his blood, Rom. 3:22, 1 John 1:7; Rev. 1:[5]. And thus those who are therewith sprinkled and washed need nothing more than that the earthly body, the evil lusts and desires of the flesh will be dead through the Spirit and conquered by him. Thus he is entirely clean out of grace and no sin will be reckoned to him, Eph. 1:4; Col. 3:5; Rom. 8:13.

The second reason why Christ has instituted foot washing is that we should humble ourselves one to another, Rom. 12:10; Phil. 2:3; 1 Pet. 5:5; James 4:10, and hold the companions of our faith in great esteem, Rom. 12:10; for this reason, that they are the saints of God and members of Jesus Christ, Col. 3:[12-]13; and that the Holy Spirit lives in them, [1] Cor. 3:16. This Christ teaches us with these words: You call me Lord and Master, and you speak truly about that, for so I am. Thus if I then your Lord and Master have washed your feet, so should you also wash one another's feet. I have given you the example that you should do the same as I have done to you. Truly, truly, I say to you, the servant is not greater than his Lord, and the apostle is not more than the one who has sent him. If you know this, blessed are you if you do that. Be now the blessed who know such and do it, John 13:[14-17].

If now those are blessed who know and do this, how unhappy are they then who boast of being apostles or messengers of the Lord, and do not know this, or knowing it, do not do that, nor teach others to do that. But their heart is all too haughty and blown up so that they will not humble themselves according to the command and example of Christ. They shame themselves, or it is for them foolishness (just as divine wisdom is always considered foolishness by the world), 1 Cor. 1:19[f.]; 3:19. But they would much rather have the honor of people, John 5:44. They like very much to be called doctors, masters, and lords rather than seek the honor that comes from God, which will be received through a true faith and holy walk. Still they want /399/ to be called the church of Christ. Yes, they want to be the only ones held as such. But God who opposes the haughty and gives his grace to the humble knows them well, [1] Pet. 5:6; James 4:10, and at the last day will certainly reveal what kind of an assembly or congregation (yes, I may properly say a sect) they have been.

The fourth ordinance is the evangelical separation, without which God's congregation may not exist. For if the unfruitful branches of the vine are not cut, they injure the good and fruitful branches, John 15:6. If one does not expel that kind of member, then the whole body must perish, Matt. 5:30, that is, if one does not exclude public sinners, trespassers, and unlawful ones, Matt. 18:17; 1 Cor. 5:10; 1 Thess. 5:14; 2 John 1:11, the entire congregation will become impure. And if one retains the false brothers, one becomes a participant in their sins, and in this regard we have many examples and testimonies in the Scripture.

In Joshua 7:1[-26] we have the terrible example of Achan who stole from the banned goods in Jericho and hid them in his tent. The Lord therefore became so angry at Israel that he allowed some in Israel to be killed in battle, and among other words said to Joshua that the children of Israel could not stand before their enemies, but must turn their backs on them, for they were under the ban. I shall from now on no more be with you, unless you separate the banned ones from you. Therefore Achan with all that belonged to him was done away with and exterminated from Israel. Joshua spoke to him: Seeing that you have brought trouble upon us, the Lord must thus afflict you on this day, etc.

In the same manner, we have in Numbers a remarkable example of Dathan, Abiram, and Korah, who opposed Moses and Aaron, Num. 16:11, and many of the principal or most honored in Israel stood with them. But Moses spoke to the congregation of the Lord: Separate from the tents or tabernacles these godless people, and touch nothing of what belongs to them, that you perhaps not be destroyed by any of their sins.

Out of such and similar history and examples of the Holy Scripture, it is well to notice and understand how no congregation or assembly may exist before God /400/ when they do not use the ban or separation in an orderly and humble manner according to the command of Christ, the teaching and example of the apostles. But the common saying applies exactly here, that a little leaven sours the whole dough, 1 Cor. 5:[6], and a scabby sheep makes the whole flock unclean. Yes, just as the priest or prophet is, so also are the people, Hos. 6:[9].

The separation must also be used in order that the one who has sinned, being chastised in the flesh and made ashamed, may amend himself and remain redeemed in the day of Jesus, 1 Cor. 5:3[-5], which is the highest love, and the best of all healing stuff or medicine for his sick soul, just as this was certainly observed with the Corinthian adulterer. Necessity requires such also, that one shall separate the fallen or evil one, so that the name of God, the gospel of Jesus Christ, and the congregation of the Lord shall not be defamed on account of it, Ps. 50:21; Ezek. 36:20; Rom. 2:24.

But which the sins are which must be punished with the ban the evangelists and apostles testify to us with explicit words, Matt. 18:15[ff.]; Rom. 16:[17ff.]; 1 Cor. 5:10; 1 Thess. 5:14; 2 Tim. 3:5; Titus 3:[10f.]; 2 John 1:10. We have also declared this well in our confession about the evangelical ban. What the congregation of the Lord thus judges with his Word is judged before God. That is why Christ has given his congregation the keys of the heavenly kingdom, Matt. 16:19, that it shall punish the evil ones, exclude and remove from itself, and to take in the repentant and believing. What the congregation thus binds on earth, that shall be bound in heaven. Conversely, what they loose on earth, that shall be loosed in heaven, which is not to be understood that people have the power to forgive and retain sins, just as some think and accept for themselves, and therefore deal with the confessional and absolution as with a peddler. But no minister of Christ shall do that, and the congregation of the Lord shall also not allow such simony.

For no prophet or apostle on earth has been authorized to forgive sins, Acts 8:21, to hear confession, and to absolve the members, although Christ has said to his disciples: Receive the Holy Spirit. Whose sins you forgive, they shall be forgiven them. Whose sins you retain, they shall be retained, John 20:[22f.]. For the holy people of God have not accepted the divine honor /401/ for themselves, but through the inspiration of the Holy Spirit they certainly have confessed that God alone forgives sins, just as the Scripture uniformly testifies, Isa. 43:25; Matt. 9:6; Ps. 51:4. But the congregation has received the Holy Spirit and the gospel from Christ, in which was declared and promised forgiveness of sins, reconciliation with God, and eternal life to all those who truly repent and believe in Jesus Christ. Conversely, disgrace, wrath, and condemnation were threatened and promised to all unbelievers, disobedient, and perverted.

This word together with the Holy Spirit is a judge in the congregation over all false brothers, over all heretical persons, 1 Cor. 5:3[ff.]; Rom. 10:16, over the disorderly and disobedient, who after sufficient admonition do not amend themselves, 2 Tim. 2:1[f.]; Titus 3:[9]; 1 Thess. 5:[14]; [2] John [10]. No other judgment will be pronounced at the last day, as the Lord himself said. And the congregation has received this word from God through which it testifies, judges, receives, and separates in the name of Jesus Christ and in the power of the Holy Spirit. What they thus bind or unbind here on earth with the Lord's Word and Spirit, that is bound or unbound in heaven.

The fifth ordinance is the commandment of love that Christ has given his disciples, saying a new commandment I give you, that you have love one for another, even as I have loved you. And hereby people will recognize that you are my disciples, if you have love for one another, just as I have loved you, John 13:34; 15:12. From this it is easy to understand that pure brotherly love is an assured sign of true faith and genuine Christianity. But true brotherly love is that we seek first of all one another's salvation, Gal. 6:[2], with our fervent prayers to God, 2 Thess. 1:11, with scriptural instruction, admonition, and discipline, James 5:19. By this we may instruct those who are overtaken in a fall to win their soul and seek it with Christian patience, by which we carry the weak and do not become well pleased with ourselves, Gal. 6:[2]; 1 John 5:16; James 5:19.

Since brotherly love is witnessed to by this, that we minister to each other with a willingly extended hand, Rom. 12:13, not only with spiritual, but also with temporal gifts which we have received from God. We accept for ourselves the poverty /402/ of the saints giving richly according to our ability, yes, that it proceed among us just as happened in that literal Israel, namely, who gathered in much heavenly bread had nothing left over; and who gathered little had no lack, Exod. 16:18; 2 Cor. 8:15. Thus the rich also who have received much in temporal goods from the Lord shall minister to the poor with it and supply their needs, so that the poor in turn come to their aid if they need it, Rom. 15:27; 2 Cor. 8:[9-]10.

Therefore Christ said in the gospel, Luke 16:9, "Make friends of unrighteous mammon so that they receive you into the eternal tabernacle if you need it." And Paul wrote to Timothy thus: "Command the rich of this world that they not be puffed up in heart, that they do not put their trust in uncertain riches, but on the living God who gives us all things richly to use, that they are held in common, give gladly, so that they acquire a treasure for the future, and that they receive eternal life, 1 Tim. 6:[17-]19. Again John wrote in his epistle: "Thereby we know love, that just as Christ has given up his life for us, we shall also give up life for the brother. If someone has the world's goods and sees his brother suffering lack and closes his heart to him, how can love abide by him? Little children, let us not have love in words or with the tongue, but with deeds and truth, 1 John 3:16[-18].

Again, how much love is needed the apostles show us everywhere in their writing, principally Paul to those from Corinth, where he thus writes, "Although I would speak with tongues of humans and angels and had not love, I am a sounding metal or clanging bell; and although I would prophesy, or could announce coming things, and knew all secrets and knowledge, and had all faith that I could remove mountains, and did not have love, I am nothing. And although I would give all my goods to the poor, and let my body be burned, and did not have love, it is of no value to me," 1 Cor. 13:[1-3].

By this it may readily be noted how far those are separated from true faith and Christianity who do not have love one for another. Their love does not show in their works for one another, but they let their poor suffer want, Deut. 15:4; Rom. 12:13; 2 Cor. 8:14; Gal. 6:8 [-10], beg for bread openly, against the command of the Lord, against all Christian nature, and against all brotherly love and faithfulness. And what is more, they cut short, hate, envy, backbite, defame, revile, slander, persecute, /403/ throttle, and kill one another, as one sees before our eyes, just as their works certainly give witness.

And although they do such things, still they nonetheless want to be called Christian and to be called God's congregation. But if they do not repent, so they shall certainly discover in that day before the judgment seat of Jesus Christ what fine Christians they have been. For where love is not present, God is not there, seeing that God is love, as John says, 1 John 4:8. And who abides in love, abides in God and God in him, 1 John 4:16. But who does not abide in love, that one remains in death, and walks in darkness, and the darkness has blinded their eyes, 1 John 2:11.

The sixth ordinance which Christ Jesus has instituted in his congregation is the keeping of all his commandments, Matt. 28:20; 1 Cor. 7:19. For he requires of all his disciples a life blessed of God, Phil. 1:27; Matt. 10:32, a walk that is worthy of the gospel, a voluntary confessing of the truth before people, a denial of self, Matt. 16:25, faithful following in his footsteps, 1 Pet. 2:12; Matt. 6:16, a voluntary taking up of his cross, Luke 9:23, an abandonment of all things, Matt. 5:3, a humble seeking after God's kingdom and his righteousness, after the invisible heavenly goods, and after eternal life, Matt. 6:20. He also teaches his disciples poverty of spirit, divine mourning, gentleness, purity of heart, mercy, peacemaking, patience in persecution for the sake of righteousness, Matt. 5:3-11; Luke 9:23, and happiness of conscience when they are despised and scorned on behalf of his name.

He also pictures for his own genuine meekness and warns them faithfully against all pride of spirit and flesh, Luke 17:33; 8:15. He remonstrates them about how they must hear and keep God's Word, John 8:47, hungering and thirsting after righteousness, Matt. 5:6, watching for the false prophets, Matt. 16:6, not to follow after the hireling, John 10:12, and to flee the strange voice. Again, how they shall fast and always pray, Matt. 6:5, how they shall watch for excesses in eating, for drunkenness, and care for the unexpected fall, how they must watch and prepare themselves for his future, Luke 21:31; Matt. 24:32[f.]; 25:13; how they should watch for the leaven of the Pharisees, Matt. 16:6, which is pretense.

They should not glory in their own works and seek a false righteousness therein, or that they do not see the chaff in another's eye, and not notice the beam in their own eye, Matt. 7:3. And do not sift out the gnats and swallow the camel, Matt. 23:23[f.]. Yes, he prescribes for his own a rule of perfection, Matt. 5:48, /404/ how they must love their enemies, Matt. 5:44, do good to those who do them evil, pray for their persecutors, bless those who curse them, forgive their debtors from their heart, Matt. 18:35, just as they have desired forgiveness from God for their guilt; do not wreak vengeance themselves, but surrender vengeance to God, Rom. 12:19.

Again, that they must watch not only for the evil public acts of the flesh as murder, adultery, false swearing, and such things, but also for anger, sarcastic words, indecent desires of the heart, and for most scornful swearing, and should not do such things in any manner, on pain of punishment of hellish fires, just as one may read in Matthew 5:22. Similarly, the apostles teach in their epistles how Christians must in all things be obedient children of the heavenly Father, as the chosen and called saints of God, Col. 3:12; 1 Pet. 1:[2], as ministers of the Lord Jesus Christ, 2 Cor. 6:4, as the instruments of the Holy Spirit, as a royal priesthood, as a chosen generation, as his own people, 1 Pet. 2:9; Eph. 5:26, who are zealous after good works, Titus 2:14, as the children of light who must walk no longer in darkness but in the light; who are therefore called out of darkness to wonderful light to proclaim God's power, and are therefore delivered from the hand of their enemies, to serve God in holiness and righteousness all the days of their life, Luke [1]:70[ff.].

And this is the heavenly philosophy which Jesus Christ, the Son of God, received from his Father, brought out of heaven, and taught to his disciples. This is the counsel and will of God, Acts 20:27, the Godblessed teaching of Jesus Christ and witness of the Holy Spirit. And in all these, so is the Lord Jesus Christ sent to his own as a master from God, Matt. 3:17; 17:5, whom they must hear, a leader whom they must follow, 1 Pet. 2:25, and an example to which they must be conformed, Rom. 8:29. And this is the rule of Christianity about which Paul wrote that all who walk in this way, Gal. 6:[16], have peace and mercy over them and over the Israel of God. But those who do not walk according to this rule are not Christians, though they boast as much as they will.

The seventh ordinance is that all Christians must suffer and be persecuted, just as Christ promised them and has also said: The world shall rejoice and you shall mourn, but your sadness will be turned into joy, John 16:33. Again, you /405/ shall be hated by everyone for my name's sake, Matt. 24:9. Again, the time shall come that those who kill you think they are doing a service to God by it, John 16:2. Therewith Paul is in accord also, saying: If we suffer with Christ, then we shall also rejoice with him, and inherit our heavenly Father's kingdom,

Rom. 8:17; 2 Tim. 2:12. Again, all those who will live blessed by God in Christ Jesus will suffer persecution, 2 Tim. 3:12. Again, Paul and Barnabas have testified in all congregations that they must go through much pressure and suffering to enter into the kingdom of heaven, Acts 13:50.

In summary, the entire Holy Scripture testifies that the righteous must suffer and possess their soul with patience, Luke 21:17. And that does not miss it, for where a pious Abel is, there is an evil Cain against him, Gen. 4:1[f.]. Where a chosen David is, there is a rejected Saul who persecuted him, 1 Sam. 18:10. Where Christ was born, there is a Herod who seeks after his life, Matt. 2:16; where he openly preached and worked, there Annas and Caiphas come together with the bloodthirsty Jews, and take counsel against him, Matt. 26:3[f.]; Mark 14:1; Luke 22:2; Acts 4:6. They could not desist until the time that they killed him and forced Pilate thereto so that he had to do their will.

Thus, the true Christian must be persecuted here for the sake of the truth and of righteousness, but they persecute no one because of their faith. For Christ sent his disciples as lambs among wolves, Matt. 10:16. But the lamb does not strangle the wolf but the wolf the lamb. Therefore, they can never more exist or be considered a congregation of the Lord who persecute others on account of their faith. For, first of all, God the heavenly Father has thus given all judgment to Christ Jesus, that he should be a judge over the souls and consciences of people, John 5:22, and should reign eternally in the congregation with the scepter of his word, Luke [1:32f.].

Second, it is thus the office or work of the Holy Spirit to punish the world for the sin of unbelief, John 16:8. And it is now clear that the Holy Spirit has not administered such punishment with violence nor with any external sword through the apostles and all pious witnesses of the truth but with God's Word and power.

Third, the Lord Jesus Christ has thus given his congregation the power and has established the ordinance that it shall separate, shun, and avoid false brothers, the unlawful and disobedient, the quarrelsome and heretical persons, yes, all who are found to be evil within the congregation, Rom. 16:[17]; 1 Cor. 5:10[f.]; 1 Thess. 5:[14]; Titus 3:[10], as was said before. /406/ What happens beyond this is not Christian, nor evangelical, nor apostolic.

Fourth, the parable of the Lord in the gospel shows us clearly that he does not permit his servant to pull out the weeds now, lest they perhaps also pull up the wheat, but they shall let the wheat and weed grow up together in the world until the Lord shall command his reapers, that is, his angels, to gather the wheat into the barn, and to cast the weeds into the fire, Matt. 13:29[f.].

Here is revealed that no congregation of the Lord may have domination over the consciences of people with an external sword, nor compel the unbeliever to faith with violence, nor kill the false prophets with sword and fire. But they must judge and exclude with the Lord's Word all who are within the congregation and found to be evil. Anything more than this that happens is neither Christian, evangelical, nor apostolic. And if someone wants to say that the authorities have not received the sword in vain, Rom. 13:1[ff.], and that God through Moses has commanded to kill the false prophets, Deut. [15], to that I answer briefly: The authority has not received the sword from God to judge over spiritual matters (for these must be judged by the spiritual only spiritually), 1 Cor. 2:13, but to keep its subjects in good order and to keep peace, protect the pious, and punish the evil.

And that God through Moses had commanded to kill the false prophets, that is a command of the Old and not the New Testament. Over against that we have received another command from the LORD, that we should watch out for false prophets, Matt. 7:15, whom we should not hear, John 10:5, that we should shun a heretical person, Titus 3:10, and we commend the judgment over them to GOD. And if one must now kill the false prophets according to the command of the Old Testament, then that must first be to those who truly are held to be false prophets and antichrists by all God-fearing and understanding people, yes, nearly by the whole world. If then the state must kill not only the false prophets, Deut. 13:5; but also all worshipers of images and servants of idols, and those who advise other people to engage in idolatry, Exod. 22:18, and all adulterers, all who blaspheme the name of the Lord, Exod. 20.7, and thereby swear falsely, all who curse father and mother, Deut. 27:[16], and all who desecrate the Sabbath. For these are all thus clearly condemned to death through the law, just as are false prophets. /407/

Therefore it is nothing more than fig leaves woven together to cover their shame that some want to adorn their tyranny with the Scripture, and object that they kill no Christians but heretics, and that God has commanded such through Moses. Yes, the world certainly holds the most pious Christians as the worst of all heretics, just as all good prophets are always considered liars by the world, Jer. 11:21, rioters, unreasonable people, and deceivers, Amos 2:[12]; Matt. 5:11; 23:30; 26:[59]. And Christ Jesus himself was accounted among the evildoers, Acts 6:14. And the apostles are presented as the least of all,

Ps. 44:[22]; 1 Cor. 4:9, and submitted to death as a curse of the world, and regarded as an animal sacrifice. And thus it still goes with all true Christians.

Nevertheless, they are certainly comforted in this; for they abandon themselves to the Lord their God, and assure themselves with the wonderful promise which they are given from God, namely, that they are saved, that the kingdom of heaven is promised to them, and the Spirit of God rests on them if they are persecuted for righteousness sake, Matt. 5:[10]; 1 Pet. 4:14. So also when people say all manner of evil against them and thereby lie about them, for Christ's name sake, when they participate in Christ's suffering and on account of him are scorned. Thereby they know that they shall also participate in his glory, Rom. 8:17; 2 Tim. 2:12.

I have thus now indicated and related briefly what the congregation of God is, how and wherewith it is built, with what ordinances it is grasped, with what signs it is portrayed, whereby it is to be known and distinguished from all sects. For such things are not to be found in all the false and anti-Christian congregations, namely, no genuine new birth, no truly differentiated teaching between law and gospel which brings forth fruit and whereby people truly repent, Matt. 3:8; Luke 3:8, and will be converted from unrighteousness to the living God; no genuine knowledge of the eternal and only God who is eternal life, John 17:3, perfect wisdom and righteousness, Wisd. of Sol. 15:3, and who is witnessed to by the keeping of the commands of Christ; no genuine confession of the pure, holy, and unblemished humanity of Jesus Christ, John 1:[19f]; no fruitful faith; no scriptural baptism; no Lord's Supper; no Christian foot washing of the saints in secrecy out of true humility; no key to the heavenly kingdom; no evangelical ban or separation; no avoidance of the temples of idols; /408/ nor of false worship services; no unfeigned brotherly love; no God-fearing life nor keeping of the commands of Christ, no persecution for the sake of righteousness. All of these ordinances and testimonies of true Christianity will not be found in a true form in any anti-Christian congregation, but everywhere the converse and opposite, just as one certainly sees clearly today if one otherwise has eyes to see, ears to hear, and a heart to understand, Matt. 13:9; Rev. 2:7; 3:6.

Furthermore, the congregation of the Lord is easy to know from her description, namely, that she is the Holy City, that New Jerusalem, having come down from God out of heaven, Rev. 21:1; prepared for her husband as an adorned bride, having the glory of God, and her light is like the most precious stone, the crystaline jasper, and it has high and great walls, and twelve gates, and on the gates twelve angels, and names are written thereon which are the twelve tribes of the children of Israel, and the construction of her walls is from jasper, and the city is from pure gold, like clear glass, and the foundation of the walls and the city is decorated with all kinds of precious stones, and the gates are twelve pearls, and each gate is a pearl, and the streets of the city are pure as transparent glass, and there is no temple in it, but the Lord God Almighty is her temple and the Lamb.

And the city needs no sun or moon to shine in it, for God's glory illuminates it, Rev. 22:5, and the Lamb and the heathen who will be saved there walk in that same light. And the gates of this city are not closed daily, and there is and shall be no night. And a pure stream of water, clear as crystal, flows from the throne of God and the Lamb, in the middle of her streets; and on both sides of the stream stands the tree of life that gives its fruit every month, and the leaves of the tree serve for the healing of the heathen. And the throne of God and the Lamb is in it, yes, God's tabernacle is by the people, and he dwells with them, and they are his people, and he himself is their God. And the glory and honor of the heathen shall be brought into the same city, and nothing that is impure may enter, anything that does abominations and lies, but [only] those who are written in the living book of the Lamb, and his servants serve him there, and his name is on their forehead, and they shall see his face and reign in eternity. /409/

This is a description or living facsimile of the Christian congregation, how it first enters there in the Spirit, and hereafter shall be perfected in the heavenly being. For the congregation is first of all the Holy City, whose citizens are the believers in Christ, and the household companions of God, Eph. 2:[12], and will therefore be called a city, because like a city it must be united; the citizens need to be firmly attached to each other, living and walking according to one kind of policy, law, and statutes so long as the city wants to remain standing. Thus it must also take place in the congregation. There must be unity in spirit and faith, 1 Cor. 1:[10]; 10:21; there one must walk according to one rule of the divine Word; there one must maintain harmoniously the divine policy which this city has received from God, Rom. 12:16. Therefore the prophet also said that Jerusalem shall be built as a city whose citizens are one, Ps. [122:3], whereby the unity of God's congregation is portrayed of which the Scripture witnesses much, Eph. 4:3; Col. 3:[15f.]; Gal. 3:28; John 17:11.

Second, thus the congregation is that New Jerusalem, Rev. 21:2. For all things are made new through Jesus Christ, Rom. 7:6; 2 Cor.

5:17. That old being of letter and flesh has passed away, and a true new being has come forth in Jesus Christ. And Jerusalem is often spoken of as a vision of peace; and therefore, the congregationy of the Lord is that true Jerusalem, for it has peace with God through Jesus Christ, Rom. 5:1, and peace is within her walls, and none who quarrel against the evangelical teaching may be allowed in or remain there, Rom. 16:[17]; Titus 3:[10]. For God is a God of peace, 1 Cor. 14:33; in all his congregations Christ is the prince of peace and has given us and left us his peace, John [14:27]; Rom. 14:[19]. The Holy Spirit gives peace and happiness to the conscience of the believers. And the apostles admonish us to this peace in all their letters, that this may gain the upper hand in our hearts, Rom. 12:[18]; Eph. 4:[3]; Heb. 12:[14]; Phil. 4:[7].

Third, this new Jerusalem has originated from heaven. For the Christian is not from the world, just as Christ is also not from this world, John 17:14. But they are born anew from above, 1 John 3:[9]. Therefore they are also not fleshly but spiritually minded, Rom. 8:5, and seek through faith the things that are above, where Christ sits on the right hand of the Father, Col. 3:1; Heb. [12]:2. They are at peace to dwell with Abraham, Isaac, and Jacob in tabernacles and to be strangers here upon earth, 1 Pet. 1:1; 2:11. For they seek another city which has one foundation, /410/ whose builder and Creator is God, Heb. 11:10. Those who are thus minded through the grace of the Lord and through the power of their faith are the congregation of God, that Jerusalem which is above, about which Paul wrote to the Galatians, 4:26.

Fourth, the congregation is prepared as an adorned bride for her husband. She is married to Christ through faith and is that gloriously beautiful bride of the Lamb, Hos. 2:[19]; 2 Cor. 11:[2], adorned with many kinds of virtues of God and gifts of the Holy Spirit. Here is the great secret about Christ and his congregation which Paul wrote about to the Ephesians, namely, that Christ is head of his congregations, Eph. 5:23; 1:22. And she is flesh of his flesh and bone of his bone. Therefore, he has loved her and gave himself for her, so that he could institute for himself a glorious congregation, and has cleansed her through that water bath in the Word, so that she would not have any blemish, wrinkle, or anything like it, but be holy and blameless. Yes, she participates in the divine nature, 2 Pet. 1:4, if she holds firmly to the end that beginning of Christ's being, Heb. 3:14. Therefore the congregation of Christ must in turn also have love. And she must surrender herself, leaving all on his behalf, Matt. 10:37[ff.]; 16:23[ff.], and attaching herself to him alone, avoiding and fleeing before all spiritual whoring, that is, idolatry, 1 Cor. 6:18; 10:14.

Fifth, this Holy City thus has the glory of God, and it does not need either sun or moon to shine on her, for God's glory illumines her, and her light is the most precious stone, like the crystaline jasper, and the heathen shall be saved who walk in that same light, that is, the congregation is the kingdom of the Most High, Dan. 7:27, elevated above all the kingdoms of the earth, in which the saints have spiritual dominion and are the conquerors of the whole world through their faith, 1 John 5:4.

And Christ Jesus, that appearance of eternal light and the exact image of the divine being, Wisd. of Sol. 7:26; Heb. 1:3, is the light of his congregation, which through his appearing illumines everything yes, with the clarity of his Word, so that we need no other light. And the heathen who shall be saved are called out of darkness into this light, 1 Pet. 2:9, and walk in that same light, as children of the light, Eph. 5:[8], and shine as a light in the world, Phil. 2:15, doing it because they hold themselves firmly to that Word of life. Therefore Tobit also said in his song of praise, "Oh, Jerusalem, you city of God, you shall /411/ shine as a clear shining light, and persons shall honor you in all the ends of the earth," Tobit 13:11.

Sixth, thus this city has great and high walls, and the construction of the walls is from jasper, and the foundation of the walls and the city is adorned with all kinds of precious stones. This signifies to us that the congregation is built upon the precious foundation of the apostles and prophets, of which Jesus Christ is the cornerstone, Eph. 2:[20]. And the same congregation has had many glorious ministers from the beginning, 1 Cor. 3:5; 1 Pet. 5:1, teachers of righteousness, adorned with high gifts of the Spirit as a wall around God's city to keep it from the enemies, and as an enclosure around the vineyard of the Lord, because of the little foxes, Song of Sol. 2:15, that is, to keep out the infiltrating false prophets that they not spoil the Lord's vineyard, Isa. 5:[1f.].

Seventh, thus twelve gates are at this city Jerusalem, and twelve angels, and their names are written thereon, which are the twelve tribes of the children of Israel, and they signify to us that the Lord's congregation has the teachings of the apostles who lead them into the heavenly Jerusalem. And one may not enter therein any other way. For the apostles have proclaimed that true gospel to us, Gal. 1:9, and aside from that no other may be preached. If we shall enter into the Lord's congregation, we must enter through this gate, Luke 13:[24].

For Christ Jesus is the only way to the Father and the only door to the sheepfold, John 10:7[ff.], that is, the only entrance into the congregation, John 14:[6], and into the kingdom of God. And seeing that the apostles preached Christ, proclaimed the gospel, and thus brought people to Christ, therefore they are called gates through which one enters the Holy City. They are also angels of the Lord, Ps. 103:20, messengers of the Most High, Mal. 3:1, sealed servants of God, and the names of the twelve tribes of the children of Israel are written upon them; for they were first sent to them by Christ, and they were first called to the fellowship of the gospel, and they take precedence, and the apostles of the Lord have come forth out of them.

Eighth, this city mentioned earlier is of pure gold, like clear glass, and it has no temple in it, for the Most High is its temple, and the Lamb /412/ which makes us know that the congregation of the Lord is clean and pure. It is refined through much tribulation, just as the Scripture clearly shows us, that God tests his holy ones as gold in fire, Wisd. of Sol. 3:6; Ecclus. 2:5, with many kinds of temptations, so that by testing their faith will be found much more precious than corruptible gold.

The congregation also needs no external temple, which is made with hands, Acts 7:48; 17:24, and counts as nothing with God. Therefore none is found in the congregation, but the tabernacle of God is with it, and the dwelling of the Most High is in her midst, Ps. [48]:9; Rev. 21:22. And, once again, thus the congregation is itself the temple of the living God, just as is written, 1 Cor. 3:16; 2 Cor. 6:16: "I will live in them and walk in them, and they shall be my people, and I will be their God, says the Lord Almighty."

Ninth, thus the gates of the city are not closed by day, and there is no night. That is, the entrance into God's congregation is always open for the repentant and believing ones to whom the door of grace always stands open, 2 Cor. 6:2, for the same ones the day of salvation always shines, and there is no darkness. For God who lives there in an eternal light, and in whom there is no change, nor changing of light or darkness, that one is in his congregation and illumines it with his divine glory here in the heart through his Word and Spirit, being accepted with a genuine faith, and hereafter in that incorruptible kingdom in which the justified shall radiate as the sun in eternity.

Tenth, thus a living stream of water flows clear as crystal, from the throne of God and the Lamb, in the middle of the streets of the heavenly Jerusalem, and on both sides of the stream stands the wood of life that bears fruit in every month, and its leaves serve for the healing of the heathen. This clear living stream of water signifies the Holy Spirit who proceeds from the eternal almighty God and Father through the Son, John 15:26, and is a Spirit of the Father and the Son. And he is in the congregation, he freshes and comforts the believing souls with the eternal comfort of divine grace, 1 Pet. 1:11; 1 Cor. 2:10; and through the same Spirit, Jesus Christ will be declared, that Word of life, John 16:13, that richly comforting gospel will be proclaimed, which is fruitful in the hearts of the believers, serviceable and profitable for eternal salvation to all who thereby are converted out /413/ of heathendom to the almighty God and will be led into his congregation.

Eleventh, thus the glory and honor of the heathen will be brought into the Holy City, Rev. 21:26, and nothing unclean may enter there, no abominations nor lies, but who are written in that living book of the Lamb, that is the heathen, who will become believers out of hearing the gospel that is preached to them through the power and working of the Holy Spirit. These have praised God (just as the prophets have testified in many places), Deut. [32]:43; Rom. 15:9, and have made God's congregation glorious, since many thousands of the heathen have been joined to the congregation.

But the unclean, the liars, and those who commit abominations may not enter into this Holy City, Rev. 21:8. For the godless (the prophet says) shall not remain standing in the judgment, nor sinners in the congregations of the righteous. Yes, their part will be with the dragon in the fiery pool, just as is written there: The cowardly, the unbelievers, the idolators, the abominators, the murderers, and liars, their part shall be in the fiery pool that burns from fire and sulfur, which is the second death. O Lord, where will they then remain who now with such proud and haughty words boast to be the Lord's congregation, and are entirely drunk in fleshly lusts, and are public servants to idols, and are liars against all truth, and do all kinds of abominations before the Lord.

Finally, thus the servants of the Lord serve the Most High in this Holy City, and his name is on their forehead, and they shall see his face and reign from eternity to eternity. These servants are the true Christians who serve the Lord faithfully in his congregation, who have yielded their members to the service of righteousness, Rom. 6:19, that they may be holy, and whose goal is to achieve the salvation of their souls, 1 Pet. 1:[9]. These are marked on their forehead with the name of their God. They confess the truth boldly as those who are sealed with the Holy Spirit. They rejoice over the mercy of the Lord, and they are not ashamed of their praise of him, Ecclus. 51:[29]. They do that which God has commanded with upright trust. /414/ Therefore, God will reward them in his time, and the Lord Jesus Christ will claim them, and they shall be like him. They shall see him face-to-face in the resurrection of the righteous and shall reign with him from eternity to eternity, John 12:28; 17:5; 1 Cor. 13:12; Phil. 3:21.

Thus the Holy Spirit has shown us the congregation of Jesus Christ in the Scripture. Out of this we may understand how the congregation must be constituted here, how glorious it is, and how it will be eternally in that heavenly being where this shall all happen and be perfected in full power and glory. And by what congregation this is now begun in the Spirit and is thereby characterized and will thereby be found, that is, the true congregation of the Lord, the city of the living God, that New Jerusalem which has descended from above. Blessed are those who keep the commandments of the Lord, so that her strength might be of that tree of life, and that they might enter the city through the gates. For outside are the dogs, the sorcerers, the idolators, and all who love lies and do them, Rev. 22:14[f.]. But God, a Father of all mercy, who has called us out of grace to this congregation of his Son keep us in it and empower us for his heavenly kingdom through Jesus Christ. AMEN.

It is God who does all that is good in everything.

THREE ADMONITIONS

No. I

Here follow three fundamental admonitions or epistles written out of brotherly love to God's congregations to strengthen and comfort their spirits, so that they might walk with a full heart in the voluntarily professed and accepted truth in genuine faith and firm trust with a pious, blameless walk blessed of God, without stumbling, to the end.

By D. P.

Therefore I will not cease to admonish you always, although you certainly know it and are strengthened in the present truth. For I deem it right so long as I am in this tent to arouse and admonish you. 2 Peter 1:[12f.] /415/

The Greeting

The bottomless grace, love, and mercy of God our heavenly Father; the peace, righteousness, and holiness of our Lord Jesus Christ, 2 Cor. 1:2; Eph. 2:4; 1 Cor. 1:3, the Son of the almighty and living God; the comfort, joy, and power of the Holy Spirit; the fellowship of the only and eternal God, with all his spiritual gifts and blessings, Rom. 14:17; Eph. 1:3, with which he endows and blesses all true Christians who believe in his name, fear and love him, be with all of you always. Amen. /416/

A Loving Admonition or Epistle to God's Congregation /417/

Dear friends in the Lord, heartily beloved brothers and sisters according to the Spirit, my companions in the grace of God, in the fellowship of the gospel, in the faith, suffering, kingdom, and patience of Jesus Christ. I thank the Lord my God with the apostle Paul, 2 Thess.

2:13, that he has chosen you as his children from the beginning, and elected you for salvation, in the sanctification of the Spirit and in true faith. He has called you to that through the teaching of the gospel, Titus 2:11 ff., as the possession of the glory of our Lord Jesus Christ.

Oh, what grace has appeared to you from God? Oh, what love the heavenly Father has shown to you in Christ Jesus? 1 John 3:1. Oh, what a treasure has been given you from God? Matt. 13:44. Oh, how precious is the pearl which you have found and is well worth selling and abandoning everything for its sake, Matt. 13:[45]. Now you may say with the prophet Baruch [4:4]: Oh, Israel, how blessed are we because God has revealed his Word to us. Remember in what ignorance, blindness, and darkness you have walked; in how great wickedness, unrighteousness, and shameful idolatry you have lived, 1 Pet. 4:3; how your course was toward eternal damnation and the way you went led toward the abyss of hell; and how graciously the merciful Father has overlooked the time of your ignorance, Acts 17:30.

He has called you out of darkness into his wonderful light, 1 Pet. 2:9, from death has made you alive, delivered you from hell, set you in the heavenly being, and has so richly had pity on you in Christ, whom he has presented to you as a throne of grace in eternity, through faith in his blood, Rom. 3:25; Rev. 1:[5]. He has washed away your sin, made your soul well, and has borne all your sickness, 1 Pet. 2:24; 1 John 4:10, with his body on the wood of /418/ the cross, and still daily takes upon himself and reconciles you before the Father with the sacrifice of his flesh and blood, Heb. 9:12; 10:11, with his persistent[1] prayer; who always nourishes and satisfies your soul with his Word through faith and renews you inwardly through the power of his Spirit. Thus you are born anew out of God, John 3:3, have become a partaker of the divine nature, 2 Pet. 1:4, [are] transformed into that immortal heavenly being, and have come to eternal life, John 3:16; 5:24; 6:40; 8:51; 11:25; 12:50.

Therefore, thank the Lord for his inexpressible grace, and do consider to what you are called from God, whereto Christ Jesus has accepted and chosen you as his disciples, namely, that you should suffer and die with him, that you might be glorified with him, Rom. 8:17; 2 Tim. 2:12. Now is the time, as I hear it, that your faith must be examined, your love tested, your long-suffering be revealed and maintained. Now is the day of temptation; which makes public each one's work, which makes the gold, silver, or precious jewels pure and clear; that burns hay, straw, and stubble, 1 Cor. 3:[12 f.].

Now is the time of joy, that all those who now suffer persecution and slander, Matt. 5:11; Luke 6:22, for God's Word and the witness of Jesus Christ, these may rejoice in the Spirit that they are worthy to suffer for the Lord's sake. For their reward is great in heaven, Matt. 5:10. Now is the day of salvation, in which all those who are persecuted for righteousness sake are saved out of grace, in which is revealed who are chosen of God and who are purged as is gold in fire, [2] Esd. 16:[73]. Now it happens to you according to the Lord's Word, according to his promise and prophecy. For he said to his disciples, Matt. 10:16: I send you as sheep among wolves. Again, you shall be hated by all people for my name's sake, [Matt. 10:22]. Again, I have spoken this to you that you may not become angry, John 16:1. They will place the ban upon you. And the time will come, that whoever kills you will think that he does a God service thereby. Such things they will do to you because they have known neither my Father nor me. Now is the time about which Christ said to his disciples, John 16:[22]: Truly, truly, I say to you, you shall weep and cry, but the world will rejoice and you will be sorrowful. Nevertheless, your sorrow will be changed to rejoicing, for whoever suffers here with Christ will rejoice with him eternally. Whoever loses his life here for the Lord's sake will find it in eternity.

Oh, my beloved in the Lord, be well comforted, and /419/ think about the comforting words with which God comforted his people and said, Isa. 41:8[ff.]: And you my servant Israel, Jacob, my chosen seed of Abraham, my beloved, whom I chose from the ends of the earth and have called from her violators and spoke to you: "You shall be my servant, I have chosen you and shall not reject you." Fear not, for I will be with you. And do not defect, for I will be your God, who strengthens you, who helps you [and] who undergirds you with my right hand. Behold, all those who set themselves against you will come to scorn and shame, and your opposition will perish and come to nothing, so that those who seek them will not find them. Your destroyers shall come to nothing and thus also those who support them in fighting you. For I, your Lord and God, will strengthen your right hand, who also says to you: "Fear not, I will help you." And be not frightened, you little worm of Jacob and you despised Israel, for I will help you, says the Lord the Holy One of Israel, your avenger.

And again, Isa. 43:1[ff.]: The Lord who has created you, oh, Jacob, and who has made you, oh, Israel, has spoken thus: "Fear not, for I will protect you. I have called you by your name, that you are mine; whenever you went into the water, I would be with you that the streams of water do not drown you. If you walk in fire that you not be burnt and the flames will not set you on fire. For I am the Lord your God, the Holy One in Israel, your Savior." And that is what the prophet said, Ps. 34:[19 f.], the righteous must suffer much, but the Lord helps them out of it all. He keeps all his bones, so that not one of them will be broken. For the body, that here is sown in dishonor, in contempt, and pain, will be resurrected in such glory immortally, and be made like the glorious body of Christ, 1 Cor. 15:43[ff.]

Therefore Christ also said in the gospel that the righteous shall radiate in the resurrection as the sun in God's kingdom, Matt. 13:43. In John's Revelation it is written that they are clothed with white clothing who have come out of great sadness and have washed their clothes and made them white in the blood of the Lamb. Therefore, they are before the throne of God and serve him in his temple day and night. And the one who sits on the throne will live above them. They will no more hunger nor thirst, and the sun or any heat will not fall upon them. For the Lamb in the midst of the throne will feed them /420/ and lead them to the fountain of living water. And God will wash off all tears from their eyes, Rev. 7:[13 ff.].

Comfort and admonish yourselves among each other with such and similar comforting passages from Holy Scripture, and do not let yourselves be frightened by the tyrants and persecutors, 1 Thess. 2:1[ff.]. But consider the word of the apostle, Phil. 1:29[f.], that it is given to you from God, not only to believe in Christ Jesus, but also to suffer on his behalf, and that you must have the same struggles which the Lord and all his followers have had. Whenever you now look upon the suffering of our Savior, Jesus Christ, then your suffering is not yet to be compared with it. For he was rich (as the apostle says), 2 Cor. 8:9, and for our sake became poor, that he had less than the birds of heaven and the foxes of the earth, Matt. 8:20; Luke 9:58, so that we through his poverty might become rich. Who can wonder then if we for his sake abandon everything and lose the temporal goods, since we have a better possession in heaven?

Christ was in the form of God and has diminished himself, taken the form of a servant and became the most despised, humbled himself, and became obedient to the Father, even unto death on the cross; how then shall his disciples be otherwise minded and not conform to his example, Phil. 2:6[ff.?]. Christ was glorified by his Father as the appearance of eternal light, Wisd. of Sol. 7:26, an exact image of the fatherly being, Heb. 1:3, a reflection of the glory of God, a spotless mirror of the divine glory, and has come to such humiliation and contempt that the prophet through the Spirit in his person thus complained and spoke, Ps. 22:[6 f.]: I am a worm and no person, despised and a mockery of the people. All who see me ridicule me, shut up their mouth and shake their head over me. And Isaiah prophesied about him, Isa. 53:[3]: We shall reckon him so despised that we will hide our face from him, etc.

Why should the world then value his disciples highly? Or why would his disciples seek and desire the honor of people? Christ is the peace of all Christians, Eph. [3:14], the wisdom of all who fear God, 1 Cor. 1:22[ff.], the righteousness, deliverance, and salvation of all believers; still the Pharisees and scribes with the Jewish people have so slandered him, calling him a riotous deceiver, a crazy person, a Samaritan, that is a banned person, and a prince of the devil, that is Beelzebub, Matt. 12:24; John 10:20; 8:48, [and] therefore scolded and accused. How can then these new Pharisees /421/ and perverted scribes, with the false Christians, do otherwise to true Christians? They must, after all, fulfill the measure of their fathers. Christ has so loved the world that he came down from heaven to save it, John 12:47, and has manifested all welfare, love, and mercy toward it. But it has hated him for it, persecuting, martyring, crucifying, and killing [him]. And thus the wicked, blind world still does. It treats all true Christians the same way still, despising them and strangling them wherever it can and may.

Notice, moreover, the conflict and suffering of all the saints from the beginning of the world, from the time of righteous Abel until the present time. Thus you will discover how all God-blessed people had to suffer so much as the apostle to the Hebrews related, Heb. 11:[35], namely, how the pious people of God were struck and did not accept deliverance, since they received the resurrection which is better. Some have suffered ridicule and scourgings, and in addition, bonds and imprisonment. They were stoned, cut into pieces, stabbed, and killed with a sword. They have gone about in furs and goat skins, with trouble, sadness, and inconveniences. The world was not worthy of them. And they went in misery into the wilderness, up the mountains, into caves and holes of the earth.

Therefore we also, says the apostle, Heb. 12:1[ff.], since we have such a crowd of witnesses around us let us put off the sin that always sticks to us and makes us slothful, and let us run with patience in the struggle that is ordained for us and look upon Jesus, the beginner and perfecter of faith, who, when he certainly might have had happiness, endured the cross and did not pay attention to the shame and has placed himself at the right hand of the throne of God. Consider him who had to bear such opposition from sinners against him, so that you not become slothful in your mind and cease and forget the comfort which speaks to you as to children: My son, do not deem the punishments of the Lord as small, and do not despair if you are punished by him, for whom the Lord loves, those he punishes, he scourges every son whom he receives, Prov. 3:11[f.]; Heb. 12:5[f.].

Dear brothers in Christ Jesus, the time has now come that the heavenly Father reveals his love and fatherly nature to you, in that he tries and chastises you as he has done to all his children and those who love him. If you now bear the chastening, Heb. 12:7, /422/ so God himself deals with you as children. For where is a son whom the father does not chasten? If you were without chastising, of which they all became partakers, then you were bastards and not children.

Therefore, you may certainly rejoice in your chastising, which is a sign that you are God's friends and children. [So] accept it with patience, knowing that it all happens to you for good and that the Father of all mercies and the God of all grace chastises you for your need, so that you might receive his sanctification and live. And though it is somewhat difficult for the flesh, it is thus a joy for the spirit, as the apostle testified and said, 2 Cor. 4:16[ff.]: We are not discouraged (namely, in our suffering for Jesus' sake) but even though our external person passes away, so the internal is still renewed from day to day. For our sadness, which is temporary and light, brings an eternal and, according to measure, a weighty glory for us, we who do not look upon the visible but upon the invisible. For what is visible is temporary, but what is invisible is eternal. In this manner also Paul wrote to the Hebrews, 12:11, that all chastising as it presently is thus is not viewed as a joy, but sadness. But afterwards it will be a peaceful fruit of righteousness to those who are thus made receptive through it.

Consider also how brief and uncertain this human life is. Why then should you seek to keep that temporary life and thereby lose eternal life? For the Lord himself said, Matt. 10:39; Mark 8:35; John 12:25, that whoever loves his life here and wants to keep it (namely, those who would rather have their life than Christ and his gospel, as the hypocrites and apostates do), they must lose it eternally. Therefore, it is always necessary to consider here what the Lord said, Luke 12:4[ff.]: I tell you my friends, you will not fear for those who kill the body and thereafter can do no more. But I shall show you for whom you should be afraid. Fear the one who after he has killed also has the power to cast into hell. Yes, I say to you, fear that one.

Does one not buy five sparrows for two pennies? And not one of them is forgotten before God. The hairs of your head are also all counted. Therefore, fear not for you are better than many sparrows. But I tell you, whoever confesses me before people, those the Son of man will also confess before God's angels. But whoever denies me before people those shall be denied before God's angels.

Therefore, do not let yourself be deceived through love and desire of temporary things, for you, of course, do not know when the Son of man /423/ will come and you must leave here. And even if the world offers and promises you life, you are not thereby assured of your life for a moment. The pious elder Eleazar certainly acknowledged that fact, 2 Macc. 6:24[ff.]. Therefore he would not save his life through pretense, and spoke to his adversaries: I will die before you, for it would scarcely be seemly for my old age that I would be hypocritical so that the youths might think: Eleazar, who is now ninety years old, is now finally gone over to an alien belief and practice, and would be deceived through my pretense and for the sake of a little perishable life, I would thereby then bring my old age into shame and scorn. But although I might by this step escape the pain and punishment of people, I thus still may not escape the power of the Almighty, neither living nor dead. Therefore I will die manfully and do as is becoming to my old age. Thereby I leave an example of bravery and manhood to the youths. So I die honorably with a courageous heart and manfully for the glorious and holy law.

Mirror yourself after this God-fearing, brave, and manful Eleazar and learn from him to despise the temporal, perishable life that is so brief, that one is not certain and secure about it for one hour. And although a person lived a hundred years, it is even so (according to the witness of Jesus Sirach, Ecclus. 18:[9ff.]), compared to the time of eternity is still only a drop of water compared to the water of the sea, and as a grain of sand compared to the sands by the sea.

Thereby consider also how your life exists in God's hands, and no one may attack and harm you without the permission of the heavenly Father, as Christ himself testified and was said above. The prophet also said the same thus, Ps. 31:[11ff.]: I have become a scorn of my enemies, to my neighbors, and to my friends a terror. Those who see me flee before me. What is mine is forgotten as if I were dead; I have become as a broken vessel. For I myself have heard the slander that is round about me. They run together against me; they consult how they may take my life. But I trust in you, oh, Lord, and say: You are my God. My time is in your hands. Deliver me from the violence of my enemies and despisers. And in another place, Ps. 37:12[f.], the godless threaten the righteous and gnash their teeth because of him. But the Lord does not let him fall into their hands and does not condemn him when he judges.

Again, Ps. 124:1[ff.]: If God was not with us, Israel shall say: If the Lord was not with us when /424/ people rebelled against us, they would have swallowed us alive when their anger was kindled against us, etc. From these and many other words of the Scripture, it is evident that people can do nothing against the Christians unless the Lord allows them, therein all is placed. Therefore, the Lord alone is also to be feared, and not people who are only ashes and earth, who pass away as grass, and are eaten by worms and moths, Ecclus. 10:11; 14:15[ff.]; Isa.40:6; James 1:10.

Also, do not be frightened by the pain and hurt of death, for the torments (although they are horrible) which the tyrants and godless may inflict upon you, accepting it as the providence and will of the Lord. But be comforted that the Lord is with you in all your needs; goes with you in prison, fire, and water; suffers with you; is with you in life and death; and never abandons you, Isa. 43:2. Thus you may say with the prophet, Ps. 27:1: The Lord is our light and our salvation, of whom shall we be afraid? The Lord is the power of our life, whom shall we fear? Again, even though life and soul languish, so are you, oh God, still the refuge of our heart and our portion, Ps. 73:26. And Paul said, Rom. 8:35[ff.], Who will separate us from the love of God? Sadness or anxiety? Or persecution? Or hunger? Or nakedness? Or peril? Or sword? As it is written, for your sake we are killed the whole day, we are counted as sheep for the slaughter. But in all this we conquer by far for the sake of the one who has loved us. For I am certain that neither death, nor life, nor angels, nor ruling powers, nor violence, nor what is present, nor what is future, nor the heighth, nor the depth, nor any other creature can separate us from the love of God who is in Christ Jesus our Lord.

I hope, my heartily beloved brothers and sisters in the Lord, that such love of God is enclosed in your heart. Therefore, do not fear and be frightened for that threatening, torture, martyring, strangling, and dying, and above all, that which the godless tyrannical persons may inflict upon you, according to what the Lord permits them, but consider how terrible it is to fall into the hands of the living God, Heb. 10:31, and how gruesome that hellish fire is that is prepared there for the devil and his angels, Matt. 25:[41], and all the unfaithful, despisers, idolators, liars, and all those who do not remain steadfast by the Lord's Word, but depart therefrom, attach themselves again to the

Babylonian whore, whose lot will be in the lake that burns with fire and sulphur, /425/ which is the second death, Rev. 21:8.

And the angel of the Lord has expressed judgment with a loud voice upon such, and also said thus, Rev. 14:[19ff.]: If anyone worships this beast and its image, and receives the mark on his forehead or in his hand (that is) who consents to idolatry, acknowledges, handles, and performs it as true in any manner, that one will drink from the wine of God's wrath, which is infused and pure in the cup of his anger, and shall be tormented with fire and sulphur, before the holy angels and before the lamb. And the smoke of their distress shall ascend from eternity to eternity. And they have no rest day and night, those who have worshiped it and its image and if anyone who has received the mark of its name. Here is the patience of the saints. Here are those who keep God's commandments and faith in Jesus.

Therefore be watchful, and do not look at the small pain and temporal death, but upon the gruesome pain of eternal death and of the fiery lake. Yes, therefore a person may properly be frightened and take as an example the rich man who, when he was in pain and distress, lifted up his eyes and saw Abraham from afar, and Lazarus in his lap, called and spoke: Father Abraham, have mercy on me and send Lazarus here that he may stick the tips of his fingers in the water and cool my tongue. For I suffer great pain in this flame. But Abraham said: Consider, son, that you received good things in your life and Lazarus by contrast the evil. But now he is comforted and you are tortured, Luke 16:23[-26]. Now consider it and suffer a little with the poor Lazarus so that as you depart out of this world you may come into Abraham's lap and there have eternal happiness and comfort. And do not, with the rich man, love the perishing desires of the flesh, so that you must not with him do penance and pay in the hellish fire, being tortured in outer darkness where the worm will not die and the fire will not be extinguished, Matt. 8:12; 22:13; 24:51; 25:[41]; [2] Esd. 9:9.

In contrast, now set [before you] the inexpressible glory and eternal kingdom that God has prepared from the beginning for those who love him. Consider always the words of comfort that speak thus: To the one who conquers, I will give to eat from the tree of life, that is in the paradise of God, Rev. 2:7. Him who conquers I will give to eat from the hidden manna, and I will give him a good /426/ witness, and with the witness a new name which no one knows except the one who receives him, Rev. 2:17. Again, who conquers and keeps my works unto the end, that one I will give power over the heathen, and he will rule them with an iron rod, and he will break them as a potter's vessel. Thus I have received from my Father, and I will give him the morning star, Rev. 2:26[f.].

Again, the one who conquers, one will be clothed with white clothes, and I will not blot his name out of the book of life. And I will confess his name before my Father and before his angels, Rev. 3:5. Again, the one who conquers, I will make a pillar in the temple of my God, and he will no more depart, and I will write on him the name of my God and the name of the new Jerusalem, the city of my God, which descends from heaven from my God, and my new name, Rev. 3:[12]. Again, the one who conquers I will give to sit with me on my throne, just as I have conquered and sat with my Father on his throne, Rev. 3:21.

In sum, who steadfastly and trustfully remains to the end and unto death, that one will be saved, that one will receive the crown of life, and that one will possess it all. The righteous shall live eternally. and the Lord is their reward, and the most high cares for them, Wisd. of Sol. 5:[17]. Therefore they will receive a glorious kingdom and a beautiful crown from the hand of the Lord. Finally, the suffering of this time is not to be compared with the glory which shall be revealed to the children of God, as the apostle writes to the Romans, 8:18[f.].

So endeavor, my dear ones, through the grace of the Lord, to bear the cross of Jesus Christ with patience, and see with the eyes of faith the happiness and glory that is prepared for you. Walk always worthy of the gospel and your requirements, according to the rule of the apostolic teaching, in one spirit and intent, and watch for the false prophets who preach soft things for you, and institute some fleshly freedoms by which the agony of the cross may be removed. And note what true Christian freedom is, namely, just as Christ said in the gospel, John 8:31, if you remain in my reason, so you are my true disciples and will acknowledge the truth, and the truth shall make you free.

Thus, there is no Christian freedom outside of the truth, which is God's Word. But that is the real Christian freedom, firstly, that Christ Jesus through his suffering and death, has freed us from the devil, hell, death, and sin, as Paul said: Since the children have flesh and blood, so has he (Christ) become similarly a partaker, so that he through death takes away the power which /427/ had forced death, that is the devil, and that he delivers those who through fear of death must be servants all their life long, Heb. 2:14[f.]. Again, we will give thanks to the Father who has qualified us for the inheritance of the saints in the light, who has delivered us from the power of darkness, and who has transported us into the kingdom of his beloved Son, through whom we have the deliverance through his blood, namely, the forgiveness of sins, Col. 1:12[f.]. And in Revelation, 5:8[ff.], it is written that the four animals and the twenty-four elders fell down before the Lamb, and each had a harp and golden bowls full of incense, which are the prayers of the saints. And they sang a new song and spoke: You are worthy to take that book and to break open its seals, for you have been killed and have purchased us with your blood out of every tribe, tongue, folk, and nation and have made God king and priest for us, etc.

Thus, in the first place, we are made free from Satan, hell, death, and sin through Christ, if we truly believe in him and remain by his Word. Secondly, we are thus through Christ made free from the law of Moses. For Christ is the end of the law for each one who believes, Rom. 10:4. Therefore Paul said, Rom. 6:14, that we are not under the law, but under grace. This freedom Paul treated very beautifully to the Romans and the Galatians, where he told about Abraham and his two sons of which the one was from the maid servant, the other from free Sarah; the one born according to the flesh, the other from the Spirit. And the two wives of Abraham signify (Paul says) the two Testaments, the two sons the two people of both Testaments, Ishmael the Jews, and Isaac the Christians. Thereupon the apostle said: So, dear brothers, we are not now children of the maidservant, but of the free one. Therefore, stand in the freedom with which Christ has freed you, and do not let yourself be captured again into the slavish yoke, Rom. 9:7[ff.]; Gal. 4:22[ff.].

This is now the freedom of God's children in which they have been placed by God through Jesus Christ, and this freedom is nowhere except where the kinship of God and the spirit of the Lord is, Rom. 8:17; 2 Cor. 3:18. Therefore this freedom does not exist in order to sin, or not to walk according to the flesh, or not to become like the world, but to serve God and the neighbors. For Christian freedom (of which it is now spoken) is actually serving God and the neighbor, as the apostle Peter said: That is God's will that you with right doing will shut up the /428/ ignorance of foolish persons, as the free ones, not as if you had freedom as a cover for wickedness but as God's servants, 1 Pet. 2:15.

Now Paul said: Do you not know to whom you commit yourself to be the servant, to be obedient that you are the servant of the one to whom you are obedient, whether it be of sin to death or of obedience to righteousness, Rom. 6:16. It follows that Christians must serve each other as the apostle said, Gal. 5:13: You were called to freedom, only see to it that through freedom you give no room for the flesh, but through love serve one another. Thus Paul himself has also done, as he said, 1 Cor. 9:19: Although I am free from anyone, nevertheless, I have made myself a servant to everyone so that I may win many of them. Again, 1 Cor. 10:32[f.], and be not an offence, neither to Jews, nor to Greeks, nor to God's congregation, just as I also make myself desirable in everything, and do not seek what works to my advantage, but what works for many and is profitable, that they might be saved.

Out of this all, it is now evident what is true Christian freedom, in what it exists, how it is a service and servanthood of God and the neighbor through love, and how false freedom is that which seeks room for the flesh, a cause of sin, their own profit and, in sum, something else than what advances God and the neighbors, the salvation of the soul and conscience. Therefore, it is a shameful error, a great ignorance, and a gruesome deception that some will signify Christian freedom thereby, that they may really go into the temple of idols, and may really listen to false teachers, and do not need to separate from the false religious services externally, but only with the heart. This is untrue and false: for one believes to righteousness with the heart (as the apostle said Rom. 10:10), but with the mouth confession occurs to salvation.

One must praise God, both with the body and the spirit which belong to God, 1 Cor. 6:20. And if one will know, hear the words of Paul, to wit: What comparison has God's temple with the temple of idols? Therefore depart out of the middle of it, separate, and do not touch anything impure, etc., 2 Cor. 6:16,[17].

To understand this rightly, one must notice his actual meaning, namely, that he said thus: You are the temple of the living God, as God spoke, 1 Cor. 3:16, I will dwell in them, /429/ and walk in them, and they shall be my people, and I will be their God. And at another place, 1 Cor. 6:19: Do you not know that your bodies are the temples of the Holy Spirit, which you have received from God, and you yourselves have no power. Again, and do you not know that your members are Christ's members? From this it is easy to measure and clearly to understand how one must separate oneself not only with the spirit and with the heart, but also with the body from idolatrous temples, from all godless preachers who stand in the pulpit and falsify the Lord's Word, and from all false religious services.

Therefore, those who present such false freedom (as was said above) lie against the truth, deceive themselves and also others, and it is of such of whom Jesus Sirach said, Ecclus. 2:[12ff.]: Woe to the discouraged heart and to the faint hands and the sinner who goes on two streets, woe to those who do not remain steadfast. How will it go with them if the Lord visits them? They are those about whom Peter said, 2 Pet. 2:17[f.]: That they are fountains without water and clouds driven around by the wind, for which is kept a darker darkness in eternity, for they speak bold words which they do not follow. They entice to fleshly lusts through lack of discipline those who had truly escaped and now walk in error, and promise them freedom although they themselves are servants of corruption.

Yes, they are vacillating and apostate Israelites that will carry [water] on both shoulders and go as cripples, those who want to serve God partly and partly Baal, 1 Kings 18:21. And they are thus misled from the beautiful appearance and whoring spirits of the prophetess Jezebel, who makes them know that sin is no sin and unrighteousness is no unrighteousness. But let everyone see that he be aware and watch for this prophetess Jezebel, and let no one be deceived by her. For the Lord will throw her with all those who practice whoredom with her into the greatest pain, so long as they do not repent. And all the congregations shall acknowledge that he is the Lord, who pays everyone according to his works, Rev. 2:20[ff.].

Therefore, pay good attention to the fear of the Lord your God, that you do not will and accept any fleshly freedom to go into the churches and listen to the false teachers. The misleading spirits will certainly attack you with greater cunning and haughtiness, especially in these oppressive and perilous times, to draw you away from the simplicity which is in Christ Jesus, 2 Cor. 11:[3]. But beware for yourself if you have love for God and your soul's salvation.

Also pay attention to those who institute quarrels and divisions against the teachings of Christ and /430/ his apostles about the ban and will not shun the apostate false brothers and sisters rightly according to the Scripture, Rom. 16:[17], but still have outward fellowship with them. But I testify to that through the Lord, out of his plainly expressed Word which he has himself spoken and through the mouths of the apostles and true messengers with the power, activity and moving of his Holy Spirit, that one separate and put in the ban those [who do not repent] after sufficient scriptural admonition from God's congregation through the power of Jesus Christ with his Word. These you must shun, avoid their person in eating and drinking, in business and daily walk.

And if someone does otherwise and scorns such commandments

of God, these should reflect on Achan, who secretly had taken a little of the banned goods at Jericho, how it went with him over it, Josh. 7:20[ff.], and do not think once that he will escape God's punishment, whether it happens here or in the hereafter. For if Achan was punished so severely because of a little banned goods that was found with him, what will then overcome the deliberate despisers of the divine ordering, who deal with the banned person apart from the Scripture?

A banned person is, after all, no less an offense before God than the banned goods. Therefore, to deal with a banned person apart from the rules of the divine Word is not less but more sinful against God than Achan had sinned, who had stolen from the banned goods. And whoever does such, that one makes him a participant in the stranger sin, and he has fellowship with the wicked works of the apostate, 2 John 11, yes, he infects the whole congregation, according to the example of Achan and Paul's word, 1 Cor. 5:[6], namely, that a little leaven sours the whole dough. If you now have love for Christ, his congregation, and your salvation, then watch out for the banned apostate, false brothers and sisters, dismiss their fellowship, and commend them to the Lord until the time of their amendment.

I have written this little [admonition] to you out of brotherly love, since you are my brothers and sisters in the Lord, and we have a fatherland both in heaven and on earth, and I love you heartily in Christ Jesus. I also hope that you will take my admonition in love, although you yourself were taught from God and established in the present truth from God, 2 Pet. 1:12. But the God of all grace, 1 Pet. 5:10, fill you with every spiritual wisdom and caution and guard you before all evil, that you may be fruitful in all good works, Col. 1:6, and walk without stumbling, and thus may appear at the last day before the judgment throne of Jesus Christ. The Lord be with you all always. AMEN.

ENDNOTES

1. *Stadich* may also be translated as steadfast, powerful, earnest.

THREE ADMONITIONS

No. II

This is the second admonition or epistle, written out of brotherly love to God's congregation.

By D. P.

Grace and peace from God our heavenly Father and from Jesus Christ his only born Son, our Lord and Savior, be multiplied in you through the power of the Holy Spirit. Amen. /432/

Blessed be God the Father of all mercy, 2 Cor. 1:[3], that he provides salvation for you from the beginning according to his measureless grace and eternal love, 2 Thess. 2:13, ordained you for eternal life, Rom. 8:[29], and now has in these last times called you out of darkness to his wonderful light, yes, chosen you as his children, Eph. 1:4, and has accepted you as heirs of all his gifts in Jesus Christ, whereby the merciful God has indicated his fatherly love to you so richly, Titus 3:[4-6]. And you have received all such benefits from him that you may say with the prophet: What shall we return to the Lord for all the good that he has done to us?

While I was there with you,[1] I have had such great joy; and my soul was quickened in the Lord when I had seen your zeal and steadfastness in the faith, your love for God and for his truth, your Christian peace, your brotherly unity, and the good ordinances that were kept by you, and God's Word that was so fruitful, and so many added to the congregation of the Lord, so that I think that a special blessing has come over my fatherland from God. Who would have thought and believed beforehand that Jerusalem, which John in the Spirit has seen descend from heaven, has placed itself there in the area /433/ so that God's tent and the tabernacle of the Lord should be erected there, Rev. 21:22? Yes, that just as Bethlehem, the little town in Judah, has become so glorious, Mic. 5:[2], because the ruler of Israel was born there and came out of it, Matt. 2:6, so also is that small despised land [the Netherlands], from a small regard as reckoned by the great kingdoms and powers, [would] come to great grace and glory before God, for the sake of the elect who are therein.

Therefore, I thank almighty God for you people, you beloved in the Lord, and I rejoice over my fatherland,[2] being delighted thereover from the bottom of my heart, because of the rich blessings of God in the heavenly things, namely, that the noble fruits of righteousness grow there, that the vineyard of the Lord blooms there, and gives off a lovely fragrance, Song of Sol. 2:13, that roses bloom in the valley, the lily stands so beautiful under the thorns, that honey and milk from the unfalsified truth flows there. In sum, there is an abundance of all kinds of fruit, yes, not only there, but also in the surrounding lands.

Oh, how great a blessing from God! Oh, what transformation and change, that from a barren wilderness such a fruitful land has come, such a blessed earthly kingdom, yes such a lovely garden of the Lord and a paradise of God! Early there was no water; now a living stream of water flows, Isa. 44:3, that has its source in eternal life. Where before no one knew of God, it is now full of the pure knowledge of God. Where before one ran after dumb idols, there one now serves the living God, the Lord of heaven and earth, 1 Thess. 1:9. Where one earlier lay captive under antichrist, one is now free there under Jesus Christ. Where one was earlier driven by false shepherds, that one must eat and drink what was trodden by feet and made impure, Ezek. 34:[3ff.], there the only Good Shepherd Jesus Christ himself now feeds his sheep, John 10:11[ff.], and leads them to the fountain of living water. Where before one must drink out of the horrible cup of the Babylonian whore who is full of all whoredom and sorcery, Rev. 18:3, there Jesus Christ gives the thirsty the clear wine of his divine Word and the water of life freely, John 4:10; Rev. 22:1.

Therefore I say once again that I thank the most high God for his inexpressible gift and pray to him with all humility in the name of Jesus Christ that he pour out on you his blessing still more abundantly, and /434/ increase your growth in righteousness to the praise of his holy name and to the salvation of your souls.

Although I hope in the mercifulness of God and have the best confidence in you people, nevertheless, I cannot refrain from writing and admonishing you a little out of duty and brotherly love which I have toward you, whereby you may recognize my inclination toward you people, for God knows how you are enclosed in my heart, and that I think about you people in my prayers to God, and will not cease through the Lord's grace to pray for you in my weakness, that the merciful eternal Father will keep you people from all evil, 1 Thess.

5:23, keep you in the true faith and save you for his heavenly kingdom.

I am concerned about you with a divine concern. For I have certainly seen and experienced over many years what is proven, how that the evil devil exercises so much diligence to destroy and spoil the congregation of God, 2 Cor. 11:[14ff.] through manifold false teachings and sects which he produces and erects, and all that under the appearance of his own chosen spirituality, that he shows off with twisted Scripture, Col. 2:18, for that is his nature, skill, and characteristic, to falsify God's Word and hide his lies under it. He does not come as a Satan in his messengers and servants, but as an angel of light, with an outward false piety and disguised with a decorated facade, 2 Cor. 11:12-16. He sends his prophets out in sheep's clothing, but inwardly they are ravenous wolves, Matt. 7:15. And they seek nothing else than to mangle the sheep of Jesus Christ.

Therefore they come to them with their high-sounding words, and let them think that they are so full of the spirit, that all genuine Christians who are taught from God and oppose them are nothing but slaves to the letter, since they are so choked in spiritual charlatanry, Tobit 3:[8ff.], which is nevertheless an origin and beginning of all perishing. And I hear that they still get a hearing from some and do harm, and that is such a pain and hurt to my soul that I cannot write about it to you. What may the miserable people still think who let themselves be so terribly deceived by the devil that they turn away from the living God, Heb. 3:15, so that they depart from the way of truth because it is narrow and is the way of the cross, and walk on the wide and broad way which leads to damnation, Matt. 7:[13f.]. And they do not once take to heart that it is written: There is a way which seems good to people to know, /435/ but its end stretches to the abyss of hell. Again, a person who yields and wanders from the way of wisdom, that one will remain in the dead congregation.

Now I certainly know that all sects claim to be right and can turn the Scriptures masterfully according to the nature of Satan to mislead its bad affairs, and to cover its roguishness, and do not notice through the blindness of their heart where they are stricken from God since they deny the acknowledged and accepted truth, that they scorn and change the unchangeable counsel of God revealed through Jesus Christ in the gospel and testified through the Holy Spirit, that they seek entirely the world's friendship which nevertheless is enmity with God, James [4:4], that they will maintain the temporal life and therefore according to the Lord's own Word lose eternal life, John

12:25, that they with Esau will sell their birthright for a meal, and by adventure nevermore may receive it, Heb. 12:16[f.]. Yes, they are in their former impurity which Jesus Christ has washed away through his blood and through the water bath in the Word now again are cursed, Rev. 1:[5]; Eph. 5:26, and that common adage applies to them: the dog turns again to that which it has vomited and the sow wallows again in her own mire from which she was washed, 2 Pet. 2:22.

Oh, it were much better if they had not known the way of the Lord, that they had remained in ignorance, that they had not come to the knowledge of the truth. But now they have come to it, now they have been enlightened, now the impure spirit is cast out, and after he has once again found the house empty (empty, I say, from the true faith, from the genuine love of God, from the pure fear of the Lord, and from other virtues, with which the house should be decorated), so he has come in again with seven other evil spirits, and the last state of the person is worse than the first was [Matt. 12:43-45].

Therefore, I bow my knee before God the Father, Col. 1:3, and before the throne of grace, praying and supplicating for you, just as the apostle has done for the Colossians and for all Christians, that you may be filled with all spiritual wisdom and understanding, so that you may test and know what is the good, the holy, and the perfect will of God, Rom. 12:[2], and that you may remain steadfast in the truth of the gospel. Watch for the boasters and renowned spirits through which the great majesty of God is blasphemed, for whosoever opposes the sanctifying teaching of Jesus Christ through fleshly intentions and human wisdom (which is foolishness before God), 1 Cor. 1:18[ff.], and despises his ordinances, that one despises God himself, /436/ just as Christ said: Who despises me, that one despises the Father who has sent me. Once again, who receives me, that one receives also the Father who has sent me, Matt. 10:40. Again, Christ says the Holy Spirit, John 16:14, shall witness of me, for he will take from what is mine and declare it to you.

From this it follows powerfully that he who despises God scorns Jesus Christ, and resists the Holy Spirit, that one breaks, changes, and acts against the only divine ordinances. Therefore, John also says in his epistle, 2 John 9: Whoever transgresses and does not remain in the teaching of Jesus Christ, that one has no God, but whoever remains therein, that one has both the Father and the Son. Mark and understand what an ugly and godless being that is before God, to transgress the teaching of Jesus Christ and not to remain in it.

Therefore, be careful yourself that you are not moved by the rash, vacillating, and apostate, and fall out of your steadfastness, but grow in the grace and knowledge of our Lord and Savior Jesus Christ, 2 Pet. 3:[18]. And consider what the apostle wrote to the Galatians, [1]:8: Even though an angel come out of heaven, or I myself, and declared to you another gospel than you have received, so must he be still accursed. Another foundation may not be laid than that is laid, which is Jesus Christ, 1 Cor. 3:[11]. On that foundation you people are constructed, on this base you are built. Look out that in the day of temptation you may not be found to be hay, straw, and stubble, but much more silver, gold, and precious stones, just as I hope on your account on the grace of the Lord.

Secondly, so I admonish you with the apostle Paul, Eph. 4:[1ff.], that you walk becoming to your calling, always pleasing to the Lord, and that you be fruitful in all good works, for that becomes those who are enlightened by God and are called to the genuine knowledge of our Lord Jesus Christ, that they walk worthily of the gospel and the heavenly calling, Heb. 3:1, and consider that the believers, just as the apostle Peter wrote, 1 Pet. 1:2, are destined from God the Father and the enlightenment from the Holy Spirit to be obedient and to be sprinkled with the blood of Jesus Christ. Thus also, dear Paul wrote to the Corinthians, 1 Cor. 6:11: You are washed, you are cleansed, you are sanctified through the name of our Lord Jesus Christ and through the Spirit of our God.

Since then you have come to this grace, look out that you have not received it in vain./437/ Consider the apostle's words, Heb. 6:7[f.], that the earth which often receives the rain and brings forth good fruit for the farmer, that one is blessed from God, but what brings forth thistles and thorns, that one is rejected, accursed, and finally will be burned. Therefore, take God's grace truly and the gifts of the Holy Spirit which you have received, and take well to heart what is written there, how that in Jesus Christ nothing is counted except the keeping of God's commandments, 1 Cor. 7:19, except faith that works through love, Gal. 5:6, and a new creature, Gal. 6:[15]; which disdains all earthly things and seeks only the heavenly things; who with Paul reckons everything in the world for loss, Phil. 3:7, when compared to the pure knowledge of our Lord Jesus Christ; who with Moses despised all the splendor and glory of Egypt and preferred to suffer the inconveniences with God's people, Heb. 11:[25].

For a new creature, Eph. 4:24, a new born person of God, who is renewed and shaped in faith through the Holy Spirit according to the image and likeness of God, Col. 3:[10], that one is spiritually minded, is one with God, and is a partaker of his nature. Therefore, he also does not sin, just as John also said, 1 John 3:7[ff.]: Thus who does right, that one is born out of God; whosoever sins, that one is from the devil, for the devil sinned from the beginning. Thereto the Son of God is revealed, that he would destroy the works of the devil. Whosoever is born out of God, that one does not sin in order that the seed of God remain in him, and therefore, he cannot sin since he is born out of God. By this the children of God and the children of the devil are revealed.

Out of these words it is certainly to be understood who are the true Christians, to wit, those who do right, who are believers, who are born out of God, who do not sin, for they are in God according to the internal person and are governed by the Lord's Spirit, Rom. 8:[14]. Yes, they are led into all truth and obedience, John 16:13, they hate all unrighteousness, as Joseph in Egypt [hated] adultery, Gen. 39:10, and the three youths and Daniel in Babylonian idolatry, Dan. 3:[17f.]; 6:10[ff.].

Yes, all God-fearers have hated and avoided the works of the flesh, and everything that is against God's Word, not only in the heart, but also with the body. For a Christian may not only be a Christian inwardly, but he must also show himself as a Christian outwardly and everywhere. A Christian's body is the temple of the Holy Spirit, 1 Cor. 3:[16]; 6:[19], a Christian's members are the members of Christ Jesus, a Christian is a spirit born out of the Spirit and united with God who is a spirit, John 3:[6]. Therefore his nature is as God's nature, 2 Pet. 1:[4]; he loves what God loves, and he hates all that God hates, for he himself has no power, /438/ but he is a possession of God, he lives for his God and not for himself, 2 Cor. 5:15.

Consider and take to heart how holy, how upright and blessed one must live in this evil world, Eph. 1:4; 1 Pet. 1:16, and watch for the return of our Lord Jesus Christ, Titus 2:12[f.], who has given himself for us since he would deliver us from all unrighteousness and cleanse us himself for a people of his own, that is zealous after good works, that is intent on heavenly things, Col. 3:[2], that seeks God's kingdom and his righteousness before all things, Matt. 6:33, and considers how all Christians must lead a holy life, Isa. 6:3, since they boast about the holy God and are called saints after him, Rom. 1:[7].

Therefore the angel said to John, Rev. 22:11, who is righteous, let that one become still more righteous, and who is holy, let that one become more holy. How should in that New Jerusalem, that is so beautiful, where the streets are pure gold, the walks and gates from precious jewels, where the throne of God is, where the most high illuminates the city with his glory, where the living stream of water flows clear as crystal from the throne of God, how should (I say) what here is impure enter there, much less remain there, just as John publicly testifies, Rev. 21:21; 22:1. Therefore let everyone cleanse himself from all defilement of the spirit and the flesh, 2 Cor. 7:1, by the fountain which stands open to the house of David and the citizens at Jerusalem and is prepared against every uncleanness, Zech. 13:1, in order to wash and make [them] an acceptable people to the Lord, that his greatly praised name may be praised thereby.

Thirdly, thus it is not only my faithful admonition to you, but also my heartfelt prayer and wish before God that you are strong in the Spirit, Col. 1:9, through the powerful working of God unto all patience and endurance with joy, for the strength and power of the faith is certainly needed by all Christians in these perilous times, in which Satan is let loose, Rev. 20:3, (as it appears) to mislead the whole world and to plague the God-fearers. He assembles every heathen to fight against the Holy City and to destroy it. No Nebuchadnezzar may compel her to pray to his image, Dan. 3:6; no Antiochus is vengeful against the Jews who remain steadfast in the faith, 2 Macc. 6:10, no Babylonians and Egyptians have dealt more mercilessly with the people of God, Exod. 4-7, than now some tyrants have raged and still rage against the Christians for a long time with persecution and all kinds of horrible torments.

Thus one may surely say with the prophet: Help, Lord, the heathen have fallen into your inheritance; /439/ they give the bodies of your servants as food for the birds under heaven, and they give the flesh of your saints to the animals of the field. They pour out innocent blood as water, the stones of your temple are scattered here and there, Ps. 79:1[ff.]. The rulers over all peoples had to mourn and weep over their children.[3] The priests and the Levites who perform the true worship service in the temple burn the incense before the Lord, prepare and offer the sacrifice on the altar, those are taken prisoner and killed. The congregation is robbed of its faithful ministers.

Oh, Lord God, have mercy over them and strengthen your servants; go before your tabernacle and lead your people through this wild wilderness, so that all those who fear you and trust in you may come to blessed rest, Heb. 4:11. And you, my most beloved in the Lord, pray almighty God faithfully for all dear brothers and companions of our most holy faith, that God empower them with his Holy

Spirit and give them endurance in the time of suffering, for endurance is needed (says the apostle), Heb. 10:36, so that one receives the promise if one has done God's will: For after a little while the Lord will come and the righteous shall live out of their faith. And if he draws back, then my soul will have no pleasure therein. We are not those who draw back to damnation, but we remain in the faith to save the soul. It is a great grace to suffer a little here with Jesus Christ, patiently and steadfastly remaining therein, so that after this time one may participate in his eternal joy and glory, Rom. 8:18; 1 Pet. 4:13; Rom. 8:17.

Therefore, all Christians glory in the cross of Jesus Christ, saying with the apostle, Gal. 6:[14]: But far be it from us that we should glory in anything [else] than in the cross of our Lord Jesus Christ, through which the world is crucified to us, and we to the world. And although the cross is not equally harsh everywhere in this time, nevertheless it can soon come, according to God's will. And therefore my admonition is to you altogether, who have bowed your neck under the sweet yoke of Jesus Christ, Matt. 11:29[f.], so that you always be ready to suffer, and possess your soul with endurance. For it will avail no one to persecute Jesus of Nazareth in his members, Acts 9:5, and to press against these pricks: Therefore, be simply strong and well comforted in the Lord, and also do not let yourselves be frightened from the opponents and apostates, Eph. 6:[10ff.], /440/ but stand manfully against them, like those who are well armed with the armor of God, for they can still not accomplish anything.

What could the godless Jeroboam do with his great separation and idolatrous multitude against King Abijah and Judah, [2 Chron.] 13:9,[4] You think (said Abijah among other words to Jeroboam and Israel) to oppose the kingdom of the Lord because you are a great crowd and have the golden calf, which you, Jeroboam, have made a god, and have you not expelled the priests of the Lord, the children of Aaron and the Levites, and you have made your own priests, just as the people in the land. But the Lord our God whom we have not abandoned is with us, and the priests who serve the Lord, the children of Aaron, and the Levites in their work, and every morning burn sacrifice to the Lord, and every evening the good incense as well, and prepare shewbread on clean tables, and the golden lampstand with its lamps that they should burn every evening. For we observe the observances of the Lord our God, but you have abandoned him. God our ruler is with us in the army, and his priests, and the trumpets, in order to sound the trumpet that the alarm will sound against you. You children of Israel, do not fight against the Lord, your father's God. You will not succeed in this.

Thus may we also glory in the Lord against all sects, namely, that the pure and clean gospel of Jesus Christ is with us, that true priesthood with its genuine worship service, the true ordinance of God, just as it has come down from heaven, Matt. 3:[16f.], given from God the Father, taught and commanded from Jesus Christ, witnessed to and established from the Holy Spirit, and practiced and proclaimed by the apostles. But the golden calves of Jeroboam and his priests with the apostates, Rev. 3, are our opposition and stand against the ordinance of God, where one made sacrifices on high places, where one served Baal, Rev. 2:14, where the prophetess Jezebel reigned with her false teaching, where one followed the teaching and the way of Balaam, who erected an offence for the children of Israel so that they whored with the Moabite daughters and served the Baal-Peor, Num. 25:5. Thus also the new Balaamiters do who there play the hypocrite to please the world, also mislead others, and exercise all zeal to pervert the congregation of God.

Therefore, let us trumpet unanimously, and blast God's horn so that the enemy is terrified as they hear the sound of God's horn; /441/ yes, thus will the prepared barley bread overtake and destroy the tents of the Midianites, Judg. 7:[13], if we blow the trumpet and break the earthen jars in pieces, and let our light be lighted, and fight manfully for God's truth. They must nevertheless come to shame, all those who stand against the truth or fall away from it and trouble and make difficulties for the congregation of the Lord.

Because Pharaoh oppressed the children of Israel, he was drowned in the sea, Exod. 14:23. Because Jannes and Jambres opposed Moses, therefore, they came to shame, 2 Tim. 3:8. And how many tyrants have been punished by God because they have tyrannized the people of God? And how many false prophets who have set themselves against the true prophets have been ashamed? For they shall certainly not accomplish it (says the apostle), but everyone's foolishness will be disclosed. Or again, they will rejoice in eternity, all those who now believe the truth, Ps. 128:[2ff.], remain by it unchangingly and have love for God's congregation. For because the ark of the covenant has been in Obed-edom's house, 2 Sam. 6:10, thus God has blessed him and his whole house. Therefore the prophet said: Greet Jerusalem friendly; it must go well with those who love you, Ps. 122:6.

Fourthly, I thus admonish you to a Christian thanksgiving, that you will thereby thank God for his inexpressible gift which he has given you. First, that he has made you eligible for the inheritance of the saints, Col. 1:3[ff.], in that eternal light, yes, that you (I say with the apostle), 1 Pet. 2:10, who earlier were no people have now become God's people, who earlier had no mercy now have received mercy and are called children of the living God. Thus you might well say with John, 1 John 3:1[ff.]: See what love the Father has given us that we are called his children. Therefore the world knows us not for they know not God. We are now God's children, but it is still not revealed what we shall become. But we know when he will reveal it, thus we shall be like him, for we shall see him just as he is.

Therefore Paul also said, Col. 3:3, that the Christians have now died and their life is hidden with Christ in God, and if Christ who is your life will reveal him, then they will also be revealed with him in glory. Thank the almighty God with the patriarch Jacob always, that he watches over your going out and your coming in and protests before the hand of Esau, Gen. 32:8, since he has richly blessed you in all heavenly goods through Jesus Christ, and nevermore forget the beneficence of your God. /442/

Now say as the prophet says, Ps. 103:1[ff.]: Praise the Lord, O my soul, and all that is within me praise his holy name. Praise the Lord my soul, and forget not what benefits he has done for me, who forgives all your sins and heals all your sicknesses, who delivers your life from destruction, who crowns you with grace and mercy, who satisfies your mouth with goods, and renews your youth just as the eagles.

All this God has done for you, he has forgiven your sins, Rom. 3, 5, 8; Matt. 9:13, he has made your soul healthy with his heavenly medicine, he has delivered you from eternal destruction. He has given you that eternal life, Rom. 6:23; Titus 3:6[-8]. The crown of righteousness is prepared for you. Your food is the bloom of the wheat, that living bread from heaven, John 6:51, that is full of all divine sweetness, that is a food of the angels and the life of all believers, Wisd. of Sol. 16:20. Your youth is renewed in the rebirth, the old being of the flesh is done away and a new being of the Spirit has now come about which is written in the letter to the Hebrews, 3:14. You have become partakers of Christ if you hold fast the beginning of his being, to the end that is, you are embodied in Christ as members of his body, 1 Cor. 12:[12f.], as branches of the vine, John 15:5, and have received from his spirit and his being (from which there is holiness, righteousness, godliness, love, peace, patience, goodness, mercy, and all of God's virtues) has begun in you since you, out of hearing God's Word through the power and illumination of the Holy Spirit, have become believers. If you remain steadfast here, thus you belong to Christ, Rom. 10:[9].

You have also become partakers of Christ and all of his heavenly goods, his grace and truth, of his eternal life and imperishable being, his divine nature and glory, 2 Pet. 1:4; 1 Thess. 5:23, here in the Spirit through faith, and hereafter in the resurrection and renewal of all things, 1 Cor. 15:53. You will still be partakers from all that is perfect, Matt. 13:43, for our conversation is in heaven, Phil. 3:20, from where we expect Jesus Christ who will glorify our despised body and make it like his glorious body, through his power with which he can make all things subordinate to him. Consider, the believers thus become partakers of Christ and will be like him and will appear with him in splendor as long as they remain in him as members of his body, as branches on his vine; and are not through unbelief and apostasy of God's Word cut away from it.

So take seriously now the admonition of the apostle, namely, that just as you have accepted the Lord Jesus Christ, /443/ so also walk in him, being rooted in him and built upon him, firm in the faith (as you were taught) and overflowing with thanksgiving, Col. 2:6, always thanking God with the prophet that he has made you so wonderful. He has kept you since birth, delivered you in these perilous times still more wonderfully from the wicked world, Gal. 1:4[f.], and has called you out of so many thousands to the fellowship of Jesus Christ. He has showed his fatherly love to you, yes, has poured out upon you the superabundant riches of his grace, [that] his name be praised therefore in eternity, Eph. 2:[7]. Amen.

Finally, thus I pray and admonish you, my very beloved and desired in the Lord, through the crucified Jesus Christ who has reconciled us with God, Eph. 2:[16], has earned an eternal peace by his Father, and has left the same for us, John 20:[21]. I pray and admonish you (I say) that you still be peaceful with one another in Jesus Christ and remember that you are children of one heavenly Father who is God, Eph. 3:15, the true Father over all, and from one mother who is the spiritual Sarah, Gal. 4:22[ff.], the New Jerusalem, the bride of the Lamb.

Therefore let this new birth be powerful in you, and be eager to keep the unity of the Spirit through the bond of peace, Eph. 4:3, and do not undertake anything outside God's Word, Isa. 30:2, neither without the counsel of the Holy Spirit, and do not consider yourself all too wise, neither all too understanding, Rom. 12:3, but fear God and ask him for true wisdom. Search the Scripture diligently, understand it properly, measuring all things with the plumbline of the gospel, testing all spirits with the character, nature, and spirit of Christ.

Thus you will easily recognize which spirit is from God, and thus you will quarrel no more. For it is impossible that where the new birth, which happens out of God's Word through faith, has thus taken place, where one through the birth has become partaker of the divine nature, John 1:14; 2 Pet. 1:4, where the fear of the Lord, the beginning of wisdom, Ecclus. 2:7, is contained in the heart, and where the unadulterated brotherly love is, 1 John 5:2, that any fleshly quarrel and division may be found there. Therefore show with your Christian peace, with your brotherly love and unity, that you are Christian. Thus will the God of peace who himself is love be with you in eternity. Amen. John 15:9; 1 John 4:[7].

I have written this to you out of pure love, as is reported above, as a friendly greeting and remembrance that you may know how my heart and mind is inclined to you all, as to my heartfelt dear brothers and sisters, and to my fatherland, yes, to all who fear God. And if I could do more for you, God knows what is in my heart. You are still my chosen ones, /444/ yes, most beloved with all the others who fear God in Christ Jesus. I should also certainly write something specially to some particular persons, but they must still have some patience, for my concern is great.

My work in the congregations is not unknown to you. Pressure and suffering, anxiety and need are also with me. God be thanked that he considers me worthy. Within me is trouble and worry; without is struggle and persecution from the world and from my enemies. Thus I may certainly say with the prophet, Oh, Lord, how many are my enemies who oppose me. Many say to my soul, it has no help in God, Ps. 3:[1-2]. And once more, Lord, see how my enemies are so many, and hate me out of evil intentions, that is out of vengefulness, wickedness and envy of their heart.

Therefore, I ask of you that you will remember my people and all ministers in your prayers to God, that God will look upon us graciously, strengthening and comforting us with his Holy Spirit, that we may fight for the truth like good soldiers, 2 Tim. 4:5, complete our course in the fear of the Lord, keep the faith, and receive the crown of righteousness from God's Son on Mount Zion with all pious confessors and conquerors, 2 Esd. 2:43[ff]; 2 Tim. 2:[2ff.].

Also pray for the authorities and all people that God, according to his good will, would be merciful and illuminate them so that they might come to the knowledge of the truth and be saved. Herewith I commend all of you to the almighty, eternal God who must empower you and me, and all those who from [their] heart desire it in his truth, making [them] fruitful in every good work and keeping [them] for his heavenly kingdom. Amen.

And just as I have written in my letter to the congregation in H. [Harlingen probably, or Holland], I thus write also to you, namely, if the Lord takes me out of time and delivers me out of the wicked world (wherein his holy will must be done), so I herewith take a Christian farewell [adieu] from you all, and rejoice that I have seen your face. I hope to see you again with joy in the kingdom of our heavenly Father. But if the Lord sees fit that we come together again in this life, so it must happen in the name of our Lord Jesus Christ to his praise and to our greatest rejoicing and quickening in the Lord. All the elders of our congregation greet you with the peace of God and also my companion, who is well known to you.[5] The grace of Jesus Christ be with you all. Amen.

ENDNOTES

1. As mentioned in the Introduction to the *Enchiridion*, this letter was likely directed to Friesland, perhaps the town of Franeker, after Dirk had returned to the Danzig area.
2. Expressions of praise for "my fatherland," albeit for the faithful in it but, nevertheless, including the nation state, are few in Anabaptist writings.
3. Dirk's Scripture reference is listed as *Trenor* 1:1, that is the *Lamentations* 1:2, usually attributed to Jeremiah. It is possible that he used his old (Roman Catholic) Latin *Vulgate* Bible, where it is listed as *Threni*, or perhaps the Septuagint (LXX), the Greek version of the Jewish Scriptures, where it is listed as *Threnoi*. An equally plausible theory might be that he used the German *Froschauer* Bible printed in Zurich, and other places, in many editions beginning in 1524, perhaps earlier. Anabaptists are known to have used this version extensively. In it the book is listed as *Threni/die klaglieder Jeremie*. A new edition of the 1536 version was printed by Amos B. Hoover of Denver, Pa., in 1975. Dirk's reference to the rulers may mean Jerusalem.
4. *2 Paralipomenon* 13:9 is *2 Chronicles 13*. The verses are not numbered in the *Froschauer* Bible referred to in the preceding note. *Paralipomenon* means "omitted things." The Hebrew tradition has considered Esdras as the author, but most authorities believe the author remains unknown.
5. Presumably a reference to his wife. See the introductory biography for further reference to her. J. ten Doornkaat Koolman, 1964, follows Karel Vos in assuming that Dirk was married even prior to his Anabaptist ordination, by his brother Obbe, on the basis of 1 Tim. 3:2 that a bishop is to be "married only once." In connection with the Frisian-Flemish dispute, Hoyte Renix wrote to Dirk on April 17, 1567: "We desire that you with your entire family come to us [from Danzig] as Jacob in Egypt, and we will take care of you in your fatherland as a beloved old father and serve you our entire life." Kühler, 1961, p. 420.

THREE ADMONITIONS

No. III

This is the third admonition or epistle, written to God's congregation.

By D. P.

Grace, peace, mercy, Christian wisdom, a genuine understanding of the divine Word, an unvarnished faith, and steadfastness of mind in the truth I wish all God-fearers and believers, the chosen saints, our beloved brothers, friends and companions, from God our heavenly Father and Jesus Christ, our Lord and Savior, who is eternally blessed. Amen. /445/

I, with the apostle Paul, 2 Thess. 1:[3], thank the Lord my God since I have not only heard but have seen presently all about your faith in God and in the Lord Jesus Christ, about your love for all the saints, about your patience in all kinds of difficulties, sadness, and persecution which comes upon you on behalf of the gospel, and about your boldness and steadfastness in the truth. The eternal almighty God be lauded and his holy name be praised, because he has thus endowed you through Jesus Christ with the power of the Holy Spirit, and has begun the good work in you. I hope [that] by his bottomless grace he will complete the same in you to his praise and your eternal salvation, Phil. 1:6; 2:13: This is the full desire of my heart before God, that it must happen.

Since the times are now so perilous, so many false prophets and antichrists arise, Matt. 24:[11]; 1 Tim. 4:1; 2 Tim. 3:1; 2 Pet. 2:1; 3:3; Jude 1:18, so many braggarts and boastful spirits are abroad who speak bravely against the Holy Scripture, who deny Jesus Christ, the only born Son of the living God, that is, oppose his eternal truth, break and change his divine ordinances, and, besides their false and blasphemous teaching, introduce a carnal freedom, therefore /446/ I cannot neglect to warn you against such haughty spirits out of an obligation to Christian love and out of an affectionate mind, and to admonish you a little with the Lord's Word, although I certainly have the confidence in you that you are taught by God himself, being grounded, firm, and immovable in the saving teaching of Jesus Christ and his apostles. Yet I must, according to the small gift which is given to me from God, renew you a little on the foundation of our Christian faith, on the covenant of God, and how we must practice a God-blessed walk therein, to the Lord's praise, and as a witness and indication that we are born believing and new out of God through faith in Jesus Christ in the power of the Holy Spirit, 1 John 1:12[f.]; 3:3; Gal. 3:22; 1 John 5:1.

For it is my greatest joy that I hear and see that it is well with the congregation of the Lord, [that it has] a genuine knowledge of Jesus Christ and acknowledges his truth properly, since no other name is given us under heaven in which we may be saved than in his name alone, Acts 4:12. Thus there is also no other truth than that which Jesus Christ brought out of heaven and has prayed to his Father for it, John 17:17[ff.], that his disciples might be sanctified therein.

For these reasons my first sincere and earnest admonition to you, out of the innermost of my soul, is to bid you through God's mercy, Rom. 12:1, that you not let yourself be moved or turned from our most holy faith, Jude 1:12, through someone's brave and high-sounding words, but believe the Scriptures and remember that it is written there that God (from whom the Holy Scripture is imparted and has come here) is alone true, and all people, who speak from themselves and do not speak the Word of the Lord through his Spirit, are liars, Ps. 116:11; Rom. 3:4. And since the true God has given his only born Son Jesus Christ to us as Lord and Master, Deliverer and Savior, John 3:16; Rom. 8:32, presented him as an example, witnessed and said about him that he is his beloved Son, Matt. 17:5, in whom he is well pleased, and that we should listen to him; therefore, do not think that a Christian shall believe and do otherwise than Jesus Christ taught, yes, [who was] brought out of heaven from his Father in the power of the Holy Spirit.

He is and remains the only way to the Father, John 14:6, and the only truth through which all believers are sanctified by God. For just as the honor of God the Father is /447/ that he is an eternal, almighty, and self-sufficient being, Exod. 3:[14], a living foundation and giver of all good, from which all that is good has its origin and being and flows here; that he is an eternal light and a Father of all light, from whom all good gifts have come and are given, James 1:17; Matt. 19:17; 1 John 1:5; that is the honor of Jesus Christ that he is the Word, John 1:1, the wisdom, and the power of God, Rom. 1:16; 1 Cor. 1:24, the truth and life, an image of the invisible God, a reprint of his being, Heb. 1:3, an appearance of the eternal light, a spotless mirror of the divine glory, which had its origin from the beginning and from eternity out of God the Father, Micah 5:[2], an only born Son of the most high and living God. Therefore he has also received from the Father a name above all names which may be named, Eph. 1:21; Phil. 2:9, not only in the present but also in the future world.

For his name is God's Word, namely, the Word which John writes about, John 1:1; Rev. 19:[13]: In the beginning was the Word and the Word was with God and God was the Word. Therefrom it follows incontrovertibly that Jesus Christ is the only born Son of the almighty God, one with his Father, and indivisible in the divine being. And therefore, every knee must bow in his name, Phil. 2:10, every tongue must praise him, all people must praise him, falling down before him, yes, he is worshiped by all the angels, Heb. 1:6, and by all creatures who are under heaven with divine honor, just as his Father, John 5:[23]. And therein he is truly honored and his heavenly Father also praised that we become his disciples, John 15:8. And those are his disciples who remain in his teaching, John 8:31, who deny themselves, take their cross upon themselves, and follow the Lord in the new birth, with a genuine faith through which they receive and obtain the promised salvation.

For that is the character and power of faith, that one believes with the whole heart and this is assured out of God's Word and promise through the sealing of the Spirit that Jesus Christ, when he was in the divine form, Phil. 2:[6], rich and glorified by the Father before the beginning of the world, 1 Pet. 1:20, who according to the providence of the Father through the action of the Holy Spirit became a person in the maiden[1] Mary, Matt. 1:20; Luke 2:7, and was born out of her a Son of the Most High. Therefore he is a heavenly person and not from the earth, yes, he is the living bread (as he himself said—John 6:51), came down from heaven, and is God's bread, and gives the world life. /448/ For he said in John: The bread that I shall give you is my flesh which I shall give for the life of the world. Oh, what a holy and heavenly, yes, divine and life-giving flesh is that flesh of Jesus Christ, God's Son, and that because it originally came out of the Word, as the evangelist testifies and says: The Word has become flesh, John 1:14. With this witness John established that Christ, with the earlier mentioned words, is the living bread come down from heaven as he said.

Now it is beyond doubt surely true that God's Word is this living bread, that spiritual manna that God let come down from heaven as food to all believing souls. This manna and bread (which Jesus Christ called his flesh, John 6:32) is (I say) from heaven and not from the earth, just as the mercy throne which stood on the ark of the covenant, Exod. 25:[17], was of pure gold. But the ark was from acacia wood and overlaid with gold.

That the ark is a figure of the congregation everyone who is taught from God well knows. That acacia wood signifies human weakness with which the congregation is seized (since they also have flesh and blood from sinful Adam). The gold signifies the purified Word of God and the power of the Holy Spirit with which the congregation, through the new birth out of God is adorned and clothed from on high. For what is born of the Spirit is Spirit, John 3:6, as Christ himself said. And Paul said if someone belongs to the Lord, that one is a spirit, with the Lord, 1 Cor. 6:17. Thus the ark, that is, the box of the covenant, was made of two substances, as an example that the congregation is also of two different substances. That is, it is from the earth through the birth from Adam, and it is from heaven through the other birth out of God; it is weak and fallible from itself, and it is wonderful and beautiful through the grace of Jesus Christ, John 3:5; 1 Cor. 15:43; Eph. 5:6; Song of Sol. 2:1.

But it is not thus with the mercy seat. That one is of one substance, of pure gold, and is Jesus Christ, the head of his congregation, the genuine mercy seat presented to us from the Father on account of belief in his blood, as the apostle said, Rom. 3:[24f.]; Heb. 5:3, through whom God spoke to us. That one is the pure Word of God inwardly and outwardly, John 1:1; 8:40, through and through, and therefore his flesh might not see nor suffer corruption. This John also indicated in his epistle expressly and said: That which was from the beginning, which we have heard, which we have seen, /449/ looked upon with our own eyes, and have touched with our hands, from the word of life, and the life is revealed, and we proclaim to you that eternal life that was with the Father and is revealed to us, 1 John 1:1[-3].

In like manner the metal serpent which Christ himself signifies and explained (as the figure to that true being, and as the letter to the spirit, John 3:14, that was made from one material, a saving sign of the grace of God. Who may now speak against it with truth? Yes, who may doubt it, since out of such and similar mysteries, figures and clear words, it is revealed that Jesus Christ is an only Christ and the indivisible Son of God; not half heavenly and half earthly, not half from God and half from Adam, yes, not half holy and half sinful, as some scholars (I may certainly say confused) have unashamedly presented and lied.

But he is entirely heavenly, John 3:13; 6:[32], entirely from God, entirely holy, who also through the only sacrifice of his unblemished flesh and precious blood has sanctified and made perfect all those who believe in his name, Heb. 10:14; Rom. 5:1. For it happened thus that the one who would pay all the guilt of the trespasser Adam with his innocence [literally, unguilt; cf. innocence], would make as nothing all our unrighteousness with his righteousness, destroying death with his life, as that only innocent Lamb of God, taking away the sins of the world, John 1:[29]; 1 John 2:1, and completed the wonderful work of our redemption, that one had to be a divine person, yes, true God and human in one person. For with his divinity he could thus help us, and according to his humanity could he thus as the only high priest of God anointed and instituted according to the order of Melchizedek, Heb. 5:1; 9:11; 10:11, offer himself for us through the Holy Spirit and set on fire that precious incense on the altar of the cross with the fire of his immeasurable love to us, a sweet smell to the Father and as a reconciliation with God and as a forgiveness of our sins, Eph. 5:[2].

Likewise that one [who] would reveal to us the fullest will and entire counsel of God, John 14:10, unlocking the treasure room of the divine hiddenness, and prepare the way to the holy of holies. In that one must lie hidden all the treasures of the wisdom and knowledge of God, Col. 2:2[f.]. Yes, in him the whole perfection of deity must dwell bodily, so that he can share out of the fullness of his grace and truth, John 1:16; Col. 1:19; 2:9, to all those who seek such from him and desire it from him. Therefore both are to be noted in him, namely, first of all, that he is the deliverer of the human race, Matt. 1:21, /450/ our reconciler with God, our righteousness, holiness and peace, our mediator and advocate, 1 John 2:2, our high priest with the Father, our one throne of grace, the horn of our salvation, and the hope of our life, Heb. 5:1; 7:22; 8:1; 9:11; 10:11. Thereafter he is thus the true teacher of truth, John 3:2, a witness to heavenly things which he has seen and heard from his Father, a living example of the nature and character of his Father, Heb. 1:3, in all his words and works. With his grace he serves us to salvation, John 1:16; Rom. 8:32, and with his truth he shows us the way to eternal life, John 14:6. And just as those are condemned, who build upon their own works, merits, and false righteousness, and comfort themselves therewith, so they are also cursed and banned who preach or accept another gospel than our Lord Jesus Christ brought out of heaven and sealed with his blood, Gal. 1:8.

The Scripture witnesses to all this in greater clarity, and faith also grasps this all, which faith is the work of God in the person, Eph. 2:8, whereby he is born anew out of God, as is written: Anyone who believes that Jesus is the Christ and the Son of God, that one is born out of God. And whoever is born out of God, that one is one spirit with God, yes, God is in him and he is in God; Jesus Christ dwells in his heart through faith, and he is sealed with the Holy Spirit, 1 John 5:1; John 3:6; Eph. 3:17. And therefore he is happy about such grace and mercy of God whom he confesses in faith, and his heart is set aflame with divine and brotherly love, since he remembers and reflects that God has so loved us and has given his only Son unto death for us, John 3:16, so that we shall live through him, and that Jesus Christ has offered himself for us, Heb. 10:11[f.]; John 17:[19], so that through his only sacrifice we may be sanctified in eternity. Therefore, I say once again, a Christian's heart is stirred to have love of God in turn, since he has loved us so heartily, and also to serve the neighbor just as Jesus has served us. And that is a true faith that is always fruitful, active in deeds, and working in love, both to God and the neighbor, Gal. 5:6. Otherwise, it is no faith.

Here now also belong the commands and institutions of the Lord, for they testify to and establish faith. Furthermore, faith thus looks to Jesus Christ alone, trusting him, because of his grace and merit. For that is without doubt a true word, which will not pass away, but is the /451/ firm foundation of God which will remain in eternity. That is also all of the Christian's greatest comfort, joy, and trust, that they are saved out of grace and that Jesus Christ is our Savior, Eph. 2:5; Matt. 1:21, and that no other name is given under heaven in which we shall be saved, Acts 4:12. And he shows us the way, John 14:6, the only Good Shepherd and Bishop of our souls, John 10:1; 1 Pet. 2:25, whose voice we must hear and follow in his footsteps. Whoever will not believe and do that, that one shall never more come to God.

This is my faith and confession before almighty God and before Jesus Christ, before his angels, and before all persons on earth, especially before those who from their heart desire to fear God and to walk in his ways.

Further, I must write to you a little about God's covenant, Gen. 17:2, in which all believers are included (in which the grace of God the Father and his only born Son is shown). From us are demanded and required faith, love, fear of the Lord, obedience to his Word, yes, also to keep the commands of God for this reason that the divine biblical Scripture speaks much of it and sets it before the eyes of all God-fearing people what his covenant actually is. And therefore, it is necessary for all Christians to know what that covenant of God is, namely, that God binds and unites himself with us, promises us every good, that he will be our God and Father, and we shall be his people, his sons and daughters, the sheep of his pasture, and receive from him the blessing through Jesus Christ. And this covenant has begun when God spoke to the serpent, Gen. 3:15: I will put enmity between you and the women, between your seed and the women's seed, and that the women's seed will itself tread upon and crush your head.

Thereafter this covenant is thus renewed and established by God with Noah the patriarch and with his sons, to whom God spoke, Gen. 9:[1]: I set up my covenant with you. Further, God had thus repeated this covenant and established it with Abraham, to whom God spoke, Gen. 17:1[f.]: I am the God Shaddai, that is, an almighty and superabundant sufficient fulness of all good; walk before me and remain firm and faithful to me. I will make my covenant between me and you. And God spoke further with Abraham: I am, and have made my covenant with you, /452/ and [you] will become a father of many peoples. Again, I will set up my covenant between me and you, and your seed after you.

Here belong all of God's promises from his grace, love, faithfulnes, mercy, clemency, and from Jesus Christ our Lord, deliverer, and Savior, through whom is assured to us blessing (in the spiritual and heavenly goods), the forgiveness of sins, and eternal salvation, Gal. 3:9; Eph. 1:3. And that is the first article in God's covenant that God initiates and is included in God's promises. The other article therein applies to us, to wit, that we accept the offered grace of God through faith, that we fear and love, honor and worship God, serve him and are obedient, keeping ourselves firmly and strictly to his Word, with firm resolve to remain there and to follow after it with God's help. And that is then the covenant and good conscience with God through Jesus Christ, 1 Pet. 3:21. And hereto all the commands of God serve, which teach and command us how we should conduct ourselves toward God.

Here to also belong both signs of the Lord, as baptism and the Lord's Supper, instituted to witness to this covenant and to admonish us thereto, John 3:14. For although that true, genuine, and saving sign from the rich grace of the covenant is Jesus Christ, and the Holy Spirit is the sealing of all the promises of God, 1 John 4:13; Eph. 4:30, nevertheless, the almighty God has always witnessed to and established his covenant with external signs. For as God comforted Adam and Eve with the promise of the coming Savior and victor over the serpent, thus he gave them garments of skins and clothed them therewith, Gen. 3:21, (and this signifies that Jesus Christ is the cloak of righteousness and the coat of salvation, with which all believers and baptized Christians are clothed and their sins covered) because they should be assured of the grace and promises of God, Gal. 3:24. For that God clothed their nakedness and shame when they had sinned was a sure and open sign that God had not turned his fatherly heart from them, but that he maintained and still cared through his bottomless mercy and love, also with bodily clothing, that they should always have a refuge in this grace of God.

In the same manner, God gave Noah the rainbow and Abraham circumcision, Gen. 9:12[f.]; 17:9[ff.] as signs of his /453/ covenant, and both of these signs image Jesus Christ for us, who is a sign of our peace in heaven, Eph. 2:13[f.], at his Father's right hand, and his circumcision is the true circumcision that occurs without hands, Col. 2:11, with the stone knife of the divine Word on the foreskin of the heart, through the laying aside of the sinful flesh, that is, all wicked lusts, desires, and works that come out of the flesh. Therefore, Paul says that he is not a Jew who is a Jew externally, Rom. 2:28. Also that is no circumcision which occurs externally in the flesh, but that one is a Jew who is hidden internally, and that is circumcision, the circumcision of the heart which happens in the spirit and does not happen in the letter, whose praise is not out of people but out of God.

In the same manner, almighty God has instituted, given, and left to us baptism and the Lord's Supper so that we thereby and through them would be admonished of the divine covenant and our debt which we once again owe to God. For the gospel, which was taught to us before baptism, reminds us and pictures for us the superabundant grace of God and the death of Jesus Christ, to wit, that God chose us as his children, Eph. 1:4; and has graciously forgiven all our sins through Jesus Christ with whose blood he has sprinkled, washed, and cleansed our consciences, Rom. 3:[24f.]; 5:1; 8:1; 1 Pet. 1:18[f.]; Heb. 9:12[ff.]; 12:2. And this was proclaimed to us in the gospel, so that we would repent, cease from sin, confessing those before God, believe the gospel, be baptized on the confession of our faith, not only internally by Jesus Christ himself with the Holy Spirit and fire, but also externally with water by a minister of Jesus Christ in his congregation in the name of the Father, and the Son, and the Holy Spirit, Matt. 28:19. [This baptism] in the name of the only God and Lord was for a witness that we then are inscribed and reckoned in the number and fellowship of all the saints and the saved, whom God the Father has accepted as his children, Rom. 8:16; 2 Cor. 6:18, whom Jesus Christ delivered with his innocent death, purchased with his precious blood, 1 Pet. 1:[19], illuminated by the Holy Spirit, and has brought to eternal salvation.

Therefore, we shall, as chosen children of the heavenly Father, as holy brothers and companions of Jesus Christ, Heb. 3:1, as those sealed with the Holy Spirit, 1 Cor. 3:16; 6:19, and marked with the sign of the living God, from that time on, having received baptism in the highly praised and worshiped name of God, /454/ serve God through the Lord's grace in his covenant with a good conscience, 1 Pet. 3:21, dying to sin, burying the old Adam, and proceeding in a new life. And that is what the apostle also meant when he wrote thus to the Romans, 6:3: And do you not know that you who are baptized in Jesus Christ are baptized in his name? The meaning of the apostle is that the believers and penitents are baptized into the fellowship of the death of Jesus Christ, first therein, that they share in his suffering and dying and everything that he has therewith fulfilled in God and extended to our salvation, and that we participate in these, and second, that they die with him, have become conformed to his suffering, and walk in a new spiritual and Christlike being.

So also the Lord's Supper is a true sign of God's love toward us and a remembrance of the suffering and death of Jesus Christ, Matt. 26:[26ff.]. And it admonishes us of the overflowing great love and the superabundant richness of the grace of God the Father, that he has given his only born Son as a reconciliation of our sins, John 3:16; Rom. 8:32; 1 John 3:16. It images for us also that bitter innocent suffering, the despised death, and painful martyrdom of Jesus Christ. With this come admonishings and imagings that we would in turn have love for God our heavenly Father and his Son Jesus Christ and be thankful for all his benefits. Thereby we are also admonished in the Lord's Supper to brotherly love, trust, and unity, and how we must be unified, peaceful, loving, and friendly in God's covenant, in the congregation of the Lord, and with all true believing Christians, serving and loving one another as Jesus Christ has served and loved us.

I have held this before you when I was there with you and have been very happy in the spirit when I have seen that so many were added to God's congregation and that you have broken the bread of the Lord in such Christian unity. The Father of all mercy and the God of all grace must strengthen all of you through his Holy Spirit, so that you go forward in the good and remain steadfast therein until the end.

And think always yet on the first love and zeal of your heart, how that the love of God and his congregation has burned within you, Rev. 2:[3]; 3:15, how zealous you were in the spirit, when you committed yourself to God's covenant, uniting with the Lord and his congregation, and there made a /455/ promise to the most high God with bowed knees of your hearts and bodies, and expressed with the full confession of your mouths that you would serve the Lord your God in his congregation with all Christians in peace and in one spirit of faith, Eph. 4:3; Gal. 6:18, walking according to every one of the rules of the divine Word, just as is seemly for all newborn children of God.

For these reasons I have told you about God's covenant so that you would always think about the inexpressible love of God through which he chose you as his children and made you his heirs in his beloved Son Jesus Christ, Eph. 1:5, and has given you the guarantees of his Spirit about the promised salvation in our heart, 2 Cor. 1:22, and how that you shall in turn thank God for such wonderful gifts and benefits, and walk and live with all those who fear God in divine unity.

Therefore, my dearest ones, since you were called from God to the genuine knowledge and fellowship of his Son Jesus Christ, and have become covenanted companions of God out of grace, I ask and admonish you through the mercy of God that you persist in all things shown to you, as is seemly to your calling, Eph. 4:1; Phil. 1:27, and remember how trustworthily the apostles of the Lord admonished all Christians to a God-blessed walk which is conformed to and worthy of the gospel, and say: You holy brothers, you who are called together through the heavenly calling, consider the apostle and the high priest whom we acknowledge, Jesus Christ, who was true to the one who ordained him, [i.e., God], Heb. 3:7[ff.]. Again, I, Paul, a prisoner in the Lord, admonish you that you walk just as belongs to your call, with all humility and gentleness, with patience and forbearing one to another in love, and be eager to keep the unity in the spirit through the bond of peace, Eph. 4:1[-3]. Again, walk worthy of the gospel of Jesus Christ so that whether I come and see you or hear about you in my absence, that you stand in one spirit and in one soul and strive with us for the faith of the gospel, Phil. 1:27.

Again, the apostle Peter has told of the benefits of God who according to his great mercy has born us anew to a living hope through the resurrection of Jesus Christ from the dead. Thereafter he admonished us thus with these words: Therefore then, gird the loins of your mind, be innocent, and set your hope entirely on the grace which was offered to you through the revelation of Jesus Christ, /456/ as obedient children, and do not present yourselves as before, when you lived according to lusts in ignorance. But since the one who has called you is holy so you should be holy in all your conduct. For it is written there: You shall be holy for I am holy, 1 Pet. 1:13[-16].

In like manner the apostle John thus admonished and said: That is the message which we have heard from him and proclaim to you, that God is light and in him is no darkness. If we say that we have fellowship with him and walk in darkness, we lie and do not the truth. But if we walk in the light as he is in the light, we thus have fellowship with one another, and the blood of his Son Jesus Christ makes us clean of all sins, 1 John 1:5[-7]. Thus the entire Holy Scripture admonishes us to a God-blessed life and testifies to us that God's kingdom does not exist in words, but in power, 1 Cor. 4:20, and that those alone who are believing Christians and do the will of God shall be saved, as Jesus Christ himself testifies explicitly in the gospel.

Therefore, my heartily dear brothers and sisters in the Lord, I ask and admonish you once again through the mercy of God that you observe carefully these and similar admonitions of the apostles so that you may walk with a good conscience in the covenant of God as rightly believing and baptized Christians, 1 Pet. 3:21, in Christian peace and in brotherly unity, and think always on the words of the apostle James who said thus: Who is wise and understanding among you, that one shows it with his good conduct, his works in gentleness and wisdom. But if you have bitter envy and hate in your heart, do not boast and lie against the truth, for this wisdom has not descended from above but it is earthly, fleshly, and of the devil. For where envy and strife is, there is disorder and idle wicked things. But the wisdom that comes from above is pure or chaste, thereafter peaceful, friendly, it speaks the truth, is full of mercy and good fruits, impartial, without insincerity. But the fruit of righteousness is sown in peace to those who keep the peace, James 3:13[-18]. God's peace (the apostle thinks), not the peace of the world.

Therefore, beware against all vacillating and rash spirits who give room to /457/ fleshly freedoms against the evangelical and apostolic admonitions, yes, against the entire godly truth, and with an insincere appearance seek peace in the world. Beware of all such for they are enemies of the cross of Jesus Christ, they serve their belly, and are concerned with earthly things, Phil. 3:18[-19]. But you yourselves reflect on all the holy people of God who have been from the beginning, and see how they have viewed all false worship, all insincere and wicked appearance, and fellowship of idolatrous servants. Consider here the encouragement, noticing the outcome of the pious and God-fearing people, and follow their faith, Heb. 13:7. Thus will the God of all grace be with you in eternity. Amen.

Finally, my beloved in the Lord, since I have heard how after our departure, persecution and oppression has come over Christians upon some places, I cannot omit to write a little about that, that you should certainly still be comforted in the Lord and be strong through the power of God, which he has shown to you when he aroused you from the dead, made you alive, and set you in that heavenly being through Jesus Christ, Eph. 1:3. Mark now that you be firmly grounded, as is Mount Zion, Ps. [125]:1, and therefore shall not be moved eternally from the foundation of the apostles and prophets, Eph. 2:[20]. Think now on the words of Jesus Christ, that you should not fear people who may kill the body and cannot kill the soul. But that you should fear the one who has the power to kill not only the body, but also the soul, and to cast it into hell, Matt. 10:28.

You certainly know well and are taught therein, not only through the Scripture, but also through the experience from God, that all who are saved by God will live in Jesus Christ and must suffer persecution, 2 Tim. 3:12, that we through much tribulation must enter the kingdom of God, Acts 14:22, and that the Father chastises all his children whom he loves and whom he receives in his arms, Heb. 12:6, and those who are without chastising, in which all true children participate, those are bastards and no children.

Therefore every Christian will take upon himself voluntarily the cross of Jesus Christ and be at peace with God's good will, and consider how that all persecution happens to the Christian unforeseen, but through the unchangeable counsel of God are added to and led thereto out of simple grace and love of God, Acts 4:28, and that all godless tyrants may do nothing to the God-fearing ones from themselves, Matt. 6:27; 10:28. For Satan might not touch the pious and simple Job, Job 1, unless the Lord permitted him to do it. /458/ Christ spoke to Pilate that he had no power over him unless it was first given to him from above, John 19:11.

How often God has shown this to his saints whom he has delivered out of death's violence and out of the tyrants' hand, as the three youths out of the fiery furnace in Babylon, Dan. 3:23, Daniel out of the lion's den, Dan. 6:19, Susanne in extreme need from shame and death, Sus. 1:44[ff.]; the city Bethulia from the haughty Holofernes through the worshiping Judith, Jth. 12:13; the Jews from the godless Haman through Esther, Esther 6:7[ff.], and Jerusalem from Sennacherib through the angel who slew so many thousand Assyrians in one night. And that is what the prophet David meant when he said: The Lord makes and destroys the counsel of the heathen and turns aside the thoughts of the people, but the counsel of the Lord endures eternally [as does] the intention of his heart. The Ziphites reported the innocent David to Saul, that they might do a high service to the king therewith, but the Lord [had] already provided an escape, [Ps. 54].

Therefore the Holy Scripture thus comforts all those saved by God who suffer persecution here, and says that the godless threaten the righteous and gnash their teeth over them, that they draw out the sword, stretch the bow, place poisonous arrows on it to shoot the pious secretly, Ps. 37:12[ff.]. But their sword will go into their own heart, their bow will break, the Lord will break in pieces the teeth of the godless, Ps. 37:[15], and it is only a little time until the godless are no more, Ps. 3:8 and their place will be nowhere to be found, Ps. 37:10; but the righteous will live in eternity, they will grow as the palm trees and stand as the olive trees in the forecourt of the Lord, Ps. 92:[12-]13.

See, my chosen friends, how comforting is God's Word to all who fear God, and how entirely nothing are all the attacks and persecutions of the tyrannical people who are scheming and directed against God's congregation. They must finally still come to shame and be nothing, Isa. 43:1[ff.], all those who fight against the Lord's will, who are wrathful therein and do him harm; they will see and discover whom they have persecuted, in what they have plundered, and whose apple of the eye they have touched, Zech. 2:8.

But you, my dear brothers and fellow companions in the faith, in the kingdom and patience of Jesus Christ, Rev. 1:9, be of good courage, and do not turn aside or vacillate, for your deliverance is near, that you who now in manifold ways are tempted and must suffer much, [for] you have /459/ whitened your clothes and have washed your robes in the blood of the Lamb, Rev. 7:14. Yes, you are marked on your forehead with the sign of the living God and therefore may not worship that ugly beast, nor receive his sign, that you, I say, will be delivered out of all sorrow and come to eternal gladness, where you will neither hunger nor thirst, and the Lamb which is in the middle of the throne will feed you and lead you to the living fountain of water, and God will dry every tear from your eyes.

Comfort each other with this, so that no one may be of little courage nor fainthearted, and that no one lose that which he has and another might receive your crown, Rev. 2:25; 3:11. And now I commend you all together to the Lord and to the Word of his grace and greet you all with the peace of Jesus Christ, out of the full desire of my heart, that you keep the peace, Eph. 4:3, and always let it have the upper hand in your heart, Col. 3:15; and that you may increase and grow up in faith, in love, and in all virtues, to God's praise and honor and to the salvation of our soul.

Written out of pure brotherly love and given as a farewell or Christian goodbye (adieu), in case I do not see you again in the flesh. Therefore I want herewith to take a God-blessed departure out of this world from all of you, and hope to see you with gladness and to find you in the resurrection of the righteous at the right hand of our Lord and only Good Shepherd Jesus Christ, as the sheep of one flock, John 10:11; Matt. 25:32. But if it is God's will that we will come together once more in this life, I hope thus on the grace of the Lord that you will find me just as I have presented to you out of God's Word according to my little simple gift, and that I will find you thus, just as you are presently, namely, that you desire with all your hearts to fear God in one spirit, one heart, and one soul, to stand with us and help us strive for the truth of the gospel, and do not let yourself be frightened by the opposing parties, as I also trust you. The Lord Jesus Christ be with your spirit. AMEN.

ENDNOTES

1. Ionckvrouwe—alternate readings given in J. Verdam, *Middelnederlandsch Handwoordenboek*. The Hague: Martinus Nijhoff, 1932: unmarried young woman, young girl, girl in good standing [trans. by the editors].

INDEX [REGISTER]

The following index of the ENCHIRIDION was prepared by Dirk Philips. It is included here as a part of his writings and because of the commentaries supplied by him in connection with the chapters of the ENCHIRIDION. Page numbers for the present volume are supplied in [ ] in addition to the folio numbers he used. A folio is simply a leaf or page number, but also a sheet of paper folded once, making two leaves and four pages. In the sixteenth century books were frequently numbered only by folio, that is, every leaf, every other page.

Text

A convenient and profitable register, whereby the reader can easily and without much difficulty find all the different booklets which are included in the preceding book, [also including] the principal contents of that which is treated in each booklet, with the folio or pages with which the different booklets have begun with the principal or main teachings.

The Faith Book	First, the book which here earlier was called the Faith Book. fol. 1 /460/ [59]
	Again, the articles where the Faith Book is treated are these:
	First, a Preface fol. 2 [59]
About God.	Second, our beliefs and feelings about God, Father, Son, and Holy Spirit. fol. 3 [62]
About creation and redemption	Third, our confession about creation, redemption, and salvation of people. fol. 7 [68]
About baptism.	Fourth, about baptism. fol. 10 [72]
Misuse of baptism	How the infant baptizers shamefully misuse baptism. fol. 20 [83]
About opinions	How many old and new writers have viewed and seen opinions without Scripture. fol. 21 [84]

428 / *The Enchiridion*

About disputed articles.	Again, about the disputed articles of infant baptizers who desire to have children baptized, each in their manner. fol. 22 [85]
About false arguments	Again, many false arguments and perverted writings are answered. fol. 24 [87]
Conclusion about the Lord's Supper	A concluding argument about baptism. fol. 43 [112]. Fifth, a very beautiful teaching and basic explanation about the Lord's Supper of our Lord and Savior Jesus Christ. fol. 44 [132]
The second booklet about the incarnation of Jesus Christ.	Second, the second booklet treating the incarnation /461/ of our Lord and Savior Jesus Christ. fol. 64 [134]
	Again, the following are the principal teachings or foundation materials, which this booklet treats about.
Confession or profession. fol. 65 [135]	First, our confession or profession about Christ Jesus, or how we hold, confess, and acknowledge him to be the firstborn and only born Son of the almighty Father and and the living God, and that Jesus Christ, our Deliverer, Savior, and Mediator is true God and man, how and in what way he is and has become such.
How Christ's flesh is not from Mary. fol. 66 [137]	Again, how that the flesh of Christ is not from Mary, as the world holds and thinks, but that he is that living bread that was come from heaven, which Christ himself calls his flesh. fol. 66 [137]
	Again, that persons in no way nor through any means may be helped than alone through the one by whom he (to wit, the person) was created. fol. 68 [138]
	Again, how God's own only born and firstborn Son, yes, God himself, was born a man, and nevertheless has also remained God, portrayed with the figure about Melchizedek. fol. 69 [139]
	Again, how, why, and in what way Christ was called a seed of the wife, also of Abraham, and a fruit of the loins of David. fol. 70 [141]

Register (Index) / 429

Again, an answer to a question. Again, the preceding profession repeated briefly. fol. 76 [149]. Herewith this booklet comes to an end.

Again, now follows the third booklet and treats about the true knowledge of Jesus Christ, which begins fol. 78 [152]

Again, these are the principal points and articles which are included in this booklet.

Again, after the word of greeting the reason of writing explained. fol. 79 [153]

Again, how one must truly know Christ, both according to his eternal deity and holy humanity, about his deity, read fol. 80 [156]

About his holy humanity. fol. 86 [160]

Again, about the unmoveable and unchangeable foundation of the sanctifying teaching of Jesus Christ. fol. 91 [169]. And herewith this booklet is completed.

The fourth booklet, an apology or response. fol. 97 [174]	Again, the fourth booklet is called an apology or response, that we (who with great injustice are accused of Anabaptism by the world) are no rebaptizers or sectarians, but that we are one with the true congregation of God, which has been from the beginning, and it begins. fol. 97 [175] /462/
Distinction about true and false worship	There in addition a distinction of the true and false worship is related and taught in the same booklet, and why a pious Christian must flee before a false worship And it begins, fol. 105 [176]
Examples about two horrible animals and furious abomination	Again, fol. 107, you find some examples of pious Israelites. [185] how earnestly they have avoided and shunned idolatry, and as further establishing of this avoidance is told about the two horrible animals which one reads about in Revelation. fol. 109 [187], page 2, reg. 3 As then you have found there about the furious abomination in the holy places. Fol. 109 [188] pag. 2. reg. 3

Solution of false arguments. fol. 110 [190]	Again, then follows a solution about some false although adorned reasoning or objections which are thus voiced, sighted, or with conscience may well exist, [namely] that one [may] hold external fellowship with idolatry if one does not cleave to it with the heart. Here to read fol. 110 [191], page 1, reg. 4 with an account of what true love is.
Conclusion. fol. 115 [194]	Finally, a concluding account of the preceding articles of this book. fol. 115 [194]
The fifth booklet about the sending of preachers. fol. 117 [198]	Again, the fifth booklet about the sending of preachers or teachers, that is, which are the true teachers, who are sent from God, and are rightly chosen and called of preachers from the Christian congregation. fol. 117 [199] Again, whereby one shall know the false prophets. fol. 120 [199]
About knowing false prophets. fol. 120 [200]	Page 1, reg. 31 Again how the calling of true teachers occurs from God and his congregation. fol. 121 [201]
A defeat of some arguments. fol. 135 [216]	Again, about two kinds of fruit of the true teacher, the one. fol. 125 [206], the second. fol. 127 [209], page 1, reg. 28 Again, an explanation or definition of some subtle objections which are thrown up or introduced by the aforementioned slanderers, from which the first begins. fol. 135 [216] The second fol. 139 [222]. The third fol. 142 [226]. With some contradictions and responses, until the end of the book.
The sixth booklet, an admonition or epistle. fol. 151 [238]	Again, now follows the sixth booklet which is a lovely admonition or epistle to the congregation of God, containing and showing how and in what way the Christian congregation shall deal with those who have committed themselves to the fellowship of the saints, and then are still found in obvious works of

	the flesh and ugly abominations. fol. 151 [239] /463/
Thanksgiving to God, how and why. fol. 151 [239]	First you find a thanksgiving to almighty God from the author, since he had heard of the congregation's faith and love to God and its saints, also with its patience and endurance in all kinds of oppression and tribulation, and admonishes the same congregation with many beautiful and comforting words and writings to remain firm thereby until the end. This lasts until fol. 154 [241].
Admonition to Christian unity and peace. Warning against quarreling. Reason why the ministers of the gospel were accused of being foolish shepherds. fol. 155 [243]	There the congregation is admonished to Christian peace and godly unity, and earnestly warned that they shall watch against all useless quarrels, for he noticed that makers of quarrels were working among them, who accused the ministers of the divine Word as foolish shepherds who do not seek the lost, and do not bind up the wounded, etc. And that otherwise for no reason but that they do not permit the ugly public disgracers, abominators, and carnal persons into the the congregation of the saints, in order to be endured, but desire them to be placed outside it with the Word of the Lord, until such time that they show true repentance, and out of such reasons you find there many beautiful teachings out of the Holy Scripture, both of the Old and New Testaments presented and which is sufficiently shown that one ought not to permit such aforementioned sinners, disgracers, and abominators in the fellowship of the saints. These materials last until fol. 159 [248].
False arguments are answered. fol. 159 [248]	And from there are some further arguments (which are beautifully adorned and shown off with fancy reasons and perverted Scriptures, in order to strengthen the unrepentant in their evilness and to comfort them in their

For him to watch from sin	evil) answered and defeated, lasting unto fol. 162 [251].
	And from there further until the end of this booklet, you find a lively admonition and brotherly warning to guard against all sins and unrighteousness.
The seventh booklet, an admonition or epistle about the knowledge of God. fol. 165 [255]	Again, now follows the seventh booklet and is, along with a lovely admonition or epistle in which the true knowledge of God is explained, demonstrated, and taught very basically, with brief words, and begins fol. 165 [255].
What is necessary to note true knowledge. fol. 167 [256]	Again, fol. 167 [256] you find that three things are very necessary to note in the knowledge of God the Father. This lasts until fol. 168 [259].
	There you find that three things are also necessary to note in the knowledge of Jesus Christ and in the knowledge of the Holy Spirit. /464/ This begins and lasts unto the end of this booklet.
The eighth book about the tabernacle of Moses. fol. 173 [264]	Again, now follows the eighth booklet and is a beautiful and true explanation or exposition of the tabernacle or tent of Moses, in which many beautiful and necessary figures of the Old and New Testaments are told and are brought to agreement with the spirit of the New Testament. Begins fol. 173. [264]
About the erecting of the tabernacle. fol. 175 [267]	Again, fol. 175 [267], you find first how almighty God had Moses build a tent or tabernacle.
Exposition of the tabernacle. fol. 179 [269]	Again the exposition starts here, fol. 176 [268] and ends fol. 179. There you find then the equipment which was in the Tabernacle, with the exposition thereby, very beautiful and instructive, lasts to fol. 182 [273].
A refutation about a false exposition. fol. 182 [273]	And from there further until the end of this booklet, a false, misleading exposition will be refuted with the power of the divine Word which will introduce and point to two kinds

of Christians with the forecourt of the holy of holies, and uses additionally Esau and Jacob and other significant figures.

The ninth booklet about the new creature. fol. 200 [293]	Again, now follows the ninth booklet about the new birth or the new creature, in which the true power, nature, and characteristics of the new birth is very basically explained, with many beautiful teachings and instructions, in the way as follows hereafter, and begin fol. 200 [293].
How a person created according to God's image has fallen and was raised up again and through whom. fol. 202 [295]	Again, fol. 201 [294] the author tells the reasons which have motivated him to write this booklet, and how God has first created persons according to his own image, how he has fallen and was raised up again, and through whom, namely, through Christ, according to whom a person is raised up again thus out of pure grace, that he also then when he has come to his understanding, again ought to be declared renewed, changed, reborn, and as the image of God, just as Christ spoke to Nicodemus. This lasts until fol. 204 [298], page 2, reg. 27.
That one may not attribute the rebirth to the children. fol. 204 [298] and fol. 206 [300]	Again, how all such power of the new birth may not be attributed to the young, unaccountable, and children without understanding, but only to the understanding, and these must first hear God's Word, accept and believe, and upon confession of faith be baptized in the name of the Lord, just as Christ himself has been an example of the same.
A warning for misleading spirits. fol. 208 [301]	Again, how they err very much and are mistaken, both those who /465/ push the internal baptism alone and despise the external, and also those who look upon the external sign alone and forget the significance or internal essence. fol. 207 [301] Again, a serious warning for such false spirits, who despise all Christian ordinances and hold them for child's play or ridicule.

A false argument is refuted. fol. 211 [303]	Again, an argument which is presented from some boasters, which is refuted with the power of the Scripture. fol. 211 [303]
How we are despised, ridiculed, and persecuted. fol. 212 [305]	Again, how we are despised and ridiculed by some, and are persecuted by some, and the reason for it, why such occurs,
Through whom we seek our salvation. fol. 213 [306]	Again, wherein and through whom we seek our salvation, and what we hold about our own selves. fol. 213 [306]
About Christ an example and pattern to all believers. fol. 217 [313]	You find here given an example of the forefathers. fol. 216 [310] And then at the last is again explained and placed before all our eyes, how Christ, the Son of the living God, is a true example and pattern, which all Christians, believing, regenerated must follow and be conformed to from the depths of their hearts, with much humility, how and in what way, and with that this booklet ends.
The tenth booklet about the spiritual restitution. fol. 220 [316]	Again, now follows the tenth booklet about the spiritual restitution, that is, how all that happened from the beginning is fulfilled, repeated, and restored in Christ Jesus spiritually, in the way which follows hereafter, and it begins. fol. 220 [316]
About the creation of heaven and earth. fol. 222 [318]	Again, how the creation of heaven and earth is first restored in Christ Jesus. fol. 222 [318]
Creation of persons. fol. 223 [319]	Again, how the creation of persons is also renewed in Christ Jesus. fol. 223, p. 2 [319]
About marriage. fol. 224 [320]	Again, how marriage is also again renewed and restored rightly in Christ Jesus. fol. 224 [320]
About Noah.	There next the treatment about Noah. fol. 226 [322]
About Abraham, Isaac, and Jacob.	Thereafter is the treatment of God with Abraham, Isaac, and Jacob, with all of Israel, also restored in the spirit and true being in Christ Jesus. Read about this from fol. 226 [323] to fol. 232 [327].

About the Passover Lamb. fol. 232 [329] About heavenly bread, etc.	Thereafter the figure about the Passover Lamb begins, also about the heavenly bread from the rock which Israel followed. Also about the angel of the Lord which went before Israel, to fol. 233 [329]. Thereafter you find about the bitter water that was sweetened. Also about the worshipers of the calf, about the whorers with the Moabites, /466/ about the Balaamites, also with Dathan, Abiram, and about the murmurers.
About the promised land, how the twelve men, etc.	Again, about the promised land, how twelve men were sent to spy upon it. fol. 235 [332]
Figures such as about judges, Samson, David, etc.	Again, about the figurative rule of the judges, and also about Samson. fol. 237 [334] Thereafter about the figurative kingdom of David and also about the figurative temple of Solomon, also about Pentecost and the Feast of Tabernacles. fol. 238 [336]
About the kingdom and glory of Solomon. fol. 240 [338]	About the kingdom and glory of Solomon, that all is also spiritually repeated and restored in Christ Jesus, with yet additionally that high song of Solomon about the queen and his bride. fol. 240 [338]
About the apostasy of his kingdom. fol. 243 [342]	Again, about the apostasy of Solomon's kingdom through Jeroboam. fol. 243 [342] How Israel has been captive twice and twice delivered. fol. 245 [343]
Building of the city of God. fol. 246 [344]	About the building of the temple and city of the living God, where the enemies of truth desired to help build, which was not proper for them, this was portrayed with the figurative temple. fol. 246 [346] Herewith this booklet is completed.
The eleventh booklet about the congregation of God. fol. 250 [350]	Again, now follows the eleventh booklet about the about the congregation of God, how it has been from the beginning, and whereby it is recognized and distinguished from all sects. fol. 250 [350] Again, the fol-

How the congregation has been from the beginning. fol. 252. [351] The first apostacy of angels.

The second through Adam and Eve. fol. 253. [353] About Abel and Cain, what is portrayed therewith. fol. 254, [354]

How God has set up his covenant with Noah and his two sons. fol. 255. [354]

New birth and whereby. fol. 258 [357]

How the pure knowledge of God belongs to the new birth fol. 261 [358]
Ordinances of the congregation. fol. 263 [363]

The second
The third
The fourth

lowing are the points and articles which are included in this booklet:
First, how God's congregation has been from the beginning, and for the first time was begun and received with the angels in heaven, and afterward with Adam and Eve, and that the first apostasy has happened with [among] the angels and otherwise through Adam and Eve, also along with them again raised up. Read about it from fol. 252 [352] to fol. 254 [354].
Again, you find afterwards how God gave Adam and Eve two sons, to wit, Abel and Cain. Abel a member of the Christian church, and Cain a member or child of the devil, with which is figured and portrayed that from that time on two kinds of people or congregations have been.
Again, thereafter fol. 255 [354] you find how God has set up his covenant with Noah and with his two sons. Also with Abraham, Isaac, and Jacob. Also along with them have been many pious from among the heathen. This lasts to fol. 258 [355].
Again, you find then about the new birth, whereby that occurs, /467/ namely, through God's Word, and how that Word is of two kinds, as Law and Gospel. This lasts to fol. 261 [358].
Again, you find next how the pure knowledge of the only, eternal, and almighty God, which is the Father, Son, and Holy Spirit, is necessary by the new birth; again, thereafter you find about the ordinances of God's congregation, whereby one recognizes it and shall distinguish from all sects, about which the first begins fol. 263 [363].
The first ordinance. fol. 263 [363]
The second. fol. 265 [365]
The third. fol. 267 [367]
The fourth. fol. 267, p. 2 [368]

Register (Index) / 437

The fifth	The fifth. fol. 269, p. 2 [370]
The sixth	The sixth. fol. 271 [372]
The seventh	The seventh. fol. 272, p. 2 [373]
That the congregation is called the Holy City, the heavenly Jerusalem. fol. 275 [376]	Again, fol. 275 [376] you find then how God's congregation well known out of its description, namely, that it is the Holy City, the New Jerusalem, come from God out of heaven, prepared as a bride for her husband, etc. Herewith the book is completed and the last folio is 280 [381]. And that which follows hereafter and here previously has never been published; thus begins the signature and again also the folio itself.
The first Epistle. fol. 1 [383]	Again, here follow three fundamental admonitions or epistles sent at diverse times to God's congregation, about which the first begins fol. 1 [383].
About the content of the first letter.	Again, an explanation of the principal foundation or content of the first letter. First, an evangelical and apostolic greeting, after which thanksgiving to almighty God, etc.
How God has overlooked the time of ignorance. fol. 2 [384]	Again, how graciously God at the time of our ignorance has overlooked it. Therefore, the congregation is admonished to give thanks for this great unspeakable grace and mercy, and that they shall consider whereto they are called from GOD, and whereby Christ has chosen and accepted them for his disciples.
Note. How God has always comforted and stood by his people fol. 3 [385]	Again, many lovely reasons and comforting writings which are very necessary for the oppressed children of God to consider, how trustworthily God has always stood by his chosen ones from the beginning and has comforted and strengthened them in their tribulation. fol. 3 [385]
That a person's life is short. fol. 6 [388] About Eleazar's bravery. fol. 7 [389]	Again, how short the time of people's lives is, with an instructive living example of the bravery and piety of the old and well-thought of Eleazar who because of /468/ a

little time of the temporal life did not desire to pretend, with many beautiful teachings serving for this purpose. fol. 7 [389]

Warning against false prophets. fol. 9 [392]
About Christian freedom
fol. 10 [392]
fol. 10 [392]
fol. 11 [394]

Again, a warning against false prophets who preach soft things to the people, thereby the people are misled and learn a false freedom, with a beautiful instruction of what true Christian freedom is. fol. 9 [392]

Again, how they err very abominably who indicate that Christian freedom whereby one may certainly go into the freedom temples and idolatrous houses in order to see and hear externally their false teachings with their adorned idolatry, if one but not believe or adhere to it with the heart, this lasts to fol. 12 [395].

Warning against those who make quarrels. fol. 12 [395]

Finally, a trusted warning for the makers of quarrels who cause quarrels and aggravations regarding the doctrine of Christ and will not shun nor avoid the apostate persons. With these matters the first letter is completed.

Here follows the second epistle and begins fol. 13 [398]. A short extract of what the letter treats. Again, after the greeting and thanksgiving, the author tells of great gladness and joy that he has had in visiting the congregations in his fatherland, how and why, etc.

fol. 17 [401]

Again, a concerned prayer for the congregation to persevere in the truth, for many braggerts and boastful spirits are found to resist and change. fol. 15 [400]. Again, how that many abandon the truth and with Esau sell their birthright for a dish of food. fol. 16 [401]. Again, an earnest plea and humble desire to walk trustworthily in the truth, because Satan is now let loose to mislead the world and to fight against all the chosen ones with many kinds of tyranny, and how one must arm oneself against it. fol. 18 [402]. A lovely plea to stand according to Christian peace and brotherly unity. fol. 22 [408]. Again, an account out of what heartfelt love the preceding letter was written. fol. 23 [409]

The third epistle. fol. 24 [412]	The third epistle begins. fol. 24 [412] Again, the following are the points and articles which this epistle treats. First, the evangelical greeting with thanksgiving to almighty God for the congregation's belief on God the Father and his Son Jesus Christ, and the love these have for one another, which the author not only heard about them, /469/ but, himself having come to them, found it thus, with still the wish [that they may] walk further thus persistently until the end, since it is a perilous time, that many false prophets and antichrists arise, and many braggarts and boastful spirits are in circulation who contradict the teaching of Jesus Christ, break and despise his ordinances. Therefore, the author is compelled to write this warning, to inform the congregation about the foundation of the true Christian faith, and about the covenant of God, how we ought to lead a God-fearing walk to the praise of the Lord, each seek in their folio.
About faith	About the true foundation of the Christian faith, a very basic instruction, and it begins fol. 25 [413].
About God's covenant. fol. 29 [418]	Again, about the covenant of God. fol. 29 [418]
About baptism and the Lord's Supper, etc.	Again, how both signs, as baptism and the Lord's Supper, were instituted from the Lord, in order to witness to this covenant. fol. 30 [418] How baptism and the Lord's Supper signifies

to all Christians to think about God's covenant and the debt of love, which we owe to God. fol. 30 [418]. A beautiful instruction to a Christian and God-fearing walk, just as befits the Christian calling. fol. 32 [423]. Finally, many trustworthy reasons and fundamental writings treating oppression and persecution. fol. 34 [424]

To the Reader

Know, dear reader, how we put annotation on the different verses and with different signs have signaled, each on its matter where it belongs, and the first number counted that followed after the indication signals the chapter which it shows, and the second number that follows the letter, which stands between both, signifies that verse, and if following after the first number counted any such follows, that signifies that the whole chapter treats the same material.

Part B

OTHER WRITINGS

ANSWER TO SEBASTIAN FRANCK

Introduction

In reaction to the abuses of the sacraments in the medieval church, some reformation leaders were inclined to reject all external forms. The Anabaptists always had to contend with those who would spiritualize the church, but were themselves commonly considered to be among the foremost spiritualizers. The tendency was reinforced by the desire to escape persecution. The visible evidence of dissent in baptism and alternatives to the mass in celebrating the Lord's Supper disclosed who the reformers were.

Already in 1533, Melchior Hoffman had suspended baptism because of the severe consequences to his followers. David Joris spiritualized the church and lived after 1544 as a respected citizen of Basel and cooperated closely with the Reformed Church while still propagating his views secretly. For Dirk Philips spiritualization was probably doubly troubling because his own brother, Obbe, had left the Anabaptist movement about 1539 and seems to have become a spiritualist while perhaps appearing to be a member of the Lutheran church in Rostock, Germany.[1]

The leading advocate of a spiritualist and individualist approach to Christianity was probably Sebastian Franck (1499-c. 1542), born in Donau-worth, Bavaria. He was a prolific writer and his writings were translated and distributed in the Netherlands. One of his foremost writings was his world *Chronicle* of 1531, an anti-Catholic history of the church, theology, and heresy.[2] Other major works available in the Dutch were his encyclopedic description of the whole earth in his *World Book*,[3] the *Golden Ark*,[4] and the *Closed Book With Seven Seals*.[5] It is probable that Dirk had access to a number of these writings. We find quotes from and references to the *Chronicle* in his writings.

Some of Sebastian Franck's writings survive only in Dutch translation. This is the case with the book *About Christ's Kingdom*, with the treatise "About the Promises of the New Testament" included in the back.[6] The same is true about the letters from Franck which Dirk wrote against.[7] According to J. ten Doornkaat Koolman, the two private letters of Franck were translated and given a foreword by Pieter Anastasius Overd'haghe (Hyperphragmus) of Zuttere in the Middle

Dutch language. They were published before 1564.⁸ They were the letters to Campanus⁹ and to "some in the Eyfelt." J. ten Doornkaat Koolman believes that Dirk Philips received a Dutch translation of the letters in 1567 and proceeded to respond immediately.¹⁰ The letters were sent to him at Emden, where he was staying, by some elders and brothers who requested that he respond for the simple who might be misled by the letters.

Franck's spiritualism and individualism threatened to undermine congregational life and discipline. There was growing resistance to the hard banning of Leenaert Bouwens (1515-1582), a fellow elder with Dirk and Menno Simons. Dirk Volkertsz Coornhert (1522-1590) of Haarlem became a powerful disciple of Franck with significant influence on the Mennonites after Dirk's death. The themes of a visible-invisible church [congregation] and the written [outer] versus spirit [inner] Word were in their seminal stages as Dirk faced the deceased Franck and the young Coornhert.¹¹

Dirk was old and sick. He was aware that his life energies were ebbing away. He apparently wrote the response and refutation hastily. The writing does not reflect his usual clear style. The sentence structure is not always clear, he introduces Germanisms, and his scriptural citations are not always accurate, perhaps because he was quoting from memory even more than usual.¹² Another uncharacteristic aspect of this writing is that he directly attacks another person, something he does not do in his other writings.

The answer to Sebastian Franck begins with a preface about the gifts of the Holy Spirit. It is directed more to the foreword of the publisher of the letters than to Franck. Dirk then proceeds to deal vigorously with the items in the letters and concludes with a brief statement of his own faith.

The intention of F. Pijper, editor of the BRN, in including the short "Appendix" here is unclear. In this translation it has been renamed "Fragment" and placed after Dirk's treatise "Omitted Writings About Ban and Avoidance" where it seems logically to belong.

The Text

A Response and Refutation to Two Epistles of Sebastian Franck, Briefly Prepared from Holy Scripture
D. P.

Philippians 3:17[-19]: Brothers, be my followers, and observe those who walk thus, just as you have us as an example, because many stray about which I have often told you; but now I also say it with weeping. They are the enemies of the cross of Christ whose end is damnation and whose belly is their God, and their honor becomes a shame, for those who are earthly minded.

2 Timothy 3:8[-9]: In the same manner as Jannes and Jambres opposed Moses, these also oppose the truth. They are persons of broken purposes, unfit for faith. But they will not succeed, for their foolishness will become evident to all people, as it was also predicted about them. /481/

Preface to the Christian Reader
D. P.

/483/ Out of grace, a fellow believer in Jesus Christ wishes all devout readers and lovers of truth, peace, mercy, and spiritual insight into the Lord's Word from God the Father, in the power and enlightenment of the Holy Spirit. Amen.

I can not hide from my dear brothers and all God-fruitful ones that a book by Sebastian Franck written some years ago has come to my hands. That same book was sent to me by some elders and brothers out of such reasons and intention that I should write an answer to it through God's grace for the sake of the naive and simple. On their behalf, although I am not well disposed for such work on account of my weakness and many tasks, and in addition have answered and developed the reasons clearly in other of my writings, especially in the "Apology or Reply" (according to my opinion), why one should separate oneself from all false worship and hypocrisy and only maintain what the Lord has commanded [I am reluctant to answer]. Nevertheless, as a clarification and establishing of all such things, and as instruction to all the good-hearted who seek to think properly, I certainly desire out of the offering of my heart to dear and chosen friends, as was said above, to answer to these booklets, so far as my God grants grace thereto. AMEN.

/484/ In the first place, the printer made a preface to the booklet, and told therein how in these dangerous perilous times the gifts of the Holy Spirit, Isa. 11 (to wit, wisdom, understanding, counsel, strength, ability, knowledge, and the fear of the Lord) is needed by every

Christian who has to distinguish various and manifold opinions and meanings in teachings and faith. The same I acknowledge with the printer, still with such distinction that Isaiah has actually spoken about Jesus Christ, the only born Son of God, since his words also announce: There shall come forth a shoot from the stump of Jesse, and a sprout out of his root will bring forth fruit on whom the Spirit of the Lord will rest, the spirit of wisdom and understanding, the spirit of counsel and strength, the spirit of the knowledge and fear of the Lord, that will enrich him in the fear of the Lord, so that he will not judge according to the sight of the eyes, nor punish according to what the ear hears, but he will judge the innocent with righteousness, and punish the poor in the land with righteousness, and he will slay the earthly kingdom with the staff of his mouth and kill the godless with the breath of his lips, Isa. 11:[1-4]; 2 Thess. 2:8.

That this prophecy applies entirely to Christ no one who is taught from God can doubt. Even so [no less] Christians must also have the same Spirit of the Lord. For while all the gifts of the Holy Spirit rest fully on Jesus Christ, which is also thereby portrayed that the Holy Spirit descended upon him in the form of the dove and remained, Matt. 3:16, and the joyfully rich oil was poured out so richly on the head /485/ of the spiritual Aaron, our only high priest from God the Father, so that it flowed on his beard and clothes; from this it is easy to understand that the Spirit of the Lord, which rests entirely on Jesus Christ without measure and in all divine fullness, the same also comes on all his Christians, and according to measure first on the ministers through whom he speaks, and his Word is in their mouth; and certainly thereafter on all his members who cling to the head, for the same Holy Spirit shares his gifts according to his will. But the gifts of the Holy Spirit about which Isaiah speaks are reported above, from which I desire to make a small explanation for all who fear God, through God's grace.

The first gift is wisdom coming out of the fear of God which distinguishes good from evil, the sweet from sour, the light from darkness, Eccles. 1; Prov. 1. Yes, the same teaches [us] to acknowledge Jesus Christ truly and to comprehend that in him lie hidden all the treasures of wisdom and the comprehension of God, that in him dwells the whole deity bodily, or essentially, that we receive from his fullness grace and truth, John 1. Thereby we recognize that eternal light, God himself, and therefore all worldly and human wisdom, philosophy, reason, and opinion are set aside and deemed foolishness compared to divine wisdom, 1 Cor. 1:[20ff.], which teaches us thus to know Jesus

Christ, the only born Son of the Father, that he has become for us from God as wisdom (that is, that we recognize God's power and truth, which knowledge is perfect wisdom), as righteousness (that is, that we through faith in his name are justified, Rom. 3:[21f.]), as deliverance (that is, that we through him are delivered and freed from sin, hell, the devil, and eternal death), and as sanctification, 1 Cor. 1:30, that is, that he has washed us through that water bath in the Word and has sanctified us through his Spirit, Luke 2:[29ff.]; Eph. 5; 1 Cor. 6, that is true wisdom which God gives to all true Christians through Jesus Christ in the Holy Spirit.

The second gift of the Holy Spirit is understanding derived out of the fear and wisdom of God, that one honors the Word of the Lord, and that one zealously observes the imprinting or imaging of the divine will through the Holy Spirit so that no error nor deceit breaks in beside the truth, 2 Cor. 11. For Satan can /486/ change himself into an angel of light, and his servants have learned that power and mastery from him. So then they come in the form of apostolic messengers, Matt. 7, and the wolf covers himself with sheep's clothing, in order that he may better and more handily show and extend his wicked rending character on the innocent sheep and lambs of Jesus Christ, Rev. 3. Therefore all Christians need to be understanding in God's words, recognize the wiles of Satan, know the mind of Jesus Christ, and always give their understanding under the mind and obedience of the Lord, yielded captive in all things, so they remain undeceived.

The apostle Paul also wrote to the Colossians about these two gifts of the Holy Spirit, Col. 1, in this manner and meaning; that he had prayed to God for them without ceasing, so that they might be filled with all kinds of spiritual wisdom and understanding. From this it was certainly clearly portrayed that wisdom and understanding belong together, although they are slightly different. For wisdom is to know God truly and fear him from the heart, but the fear of God, Jesus Sirach says, Ecclus. 18, causes one to do wisely in all matters, and learn to walk cleverly according to God's commands in all affairs. Guile is not wisdom, and godless vanity is not cleverness, for it is wickedness and idolatry, and vain foolishness and not wisdom. Understand that who applies the received wisdom of God rightly and puts it to work and earns profit with the Lord's pound, Matt. 25:[14-30], that one is called an understanding and faithful servant of the Lord.

In contrast, worldly wisdom and understanding is ignorance and folly, stubbornness, and contempt against God's Word. Of such wisdom and understanding, Christ spoke in his prayer of thanksgiving with which he thanked his Father, the Lord of heaven and earth, Matt. 11:25: that he concealed the hiddenness of faith and the truth of the gospel from the wise and understanding, and according to his divine will and pleasure revealed it to the small and simple ones. For they, through God's grace, are fit to learn wisdom and discipline, understanding, cleverness, righteousness, right and wrong, just as Solomon in the preface to his Proverbs said, Prov. 4, those who let themselves also be advised (understand with God's Word), that they hear the proverbs /487/ and their explanation, the teaching of the wise and their opposite.

Therefore [now] follows the third gift of the Holy Spirit, and it is counsel, that is, that the wise and understanding are sober and cautious in all matters, principally asking God's counsel and doing nothing outside of divine counsel. We have many beautiful figures and examples of this in the Old Testament, how the God-fruitful fathers, whenever they wished to begin and do something special, they first asked the Lord's counsel. For that the throne of grace was also foreordained by God, Exod. 37, and placed in the most holy place [so] that God himself would speak and answer them, Rom. 3. So Jesus Christ is now our throne of grace, set by the Father for us in the most holy place, that is in the time of grace, Heb. 5; Col. 3. Yes, [set] in heaven itself at the right hand of God's majesty, 1 Pet. 3, who has spoken to us through him, and given him a name which is called wonderful, counselor or counsel giver, strong God, eternal Father, Prince of Peace, Isa. 9:[6]. That now the name of the Son was given us from the Father, also counselor or counsel giver, signifies that wisdom counseled with God in the creation of all creatures and foreordaining of all things, and God through his wisdom, Prov. 8, has made all things well.

Therefore it is after all reasonable and right that all who fear God and who love righteousness and truth, that they also be advised with this wisdom, and that they not accept anything except what this wisdom (which is Jesus Christ) has taught and commanded. For all is included in him, and it has pleased the Father that in him all fullness dwells, and no one would come to God except through him; who rightly reflects on this has certainly taken counsel with God in Jesus Christ through the imparting of the Holy Spirit. Whoever does otherwise will experience, just as wisdom spoke, that those who despise as well as threaten, to wit, whenever it comes over them as a storm, that they will fear and will perish as the onrushing water will fall upon them whenever anxiety and need arrive. For they will (wisdom says) call upon me, but I will not hear them; they will seek me early and not find me, for they have hated the teaching, and the fear of the Lord has no value for them; they will not accept having his counsel, and they have despised his punishment. Therefore, they will also eat of the fruit of their being and be tired of their own counsels.

From this it is easy to understand that it will go badly with /488/ the despiser of wisdom, and how they come to eternal shame, although they are wise in their own eyes and understanding by themselves. There nothing comes to pass. So they are still, and especially all those who once acknowledge the truth and had accepted it. They are to be compared with the foolish and unwise maidens (who have lamps without oil), who thought they would enter in, understood through the door of grace, so it will be closed before them because they neglected the grace of the Lord or have received it in vain.

The fourth gift of the Holy Spirit is strength. That is, that one is strengthened with God's power in the inner person, about which strength the Holy Scripture relates and testifies in many places, both in figure and true being. It is painted many ways in the figure, especially in the example of the children of Israel, Exod. 16, and of the prophet Elijah. For just as the children of Israel were fed through that figurative heavenly bread many years in the wilderness, and thereby strengthened to come into the promised land, and just as the prophet Elijah wandered forty days and nights through the wilderness in the power of the food (brought to him by the angel) until he came to the mountain of God's Horeb, [1] Kings 19, so also the true Israelites are strengthened through that living bread, John 6, and through that baked bread that the angel of the Lord had laid by the head of Elijah, and through the water pitcher, that is, through the gospel of Jesus Christ (that once was regarded small, yes, despised by the self-directed and haughty of this world), and through the power of the Holy Spirit to come into the promised saving rest of God's kingdom, Heb. 4.

Here it serves well to notice the figure from the sixty strong ones who stood around the bed of Solomon, of the strong ones in Israel, and each one had his sword at his side on account of the fear in the night, Song of Sol. 3:[6f.]; which signifies that round about the congregation of the Lord Jesus Christ stand those who are strong in the faith, who are equipped with the armour of God to protect the congregation through the help of God before all the horrors of the night, that is, before the errors and spirits of darkness which are secretly round about to deceive the simple.

Further, it is necessary to notice here and to consider how the spiritual new birth has three states, John 2[3], to wit, childhood, youth, and mature age. Childhood signifies Christian simplicity, about which Jesus Christ /489/ talked in the gospel and spoke to his disciples: Truly, truly, I say to you, unless you be converted and become like little children, you shall not enter into the kingdom of heaven, Matt. 18:[3]. Paul agrees with that in writing to the Corinthians, 1 Cor. 14:20: Dear brothers, be not children in understanding, but in wickedness. And the apostle Peter called the Christians the firstborn children of God who should be desiring for that understanding, unadulterated milk, that they may grow up through it [1 Peter 2:2].

Youth signifies the power of faith, as the apostle John says: I have written to you, youths, for you are strong and the Word of God remains in you, and you have overcome the evil one, [1 John 2:14]. Mature age signifies the experienced minds which are inclined to acknowledge and to test good and evil, about which Paul reported and witnessed to the Corinthians and Hebrews, Heb. 5:[14]; Eph. 5:[15].

So now these three grades or stages must be found in Christianity and found in every Christian, that is childlike simplicity with regard to evil, the power of youth in faith and truth, and mature-aged wisdom and experience to recognize and judge everything individually.

The fifth gift of the Holy Spirit is knowledge or recognition, namely, that one profess and know that all good gifts come from above, that is, from the Father of eternal light through Jesus Christ in the Holy Spirit, James 1:[17], and on that account brought to their original source. Yes, to the foundation of all good, that is brought again to the eternal and only God, Jer. 2:[13ff.], and must be ascribed to him alone.

That says and means this much, that the gift of the Spirit exists in that one gives honor to God alone, Ps. 115, and that no creature accepts anything outside of God and the Word of his grace, but everyone says with the prophet at all times: Not us, Lord, not us, but give honor to your name. Also that is the true knowledge of the Holy Spirit, that one knows God in his eternal wisdom and ordaining, through opposition or contrast, that is recognized through paradox, thus one sets good against evil, the spirit against the flesh, righteousness against unrighteousness, light against darkness, belief against unbelief, Christ against Belial, and the temple of God against idols, 2 Cor. 6:[14-16]. Everything is distinguished well, and that is especially needed in these dangerously perilous times, since now so many /490/ lost spirits are abroad who mix up and confuse everything without understanding and distinction. Therefore a Christian cannot do better than that

Answer to Sebastian Franck / 453

he lays it all on the golden scale of the Holy Scripture and tests what is true or untrue, what conforms to or is against the truth. Thus he remains unchanged in his simplicity.

The sixth gift of the Holy Spirit is the fear of the Lord, about which the Holy Scripture testifies much. Especially Ecclesiasticus writes much in his book, Ecclus. 2, about it, and that all may be contained thus in a short summary: The fear of the Lord is the beginning of wisdom and is the foundation of the heart alone with the righteous and the believers. The fear of the Lord is the true worship of God. It keeps and makes the heart pious and happy, gives joy and blessing eternally. Fearing God is the wisdom which makes one rich and brings every good thing with it. It fills the whole house with its gifts and all the rooms with its treasures. The fear of the Lord is a crown of wisdom and gives peace and righteousness abundantly. This wisdom makes people truly wise. To fear the Lord is the true root of wisdom, and its branches grow or bloom eternally. The fear of the Lord drives out sin, but who is without this fear is not loved of God.

But that is now the true fear of the Lord, a serious questioning, reflecting on, and seeking for the good, holy, and perfect will of God, Rom. [12:1-2], and that a person observe himself carefully in all his thoughts, words, and deeds, so that he may be pleasing to his God. For the nature and character of the fear of the Lord is to avoid evil and to pursue the good. Such fear of the Lord brings the clean and perfectly pure recognition of the only and eternal almighty God and his divine being, that is, that one truly recognize God the Father and his only born son Jesus Christ, our Lord, and his Holy Spirit in name, power, office, and activity. Out of such acknowledgement comes faith, to wit, that blessed, dear and firm faith in God and his Word, a certain comprehension of heavenly and invisible matters, Heb. 11:[1], through which faith we become God's children, formed according to him through Jesus Christ in the Holy Spirit and being partakers of the divine nature, Gal. 3, Eph. 4 /491/. And when we are thus united with God, we must love him as the highest good, in certain confidence and living hope that God is the rewarder of all those who seek him in truth, Deut. 6:[5]; Matt. 22:[37]; Heb. 11:[6].

Therefore the fear of the Lord is truly the beginning of wisdom, Prov. 1:[7], and teaches persons to deny themselves, Matt. 16:[24] and with childlike reverence, worshiping and obedience, serving God in holiness and righteousness which is pleasing to him, and in complete surrender setting their entire hope on the living God and waiting in all patience for what God will do and work, Luke 1; 1 Pet.

1:[14]. Just as Abraham did when he offered his son to the Lord out of the fear of God through his faith in an undoubting hope, Gen. 22:[9ff.]; Heb. 11:[17ff.], that he, because of the promise of God, would receive him [i.e., his son] again. Therefore he was given to him from God as an example of the resurrection, with such witness that he certainly feared the Lord, while he had not spared his only son for the Lord's sake. Out of all this it is now easy to notice how much good the fear of the Lord accomplishes.

Whatever person now has these above mentioned gifts of the Holy Spirit, 1 Cor. 12, this one is in every way spiritually minded, and therefore can judge everything with God's Word and Spirit. Thus, the old crooked serpent, however deceitful it is, cannot deceive him or turn him aside from the simplicity which is there in Christ Jesus. For wherever this happens, there the Word of God is written with his finger in the table of the heart and imprinted there with the Holy Spirit. There the light is turned on and set upon the lampstand, Matt. 5:[15], and for its glory the darkness must give way. The mustard seed is put there in the garden or yard, Matt. 13:3[ff.], and thus grows up, that the birds of the air nest under its branches and live secure, Matt. 13:[31f.]. There the precious pearl is bought with the loss and forsaking of all temporal things, so they cannot therefore be taken back again. There the precious treasure is hidden in the field under the seed of God, that keeps the born-again person from all evil, Matt. 13:[44]; 1 Pet. 1:23.

In sum, there the person is united with God, 1 John 3:9, taught by God, comes to Jesus Christ as the only Shepherd and Bishop of our souls, 1 Pet. 2:[25]; John 10. His voice he knows well [over against] the stranger's voice, yes, and can distinguish it from the howling wolves. I mean the false scribes, teachers, and poets, /492/ they may be called whatever they are called, who embellish their works with high-sounding, flourishing words, and mislead with darker words. Therefore, neither Sebastian Franck nor any other subtle spirit can easily mislead a true Christian, for his trust rests in God. He sits under the protection of the Most High and rests under the shadow of the Almighty, Ps. 91:[1], the truth is his shield. Thus the fear of the night does not terrify him, nor the arrows that fly by day, nor the pestilence which sneaks in the darkness, [nor does he fear] the shadow which ruins the bright, clear day, nor the devil, that is, for the self-chosen spirituality and assumed form of holiness which appears beautiful externally, and yet is ugly before God.

So much I have wanted to indicate in Christian good intentions to good-hearted readers of the preface of the booklet, as an introduction so that the following might be better understood. Thereto may God give his grace. Amen.

Answer to the Two Letters of Sebastian Franck

/493/ But before I begin to answer these booklets, it is (according to my understanding) very necessary that one has a true touchstone to test everything, a plumbline to measure everything by, 1 Cor. 1, yes, to lay a good foundation upon which all may be well built and founded. But the only touchstone and the only plumbline is God's Word, and the only foundation is Jesus Christ, 1 Cor. 3:[11]. Therefore, for a person who seeks and loves his salvation, nothing is better nor more certain than to confess and to believe out of God's Word, that through Jesus Christ the healing grace, the perpetual unchangeable truth, an upright and perfect being has arisen and appeared, John 1; Titus 2:[11ff]., and that no change in any way may occur therein than his Word, his Spirit, and life, John 6; 15; Acts 20. And God, the heavenly Father, has revealed to us thereby his innermost will and entire counsel, and it may not be put forward in any other way, neither by angels, nor through persons (that the teaching of Jesus Christ is against or not in conformity—Gal. 1:[8]), or it will be accursed, as Paul explicitly said. Beyond this also no misuse of the Lord's ordinance can take it away entirely or make it to be suspended, for heaven and earth (the Lord himself says in the gospel) will pass away, but my Word will not pass away.

Therefore, it is unjust and false what Sebastian Franck presented, to wit, after the early and apostolic church has fallen, and the antichrist has destroyed everything and changed it into a misuse, thus now all ordinances of the Lord (which Sebastian Franck calls ceremonies or sacraments) should be suspended and are not to be respected. To that I answer in Christian /494/ simplicity that I rightly respect much less such audacious and blasphemous words of Sebastian Franck than he unjustly, yes, through puffed up self-conceit despises and rejects the ordinances of the Lord Jesus Christ and testifies with the Lord's own words, Matt. 5:18.

Furthermore, it is well to note that God blessed all his works from the beginning and viewed them as good, Gen. 2:[3], but the misuse which was introduced and came through the devil's guile and envy upon God's work, Wisd. of Sol. 2:[24], has certainly in part destroyed and defiled God's work, but has not entirely taken it away. For human beings are also God's work, Gen. 2:[7], originally created upright by God, made according to his image and likeness. But the person was deceived through the serpent's lie, Gen. 3:[1ff.], and came to ruin, Eph. 2:[2]. So God, therefore, has now not entirely rejected humanity, nor let the ruin remain, since it is his work. Rather he has reformed him and made him new according to the first creation through Jesus Christ and the Holy Spirit in the new birth through faith. Thus he is once again made in the image of God according to the inner person, in righteousness and truth, John 3:[1ff.]; Titus 3:[5]; 1 John [4:1ff.].

In the same way circumcision was given to Abraham from God as a sign of his covenant, Gen. [17:2, 9-14], but afterward through misunderstanding became a Jewish superstition or was not rightly used nor viewed by the pompousness of many, for they sought righteousness thereby, as the prophets complain over it in many places, and the Epistle to the Romans testifies to it, Rom. 2:[25ff.]. For circumcision has still remained according to its original institution and was used orderly according to the purpose of God in their children. For that is clearly to be noted that John the Baptist, yes, the child Jesus himself was circumcised on the eighth day according to the will of his heavenly Father and according to his ordinance. Luke 2:27.

Therefore, no one may reject or let fall into disuse any ordinance of God on account of misuse. But one is to deal rightly therewith according to the Lord's command and first formulation, for if circumcision (which was certainly figurative) had remained in its proper use by the God-fearing (as related above) until Christ fulfilled the law, took away the figures and shadows and in their place established the true being, how much more must then the ordinances of the Lord (which are certainly genuine) have their continuance and remain in existence since no one will come after Jesus Christ /495/ who with right will be able to change one tittle in his teaching, in his work and commands. For Jesus Christ (the apostle says, Heb. 13:8) is today and yesterday, and also eternally. Do not let yourself be misled by various and strange teachings.

Out of such reasons baptism and the Lord's Supper were restored to the former divine institution through God's grace, and it is fitting for all repentants and believers to receive it thus, just as John and Christ himself accepted circumcision.

It also says something more abominable in the booklet, yes, it has ascended out of the pit of the abyss as a smoke to darken the glory of the sun, Rev. 9:2, to wit, that according to Sebastian Franck's meaning, the ordinances of the Lord, especially baptism and the Lord's Supper, are doll's things and child's play (for these are his words), and that nothing is taken from the child but the doll and child's play, with which they have now played long enough, and God certainly permitted, yes, has given as an external sign a doll's play to the childish congregation; not that they were necessary for the kingdom of God, but since God himself has baptized for so many years with his Spirit and has fed us, the weak element need no longer be repeated—End, citation of Franck.

To that I say thus: It saddens my heart that I must relate and answer such awkward, blasphemous words. Nevertheless, on this account if I perhaps through God's grace may be of some service, I desire with the Lord's help to answer to it briefly. First, it is certainly and undoubtedly true that Jesus Christ is a born Son of the living God, John 1, a ray of the eternal light, an exact image of the Father, Heb. 1:[3]; Col. 1:[15], a reprint of his being, and a mirror of his divine glory, for the Father has expressly imaged himself in the Son and will be seen and acknowledged in him, Wisd. of Sol. 1. Therefore, the Lord spoke to Philip, who sees me, sees my Father also, John [14]; Rom. 5:8.

This Jesus Christ the Father has presented to us as a throne of grace and example to which we should conform, Matt. 3:17. God the Father has given him to us as Lord and Master, /496/ and witnessed about him, that he is his beloved Son in whom he is well pleased. Him we shall hear as the only born from the Father, who is full of grace and truth, and from his fullness we receive grace upon grace.

This one is the firstborn of all creatures, a Lord over all principalities and powers which were created through him, a head of his congregation, a light of the world. Who follows him shall not walk in darkness, but will have the light of eternal life.

Out of these reasons the apostle Paul has told so thoroughly in his epistles that in Jesus Christ the full deity suffered, dwelt bodily, Col. 2:9; 1:19, John 1:14, and that he has been from the very beginning, and that everything exists through him, John 1, that he is a Savior of his body and a finisher of our salvation. Therewith he lets us know that neither angels, nor persons, nor any creature, 1 Cor. 1 [?] is able to do anything against the Son of God, the Almighty Father's Word, wisdom and might, for everything was created through the Son, Heb. 1. He is the beginning, as was related above. He rules and maintains everything with his mighty Word. Therefore no wisdom, nor truth, nor righteousness, nor help, nor comfort for salvation is to be sought outside of him, much less to be found, John 16.

This Jesus Christ also said himself, that he is the way, the truth and the life, and that no one comes to the Father except through him. From this it follows that no one may come to God nor be saved unless he must accept the Lord Jesus Christ, believe in him, and follow in his footsteps. For he is the way with his holy life and example, showing us that we should be his followers. He is the truth with his sanctifying teaching which he has brought out of heaven from his Father. He is life with his grace, with his merit, yes, with his guiltless death (that is our life), and with his precious blood through which we obtain the forgiveness of sins, John 17; Col. 1; Eph. 1; John 1.

And herewith enough is shown and testified that Sebastian Franck, as a thoughtless and irresponsible person, called the signs and sacraments of the Lord doll's work and child's play. And in addition to this he writes that since the external services and sacraments (through the antichrist who destroys everything) after the apostles were not entirely observed, but rather were /497/ misused and defiled. Thus God has begun to judge everything through the Spirit in the truth with his spiritual churches which alone have signified the preceding signs instituted from the Lord. And [he] has permitted the external devil to do his will with the external and misused sacraments.

Answer

How has any God-fruitful person who was taught from God and has received anointing from him ever spoken and written so shamefully and blasphemously about the holy commandments as this Sebastian Franck does here? Or how has God ever permitted the external devil to complete his willfulness with the external and misused sacraments? Or how has God ever willed that after his ordinances were defiled or misused by the antichrist, that therefore a Christian should be allowed to maintain such unclean misuse or have fellowship with it? 1 Cor. 6; Gal. 5. What does the Scripture say about idolatry and limping about those who practice hypocrisy because of their belly? Will their part not be in the fiery lake which burns from fire and sulphur? Rev. 11:[7ff.]. This is the second death.

I now know certainly that many years ago I have seen, and read, and well understood a letter from Sebastian Franck (written to one of his particular and special friends) in which he allowed freedom for infant baptism and all hypocrisy with the world. And that out of a fear of people, that is, in order to keep peace with the world, John 12:[42]. It is impossible thus to please both God and people, to keep peace with

Jesus Christ and the world, Matt. 12:[25ff.], as Christ himself said to his disciples: My peace I give to you, my peace I leave with you, not as the world I give it to you, [John 14:27]; and at another place he said to his disciples: In me you have peace, in the world you have fear, [John 16:33]. And the apostle James testified with explicit words that friendship with the world is enmity with God, and whoever will be a friend of the world must be God's enemy, James 4:4.

But this is entirely against the feeling of the ingratiating Sebastian Franck, who places pillows under the heads of people /498/ and cushions under their arms, [Ezek. 13, 18]. He strengthens the hands of the wicked, so that no one turns away from his unrighteousness. He proclaims peace to those who have no peace, Jer. 6:14; Ezek. 13:10, and promises life to those who still have no life as long as they do not repent of their idolatry, dissimulation, and other unfruitful works of darkness which they have committed, Eph. 6:[6].

He teaches people a wide and broad way, and he is himself the pioneer and leader of the same which pleases the flesh well. Therefore he has so many followers, readers, and pupils who incline their ears after false freedom and seek to be fed according to the flesh. But what does Solomon say: It is a way which the people think is good, but it leads to the abyss. To this both Ecclesiasticus and the Lord Jesus Christ himself testify, and Solomon says further: It is a nature or tribe that lets itself think it is clean, and yet is not washed from its uncleanness. These are the false prophets about which Peter the apostle wrote who speak high-sounding and puffed-up words which they do not follow, who promise others freedom, and themselves are slaves of destruction, 2 Pet. 2:18, 19; they draw or entice to themselves the light-minded who once had escaped the impurity of the world but were once more cursed and won to the same thing, 2 Pet. 2:20. It thus happens to them according to the common adage, that the dog eats its own vomit again, and the sow wallows again in the muck when she was washed. Oh, how many (regretfully) experience this in our times! Prov. 16:18; Ecclus. 30, 31.

But now the crooked serpent comes and presents the passionate easy life with flowery words and excuses, hiding and deceiving to the flesh that flees the cross, that God does not need external things, but judges everything now in spirit and truth, baptizes and feeds everyone with Spirit and Word, and nothing is taken from the child except the doll, with which one has played long enough.

Answer

I certainly acknowledge that God is a spirit, and if someone would worship him, he must do it in spirit and truth. But just there is the question, whether the words of Jesus Christ are not spirit /499/ and life. If now the Word of the Lord is spirit and truth, then it follows that everything is spiritual and truthful which the Word of Jesus Christ teaches, and thereafter is rightly dealt with and done, John 5:[24], for what comes from the Spirit must of course be spiritual, and what the New Testament produces as truth, that is true and abiding, Luke 12:[8ff.].

Again, the forerunner and messenger John the Baptist, has he not from his mother's body been gifted and filled with the Holy Spirit? Has he not walked in the spirit and power of Elijah, so that he makes everything right, smoothing the way of the Lord, converting the heart because he should prepare an acceptable people for the Lord? Thus also he was sent from God to baptize with water to repentance and to teach belief in the Lord Jesus, Acts 1:[5]; Matt. 3. Yes, was not the Lord Jesus Christ himself baptized by John? And his apostles in the same way, which the Lord has also seriously commanded to baptize the repentant and believing, and to teach the baptized to keep all things that he had commanded? Matt. 28:[19]; Mark 16:[16]. Was the Lord Jesus Christ, during the time he was teacher, baptizer, feeder, and everything, not also in and by the believers as he is now, or might be at any time? Luke 3. Did the apostles not lay hands on the baptized and believers and they received the Holy Spirit? Acts 8:19. Has not the apostle Paul repeated the command to baptize those who were thus baptized by John? And still had they not been acknowledged and received by the Holy Spirit so that they might receive the gift of the Holy Spirit through the laying on of hands after the more acceptable baptism, as the apostle Peter testified? And why does one need many words since the Lord Jesus Christ himself, in whom the fullness of the Spirit dwells, and his messengers who were the first to receive the Spirit, and were confirmed with great power from on high, have received the sacramental sign of the Lord, used it, and commanded the believers to use it? Acts 2:[38]; John 1:[31]; Col. 2:[12]; Rom. 8; James 1.

Therefore, it is an intolerable blasphemy of God that Sebastian Franck, a mocker of God and his ordinances, writes out of the presumption of his heart that a child is not deprived of anything but a doll, considers the early apostolic church as children who played with dolls, but he attributes to himself adult wisdom, valor, and perfection, /500/ as though no such spirit of truth had been with John, or Jesus Christ himself, or with the early apostolic congregation because they used external signs. If then the Lord's signs are thus nothing and powerless, so that neither Spirit nor truth is in them to the extent that they were used rightly with genuine faith and everything that belongs to it, what abominable pomposity, presumption, and blindness that is. Which presumption is but dust and ashes?

The faithful and pious Abraham feared to speak to the Lord in the manner of prayer and supplication since he certainly recognized his own nothingness compared to the most high divine majesty. But this Sebastian Franck is wise in his own eyes. Nevertheless, before God and every right understanding person, [he is] unwise. And he criticizes every person but neither sees nor knows his own weaknesses. He does not fear to contradict the Lord Jesus Christ and to reject his ordinances or to consider them child's play. Oh, bold presumption, yes, nonsense of the heart.

Further, the booklet of Sebastian Franck reports that the congregation of the Lord which existed after the apostles' time has fallen and thereby the antichrist has destroyed everything. Still, no one must undertake to set the fallen worship up again except he has a special call from God to do it. And since no one (according to his opinion) has such a call, it will remain with the antichristian and idolatrous misuse of the signs and the devil may have his way with them. Thus far Sebastian Franck, Matt. 24; 2 Pet. 2; 1 Tim. 4:[1ff.].

Answer

That the congregation of the Lord fell after the apostles' time I certainly acknowledge, for the Holy Scripture testifies to that in many places, 2 Tim. 3; 2 Pet. 2; 1 John [2:18ff.]; Acts 20:[20f.], but that therefore persons will remain [with] and maintain the false worship, that is untrue and a root of idolatry. The reason is this: What God has commanded that he will have observed, as it is written, Ps. 118; Deut. 4:12[f.], that God has firmly commanded the ordering of his commandments, and that one should neither add to nor subtract from God's Word, Prov. 30:[6]. From this it follows that God permits no misuse of his ordinances, and that no Christian may have any fellowship therewith since such misuse is contrary to the Word and command of God, which is from the evil one, Eph. 5. For who is not with me, says the Lord in the Gospel, /501/ that one is against me, and who does not remain with me, that one scatters, Matt. 12:[30]. No one can serve two masters, for he must love one and hate the other; he must be devoted to one and despise the other, [Matt. 6:24].

Again, they serve God in vain with human teachings and commandments, Luke 18:[18ff.]. Yes, it is an abomination before the Lord, for what is highly prized by people is an abomination before God. Now human teachings and commandments are also highly prized by the world, for on its behalf God's commands are put back, just as the Lord remonstrated the Pharisees; therefore, they are an abomination before God, Matt. 15:[1-9]. The history of Saul and many other biblical and scriptural histories testify to this very clearly, 1 Kings 15. Therefore it is not necessary to write much about it.

To continue, as far as the divine calling is concerned, as is brought up by Sebastian Franck, my simple answer that must be acknowledged and observed thereby is whether a minister of God was sent or not when he was called in orderly fashion by his congregation, so that he is fiery in love along with Jeremiah and Paul through the moving of the Holy Spirit and cannot be silent, when he teaches God's Word truly, produces fruit from it, and himself walks according to it in his weakness through the Lord's grace.

As I, with the aid of God Almighty, have shown out of his Word well enough in my booklet about the "Sending of Preachers," I will let it remain with that, for those of understanding will certainly be at peace with the simple truth. But the quarrelsome, the conceited and spoiled ones cannot be satisfied. Therefore I let them go and say with the prophet, what will die, will die. And as is written in the Revelation of John, Rev. [22:11], he who does evil is still evil, and whoever is dirty, he will become still more dirty.

Again, Sebastian Franck has mentioned Elijah several times /502/ in his writings, as if he did not reinstitute the fallen worship in Israel without the special command of God. To that is answered: that Elijah did not do anymore than he had testified and pointed apostate Israel to God who is Lord, pointing, to wit, to the God of Abraham, Isaac, and Jacob, and that they ought to serve him alone as he had commanded, [1 Kings 18]. Now it had to do with external sacrifices in Elijah's time, which were instituted from God as a figure of the true being. Elijah reinstated the same worship and no other and testified thus to Israel that the God of Abraham, Isaac (and Jacob) is the only, true, living God and Lord, and that Baal was an idol. All his prophets and priests were false.

All who now follow the example and model of Elijah out of divine zeal and calling seek the honor of God and the salvation of souls. How can anyone with any scriptural modesty and truth judge otherwise than that they are commissioned from God and are motivated thereto by his Spirit? Has it ever in truth been heard or found from the beginning of the world that a false prophet who runs of his own accord[13] has taught rightly and sought the honor of God therewith rightly? Does not the Lord compare the false prophets to ravenous wolves who come in sheep's clothing, that is, under a pious appearance [but] seek nothing other than to rend the sheep? Matt. 7:[15]. For a thief (that is, a false prophet), says the Lord, does not come except to steal, to murder, and to destroy, John 10:[10]. In summary, the intention of a false prophet is and always remains to take the people away from the living God and to lead them to idolatry. In contrast, the true prophets intend to demolish and root out every planting which God the Father has not planted, and to rebuild and plant everything which God has commanded, Jer. 1:[10]; Matt. 15:[13ff.].

Finally, he [Sebastian Franck] would thus have God's congregation invisible among all peoples, that is, scattered under the name of Christians, Jews, /503/ heathen, and Turks. And he admonishes Johan Campanus and those in Eyfel that they shall hold as a brother everyone who fears God among all people, although they certainly have not heard the word baptism, yes, even if he knows nothing about the history or Scripture of the Lord Jesus Christ. Anyone who wants to may read the words of Sebastian Franck himself, for I am sorry to relate them, since they are such an abomination to me, and I thus answer them briefly.

The congregation of the Lord, although it is certainly based in the Spirit and truth, is nevertheless visible, as I have also explained in the booklet about the "Sending of Preachers," and still declare. The reasons are as follows: First, the name congregation thus shows that it is not only invisible but also visible, Eccles. 1; 1 Tim. 3:16. For it [is called] "ecclesia," that is, a gathering or meeting, and those who speak to the meeting are called "Ecclesiastes." Therefore, Solomon is also called "Ecclesiastes" since he spoke to the assembly or congregation of Israel. Now it is certain and incontrovertible that just as Solomon the preacher was visible, the congregation has also been visible, to which he has spoken.

Second, Christ Jesus himself chose his apostles and disciples and gathered them as a congregation, John 15:[16]. And he was, after all, not invisible to Jerusalem and Judah.

Third, the apostles gathered a congregation according to the command of the Lord out of all the people through the preaching of the gospel in faith and truth, Matt. 28:[19-20]; Mark 16:[15-16], and through the true Christian baptism, power, and unity of the Holy Spirit. It has not been invisible, for it has not sent its letters in general, to all peoples, neither wrote in such manner, but in specifics or addressed by name to the believers and God-fearing, and called the places and many persons addressed by name. How is it then possible that it would all be invisible?

Furthermore, some gospel parables testify to everything that was said earlier, to wit, from the seine or net which was cast into the sea, and captured therein all /504/ kinds of desirable fish, Matt. 13:[47-50]. Again, about the king who prepared a wedding party for his son and sent out his servants to call so many people (yes, the good and the bad) so that his house would be full, Matt. 22:[1ff.]. Again, about the noble who traveled into far lands. He called his servants and gave them his goods, saying, deal with these or put them to work until the time that I return. Yet one servant was lazy or slothful or a knave, and hid the Lord's money in the earth, Matt. 25:[14ff.]. Again, about the ten maidens, of whom five were wise and five foolish, Matt. 25:[1ff.].

Since now the Lord Jesus Christ himself compared the kingdom of heaven, that is, the preaching of the gospel, the congregation, and the trustworthy grace of God, to the above mentioned parables or thereby expressed and indicated it, it thus follows from it incontrovertibly that not only the pious but also the evil ones were found in the congregation, Ps. 12. But they shall not remain therein, for here on earth they must be excluded and separated through God's Word as much as is possible for the congregation, 1 Cor. 5:[12f.] and hereafter in perfection when the sheep shall stand at the right hand and the goats on the opposite or left hand. Then they shall hear the sentence and judgment which will differ so much from each other, Matt. 25:[31ff.]. Therefore the congregation of the Lord cannot be invisible, since the bad or wicked are separated therefrom and the pious remain therein.

About all this the almighty God sent his only born Son into the world so that whoever believes in him will be saved and have eternal life, John 3:[16]; 1 John 3:6. But whoever does not believe in him, that one is already judged and will not see that life, for the wrath of God remains on him. One reads about this in the evangelist John, John 14:[8ff.], yes, the entire Holy Scripture of the New Testament which would be too long to relate. Thus one will discover that no one may come to God and be saved except through Jesus Christ, that is, through a true faith in his name, Heb. 11; John 3:[36].

From this it follows then that it is nothing but nonsense that Sebastian Franck presents and advises that one must acknowledge as brothers the heathen, Turks, Jews, and also those who know no history or Scripture about the Lord Jesus Christ so long as they fear God. Yes, dear reader, how shall anyone fear God whom he does not know? Or how can anyone fear and confess God /505/ the Father who does not believe in Jesus Christ whom the Father has given as a Savior and Reconciler? Or how will anyone be born out of God except through faith in Jesus Christ? John 1; 1 John 5. Or how will anyone become a brother and member in Christ Jesus who was not born out of God, which birth cannot occur except as already was reported, to wit, that as many of them as have accepted the Word and light of Jesus Christ, these he has given power to become children of God, [1] John 2. And at another time: everyone who believes that Jesus is the Christ and the Son of God, that one is born out of God, 1 John 5:[1].

Out of all this it is easy to understand that the two letters of Sebastian Franck are nothing but slanderous writings and are entirely contrary to the truth and faith, full of deadly poisons, gathered together from many cunning and subtle Turks out of a high flying spirit which will tramp over all others here.

Finally, thus the sum and meaning of all that has been said is, first, that the gospel of Jesus Christ is the right truth and the only basis on which everything must be built and constructed, 1 Cor. [3:11]. Outside of the truth and this foundation there is also nothing which may exist before the Lord.

Second, that faith and a right confession of God and Jesus Christ is that one keep his commandments, and walk as he walked, and that one remain in his teaching, for whoever trespasses and does not remain in the teaching of Jesus Christ has no God, John 17:[6ff.]; 1 John 2:[3ff.]; 2 John 2[ff.].

Third, thus Jesus Christ with his teaching, life, and example is our Teacher, Leader, and Pioneer. We must hear the same and follow him. He is the true light come into the world. Whoever follows him will not walk in darkness, but will have the light of eternal life, John 14; Matt. 15; John 18; Luke 12.

Fourth, thus the words of the Lord Jesus Christ are spirit and life. Therefore, they also show their nature in all believers, bringing the Holy Spirit into the heart and giving eternal life, John 6. For the Spirit makes alive, and in that Word is life, and that life is the light of the salvation of humanity. Thus anyone who now accepts that Word would be /506/ through it enlightened by God. That one is saved and an heir of eternal life, John 6.

Fifth, the congregation is then an assembly of the repentant, God-fearing, believing, and born-again people of God who are obedient to the gospel and baptized as one body through one Spirit, 1 Cor. 12:[12f.], the spiritual Eve from the heavenly Adam, Gen. 3:20, the free Sarah who receives from God the Father the true Abraham, Rom. [4-5]; Gal. 3:[6ff.], the seed of the godly Word out of which the children of the marriage were born through a right belief in Jesus Christ, without which no one may please God nor be saved. That is certain and true.

Herewith I command all God-fearing readers, my dear brothers and friends in the Lord Jesus Christ, and desire in friendliness that they will take my simple answer to the two slanderous letters of Sebastian Franck with good intentions, reading with a devout heart, judging everything with the Lord's Word and Spirit. The God of all grace and the only wise God give wisdom and understanding in all godly affairs to all those who desire it from their heart, 1 Pet. 5:[10]; 1 Tim. 1. AMEN.

D.P.

ENDNOTES

1. See Williams and Mergal, *Spiritual and Anabaptist Writers*, pp. 204-225.
2. *Chronica, Tijtboeck ende geschiet bibel, van aenbegin Tot in dit teghenwoordich. MDXXVI jaar . . . Door Sebastanum Franck van Word, . . . An. MDXXXI.* The 1595 edition has been used in the preparation of this document.
3. *VVerelt-Boeck, Spieghel ende Beeltenisse des gheheelen Aerdtbodems, van Sebastiaen Franck van Word in vier Boecken (te weten, in Asiam, Aphricam, Europam, ende Americam) ghestelt ende afghedeylt. . . . Delft, Aelbert Heyndrickxz. . . . Anno MDLXXXIII.* This was included in one volume with the *Chronicle* in the 1595 edition.
4. *Die Gulden Arcke waer in de keern ende beste hooftsprueken der Heyliger Scrift, der ouder Leeraers ende Vaders der Kercken: oock der verlichte Heydenen ende Philosophen (daer aen den knoop ende steck onser salicheyt leyt:) Ende daer in der Christenen gelooue, als in eenen angel gaet) gedragen, veruaet ende Ingelijft zijn. Seer nut voor alle menschen. Door Sebastianum Frank van Word, 'tsamen ghestelt . . . . An. MDLX.*
5. *Concordantie Sebastiani Franck, Ofte het Verseghelde met seuen Seghelen besloten Boeck, dat rechts niemandt op doen, verstaen ofte lesen kan, dan het Lam, ende die met Teecken thau geteykent sijn. . . . . Ende nu eerstmael in Nederduyts vertaeld door D.W.C. . . . . Tot Haarlem, by Francoys Beyts, Anno 1618.*
6. *Van het rijcke Christi, Een stichtelyck Tractaet, allen eenvoudighen Christenen tot onderwijsinghe, ende den Gheestelijcken verlichteden Menschen, te oordeelen int Licht ghegheven, door den verlichteden ende van Godt-gheleerden Sebastaen Franck van Werdt, ...Tot Goude, bij Jasper Tournay. Anno 1611.* In the back placed on fol. 78-81: *Vande beloftenissen des nieuwen Testaments ende van het Rijck Christi.* Cf. A. Hegler, *Sebastian Franck*, in the *Realencyclopadie für protestantische Theologie*, Leipzig, 1899, Bd. VI, pp. 142-150
7. F. Latendorf, *Sebastian Franck's erste namenlose sprichwörtersammlung*, Paesnek, 1876, p. 365.
8. See Koolman, p. 174, especially notes 63-64.
9. The letter to Johannes Campanus (c. 1500-1575) is dated February 4, 1531. The Dutch version lists February 7 as date. It is reprinted in both Dutch and High German texts in Manfred Krebs and Hans Georg Rott, *Quellen zur Geschichte der Täufer*, I. Teil, Bd. VII, 1959, pp. 302-325. Of importance are the critical textual observations of Hegler-Koehler in *Beiträge zur Geschichte der Mystik*, Berlin, 1906, pp. 90-97. The letter to Campanus was translated by Heinold Fast into modern German in *Der Linke Flügel der Reformation*, Bremen, 1962, pp. 219-233 and into English by Williams in *Spiritual and Anabaptist Writers*, pp. 145-160. Details about where the original or translated versions of Franck's letters can be found are listed in Williams' volume, pp. 147-148. See also Koolman, p. 189, note 65. It is not clear whether Campanus was an Anabaptist or not, but his influence on the Wassenburg preachers and the events of Münster was significant. He seems to have been antitrinitarian.
10. Koolman, p. 175.
11. For a helpful treatise on Franck-Mennonite relationships, see Toews, *Sebastian Franck.*, especially pp. 266ff. Also Hegler, *Geist und Schrift bei Sebastian Franck*, and Teufel, *Landräumig*.
12. Examples of the Germanisms include hercomen, rijtenden, daerom so, aen vele plaetsen, daer met stemt [stimmt], ghebeeldet, etc. The fact that he had spent many years in the Danzig (Gdansk) area will have contributed to this. See also BRN X, p. 478, notes 2 and 1.
13. *Van sick selfs gheloopen*, i.e. without being sent. The accountability of a minister to a congregation(s) was important to Dirk.

THE FRISIAN—FLEMISH DIVISION

A. Introduction

Dirk Philips' last days were disturbed by a growing conflict within the Dutch Anabaptist movement. The conflict began between the Flemish who had fled from Flanders to Friesland and the native Frisians; in that process the different economic, cultural, and spiritual traditions were forced to merge.

One example, among others, may illustrate the problem. Flanders was a primary weaving center for sheeps' wool from England. The center also dyed cloth. Flemish people thus seemed to prefer brightly colored clothing. The more stolid Frisians, on the other hand, were famous for their agriculture and large farms. Consequently Flemish Mennonite immigrants tended to ask why their Frisian hosts had such large farms, while the Frisians wondered about the worldly clothing of the Flemish.[1]

But there were deeper causes involving personality conflicts, power in decision making in the congregations, and different views about the function and authority of leadership. Would Leenaert Bouwens or Dirk Philips inherit the "mantle" of Menno Simons (d. 1561), especially with Dirk spending most of his time in distant Danzig-Prussia? For Dirk the central issue was the authority of the Bible itself.[2] A certain anti-clericalism was evident; any tendency towards hierarchy or episcopacy was suspect within the congregations. Positively this might be stated as an affirmation of the priesthood of all believers. In any case, the events of the division soon led to where "Frisian" and "Flemish" no longer referred to geographic origins but to ideological group and party loyalties.

The account may best begin in 1560.[3] In that year the ministers and church councils of four Frisian congregations (which included many Flemish members) in Franeker, Harlingen, Leeuwarden, and Dokkum, for reasons of unity and combined strength and, perhaps, simply the result of an "old boy" network, drafted a nineteen-point statement of cooperation known as the *Covenant* (Verbond der vier steden), also called *Ordinantie* (ordinance).[4] It provided for the sharing of ministers, relief aid to the poor, and other channels of cooperation. This arrangement was arrived at by the ministers and church councils alone, without the knowledge of the congregations involved and without invitations to other congregations.

Subsequently the Flemish in Franeker wanted their own ministerial worker and installed Jeroen Tinnegieter, formerly of Flanders. The Harlingen, Leeuwarden and Dokkum leaders, especially Ebbe Pieters, the elder of Harlingen, felt him to be unqualified. This led Franeker to have a grievance against Ebbe Pieters, feeling that he had rejected the Flemish as a group. Under the earlier polity of congregational autonomy this would have made little difference, but now the covenant gave the other congregations powers to intervene. This led Jeroen and others at Franeker to decide to withdraw from the covenant. At an evening meeting in early spring in 1566, Jeroen and his colleagues suspended six council members who opposed withdrawal. All of this was to remain secret.

The following morning Ebbe Pieters traveled with the tow boat to Leeuwarden through Franeker. When a member of the Franeker council came on board, he told Pieters of what had happened the night before. Pieters, in turn, spread the news in Leeuwarden. The Flemish now had two accusations against Pieters—first that he had lied when he reported that the six council members had been banned when, in fact, they had only been suspended and, second, that he was inciting to quarrels and disunity.[5]

The accusations were presented to Ebbe Pieters in writing on May 13, 1566. He was summoned to appear before Jeroen and his colleagues to defend himself. After considerable negotiation, Pieters indicated a readiness to appear before a small group in Harlingen. Hoyte Renix of Bolsward was to lead the hearing and, with a few ministers, pronounce judgment. It needs to be noted that Hoyte Renix had no assignment from his congregation to undertake the task.[6]

An assembly of forty persons, in part from Franeker and in part from other places, heard the response of Pieters and declared him innocent by a vote of twenty-five to fifteen. Jeroen had meanwhile made a quick trip to Flanders and on his return decided to overturn the verdict by having a trial before the entire congregation. The meeting took place on August 7, 1566, but not more than thirty persons appeared out of a membership of four hundred. The meeting was inconclusive. After Pieters left the meeting, those remaining proceeded to ban him that same night. Six men were appointed to announce this to him, which they did early the next morning. They aroused him from his bed and "declared all such ban and separation under his eyes." The Frisian party responded by excluding a few adherents of the Flemish at Harlingen and at Franeker.[7]

The controversy was not simply a personal conflict or a conflict between the Frisians and the Flemish, though that certainly complicated the problem. It was also a conflict over the relationship between a minister and the congregation. The defenders of the Covenant of the Four Cities stood over against those who believed in the autonomy of the local congregation and in congregational, rather than clerical, control. They objected to the secrecy with which the covenant was surrounded. Ebbe Pieters belonged to those who supported the covenant.

The issue was illustrated more clearly in the case of Leenaert Bouwens and his congregation at Emden. Leenaert traveled to Friesland, leaving his congregation repeatedly on his own authority. He apparently liked the hospitality he found in Friesland and enjoyed being entertained by the people there. When the congregation at Emden became aware of his frequent absences and tried to set some limits to his travel, he refused to submit to their desires. He told them he would travel to Friesland as often as he was invited, whether they approved of it or not. His view of the relationship between a minister and the congregation was not shared by others. For this reason a gathering of seven teachers, including Dirk Philips, met at Emden in 1565 and removed the teaching and baptizing office from him. He accepted the suspension, but it is noteworthy that he left Emden and took up residence at Harlingen, that is, in the immediate neighborhood of his friend Ebbe Pieters. Although he lived at Harlingen with no official function, he gained a significant following.[8]

The dispute escalated with all kinds of other issues entering into it. One banning followed another. Dirk Philips wrote his "epistle written to the four cities out of pure brotherly love in order to admonish the quarrelers to a Christian peace and a God-saved life" to try to minister to the situation as reports of the disturbances reached him in Danzig.[9] The tone of the letter is conciliatory. He had reflected long and hard on the best means to improve the situation. He certainly entreated the brothers in Friesland to make peace with one another. Earlier persons had praised the fatherland because of the growth of the congregations. Now, if the quarreling did not cease, he wrote, the opposite would be heard, to the great sorrow of many pious ones.

Dirk also appended a copy of the 1565 agreement to his epistle.

It is the general declaration signed by the six ministers (plus Dirk) who had participated in the decision regarding Leenaert Bouwens in 1565. He thought it had relevance because it dealt with the calling and election of ministers and teachers. The call and election is of two sorts: "The first and principal one is from God, through his Word and Spirit, through which he as the Father of his household sends forth his servants and impels them into his harvest, that they gather the wheat into his barn." "The second calling and election of teachers and ministers happens by the congregation, through God's inspiration and command, with unanimous vote of the congregation, also with fasting and praying. Such chosen ministers are established by the elders with the laying on of hands."[10]

Dirk Philips no doubt saw a close connection between the conflict of Leenaert Bouwens with his congregation at Emden and the dispute between Jeroen Tinnegieter with his Flemish colleagues and Ebbe Pieters with the Frisian party. As events were to demonstrate, his letter did not accomplish its purposes, for the conflict deepened and eventually the split widened.

In December of 1566, two mediators from Hoorn, Jan Willems and Lubbert Gerrits, both elders ordained by Dirk, were summoned and managed to work out a four point "Compromise," based on what might be called "binding arbitration." It was signed on the nineteenth of that month. They had worked patiently and carefully, but their sympathies were probably more with the Frisians than with the Flemish. Finally reconciliation was achieved, and a meeting to publically finalize the new unity was convened at Harlingen on Saturday, February 1, 1567, with many congregations sending representatives. In an opening statement, Willems admonished those present not to weigh every issue on a golden scale for right or wrong, but to forgive and ask forgiveness. The leading Frisians and Flemish were then asked to kneel as the final and formal act, presumably to have forgiveness pronounced and celebrated. This they did, asking each other for forgiveness and forgiving each other. Then the Frisians arose. As the Flemish were about to do likewise, Willems said no, that since they had begun the quarrel, they needed to be helped up, presumably by himself and the Frisians. This unexpected accusation led to complete confusion, anger, and chaos, tragically ending the "Compromise."[11]

It seemed to some, finally, that the only remaining hope was to invite their senior elder Dirk Philips, who had been working in Prussia since about 1550, to come as mediator. It appears that Dirk had been waiting for just such an invitation. In a letter of 17 April 1567,

Hoyte Renix, presumably writing in the name of the Frisians and perhaps others, invited Dirk to come to Emden. He and his family will receive a most cordial welcome provided that he agrees with the Frisians; if not, he would be of no help.[12] There is reason to believe that Dirk was neutral on the "Covenant" (Ordinance) and, perhaps, on the "Compromise" issues. If he was suspect, would Hoyte Renix and the Frisians have invited him at all? Their stipulation for his coming, however, indicates some uncertainty about his position. Outerman reports that Dirk had earlier said of the "Covenant" that "the congregation of God can be built by [through] it."[13] It does seem that Dirk changed his mind, which may have happened when he came to Emden and found new information.

J. ten Doornkaat Koolman believes that Dirk came as early as May 1567. He ends his 7 June 1567 letter to Hoyte Renix with the words "written and sent in Friesland," presumably Emden.[14] Meanwhile he asks, even demands, that Hoyte and all key leaders involved in the dispute cease their acts of ministry, that is, receiving or disciplining members, etc., until they have explained their actions ("purged themselves") before him and have been exonerated. The congregations in Prussia gave him and his two traveling companions their blessing and specific instructions on how to proceed, particularly that they should listen carefully to both groups. His insistence that they meet together, meet face-to-face, seems to have been a part of his own strategy conviction.

On Dirk's arrival at Emden, the Franeker and Harlingen leaders urged him to come to Harlingen but he refused, insisting that Willems, Gerrits, and others come to Emden. It may have been that fear of the Inquisition led him to this; or that he was old (63), tired, and had already come a long way; or it may have been part of his strategy to have the relevant parties come to Emden, which they eventually did after at least three letters from Dirk. In fact at least thirteen men came to Emden, but Dirk refused to see most of them, referring to them as "a large group" (een grooten hoop), perhaps perceived by them as a derogatory remark. His writings leave no doubt that whatever his early view of the issues may have been, he now asserted unequivocally that the covenant, the "Compromise" which Willems and Gerrits had achieved, and the judgment (sentence) they had passed were all unscriptural and to be rejected. There was, he asserted, only one covenant, the divine one, and nothing should be allowed to take its place.

The end result was tragic. Dirk was unable to initiate helpful discussions. It became clear that he had sided with the Flemish though his long-standing position would seem to be closer to the Frisian preference for centralized authority, which he himself also represented. Two years earlier (1565) he, with six others, had silenced the powerful Frisian elder Leenaert Bouwens;[15] now he banned the others, in particular Willems and Gerrits, as well as his former friend Hoyte Renix. The Frisians followed suit and banned the Flemish and, in a letter dated July 8, 1567, Dirk himself. Congregations who tried to remain neutral were banned by both parties.

This division was the most serious among the Dutch Mennonites (Doopsgezinden) and spawned other schisms. Efforts to heal it were made in 1569, with the 1574 Peace of Humster (Humstervrede), at Hoorn in 1576, at Emden in 1578, and at Haarlem in 1582. Even a confession of guilt by ministers of both parties in 1589 failed to bring unity. Nanne van der Zijpp wrote, "In the Netherlands it took 200 years to wipe out the last signs of the division."[16] But the ripple effects continued. It has been claimed by P. M. Friesen that traces of the dispute could be found among the Mennonites who left for the Ukraine in 1789.[17] Dirk died within a year in the Emden area in March 1568.[18]

ENDNOTES

1. I. H. V. P. N. [Carel van Ghendt], *Het beginsel en voortganck der geschillen, scheuringen, en verdeeltheden onder de gene die Doops-Gesinden Genoemt worden.* (1615) Amsterdam: Tymon Houthaak, 1658, in BRN VII (1910), p. 535.

2. Kühler, *Geschiedenis* I, pp. 395ff. believed that the origin of the entire Frisian—Flemish division lay in a power struggle between Leenaert Bouwens and Dirk Philips. His sources, as he himself argues, are reliable including especially Jacques Outerman, *Onder verbeteringhe. Verclaringhe met bewijs* ... (1609). idem, *Copye eens briefs* ... (1634). Syvaert Pieters, *Corte aenwijsinghe* ... (1634).

3. The fullest account of the origins of the division is found in J. G. de Hoop Scheffer, "Het verbond der vier steden," DB (1893) 1-90. The exact time, even year, of this event is not fully clear, but 1560 seems most probable. See also "Flemish Mennonites" and "Frisian Mennonites" in ME 2:337ff. and 413ff. respectively. It is instructive, for example, to compare the different worship patterns as described in the two ME articles, patterns which have continued among some Mennonites to the present time.

4. In part to avoid comparison with the increasingly dominant Covenant theology of the Reformed Church (Bullinger), but also to deny any comparison with Anabaptist radicals who had called themselves "Covenanters" (bondgenooten) even before the Münster 1534-1535 episode. Soon a particular criticism of using the term Covenant came from those who believed it was being elevated to a status comparable to the Old and New Testament covenants. I. H. V. P. N. [Carel van Ghendt], *Het beginsel en voortganck der geschillen,* BRN VII, p. 536; cf.: Dirk below, pp. 487-519, in *A Short But Fundamental Account.*

5. I. H. V. P. N. *Het beginsel,* p. 25, BRN VII, p. 537f. Jacques Outerman, *Noodtwendighe Verklaringhe* ... (1596), Haerlem: 1634, p. 15. Idem, *Onder verbeteringhe.* (1609), art. 95, 99, 100, 119.

6. J. Outerman, *Noodtwendighe Verklaringhe,* p. 24. Idem. *Onder verbeteringhe* (1609), art. 120-126. BRN X, pp. 512ff.

7. I. H. V. P. N. *Het beginsel der scheuringen,* p. 26, cf.: BRN VII, p. 538. Cf: BRN X, p. 513. Syvaert Pieters, *Corte aenwijsinghe,* p. 20f.

8. I. H. V. P. N. *Het Beginsel der scheuringen,* p. 21. cf.: BRN VII, p. 532ff. Bouwens sided strongly with the Frisians. He was a talented and "charismatic" leader, unduly harsh in his banning and given to working rather independently. He did not seem to acknowledge accountability to any one congregation but saw himself as "everybody's minister." He normally did not consult with a congregation before placing someone under the ban. Nevertheless, he kept a record of having baptized 10,252 persons, a listing which is still extant.

9. Dirk's Epistle [letter], which is dated September 19, 1566, is lost. Its first printing of 1567 was not available to the editors of the BRN X, but seems to have been found, though it has no date or place of publication and may, in fact, be a later printing. The following translation has been made from that copy (IDC microfiche) with a careful comparison to the BRN X:517ff. text.

10. See below pp. 482-485 translated from BRN X, pp. 530-534.

11. I. H. V. P. N., *Het beginsel der scheuringen,* in BRN VII, pp. 540-541ff.

12. Syvaert Pieters, *Corte aenwijsinghe, Voorgestelt in eenighe Vraghen, vande voornaemste mishandelinghen der Vlamingen ende Vriesen, in 1566.* Hoorn: 1634, p. 21. Cf.: De Hoop Scheffer, "Het verbond der vier steden." DB (1893), p. 53.

13. Outerman, *Verclaringhe,* para. 17 and 313. See also Koolman, pp. 134ff. and p. 141, where he asks whether a theologian, after careful study, cannot change his mind.

14. See pp. 542-546 below. "Door Dirck Philipsen geschreven en gesonden in Vrieslant." Koolman, p. 204.

15. See pp. 482-485 below for the 1565 Agreement.

16. "Flemish Mennonites," ME 2:338.
17. P. M. Friesen, *Die Alt-Evangelische Mennonitische Bruderschaft in Russland (1789-1910)*. Halbstadt: Raduga, 1911., pp. 46ff., 138f. Translated as *The Mennonite Brotherhood in Russia (1789-1910)*. Fresno: Board of Christian Literature. General Conference of Mennonite Brethren Churches, 1978.
18. I. H. V. P. N. [Carel van Ghendt], *Het beginsel der scheuringen onder de Doops-gesinden*. (1615) Amsterdam: Tymon Houthaak, 1658, in BRN VII (1910), pp. 508ff. V. P. (Simon Walrave?), *Successio Anabaptistica, Dat is Babel der Wederdopers*. Cologne: S. B. Gualtheri, 1603 (Cf.: BRN VII, pp. 16-87). Jacques Outerman, *Onder verbeteringhe. Verclaringhe met bewijs wt den droevigen handel van Vr. ende Vlam.*, n.p., 1609, (See *Catalogus*, p. 103). Idem. *Appendix, dienende tot Conclusie van de verclaringhe, 1609*. Idem, *Copye eens Briefs*. . . . Haerlem: Th. Fonteyn, 1634. Idem, *Noodtwendighe verklaringhe*. . . . Haerlem: H. P. v. Wesbusch, 1634. Syvaert Pieters, *Corte aenwijsinghe, Voorgestelt in eenighe Vraghen, vande voornaemste mishandelinghen der Vlamingen ende Vriesen in 1566*. Hoorn, 1634, pp. 12-14. S. Blaupot ten Cate, *Geschiedenis der Doopsgezinden in Friesland*. pp. 96ff. J. G. de Hoop Scheffer, "Het verbond der vier steden," DB (1893), 1-90. Kühler, *Geschiedenis* I, pp. 395-436. N. van der Zijpp, "Flemish Mennonites," ME II:337-338 and "Frisian Mennonites," ME II:413ff. Koolman, pp. 131ff. Keeney, *Dutch Anabaptist Thought*. Krahn, *Dutch Anabaptism*.

B. EPISTLE TO FOUR CITIES[1]

An epistle written out of pure brotherly love to the four cities to admonish the quarrelsome to Christian peace and a life blessed of God.

Mark 9:[50] Have salt in you, and peace among you, the Lord said to his disciples. And once more: My peace I give to you. My peace I leave with you. [John 14:27]

Heb. 12:[15] Pursue peace, and for that which sanctifies, without which no one shall see God. And let no one neglect God's grace. Let no root of bitterness grow up among you through which many become impure.

[The BRN X edition carries Dirk's initials and the following three lines on the title page.]

D. P.

According to the copy printed in the year 1567.

Printed at Haarlem by Vincent Kasteleyn on the Marckt-veldt in the Book Press, Anno 1619. /517/

To the Christian Reader, Salute. Grace and Peace.

/519/ We cannot with good intention hide from you, dear reader, how we have for a long time had great sorrow and difficulty on account of the miserable and distressing quarrel which has arisen in Fr.[iesland] in the cong.[regation], and [which] has done very much harm, just as experience teaches and shows. Also the apostle James said that where quarrels, envy, and division is, there is disorder and every wicked affair, James 3:16.

Again, where peace, love, and unity in Jesus Christ are, progress and take the upper hand, there it proceeds well; there is steadfastness in the faith and all Christian being. Yes, there people serve God in holiness and righteousness, which is well pleasing before him. There people consider that God is a God of peace in his congregation, that he has also called us in peace, Luke 2:[14], and that we were admonished so heartily thereto by the Lord Jesus Christ himself, as also by his apostles, John 20:[21]; Col. 3:[15].

Therefore we wrote this letter last year to the four ci[ties], out of pure Christian love.[2] Therein each may read and note our inclination of mind to our fatherland, our trust and brotherly admonishing and warning to the God-fearing, to watch against all quarreling and strife. [We] protest and witness here to all impartial brothers and fellow companions of our faith that we have always sought peace and worked for it, and that we are innocent of all this unpeacefulness, schism, and /520/ destruction of the congregations, but that we in our weakness through the Lord's grace would much rather repair, improve and build again the temple and the fallen walls of Jerusalem. [We] pray and sigh daily to God, in the name of Jesus Christ, that he will attend to his people graciously, will take to heart the misery, sorrow, and burden of Zion, yes, that he will release the captives, lift up those who are fallen, bring the lost onto the right way, and keep to a God-saving end those who stand in his grace and truth. The peace of God be with you. Amen.

/521/ To all the God-fearing companions of our Christian faith in H.[arlingen], F.[raneker], L.[eeuwarden], D.[okkum], beloved in the Lord, for the sake of truth I, D. P., your brother and servant in the gospel and the least among the saints, as also the brothers who are with me, wish you much grace and peace, much wisdom and understanding, much humility, gentleness, and patience, much caution, cleverness, and simplicity, yes, a God-saving result in all the temptations and struggles, which come upon you as a testing of your faith. We wish you all this and even more of the other virtues of God, from God the heavenly Father and Jesus Christ, his only born Son, our Lord and Savior, through the power of the Holy Spirit. Amen, 1 Pet. 1; 2:1.

Heartily beloved brothers, our beloved in the Lord, and in the fellowship of the gospel, we thank almighty God, and rejoice in our heart therein, Phil. 1, as we remember wherewith you were called by God out of darkness into his wonderful light, 1 Pet. 2:9. Yes, you were delivered out of Egypt and have gone through that sea, baptized in Jesus Christ and in his death, clothed with the power of God, and have eaten from the spiritual meal, and have drunk from the spiritual drink, 1 Cor. 10:1ff., the fruit out of the promised land, that is, out of the heavenly kingdom from the true vine, John 15:1ff. Through the prevenient figures of the Old Testament and the succeeding truth of the gospel delivered to you, you have tasted and found how friendly the

Lord is, and how blessed the person is who hopes in him, 2 Cor. 6.

The full wish of our heart before God is that you truly know this inexpressible love of God and the grace of Jesus Christ, [that it] keep and motivate you, /522/ and that you be not led away from brotherly love and unity, from Christian simplicity and truth, yes, that the waters of Marah [Exod. 15:23] not be too bitter to you, that the heavenly bread not lose its sweetness, nor that the Amalekites gain dominance [Exod. 17:11], nor that any murmuring occur against Moses and Aaron, 1 Cor. 10:10, that no golden calf be erected, or that anyone let himself be deceived by the beauty of the Moabite daughters [Num. 25:1].[3]

We wish this for all of you, also for ourselves, from the depth of our hearts. For you are now also put to the test, as we hear. Therefore, although we are not present with you bodily at this time, nevertheless, our heart is with you, Col. 2:5, and we remember you in our gathering, admonishing, and prayer, praying and pleading with God, before the throne of grace [Heb. 5:7], that he keep you and us with each other in the right faith and peace, Rom. 3, that he allow all quarrels and divisions to be far from us since he is a God of peace in all of his congregations, Rom. 15:5; 1 Cor. 7:15.

Therefore our hearts are troubled since we hear and understand that there is great sorrow among you, that one brother strives against the other, that the love of many has grown cold, that the peace was broken, and that disunity breaks in as a flood. Yes, that Jerusalem about which is written that God made the locks or bolts of her gates closed, that he sets her frontiers or borders at peace, Ps. 147:13f., and that on her streets hallelujah is being sung, Tob. 13:18, that Jerusalem we mean, appears now to wobble among some [of you] and moving from its firmness, Ps. 47. There is strife and complaining within her walls, there that happy hallelujah is now not heard by many. [May] the merciful God have pity over this and mend it according to the richness of his grace.

Oh, how sad of heart we are and troubled about the quarrel that is among you there. How many times we have thought about how one might handle it in the best manner. We are all on this account oppressed, anxious, and burdened in our consciences, whether we should write something, yes, much more plead with you that you might make peace with each other. For that you are quarrelsome, splintering, and divisive among yourselves is a great heartbreak for us, and if we through God's grace can do some good which would serve peace, how completely willing we are to do that.[4]

For this reason we have /523/at last, as we have taken counsel with the Lord through praying and sighing, yes, with tears, and have also spoken with some God-fearing people, emboldened ourselves, have taken courage, and risked in the name of the Lord, out of the deep sorrow of our hearts, and out of pure sincere love, to write a little with good intentions and hopes, that our limited labor might be acceptable and serviceable to you, Rom. 12. For this God give us his grace. Amen.

First, consider well the beginning of your faith, namely with what devotion, celebration of the Spirit, 1 Thess. 1:5, and gladness of heart, you have accepted the Word, how you have come into the covenant of God, what you then promised the Lord, to serve your God in holiness and righteousness all the days of your life, to walk with a good conscience before him, 1 Pet. 3; Luke 2, no longer to live for yourself, but for the Lord and his congregation, Rom. 14:7f. Yes, all that your heavenly calling taught you and brings with it, Gal. 2, take that to heart.

Thus we admonish you with the apostle: just as you have accepted the Lord Jesus Christ, so also walk in him, and be rooted in him, and built upon him, just as you were taught through the faith, and be overflowing in the same faith with thanksgiving, Col. 2:6f. Look out that no one robs you through philosophy [Col. 2:8] and misleads you according to human teaching of the world and not of Jesus Christ. What John wrote agrees with that. Let what you heard from the beginning remain with you; if that remains with you that you have heard from the beginning, you will remain with the Father and with his Son, 1 John 2:24. And that is the promise which he has given us, that eternal life, with such answers, if we remain therein, but who transgresses, that one has no God. But who remains therein has both the Father and the Son.

And this is now the principal teaching and the highest command of our Lord Jesus Christ, that we shall have love one for another just as he has loved us, John 15:12. And this love is not only in words, but lies in power and truth and must be shown in deeds, 1 John 3:18. /524/ For since God is love, as John says, 1 John 4:[7], so it is powerful and according to Solomon's word, stronger than death and firmer than hell, for love is fiery and a flame of the Lord, that waters also cannot extinguish love, nor streams drown it, Song of Sol. 8:6[f.]. And if someone wanted to give all his goods for love, he cannot buy it with them, for it is a gift of the Lord and a special power of God, 1 Cor. 1. It comes into the heart of believers through the Holy Spirit, Rom. 5:5, and apart from love nothing counts that a person does; as little as anything counts that is outside of God, 1 Cor. 13:1-2.

Therefore the Scripture also witnesses that anyone who does not love his brother remains in death, and he walks in darkness, and his eyes are blinded, and he does not know where he is going, 1 John 2:11. He has also forgotten the purification and washing off of his sins, 2 Pet. 1:9. Again, if anyone hates his brother, that one is a murderer and does not have life remaining in him, 1 John 3:15. Again, what the Lord Jesus Christ also told so often about love in the gospel and how abundantly the apostles write about it in their letters, how heartily they admonish us to it, that anyone who loves his soul may well consider and reflect upon, Rom. 11; 1 Cor. 13; Eph. 4; Col. 3; 1 Pet. 3.

Second, notice carefully how harmful is quarreling and disunity. If you observe the example of Scripture, you will find how damage and destruction has come from division, of which both literal and figurative Israel is certainly an instructive and terrible example. Reflect on it that you do not fall [into the same pattern] and become just like all such people, Num. 16; Judg. 11. Again, if you pay attention to what has happened in our time you may well shudder before such quarreling and division, Heb. 4. It is unnecessary to tell their history, for they are well known and all such things result from them, as James says, from where does strife and quarreling come among you? Is it not out of your passion which fights there in your members? James 4:1. You are covetous but do not receive therewith. You envy and hate, and yet cannot acquire; you wrangle and fight, and have not; you pray and do not receive because you pray wrongly, /525/ to wit, because you devour it in your passions. Note from where the quarrel comes among the brothers and how harmful it is.

Therefore, the same apostle also admonishes all Christians and says: Be submissive to God and resist the devil (for he is a troublemaker), then he flees from you. Draw near to God and God will draw near to you [James 4:7-8]. Cleanse your hands, oh, sinners, and purify your hearts, you who vacillate. And still once more: who is wise and understanding among you? That one shows his good works with gentleness and wisdom. But if you have bitter envy and quarreling in your heart, do not boast of it and do not lie against the truth, for that is not the wisdom which comes from above, but that wisdom is earthly, human, and devilish. For where jealousy and quarreling is, there is a disorderly being and every evil practice. But the wisdom which is from above is first pure [chaste], thereafter peaceful, friendly, courteous, readily receives counsel, it is full of mercy and good fruits, without partisanship and hypocrisy. For the fruit of righteousness is sown in peace to those who keep the peace, James 3:13-18.

These words of the apostle show us clearly whereby a Christian shows his Christianity and godly wisdom, and how much evil results out of partisan practice. Yes, that nothing other than every ineptitude, offence, lying against the truth, and false boasting was found there. Therefore, anyone who wants to be a Christian is advised that he guard himself from quarreling and division and show his Christian nature with a gentle spirit and God-saving life. But with disputing, quarreling, and wrangling, little good has been done in all time and at all places where it has happened.

Third, take to heart what great gladness and profit, according to the Spirit, brotherly love and unity brings with it. For so says the prophet: see how lovely and fine it is where brothers live together in unity with one another. Just as the precious balsam which flowed off the head of Aaron into his whole beard, which flowed down into his cloak, just as the dew flowed from Hermon onto Mount Zion. For there God the Lord himself promised life and blessing /526/ in eternity. Look and see how the blessing of God comes over a peaceful congregation, and God himself desires to live there. Therefore, the Lord Jesus Christ himself praised the peacemakers as happy, for those will be called God's children, Matt. 5:9. On the other hand, the makers of quarrels must not be blessed and [are] children of the evil one who at all times is a maker of quarrels, John 8:44ff.

Again, the words of the Lord testify how unified and at one the congregation of God is to be, namely, that he prays for all those who believe through his Word and the service of the apostles, that they will be one, just as the Father is in him and he in the Father, so that they are fully one, and the world recognizes that God so loves such Christians, just as he loved his Son Jesus Christ and still loves in eternity, John 17:21ff.

Such unity must be found in the congregation of God at all times, just as between God the Father and his Son, a perfect unity in the Holy Spirit. The apostle Paul admonishes us to this unity, and says, I admonish you that you walk fitting to the calling to which you are called, with all humility and gentleness, with patience, and forebear one another in love and be eager to hold the unity in the Spirit through the bond of peace, one body in the Spirit, just as you are also called in one hope of your calling: One Lord, one faith, one baptism, one God and Father of us all who is over you all, through all, and in you all, [Eph. 4:1-6].

And once more, all bitterness, rage, anger, clamor, and slander, they are far from you [as is] all wickedness. But be friendly among one another, tenderhearted, and forgive one another, just as God in Jesus Christ has forgiven you [Eph. 4:31f.] And again the same apostle teaches us and said: Put on as the elect and beloved of God, heartfelt mercy, friendliness, humility, patience, and forbear one another, and forgive among each other if anyone has a complaint against the other, just as Christ has forgiven you, do you also thus. But above all these, put on love which is the bond of perfection, Col. 3:12ff. And the peace of God take the upper hand in your heart, to which you are called in one body, and be thankful, Phil. 4.

In addition, the Lord Jesus reprimanded his disciples who argued and disputed with one another about who should be greatest in the /527/ kingdom of heaven and said: Truly, truly, I say to you, except you turn around and become as children, you will not come into the kingdom of heaven. Whoever humbles himself as this child (which he had set in the midst of his disciples), that one is the greatest in the kingdom of heaven. And whoever accepts such a child in my name, that one accepts me. For if anyone confuses one of the least of these who believe in me, it would be better for him that a millstone be bound on his neck and he would be drowned in the deepest of the sea. Woe to the world because of aggravation, yet aggravation must come, but woe to the person through whom it comes, Matt. 18:[1-7].

Read this with understanding of what the Lord's meaning is. When the mother of the children of Zebedee desired from the Lord that her two sons might sit beside him in his kingdom, the one on the right and the other on the left hand, and as the ten disciples heard that, they became indignant at her. Then Jesus called them to himself and spoke; you know that the worldly princes rule and the authorities have power, but it shall not be so among you; rather if someone wants to be the greatest among you, that one will be your servant. And whoever will be the chief, that one is your servant. Just as the Son of Man did not come to be served but to serve, and he gave his life as a deliverance for many, Matt. 20:20-21; 24-27; Luke 22:24-27. Oh, that all these words would be always well considered by every Christian; it would be much better among us.

Fourth, consider well and take to heart what great sorrow and aggravation comes out of your quarreling and division, and may yet come. Yes, that not only you there but all congregations will be troubled by it. For after all it thus affects all true Christians, just as the apostle said: Who is weakened, and I will not be weakened? Who aggravates himself, and I am not burned? [2 Cor. 11:29]. Therefore, consider well what trouble and sorrow your quarreling in this regard is causing among the God-fearing.

Before this time, there was much boasting about our fatherland, about the growth of God's congregations, yes, that honey and milk flowed therein, that there one sat under the vine of Jesus Christ, that one enjoyed the figs, olives, and pomegranates; we mean the /528/ spiritual gifts, namely, that the sweetness of the divine Word has flowed there, that one has received the beautiful gifts of the Holy Spirit. One is fed with the flower of the meal and is satisfied. But now we fear that if this quarreling is not laid down that one would have heard the opposite, to the great sadness of many pious and devout hearts. In addition, [these divisions] will lead to the happiness and glory of the enemies and adversaries of the truth, who as Ishmael mocked Isaac, and as Esau hated Jacob, Gal. 4:21[ff.], wish the destruction of God's congregations and would like to see that the foundations of Jerusalem might be uprooted. Still we hope for the grace of God that he will preserve his congregation, and deliver [us] from all hindrances, and make all wicked attacks as nothing, Ps. 52.

Thus we beg you and admonish you through the mercy of God, Rom. 12:1, and through the love of the Lord Jesus Christ, who with his innocent death and precious blood has made and received for us peace from God his father, Rom. 3, 8; Eph. 1, 2; Col. 1. We beg and admonish you, and say in conclusion with the apostle thus: [if there] is now with you any admonition in Jesus Christ; [if there] is heartfelt love and mercy, so fulfill my joy therein that you be of one mind, having the same love, being harmonious and one, not acting through quarreling and empty honor, but through humility, honoring one another as higher than himself. [Let] no one seek what is his own but what profits another, everyone being so minded as Jesus Christ was also minded, etc. [cf. Phil. 2:1-5].

Thus you now observe the crucified Jesus Christ and are eager to be conformed to his likeness, so we hope in the grace of the Lord that he will still grant a good outcome. Once again we beg and admonish you through the love of the Spirit, that you will take to heart and consider everything that is reported [here], and what the Scripture still more so abundantly testifies about it. Take our simple writing for the best, for we have written out of pure /529/ sincere love, that the Lord knows who knows all hearts, Ps. 7:9; Jer. 17:9. And if we can serve you in any manner for peace, for improvement and edification of the congregation, how willingly we (as much as God gives us grace and concern) will do and complete such.⁵ Herewith we commend you to almighty God and the Lord Jesus Christ who is powerful to teach you, to admonish, and to give you his peace, to increase love in you, and to preserve you for his heavenly kingdom. Amen.

Many God-fearers who are with us greet you. Oh, that you might truly greet each other with the holy kiss of peace. The grace of our Lord Jesus Christ and the peace of God be with you all who seek peace and have love. Written out of great sorrow and anxiety of heart. Anno 1566, the nineteenth of September.

We desire that you read this letter at H.[arlingen], and then immediately send it on to Fr.[aneker], L.[eeuwarden], D.[okkum], that the letter be read there also.

a. Attachment: 1565 Agreement
D.[irk[P.[hilips] Y[our] B.[rother]
I[in the] L[ord].

The 1565 agreement among the ministers concerning the calling to ministry, the occasion for which had been the disruptions caused by Leenaert Bouwens.⁶

To The Christian Reader, Grace and Peace.

/530/ Since now (alas) much quarreling and division has come into the congregation of the Lord, and some have taken upon themselves to lord it over the congregation of God; against their own discussion, agreement, and decision made with all the m.[inisters] about how to act, they boast of the great power and authority which they think they have. Still, according to the Lord's parable, all is taken from them and given to the faithful servants.

Therefore, we are compelled to bring into the light the decision all of us m[inisters] arrived at in 1565. We arrived at [this decision] harmoniously out of God's Word, from which everyone may understand how a m[inister] is to conduct himself in relation to the congregation which has been entrusted to him, and how a congregation shall act towards its m[inister], that which we through God's help at this time hope to clarify still more broadly. Therefore, we set that [before you] simply as much as the m[inisters] concluded in unity, having been read before the congregation and approved [by them].

/531/ 1 Timothy 3:14f. This I write to you so that you may know how you shall walk in the house of God, which is the congregation of the living God, a pillar and foundation stone of the truth.

2 Timothy 2:15. Be anxious that you show yourself to God to be a proven worker, who dares not shame him, who correctly cuts the word of truth.

/532/ With regard to the calling and election of bishops and ministers, we acknowledge m[inisters] and elders for the Lord and all congregations that the calling and election of m[inisters] and teachers is twofold.

The first and most important is from God, through his Word and Spirit, through which he as father of the household sends forth his servants and urges them into his harvest that they gather the wheat into his barns.

Again, the parable of the gospel about the fishers, nets, and all kinds of fish which are caught therein, about the nobleman who went on a journey and gave his servants gold that they should make money with it, and about the faithful servant which the Lord set over his family and household to give them food at the right time. All [of] these parables testify to us clearly that the Lord is the right and principal commissioner who according to his providence endows his servants with his Spirit and lays his Word in their mouths; he speaks, teaches, admonishes, and works through them. Therefore the m[inisters] actually serve out of God's strength, just as the apostle Peter says: if anyone serves, let them serve out of the power which God supplies, 1 Pet. 4:11.

This was established in Acts 13:[2-3], for there it is written that the H[oly] Spirit spoke to the congregation at Antioch; separate for me Paul and Barnabas for the work to which I have chosen them. And as they had fasted, prayed, and laid hands upon them, they set forth and were commissioned by the Holy Spirit.

Again, Acts 20:28, Paul spoke to the elders of the congregation: Pay attention to yourselves and to the entire flock over which the Holy Spirit has placed you, to pasture the congregation of God, /533/ which he has earned with his blood. From this it is clear that the principal commissioning of true ministers is from God who prepares and quickens people's hearts through his Spirit, and makes them eager and able for his service and work.

The second calling and election of t[eachers] and m[inisters] occurs from the congregation, through God's inspiration and command, with the single voice [i.e., unanimously] of the congregation, also with fasting and praying. And the same elected ministers were ordained by the elders through the laying on of hands, Acts 14:23. For it is also written there that Paul and Barnabas placed elders in all the congregations as they had fasted and prayed.

Again, the apostle wrote to Titus, therefore I left you in Crete that you should complete what I have left there, namely, that you [should] install elders in all cities, Titus 1:5. He has also portrayed and described the elders, how they shall be qualified.

These two kinds of calling and election Paul included in the words which he wrote to Timothy, namely, that he should not despise the gift which was given him through prophetic utterance (that is, to understand the Scripture through God's grace and Spirit) with the laying on of hands by the elders [1 Tim. 4:14].

From all this it follows clearly that a true minister must have both this calling and election, that is, the calling from God and the orderly election of the congregation of the Lord. According to the first election and godly calling, he is obligated to the entire church. According to the other election he is the minister of the congregation that has chosen him and in which he was ordained.[7] Thus the congregation at Philippi had bishops and deacons, Phil. 1:1. And every congregation in Asia also had a bishop and a messenger, that is, a teacher, Rev. 2:3.

Again, Paul and Barnabas came to agreement with Cephas, James, and John that these three should serve the apostolic office among the Jews, and the other two among the heathen, only that they should consider the poor. Therefore, it is proper for a minister to have a special place and congregation where he has his career and serves, yet always under the condition that the whole flock is cared for, that the congregation is also served, and that the entire body of the Lord be built up and improved, John 10:[1-18]; Acts 20:[28f.]; Eph. 4:[1-16]. And all this must be done with peace and in love, /534/ with the advice and consent of the congregation which has chosen him and in which he lives. For that a congregation shall also send out a minister in peace is revealed by this that the apostles, when they heard that Samaria had accepted the gospel, they sent Peter and John to them that they should pray for the Samaritans and lay hands upon them that they might receive the H[oly] Spirit, Acts 8:14f.

Again, Paul and Barnabas, although they were required and sent forth by the Holy Spirit, were equally ordained and commissioned by the congregation at Antioch, Acts 13:[1-3]. In addition, the congregation at Jerusalem sent men out with Paul and Barnabas, which makes us understand that it is still to happen in that way, so that everything may transpire orderly and according to Scripture. And no one runs lightly from himself outside of the election and ordination of the congregation.[8]

All this is clearly to be shown by the fact that the apostle Paul wrote to the Corinthians: We have admonished Titus that he came to you voluntarily and have sent a brother with him who is being praised through all the congregations in the work of the gospel. Thus he was ordained through the congregational vote as a companion in our travel, in this [is the] benefit that will be served by us to God's honor and your happiness.

The apostle to the Ephesians also laid this foundation that the Lord has appointed some as apostles, some as prophets, some as evangelists, some as shepherds and teachers, that thereby the saints might be joined together, through common service, to improve the body of Christ, until we all come to one faith of the Son of God and become a perfect man in the measure of the perfect maturity of Jesus Christ, Eph. 4:11-13.

And following this the apostle said that we shall be accountable in love, that is, that we should keep together what is right in love and grow in every way unto him who is the head, Christ, out of which the whole body is joined together. And one member is bonded together with [depends on] the other, through that total joining together whereby one reaches a helping hand to the other, so that the body grows to its own improvement, and all of that in love. Therefore, where love is not powerful, no service nor work of the Lord can proceed in its true purpose.

This briefly now is our confession about the calling and election of bishops and teachers.

ENDNOTES

1. *Sendtbrief, uyt reynder Broederlycker Liefde, aen de vier St. gheschreven, [Door] D. P.* (1567). IDC microfiche; BRN X, pp. 516-529; attachment: The 1565 agreement among the ministers about the call to ministry, the occasion for which had been the disruptions caused by Leenaert Bouwens, pp. 530-534.

2. We assume that he sent the letter to the four cities after he had written it on 19 September 1566. The present 30 June 1567 (?) letter then may be a copy of the earlier one, with a new introduction, in anticipation of his coming there as requested in the 17 April 1567 letter of Hoyte Renix. However, neither the introduction to the letter nor the letter itself assumes that they had seen it before. We note in the Epistle that he offers to come if he can be of help.

3. In his "Short Account" of events in Friesland, written also in defense of his letters, Dirk seems to identify the Frisians with the Amalekites. This seems to be a similar veiled reference though we are familiar with Dirk's fondness for typology. He regrets having ordained Jan Willems and Lubbert Gerrits even as God regretted having made Saul king. See pp. 507-508 below. Cf.: BRN X p. 567.

4. This seems to be an offer to come to Friesland to help mediate.

5. Another expression of concern or a longing to become involved in the resolution of the growing division?

6. *Aengaende de Beroepinghe ende Verkiesinghe der Bisschoppen ende Leeraers* (1565). Bouwens was a vigorous apostle. Ordained in 1551 by Menno Simons, he was younger than either Menno or Dirk and apparently more active. He baptized a total of 10,252, keeping a record himself. See Karel Vos, "De dooplijst van Leenaert Bouwens," in *Bijdragen en Mededeelingen van het Historisch Gennootschap*, Vol. 36 (1915), pp. 39ff. Cf: Kühler, *Geschiedenis* I, p. 311, note 2. He was extremely rigourous in discipline, but himself enjoyed certain luxuries like a glass of wine on a cold night. While Emden was his home congregation, he refused to be accountable to anyone but God. Apparently six ministers and Dirk were present at this meeting. See also n. 8, p. 470 of A. Introduction above.

7. These two sentences seem to have Leenaert Bouwens in mind.

8. This again seems to have Bouwens in mind, yet Menno Simons himself encouraged his itineration; "Sincere Appeal to Leonard Bouwens' Wife," (1553) CWMS, pp. 1038-1040.

C. A SHORT BUT FUNDAMENTAL ACCOUNT

Introduction

This "Short But Fundamental Account" was written by Dirk in 1567 to explain and justify his position in the dispute between the Frisians and the Flemish. It was clearly written in Emden and, therefore, also served as a report to his home congregation in Prussia, as well as a rather thorough defense of his actions in the dispute. A few passages seem to imply that Dirk was still working at the issues, but it is probably the final report of a failed mission. This means it was written in July or later.

The first part of Dirk's "Account" deals with the sentence passed at the 1 February 1567 meeting in Harlingen under the mediation of Jan Willems and Lubbert Gerrits. He cannot accept it because he considers the arbitrators unworthy. We note that Dirk's feelings toward the two Hoorn elders must have been similar to the disappointment of Samuel with Saul. Dirk believed that they had not acted according to the apostolic example and had not followed divine truth. Most importantly, they failed to support their decision with Scripture. If they had done so, he could have accepted it, but now he must view it as an unjustified judgment. He implies that they were too young and inexperienced. His comment that they should have chosen "the oldest and most experienced" as their helpers seems to indicate that he himself wanted to be involved.[1] As a consequence of their action, many innocent persons were put outside of the congregation.

In the second part Dirk deals with the covenant of God. He had done that in earlier writings, but now he does it more from the viewpoint of principle. There is only one covenant from God. That is the one which God offered and which people had accepted. God had promised to be their Father, and the people had responded as ready to walk according to his will. Now they have placed a human covenant in place of God's with its demands and promises. It was introduced under the appearance of being from God. Thus Dirk likens it to the golden calf set up by Aaron in the wilderness and two similar ones set up later by Jeroboam. They call this new covenant "The Ordinance of the Four Cities." If it were God's ordinance, then it would not be just for four cities but for everyone.

The next section deals with what Dirk considers to be a second golden calf, parallel to that which Jeroboam set up at Dan. It was the Compromise which the judges had required to be signed before they rendered their decision. The first article of the Compromise read: "That we voluntarily with a pure heart entirely and fully dedicate and surrender into the hands of our dear brothers and ministers Jan Willemssoon and Lubbert Geritsoon, with their companions and all those whom they will add to themselves, and covenant with these mentioned Christians, as befits men of their faith, all discord which has come forth among us, including the matters and issues which are dealt with as well as over those still not treated. And we bind ourselves to fulfill and to obey everything unconditionally, without any opposition, how and in whatever manner that also implies, however they thus lead in the handling of our quarrel or our issues, or the verdict they make, promising therewith to be entirely satisfied and to submit ourselves to it."[2]

Dirk found the Compromise unsatisfactory because it bound the conscience of people to human judgment. It did not allow for disagreement if the persons felt that the arbitrators' decision was contrary to Scripture. Since the judges in the Frisian-Flemish dispute did not support their finding with Scripture, Dirk found the Compromise an unjust commitment. God alone could be the judge over people. Dirk felt that the judges had placed human opinion above the judgment of God and, therefore, when the Flemish had objection to the decision, they felt justified in rejecting it.

The section which then follows is Dirk's response about his letter to Hoyte Renix and to the ministers from Hoorn.[3] J. ten Doornkaat Koolman believes that this material was already prepared by Dirk and simply inserted into the account here.[4] Because of the unwillingness of the Frisians to respond in the presence of the Flemish, Dirk was convinced that they were the primary guilty ones. In his opinion, the Frisians had broken the peace with their "Covenant of the Four Cities," the Compromise, and the sentence rendered at Harlingen.

Because of these experiences, Dirk has often been characterized as stubborn, as lacking in moderation. He was firm indeed. He sounds more contentious, perhaps, in this document than in any other, but there are beautiful passages eloquent with spiritual concern and a profound faith in the reliability of Scripture. "We have placed our soul in the Lord's hands, and on that account we are comforted, that our friends became enemies because we spoke the truth."[5]

Yet his pain over the failure of negotiations is palpable: "It would be better and preferred by us to depart into the wilderness with

Elijah, and to wish from the Lord that our soul might die, than that we must see that the prophetess Jezebel should dominate the congregation and mislead the servants of the Lord."[6] He became involved from distant Danzig because of his love for God and the people of God: "Since we are old and full of years [63], and expect our release at any moment, we desire still before our end to warn all God-fearers about all philosophies and the traditions of people. In addition, we desire to admonish each one in our simplicity, that they hold firmly to Jesus Christ in whom all the treasures and knowledge of God lie hidden."[7]

The reliability of Dirk's account is confirmed by many near contemporary sources, especially *Successio Anabaptistica, Dat is Babel der Wederdopers,* and *Het beginsel der scheuringen onder de Doopsgesinden, 1658.*[8] In his conclusion to the introduction of the document the editor of BRN X aptly writes: "See here the tragedy of history. . . . At the end of his life Dirk Philips became the sacrificial victim of a collision which could not be avoided."[9] The inevitability of this collision remains subject to the judgment call of the historian, theologian, and general reader.

A SHORT BUT FUNDAMENTAL ACCOUNT[10]

A short but fundamental account about the quarrelsome affair and unscriptural judgment that was given in Fr.[iesland] over [about] some whom people call Flemish. With a clear confession about the only covenant and Word of God, and thereby a refutation and counter-argument that a human covenant and compromise is not valid before God, yes, is an abomination before him. /545/

Gen. 17. God spoke to Abraham: Sarah, your wife, shall bear you a son whom you shall name Isaac, for with him I will make an eternal covenant, and with his seed after him. In Isaac you shall be called that seed, and Sarah is the mother of us all. Rom. 9, Gal. 4

John 12. The Word that I have spoken, that will judge in the last day.

1 Cor. 3. The Lord catches the clever in their cleverness and cunning, for there is no cleverness, no counsel, no strength contrary to the Lord. /546/

1 Cor. 4. The kingdom of God does not exist in words, but in power.

Matt. 15. Why do you break God's command on behalf of your traditions?

/547/ Dirk Philips, out of grace a companion of the faith in Jesus Christ and a minister of his congregation, offers his brotherly, Christian and friendly greeting or salutation, to all God-fruitful ones living here and there, scattered and pilgrims on earth for the witness to the truth, 1 Pet. 2:[11], according to the providence of God the Father, in the sanctifying of the Spirit and in obedience to the gospel and the sprinkling of the blood of Jesus Christ. 1 Pet. 1:[2]. Grace, peace, and mercy from God the Father and Jesus Christ our Lord be multiplied in all of you, through the power of the Holy Spirit. Amen. Rom. 1:[7].

Heartily beloved brothers and friends, co-participants of the grace of God in patience and in the kingdom of Jesus Christ, Rev. 1; we thank the almighty God and Father through Jesus Christ that you were called by him to the acknowledgement of the truth and were chosen to salvation, 2 Thess. 2:[13]. And we pray almighty God that he keep you in his grace eternally, that you bring your faith to the end, [even] the salvation of your soul, 1 Pet. 1:[3-5]. Furthermore, we so pray and admonish all God-fruitful ones who come upon or get in hand this our letter, this our confession of the distressing and grievous affair in Friesland (with which all congregations have been troubled), that they will read all this with a pure, nonpartisan heart, understand well, and test with the true touchstone, that is, God's Word.

If that happens, we hope that many persons' eyes will be opened through God's grace /548/, that they may see the blindness which has overcome some, and that many have surrendered to a mistaken understanding of God, 2 Thess 2:[4], because they have not walked in the truth nor remained in it; that they have not pursued the peace of God nor [sought] after holiness and righteousness, without which no one shall see God, that they have neglected the grace of God and received it in vain and have become a bitter root, whereby many were defiled and many more may be defiled, Heb. 12:[14-15].

We write this because of the present deed and need, namely, that unrighteousness is taking the upper hand, on which account love has grown cold in many, Matt. 24:[12], that poisonous and false tongues do much damage and make the peaceful restless; that robbers of reputations, gossip,[11] lying, and deceiving has full sway and is entirely common with some, through which many innocent hearts may be led astray from the simplicity which is in Jesus Christ, 2 Cor.

11:[3]. Yes, it now proceeds thus that one may say with the prophet: Help, oh Lord; the saints have departed, the believers are few among the children of humanity; [they] speak useless things with one another; they speak and deceive with a divided heart.

[Oh, that the] Lord would root out all deceitfulness and the tongue that speaks so boldly: who say, our tongue shall have the upper hand, it belongs to us to speak, who is it who will master us, or who is our Lord? Meanwhile the distressed are disturbed and the poor sigh; will I make ready, says the Lord. I will send help, that people will teach willingly. The reason of the Lord is pure, just as refined silver in an earthen furnace tested seven times. Oh, Lord, will you still keep them, and protect us eternally from this generation? For it is everywhere full of the godless where such cunning people lord it over people, Ps. 12.

This one sees clearly, that it still proceeds thus today, just as the prophet has spoken, just as the apostle Paul saw before in the Spirit and said to the elders of the congregations: take heed for yourselves and for the flock over which the Holy Spirit has placed you, to pasture the congregation of God which he has earned or received with his blood. For I know that after my departure /549/, vicious wolves will come among you who will not spare the flock, and men shall arise among you who will speak perverted things to draw the disciples away and bring them to themselves, Acts 20:[28-30].

And John said that in his time antichrists were already in circulation and came from the congregation, but they were not of us. For if they had been from us they would have remained with us. But since they were revealed, [it is clear] that they all are not from us, 1 John 2:[18-19]. Therefore, it is no wonder that now at this time such still happens, that devouring, grasping wolves come among the sheep (nevertheless they come in sheep's clothing), Matt. 7:[15], that perverse men arise in the congregation (nevertheless, they present themselves as angels of light), that antichrists go forth from the congregation (and still want to be called Christians), who forsake the Lord Jesus Christ in that they do not remain in his teaching, his love, nor in his peace, 2 Cor. 10; 1 John 2:[18-19]. For whoever transgresses, John says, and does not remain in the teaching of Jesus Christ, that one has no God; but whoever remains therein, that one has both the Father and the Son, 2 John 1:[9].

And once more: What you have heard from the beginning, let it remain with you; if it remains with you [that] which you have heard from the beginning, [then] you will remain with the Father and with his Son Jesus Christ. And that is the promise which he has given us, eternal life, 1 John 2:[24-25]. From this it is easy to understand how one must persistently and wholeheartedly remain in the sanctifying and saving teaching of our Lord Jesus Christ and in the faith that was given us once [for all] from God, Jude 1:[17-21].

Since we then are old and full of years and always expect our deliverance, therefore, we still desire before our end to warn all who fear God against all philosophy, against all human traditions, and [against] cunning deceptions, Col. 2:[8]. Furthermore, we so desire to admonish each one in our simplicity that he hold firmly to Jesus Christ in which all treasures of wisdom and knowledge of God lie hidden, yes, in whom the entire fullness of God dwells bodily, that we may receive from his fullness grace upon grace, John 1:[16], and everything that is needed for the salvation of our soul.

This is the reason for our writing. The eternal and only wise God give us wisdom and understanding for it, so that his highly praised name may be praised, the bound and restricted conscience may be unbound and freed, and the elect may be kept from all evil, comforted, and strengthened. Amen.

Accounting and explanation about our trip, namely, why we traveled out of P.[russia] delegated by our congregation and have come here [Emden] with the help of the Lord.

We cannot with good intention hide from you how that we have for a long time had great sorrow in our heart about the disturbance and destruction of God's congregation. Yes, not only we, but the congregation in P.[russia] has concerned itself, has become sad and troubled about it, since it has received letters and supplications from which it could easily note and understand the distressing present need which is everywhere in the congregations. Therefore, it has also been moved to send us out to listen to both parties, to investigate and determine where the truth is and where it [may be] found. With those we should agree upon what is right and true and should accept and support it.

Thus we have come here, delegated out of such reasons by our brothers, yes, out of the power of our commission which we have from God, out of duty to our calling which we have from the congregation, and [out of] our debt to our ministry. So we have taken every care to get both parties together so that we might finally hear and thoroughly understand the disputed matter. But we could not succeed in that. For the Flemish (as they are called) were certainly prepared for that, yes, they have had a longing for it, that their matter might finally truly come to the light of day. But the Frisians (as they are called) did not wish to do it that way; they have not wanted to accept our reasonable, friendly, and Christian request and desire. That saddens us much, that such unreasonableness, unrighteousness, and stubbornness, without any modesty is found among them. For since they are accused so much and in many ways by so many, they are obligated to purge [themselves] and respond before all their complainants and accusers, and let everything be judged with God's Word.

But the Fr.[isians] /551/ have not wanted to do that, which is a sure sign that they are wrong.[12] For the Lord said in the Gospel: Whoever does evil, that one hates the light and does not come to the light so that his works will not be punished. But whoever does the truth, that one comes to the light so that his works will be revealed, for they are done in God, John 3:[20-21]. Of this we have a clear example in the biblical Scripture, to wit, that Moses saw two Hebrew men who were quarreling and wrangling and spoke to the unrighteous one: Why do you strike your neighbor? But he said, Who has placed you as a supervisor or judge over us? Will you also murder me just as you murdered the Egyptian? And thus brought the hidden matter of Moses to be known so that it came before Pharoah who sought to kill Moses. Therefore, Moses had to flee out of Egypt, Exod. 2:[13-15]. Notice that the innocent one did not address Moses, but the unjust one [did]; he did not want to be punished or judged by Moses.

It still happens that way. Those who are and will be oppressed desire and seek help. But the unrighteous, who do not fear God and who do wrong and violence to their neighbors, those do not want to appear before the truth nor be held to account; they prefer proudly and stubbornly to stare down their accusers, adversaries, and punishers, and do still more, just as we and many others have often experienced from such people.

And if anyone will say that the quarrelsome matter between the Fr.[isians] and the Fl.[emish] is already judged, we answer thus to it: Since we could not get both parties together, and the guilt is actually with the Fr.[isians] whom we have presented more than enough, invited, pleaded, and begged through the crucified Jesus Christ, that they would respond before their adversaries in our presence (still we could not succeed in having them do this), therefore, we must now free our conscience before God and reveal and make known to all

God-fearers our concern over the judgment, decided and expressed in Fr.[iesland] by some: that we do not consent with that judgment nor are we able to accept it without more evidence out of God's Word.[13] /552/ [For] we do not understand, nor does it appear that it was judged orderly according to Holy Scripture, according to godly truth and righteousness, but much more according to the contrary. The reasons why we have such insight therein are as follows:

Reasons why we hold the Judgment [to be] Suspect

First, Ho.[yte] R.[enix] received the ministers, when they first came to Fr.[iesland] last year [1566], calling them welcome. But when he noted [that] the ministers could not agree with him, that the ministers of the cities might be the competent or appropriate judges between the Fr.[isians] and their adversaries (as they were also understood to be in the human covenant out of which the quarrel has come, as well as the others), therefore the ministers were held outside and excluded from the judgment that Ho.[yte] R.[enix] with his second examiners have given to Fr.[iesland.] Yes, they were also accused with regard to their arrival, although their arrival was right and evangelical, for they had come in the name of the Lord out of the power of their calling from God, because of their ministry, sent from their congregation out of brotherly love to seek peace between both parties and to find out after the quarrel with whom the guilt was. Still they were accused and set back as partisan.

Notice the great impropriety and the wrong that has been done to the men, for there is boasting that they traveled back out of the country with shame. Thus Ho.[yte] R.[enix] has said, which is proof that he did not anticipate any good could come of it, or that one should describe [this] or offer it to us; [that] he would rather seek and use means to hinder or to warn us. And if we came anyway, we would be received as little as the others, /553/ out of which is plainly to be noted that he did not have good intentions at the time and was planning even worse difficulties which he bore after that time.

Second, as the t.[eachers] and m.[inisters] noted that they could not progress in Fr.[iesland], but were always hindered in their good resolves by H.[oyte] R.[enix], they prepared to leave; and before their departure they admonished and warned H.[oyte] R.[enix] that he should use no sharpness for they did not approve of it, but they wanted to write to us and desired of him that he should do so also, but he rejected that and spoke as is related above, and has continued in his stubbornness.

In addition, H.[oyte] R.[enix] has been accused by the brothers at Fr.[aneker] about Nette, our dear b.[rother] who has died in the Lord, with banworthy matters and has not cleared himself thereof, nor does he want to clear himself.[14] Furthermore, he has thus judged, which is clear proof of his presumption and wrongness, that he does not respect the word of the ministers, that he wants to judge others, though he himself was punishable and perhaps was much more guilty before the Lord than those with whom he has dealt so severely, according to the example of the roguish servant, therefore the righteous judgment of God has stricken him, Matt. 18:[34-35].

Third, the Ho.[llander] men were already defiled through the unscriptural action and undertaking of an undisciplined man, which undertaking is entirely contrary to God's Word, also contrary to the intention of our congregation, wherein the misdeed was begun and in part occurred. Persons had written to us for counsel but before our answer came the apostate was already received [into the congregation]. Therefore, thus we have also afterward written /554/ to the assembly at H.[oorn] that our and many God-fearing souls could not agree to that action, for many reasons which we have about it and which are well known also at H.[oorn], for it was written to them modestly enough. They must be careful in what they have done and what they still maintain, whether they are not in the ban just as Israel was in the ban on account of Achan [Joshua 7], and that a little leaven has not already soured the whole dough.[15]

Fourth, there are brothers who want to prove and with sufficient witnesses convey to J.[an] W.[illems] that he was a liar already before he and his companions traveled to Fr.[iesland] and accepted the [task of] mediation. He was also here at this place [namely, Emden] clearly told to respond in the presence of his adversaries for [the sake of] the men who would convince him of the lies, but he has not done that. We also suspect that he will never do it nor can he; from which it is easy to understand how his judgment may stand, according to the word of Ecclesiasticus: What can be cleaned by the unclean and what truth will be said by liars, Ecclus. 34:[4].

Fifth, thus the five teachers with their co-helpers again came to Fr.[iesland] last December [1566], and [were] once again kept from working at mediation, and accused afterwards as before for [the motives?] of their coming. But persons did set up two of the youngest teachers as judges, who because of their age may not have had such a difficult assignment before. And since they could take as co-judges whom they wanted, /555/ many God-fearers thought and did not doubt but that they would [choose] the oldest and most experienced as co-helpers.[16] But they have not done that (and thus have become untrustworthy and have not kept their promise), but they have followed Rehoboam's example, and have chosen men according to their own purpose and liking, 1 Kings 12:[8], of whom some, after all, were incompetent for it that they should be judges, about which we know enough.

And although this is altogether contrary to reasonableness and justice, as also contrary to the plain Word and command of God, nevertheless, it must thus all be called done, Deut. 17. Still persons speak so boldly: It is a judgment and shall remain a judgment. Another said: We do not want to be dominated. The third said: We certainly have understanding about godly and worldly justice, although we [might be] taken from the cradle not long ago. And many such bold, haughty words are spoken there, which we know well, although we are still silent about them. Oh, Lord, have mercy for your people and see the spite and pride which reigns and has taken the upper hand in the congregation under the appearance of your Word.

And if anyone wants to identify us with any party, we answer and confess with Paul, 2 Cor. 5:[16], that we know no one after the flesh, that we agree with the truth and are partisan against the lie and unrighteousness. Otherwise we know of no partisanship.[17] But if persons want to speak about parties, that is proof that the principal judges were full of parties already before they came to Fr.[iesland.] But we take sides with no party; we also judge no one, but we hold ourselves to that which the Lord Jesus Christ said in the Gospel: Whoever hears my word and does not believe, I will not judge that one, for I have not come to judge the world, but to save the world. Whoever despises me and does not accept my words, that one already has one who judges him. The word which I have spoken, that will judge him in /556/ the last day. For I have not spoken about myself but of the Father who has sent me. He has given me a commandment of what I shall do and speak. And I know that his commandment is eternal life. Therefore what I speak, that I speak just as the Father has said to me, John 12:[47-50]

Shall the Lord Jesus Christ now not judge, since all authority and judgment on earth and in heaven are given him from God his Father, Matt. 28:[18]; John 5:[19ff.], but if his Word will judge, where do the judges with their Compromise remain, who have set themselves in place of God's Word and judge according to [that standard]? Oh, woe the unrighteous judgment, the distressing and mournful dealing, with which the congregation of the Lord is so disturbed and destroyed. The judgment and dealing makes us afraid, calling to heaven over those who expressed and handled it. Therefore, we would rather die with the Lord's help than that we would express or consent to such a judgment. If persons could support that judgment with God's Word, we would reasonably have accepted it. Yes, we were truly obligated to accept it. But now [even] with much admonition and praying, with great patience and long-suffering, we could not get so much that the persons will respond to their accusers and complainants. So much reasonableness, modesty, yes, fear of the Lord, Christian nature, and brotherly love was not found among [those] people that they did what they should have wanted to do. We, who with right accuse and shall accuse [them] before God, the God and judge over all, before his angels, Heb. 12:[22ff.], and before all understanding and nonpartisan brothers and friends, as long as the controversial and hard-necked do not repent therefrom; that they (according to our opinion) will hardly do. For it is to be suspected and [we are concerned] also that they are already hardened and that they are already struck blind by God and that they have surrendered to perverted senses, 2 Pet. 1:[9], because they have set themselves stubbornly against God's Word and strive with force against it, 1 John 1:[1ff.]; 2 Thess. 2:[4].

See, dear brothers, you who love righteousness and hate the ungodly being, we speak with you before God, and we confess to you that those reasons which we related above, and still many others which are too long to write about here, move us, yes, compel us that we hold that judgment or declaration to be unjust, as that [which was] given and expressed from lack of understanding, partisan, /557/ and corrupted judges who in the context following the Scriptures may not be judges. God keep every pious and simple heart from that. Amen.

Further, since these earlier disturbing quarrels originally had come out of the human covenant, therefore, we were through the love of the Spirit which we have to the brotherhood of the Lord Jesus Christ, forced and could not do otherwise than that we must reveal our mind and understanding to the true Christians; first, what we hold as the only covenant of God; thereafter what we feel, understand, and acknowledge about the human covenant.

About God's Covenant

The covenant of God is that God binds himself with us, that is, our promise and commitment that he wants to be our God and Father, just as God spoke to Abraham: I am the God Shaddai, that is, an almighty and superabundant sufficient fullness of all good; walk before me and be [lean] firmly and trustingly on me. And I will make my covenant between me and you, and I will multiply you steadily, Gen. 17:[1-2]. These words of God we understand thus, that God obligated himself with Abraham and with his seed, that is, with the believers, and has promised them that he will be their God and Father, their protector and keeper, for in him is complete almightiness, thus, that no one may withstand him nor take anything out of his hand. In him is the fullness and superabundance of all good. In him is the fountain of life out of which the thirsty souls shall drink and not out of an unclean cistern or mud hole. He feeds his people with the flower of the meel, and satisfies with honey and drippings of the honeycomb, that is, with his godly Word, Deut. 33; Isa. 40; 44; John 10; Jer. 2; 17; Ps. 19; 118. In summary, the covenanted companions of God lack nothing good. For they say with the prophet: Oh, Lord, whenever we just have you, we do not ask after heaven nor after earth; yes, whenever also our body and soul languish, you are even so our heart's comfort and our share.

And that is the first part of God's covenant, /558/ for although God's covenant is the single and eternal covenant, two parts are included in it: the first relates to God, and about it [we have just] said; the other relates to the believer, and it exists therein that God spoke to Abraham: Walk before me, hold yourself firmly and trust in me, Gen. 17:[1]; therewith all covenanted companions of God and true children of Abraham are admonished by God that they should lead a God-saving walk, serve the Lord in holiness and righteousness, remain by his Word firmly and unmoveably, Luke 2; Col. 2; Matt. 24. These children of Abraham and covenanted companions of God must also have the sign of the covenant, that is they must be circumcised on the foreskin of the heart with the spiritual circumcision of Jesus Christ, through the putting off of the sinful body and fleshly lusts: they must also be buried with him through baptism and also raised up with him to a new life through the faith that God works in them, Col. 2:[11ff.]; Deut. 30:[6]; Rom. 6:[4]; Col. 3:[5ff.].

Oh, that all they, who now at the time of God, are called with Abraham out of Chaldea to that true promised land Canaan, that is, from the unbelieving and idolatrous world to that kingdom of God, to that new Jerusalem, [would] observe their calling well and not entrust themselves too much to external signs. Still, as it appears according to the Lord's Word, few are chosen, for in Christ Jesus neither circumcision nor foreskin are valid, but the keeping of God's commandments, 1 Cor. 7:[19].

Now the chief summary of the commandments is, as the apostle said, love out of a pure heart, out of a good conscience, and out of a sincere faith—*a quibus, nempe a charitate, corde puro, bona Conscientia et fide non simulata*—[out of love, a pure heart, a good conscience, and authentic faith] from which some have strayed and thus given themselves to useless chattering, 1 Tim.1:[5]. Thus they want to be teachers and masters of the Scripture or the law, and do not know what they present, affirm, and establish. Just so it now happens with many. For many now speak little about the faith that works through love, and about the rebirth out of God, about the new creature, which is in Christ Jesus. But they talk and glory much about a human covenant and Compromise, which nevertheless do not count before God. For the blessing is not thereby promised from God. But that one is from God, out of his eternal love and bottomless mercy to all true Christians offered in Christ Jesus, Gal. 3:[14,15], /559/ whom God the Father has given us as a Lord, Deliverer, and Savior, who is full of grace and truth, and from his fullness we receive everything, so that we are completed in him, etc., 1 John 4:[14]; John 1:[16ff.]; Col. 2:[10ff.].

Now the covenant of God exists therein that we are children and inheritors of all his heavenly goods through faith in Jesus Christ. Through this covenant we are united with God. Therein and thereby God has accepted us and has chosen us to salvation in the sanctification of the Spirit and in the faith in truth, so that we should walk therein and serve him in the Spirit and truth. This covenant also teaches us how we shall pursue peace, that we should keep love and unity in the Holy Spirit with all true Christians and pay God the promise that we have made to him in baptism. That is, then, the covenant of the good conscience with God through the resurrection of our Lord Jesus Christ. This is an eternal, single, powerful, and unchangeable covenant of God that the almighty God himself has made, and no human being, which binds and unites God with all true believers and the believers with God. In summary, just as there is not more than one gospel and one New Testament (in which the covenant of God is stated), so also not more than that one covenant of God is valid in God's congregation. Of that a little has now been related.

We should love and hold this covenant as the Lord said through the prophet: Assemble for me my saints who love the covenant more than sacrifice. And once more: The grace of the Lord remains and endures from eternity to eternity, and his righteousness to the children's children, with those who keep his covenant and remember his commandments, that they then do accordingly. Therefore, Christians should concern themselves with this covenant of God, reflect and discuss it at all times, and think how they should serve God in his covenant with a good conscience and walk before him.

But as for the human covenant, everyone should watch himself who loves his soul, for that has no basis in God's Word; it has made and produced much trouble, irritation, and division. /560/ Therefore, it may certainly be called an abomination and idol and be compared with the golden calf that first Aaron, and following his example, Jeroboam thereafter, made and placed at Beth-El. This golden calf was put in the place of God's Word and service, Exod. 32. Moreover, as the people were to honor, worship, and show fear before it, it had to be called the Lord's feast, and those persons had to worship the God of Israel, for that one had led and delivered Israel out of Egypt. And Israel boasted always about this God, regardless of how many idols they had externally and internally in addition.

This is still happening, for persons certainly boast about God's covenant, about the gospel and the New Testament, but with it is that human covenant which is introduced under the appearance of God's Word. And [regardless of] how much evil has come out of it, it must still be called a good ordinance (that is, a new name) and the righteousness of the four cities (with which it is a human righteousness that is not honored before God); yes, one might truly say unrighteousness. For is there any righteousness other than that which comes from God and out of faith? Roms. 3, 4; Gal. 3. Where has God in his Word instituted or commanded to make such a covenant? Where is God's Word out of which that faith will come that persons will have to acknowledge and admit the human covenant as good and that it has any righteousness and power? Therefore, we say another time, that it is no righteousness and nothing other than unrighteousness.

In addition, we acknowledge that just as the worshipers of the golden calf, out of the command of the Lord given through Moses to the Levites, are reprimanded for the same thing, Exod. 32; Deut. 33, so also are the discoverers, establishers, and maintainers of the deceitful human covenant defeated through the sword of the Spirit, by the true Levites who have given themselves to the service of God, and [the former] have no more power than to puff and blow, yes, to lie and deceive, presumptious and banning, these are the weapons of their fight, and therewith they must help themselves, /561/ yet finally come to shame, just as has already happened.

And as we understand, they also seek praise because of us, or much more disgrace us therewith, as if we should have earlier praised the human covenant in our epistle to the c.[ongregations] in Fr.[iesland] and have acknowledged it for a good ordinance.[18] To this we say that in our writings we have everywhere (to our knowledge) written about the godly and not the human covenant. Without detracting from these, we praise all the good ordinances of God's congregation which were contained in and based on the Scripture, which are in accord and agree with God's Word and with the faith which Paul also wrote much about in his epistles, Col. 2; 1 Thess. 4, which also are not bound to a particular place, but just as the kingdom of God and its righteousness is with all true Christians, thus is also every good ordinance of the Lord with his congregation everywhere, and not alone in four cities. But one certainly knows what [they] had in mind with the human covenant, and it will certainly be revealed even more, etc.

About the Compromise

In the same measure persons have set up still another golden calf, namely that crafty Compromise. And this golden calf is placed at Dan for they judged according to it, the people were pointed to it, under it brothers were attached and taken captive as under a slavish yoke, 1 Kings [13:28ff.]. We have said above that God's Word alone is the judge, and that everything must be judged therewith. Is it not then well to complain that persons have set God's Word back and have judged according to an idolatrous Compromise? How is that any different than what the Pharisees did, who made God's commands as nothing on account of their traditions? For God had commanded: Honor your father and mother that it goes well for you, and you will live long in the land the Lord your God will give you. But the Pharisees taught the people otherwise, namely, that one should say to father and mother, Corban, that is what one should give to you is given to God, and thus they make God's commandments as nothing on account of their traditions. Therefore, /562/ the Lord has scolded them as hypocrites, Matt. 15:[4-7]. Beloved, what has been done otherwise with the covenant and the Compromise?

But now perhaps someone may say or think that we blaspheme, because we compare the covenant and Compromise with the two golden calves and call them idols. We answer thus to that, that we do not thereby blaspheme, but we say and witness to the truth. For everything that will be instituted, accepted, and held by persons out of their own thinking, and (as one says) instituted, accepted, and practiced with good intentions but as a disadvantage to the Word of God, as a burden to consciences, and to the destruction of God's congregation which is called in peace, is an idol, that is a loose confusing and destruction of the soul, even if it appears so beautiful, so worshipful, and as holy as possible, for through that God's Word and command is destroyed. And if anyone will ask wherein God's Word and command have been destroyed through the covenant and Compromise, thereto we answer that it is sufficiently explained and testified to above. And as further explanation we say once more that persons transgress God's Word and command about love and peace with it, restrict the conscience therewith, and have brought great disunity and division in the congregation of the Lord. Therefore it is an abomination before the Lord to act thus, John 15:[12ff.]; Col. 3:[14f.]; Eph. 5; 4; 1 Pet. 1:[22]; 3:[8ff.]; 1 John 2:[4ff.]; 4:[21]; 5:[2f.].

But we hope simply to remain by that Word that Jesus Christ said in the gospel: Who is not with me, that one is against me; and who does not gather with me, that one scatters, Matt. 12:[30]. From this it is easy to understand that one must be with Christ and gather with him. Or one must be against Christ, that is, an antichrist, and from him scatter. With Christ one gathers through his Word. Christ is scattered with human teachings, traditions, and commands. Therefore, Christ said in the Gospel: Set the tree well and its fruit will be good, or set the tree badly, and its fruit will be bad, for the tree will be known by its fruit, Matt. 12:[33]. From this it is revealed that everything is divided into two parts, and that one is against the other, the good is against the bad; yes, Christ against Belial, light against darkness, righteousness against unrighteousness, the truth against the lie, belief against unbelief, the temple of God against idols. What the one is, that the /563/ other and the opposite cannot be. Thus it is also with God's Word and the Compromise. For God's Word is the truth, and that must judge. For that one does not need any Compromise. For that one makes a Compromise is a certain sign that one neither cares to judge nor to act according to God's Word.

Here it is also well to note that God alone will be the Lord and master. Therefore he will not have anything added or taken away from his Word, Deut. 4:[2]; 12:[32]. He does not want one to turn aside from it to the right hand or to the left, Deut. [17:20]. Everyone turns off to the right hand who adds to God's Word; to the right as if the gospel is not sufficient to our salvation, that it is still a power of God and makes the believing ones saved. Those turn aside to the left hand who take something away from God's Word, who do not keep all the words and commands of God, who make themselves free to do what God forbids, 1 Cor. 1. Both are wrong, and those who do such are altogether liars, Prov. 20.

And to establish these even more, namely, that no human devotion, thought, or good intentions count before God, the example of Gideon teaches us well: For as the people spoke to Gideon, that he and his son should be lords over them since he had delivered them from the Midianite's hand, he spoke thus: I will be no lord over you, neither shall my son be lord over you, but the Lord shall be lord over you. But one thing I desire from you, that you give me the earrings or the head pendants which you have robbed from the Midianites or Ishmaelites. And they gave him the earrings and he made a body garment [ephod?] from them, and put them in his city, Ophrah. And all Israel practiced whoredom therewith. And it became a vexation to Gideon and his house. For since God had not commanded that, therefore, it was no worship of God, but idolatry, Judg. 8:[22ff.].

Yes, if God himself has already given some command or a sign, and it becomes misused, then an idol can result from it. And that is revealed therein that God had commanded Moses to set up a metal snake in the wilderness as a sign of the healing of the Israelites who were bitten by the fiery snakes, Num. 21:[8ff.]. This snake signified Jesus Christ, as he himself pointed to that sign, John 3:[14]. Nevertheless, the children of Israel burned incense and named it Nehushtan, thus it was broken by King Hezekiah and destroyed, 2 Kings 18:[4f.]. How much more /564/ shall the human covenant and Compromise be entirely destroyed, since so much discord, quarreling, and mishandling, moreover, parties and separations resulted from it, while so many God-fearing people are sadly deceived thereby, and also became the occasion of much slander by the adversaries. That is our confession about the covenant and God's Word, followed [by our account] about the human covenant and Compromise, by which with the Lord's help we hope to live and strive, and to appear and be before the judgment throne of Jesus Christ with it, yet all through the grace of the Lord.

Response to Our Letters Written to H.[oyte] R.[enix], J.[an] W.[illems], and L.[ubbert] G.[errits][19]

With regard to our letters, we hear that they have been interpreted and signified in the worst and most poisonous manner, just as is the nature of the perverted heart and false tongue. But we confess openly before God and every person that we have written the letters to the men mentioned before and the reason why we have written thus are many, of which we will relate some as follows.

First, we have shown enough above that the three principal judges with still others of their helpers were not competent [for the task] since they themselves were unclean and should not rightly sit in the chair of judgment. In addition it was said of them, and that one had wanted to prove to them, that they promised much by the Compromise, how they would judge everything with God's Word, so that no congregation would be troubled with it, but they have not done that.

They also had no commission from their congregation /565/ to use sharpness in Fr.[iesland], but they had a contrary command, not to do that without us. Yes, they were admonished and urged through the Lord Jesus Christ by our d.[ear] b.[rother] G.[illis] S.[cribe] that they should not do it, for they would have to give an accounting thereof. But they did it nevertheless and paid no attention to how many persons warned, admonished, and pleaded with them. Oh, bold presumption and pride that never does good and out of which nothing but evil can grow. While all this and still more has been repeated to them and they were required to respond to their accusers and complainants they still did not come. They would or could not respond to them. Therefore, they may not remain [active] ministers nor brothers in the congregation of the Lord so long as that does not happen, that is, so long as they have not been accountable to them.

Second, the two H.[ollander] m.[en] knew well that not only the brothers but many congregations were saddened by their activity and judgment. Nevertheless, they have broken the bread (but we say not the Lord's bread) here and there. Now the Lord said in the Gospel: If you bring your gift to God's altar, and there remember that your brother has something against you, so leave your gift at the altar and be reconciled with your brother, and then offer your gift, Matt. 5:[23-24]. Note how before all things quarrels and division between the brothers must be settled, peace and reconciliation made if they otherwise will serve God and proclaim peace. If these men had done this, they might also have made offerings [that is, served the Lord's Supper]. But since this has not happened, they could not make offerings, although they have appeared to make offerings, but it has certainly not pleased God.

Third, the judges, and at that time called t.[eachers], acted entirely unlike the apostolic example of how a bishop is to behave, 1 Tim. 3; Titus 1. There our opinion is sufficiently /566/ expressed, and to say that we have reason enough: But that we are silent about the reasons, that we do out of courtesy. We would otherwise certainly paint with their own colors that everyone might learn to recognize them as we now certainly know them, namely, as those who have served in the congregation for a short time and have saddened so many devout hearts with their guilt and have not yet repented of it. Yes, they have also through their haughtiness brought about that they cannot give account before any understanding and reasonable people. They may boast as highly and as much as they want, God knows them well.

Fourth, they have judged many innocents, banned and separated them, of which we have enough information. Yes, they have so acted that it may grieve a Christian heart that one lightly judges and rejects the pious, the God-fearing, and those who only desire to remain with God's Word. Therefore, as we observed such things, we put our soul into the Lord's hands and comforted ourselves with this, that our friends [would] become our enemies because we tell the truth.

Still we risked it in the name of the Lord to set truth up again in Israel (that no one should act according to his own good intentions, but alone according to God's Word), to comfort the saddened hearts, to strengthen the burdened conscience with the gospel, to release the captive, to declare peace to the oppressed and suffering, and to speak of the acceptable year of the Lord, that the unrighteous be punished, the discord be removed; righteousness and peace should be planted again, grow and bloom to the Lord's praise and the salvation of souls. If it does not happen with the perverted, apostate, and willful who have judged themselves, it shall still happen among the chosen, those who are left out of grace, among the small flock, Rom. 11:[5f.], the simple lambs of Jesus Christ who know their shepherd, hear his voice and follow him, Luke 12:[32]; John 10:[1ff.]. Therefore he also gives them eternal life and no one may take them out of his hand. He will certainly keep them from the biting wolves; he will turn aside the foxes sneaking in that they do not come into his vineyard and destroy it, Song of Sol. 2:[15].

We have also thought of the proverbs of Solomon, which go thus: Rescue those whom people want to kill, and do not withdraw from those whom persons want to murder. You say, /567/ we do not understand; do you not believe that he who knows the hearts notices this, and that he who watches over the souls, knows that? And rewards a person according to his works, Prov. 24:[11f.]. We have been guided by this proverb with the Lord's help and are of good courage, whether pressure or suffering, scorn and despising comes upon us from the apostates for it. We have often had to bear these in the time of our faith and service and have overcome through God's grace. We also do not doubt that the almighty God is with us, he will help us and give the victory through our Lord Jesus Christ. Amen.

Look, dear br.[others] and friends, we have here briefly related some reasons why we have written the letters to H.[oyte] R.[enix] and the H.[ollander] m.[en]. And we do not regret that, but we may well regret that we were silent and did not oppose nor reprimand the men in their wrong and willfulness. For we have clearly seen and observed that it has gone for us with both Hollander men, just as it went for the Lord with Saul, namely, that Saul quickly turned aside from the Lord, undertook to make a sacrifice above and against God's Word which was not commanded him, but he did it out of fear that the people would turn away from him and did not expect the prophet Samuel. Therefore, the kingdom was taken from him already at that time, since he had acted foolishly, 1 Sam. 13:[8ff.]. And the Lord regretted that he had made Saul king, 1 Sam. 15:[11].

So also we may well regret that we confirmed the two H.[ollander] m.[en] in the ministry, since in the beginning of their ministry they so quickly offered with strange fire, taking back [into the congregation] a godless and apostate one, and have brought that banned one into Israel out of fear of the people who murmured and would have the apostate restored as was said above. Notice how closely it conforms to the example of Saul, just as the other example of the Amalekites conforms entirely with the affair in Fr.[iesland]. Therefore they have, according to the example of Saul, through that righteous judgment of God, fallen on their own /568/ sword and thus perished, just as the prophet also said; the godless draw the sword out and bend the bow so that they might shoot the pious in the land. But their sword will enter into their own heart and their bow will break, Ps. 37:[14f.].

It would be better for us, and preferred, to go into the wilderness with Elijah, and to wish from the Lord that our soul might die than that we should see that the prophetess Jezebel would dominate in the congregation of the Lord, 1 Kings 19:[4ff.] and mislead the servants of the Lord. From the wicked Jezebel, although she is whitened, gaudy, and painted up nicely with false colors, the Lord will keep us and send to us in our sadness and loneliness that ashen bread and the water jar that we might be strengthened thereby to walk in the way of the Lord through the wilderness of this world until we come to God's Mount Horeb.

The same God will also sustain us with Elijah [as with] the widow in Zarephath, 1 Kings 17:[10ff.]; Luke 4:[25-26], through a little flour and oil in those troubled times, not through natural bread, but from God's Word which many will seek and not find. Yes, they will eat sourdough for sweet bread, must eat hogwash [or slop—Verckens draf] for the flour of the meal, and must drink unclean water that is defiled by people's feet. And that their shepherds do who lead them thus. But the Lord will have mercy over that just and simple people without any doubt, and himself care for his sheep and deliver them from all false shepherds. Amen.

Explanation of what we are accused of, that we did not want to speak with the Fr.[isians] and H.[ollanders]

Since we note, hear, and understand that we are accused and criticized as if we did not wish to speak with the Fr.[isians] and H.[ollanders], we say first of all about it, that the prophet speaks rightly of such people: it is spoken out of the depths of my heart about the way of the godless, that no fear of God is in them. They adorn themselves among each other to promote their wicked affairs and speak badly of others or despise them. All their teaching is damaging and lies. They do not let themselves be instructed, so that they might do something good. /569/ On their bed they think to do damage and stand firmly on the wicked way, and they spurn no evil, Ps. 36. Our adversaries may well consider and reflect upon these words.

But on the earlier mentioned accusation, we answer with the truth thus, that we spoke with the messengers out of Fr.[iesland] and H.[olland] six times at diverse times and have always desired, according to God's Word and our commission from our congregation, that both parties who were quarreling might come to each other, [in order that] the judges might put them before their complainants and accusers. But as was often related, we could not get an answer once [at all] that they wanted to do that. Moreover, we must let the God-fearers know how we have often written and invited the two H.[ollander] m.[en] that they should come to us. But they have not wanted to come [in response to] our writing and desire, but afterward they came with a great crowd.[20] When we learned of that, our two brothers H.[ans]

S.[ikken] and G.[eert] H.[arms] went to them to bring these two men to us. But they did not succeed in getting it done, neither from I.[?] S.[?] [21] nor from anyone else where they were in the inn, although they tried twice. We are silent then that at our desire they would have wanted to speak with us.

In addition to all that, we must also relate that four men out of N.[orth] H.[olland] have come and brought us a letter which had the same contents and meaning, namely, that the m.[inisters] in N.[orth Holland] could not consent that J.[an] W.[illems] and L.[ubbert] G.[errits] should come to us, /570/ but they have desired and required, after as before, that we should come to H.[oorn]. In the same manner, five men came from Fr.[iesland] at that time who desired that we should come to Fr.[iesland]. And they had already decided among themselves that they should travel to us as the present deed has shown. Is that spoken according to the truth, and dealt with according to Christian nature, that we give to the God-fearing reader to consider.

Afterward, when we noted that they did not want to come to us, we said that we rather wanted to come to meet the H.[ollander] m.[en] over [on?] the Ems [River] so that our meeting and discussion might remain private. In this manner and intention, we have spoken whereupon the Fr.[isians] and H.[ollanders] have answered, they wanted to make every effort to have the men who were named earlier, willing that they should meet us, whether it was at D.[illum?], or at C.[?], or at Gr.[oningen], or in the D.[am, i.e., Appingedam], or finally at E.[mden]. And as the nine men and emissaries out of Fr.[iesland] and No.[rth Holland], who had come to us departed from us and would thereafter work as was said above, the Fr.[isians] and H.[ollanders] were already traveling, yes, perhaps had already come to D.[am, i.e., Appingedam] and expected the emissaries there. Is that handled truthfully as it behooves one to act? That we could not understand, but we certainly know how we see [think of] such activity, etc.

After we now have known and experienced all of this, with what cunning persons dealt and related with us, we have canceled entirely rightly every appointment, message, and activity as long as both quarreling parties have not spoken with each other, have accused each other, /571/ [and not] responded or explained everything according to the reported format.

For it was still (as we said) impossible to promote and administer something good in the matter as long as that had not happened. Therefore we must be called fugitives (deserters) from the field by them, as if we were ashamed to show ourselves during the day, even though we often desired to have an open discussion as was related sufficiently above, but it is always refused us and [they will] not consent.

Beyond this persons want to admonish us that we should consider what we have written earlier to our dear b.[rother] M.[enno] S.[imons]'s memory. *Audi alteram partem.* [To hear the other party]. And, therefore, that we desire such with all our heart and hold this to be right, are still unchanged in our mind, honoring reasonableness and right, that it happen thus. Thus we are now highly accused and must be scolded as fugitives (deserters) from the field. Yet God knows which are the fugitives (deserters), and who hates the light because their works are evil. And thus we must be scolded after all by the bold Ephraimites, who left them at their boasting, at their strength and multitude (for the name Ephraim includes that) as the fugitive (deserters) Gileadites, Judg. [12:1-6]. But we comfort ourselves against it with the example of the biblical Scripture that God punished haughty Ephraim and elevated the despised Gileadites according to the proverb: God opposes the haughty and gives the humble his grace. Amen.

Now as the Fr.[isians] and H.[ollanders] noted that they were captured by our proposition or proposal (for they say that they will purge themselves, they found themselves burdened as they themselves have confessed, for they well knew that they could not continue; and they said that they did want to do it; thus they certainly thought they must come to shame before all the God-fearing and reasonable ones). Therefore, they have thus produced the advice of Ahithophels, 2 Sam. 17:[21-23] (Ahithophel means an apostate brother) and have wanted to oppress us. But the grace of God through the Chusai [their choice] already provided something better for us. For in that they have wanted to judge us, they have judged themselves, just as Absalom /572/ wanted to slay his father, David, and himself remained hanging on the oak tree with his beautiful hair. Thus these people also stumbled in their haughtiness, and as Peter said, died in their snare, having separated themselves from the Lord and from his congregation, just as we have sufficiently told and witnessed to both in writing and orally.

We relate this, therefore, that any God-fearing one may know how these people have judged themselves and actually not us. For we had not come to judge, but to make peace as much as was possible for us through the Lord's grace. Therefore we have borne with them with all Christian patience and expected their improvement, just as is fitting for Christians. It is for this reason that we have also shown all long-suffering to the malevolent and contrary, so that we should measure them with the fullest measure. But they could no longer hide their evil and perverted nature, but they have wanted to judge us, and thereby have they judged themselves, as was said above. And we hold them for apostate and separated people whom one must avoid according to the apostles' word, knowing well that they are perverted and sinful, as they have condemned themselves, Titus 3:[10f.]. We also do not doubt this; their own conscience (if they otherwise still have and feel any conscience) certainly accuses them in any case, that they have not acted rightly. But it appears that they are of the nature of which Sirach speaks, namely, that many a person prefers to do his worst rather than that he would lose his honor, and do such on account of the godless people.

We also understand that we were slandered very much because we opposed and rejected that which so many wanted, accepted, yes, have undersigned, and have then separated in peace. To that we answer thus: we certainly acknowledge that we have not wanted to accept the Compromise and acknowledge it as right, even if many hundreds, yes, thousands, [had] willed and signed it. For what we hold about it is said above, and that we have already acknowledged in P.[russia].[22] We have also not come here to consent to and support that Compromise or that judgment (one had to first prove that to us with the truth) /573/ but we keep to God's Word, that is our judge; and we hope with the Lord's help to do as Moses taught us and said, You shall not believe a false complaint, that a godless one confirms, and is a false tongue; you shall not follow the multitude to evil, and not answer before the court that you run aside from the right (following after) the multitude, Exod. 23:[1f.]. And Jesus Sirach said, Do not rely on the multitude that thereby you do wrong, but fear the Lord. Do not let any wind move you and do not follow any way, just as the wavering heart does, Ecclus. 7. Therefore we desire hereafter to be guided by this, and not let us be intimidated by anyone (through God's grace), nor move us from our firmness which is in Christ Jesus, 2 Pet. 3.

Afterwards persons called us troublemakers, breaking the peace and destroying God's congregations. To that we answered that we are not those people but they themselves have over a long time disturbed and destroyed the congregation of the Lord not a little, now with their human covenant, now with their Compromise and judgment. In the meantime we have held to our congregation in good peace and have stayed outside of the quarrel. Yet they want to be called the peacemakers and blame us as peacebreakers, and that because we cannot consent to nor accept the Compromise and judgment. But if we had wanted to do that, we would be the dearest friends.

Thus persons portray us with our entire family as an old father to be cared for in old age. That is the bread that persons have shown us with the one hand. But now that we out of the fear of the Lord and on account of our conscience cannot do so, we are accounted as the most evil enemy and are most atrociously disgraced. Those are the stones which persons throw at us now, and do not consider that whoever throws a stone high into the air, it will fall on that one's head, Prov. 28; Ecclus. 27:[25]. But we through the Lord's grace, with the old Eleazar, would still rather die honorably for the truth than that we should be hypocritical on behalf of someone else's will and thus live in pretense and shame. If then sadness and misery will overcome us and abuse us, we know why we suffer such, and that it befalls us from the perverse, apostate, /574/ and godless people, just as we have also written to H.[oyte] R.[enix].

But they that revile and slander us, causing suffering and sorrow (as much as they can), that saddens us on their behalf, but on our behalf we thank God that we are delivered from these perverse and wicked persons, 2 Thess. 3, since they will not improve themselves so that God's Word might run true. We have often prayed that out of the simplicity of our heart, and said with the prophet, Deliver us, Oh, Lord, from evil persons; keep us from spiteful people who think evil in their hearts, daily engage in strife; they sharpen their tongue as a snake, the poison of adders is under their lips. The proud lay ropes for the pious, prepare nets, place traps on the way; they dig pits and fall into them themselves, Ps. 140:[1-5]. They weave spider webs, and hatch snake's eggs, Isa. 59:[5].

But God has kept us from that, that they have not taken us captive and we have not eaten from their eggs. For if persons eat from them, they must die. Therefore, we would rather with the Lord's help want to tread thereon, not being afraid although a basilicus[23] comes out of there. For when they blow the most poisonous and revile most atrociously, we trust ourselves with this, that the Lord will not let the godless have their desires and does not strengthen their willfulness. They may pride themselves in this. And a perverse mouth will have no luck upon earth, and a spiteful evil person will be expelled and dumped. For we know that the Lord will carry out the affairs of the miserable and the poor rightly. Also the righteous will thank the name of the Lord and the pious remain before his face, Ps. 140:[12ff.].

Again, what is an evil tongue and what can they execute? It is like a fire in genever wood, that at first will blaze up high because of the oil in it, but afterward dies down and goes out, Ps. 120:[4]. Thus will their slanders also disappear and melt and die with shame in themselves. But the truth will triumph and the righteous will remain as an olive tree in the house of the Lord and rely on his goodness eternally, Ps. 52:[5ff.].

Again, persons boast of many congregations in Fr.[iesland] and N.[orth Holland], but that is no more than idle boasting. If boasting /575/ should count, we also certainly want to boast in the Lord. But now we would rather say with the prophet: Oh, Lord, how are our enemies so many, and so many are against us and say about our soul that it has no help from God. But you, Lord, are the shield for us, which gives us respect, which blesses us, as the Bileamiters, [1 Chron. 6:70], want to curse us. Therefore we are not afraid for many hundred thousand who oppose us with all their purposes. For the Lord strikes all of our enemies on the jawbone and breaks the teeth of the godless in pieces. With the Lord is help and his blessing is over his people, Ps. 3:[1-8].

The apostle Paul says that in his first response no one stood with him but the Lord alone, that Phigelus and Hermogenes with all those in Asia have turned away from him, 2 Tim. 1:[15], that the Galatians have fallen away from the gospel and also from Paul, Gal. 1:[6ff.]; 3:[1ff.]; 4:[8ff.], that Hymaneus and Philetus have deviated from the faith and also perverted the faith of some; that Alexander, the coppersmith, opposed him severely and did much harm. Diotrephes also ruled over the congregation with force and chattered much about John, as some still have the nature of Diotrephes, [3] John [9-10].[24] Again, in Revelation one reads about many false teachings and sectarians, yes, that in entire congregations not much good was found, as in the congregations at Sardis and at Laodicea, Rev. 2; 3:[1-6]; [14-22]. The one was living dead; the other was neither cold nor warm, but lukewarm. Nevertheless, there were still a few names at Sardis who had not dirtied their clothes, who will walk with the Lord in white clothes, for they are worthy of it. We hope that of such names many will still be found who will not have wanted to soil their clothes, but wear and keep the true wedding dress, Matt. 22:[1-14].

Conclusion, With an Admonition to the God-fearing

We have now briefly related our confession about the quarrelsome affair in Fr.[iesland] out of which has come so much harm, as we hope to present ourselves before the Lord with it in his grace. Moreover, we so desire that everyone who desires to keep his soul observes and takes to heart the admonition of the apostles, namely, that we should not have received God's grace in vain nor neglect it, /576/ that an evil, unbelieving heart be not found in any of us, [a heart] that turns aside from the living God, but that we admonish each other daily, that we may not be carried away through the deceptions of sin. For we have become partakers of Christ as long as we keep the beginning of his being unto the end, Heb. 3:[1-15]; 12. That being of Christ is a truly created being, a spiritual mindedness, a godly nature, and all believers have become partakers of the same through the promise of the Father in the new birth, as long as they flee the passing lusts of the world, Eph. 4:[17-24]; 2 Pet. 1:[4]; John 3:[3ff.]. But such Christians are few to be found, according to the witness of the Scripture and the evangelical parables, which clearly show us that they are not all Christians who have the name of Christ and boast of the Lord's sign, Matt. 13; 22:[1-14], 25.

So let us now watch that in these perilous and evil days, we lay a firm foundation of faith and always have concern in God's Word, admonish one another mutually about the faith, about the obedience of the gospel, about Christian peace, about godly and human love, and about the new birth to God, Ps. 1; 118. For that is the real issue, not a human covenant and Compromise. About those we let the bold speak and the boastful spirits who now rise up in the congregation, who want to be more clever than God's Word teaches. Therefore, they are already rejected by the Lord and thrust from the throne, and the humble will sit in their place, 1 Sam. 2:[1-10]; Luke 2[?]. For we notice that it will now happen just as the Lord said through the prophet: Behold, I will turn my hand to the small ones, and it will occur that in whatever land (says the Lord) there are two parts, they will be uprooted and perish. And the third part will persist there. And I will lead and purify that same third part through fire, just as one purifies and tests silver, just as one tests gold. They will then call on my name, and I will hear them. I will say, it is my people. And they will say, Lord, my God, Zech. 13:[8-9].

The Lord also said through another prophet that he will take away the bold saints, that they will no more boast on account of his holy mountain, but he will let a poor, simple people remain who trusts in the Lord. The remnant in Israel will not do any wickedness nor speak lies, and one will find in their mouth /577/ no deceitful tongue, but they will pasture and rest without any fear, Zeph. 3:[11-13].

Dear brothers and friends, observe these and similar sayings of Holy Scripture which are very comforting, and consider which are these bold saints, namely, those who let themselves think that everything they present must have come down from heaven; who boast about great wisdom, of great might, authority, and calling from the four cities to full ministry, yet are not accepted[25] (note an idle, rash boast), yes, they speak as those who do not know about God, Ps. 73. For just as one who fears God from the heart and believes his Word knows God (what one must know and is necessary to salvation), that one is able to do everything through the Lord Jesus Christ who is the master and judge of all the words and works, Phil. 4, according to the word of Paul: the spiritual judge all things and are judged by no one, 1 Cor. 2:[14]. Thus again, who does not fear the Lord heartily and does not avoid evil (for that is a beginning of wisdom and the right understanding in God's Word), who is proud and puffed up, that one knows nothing, is able to make nothing, that one can do nothing, that one has nothing, although he thinks that he has much and has become rich and needs no one, Prov. 1; Ecclus. 1, 2; 1 Cor. 8:(1-3], yet everything has been taken from him and is given to the trustworthy servant, Matt. 24:[45-51].

Therefore, the bold and haughty spirits have nothing of the character and nature of Jesus Christ, but what they have, know, and speak, that is from him who as lightning is fallen out of heaven, because he was bold and untrue against his creator and has not remained in the truth, Luke [10:18], but has turned aside from it. He is a father of lies, John 8:[44], an adversary of God, an opponent of his godly Word, a misleader of people, an Apollion [Rev. 9:11], that is, a destroyer and killer of souls, who also sends out his servants under a hypocritical appearance, who have the form of God's salvation but they deny his power, 2 Cor. 10[?]; 2 Tim. 3. Their words are sometimes smoother and softer than oil and butter, and yet are bare swords, arrows, and daggers, Ps. 55:[21].

One must be on guard against such spirits and /578/ not be afraid of them, but on the contrary one must arm oneself with the armor of God, that is, with the breastplate of righteousness, with the helmet of salvation, with an evangelical, peaceful, and God-saving walk, with the shield of faith, and with the sword of the Spirit, and, in addition, a fiery prayer to God, Eph. 6:[13-18]. Against such knights of Jesus Christ, all proud spirits are able to do nothing. For the weapons of this knighthood are powerful before God, as the apostle said, 2 Cor.

10:[3ff.], to break all pride which arises against the acknowledging of Jesus Christ, and to punish all disobedience with the sharpness of the divine Word, without regard to persons, not minding that the world, the apostates, and the sectarians are against it.

For while they rave and slander and their mouth is so full of curses that they cannot prove or subscribe to the Scripture, we sit under the protection of the Most High (as the prophet said), and remain under the shadow of the Almighty. We say to the Lord, "Our refuge, our fortress, our God in whom we hope." For he delivers us from the snare of the hunter and from the harmful pestilence. He will cover us with his feathers, our refuge will be under his wings. His truth is shield and protection so that we do not fear before the terror of the night, for the arrows which fly in the day, for the pestilence which creeps in the dark, for the sickness which destroys in the midday. When thousands fall at our side and 10,000 at our right hand, still it will not touch us. Yes, we will see our joy with our eyes and observe how the godless are recompensed. For the Lord is our refuge, the highest is our sanctuary. No evil shall befall us, and no plague will come near our tent, Ps. 91:[1-10]. Yes, the Lord is our Shepherd, we will lack nothing. He pastures us on a precious landscape and leads us to fresh water. He quickens our soul. He leads us in the right way for his name's sake. And if we also walk in the dark valley, we still fear no accident, for you, Lord, are beside us, your rod and staff comfort us. You prepare a table before us against all our enemies. You anoint our head with oil, and pour our cup full. Goodness and mercy will follow us our life long and we will remain in the house of the Lord eternally, Ps. 23.

So be now well comforted in the Lord, dear brothers, for the /579/ almighty God is our strength and help in all temptations and need, Ps. 22. Jesus Christ, with his sanctifying teaching, is our only foundation, Rom. 8. We have built upon it, our only wisdom, righteousness, deliverance, holiness, reconciliation, and salvation, and we are not outside of him, 1 Cor. 3:[11]. The H.[oly] Spirit is our Comforter and Teacher who leads us into all truth and comforts us with the only eternal comfort and good hope through grace, John 15:[26]; 16:[7 ff.]; 2 Thess. 2:[13ff.]. The angels of God with the apostles are our witnesses and fellow servants who declared and left the gospel to us on which we believe and desire to remain in it with the Lord's help in eternity, 1 Pet. 1:[10ff.]; Luke 24:[44ff.]. The almighty God strengthen and empower us therein that we may hold firmly to the Word of truth, and do not forget to pray to God for each other in all prayers. For true Christians are still one body in Christ Jesus, one congregation of God, which has one God and Father, which confesses one Lord Jesus Christ who is the only born Son of the Father, endowed with one Spirit of faith, bought with one treasure, and are bound together with the bond of perfection, that is, with sincere love, Rom. 12:[4ff.]; 1 Cor. 10; 12; Eph. 4:[4-5]; John 17; 2 Cor. 4; Eph. 5.

And if now already through Jeroboam, many turn aside from the house of David and become an apostate Israel, 1 Kings 12, that does not weaken us. For they have turned aside from the living God. They fight for the human covenant and Compromise which they have. Therefore, they quarrel; with it they made separations and divisions and arouse such aggravation that it is without doubt that the Word of the Lord in the Gospel has spoken about him, through whom aggravation comes, such people are dealt with hard, they may think and encourage what they will, Matt. 18.

But with us is that only eternal covenant of God, and the Word of the Lord, a judge over everyone. With us is the ark of the covenant with the throne of grace, cherubims and altars to offer the burnt sacrifice and the full sacrifice to the living God, 2 Chron. 13; Ps. 51:[15ff.]. With us are the priests and Levites, yes, with us is our king Jesus Christ, who will slay all our enemies with the sword of his mouth and with the breath of his lips, Isa. 11; Rev. 19. We also do not doubt that everyone who fears God from heart and mind will abandon apostate Israel, [and] will not want to worship before the golden calves of Jeroboam, 1 Kings 12:[28ff.], but they will /580/ journey to Jerusalem to pray in the temple there and to bring their sacrifices to the Lord, Tob. 1:[6ff.]; 2 Chron. 12. We will herewith abbreviate our writing and conclude in the name of the Lord.

We hope that through God's grace still more reports about this affair and about the scandalous lies which our adversary spreads here and there will be brought to light in due time. But this little we have written hastily with a true heart and out of Christian compassion, which we have with the simple for their good and as a direction, and therewith we hope to stand before the Lord in his great day.

With this we also testify to everyone that we are innocent of all this quarreling, that we have not sought other than God's honor, the salvation of souls, and the welfare of the congregation, that we are unchangeably in the teaching of the gospel and in behalf of the truth, thanks be to God. We stand for the right; therefore we have become the enemies of the false ones, who deal perversely with their worldly statutes and human cleverness. [This is] for themselves an eternal shame with every God-fearing and understanding one (as long as they do not improve themselves, which will hardly happen according to our opinion) and as a greater sadness, aggravation, and burdening of many congregations of God.

Yet the Lord will certainly save his own, and the firm foundation of God always remains and has this seal: God knows his own, 2 Tim. 2:[19]. But if anyone will not accept our true and brotherly admonition and warning, but is hard-necked, unbelieving, and controversial, and will not let himself be helped from that evil generation, Acts 2:[40], of his blood we are innocent and go clean from him to our dear brothers and companions of faith, with whom we desire to walk in good peace and unity of the spirit all our life, Ps. 55, and to say with the prophet: behold how fine and lovely it is that brothers live with one another, just as the precious ointment which was poured out on the head of Aaron, which flowed down on his beard and garments, just as the dew which fell down upon Mount Hermon and made Mount Zion fruitful, for there God the Lord has commanded the blessing and life eternal, Ps. 133. Note, where brotherly love and unity is, there is God's blessing and eternal life, which God the Father gives to every God-fruitful one, through Jesus Christ, in the power of his Holy Spirit. Amen. The grace of the Lord be with us all. Amen.

D. P.

Printed in the year 1567

ENDNOTES

1. Cf.: Kühler, *Geschiedenis* I, p. 416, note 1.
2. The entire text of the Compromise was published by V.P., *Successio Anabaptistica, Dat is Babel der Wederdopers...*, Cologne, 1603, with a reprint 1612. This is one of several extant accounts of sixteenth-century Dutch Anabaptism written by an outsider of the movement. It was probably written to counteract a treatise by Mennonite Jacob Pietersz van der Meulen attacking apostolic succession. It was likely printed first in the 1578 Emden debate volume, *Protocol. Dat is Alle handelinge des Gesprecks tot Embden... met den Wederdooperen anno 1578*. Embden, 1579, fol. 371b. Samuel Cramer published the *Successio*, and therefore. the Compromise in BRN VII, 1910, pp. 62-64. See also ME 4:652.
3. See pp. 544ff. below. Hoyte Renix was an elder in Bolsward (Friesland) and a close follower of Leenaert Bouwens, both of whom sided with the Frisians, against Dirk, in the Frisian-Flemish controversy.
4. Koolman, p. 152.
5. Present text p. 507 (IDC microfiche), BRN X, p. 566.
6. Ibid., p. 508f. (IDC microfiche), BRN X, p. 568.
7. Ibid., p. 493 (IDC microfiche), BRN X, p. 549.
8. See the notes in A. Introduction, pp. 474-475 above, especially n. 18, where the original documents used for this section are listed. These were also used, of course, by the editors of the BRN. See BRN VII, pp. 1-87 and 489-564 respectively, as also BRN X, pp. 537-543 and, for some parts, IDC microfiche.
9. BRN X, p. 543.
10. Dirk's 1567 edition and the BRN X pp. 545ff. were used for this document. See also note 8 above. The Dutch title is: *Een cort, doch grondtlich verhael vanden twistigen handel ende onschrifmetigen Ordeel, dat in Fr. over sommighen, diemen de Vlamingen noemt, ghegheven is....*
11. *oorblasen*, literally ear blowing.
12. Dirk wanted to have both the Frisian and Flemish representatives meet together with him and his helpers at Emden, but the Frisians insisted on a separate meeting. Dirk had apparently been encouraged by his congregation in Prussia to hear both sides carefully. See above, also cf.: BRN X:569.
13. The sentence (judgment) which Jan Willems and Lubbert Gerrits announced was as follows: "That the Frisians, and also the Flemish, should kneel, confess their mistakes and guilt, ask each other for forgiveness, and henceforth live and walk in peace and brotherly love." The Frisians did this first, then arose. Then the Flemish, but as they were about to arise, the moderator said, "As erring brothers you may not arise on your own but must be given the hand of fellowship [forgiveness?] to arise." Outerman, *Onder verbeteringhe*, par. 216; cf. Koolman, p. 138.
14. Nette Lipkes (d. 1567), was an Anabaptist elder in the Dutch province of Overijssel who had just died before Dirk wrote this account. In 1566 he had been asked to help mediate the Frisian-Flemish dispute, eventually siding with the Flemish. He had participated with Menno Simons and others in Harlingen in the earlier discussions about the ban. It was in that context where the report originated that Menno had been threatened with the ban by Leenaert Bouwens unless he agreed with the rigorists, including Dirk. As the elders were discussing the ban, a woman by the name of Aplonij Ottes had listened outside the door and heard Bouwens say, "Menno has not yet grown above our head, and if he cannot follow us, we must do to him as we have done with the other ministers." She, in turn, had reported this to minister Alle Visscher who, later in Emden reported this together with Menno's personal admonition to him: "Do not become a slave of people as I have been." Hans Alenson's "Tegen-Bericht..." BRN VII, pp. 63, 258-259. On Lipkes see DB 1893, pp. 12ff, ME III:844, CWMS, 1010.
15. The reference appears to be to Jasper van Cocmen who had been excommu-

nicated by Dirk in Danzig and, on returning to the Netherlands, had asked for membership in the Hoorn congregation where Jan Willems and Lubbert Gerrits were ministers. They had written to Danzig for a reference, but received him as a member before they received the Danzig reply. Willems and Gerrits were also mediators in the Frisian-Flemish dispute. BRN X, p. 553, n. 8 and DB 1893, pp. 54-55.

16. Dirk again seems to imply that he was disappointed at not having been called to help at that time. He was clearly the oldest.

17. Dirk did accuse the Frisians of being guilty, as we noted above. How then shall we understand this claim to objectivity? Dirk did change sides as indicated above. On first hearing of the "Ordinance" he called it scriptural, saying that "the congregation of God can be built by [through] it." Outerman, *Onder verbeteringhe*, par. 17 and 313. He apparently became convinced later, when he came to Emden in June 1567, that he had been wrong, that this "covenant" was being seen as equal to the covenant of God.

18. The reference is likely to Dirk's Letter to the Four Cities, above. See also A. "Introduction" above for references to the possibility of Dirk having changed his mind about the "Covenant of the Four Cities."

19. See below pp. 544ff. The letters were also printed by Jacques Outerman in *Onder verbeteringhe. Verclaringhe met bewijs, wt den droevighen handel, van Vr. ende Vlam. . . . n. p.*, 1609. It seems clear that three or more letters have been lost. In this document Dirk refers several times to H.[ollander] m.[en]. Willems and Gerrits were from the province of Holland. His reference to ordaining an unfit person [Egbert Cuijper] is addressed to Hoyte Renix (see the following 7/8 June 1567 letter, Ibid.). The question was not so much about Cuyper's qualifications, though Dirk had problems with him, but that Renix had written Dirk for a reference but then proceeded to ordain him at Harlingen without waiting for Dirk's reply. Willems, Gerrits, and Renix were all ordained by Dirk.

20. Nine persons had been sent to Dirk at Emden from North Holland. He would not meet with them. On their way back, they met a new delegation, including Jan Willems and Lubbert Gerrits of Hoorn. Thereupon they all went back to Emden together. Dirk agreed to meet with two representatives but not with the entire group. He may have met informally with the larger group; the text is not clear. They spoke "six times," he states. His non-negotiable requirement, however, was that the two parties meet *together*. cf.: BRN X, p. 569, n. 5.

21. As noted earlier, initials were used to provide anonymity should state persecutors see these documents. It is not always possible to trace these identities now.

22. This statement would imply that he had already made up his mind before leaving home.

23. "A legendary reptile with fatal breath and glance." (Webster).

24. For Hymenaeus and Alexander, cf. 1 Tim. 1:20; for Hymenaeus and Philetus, 2 Tim. 2:17; for Alexander, 2 Tim. 4:14; for Diotrephes, 3 John 9.

25. The reference may be to Egbert Cuyper, chosen elder at Harlingen but not accepted by Dirk. He was among the 1567 delegation to Emden and the first to announce to Dirk that he (Dirk) had been placed under the ban. So F. Pijper, BRN X, p. 577, n. 1, based on Outerman, op. cit., 1609.

D. AN APPENDIX ABOUT THE FRISIAN—FLEMISH AFFAIR[1]

Introduction

A second delegation of North Holland and Frisian teachers arrived in Emden in early July 1567. Among them were Jan Willems and Lubbert Gerrits of Hoorn, Pieter Willems Bogaert of Monnikendam, and Hoyte Renix of Bolsward.[2] Nothing had changed for the better. Dirk would not change his position. He held to his requirement that both parties should respond before him in each other's presence.

The Frisians and Hollanders continued to object to that arrangement. The result was that they mutually denied each other fellowship.[3] A formal banning sentence was sent in writing to Dirk Philips and the two teachers of Danzig who accompanied him, Hans Sikken and Geert H[arms].[4]

The delegation did not limit themselves to this action. They sent a report about the judgment to the congregations at Groningen and Appingedam in a grave "Epistola."[5] The contents offended Dirk and the Flemish greatly. The substance of the report is known from the minutes of a hearing about the quarrel held in Hoorn in 1622, at which the letter was read, but the letter itself is lost. Following are some of the excerpts from the minutes (letter) based on the BRN X document, pp. 586 and the literature cited in note 5:

Par. 59. Again the letter from Groningen, 12 July, 1567, also testifies to that in which they themselves acknowledge that the judgment which Hoyte rendered over the Flemish was acknowledged as good by them (that is, the judges) which were nevertheless presented to the Flemish to prove that they cannot exist either according to heathen or evangelical truth.

Par. 64. Furthermore, the abominable [terrible—*grouwelicke*] letter, written to those at Groningen and the Dam [Appingedam] dated 12 July 1567, signed by Lubbert Gerrits, Jan Willems, Pieter Willems and Hoyte Renix, etc., was read.

Par. 65. In which they so abominably scold and blaspheme the Flemish and call them dishonorable, unbelievable, disturbers of the peace, and tumultuous people, who against all reasonableness, right and truth, against their own hand and mouth, promised, passed [a] contract, and agreed to freedom [in order] not to avoid the separated ones, thus violating the congregations' service, sacraments, and practices.

Par. 66. In sum, they write in the same letter that they are burdened with still more burdens.

Par. 67. Still, in the same [letter] they write about Dirk Philips, but without proof, the reason why he was given his farewell, that is, because of his tumultuous and bold madness, scandal, and shamefully spotted will, as one who rejects congregational service; who attacks, overburdens, and seeks to oppress the ministers with pride, without judgment, right, and modesty; who shames and scandalizes their honor, name, and fame very much with all the people.

Par. 68. Who reviles God's h.[oly] sacraments and practices without judgment and investigation, who blasphemes the godly ordinances, etc.[6]

After the banning sentence and this letter were known to him, Dirk Philips wrote the present document, "An Appendix to our Book about the quarrelsome affair in Fr.[iesland] between the Fr.[isians] and the Fl.[emish]." According to the literature cited, Dirk was pressed daily with demands from his adversaries to hold a disputation, but he saw little good coming from such an encounter. On the other hand his friends urged him to reply to it as the many references in the "Appendix" show.

He objected to further negotiations particularly because he felt his opponents did not take the Scriptures seriously. Yet he regretted the quarreling deeply. We note that he was even ready to offer his own blood to heal the division. Nevertheless, he also wanted to be clear about the unchanging character of his requirements for continuing the discussion, as we note at the end of his writing. He declares himself prepared for it as well as to hear the response of the Frisians on two conditions. First, they must rescind the banning sentence. Second, the requirement, from which he had never departed, must be met that both parties be heard equally and in each other's presence.

It is evident again from this "Appendix" that Dirk saw the cause of all the misery that had come upon the [Doopsgezinde] Mennonite world in the "Covenant of the Four Cities" and in the subsequent Compromise, which they had substituted for God's Word.[7]

An Appendix /589/

Written to our booklet about the quarrelsome matter in Fr.[iesland] between the Fr.[isians] and the Fl.[emish] (as both parties are named), with an apology, that is, reasons in defense of, or accounting of, why we at this time do not desire to hold any meeting with the apostates, the adversaries of the truth and of the congregations of God, in the manner they propose, but according to the Scripture, in all Christian modesty, truth, and love we hope through God's grace always to be found willing.

I pray you, dear brothers, that you take note of those who make and execute division and offense against the teachings which you have heard, and separate yourself from them, for those who are thus do not serve the Lord Jesus Christ but their belly, and through sweet preaching and flattering words mislead the simple hearts. Rom. 16:[17-18].

/590/ An heretic, that is a factious person when he has been admonished once or twice, avoid him, knowing that he is perverted and sinful as one who judges himself. Titus 3:[10, 11].

The second letter to Timothy in the second chapter [16-17]. Avoid unspiritual, useless chatter, for it very much promotes an ungodly being, and their words bite and tear around him as a cancerous sickness.

Ecclus. 23:[15]. Do not rely on a slanderous one so that he not pervert your words, for a cunning man spies upon his neighbors, and who accustoms himself to slander will not be corrected all his life.

D. P.

/591/ Grace, peace, mercy with a true understanding of God's Word, and a clear vision in all godly manners and activities, we wish all God-fruitful brothers and friends, fellow companions of faith [and] lovers of truth, from God the Father and Jesus Christ our Lord, Deliverer and Savior, through the power of the Holy Spirit, Rom. 1:[7]; Gal. 1:[3]. AMEN.

You most beloved in the Lord, we pray almighty God for you out of the depth of our hearts, that it may go with all of you as Paul wrote to the Colossians, Col. 1:[9-13], namely, that you may be filled with all spiritual wisdom and understanding, that you please God, and be strengthened from him through his great power to all patience and long-suffering, with the joy of the Spirit, and be fruitful in all good works and thanksgiving. [Through] God the Father, who has made you qualified for the inheritance of the saints in light, who delivers you out of the power of darkness and has transferred you into the kingdom of his Son Jesus Christ.

Therefore, we admonish you and pray through the mercy of God that you remain steadfast in your faith that was once given to you from God, Judg. 1; Matt. 24; Eph. 3; 1 Pet. [2], yes, daily increase and grow therein, that you may be wise and understanding, not in human wisdom and subtlety, (in which some now study more, [and are] also more experienced [in it] than in God's Word), but in divine wisdom about which the apostle James writes, James 3:[13f.]. Oh, that this would be well considered by many, there would then not be so many quarrels among them who boast of being Christian.

It would also have been better and more precious before God that one had troubled and disturbed him with how one should live God-saved in JESUS CHRIST and please GOD, 1 Tim. 3, how that /592/ one may increase and grow inwardly, how one must be meek and patient, humble and gentle, joyful in the Spirit, and thankful to GOD for his unspeakable gifts, Eph. 4, that he called us out of darkness to his wonderful light, 1 Pet. 2:[9], yes, out of his bottomless grace and mercy has saved us, through that bath of the new birth and renewing of the Holy Spirit, which he richly pours out over his children, so that they believe in Jesus Christ and out of grace might become inheriters of eternal life according to their hope, Titus 3:[4f.].

If one took this to heart and everything that the Scripture teaches us and belongs to being God-saved spoken about here, and had examined himself herein day and night, it would have gone better in the congregations. But now quarreling and disputing has neither limit nor end, which must have grieved God in heaven and all peaceful children of God, Matt. 5:[9], on earth and still grieves, and how entirely that has all happened against our heart and mind, that the Lord knows. We have certainly proved this [love] by our service which we have done in every way, with admonition when present and in writing when absent, to the congregations in Fr.[iesland] more than once, out of a faithful heart and pure brotherly love.

God be thanked, who has given us the purpose and the courage, and we trust him also that he is powerful to guard the pound that he has entrusted to us, Matt. 25:[14ff.]; 2 Tim. 1:[12]. [This until] the day of his glory, in which he will appear with his angels and his flaming fire to wreak his vengeance over the unbelievers and those who have not been obedient to the gospel of our Lord Jesus Christ. Those will suffer pain and eternal destruction from the face of the Lord, when he will come to be glorified in the saints, and to appear marvelously in all the believers, etc., 2 Thess. 1:[7ff.].

We await this future of the Lord, longing for it; we comfort ourselves with it, and do not mind what /593/ suffering, reviling, and despising comes upon us from our unfavorable and opposing parties, but on the contrary, we are of good courage in the Lord, Rom. 7:[21ff.]. For we do not doubt at all about whether we are right, and hope to remain in it all our life, praying and humbly desiring from the most high GOD, our heavenly Father through JESUS CHRIST, that he help, strengthen, and empower us thereto with the power of his Holy Spirit, and to do everything that is pleasing to him, until the very end. Amen. 1 Pet. 5:[10f.].

But although we are comforted in our conscience, let us be content with the grace of God and do according to the prophet's word which says: *In silentio et spe erit fortitudo vestra*, Isa. [30:15]; that is, in quietness and hope shall be your strength. Yet we can nevertheless have no peace from the apostate and perverted ones, who now at this unseasonable time come with presentations and supplications (thus they must be called) and insist of us holding a meeting, wanting to show us that we have not written correctly in our booklet, that their ungodly and unjustified judgment rendered over us is true, even though it is as far from the truth as heaven is from the earth.

Therefore, we were so compelled in our own mind, also invited thereto by many God-fruitful ones to make a short response to them, although we would rather remain silent and unsuspected by everyone, as if we had any desire for such writing, in which we are nevertheless guiltless. For it has never been our manner, but now we must respond somewhat out of necessity. Yes, we must much more confess the right and the truth and strive for it. We know also that the Lord shall strive for us, Ecclus. 4:[28].

First, we have explained sufficiently in our booklet how we, on account of our calling from God, on account of our ministry, out of the duty of Christian love, and on account of our appointment and commission from our congregations, thus often, with much writing, praying, and admonishing, /594/ have sought and attempted to get both parties together so that we might hear and know where the truth was that we might support it. But we have not been able to gain nor receive that from one part (the Fr.[isians]).

From this it is plain that if our opposing parties, in any case, had desired to deal with us in a brotherly manner; yes, had wanted to show us in their faith any Christian courtesy and modesty (this they boast about, but God knows with what right), they should then not, after all, have objected to our little appeal and scriptural requirement. But now that they have shown their stubbornness toward us and others also, now they want to have a discussion with us and have not considered well that Solomon said: Who moves incautiously here pierces as a sword. And still once more: A bitter person tries to do damage there, but a horrible angel shall come over him. Again, the wise have their mouth in their heart, and weigh their words, but the unwise have their heart in their mouth [cf: Ecclus. 21:26].[8] For thus a word in an unwise heart pierces just like an arrow, which is placed upon the stretched bow, Prov. [25:18].

If our adversaries had noted and taken to heart these and similar passages of Scripture, they would probably have been more careful. We rightly had many [passages] to allude to that served this purpose out of the prophets, Ezek. 13, evangelists, Matt. 12, 14, apostles, 2 Tim. 3, and John's revelation, Rev. 2, 3, 12, 19, 22, but we will let these lie for the time being. If God wills and we live, they can still appear.

But now we must yet show to the good-hearted that these people were after all, according to the words of Jesus Christ, Matt. 15; John 12; Moses, Deut. 28; Peter, 1 Pet. 1; and John, 1 John 1, struck with great blindness from God, for when they were still called our brothers, they not only declined the before mentioned requirement, but they also, according to their perverted nature, wanted to judge us. Note all of you who fear God and are taught by him what blindness has overcome these people, John 6. For now that they have dealt with us and many others so stubbornly and godlessly, now they come to us in order to have a discussion with us, and we must be called their apostates (but with violence and injustice), yet they are the truly apostate before God and his congregation and held as such. /595/ With that they make themselves entirely a scandal. For if their presentation is now right, our before mentioned requirement is even more right, since we have made it to them when they were still called our brothers.

But now they have departed from the truth, and have declined our reasonable requirement, and proposed that it was unreasonable to deal with apostates, so each one must now consider how much more unreasonable it is that they want to deal with those whom they themselves have judged, and require and demand of us what they themselves did not nor have wanted to do. They cannot speak contrary to that in truth, as will be explained here more broadly in the following.

The reason that we cannot now agree to any meeting with the apostates in the form and setting they propose comes out of important and scriptural reasons. Since we sought by all means (in order to promote peace in the congregations) and could not carry it out because of their unwillingness, therefore, we must now act according to the counsel of the Holy Spirit, given to us by Paul, that is, that we will shun a separated person after sufficient admonition, for every Christian certainly knows that such a one is perverted and sinful as he has judged himself, Titus 3:[10].

Again, the principle troublemakers are portrayed by Solomon thus: whoever separates himself seeks what he desires and sets himself against everything that is good, [Prov. 11:6]. Now God's Word is the eternal and only good that all true Christians with Mary[9] have chosen, John 12:[2-8]; [Luke 10:42]. Contrary to that some have introduced a human covenant and Compromise from which have come these great difficulties and divisions in God's congregation. And if one speaks something against it and wants to instruct the teachers of these matters with God's Word, then it happens just as Jesus Sirach said, to wit: when one wants to teach an unwise person, he places himself as if one will shackle him hand and foot, [Ecclus. 21:19]. On this account Solomon also said that it is better to meet a bear when the young are taken from him than an adult who is left to his foolishness, Prov. 17:[12]. And once again: Behold, one who lets himself think he is wise, more hope is in a fool than in him, [Prov. 26:12]. For it is written: Woe to those who are wise in their own eyes and understanding by themselves, Isa. 5[:21]. /596/ Out of this it is plain how damaging one's own and human wisdom is.

In addition we see and note openly that these people proceed just as the Lord said through the prophet: Can a Moor change his skin or a leopard his spots? Even so this folk can do nothing good after they have been accustomed to evil, Jer. 13:[23]. In the same measure our adversaries are so used to blasphemies and scolding, to backbiting and robbing of reputations, and to lying, that these have become their refuge and help, and the truth has no place with them. Yes, these people now proceed just as the prophet said: Justice is turned back and righteousness has traveled far away. Truth that is pure and bright lies fallen down in the street and may not appear, Isa. 59:[14f.]. Yes, truth is led captive, and who turns aside from evil must be everyone's victim and [fall under] these people's yoke and despising. But God is trustworthy, says the apostle, who will not let us be tempted above our ability, but will give us an escape so that we can bear it, 1 Cor. [10:13].

Second, our opponents are not only apostates but also open liars and slanderers, just as their letter written to those at Gr.[oningen] and in den D.[am, that is Appingedam] testifies sufficiently. Yes, a more horribly slanderous letter we have neither seen nor read in our lifetime. We will remain silent about the other slanderous writings which have been made about us. On this account we desire neither to speak or deal with such committed slanderers. But we desire to judge ourselves according to the Scripture which teaches us that we should not blow on the godless in their fire so that we are not burned, Ecclus. 8:[10], and that we shall not depend on a slanderer so that he does not pervert our words.

Again: drive the scornful out; then the quarrel stops. For when the wood is no longer available, the fire goes out. /597/ Thus if the backbiter is gone, the quarrel comes to an end. Also, experience teaches us that one can not work anything good with the perverted, and it is impossible to do right with him who is intent on evil, but it proceeds just as the Lord Jesus Christ presented in a parable to the Jewish people about the children who said two kinds of things in the market to their playmates, still not getting or receiving, which parable the Lord himself explained: that neither John the Baptist, with the strictness of his living, nor he with his friendliness and fellowship could satisfy the perverted generation. But the wisdom must be justified by their children. Let him who has received understanding from God consider this, how wisdom from their children must be justified, Matt. [11:16ff.].

Since then no one, neither prophet nor apostle, yes, neither John nor the Lord Jesus Christ himself can satisfy the opponents, but they have always sought excuses to slander, what are we poor, insignificant people able to do? On this account we have rather followed Holy Scripture to remain untroubled than that we should act against God's Word; that [brings] nothing but trouble and work in vain with it. That warning and trustworthy admonition to the God-fruitful ones we hope with the Lord's help always to observe, so that we do not misuse or transgress upon the Lord, and also remain untroubled. For we find that our experience with our opponents is just as Jesus Sirach said: A false heart is as a decoy bird in a trap lying in wait to see how he may capture them, Ecclus. [11:30]; for what he sees as good he signifies as the worst of all, and the best of all he defaces to the utmost.

On this account it is not possible to speak nor to deal with such people, for if one speaks with them they turn the words around and change the truth into lies, as has been experienced by us from them more than once in our presence. What shall they then do in our absence? If we keep quiet, they pervert that also and interpret that as badly as they can. For their way is wrong, and those who [walk in] it will not know about peace. But with the true Christian it happens otherwise, namely, [that] there the peace of God /598/ has dominance in their heart, to which they were called in one body, and they thank God the Father through Jesus Christ, Isa. 59:[8]; Phil. 4:[7]; Eph. 4:[3f.]; Col. 3:[15].

Third, it often seems to us that we should consent to a meeting with our opponents (yes, much more with our judges, as they think of themselves) for the sake of the simple ones, so that they might be [safe]. To it we give this answer: that we value Christian simplicity, but let us examine what true Christian simplicity is, namely, that one is right and wrong as Job, fears God, and avoids evil. In this regard Ecclesiasticus said: [A] little cleverness with the fear of God is better than great wisdom with [a] despising of God, Ecclus. [19:24].

From this it follows surely that where true simplicity is, there is [also] the fear of the Lord which is the beginning of wisdom and [which] teaches cleverness to deal with every matter and prevents sin, Ecclus. 1:[14]. For where the fear of the Lord is, there the commandments of God are kept, there persons live holy and right (yet in weakness), Wisd. of Sol. [6:10]. Yes, there the person does not live anymore, but Jesus Christ lives in him through faith, Gal. [2:20]. There is the true simplicity of the dove to which the Lord pointed us. There is the innocence of sheep which follow their trusted and only Shepherd Jesus Christ and flee before strangers, John 10:[4f.]. That is what the prophet said: Oh, Lord, protect me for better or worse, for I wait upon you, Ps. 35.

Those are the truly simple who are not easily led into error, and if they are already deceived (since Satan still desires to sift the Christians as wheat), so will their faith still (through the intercession of Jesus Christ before God the Father) not cease, neither be entirely lost, but they will once more be converted to the Lord their God, and return again to the only Shepherd and Bishop of their souls, on this account, that they have feared the Lord and walked simply in his ways, 1 Pet. 2:[25].

But what shall we say to that, if it proceeds just as the Lord said through the prophet: It is horrible and terrible in the land. The prophets teach lies and the priests rule in their office, and my people like to have it that way. What will at last come of it? Jer. 5:[30f.]. And once more: My people are lost because they will not be taught, for they do not respect God's Word; thus I will also not respect you that you shall be my priest. You forget God's law, /599/ therefore, I will also forget your children, that they will be more, that they [will] sin more against me. Therefore, I will bring them to great shame, just as they have been great in glory. They eat the sins of my people and are entangled with the same misdeeds in their hearts. Thus the prophet is just like the people, etc., Hos. 4:[6ff.].

When it now happens that way, and the unwise people lie [as do] the false prophets and are satisfied with the godless priests' rule, and will have it that way, and are even like the lying prophets and the violent priests, what more is there to do against it than that one punishes with God's Word? We want, after all, to win many souls to Jesus Christ, yes, that all people may come to the knowledge of the truth and be saved. Therefore, we also pray for all people, just as the apostle Paul admonishes us. But what can a poor, weak, and miserable person do about it if the grace offered by God is despised by the thankless, disobedient, and contrary and will not be accepted? What more can the servant of the king do that the guests who were invited will not come to the banquet or wedding, objecting to it and seeking excuses? Matt. 22:[1ff.].

Moses desired of God to be taken out of his book if he did not want to forgive Israel the sin committed with the golden calf. Nevertheless, Israel had to bear its sin until the time of God's visitation, Exod. 32:[32ff.]. Paul wished to be banned by Christ for his brothers according to the flesh, that is for the Jews that they also might be saved, Rom. 9:[3]. Nevertheless, many unbelievers still remained and could not escape the wrath of God, Matt. 3:[10]. Yes, our Lord Jesus Christ himself said in the Gospel that he often wanted to gather Jerusalem under his wings (according to the word of the prophet: Lord, keep us as the apple of your eye, shelter us under the shadow of your wings, [Ps. 17:8]), but they had not wanted it [Matt. 23:37; Luke 13:34].

Also the Lord Jesus Christ himself could not keep his own disciples with him when they could not hear and bear his words, John 6:[66-70]. How much less can a person (who is of himself nothing, for what he is and enabled to do, that is through God's grace) do such? God knows if we could have prevented this miserable division in the congregation with our blood, how willingly we would have committed ourselves to it through the Lord's grace. For what have we [sought] in the time /600/ of our faith and service, according to our weak abilities, with simple heart, as much as the merciful God has given strength, other than God's praise, the honor of his highly praised name, and the improvement and upbuilding of his congregation? For that we have had to suffer so much from our opponents and enemies. Yes, has any sect arisen in many years that we have not striven against with God's Word who have not hated, slandered, and caused much suffering to us? Still the almighty God has delivered us out of all this, and will also keep us from all evil according to his good pleasure, and keep us for his heavenly kingdom. That we trust him to do. Amen. 1 Tim. 6:[3ff.]; 2 Tim. 4:[3ff.].

We also pray and admonish all those who fear the Lord in their heart and love the truth, that they will not misinterpret nor take amiss (for love thinks no evil) that we now neither can nor may commit ourselves to any meeting and dealing with the apostates who have dealt with us in such an unchristian way. For we do that out of no other reason than out of a pure fear of the Lord, out of the direction of his divine words, and out of the witness of our conscience, as is related above. Otherwise we would speak with our adversaries as long and as much as pleases them, and say with the prophet: Ps. [27:1], The Lord is our light and salvation, of whom shall we be afraid? The Lord is the power of life, before whom shall we be terrified. Again, the Lord is with us to help us, what can people do to us? etc., Ps. 107.

We are still convinced in this issue, through God's grace, just as we have often professed. We are comforted with that and do not deny anything, even if persons scold us; thus we suffer. If they threaten us, we live in the hope of God, 1 Cor. 4. If we are abused, insulted, and scolded as are those who sit in corners and shops (thus the world blasphemes us through insults from others), as those who come running over a field, so we do not regard that; God knows what we are and seek.

We say with the apostle that it is a small thing that we are judged by people (note, by the perverted) or by a human court. /601/ But it is the Lord who will judge us and bring into the light what now is still hidden and will reveal the counsels of the heart, 1 Cor. 4. And then each one will experience praise from God, 1 Cor. 4:[5]. We comfort ourselves with that, saying and witnessing before the Lord, who knows every heart and hears every word, that if we could do some good to improve the matter of the quarrel according to God's Word and will, we would certainly enter the field openly, and with the Lord's help show and defend our entire activity with the Scripture.

But everything has its time, says Ecclesiasticus: there is a time for speaking, and a time for silence, for where no one listens, there one shall not speak much in vain, Ecclus. 32, Ecclus. [22:6]. But one word spoken in its time is like golden apples in silver bowls, Prov. [25:11]. Therefore we cannot enter into conversation with our judges at the wrong time. For we are not so lacking in understanding (God be thanked) that we abandon the first [condition] that we with right have required, and that what in the past was not done orderly should now be ignored and [we should begin at the end] with the last. We are also not so unthinking, that we would accept the judgment of such people and require proof of it afterwards, since we well know and the present action testifies sufficiently what judges they are, namely, who have not judged a trusted matter in the congregation with the Lord's Word, but according to human fabrication, compromise, and their own opinions, not considering that it is written: He who shows violence in judgment is like a steward who shames a maiden who is entrusted to him, Ecclus. [20:4].

And if one then asks us and proposes whether one may not speak to the apostates we answer briefly thus: We are certainly free and permitted to speak with the apostates and to admonish them as brothers who want to be admonished, [2] Thess. 3:[14f.], according to the teaching of the apostle Paul. But the apostates who come in order to maintain their injustice, to speak against the truth, to deceive the God-fruitful ones and to change the listeners [minds], to speak much with them is not only unprofitable and in vain, but is also openly against God's Word, as was said above. And if anyone wants /602/ to say that we still wanted to have the Flemish [seen as right] who were already judged by the action between both parties, we answer that we could not acknowledge nor accept as right the judgment given to the Flemish so long as that was not proven [to us] with God's Word. And for that we have important reasons, as our booklet reported in part; otherwise we would not have done that.

In addition, there were many complainants, accusers, and witnesses against H.[oyte] R.[enix] and many other pious and honest people, ministers of the congregations, who had strong complaints against the judges. They should have reasonably responded before them. Therefore their proposal cannot be compared with our requirement and does not entirely agree with it, [1] Tim. 5:[20f.]. Also there is a great difference between apostasy: for one is repentant, desires to hear the admonition, subjects himself to instruction, confesses his guilt, and proves his yieldedness; on the contrary the other is bold, puffed up and controversial; yes, blasphemes, scolds, ruins reputations, backbites, will hear no admonition, nor confess his wrong or repent of it. Thus they are very different, as anyone with understanding and modesty can see.

In addition to all that, we understand that H.[oyte] R.[enix] has recanted the judgment over L.[eenaert] B.[ouwens] he agreed to with us and supported with many words at E.[mden], and acknowledged his guilt over it. Yet he still so many times expressly and openly after that time at different places confirmed the same and acknowledged it for right, and now he recalls it, now he demonstrates sorrow for it, as we are informed by the praiseworthy b.[rothers], and have also heard and inquired from his own b.[rother] whether we may repeat that; the answer to it was yes. Oh, what great frivolity, vacillation, and pretence; with such a hypocrite we do not wish to deal, but we would rather follow the advice of Ecclesiasticus, who teaches us that we shall not speak much with a fool (that is, with one who has abandoned God's Word) and not associate much with one lacking understanding; that we should keep ourselves from him, so that we not be led into difficulties by him, nor be smeared by his foulness, that we should avoid him. /603/ Thus we remain at peace and shall not come into anxiety and need through his foolishness.

But now someone may accuse us that the m.[inisters] have also signed but not kept the Compromise. To that we answer first that the m.[inisters] (as they say) have signed the Compromise not in the letter of the Compromise but upon the promise which was made by the H.[ollander] m.[en], [i.e., Jan Willems, Lubbert Gerrits, etc.], namely, that they would judge everything with God's Word and not deprive any congregation of its right. But how they have kept their promise, that God will judge, Heb. 12:[22f.].

Afterward, the ministers have not judged, but they have listened and when the judgment was spoken, they were sad at heart, having also said that they could not defend that judgment, nor anyone who was not satisfied with it, who could interpret it or seek punishment, for they were themselves untaught in it. This has been their confession before God and us. Nevertheless, H.[oyte] R.[enix] with his associates has so horribly portrayed, signified, and written of some of whom have signed the Compromise in his Epistle (as it is called by him), which is inhuman and too shameful to repeat or write [about]. Still he has brought all the scandalous words (as they would apply) upon himself. For are they to be accused and worthy of such scandal (although we acknowledge such scandalous charges for wrong, yes, for an abomination) who signed the Compromise and yet have not judged, but they were deceived with beautiful words and thereby brought [to it]? How much more is he guilty of all and much more, who himself has been judged with us, and he has included and established his own judgment many times and responded with us out of premeditated counsel, [but] now reversed, recalled, and himself complains about it? Oh, shameful hypocrisy.

To those who want to accuse the m.[inisters] so severely for signing the Compromise (but no one should think that we will respond to them in a wrong way, that be far from us), [we say thus] that all of the m.[inisters] of the four c.[ities—i.e., Harlingen, Franeker, Dokkum, and Leeuwarden] are as guilty and punishable after all in the same measure as the other before mentioned m.[inisters], 1 Thess. 4:[9ff.]. For we testify to that before the Lord, before his angels, and before his congregation, that the m.[inisters] of the four c.[ities], as many as were there with us at E.[mden] have yielded to and trusted us entirely in that judgment between the c.[ongregation] at E.[mden] and L.[eenaert] B.[ouwens] regarding their quarrel, except for E.[bbe] P.[ieters] alone, who made a speech which proved nothing and about which something else shall certainly be said about him justly whenever, for the sake of peace, it does remain at issue. Yet he promised us to keep quiet and not to make any difficulty for us, and the less he says the better, for his word is powerless in part because he objected to, rejected, and did not accept the election of the congregation. Yes, we may well say he has rejected it, as the apparent deed proves; in part also because he has not followed his word, just as the present experience and also previous experience clearly and obviously shows.

After that time the m.[inisters] from H.[arlingen] promised us again that they would keep the peace with us over the action and over the judgment that was issued over L.[eenaert] B.[ouwens] at E.[mden], but they have not done that. If one now accuses and blasphemes the before mentioned men and m.[inisters] (which is a shame to repeat) because they have signed the Compromise, in the form as was told above, where with shall they prove their guilt that they have twice accepted, promised to have peace with us, but have not kept anything?

But it is now the time that many see a splinter in another's eye, but do not see the log that is in their own eye, Matt. 7:[4f.]; many now strain at the gnat and swallow the camel, Matt. 23:[24]. (Oh, alas), it has now come this far with many of our opponents.

Thus we cannot hide from the God-fruitful ones more widely how a rumor runs here and there, also has already come to us out of P.[russia] /605/, and we know more details through it than we plan to tell here (but at this time we will let it remain for what it is worth) that letters were written by H.[oyte] R.[enix], or by his adherents, to the apostates in P.[russia], or messages were sent to them, in order to learn if there were also any other charges against us there on account of the quarrels which have been there between us and some others. This they could never do rightly to us, but much more to themselves. For they themselves have been judges over the matter of quarrels and have separated the troublemakers from the congregation. If they have now judged rightly, what is there more to say since they themselves have acknowledged their judgment as right so often?

But they now want to twist, change, and disguise (we say that at its softest) their judgment, thus they make themselves into false judges and must bear an eternal shame because of it, and also have no more words to speak and may not raise up their face before reasonable, honorable, and pious persons. But it appears and may be sensed that the Spirit of the Lord has departed from them entirely. Therefore, they go with Saul to those who may not consult with anyone, whom God will have expelled out of his congregation, yes, who also have expelled themselves and will seek help, comfort, and counsel there, and what is more, ask the truth from the dead, which God has so severely forbidden. But they must fulfill the measure of their Father.

Oh, Lord, where have these people come to? On our behalf, we are unencumbered, and the witness of our conscience before God is our sufficient defense. If our adversaries have no more shame and will wipe away their own shame (as the apostle says), they may do whatever they want in whatever God permits. They can do us no harm, but [only] to themselves; when they have first purged themselves, they may see if they have accused us rightly, Prov. 11:[5ff.], yes, [see] if they are not of the nature or race that lets them think that it [the nature] is pure, and yet is not washed of its uncleanness. Or that they are not much more those who once have escaped the uncleanness of this world but were once again soiled in the same, /606/ so that the last has become worse than the first, and the common proverb of Solomon and Peter applies to them, 2 Pet. 2:[20f.].

With regard to our booklet,[10] we acknowledge that we have written it with the Lord's help, knowing and not confessing that there is anything in it that does not agree and accord with the truth. For we have well compared, weighed, and tested everything in our simplicity beforehand with God's Word, and also do not doubt that the pious who fear GOD, the impartial who ask after the truth, and who have love, are satisfied with it. Yet if anyone of the God-fruitful ones has any lack therewith, they should speak to us in a brotherly way, [and] we hope through God's grace to give them a good report. We are not ashamed that we have written, although our opponents [find it] somewhat hard, but we have acted according to the teaching of Jesus Sirach, namely, that one shall strive unto death for the truth, Ecclus. 4:[28], that one shall freely acknowledge the right, if one will help the people, that one shall let himself be moved by no persons, nor shall let himself be afraid of any multitude or quantity, but one will maintain the right without regard to any person.

For these reasons we have made the booklet and given it the light of day with the Lord's help. And we do not regret it, although our opponents regret it, and although they complain about it. That does not matter. It is an old proverb, *obsequium amicos, veritas odium parit* [the full sentence reads: *Namque hoc tempore obsequium amicos, veritas odium parit*, meaning "Nowadays complaisance makes friends and truth ill will"][11] if we with them had wanted to supplicate and pretend, thus we had been and remained their friends. But in behalf of the truth which we hold before them, they have become our enemies. For wisdom is a hard touchstone for the unwise and the reckless casts it from him, Gal. 3, *et amara est veritas inquit Hieronimus, et qui predicant eam, replentur amaritudine* [Not only is truth bitter, says Jerome, but also those who preach it will be filled with bitterness].[12]

And that we are accused that we have given the names of our opponents to the authorities and report through our booklet, by the fact that their names were told therein, we reply that we have put our own name expressly at the front and the other names we put with initials [only]. If now any difficulties should come from the booklet, we would be identified first, and of that we are certainly comforted in the Lord. And if that was done badly that we have named our adversaries out of necessity /607/ (for one must, of course, know what and which persons we mean) we have put them with initials. How much more [damage] may have been done by those who have put the name and surname of pious men, also the place of residence with complete words in an epistle to the c.[ongregation] at Gr.[oningen] and written [sent] it into the land, to the great disadvantage of the pious and God-fruitful ones, but to themselves an eternal shame, as anyone who fears God well understands.

Again, with regard to J.[acob] F.[reerks][13] that he has complained about us that we have accused the Compromise as very sly and idolatrous, to this our answer is that we are not sorry about that for we know, and are certain from God's Word, that we have written rightly, and that J.[acob] F.[reerks] shall never prove his Compromise with the truth (since he himself accepts it.) Therefore, we do not desire to hear his unprofitable words but if J.[acob] F.[reerks] wishes to prove something, let him prove his untruthful words which he has spoken more than once at E.[mden], and was convinced of that by sufficient witnesses, and if he can defend his Compromise, let him see to it that he may defend it in the day of the Lord, before the supreme judge, Jesus Christ, Matt. 16:[27f.]; 25:[31f.]; 2 Cor. 5:[10]. We desire no proof of this, for we have acknowledged it, and acknowledge it still out of the depths of our hearts as wrong, and we hope by the grace of the Lord that we have received so much vision from God that one will not make us wise to where white is black, and black white.

Also we wish everyone to consider that the author of the Compromise reports himself, for we have been silent about his name out of courtesy, but he himself cannot be silent. What he means thereby he may consider [himself], if he will with his Compromise (which he himself accepts) achieve honor as it appears, which he may seek from others and not from us; but if he wants shame from it, he may not reckon that to us, but much more to himself. Therefore, the Scripture says rightly that if an unwise [one] could remain silent, he might be viewed as wise and clever, [Prov. 17:28].

We also understand that there is more than one author of the Compromise and [that they] boast about it. What shall we say much about these authors except what Horatius said in *Arte Poetica*: *Grammatici certant, et adhuc sub Iudice lis est* [Scholars disagree and the case is still before the court].[14] /608/ Do not hold that against us, that we allege so much out of the before mentioned poet. For the apostle Paul also alluded to and referred to Menandrum and Epimenidem according to the opportunity of the affair and the time, 1 Cor. 15:[33]; Titus 1:[12].

In addition to all that H.[oyte] R.[enix] has a false basis for the

God-saving teaching of Jesus Christ, for faith and the congregation of God, which is wrong in more than one article. All of this we wish to explain to them through the Lord's grace, if the quarrel between the Fr.[isians] and Fl.[emish] had not been or had already been resolved, and that is also in part the reason why we could not consent to the ministry of E.[gbert] K.[uyper], on behalf of which we have still more to say out of important reasons.

Therefore, our meaning is actually that we do not plan to hold any meeting with these people. They must first recall that ungodly judgment which they have issued over us and others more, and to repent from it in a way that may stand before God and his congregation. If that has happened, the congregation of the Lord will see everything with modesty and what one shall best do in the matter. And if it then appears good that a discussion shall be held, it must then happen according to the before mentioned form, namely, that both parties come together and explain everything that has contributed to the quarrel from the beginning.

After that we are prepared to appear before all the God-fruitful ones, and if anyone has any complaint against us, we are ready in the name of the Lord to give a good account of it, although we do not know that we have deprived anyone in any manner. We have always been desirous of the peace of God and heartily longed for Christian and brotherly unity. Yet we do not want to praise ourselves /609/ (for that is foolishness), nor justify [ourselves], but we commend our affair to the Lord, in the certain confidence that he will see it through for us, Ps. 1.

Finally, we could not refrain from asking all God-fruitful ones, all lovers of the truth through the mercy of God to pray, to admonish, and to warn them that they be careful, and that they have nothing to do with impurity, just as Paul wrote to the Corinthians and thus admonishes us: Do not pull on an alien yoke with an unbeliever. For what fellowship does righteousness have with unrighteousness? What fellowship does light have with darkness? How does Christ agree with Belial? What part does faith have with unfaith? Or what similarity has the temple of God with idols? You are the temple of the living God, just as God said: I will dwell in them, and walk in them, and I will be their GOD, and they will be my people. Therefore, go out from among them, separate yourself and do not touch anything unclean. Then I will receive you and be your Father and you will be my sons and daughters, says the almighty Lord, [2] Cor. 6:[14-18].

It is plain from these words that one must separate himself from the unclean, apostate, and idolaters so that one does not participate in their sin. For although a person himself is innocent of any misdeed, he can thereby dirty and soil himself through fellowship and consenting to it. Of this we have sufficient clear examples and witnesses in the Scripture, as also the express word of the apostle which says: A little leaven sours the whole dough, 1 Cor. 5:[6]; Gal. 5:[9].

For this reason we have been compelled to give you a little indication of how one is obligated to avoid altogether those who do not agree with the Lord's congregation but have departed from the truth. For it is now time that one must separate the clean from the unclean, yes, that one must stand with Jeremiah against the unrighteous as an iron wall and metal pillar, Jer. 1:[18]; for one may not agree with unrighteousness but they must agree much more with the righteous and pious, and be converted from all unrighteousness to the living God who is gracious and merciful, /610/ to forgive sins, if one confesses them from the heart and improves himself, Jer. 20.

Thus we give the God-fruitful ones the following points to consider, so that they, for better or worse, walk securely on the way of the Lord according to the teaching of Solomon. First, some of the judges were accused of things worthy of the ban already before they committed themselves in this judgment. What fine judges have they then been? All who now join themselves with such people take upon themselves [their] strange [unknown] sins and cannot remain clean from them. For whoever touches dirt soils himself with it. And who touches the dead becomes impure, etc.

Second, one must thus accept, approve, and support the human covenant, or as it is now called, the ordinance of the four c.[ities], and through such acceptance one is obligated to respond to everything evil that has come out of it and still may come, namely, quarrels, division, and [the] splitting up of God's congregations, just as one sees before [our] eyes, [so] that a Christian who takes to heart the salvation of his soul would rather die with the Lord's help than lay upon himself such a burden.

Third, if one must consent to the Compromise and acknowledge it as right, [then one must know that this] Compromise has been put in the place of God's Word and therefore is an abomination before him, as we have confessed and explained in our booklet. For quarrelsome affairs, those which raise themselves up in the congregation, those one needs to judge with God's Word. That is the only plumbline by which it all must be measured. Therefore, one has done a great dishonor to the most high God, yes, one has interfered in God's judgment since one has judged not according to the Lord's Word, which is the only judge, but according to a Compromise (which was made according to the manner of the world and not according to the rule of God's congregation), John 12:[44f.].

Fourth, then one must assume and lay upon oneself all the difficulties which have come out of the judgment given according to that Compromise, /611/ which is very difficult to do for a God-fruitful conscience, if one otherwise thinks the matter right; for if one himself gives an unrighteous judgment or consents to it and maintains it, what difference is there between the two?

Therefore, we cannot neglect to free our conscience before God against anyone, and want herewith to excuse ourselves before the Lord that we are clean [innocent] of anyone's destruction, if anyone will after all destroy himself and does not desire to be helped. For the Lord knows that in order to seek and promote peace, we have done everything that is possible for us through the Lord's grace, Heb. [12:14ff.]; Phil. 4:[8ff.]. But now that all this cannot help at this time, yes, is resented and misinterpreted, we say with the prophet: What will die will die, and what will be lost will be lost, although it is God's will that all people shall be saved and come to the acknowledging of the truth, as it is written, Zech. 11:[9]; 2 Pet. 3:[9]. The Lord also says to Israel: Why do you want to die, you from the house of Israel? Turn to me, and I will turn to you, and be gracious to you, says the almighty Lord, Ezek. [18:31f.].

But it can appear as though it were deserved (God knows whereby and with what) that God's shepherds are indulgent in the land, who do not seek the lost and do not ask after the strayed, who do not heal the wounded and do not care for the healthy who eat the flesh of the fattest sheep and would cut off their claws. But such shepherds have to observe that which is written there: *Oh, Pastor et idul,*[15] Oh, you useless, foolish shepherd, the sword will come upon your right arm and upon your right eye, so that your arm shall wither and your right eye shall be blinded, Zech. 11:17.

For just as God is in his divine character and nature, thus he deals with people also, that is, with the good he is good, with the holy he is holy, and the perverted he treats also according to their perverseness, /612/ that is, he gives them over to perverted purposes, because they do not believe the truth but value unrighteousness much more, 1 Thess. 2. For one of both must happen, either one wins or loses, according to the parable of the gospel. And still the spirit of the prophet says: Who does damage, that one damages still more; and who is unclean, that one becomes still more unclean. But who is righteous, that one becomes more righteous, and who is holy, that one becomes still more holy, Rev. 22:[10ff.].

The God of all grace and the Father of all mercy, 1 Pet. 5:[10]; 2 Cor. 1:[2], give you all together to be of one mind in Christ Jesus, so that you may praise God in unity and walk in peace with one another, Rom. 15:[5ff.], to the praise of his holy name, and to his eternal glory, and to your salvation. The grace of our Lord Jesus Christ be with you all. AMEN.

D. P.

ENDNOTES

1. Complete title: *An Appendix to our book about the quarrelsome affair between the Fr.[isians] and the Fl.[emish]*. D. P. [*Een Appendix aen ons Boecxken vanden twistigen handel in Vr. tusschen die Vr. ende Vl.* 1567/1568. BRN X, pp. 589-612.] IDC. Again, comparison of the 1567/1568 text with the BRN X text shows only minor spelling variations, with which we are now familiar, namely: Heere in the BRN in place of Here, Broederlycke in place of broederlicke, koemt in place of coemt in the 1567/1568, etc. Textual variations were not found.
2. Outerman, *Onder verbeteringhe* (1609), par. 278, 287. De Hoop Scheffer, *Het verbond der vier steden* in DB (1893), p. 62ff.
3. Outerman, *Onder verbeteringhe*. (1609), par. 285, 343.
4. The man's full name was not known but now is believed to have been Geert Harms. See BRN X, p. 41, 569, n. 6, and De Hoop Scheffer, op. cit., p. 54. About the banning see J. O.[uterman]. op. cit., par. 285, 343., and De Hoop Scheffer, op. cit., p. 66ff. Initials were used for reasons of security. When Dirk used full given names at times, he was accused of helping to deliver persons to the authorities for persecution and death.
5. The letter was probably sent to Appingedam because Dirk had first been named elder for that congregation. Syvaert Pieters, *Corte aenwijsinghe*, p. 9. P. Verkindert, *Brief, Dienende om te bewijsen* . . . (1634). Outerman, *Noodtwendighe Verclaringhe* . . . p. 24. Bespreck binnen Hoorn tusschen Jan Lues van die Vlaemsche mennichte, ende Pieter Jansen Twisck van die Oude Vriesen, 1622, par. 156-161. See also BRN X, p. 512, n. 7, and p. 539, n. 6.
6. This letter was dealt with in Syvaert Pieters, *Corte aenwijsinghe vande mishandelinghen der Vlaminghen end Vriesen in 1566*, Hoorn, 1634, p. 26f.
7. This introduction is particularly indebted to the editor of BRN X, pp. 585-586.
8. Today *heart* is interpreted as *mind*.
9. An unusual reference, reflecting his Roman Catholic background. Anabaptists tended to see Mariology as idolatry. See, for example, interrogations in the *Martyrs Mirror*.
10. *A Short but Fundamental Account*.
11. This "old proverb," as Dirk calls it, comes from Terence, *The Lady of Andros*, Act 1, lines 68-69. Publius Terentius was a Roman dramatist who lived in the second century before Christ.
12. (Saint) Jerome, known in Latin as Eusebius Hieronymus, is known as a "church father," living first in Rome, then in Jerusalem. He is known best for his translation of the *Vulgate*, the Latin Bible, used by Roman Catholicism even to the present, from ancient original documents. He died about 420.
13. A minister in Harlingen with Ebbe Pieters.
14. From Horace, a Roman poet 65-8 B.C., *Ars Poetica*, line 78.
15. Zechariah 11:17: *Vae stulto meo pastori derelinquenti gregem! Gladius super brachium eius et super oculum dextrum eius; brachium eius ariditate siccetur, et oculus dexter eius tenebrescens obscuretur* [from the Latin Vulgate].

E. RELATED LETTERS

The first extant letter relating to the division, not counting the above documents B, C and D, is Dirk Philips' letter of 7 June 1567 to Hoyte Renix. Following the impasse of 1 February between the Flemish and the Frisians, Hoyte Renix wrote to Dirk, in the name of the others and himself, inviting him to come to Friesland as adjudicator of the dispute. That letter is lost, but the date was 17 April 1567. We gather from the contents of this letter from Dirk that it is a reply to the April invitation. In the letter Dirk refers to an earlier copy, which we assume was a copy of this same letter but which Hoyte may have believed to have been lost. It might, however, have been another letter.

Hoyte Renix served as elder of the congregation at Bolsward. He had probably been involved with Willems and Gerrits as helper and adjudicator of their ill-fated attempt at reconciliation. His letter now invites Dirk most cordially, "We desire you with all our heart, that you come to us with your entire family, as Jacob in Egypt, and we will care for you and serve you as a dear old father here with us in our fatherland all our life long." But Hoyte adds that if Dirk did not find in their favor "we should not only not desire you; you would be useless to us."[1]

ND Dirk was obviously aware of what Hoyte had in mind. Thus he asks, actually demands, that Hoyte suspend all ministerial activities until he "had cleansed [himself] and responded before the Lord, before us, and with others, in the presence of your accusers and complainants."[2] While declaring that there is only one covenant for believers, Dirk remains evenhanded when he writes: "Who has the guilt, God will still reveal and judge." The preceding treatises have clarified what eventually happened.

The translation of this letter is based upon the Dutch edition found in J. ten Doornkaat Koolman, *Dirk Philips...* pp. 200-205. A fragment of the letter is also found in BRN X, pp. 689-690, dated 8 June 1567. No explanation has been found for the one day difference. Ten Doornkaat Koolman found this letter in the *Urkundenbuch der Gemeinde Heubuden*. It is dated 7 June 1567. Elder Gerhard Wiebe (1723-1796) had an important collection of documents transcribed by one Isaac Wiebe. Included in the transcription were also Menno Simons' letter of 7 October 1549 to the congregation in Prussia, the confession of Obbe Philips (Dirk's brother), as well as reports about Obbe, and other documents.

Ten Doornkaat Koolman examined and copied parts of the document collection of 376 pages in Hamburg in August and September 1914. He later compared his copy with one sent to him by Mrs. Rose Crous in 1963 from Krefeld, where the Mennonite research center was then located. He used the 1914 copy for this printing, it being in better condition.[3] The *Urkundenbuch* is now located at the Mennonitische Forschungsstelle (research center) at the Weierhof, Palatinate.

No. 1 Dirk Philips to Hoyte Renix [4]
7 June 1567

A copy of a letter which Dirk Philips wrote to Hoyte Renix, an elder in Friesland. /200/

God is with us if we are with him, and if God is with us, who then can be against us, Rom. 8:31.

I can not hide from you, dear Hoyte, brother and friend, how I earlier have had much friendship with you, especially about six years ago in our fatherland, and I have many times out of the depth of my heart wished and prayed to God that we and all fellow companions of our Christian faith might have remained in the joy of the spirit and in brotherly unity and love with one another, and still remain eternally. I also hope in the grace of God and do not know, between God and my conscience, that I have been changed [in this] time in any quarrel or any manner, for which I thank the very highest that he has kept me.

[So as] I was then minded after Jesus Christ in my weakness, so I am still minded through God's grace, and just as I then sought the peace of God which goes above all understanding and [that] the believing heart and mind might be kept in Christ Jesus, so I still seek that peace. Yes, just as I always with the Lord's help in my simplicity have liked to seek, see, and promote with much work the improvement, upbuilding, and keeping of God's congregation, so my mind and hope still rest in the Lord, that he will strengthen, empower, establish and still keep me from all evil for his heavenly kingdom. Amen.

But now I can no longer keep my well-meaning Christian [intention] from you, that I have been greatly burdened and troubled over you and your adherents for a long time, about which I received and understand from praiseworthy and God-fearing ones already in Prussia, through words and writings, that persons in Friesland may have driven that human covenant very hard (although it may not have been called or said that way), that it is the only covenant of God, and that there is no other that is valid before God, and which [the latter] was partly forgotten and put back [because of it]. But I do not accept this further than that a good explanation will be given to us in due time, which thus needs to happen.

/201/ Thereafter it happened that you sent me a copy of your writing over which I sorrow very much, yes, [about which I feel I should] complain before God and all the God-fruitful [ones]. For according to the common proverb, you show me bread with one hand and entice me with it, and with or in the other hand you have a stone to strike me with it, if I cannot follow or agree with you; yes, you pressured me so hard and meant to frighten me therewith, that according to my knowledge, I have not been threatened so hard by a pious one in my [whole] life.[5]

Nevertheless, I have had [so many] adversaries and opponents in my lifetime that the Lord, who rightly guides the affairs of the miserable and the poor and who has always stood by me, [will] also now according to his certain hope view my simplicity graciously. For he knows, since he knows all hearts and tests all kidneys,[6] that I have pursued peace in every way and still pursue it, and that I am innocent of the quarrel, suspension, strife, and partisanship which has taken place there. Who has the guilt, God will still reveal and judge. But I desire through God's grace to remain by the truth which I have once accepted and acknowledged, and trust in the Lord with the prophet [when he says that] although 1,000 fall at one side and 10,000 on the other side, still misfortune will not come upon the pious, [Ps. 91:7]. Therefore, I pay no attention to your threatening and that you tell about Absalom and the rioting.[7] I am ashamed on your account that you make such an impious, unbiblical interprepation of Scripture.

Again, you write to me, "If I despise and do not accept the actions and judgment of the true servants who have risked all for the Lord's praise and the people's salvation, which you do not suspect, so that I should drive away from me every pious heart thereby, which then should be hard and sad, that all misery has been treated, which I have never had."[8] But, dear Hoyt, I renounce nothing of it; it saddens and disturbs me that you write so thoughtlessly. For what is true and so proven to me, that I desire to accept and maintain. God help me to do that. I have never driven pious hearts away from me into the world, rather they have always liked to be with me, and I with them, God be thanked. For I say with the prophet, "that perverted hearts may turn from me, /202/ the wicked I do not tolerate and do not like those who have high counsel and a proud bearing." [Ps. 101:4 ff.]

I am as certain of this as when I [the Lord allowing it] have difficulty or sadness, as I have often had, that I will not have this on account of the pious nor on their behalf, to wit, that they should cause me any suffering or heartache. So I will not drive the pious away [from God], nor drive them away from me. I hope with the Lord's help rather that a few [more] remain than ten who do not walk truly.[9] I do not desire to agree with these, God helping me. For "the Lord was never with the chair of the pestilent who should indicate judgment falsely," [Ps. 94:20]; "What is right must remain right, and all pious hearts will agree," [Ps. 94:15], as the prophet says. If I will have some misery or trouble, I will experience that from the perverted apostates and godless, as has happened at this time.

You have referred to all of this in your earlier mentioned copy, as also that you want to ordain and install Egbert Cuijper into full service [ministry], which I have denied [forbidden] to you at this time for many different reasons, of which I am ready to give an account. Nevertheless I hear, and have many reports from sufficient witnesses, that you have proceeded with it, which makes me wonder much that you are so bold; you should understand that to my knowledge and in my time in the B.B. [Beminde Broederschap, that is "beloved brotherhood,"] this has not [been done] by a true servant.

Since you are then so bold and dare to act so brashly, as it appears, and do not ask about us, while judging and banning happens so much among you that many pious ones sigh and complain about it, on this account the great and present need compels us to make a brotherly appeal and admonition to you, friendly at first, through the mercy of God and the love of the Spirit, that you suspend your ministry for the sake of greater peace and to avoid all the aggravation and affliction.[10]

But if our friendly appeal and brotherly desire is not valid for you and is not heard and you [do not] accept it, then we say to you in the name of the Lord Jesus and in the authority which he has given to his congregation and to us, that you shall suspend your ministry and not accept any activity of the congregation, not to receive anyone, /203/ not to separate anyone until you have purged yourself and answered [the charges] before the Lord and before us in the presence of your accusers. We also hope, if the Lord wills and we live, according to opportunity, time, and place, to determine and then to invite you, when and where we will come together. But if you do not accept this from us and proceed in your ministry, then you should know that we hold that of no worth; also [that we] are not satisfied with you, will not acknowledge you before any brothers, but renounce our brotherhood with you on the condition indicated. Still we hope for the better and that it will work out better, even if it is that we write thus, and that you will consider this well, make yourself responsible, and do not strive against the stream.

In the same measure we do not consent yet to the ordination of Egbert Cuijper, but hold it for improper and powerless and do not recognize him as a co-worker in the service of the gospel. So also, if someone will support you therein, that you should not want to act accordingly and just continue in your ministry, then we say and command them the same as you to desist and stand still, be he whoever he might be, whether resident there or in another place. We tolerate of the same no activity in the congregation until you have purged yourself, and he also whom you permitted not to hold still, but much more has strengthened and supported you therein. But the simple people, that is good and bad, fearing God and avoiding evil, are not meant herewith.[11]

We hope through the grace of God that he will keep the sheep of his pasture and not abandon them, and will no longer [permit the Lord's sheep to the congregation].[12] It also distresses us very much that the souls whom Jesus Christ, the Son of God, has bought with his blood, are no longer honored nor taken seriously. The Lord have mercy over his own in this and help us through the freedom of his Spirit that we remain in the truth, "that we do not follow the multitudes to evil and not agree with the judgment of many multitudes," [Exod. 23:2], so that we may not depart from the truth.

At this time no more. If then my letter saddens you, let it be godly sadness, for that works to salvation,[13] and remember that I have written it out of great anguish and that you, without anguish or cause, have saddened me not a little with your writing. Herewith commended to the Lord; may he give you wisdom and do in you what is well pleasing to him and [what] is serviceable and profitable to your soul.

The 7 June, year 1567.

Written and sent in Friesland by Dirk Philipsen.

No. 2. Dirk Philips to Jan Willems and Lubbert Gerrits[14] 30 June 1567

Since Jan Willems, Lubbert Gerrits, and their companions did not go to Emden at that time [though they went later] as Dirk Philips had requested, hoping that he would come to them at Hoorn, Dirk wrote to them and to their congregation in letters 2 and 3. He demands that the two men must be viewed as suspended from their offices (that they must "remain silent") until their guilt or innocence has been determined. The reason underlying this demand was their support of the Covenant, the Compromise and the Sentence, which was primarily their work. Dirk wrote four letters urging them to come, of which we have the following two. The congregation did not let them go at first, apparently.

As we read these letters we need to keep in mind that we have only excerpts. If we knew the full contents, the impression which they give might be different. Further, the suspension was only temporary and conditional, which was normal practice at that time. Beyond that, Dirk was not acting on his own authority but as an elder, and that primarily on the basis of the mandate he and his two companions (Hans Sikken and Geert Harms) had received from their Danzig congregation.[15]

Further I cannot conceal from you how our brotherly prayer and desire is (that you come to us as was written above). In addition, we admonish and remind you that you know how to direct your ministry according to our writing, that you do not undertake to serve, nor receive [members], nor act to separate [ban], until you have purged [exonerated] yourself. [But] if you do not honor that, and still proceed in your ministry, or do not pay attention to our writing [you to stop], then remember that it is written that a presumptious person ends up amiss, a presumptious person brings much bad luck upon himself and executes one trouble after the other, for pride never does any good, and nothing but evil can grow out of it. We address that to you if you still accept the ministry of the cong.[regation].

Thus we dismiss you from the brotherhood in the name of the Lord, for we do not desire to serve [with] nor to have fellowship with all such [persons]. That is the innermost meaning of our heart. Herewith [you are] commended to the Lord, and know [how] to conduct yourself lest greater sadness and punishment come over you from the Lord. The peace of God be with all those who love the Lord Jesus Christ out of a pure heart. Amen. Anno [year] 1567. The thirtieth of June. Signed, Dirk Philips.

We also command in the name of the Lord Jesus Christ all of your ministers, elders, and bro[thers] that they stand still, and not to undertake to separate [ban] anyone, or to accept [receive as a member], until you as well as they, and they as well as you, have all purged [exonerated] yourselves. (And everything that you do beyond this and against it, that we hold as nothing and of no worth).[16]

No. 3. Dirk Philips to the congregation at Hoorn [17]

I have also written and commanded your ministers and elders and all the brothers that they [stand] still and separate [ban] no one until the time that they have purged [exonerated] themselves. That is, [until] both men J.[an] W.[illems] and L.[ubbert] G.[errits], the ministers and brothers have all purged [exonerated] themselves before God and us and others more; desire also, yes, command through the Lord Jesus Christ, that you let this letter be read in North Holland in all the congregations.[18]

ENDNOTES

1. Excerpt from a letter as reprinted by Syvaert Pieters, *Corte aenwijsinghe, Voorgestelt in eenighe Vraghen, vande voornaemste mishandelinghen der Vlamingen ende Vriesen in 1566*. Hoorn, 1634, pp. 21-22. Cf: De Hoop Scheffer, "Het verbond der vier steden." DB (1893), p. 53.
2. De Hoop Scheffer, "Het verbond..." p. 57.
3. Koolman, p. 204, note 1.
4. The date given in the Heubuden document is 7 June 1567. A fragment of the letter is also printed in BRN X, pp. 689-690, where the date is given as 8 June, based on J. O. Outerman's, *Onder verbeteringhe*... n.p., 1609, art. 267 and 268. *Catalogus*... p. 103. No explanation for the one day disparity has been found. Renix sided with the Frisians in the 1565ff dispute, Dirk with the Flemish.

Renix, who was also called Hoyte Renix Santvoort, was baptized by Leenaert Bouwens and ordained by him as elder in 1555. He served the congregation at Bolsward in Friesland. The date of his death is not known, but it was after 1600. See also ME 2:824 and BRN VII, 51, 62, 67f.

5. Dirk is referring to the 17 April 1567 letter inviting him to come to Emden, but only if he agrees with Hoyte.
6. In older Dutch (and German) versions e.g., Ps. 7:10; 26:2; Jer. 11:20; 17:10; 20:12, etc., [nieren=kidneys] more recently translated as "heart and mind." Kidneys were considered central to personality.
7. See *An Appendix*... above, pp. 522ff. cf.: Kühler, *Geschiedenis*, pp. 420-421.
8. J. G. de Hoop Scheffer believes that the last half of the text is garbled here and cites Hoyte's later correspondence with Syvaert Pieters, an Old Frisian minister from Hoorn, as follows: "which would be harder and more painful for you than all the misery you have experienced in your entire life" (p. 204, note 20).
9. This may refer to the findings committee from Harlingen, of whom two of the twelve withdrew their cooperation, Koolman, p. 204, note 26, based on J. G. de Hoop Scheffer, "Het verbond der vier steden," DB, 1893, p. 51.
10. The BRN X, p. 689-690 fragment begins with this paragraph. Textual variations are slight and do not affect its meaning. This translation follows the ten Doornkaat Koolman text throughout. The request is for a temporary suspension.
11. The expression "simple people... good and bad," is idiomatic [recht ende schlecht] and not meant pejoratively. The BRN X text of this letter ends here.
12. The text in [ ] has been corrupted, presumably by the copyist. What may have been meant is that the Lord would not permit a shepherd or hireling to mislead the sheep, i.e., the congregation.
13. Cf: 2 Cor. 7:8-10.
14. Jacques Outerman, *Onder verbeteringhe*. 1609. Fol. 272. BRN X, 690-691, 692-693.
15. J. Outerman, *Onder verbeteringhe*. (1609), art. 269, 279. Koolman, p. 149. Translated from BRN X, p. 692, identical with P. Verkindert, *Brief dienende om te bewijsen*... (1634), reprinted also in de Hoop Scheffer, *Het verbond*..., DB 1893, pp. 58-59.
16. There are three sources [fragments] of this letter, two by Jacques Outerman, *Copye eens briefs*..., Haarlem, 1634, fol. 272; the other by P. V[er] K[indert], *Brief, dienende om te bewijsen*..., Haerlem, 1634, pp. 21f. The fullest text possible has been created by merging these nearly identical versions. Duplications have not been indicated but the ( ) indicate additions from Verkindert to the Outerman version. See also BRN X, p. 692.
17. Only the following extract is available. BRN X, p. 692.
18. From BRN X, 692. Reprinted also in de Hoop Scheffer, *Het verbond der vier steden*, DB 1893, pp. 58-59.

ABOUT THE MARRIAGE OF CHRISTIANS

Introduction

As far as we know this is the last treatise Dirk Philips wrote before his death. In it he says that he is old, weak, sick, and awaiting his deliverance in death. He finished writing it on March 7, 1568, and died shortly thereafter in the same month.[1]

The treatise is referred to extensively by the anonymous author of *The Beginning of the Divisions*,[2] where he discusses the practices of the Mennonites and says, "No brother or sister may marry outside of the congregation. For whoever marries outside of the congregation, [no matter] how pious, believing, and God-fearing the person [from outside of the congregation] may be, it must nevertheless be called outside of the Lord. If on the other hand, one married within the congregation, that one surely, without doubt, worry, and further consideration . . . married in the Lord. . . . Whoever oversteps this canon or rule . . . is punished with the ban and neither can nor may ever come to forgiveness and re-admission into the congregation, however much he sought, begged, and desired with tears, wails, and groans except the outside-married party die or the banned party [succeeds in] bringing her to the congregation."[3] He says further that this all is "just as Dirck Philipsz. has ruled and written, taught and left afterward in a booklet about the marriage of Christians as his last jewel."[4]

The title of the treatise is somewhat misleading. It actually deals with the question of mixed marriages, marrying "outside of the faith" [*buitentrouw*] that is, a Mennonite marrying a non-Mennonite. Dirk begins with several assumptions. One is the absolute authority of the Scriptures. He presents a number of evidences from the Old Testament about the rejection of mixed marriages. He then proceeds to the New Testament and finds that the Old Testament view of mixed marriages is maintained. His entire approach to the issue is derived from this basic assumption.

His second major assumption concerns the need for keeping the congregation pure. He is fearful that mixed marriages will eventually lead to the destruction of the congregations since it brings into the fellowship persons who are not believers. The treatise was written during a time of great stress within the congregations and threat from the outside. The division with the Waterlanders had already occurred. They were inclined toward a more moderate interpretation of the issue of banning and separation than was Dirk. This was also the time of the division between the Frisians and the Flemish. The Calvinists were also gaining ascendancy as a major Protestant group in the Netherlands. Dirk was wary lest these pressures should bring in persons who were not ready to maintain the purity of the congregations he had struggled so mightily to establish.

Dirk assumed that only two types of marriages were considered legitimate in the Scriptures. The prototype for marriage was Adam and Eve prior to the fall. Thus all marriages were to be between believers. A second type of marriage occurred after the fall. That was a marriage between two worldly persons, which was not a Christian marriage, but one recognized by the world. A mixed marriage of a worldly person and a Christian person was not one to be recognized by the congregations as a true marriage.

The person who was a believer and married outside of the congregation was presumed to be pursuing fleshly rather than spiritual desires. Such action was evidence that persons who had given their bodies to Christ were now giving them to the world again, and that was a sign of unfaithfulness. Such a person needed to be brought to repentance and renewal. But repentance required evidence in behavior of a changed attitude. To remain with the worldly partner would be to continue in sin. Therefore, one had to be separated from the worldly partner.[5]

The only way to come back into full fellowship without separation from the partner was to have the partner become a believer and be joined to the congregation, or for the partner to die. Otherwise the person was to be separated from the partner. But some recognition of the reality of a marriage was acknowledged. The conditions on which the person was to be restored were that the believing husband was to provide for the support of the unbelieving wife and was also not free to marry another person. Underlying the latter condition apparently was the hope that the true Christian marriage might be realized by the partner becoming a believer as a consequence of the action.

It was possible, however, for a person who had contracted a worldly marriage while still in the world to become a believer and to be accepted into the congregation of believers without having to put away his worldly spouse. That was possible so long as the worldly spouse was not a hindrance to the believer in leading a Christian life. The allowance for this relationship was based on Paul's teaching in 1 Corinthians 7:12[ff.].

The issue also indicated the importance with which Dirk held the relationship in the fellowship of believers. He did not consider a marriage to be simply a concern between the two persons wanting to marry. They could make promises to each other, but for the Christian believer, the promise was not a true marriage unless the congregation also gave its consent and approval to the marriage. This became evident in response to the argument from some that if the believer had given a promise to another for marriage, that person was already bound by the promise. Dirk did not consider it binding until it was confirmed by the congregation also.

Dirk also had a high regard for a consensus process for making decisions about controversial matters. He thought it improper for a leader of a congregation to make a decision on such matters alone. When such issues arose, the leader of the congregation was to gather as many other ministers and teachers as were available for a consultation. Out of the joint consideration, the correct understanding for the application of the Scripture would come.

The consultation of ministers and teachers was the way in which Dirk, Menno, and others had proceeded when the issue of mixed marriages first arose, some twenty years earlier, according to Dirk's statement. He probably had reference to a gathering of seven leaders of the movement in 1547 in Emden[6] when they first took a stand against mixed marriages (or marriages outside the faith, as they called them.)

In this treatise on marriage, Dirk did show some pastoral concern in stipulating that the unbelieving spouse be cared for by the believer. In his view this did not violate scriptural teaching. The treatise was published in 1569, a year after Dirk's death. It was reprinted many times without alteration.[7]

About the Marriage of Christians

About the marriage of Christians, how it is commanded by God, and must be kept and practiced by believers according to the Scriptures: scriptural proof, to the service of all believers and against all those who oppose the truth, written by

D. P.

1 Cor. 6:15, Brothers, do you not know that your bodies are members of Christ? Will I then take the members of Christ, and make them members of a whore? That be far from us.

1 Cor. 7:39 A wife is bound to the law, as long as her husband lives. But if her husband dies, then she is free to marry whom she will, provided that it happens in the Lord. /623/

Preface

[To] all believers and God-fruitful ones who are in Jesus Christ, our heartfelt dear brothers and friends in the Lord, companions in our Christian faith, and participants [with us] in the fellowship of the gospel, we wish much grace, peace, 1 Thess. 1:[1]; 1 Cor. 1:[3], mercy, and spiritual insight in God's Word, ears to hear, an understanding heart to comprehend what God's will is, Matt. 13:[14ff.], and all of that from God the heavenly Father, from whom come all good gifts, James 1:[17]; John 1; 1 Cor. 1:[4ff.]; John 14:[12ff.], from Jesus Christ our Lord who is the Father's Word, wisdom, and truth, through the power of the Holy Spirit. Amen. /625/

We thank almighty God for you, dear brothers and friends, for we hope that, according to the providence of God the Father, you have come to the knowledge of his only born Son Jesus Christ, Rom. 8; 2 Thess. 2:[13ff.]. We also pray the eternal God for you and for all believers, that you together with one another may wholeheartedly remain therein, Matt. 24:[13], and that the most high God will preserve and keep you from all evil in his grace and truth eternally in these perilous times, especially [your] soul. For it appears and surely seems that the quarrels and disunity, the lostness and departures from God's Word on both sides, to the right and to the left, has neither control nor end, yes, that now the words of Jesus Christ come fully into their own, namely, if it were possible, even the chosen would be led into error, Matt. 24:[24]. Again, when the Son of man shall come (he himself asks), will he also find faith on earth?, Luke 18:[18]. /626/

One sees it and also experiences daily that it happens, that there are certainly many who have been called but it is of great concern that according to the Lord's own words, few are chosen and shall be saved, Matt. 22:[14]. For the kingdom of God does not exist in words, but in power, in the righteousness, peace, and joy of the Holy Spirit. The one who serves God thereby is well pleasing to him, 1 Cor. 4:[20]; Rom. 14:[17f.]. But many boast about the kingdom of God, yet nevertheless know little about it. Many let themselves believe that they seriously serve God, yet the concern remains that many of those are people about whom the Lord said in the Gospel: namely, that those will work to go in through the narrow gate, and yet still will not be allowed to come in there, because they do not begin in the right way, much less can [they] endure and complete [it], Luke 13:[24].

For who will come to the Lord Jesus Christ, that one must first hear and learn from God the Father, John 6:[45], that one must be hungry and thirst for righteousness, Matt. 5:[6], not seeking anything other than God's praise and the salvation of his soul. Who thus comes to the Lord, that one he will certainly accept and bring into the sheepfold through the right door, lead out and in, that he finds the pasture of eternal life, John 10:[3ff.], that is, that pure unfalsified word of the gospel, through that faith, accepted in the power of the Holy Spirit, which is his salvation and eternal life, 1 Cor. 1:[18].

Oh, that they were all thus minded who boast themselves to be Christians, how [wonderful] it would be in the congregation of the Lord! But it may be assumed that many now, as in the time of Paul, seek themselves more than Jesus Christ, and that they prefer their own honor rather than the honor of God and the welfare, improvement, and upbuilding of his congregations, Phil. 2:[4ff.]. For they want to introduce, from the outside, a strange and false freedom about marriage into the congregation, and if that were to proceed, then the congregation would be ruined in its foundations and disappear. Therefore, we cannot let that get underway and must share our innermost understanding [of what happens] if a brother or sister takes [marries] a worldly person, and make it known to all good-hearted lovers of the truth. For we have in the time of our ministry often had great temptations, difficulties, and troubles over it, and decided unanimously out of God's Word with seven teachers more than twenty years ago,[8] just as is still our understanding, /627/ and we hope through God's grace to explain still further in the following.

[We are] praying and admonishing humbly all God-fruitful ones, through the Lord Jesus Christ and through the love of the Spirit, that you will take, understand, and interpret our modest and simple writing at its best, according to unfalsified love and scriptural truth, excluding all human opinion, reason, and subtlety, Rom. 12:[3], and consulting alone with God's Word, just as we trust in all the good-hearted who fear the Lord. For God knows that we have written this out of a pure heart and out of constraint of conscience since we see that unrighteousness gains dominance over some, which we would like to prevent with the Lord's help, and [also to] defend righteousness, Matt. 24.

Besides this we are old, weak, and sick in the flesh, expecting our deliverance from the Lord, that we may come to the blessed rest. We have many times treated this subject, spoken, testified in the assembly, admonished, also many years ago wrote about it; thus no one will suspect us as if we had just accepted and presented this recently.[9] Therefore we desire, if it is God's will and he gives us understanding, strength, and power, that we may bring up this matter yet once more before our death in order to reveal, to free us before all consciences, and to witness to the truth of our mind before God. Therewith we desire to appear before the judgment seat of Jesus Christ, and do not doubt that we will be acceptable therewith in his grace, Matt. 16:[24-28]; for God knows that we do not seek other than his praise and the salvation of his congregation. Thereto the most high and only wise God help us, through Jesus Christ, with the power of his Holy Spirit. Amen. 2 Cor. 5:[10].

About the Marriage of Christians

First, it is to be noted how God himself instituted marriage with two persons in paradise, Gen. 2:[18ff.], namely, with one husband and one wife, both of whom were created according to the image of God. /628/ Those God has joined together, blessed, and made fruitful. It is also still his will to the present day, yes, as long as children of God are on earth, that among them marriage should begin and be kept according to this example. For God does not will, yes, it is an abomination before him that one should break or change his ordinance for any fleshly purpose, Matt. 15:[1-9]. And that is what God meant when he said through Moses and in many other places that one shall not add to his Word nor subtract therefrom, but one shall maintain everything he has commanded, so that one be not punished nor found a liar, Deut. 4:[2]; 12:[32]; Prov. 30:[6].

Therefore it is very necessary that by an ordinance of the Lord these following points are noted and encouraged: first, who the author and institution of the ordinance is; thereafter, what the ordinance in itself is; and, finally, why God has made the ordinance. Thereby it must remain, and there may be no change in it, for it is a real pharisaical nature to change God's institution, ordinance, and command, and to set them upon a wrong basis, Matt. 15:[1ff.]. Nothing but evil can come from that. For through such changes the good is changed into bad, light into darkness, divine into human, and the spiritual into carnal, and thus misused. And misuse destroys everything that is good. Notice to what other ordinances of the Lord have come through misuse, yes, what abominable idolatry has been motivated therewith and is still [being] motivated.

Therefore [let] everyone observe and consider that the almighty and eternal God will be mastered by no one nor have his ordinances broken and changed, for he alone is wise, teacher, and judge, 1 Tim. 1; John 6:[45ff.]; Heb. 12:[18ff.]. This same God is the author of these ordinances about marriage of which we speak. The ordinance is the divine uniting of two persons who are born pure and holy out of God the Father, through faith in Jesus Christ in the Holy Spirit, 1 John 2; 5; Gal. 3; John 3. The reason, cause, and effect of this ordinance is the growth and increase through the blessing of the LORD, Gen. 2:[18ff.]. That is then a true Christian marriage which may stand before the LORD in his congregation. For thus it was instituted in the beginning by God himself in paradise, but that after time this good divine ordinance has come into great misuse, that flesh and blood has done, as follows hereafter, Gen. 6. /629/

Second, the misuse of the ordinance of God about marriage has come from this: that the children of God looked upon the daughters of humanity, that they were beautiful and fair, and took as wives those whom they wanted and did not observe the first ordinance God made with Adam and Eve in Paradise, but looked much more on the beauty of the daughters, for they were all spoiled and became flesh. Therefore, they followed the desires of their evil flesh, Gen. 6:[1-2]. Now when God saw that he said: My spirit will not always be judge among people, for they are fleshly. I will give them a respite of 120 years, Gen. 6:[3]. And yet once more: When the Lord saw that human evil was great upon the earth and all the intent and thoughts of their hearts were always inclined to evil, then he regretted that he had made human beings on earth, and it troubled him in his heart, and [he] said: I will eliminate the people whom I have created, or remove them from the earth, beginning with the people to the beasts and to the worms and the birds under heaven. For I regret that I have made them. But Noah found grace before the LORD, Gen. 6:[5-8].

From this it is clear what an abomination it is before the Lord to break his ordinance and to act against it. And it is amazing that we know and have before our eyes such clear, striking, and terrible examples and witnesses from Holy Scripture about God's anger and disfavor over the transgressions of his divine ordinances, that still anyone who boasts of being Christian does not honor everything but dares to act against God and his Word deliberately, boldly, and with evil intention, out of evil desires of his self-willed flesh; [that he dares] to commit such irritation, to sadden and trouble thus the congregation of the Lord, that which a true God-fearing Christian should not want to do because of all that is under heaven. But he should rather prefer to die with the Lord's help, and consider how abominable it is to bring God's anger into the congregation by his offense, Matt. 18:[7-9].

Therefore, one may well say that the person who does such has traveled far enough from God and is alienated, yes, that one may complain and sigh over such ones with these kinds of words: Where is your fear of God? Where is your faith in Jesus Christ? /630/ Where remains the promise you have made to him? Where is your love to the congregation of the Lord with which you joined and dedicated yourself in peace, love, and unity of the spirit to walk therein all the days of your life? Where is your care for your own soul and salvation? How shamefully do you sell your birthright with the fleshly Esau for an inferior meal? Heb. 12:[16]. When this and similar things are well considered and taken to heart, it should nevermore come to where anyone called a brother or sister should take an unbelieving person [as a spouse] from the world if they hope to be saved, nor should such be found [among them].

Third, thus has God from all this [which we have] already told, revealed and established his holy divine will still further through his trusted servant Moses, who out of that command of the Lord spoke thus to Israel: You shall not give your daughters to their sons (understand to the heathen and inhabitants of the land of Canaan), and you shall not take their daughters to your sons, for they should mislead your sons and then should the Lord's anger be kindled over you, and he should destroy you, Deut. 7:[3f.].

From these words it is, after all, clear to note what a great sin and peril of the soul lies in that a believer accepts a heathen, that is an unbelieving person. For here God himself said through Moses explicitly that the unbeliever misleads and wins over the believer who once had acknowledged and accepted the truth and was recorded in the number of the saints, that should the heathen daughters win [them] over, they would be turned from the living God to idols. This is also revealed in that the Moabite wives brought the children of Israel to where they served the Baal Peor, made sacrifices, and subjected them to him, as proof that they were one flesh, one folk, and had one worship with the Moabites, Num. 25. And that is, for the second time, a terrible example for those who look outside the congregation of God to an unbelieving person and accept that carnal one. Those may certainly be portrayed here, etc.

Fourth, thus all that which has been said before is yet more established in Ezra when he heard from the authorities /631/ that the people of Israel had not separated themselves from the abomination of the Lord. For they had the same daughters, themselves and their sons, and have thus made that holy seed common with the people in the land, etc., Ezra 9. So he tore his garments, plucked the hair from his head and out of his beard, lamented and moaned terribly before the Lord, prayed and spoke among many others also these following words: What shall we say after this, Oh, Lord our God? That we have abandoned your commandments that you have given and told through your servant, the prophet: the land which you came to inherit is an unclean land through the uncleanness of the people in the land, therewith they have defiled it here and there. Thus you shall not give your daughters to their sons, and their daughters you shall not take for your sons, and seek no peace with them, etc., Deut. 7:[3].

Here one may see, note, and hear how it has been taken to heart and vexed the pious and God-fruitful ones that anyone who boasted of faith or has the name of being a Christian takes a strange, unbelieving person against God's expressed Word. For that is a plain despising of the ordinance of God and a transgressing of his holy commandments. And that some highly reputable and important persons were deceived thereby and have departed from God, that each one may well consider.

Thus we have now presented our reasons [against] marrying outside of the faith based on the Old Testament, and proved powerfully with Scripture how God himself has instituted marriage in paradise, Gen. 2:[18ff.] and [it] is still his will that marriage shall be performed according to his ordinance and institution, in his fruit and in faith, between two persons who are of one mind according to Jesus Christ, according to the example of Adam and Eve, which God himself has presented to us in paradise. Thereafter we have thus witnessed how severely God has punished the transgressors of his ordinances, Gen. 8:[19-20]. Again, how God established his ordinance with an explicit command through Moses, over which Ezra thus complained that the children of Israel had transgressed against this commandment of the Lord and had taken heathen wives, Deut. 7:[3]; Ezra 9:[2ff.].

About the Marriage of Christians / 561

Here it is well to remember the educational example of Tobias and Sarah who were also under the law, but remain still today a clear reflection to all married people of how marriage shall begin and also be maintained, Tobit 3:[7ff.]. In addition, it is also well to take to heart what God had allowed to come over the seven men whom Sarah /632/ desired out of evil lust and God had excluded from her heart, and what violence Asmodeus had about it. That anyone who loves his salvation may well consider. And that is certainly, for the third time, a terrible example for those who do and have done this sin outside of marriage. And those who maintain it shall also not remain unpunished. Now in order that no one thinks we support the before mentioned position only with the Old Testament and otherwise have no scriptural proof, we hope also to prove and witness to this matter out of the New Testament with God's help.

Fifth, our Lord Jesus Christ has directed us in the gospel to the first creation of one husband and one wife who are joined together by God as a certain testimony that we must always look upon that example, Gen. 2:[18ff.]; that marriage may now not be begun otherwise by the faithful than it was begun and instituted by God himself. In addition, it is well to remember that the Old Testament was certainly incomplete, could not exist before God, much less can it now in the time of the gospel exist before God, Heb. 8:[4ff.]; 10:[1ff.]. For the gospel of our Lord Jesus Christ teaches us all perfection and completeness so that the people of God be complete, fitted for all good works, Matt. 6:[32f.]; 2 Tim. 3:[17].

Since then the Lord Jesus Christ has reinstituted and reformed marriage in its first form as it was made in paradise by the eternal God, his heavenly Father, therefore, thus now no other marriage must be accepted by the faithful than according to the first marriage which was instituted by God in paradise and thereafter was renewed and established through his Son Jesus Christ, that is with one husband and one wife, with two believing persons whom God himself joins together, Gen. 2:[18]; Matt. 19:[3ff.]. That is a true marriage and from it anyone who fears God may then understand how unreasonable, how untrue, yes, how entirely godless it is that one dare act against the pure, good, and holy ordinance of the Lord, that is, [against] the eternal heavenly Father and his only born Son Jesus Christ, so boldly and evil out of flesh and blood.

And if that has happened, then one attempts to cover that great sin and shame with a fig leaf, /633/ that is, with twisted Scripture, showing off and covering up the ugly affair. Then cleverness, cunning, and subtlety is used but it can still not solve anything. For the truth still triumphs everywhere. It must be pure if it shall survive before God in his congregation. Because there shall not enter unclean, nor lying, nor abominable persons into the New Jerusalem but those who are recorded in the book of life, Eph. 5:[4ff.]; Col. 1:[21ff.]. And no one may live by the eternal and consuming fire except those who fear the Lord from the heart, have his word before their eyes and have a humble spirit, Isa. 53; 57; 66.

One reads about this in the Psalms, Ps. 15:[1ff.], the prophet Micah, Mic. 6:[8], and many other Holy Scriptures. It does not pay to deal with God scoffingly for he is a judge and avenger [of such conduct], in this life or hereafter eternally. And after that everyone will need to shift for himself. What he now sows (as the apostle says), that he will also reap. If he sows through the flesh, he will reap destruction from the flesh. But if he sows through the Spirit, he will reap eternal life from the Spirit. After all those sow through the flesh who are fleshly minded and live according to the flesh, Gal. 6:[7ff.]. And those sow through the Spirit who are spiritually minded, and crucify and kill the flesh through the Spirit with all evil desires which strive against the soul, etc., Rom. 8:[5ff.]; Gal. 5:[16ff.]; 1 Pet. 2:[11ff.].

Sixth, we refer to the word of Paul to the Romans, namely, that the woman is bound to the law of the husband as long as he lives, Rom. 7:[1ff.]. But if the husband dies, she is free from the law of the husband, in order to wed, and to give herself in marriage with whomever she wills, only that it must happen in the Lord, 1 Cor. 7. We put this apostolic word there as a foundation from our earlier explanation. Yes, we put it as an irrefutable testimony to the truth which we believe as an unconquerable argument against all our opposition. The reason is this: the apostle presents the free, unbound person with the freedom to change, but with the condition that it happen in the Lord. What now happens in the Lord, that cannot be done against his Word and will. Here Paul's words to the Corinthians serve well, noted and taken to heart, namely, /634/ that one shall not pull together on a strange yoke with unbelievers, etc., 2 Cor. 6:[14ff.]. Read the text and understand it well.

Likewise he admonishes us [in his letter] to the Ephesians where he writes in other words, Eph. 5:[5-6]. Let no one mislead you with useless words. For on account of the same, the wrath of God comes over the children of unbelief; therefore, do not be their companion, for you earlier were in darkness, but now you have become a light in the Lord. Walk as children of the light (for the fruit of the Spirit is all kinds of goodness, righteousness, and truth), and have no fellowship with the unfruitful works of darkness, but punish them much more, etc. This agrees with what the apostle also wrote to the Romans: the night is past, and the day has arrived; so let us lay aside the works of darkness and put on the weapons of light. Let us walk honorably, as in the day, not in reveling and drinking, not in debauchery and dishonor, not in wrangling and jealousy, but put on the Lord Jesus Christ, and do not do according to fleshly cleverness in order to gratify its desires, Rom. 13:[12-14].

Now every one who fears God, who seeks and has love for God's honor and the welfare and improvement of the congregation, consider how openly and stubbornly outside marriages work against other marriage admonitions and warnings of the apostles, 1 Thess. 4:[3ff.]. And if one will confess the truth rightly, what is being sought with the outside marriages and what is otherwise contained in them than that one gives room for the evil stubborn flesh (that will not be obedient to the Spirit because it has not been sufficiently disciplined but much more bound to sensuality) to complete its evil and unbecoming lusts? And what can result from it but aggravation and evil examples? Now the Lord said in the Gospel: if anyone offends one of the least of those who believe, it were better that a millstone be bound to his neck and he be sunk and drowned in the deepest of the sea, Matt. 18:[6-7]; Luke 17:[2]; Mark 9:[42]. From this is to be noted: If it is such an abominable and blameworthy sin to offend one of the littlest of the Christian believers, how much more is it an abomination that one offends, saddens, and burdens to death not one but so many God-fearing hearts with [the practice of] outside marriage?

In addition, the Scripture says that bad examples destroy the good and lead astray the guiltless heart, Wisd. of Sol. 4:[12]. If now brothers and sisters who have been in the faith for a time do this and accept the unbelievers outside of God and his congregation, does this not /635/ open both a window and a door for young brothers and sisters also to commit such sin before the Lord? That the old Eleazar certainly thought through. Therefore, he would not pretend but would rather die than that he should offend the young brothers and leave a bad example for posterity, 2 Macc. 6:[18ff.]. [Let] each one consider this well.

And that is actually the intention, that Christians have no freedom to attack marriage for [except] as Paul said, that it should occur in the Lord, 1 Cor. 7:[39]. What now occurs in the Lord, that occurs and must occur according to his divine will. Once more, what occurs outside the Lord, that is wrong. And all wrong is sin, and it is from the devil, who sinned from the beginning, 1 John 3:[8]. But the Son of God was revealed to take away sin, and sin is not from him. Whoever remains in him does not sin. Whoever sins has not seen nor known him, as John openly confesses.

Seventh, therefore we establish this as an immoveable basis of truth that the apostle said: Do you not know that your bodies are temples of the Holy Spirit which you have received from God, and you are not fully in control of yourselves? 1 Cor. 3:[16]. And again, do you not know that your members are members of Jesus Christ? 1 Cor. 6:[15]. From this it then follows powerfully that a Christian has no power over his own body in order to take that from the Lord and give it to an unbeliever. For since a Christian's body belongs to the Lord and is a temple of the Holy Spirit, how can that be given to an unbeliever outside of Jesus Christ, outside his word and will, and outside his congregation?

That a Christian's body is the Lord Jesus Christ's body, that the aforementioned words of the apostle clearly testify, and from this is also certainly evident and plain that it is united and married to the Lord through faith, just as many beautiful histories, figures, and sayings tell and witness in both testaments with great clarity. And what requires many words? The congregation is generally the bride who is married to the husband, the bride and wife of the Lamb, this is each pious Christian in particular, Hos. 2:[19ff.]. Now a married maiden, bride and wife has no authority to give her body to another, for she is not, according to Paul's words, ruler over her body, /636/ but the husband, 1 Cor. 7:[4]. How much less then is a Christian ruler over his body, but the Lord is the ruler, Eph. 1:[22ff.]; 1 Cor. 7:[4]. For a Christian is the Lord's possession and belongs to the Lord with all that he has received from God, for the Lord Jesus Christ has accepted him out of grace when he was miserable, naked, blind, and poor, Rev. 3:[17]; Ezek. 7. He has spread the cloak of his righteousness and salvation over him when he lay in the blood of his sin; he has married him in faith, yes, delivered, bought, and helped him from all unrighteousness of this world, according to the will of his Father, and joined him to himself as a chosen bride, Hos. 2:[19ff.]; 1 Pet. 1:[18ff.]; Rev. 1:[5]; Eph. 5:[23ff.].

Therefore, then the bride has no authority to give herself or her body to a strange unbeliever against the will of her bridegroom. For whoever takes from the Lord what is his, that one does him violence and wrong. Thus if one violently takes from a person what is his, that will be seen as violence and punished. How much more is that worthy of punishment if one takes from Jesus Christ what is his and gives it to a stranger, yes, to a heathen? That each one must certainly consider. But a believer may accept a believer as a spouse in the fear of the Lord and present his body to him. For the spiritual marriage between Jesus Christ and his bride does not take away the freedom between two believing persons to be legally married, but it must be in Christian freedom. But the fleshly and stubborn intention to look around for a strange flesh it [the Scripture] forbids so firmly that it may not be more strictly forbidden.

As a further explanation and establishment of all that has been said, we establish this as an irrefutable argument of our concern about outside marriage: that it is so wrong and unclean in itself that it will be punished with the ban. And why will it be punished with the ban? Is it not because of the transgression of the divine commandments? Wherein now lies the transgression? Is it not therein that the believer binds himself with the unbeliever and thereby becomes one flesh against God's ordinance? Ezra 9:[10ff.] So long now as the transgressor is one flesh with the unbeliever, thereby acting as if she were his rightly genuine wife given to him from God, but nevertheless God had nothing to do with it, how can he then repent, since he still remains lying in the sin and trespass? Therefore, he is punished rightly by God and his congregation with separation.

Could Miriam /637/ come to the camp of Israel and be admitted except she was first cleansed of her leprosy? Num. 12:[1ff.]. And if one would then present to us that the transgressor is cleansed through repentance, through his sorrowful lament and confession of his guilt, we answer to it that no one can repent and still live in sin, Rom. [6:1-4]; Ezek. 18:[21-22]. The reason for this is: true repentance always has these following points or characteristics (which one calls properties), and which cannot be separated from it, namely: a proper sadness and sorrowful state about the preceding sin, Matt. 3:[1-2]; after that a true confession of the sin before God, Ps. 32:[1-2]; praying and sighing before the throne of grace with a genuine faith for the forgiveness of sin and with a firm trust in God's bottomless mercy, Rom. 3:[21-25]; Heb. 5:[7-8]. But above all there must be a good and firm resolve to sin no more and to refrain from the sin. That is then true repentance which is valid before God, that one refrains from sin, yes, that is the true worship which pleases the Lord. And that one ceases from unrighteousness, that is a true atonement for sin, Ecclus. 35:[1ff.].

From this we thus conclude: Is the transgression of the outside marriage not so great that it is worthy of the ban, then one may also not separate the transgressor [from the congregation]. But is it an affair worthy of the ban (just as all God-fruitful hearts confess and allow), then it is impossible that the apostate may come into the congregation again so long as he still remains in his uncleanness for which he was banned and is not cleansed from it.

Behold, dear brothers, friends, and companions in Christ Jesus, you who fear God and love the truth, here you have our highest understanding, heartfelt understanding, and public confession about outside marriage, and thereby we desire to live and die in the Lord's grace, and hope without any doubt to stand with [it] with his help in the great and terrible day of the Lord. Now we will also set forth the arguments and counter arguments or accusations and answer them to the extent to which God gives grace.

First, our adversaries declare that the children of God have taken as wives the daughters of humanity /638/ because of their beauty, which they wanted, Gen. 6:[1-2]. Thereby they allege that the Lord says in the Gospel that in the time of Noah the people ate, drank, married, and let themselves be married, Luke 17:[26-27]. From this they want to conclude and decide that if a brother takes an unbelieving person as his wife (although against God's will and ordinance), then she is nevertheless his real wife. They want to prove this with the aforementioned texts of Scripture that the two different persons, one believing and one unbelieving, who have come together in unrighteousness must remain with each other, for they are married people. Thus they comfort the people in their unrighteousness and strengthen the hands of the godless, so that no one is converted from his wickedness, Ezek. 13:[22].

To this the following is our simple answer: Since our adversaries openly confess that there is a wrong and unclean marriage, we are greatly surprised that they use an unjust issue, which is also unclean, in their defense since they can only come to shame with it. For if it is wrong, it may not stand before the righteous God, who hates all godless beings and is an enemy of all unrighteousness, Ps. 7:[11-13]; [45:7]; Heb. 1:[9]. Therefore, the apostle John also wrote: If you know that God is just, then know also that whoever does right is born out of God; but whoever does sin, that one is from the devil, 1 John [3:7-9]. If it is unclean, it may not exist nor be allowed nor introduced into the congregation. For the congregation is clean and holy.

Therefore, we are greatly puzzled that brothers were found who seek and use all cunning, cleverness, and subtlety to varnish over the ugly affair. Yes, they [attempt] to make wrong into right and unclean, clean. That is, they claim that the children of God took the daughters of the people as wives, which they simply wanted, Gen. 6:[1-2]; Luke 17:[27]. With that they want to say that such a marriage is based first on Moses, after that on the Lord Jesus Christ. Therefore, it is a wedding and marriage, and thus must remain.

Oh, Lord, what kind of a marriage that has been is seen in the terrible example and the severe punishment of the Lord which has come over all flesh and destroyed it. If the marriage could have existed before the Lord, it would not have been so severely punished by God. But now it is punished by the Lord because it is an abomination before him. And that the Lord Jesus refers in the Gospel to the example from the time of Noah, Luke 17:[26ff.], about marrying and being married, that /639/ has this meaning: That just as the world was destroyed in the time of Noah and few pious ones survived who were kept in the ark, so also shall the world be destroyed in every manner in the coming of the Son of man, and few righteous shall then be found, Luke 17:[26f.]; [1] Pet. 3:[10]; Luke 18:[8].

And if one would hold ever so firmly to that word promised, though still with immodesty and wrongly, then we set against it that Esau also took the Hittite daughters as wives, and both were disobedient to Isaac and Rebekah, Gen. 26:[34f.]. Then Rebekah spoke to Isaac: I regret to live because of the Hittite daughters; if Jacob takes a wife from the Hittite's daughters which are like the daughters of the land, then what use is life to me? Gen. 27:[46]. Here everyone hears and understands that Esau had taken the Hittite daughters for his wives. But what kind of a marriage it was, and what kind of example Esau is, the letter to the Hebrews testifies where it is written: Pursue peace and sanctification, without which no one shall see God, and [let] no one neglect the grace of God; let no root of bitterness grow up among you, through which many are defiled, and no one be a whorer or unspiritual, just as Esau was who for a little food sold his birthright, and when he sought it again with tears, did not find it, Heb. 12:[14-17].

From this it is plain to understand what a marriage it was before God and for Isaac and Rebekah that Esau took the Hittite daughters. Again, that one proposes to us about Herodias, the housewife of Philip, that John the Baptist therefore punished (reprimanded) Herod, and said to him: It does not become you to have your brother's housewife, that is not against us, and we have nothing against it also, Matt.

14:[3-4]. For we let the marriage of this world remain there, as Paul has written to the Corinthians about it, 1 Cor. 7:[17-18]. But we are not dealing with that now, but we are dealing with this, what one shall do with those who in the time of their belief and their brotherhood take an unbelieving person in the world and unite with them: what repentance they need to do, etc.

Second, our adversaries accuse us (although with all lack of understanding) with that which they want to defend the wrong and /640/ unclean marriage (according to their own confession), namely, that the Lord Jesus Christ said in the gospel: That from the beginning God created one man and one woman, and that a person shall leave father and mother and adhere to his housewife, which two shall be one flesh, etc., Gen. 2:[23-24]; Matt. 19:[4-5]. Answer: We acknowledge that all as right and as the truth. But it saddens us in our hearts that one sets the holy ordinance of God [together with] an entirely fleshly and ungodly act. Is it not a blasphemy of God which each one of us should consider? For the Lord Jesus said by the aforementioned words: What God has joined together, that people shall not separate, Matt. 19:[6]. If now anyone says that this fleshly action (namely, that a believer accepts an unbeliever) is a union [brought about] by God, that one may step forward and defend it. But we think, yes, we certainly know well, that no one can do that with the truth. But we confess openly before God and all the God-fruitful ones, that it is no uniting [brought about] by God but a fleshly joining and uniting. God has nothing to do with it. For it is an abomination before him, just as he has shown in the first world with the punishment of the flood.

In addition, it is well to consider what the apostle wrote to the Corinthians: To the married, not I but the Lord command, that the woman shall not allow herself to be separated from the husband, and if they let her separate, that she remain alone or be reconciled to her husband, and the husband shall not leave the woman, 1 Cor. 7:[10]. From this it is easy to understand that the Lord spoke of two believing persons. To allege on this basis and thereby compare thus that these words of the Lord also apply when a believer takes an unbeliever is not further spoken to, but only about two believers. To apply these words to an apostate and unbeliever, that is a great misunderstanding. God grant that no stubborn perversion be found at any time.

Again, to compare a marriage which is contracted in the time of unbelief and ignorance between two unbelievers, after the custom of the world, with one contracted by a person who lets himself be called a brother and who takes a worldly person, that does violence to the

Scripture. For one can out of the whole New /641/ Testament not prove with one word that there is more than the marriage between two believers, of which the Lord said: And the marriage which is made in unbelief by two unbelievers according to the world's manner, when after a time one of them comes to faith, the believer may then remain and live with the unbeliever, (for Paul acknowledges it for a marriage) but still with such condition as the apostle declares, 1 Cor. 7:[12ff.]. But about a marriage where a believer takes an unbeliever, the whole New Testament says nothing, and is [therefore] not good human thinking [but] subtlety, and a plain twisting of the divine Scripture, and we hope not to consent therein all the days of our life.

Third, the word of our adversaries is that only the promise actually makes the marriage, and want to prove that with Moses, namely: If anyone sleeps with a married or promised person, that one is punished as a fornicator, Num. [5:11-31]. Thereafter their proof is also that Mary, the virgin, was betrothed to Joseph, and, nevertheless, it was counted as a marriage, Matt. 1:[18ff.]; Luke 2:[5]. Answer: We do not speak against that, also cannot justly do so, but it is well to note that not the wedding alone makes the marriage and binds so firmly, for hidden things can lie there which make such a wedding powerless. But this we certainly confess, that the marriage exists principally therein that the hearts of both persons are inclined and purposed thereto, and they have prayed to God with fasting and meditation, not further surrendered themselves than so far as the Lord and his congregation permitted it; thus they are satisfied on both sides, still with this condition, that in the meantime, before they are united and joined together by God, remain in Christian yieldedness.

In order to understand this still better, note this analogy: A prospect who desires and hopes to give himself to God's congregation and to unite therewith, that one may not do or act otherwise in all that is against faith and God's Word than as if he had already been accepted. Thus also may a person who is promised or engaged not do otherwise than as if the marriage was already entirely established with her and her future bridegroom. And just as now a prospect is not counted as a companion of the faith nor as a full member /642/ of the body, but he must first receive the Lord's sign and be accepted orderly by the congregation as a covenanted companion with the hand and the kiss of peace and love. Thus also the promise certainly is one part of the marriage and is its beginning, and without it the marriage is not established. But a complete marriage is actually the consenting of both parties out of the depth of the heart with the promise and the conditions, as was said above, with all that the Lord put with it and according to whose will the ordinance of marriage has been made.

Therefore, the word is without power when it is said: The wedding or the promise makes the marriage. And if that already were thus, and we permitted it, our adversaries are still not helped therewith. For what they allege, that was in Israel and Judah, that is, in the congregation of God, and therefore does not affect the heathenish daughters. What similarity then has the allegation with this affair of which is spoken? Still Solomon said that who separates himself seeks what he lusts after, and places himself against all that is good, Prov. 18:[1]. But who walks simply walks safely. For if one has acted somewhat against God's Word, it generally happens just as Sirach said: Some would rather do their worst than that they should lose their honor, and do such for the sake of godless people, Ecclus. 20. Therefore, each one may watch that he always acts rightly through God's grace; thus he may not pretend [in order] to please the godless and apostates, etc.

Fourth, our adversaries allege that Paul permitted to the Corinthians that a believer may live with an unbeliever as long as the unbeliever consents to live with the believer in peace, that is, that the conscience of the believer remains clear, 1 Cor. 7:[12-13]. And that the unbeliever is sanctified through the believer. Hereby they want to compare it as if a brother or sister takes an unbeliever and unites with him, then shall the unbeliever, through such apostasy which has acted so stubbornly against God's Word and against the congregation, thereafter accuses him, shows sorrow, and promises improvement, also be sanctified. We oppose this as a false basis and with this evidence and proof that the apostle has not written wider than that, namely: If two persons, /643/ a man and woman, in the time of ignorance and unbelief had come together, promised each other to marry, and had lived together as married persons with each other, that these, on account of the gospel and faith, shall not separate nor break the promise which they, the one to the other, had made, although in unbelief, still always with the aforementioned condition. But that anyone who lets themselves be called brother or sister in the congregation of the Lord accepts an unbelieving person in the world, that is far from the apostle Paul's early word and meaning. For what happens in ignorance, that God accounts to that ignorance. But that after the acknowledged and accepted truth it is mishandled and stubbornly sinned against, that is an abomination before him. We think that no one is so ignorant that they do not understand and know that, if he otherwise will not speak or act stubbornly against the Lord's Word, against plain truth, and against his own conscience. From this we conclude and decide that it is a wrong and unscriptural comparison that one will compare such by each other as was said before.

And that the unbeliever will be sanctified by the believer, that is not to be understood wider than applies to the married practice and action, as all God-fruitful ones also certainly know and are taught therein from God, and may nevermore be interpreted that an unbelieving person be accepted by a brother or sister in the world, that then they who acted and worked so openly against God's Word should be clean and holy in their being. For we have in the entire New Testament not more than two kinds of marriages, namely, of two believing persons whom God joined together, and two persons who have come together in unbelief and one of them comes to faith, how that case will be in the congregation, and the marriage on account of faith shall not be broken but be kept, still always with such condition as the apostle writes, Matt. 19:[3-6]; 1 Cor. 7:[26-27].

Finally, it is meant that as little as an apostate woman is clean and free on account of her apostacy, though a brother is her husband, so little is an unbelieving worldly person clean and free [because] /644/ he has taken her in the time of his faith. And if he will repent, he must cease from that which was begun by him against God's Word, and sin no more. For what was not begun rightly in the Lord, that can hardly be brought to a good end.

Also some claim that they have a concern in this, namely, that if someone in the time of their apostasy errs still farther and takes a worldly person, that shall not be compared to what happened in the time of faith. Answer: That one sins even more in the time of apostasy, that does not excuse the apostate but burdens his apostasy even more. Reason: The one sin cannot lighten or improve the other, but makes it much worse. For Ecclesiasticus said: To sin once is much, because the sin was done against the most high and righteous God who is not pleased with all godless beings, who hates all unrighteousness and loves righteousness, Ps. 7:[11-13]. Therefore, sin has been an abomination before him from the beginning, severely punished, both in heaven among the angels and by people upon earth, although they were created according to his image, Ps. 45:[7]; Heb. 1:[9-12]; 2 Pet. 2:[4-10]; Gen. [1:26-28]. But to sin twice makes it still more difficult. And to sin three times brings the punishment with it, Ecclus. 23:16.

From this a Christian shall consider and take to heart that to fall away from God and his Word is a great and terrible abomination. And if one sins still more in the time of the apostasy, that is still more abominable. This is plain to see in the figurative Israel for it was disobedient and rebellious to God so many times. Now that they wanted to have a golden calf, Exod. 32:[2ff.]. Now that the heavenly bread was a light food. Now that they followed the godless band of Korah, Num. 16:[1ff.]. Now that they wanted to stone Joshua and Caleb because they stood against the other spies and were well comforted in the Lord, Num. 14:[6-10]. Now that they murmured against Moses and Aaron, and did many more such things that are unnecessary to relate, Exod. 16:[2-3]; 17:[2-4]; Num. 11:[1ff.].

But when they above all that took the Moabite daughters and slept with them, then they thus did [added] still much more evil thereto before the Lord, so that they were more severely punished by him, Num. 25:[1ff.]. When Balaam loved the presents of King Balak and therefore traveled to the Moabite land and had evil in mind, then his way was already wrong and /645/ his heart already turned away from God. But when God hindered the evil attack of Balaam against his own (to wit) his curse which he had in mind changed into a benediction, then he still gave in his farewell the false counsel how Moab would deceive Israel. Therefore, he must also die and out of the Lord's command through Moses was killed by Israel, Num. 22; 24; 31. From this is to be noted that his last misdeed was not smaller, but (according to our opinion) greater than the earlier one was.

Saul, the first king over Israel, was already turning away from God at Gilgal when he sacrificed out of fear that the people would turn away from him, and he did not stay for the prophet Samuel; that was the beginning of his falling away, 1 Sam. 13:[8ff.]. Thereafter he turned still farther away from God when he did not carry out the Lord's Word against the Amalekites. And that was still certainly difficult since he was a hypocrite before Samuel and wanted to keep his honor with the people, 1 Sam. 15:[1ff.]. And we could relate many more such examples from which it is easy to understand that every evil and nothing good comes out of apostasy from God, and that one sin follows another just as also the experience and daily occurrences teach us well.

Now there is still an objection from our adversaries, namely, if someone forgot himself so that he took, in the time of his faith, a worldly person and afterwards he comes to sadness and sorrow, desires from his heart to improve, and he cannot move the unbeliever nor bring [her] to the congregation, what counsel is there then for such a repentant and apostate? Answer: We acknowledge before God and have openly acknowledged many times before this that in our time in the faith and in our service, with our knowledge and consent, no one who has thus run away to the world, that that one coming once again to the congregation of God, is taken in unless the unbeliever is first converted, has become a believer, and is received as a Christian and companion in the faith.

While we have not seen otherwise in the congregation of God, we thus had the right and reason to reject such a useless question. But what was sought and intended therewith, the Lord knows, and the God-fruitful also notice that. /646/ It would be time enough to speak about it when the matter is present and suspend it until one has sought help, advice, and comfort from God. Thereafter [we could] hold a general discussion with all teachers, elders, and ministers (as many as one can get) agreeing and deciding out of God's Word how one shall act in this matter. And not that some brothers carry it out by themselves without any teachers according to their own opinion. That simply has no parallel in Scripture, but it lets him appear much more stubborn, puffed up, and conceited.

As long as the congregation of God acted thus, as was said above, according to the example shown us in Israel, Deut. 17:[8ff.], and according to the example of the apostolic congregation, Acts 15:[1-2], it went reasonably well, then there was fairly good peace. But if one, or some congregation, was stubborn to deal with any difficult matter outside of the teachers, elders, ministers, and other congregations, then everything resulted in aggravation and sadness, yes, disturbance, division, and destruction of God's congregation, just as one may observe today with sorrowful eyes that many have fallen short over it [marriage and the ban], and that it is certainly high time to consider and to reflect [on these things].

Now we want to return to the former proposal, namely, to the question of our opposition, which is this: if the unbeliever is stiff-necked, and the repentant one will not follow, if then the repentant one therefore shall always remain outside of the congregation? Whether his repentance will remain bound to the unbeliever? Answer: Such genuine, patient, and steadfast repentance may be found in the one who has transgressed that one cannot deny or reject the acceptance of him with humility, nevertheless, always with the condition that he shall leave the person which he has taken against God and his Word; shall have no freedom to take another for himself; shall take care of the abandoned person with regard to her necessities; and pray for her to God trustfully and worshipfully, that God may open her eyes of understanding that she may acknowledge the truth and convert to the living God, 2 Tim. 2:25. But if someone would understand us herein to say that we herewith acknowledge it as a marriage that a brother or sister thus takes and an unbelieving person thus made, then we respond that this was sufficiently answered and explained above. /647/ And since our own opponents themselves acknowledge that it is a wrong and impure marriage, we let it remain thereby.

But if someone will be subtle, that one should reflect that all human wisdom and subtlety is foolishness and folly before God, 1 Cor. 1:[19ff.]. Let anyone imagine to himself that he knows something, that one [should] reflect on the apostle's word, that he does not yet know as one ought to know, 1 Cor. 8:[2]. Will someone ascend high [be someone], we desire to place ourselves equal with the humble and downcast, and to say with Paul, that we do not boast of knowing anything other than Jesus Christ and him crucified, whose footsteps we desire to follow and to walk according to the certain rules of his godly Word, Gal. 4:[21]; Rom. 12:[3]; 1 Cor. 2:[2]. In summary, if someone likes to argue, that one shall know that we do not have that style, nor does the congregation of God, 1 Cor. 11:[17-20].

Behold, these are the main arguments (so many as we have remembered) wherewith our opponents, in the before mentioned matter, want to maintain about those whom one accepts as an unbeliever outside of the Lord and his congregation. But we hope that we through the grace of the Lord have established the matter so clearly, proven with godly Scripture, also thus have answered the arguments of the opponents so that any God-fruitful ones shall be well satisfied with it. Nevertheless, what we now by chance have not been able to do so perfectly by reason of the sickness of our flesh, that the almighty God can still give more clearly in his time, be it through us or through another, although we hope that we have fully herewith [helped] all God-fruitful lovers of the truth and fellow companions of our Christian faith.

Finally, this is the sum and conclusion about that which was said, that marriage is a pure, good and holy ordinance of God, Gen. 2:[18-25]; 5:[1-2], and nothing otherwise may be begun, accepted, and held by the believers than according to the expressed Word of the Lord, according to the witness of the Holy Scripture, yes, according to the example of Jesus Christ who accepts no bride other than the believer, yes, who is flesh born from him in the Spirit, Rom. 7:[2-3]; Eph. 5:[21-33]. Thus also a brother may accept no person other than those who are a member of Jesus Christ with him, his same sister according to the spirit, in the faith, like-minded with him in the truth, 1 Cor. 6:[15-16]; 12:[12-13]; and just as he /648/ has become a son of God out of grace through the acceptance of the eternal Father in the knowledge of his Son Jesus Christ, thus he must also accept a God-fruitful sister who is a daughter of the almighty heavenly Father as his wife in the fear of the Lord.

That is then called done and married in the Lord. Otherwise, there is no marriage which is valid before God than [that which] the apostle Paul allows for the marriage of this world (that two unbelieving persons have come together in unbelief), and lets it remain a marriage with such condition that the unbeliever consents to live with the believer, not wanting to dominate over his faith which God has wrought in him, wanting to leave him undisturbed, unburdened, and unhindered, 1 Cor. 7:[12-16]. Thus may such living together certainly happen. For the unbeliever is then pure and holy for the believer so far as the marriage activities are concerned, and to such an unbeliever who allows himself to be found in such circumstances there is still hope that he may come to faith through God's grace.

But one cannot produce a single saying for us in the New Testament wherewith this third marriage (that is how our opponents wish a marriage to be called) will be accounted and established as free, pure, and in such a manner as the marriage between a believer and unbeliever who have come together in unbelief. And that one wants to so twist the words of Paul to the Corinthians, 1 Cor. 7:[12-16], does open violence to the Scripture, and has no more power than what the pedobaptists or child baptizers allege that households were baptized by the apostles, from which they seek to prove that children were there and baptized also. But that is now a powerless proof about the false basis of infant baptism against the firm basis of truth, the true baptism of the repentant and believers. After all, it is so powerless that one will prove out of the words of Paul to the Corinthians about marriage between a believer and an unbeliever who have come together in unbelief, that thus if a believer accepts a worldly person that that living together and marriage fellowship shall be pure. No, never. But if the apostate who was separated from God and his congregation through his trespass will do and show repentance, he must before all else leave that which he has done against God's Word and will, as was explained above.

And as further explanation about all of this, so everyone may notice that this matter about outside marriage is in itself so wrong, so impure, and so godless that they were punished with the ban from the congregation of the Lord, /649/ how then shall the transgressor be able to repent so long as he remains in sin and transgression for which he was punished with the separation from God and his congregation? Does not true repentance have these following characteristics: namely, a true sorrow and pain about the previous sin; thereafter a true confession of the sin before God; praying and sighing before the throne of grace for forgiveness of sins, with a firm trust in God's mercy and with a good intent to sin no more, but to cease from it, Matt. 3:[8ff.]; Acts 2:[38]; Ps. [32:1-5]. For that is true repentance and worship, that one cease from sinning and stop doing wrong, Ecclus. 35:[3-4].

From this it follows indisputably that if the transgression and misdeed from the outside marriage is so great in itself that it is worthy of the ban, then it is impossible that the apostate may again come to the congregation. When he still remains in his uncleanness and sin, the impure, godless, and banned party must first be put aside before he can show true repentance. In addition, each one [should] consider the words of Paul that one may not marry other than in the Lord, 1 Cor. 7:[12-16]. And that a Christian does not rule over his body, but the Lord [does], 1 Cor. 3:[16-17]; 6:[15-20]. Each one should reflect upon these words in his heart.

Herewith we close our writing at this time about these matters, and admonish the God-fruitful reader that he read thoughtfully, take to heart, lay upon the golden scale of the divine words, thus weighing, testing, and researching if it is not the simple truth and the most certain way to walk and come to a God-saving end, all that we have written through God's grace with great difficulty in our sickness of body. For there is certainly a way which persons think to be good, but its end leads to the abyss of hell, Prov. 14:[12]. Again, there is a narrow and straight street, and who walks it, that one walks securely, Prov. 10:[9].

The almighty God and Lord give you and all of us understanding and wisdom always to act according to his godly will, which is well-pleasing before his eyes. Written and completed the seventh of March in the year [anno] 1568.

D. P.

ENDNOTES

1. BRN X, p. 649 and BRN VII, p. 462, note 2. Also Keeney 1958, pp.171-191. Koolman, p. 183.

2. I. H. V. P. N. [Carel van Ghendt], *Het beginsel der scheuringen onder de Doopsgesinden.* (1615) 1658. BRN VII, pp. 489ff.

3. Ibid., p. 531.

4. Ibid., p. 532.

5. The assertion that Dirk did not shrink back from letting his teaching lead to divorce, as the editor of the BRN document seems to imply [p. 619], is probably overstated though it may, in fact, have led to that in some instances. Loss of members may have been the more likely result. Menno Simons reports that some 300 spouses did not obey the excommunication order to shun their partner. CWMS 1956, p. 972.

6. In addition to Dirk, the meeting included Menno Simons, Adam Pastor, Frans de Kuiper, Hendrik van Vreden, Antonius of Cologne, and Gillis van Aken. ME II:194ff. ME III:502ff. Vos, *Menno Simons, 1496-1561.* pp. 91f., 197ff. BRN VII, pp. 524ff. Koolman, pp. 35ff., 49. A similar meeting was held in Wismar in 1554 where nine articles were adopted, of which the first five deal with the ban and marriage, but go further than Emden 1547 in apparently authorizing remarriage of the believer subject to congregational approval. BRN VII, pp. 52-53. ME IV:966.

7. The original 1569 edition is the basis for the following text, based on the IDC microfiche and BRN X, pp. 623-649. For a listing of editions and photocopies of title pages, see Keyser 1975, pp. 138ff.

8. See note 6 above.

9. See note 6 above.

OMITTED WRITING ABOUT THE BAN AND AVOIDANCE

Introduction

J. ten Doornkaat Koolman reports that in the introduction to the French edition of this book it is reported that it was found in manuscript form in Dirk Philips' handwriting.[1] Thus it was not discovered until after his death. It was probably preserved by his most faithful followers, the Flemish Anabaptists. Since many of them did not read the Dutch, in which it was written, it was translated into French. It may have been translated prior to 1602 and circulated in handwritten form, but if so, no copies are known to exist. Ten Doornkaat Koolman suggests that it was done by Carel van Mander upon the assignment by P. van Wesbusch who published it together with "About the Marriage of Christians" and the "Answer to Sebastian Franck" [against S. Franck].[2]

Ten Doornkaat Koolman presumes Dirk wrote the copy in 1567. Many of the same thoughts and even identical wording appear in the new or "Second Banbook," which is known only in a French translation.[3]

The introduction to the present treatise is shorter and the biblical teachings are fewer than in the new or "Second Banbook." The answers to objections raised by opponents are more succinctly stated, especially with regard to the love of God and the neighbor. He does not deal with the issue of whether the ban applies only to those who are stubbornly public sinners, or to those who are grasped by human weakness. He applied it explicitly only to the former in the "First Banbook" which appeared in the *Enchiridion*.

It also appears that Dirk puts more stress on the importance of discipline as a means of restoring the sinner to fellowship than upon the danger to the reputation of the congregation as appeared in the earlier writing. In this later writing, the prime emphasis seems to have shifted; a concern for the reputation of the congregations is there, but together with a desire to protect the members from the infection of the defecting person.

The appended "Fragment," from pp. 507-508 of BRN X is an enigma in terms of original context but it fits into the theology of church discipline expounded by Dirk and is, therefore, included here rather than after the response to Erasmus, where the editor of BRN X placed it, albeit with a similar question about what to do with it.[4]

It is a defensive, polemical, and unfinished short piece, apparently written against the Swiss Brethren, who had admonished the Dutch to greater love and moderation in using the ban and avoidance. The editors-translaters here follow Marja Keyser in her judgment that Dirk did not write this document. It is included here, however, since some believe he may, in fact, be the author. The German document referred to was likely Menno Simons' *Reply to Sylis and Lemke*, Swiss Brethren who had admonished the Dutch about their harsh use of the ban.[5] This short document seems to have been added to the former in a 1587 printing by an anonymous author who used the pseudonym Gherit Andrieszoon.[6]

Omitted Writing [published posthumously] About the Evangelical Ban and Avoidance Through S.[aving] M.[emory]

Dierick Philips.

Translated from the French by C.[arel] v.[an] M.[ander] [?]

Matt. 28:20, Teach to keep all that I have commanded you.

2 Cor. 2:11, Therefore I have also written, so that I acknowledge and should prove whether you are obedient in every part.

Printed for Passchier from Wesbusch, bookseller, at Haarlem
Anno 1602 /657/

The translator to the truth-loving reader: /658/

That the truth constantly suffers much struggle, that passion of the beloved flesh is the enemy of the Lord's sweet yoke and is inclined to the broad way, that also earnest love of the truth appears [only] in a few, we see, alas, all too abundantly in these last times. The Lord's commands are perverted, slandered, and called into question for people; among others what the Holy Spirit teaches about separation and avoidance of the sinner, the flesh is there to defend against it with its reason; for it is painfully difficult for him to suffer for his favorite sin and to be punished and to bear shame [because of it]. In order then to teach a good distinction in this, I thought it not unuseful to translate this omitted document [left by] so pious a predecessor and to let it come to the light. Thus may everyone look at his understanding of Scripture and recognize that there is a distinction between unbelief and apostasy, which are portrayed as unequal in the Lord's Word. My desire is only that this my well-meant service may be acceptable and useful to all lovers of the truth.

C.[arel] v.[an] M.[ander]

Omitted Writing [published posthumously] and Treatment of Blessed Memory.
D. P. Regarding the Evangelical Ban and Avoidance

/659/ The Christian congregation must be diligent in attention and always have the Word of God before it, so that everything it judges will be done and directed after that same Word, which must also happen in [connection with the issue of] separation, and where one must exercise it, the sin will be shown clearly in the Holy Scripture beforehand.

First Christ says: If your brother sins against you, go and reprimand him between him and you alone. If he listens to you, you have won your brother. But if he will not listen to you, take one or two to you, Deut. 17:11; 19:15; John 8:17; 2 Cor. 13:1, so that the whole matter may be known [in the mouth of] to two or three witnesses. If he does not listen to them, report it to the congregation. If he does not listen to the congregation, hold him as a tax collector, Matt. 18:15ff.

Similarly the apostle wrote to the Romans in this manner: I pray you, dear brothers, that you will watch those who make division and aggravation among the teachings which you have learned and separate yourself from them, Rom. 16:17. He taught the same thing to Timothy and Titus, 1 Tim. 6:3ff.; 2 Tim. 3:5; Titus 3:2. John also did the same in his letter, 2 John 10[f.]. Again, the holy Paul writing to the Corinthians admonished them saying: If anyone lets himself be called a brother, and nevertheless is an adulterer, or greedy, or a servant of idols, or a slanderer, or drunkard, or robber, with all such you shall not eat, 1 Cor. 5:10.

He also wrote to the Thessalonians: We bid you, dear brothers, in the name of our Lord Jesus Christ, that you withdraw from all brothers who walk unseemly there, and not according to the tradition which you have received from us, 2 Thess. 3:6, and if there is someone who is not obedient to our words, he be notified through a letter and have nothing to do with him, so that he might be ashamed. /660/ Nevertheless, do not hold him as an enemy, but admonish him as a brother. This is a plain and general rule in Holy Scripture, to which the Christian must conform and comply without doing anything against it: for it is an established commandment from the Lord and through his apostles, by which it is of much importance, just as is to be observed clearly in the previous words. Therefore, it must be maintained and taken as true by all believing Christians, along with the fact that there are weighty reasons and causes why this separation must be practiced and maintained among the believers.

First of all, so that the congregation or assembly of the Lord should not be defiled through the unrighteous, for the Lord does not want that the unhealthy scabby sheep shall remain in his fold, in order that the whole flock may not be spoiled, about which we have a clear example in the books Joshua and Numbers, Josh. 7; Num. 16. About the same in Paul's letter to the Corinthians: Do you not know that a little leaven sours the whole dough? 1 Cor. 5:6. The apostle John admonished the believers about the same, saying, If some one comes to you and does not bring these teachings, do not take that one into the house, and also do not greet him, for who so greets him, that one has fellowship with his evil works, 2 John 10[f.].

Second, so that the sinner or trespasser would be ashamed, humbles himself, comes to confession, and amends himself, just as Paul taught in the first letter to the Corinthians and the second to the Thessalonians, 1 Cor. 5; 2 Thess. 3:14.

This evangelical separation thus rightly exercised and maintained is very useful and necessary, and that in a twofold manner: First, on this account, that through this means the congregation of the Lord be kept clean. Second, so that the sinner will repent and may himself thereby begin improvement.

It is also a medicine which is very strong and corrosive in order to heal the festering wounds which may not be healed through soft plasters, but through their infection the whole body may be destroyed, and where it was not attended with this hard, severe physic or medicine: still it needs to be intermingled with such sweetness and additive as the Holy Scripture teaches us. /661/ For otherwise it may cause more harm than good, which is why one shall pay attention to the rule which is given to us through God's Word.

In instituting separation Jesus Christ wanted that one hold the separated one just as a heathen or tax collector. Now the Jews have avoided these in such joining, as that they did not eat with them, neither drink, yes, also did not come into their houses, as can be seen sufficiently in Holy Scripture, for they also considered them to be equal to dogs, thus they also were as long as they remained in their unbelief, for Christ said to the Canaanite woman that it was not good to take the bread from the children and give it to the dogs, with which children the Lord has wanted to make known the Jews, and with the dogs, the heathen, Matt. 15:26; Rev. 22:[15].

In the same way the Holy Spirit also called dogs those who are outside the Christian congregation. Also, the Samaritan woman said to Jesus Christ, How do you, who are a Jew, desire to drink from me, who am a Samaritan woman? For the Jews have nothing to do with the Samaritans, John 4:9. Now the apostles declared to us plainly enough the before related words of Jesus Christ regarding the separation when they taught us and expressly commanded us to withdraw ourselves from all brothers who walk unseemly, not to eat with him, not to receive him in the house, to have no fellowship with him, neither to greet him, 2 Thess. 3:6; 1 Cor. 10; 2 John 10f. Following which teachings we have to conform ourselves, without going a longer or shorter way, or to make the burden heavier or lighter, as was taught to us earlier.

To this some say that one may certainly deal out of friendliness and love, speaking, eating, and drinking with an apostate or separated one, and that so he may come to repentance. Whereto we answer that we certainly permit and agree therein that one shall speak with him, and admonish him with God's Word, for the apostle taught such through the Spirit of God, but to deal with him, eating, and drinking, that we do not permit, since there is not a single word in the Holy Scripture through which it can be proved to us. For the apostle says that we should have no fellowship with such, nor even eat with them, saying in addition yet that the kingdom of God is not in eating or drinking, but in righteousness, peace, and joy in the Holy Spirit.

In the same manner Christian love does not exist in eating and drinking, /662/ but in deed and truth, Rom. 14:17; 1 John 3:18; neither will the apostates be moved to repentance through eating and drinking, but through a genuine displeasure and sadness about their sin, which brings in them a true suffering, through the pangs of conscience, which will be instructed and punished with God's Word.

Why does the apostle say admonish him as a brother, and does not say eat and drink with him? Thus it is then but human opinion and reasoning. Yes, such love must be considered as false, not agreeing with the truth and being against the evangelical separation.

Who then desires to walk in the love of God and his neighbor, that one [should] observe the Lord's Word and seek his neighbor's salvation. Then he shall certainly see that it is a commandment of God to put away the unrighteous or evil one from his congregation, that the love of God also exists in the keeping of his commandments, and that genuine brotherly love actually exists in seeking and promising in everything according to ability, the protection, and salvation of his brothers. Now then separation thus serves to bring the sinner to shame and to recognize himself; whereto from the same the instruction which was made to him out of God's Word serves to the recreating of his soul which will not be consoled through eating or drinking.

Further, it was asked if one may give no help or assistance to a brother who was apostate and separated from the congregation in the event that he has need or want. We answer thereto, according to the understanding that our God, the Lord, has given through his Holy Word; the separation commanded by Christ Jesus is not instituted for destruction but for improvement, 1 Cor. 10:8. Therefore, the Christian must not use separation as the Jews earlier used the Sabbath [where they would] sooner have let a person die than help him on that day, for we no more serve in the ancient [spirit] of the letter, although they previously have broken the Sabbath in order to escape their own injury, Matt. 12:10; 24:20[ff.]. Thus the Christian does not break the separation which was instituted by Christ whenever they give assistance to the separated in their need, for to show love in mercy or to give welfare to the poor is not forbidden, but in many places in the Scripture is deemed good and commanded. In short, in case someone being cut off from the congregation fellowships with a brother in the time of his need, just as the Samaritan did with /663/ the one who had fallen among the murderers, we hope that God shall be well pleased with that, Luke 10:30[ff.]. Thus we had much rather to show mercy to the poor with the Samaritan than to pass by with the sacrificing priest or Levite.

Again, it was asked in case two believers were joined in the married state and one of the two became apostate and thereby was separated from the congregation, whether the spouse who stands firm must withdraw from the other in avoidance. To that we answer that the separation is a general rule which one must use rightly, without regard to or exception of person, even if father, son, mother, daughter, husband, and wife give judgment against each other, for a Christian does not look upon the flesh or to excuse anyone herein.

If someone contradicts this, yet consents that the husband gives his judgment from his side with the Word of God against his blameworthy wife, and helps to place her outside of the Christian assembly, but wills additionally that [the husband] should not oppose her nor associate or be in fellowship with her as his wife just as before? Hereto [I give] this answer: the congregation cuts off, with the authority Jesus Christ has given it, the sister who has sinned or has become apostate, and that in such a manner that one shall have no external fellowship with her until the time that she through improvement and sorrow is readmitted into the congregation. The same must also happen with the husband, seeing that he is not his own but God's and his congregation's, to which he must be more attached and bear more love than to his own wife, 1 Cor. 6:9[f.]; 3:23.

If one says thereto that the husband is bound and united through marriage with his wife, being one body and flesh with her, which he is not with the congregation? Answer: Since the believing husband is united with his wife through marriage, so he is also united spiritually with Christ, who is the genuine bridegroom of the congregation. Moreover, since the believer is one body and one flesh with the congregation of Jesus Christ, the spiritual union is and must be firmer and more binding than the fleshly, Eph. 5:3ff.

About the same [some]one will say that the husband may certainly be united with Christ and [yet] remain with his wife, although she has /664/ fallen away from the truth. The answer [to this] is that this may not happen, noting that it is against the teaching of the Lord and his apostles, since in so doing he does not maintain the separation as it was instituted, for where shall this freedom come from? Should it be on this account that it is his wife? No, know that just as we have related, the fleshly intermingling may not nullify the evangelical separation.

But someone might say that the separation was not broken since the husband holds his wife for his wife and not for a sister in the congregation although he is living with her. One answers to this that by all this the separation of the person was nothing but spiritual, and external fellowship is not forbidden, one might certainly permit that, but we have proven the opposite.

If someone says that separation according to the spirit is sufficient here, and the [denial of the] bodily fellowship of marriage is not required and does not permit the external withdrawal. Answer: The fleshly intermingling may not be permitted to break the evangelical separation, as earlier related, for the commandment of separation is greater than that of marriage, noting the one applies to humans, and the other to God: And herein is proven what faith and love one has to God the Lord, when we withdraw from our wife on behalf of his Word and command. For it is an explicit command that the congregation must put away and cut off from itself every apostate and trespasser of truth without regard to persons, 1 Cor. 5, wherefore the command and the intermingling of the marriage must give way.

Of this we have a plain example or witness in the Holy Scripture, since God commanded the Israelites to stone their wives who invited or aroused them to go worship strange gods, Deut. 17:5, yes, that they also might not be spared by their own husbands, but that they must themselves throw the first stone at her, Deut. 13:9, through which we discover that marriage and fleshly union may not remain against the figurative separation. [Marginal note: Apostates and trespassers of the teachings have no God. 1 John 1.]

The Israelites also could not excuse or deliver their wives with the institution of the marriage union, but they must themselves denounce, accuse, and judge according to the law. Similarly Christians must also maintain evangelical separation. To wit, to avoid their wives for a time, until they return to repentance and sorrow, /665/ which punishment is easier to bear than that instituted in the law of Moses. Moreover, we must note that God has commanded to honor father and mother, Exod. 20:12, nevertheless, that command must give way before the other word or command, saying that a person shall leave father and mother in order to join with his wife, and they two shall be one flesh, Gen. 2:24. Notice now that this union was higher and narrower, Matt. 19:5, thus the love of the wife and the union of marriage must also give way and place to the love of Christ and of the gospel.

If someone contradicts this, saying that the husband does not rightly leave his wife because of the name of God, because of the love of Christ and the gospel, if he but withdraws himself from her because of the separation, except only when he is rejected, persecuted, or imprisoned because of faith. Answer: And is it not the Word of God and his command to hold just like heathen and tax collectors those who are separated and cut off from the congregation? And that one shall have no business or fellowship with them, not even eating with them? If then a Christian withdraws himself from his wife for this reason, 1 Cor. 5:11, does he not do that because of God's love and of the gospel? Thus also certainly when he has left her, because he will not live in idolatry or trespass a command of God? The preceeding words of Jesus Christ and his apostles, are they not held for the Word of God and the Holy Scripture, or are they untrue?

[But] if one again introduces that Christ has forbidden [a husband] to leave his wife except for adultery. Answer: Take notice how Christ wanted therewith to forbid the separation and rejection which the Jews practiced with their wives because of all kinds of reasons which they thought good or preferred, and that in order to marry another, which nevertheless the Lord had permitted them because of the hardness of their hearts, Deut. 24:1ff., and that such separation was not instituted or permitted from the beginning. Thus the Lord willed and commanded that one should do that no more except in the case of an act of adultery, which is the only and true reason for which a husband may leave or reject his wife and take another, Gen. 2:24; Matt. 19:3[ff.]; Matt. 5:32.

Now the believer does not misuse the command of Jesus Christ if he withdraw from his wife because of the separation, for it is not in order to take another, as the Jews did because of the hardness of their heart, but expecting patiently with prayer, fasting, and sighing to God /666/ for the gift of abstinence until the time that his spouse, being cut off from the congregation, has come again to sorrow and improvement and is once again accepted there. Then she would be received again by her believing husband or spouse, and thus the marriage is neither broken nor defiled during the time of the separation, of which the believer is neither the cause nor factious, rather the one who has fellowship with sin or transgression because of which she has been cut off to maintain the purity of the congregation, to the fear of others, and after sufficient improvement, to again be accepted into the congregation of the Lord, Num. 12:14. The end.

1 Cor. 2:14

A natural person does not enjoy the taste of that which comes from the Spirit of the Lord; but the one who is spiritual judges all things spiritually and will be judged by no one.

FRAGMENT

To the abominable bitter slanders of some (also principal) Swiss brothers. Since they still today decry and scold, yes, with intemperate blasphemy despise the serious apostolic command about avoidance (as it is carried out in its own strength among us), [calling it] an inhuman abominable and tyrannical ban (so also the people have rumored in some sense), but regretfully to their own much greater hurt and destruction, 2 Pet. 2; Judg. 1. For this reason alone, since one will not sow to the flesh out of the pure fear of God. Galatians. Final. Nor can [they] be acknowledged here as edifying members, 1 Esd. 4. A very short summarizing extract out of another similar writing to the Swiss brothers is found by them (with the Overlanders [Germans, others]) as well as in Moravia, written more than eighteen years ago, in good, clear high German. From this every good-hearted and well-intended [person] can easily see how tyrannical and inhuman, etc., our ban and avoidance is.

Perhaps these [people] will even blush with shame and learn better to fear the righteous judgment of God. And Saul's spirit must be quieted somewhat with David's harp, and finally confess that the Lord had given David the kingdom, and as such is the kingdom of the Lord, Abdi 1 [Obadiah]. Also consider what happened to the perverse and haughty Chancellor Heliodorus, 2 Macc. 3, who after enough scourging said to his king, the one who had sent him: Do you have an enemy, or [one] who is against your kingdom, send that one there; he will be beaten enough for you, the beating will be such that he will [barely] remain alive. For at that place there is no doubt a /508/ special power and activity of God, for he who has his dwelling in heaven is an overseer and protector of this place, and punishes all those who come there to do evil.[7] The end.

ENDNOTES

1. Koolman, p. 173. Much of the following discussion is dependent upon his account of the publication of this treatise.
2. Ibid.
3. See the following document, "Evangelical Excommunication," pp. 591ff. For a comparison of parallel passages in the Dutch between the "Lieflicke vermaninghe" of 1558, known as the "First Banbook," see the "Second Banbook," which is known only in the fragment in Gerardus Nicolai's "Inlasschingen," [insertions into Heinrich Bullinger's treatise *Against the Anabaptists*], BRN VII, pp. 437-444, but exists in its entirety in a French translation published in 1626 as "Claire et manifeste remonstrance de l'excommunication," and the treatise which follows here, see Keyser, pp. 26-28. Thus Dirk actually wrote four documents on church discipline: the first one in the *Enchiridion*, pp. 238-254, the present one pp. 578-588, the following document pp. 591-610, and "A Confession About Separation," pp. 611-617.
4. BRN X, p. 507 n. 1.
5. CWMS pp. 1001-1015.
6. As indicated in the introduction to this document, the editors-translators follow Marja Keyser in believing that the "Fragment" was not written by Dirk. Neither the style [which has been smoothed in translation to make it intelligible] nor the contents fit Dirk's writing and spirit. Keyser's thesis that the reference to the German document is to Menno Simons' *Reply to Sylis and Lemke*, CWMS, pp. 1001-1015, seems right [Zylis Jacobs of Monschau (Eifel) and Lemke Bruerren of Maastricht]. See Keyser, pp. 19-28, for a full discussion of the issues as well as a copy of the document and a comparative tabulation of the editions of 1587, 1626, and 1602. According to Keyser the note in the margin, "Written by D. P., also of an equal office with Menno," does not refer to this document, but to the one on the next page, bound with it, which was by Dirk but the note itself is not by him. Dirk would not identify himself that way.
7. A paraphrase of 2 Maccabees 3:38-39, apparently meaning that those who do not respect the ban will be judged from heaven.

CLAIRE ET MANIFESTE REMONSTRANCE DE L'EXCOMMVNICATION EUANGELIQUE,

& institution d'icelle:

Comment elle se doit vrayement observer:
& quel est l'effet & fruit d'icelle.

Composée & extraite de la Sainte Escriture.

PAR

THEODORE PHILIPPE.

Ierem. 15. vers. 19.
Si tu separe la chose precieuse de la vile, tu seras ma bouche.

2 Timoth. 2. vers. 21.
Si aucun se nettoye soy-mesme de ceux-là, (qu'est des mauvais, & des faillans de la verité) il sera vaisseau sanctifié à honneur, duisant au Seigneur, & appareillé à toute bonne œuvre.

EVANGELICAL EXCOMMUNICATION

[A] Clear and Manifest Exposition
of Evangelical Excommunication and [an] Explanation of It.
How It Should Be Validly Observed
and What Is the Effect and Fruit of It.
Composed and Extended from Holy Scripture.

By

Theodore Philippe

INTRODUCTION

Dirk Philips apparently became dissatisfied with his earlier work on the ban which appeared in the *Enchiridion* of 1564. He proceeded to write a "second"[1] or "new"[2] treatise on the ban. Except for a few unreliable fragments, according to Marja Keyser, the only complete copy (as far as can be known without having the Dutch original) is a French translation, found by J. ten Doornkaat Koolman, which appeared in 1626 under the title *A Clear and Manifest Exposition about Evangelical Excommunication.*[3]

The exact date of the writing is uncertain. The best evidence seems to point toward 1567, about a year before the death of Dirk. In the treatise he makes reference to the fact that he wants to write a more satisfactory explanation of the topic since his end is near. He also refers to earlier treatments of the topics as having been done twenty-four and sixteen years earlier, which would make the dates 1543 and 1551. Those dates do not seem to accord with any known publications, though he may have written some manuscripts that circulated in handwritten copies and were later incorporated in published works. Parts of the present document do appear in the preceding *Omitted Writings About the Ban and Avoidance*. Some of his writings may also have been lost. The first use of the materials would require that the work be written no later than 1567.[4]

Dirk indicates clearly that this treatise on the topic is his preferred one. He asks that it be attached to the *Enchiridion* as an appendix in place of his earlier work which was published with the 1564 edition. That was only done in the 1626 French edition, which J. ten Doornkaat Koolman attributes to Virgile de Las about whom neither he nor we know anything more.[5]

The writing is also confirmed as a late writing of Dirk Philips by the style. At the conclusion of the treatise he has a section of questions raised by his adversaries and proceeds to give answer to them. That particular literary style is found in other late writings.

A major difference between this treatise and the earlier one is much greater detail with regard to the scriptural support for excommunication. He particularly added many more incidences from the Old Testament.

The treatise also shows the shift which occurred otherwise in Dirk's and Menno's writings. The reason for the ban is shifted from the first concern as redemption of the person to a first concern for the effect of the apostasy of the person on the church. The concern becomes primarily one of protecting the church from infection of the bad practices and to protect the reputation of the church.

Dirk makes clearer that he is not in favor of divorce in the case of one partner in the marriage being under the ban. He was accused of being a marriage breaker. He affirms that the only valid reason for divorce is adultery. He makes a distinction between avoidance of the banned partner and divorce. He expects that the couple will have the marriage relationship fully restored in the event of repentance and a return to fellowship of the excommunicated person.

While Dirk continues to oppose any strictly social relationships with the excommunicated person, he is more positive in his expression of the need to render help to the person in the event of need. The only conversation a member should have with the excommunicated person is to admonish the person with Scripture so as to bring the person to repentance, except when the person is in need.

The Text

If you separate the precious from the vile, you shall be as my mouth, Jer. 15:19.

If anyone cleanse himself from them (that is of evil and defiling of the truth), he shall be a holy vessel of honor, dedicated to the Lord, and prepared for all good works, 2 Tim. 2:21.

Preface of the Author /208/

Theodore Philippe,[6] brother of all true Christians by the grace of God in believing the truth and in the communion of the gospel, wishes the faithful reader mercy, peace, and true spiritual wisdom of God the Father, and of Jesus Christ his only Son, our Lord and Savior, through the virtue and working of the Holy Spirit. Amen.

I give thanks to the Lord my God from the depth of my heart, who calls me (a man always unworthy and of no value) to the true knowledge of his Son Jesus Christ and has till now kept and held me in his doctrine. Hoping that by his immeasurable goodness he will keep me persevering in the cause until the end of my days. Whereby, since such grace has been done to me, I would wish or would desire perfectly before the Lord, that each one might know the truth by the illumination of the Holy Spirit and thereby be saved.

Wherefore I have written in my *Enchiridion*, or *Handbook*,[7] the principal articles of our Christian faith: Where there lay the most ambiguity and contention concerning religion, I have declared and explained it fully. In order that with my small powers I may be able to satisfy people of good will and by the grace of God to give them some instruction about thinking of matters more profoundly. I hope with his help always to persist in that confession of truth, (established on the foundation of the Holy Scripture) which I have confessed and included in my booklet. Wherein I intend by no means ever to depart from it.

But since I perceive that my days are henceforth almost over and that their end is near, and when I see daily with what pride and daring the world and those who have fallen away from the truth, and all other sects defame our very holy faith, and especially this matter of evangelical excommunication (which, however, was instituted by the Lord, and thus practiced in our /209/ church or congregation) by words and blasphemies, naming said excommunication (by which nevertheless, according to the word and commandment of the apostles, the bad are separated from the church) a new pharisaical doctrine. They attribute to us the title of being separators from marriages and accuse us of being a people without mercy in the usage of such excommunication. Thus they ignore departing in what ugly manner they so awfully wish to deny us.

Thus being compelled by my conscience, I have illuminated what I have felt, known, and understood (according to my simple knowledge) by the grace of God, from his Word, partly twenty-four years ago and partly sixteen years ago. That I have also confirmed and confessed in writing, to the end that no one could think that in the church was ever taught otherwise than now or that excommunication should ever be otherwise observed than it is at present in the source. In some of my books, I have touched this in several passages. I am also assured that the church of the Lord is rather adequately instructed on this point.

Nevertheless, in order to testify to my faith and to confess the truth, I desire before my death (if the Lord permits) to confess entirely what, concerning excommunication, I am myself able to feel totally. For I am not ashamed of the evangelical and apostolic doctrine, despite what all sects say against the same. That makes no difference: FORTISSIMA OMNIUM VERITAS, that is to say, "The truth is stronger than any other thing and overcomes all." The Lord be blessed and praised, who opened the eyes of our understanding by his unspeakable charity and profound mercy, so that we might know his ways on earth, his good, holy, and perfect will in all that which we need to know, to believe, and to accomplish to the end that by the grace of Jesus Christ we may be saved. AMEN.

Of Evangelical Excommunication /210/

The eternal and very powerful God, jealous, Exod. 20:5, and lover of justice and of all the truly faithful, elected from the beginning by grace Adam, Gen. 2:15; 3:22; 4:26; 5:1; Shem, Gen. 5:[32]; Enoch, Gen. 5:21; Noah, Gen. 6:9; 9:9, and then afterward the patriarch Abraham, Gen. 12:3, with his posterity, to be his own particular people, Exod. 3:8, having loved them from an eternal love, working miraculously with them, Exod. 8; 10; 11; 12, (read all the chapters), whom he has also endowed abundantly and singularly out of all other nations. That is of the kind that he called the royal priesthood, Exod. 19:6, the holy people, exhorting them to sanctity thus: "You shall be holy for I am holy, says the Lord," Lev. 19:2. Therefore, they must be punished and amended and corrected for all the sins and transgressions, Heb. 2:2, in Israel.

All this is a figure and example of the true essence which must come, and the introduction of a better hope (which is in Jesus Christ), to wit, that our Lord Jesus Christ has elected by grace, without regard to persons, in the same faith, to be to himself a faithful church, which he has gathered by the preaching, Matt. 28:19; Mark 16:15, of the gospel. Primarily by himself, John 15:5, and then afterward by his apostles, Luke 24:[48], who were his true witnesses.

Now this church must be entirely, Eph. 5:27, pure, holy and without blemish, as Paul said. She is the bride, Rev. 19:7, of the Lamb, the Holy City, Rev. 21:2, the New Jerusalem descending from heaven adorned to meet her husband. Such that in her nothing that is unclean can enter, Rev. 21:27, or which commits abominations and falsehood, thus only those who truly repent, believe the gospel, hear the living Word of God, receive and keep it, forsaking totally Satan, the antichrist and the world, renouncing, Matt. 10:39; 16:24, themselves and desiring daily to carry their cross, following Christ in the new birth. These are those who enter into the new Jerusalem and are received by God by grace in the Christian church as his beloved children, being baptized to be one body, 1 Cor. 12:13, on the confession of their faith, Matt. 28:19, in the name of the Father, the Son and Holy Spirit.

In these was announced the remission of sins, Luke 24:[47];

Rom. 3:25; Col. 1:14, by the precious blood of Jesus Christ, and to them have been given by the Father the earnest of the Spirit, 2 Cor. 1:22. By these they are marked unto the day of redemption, Eph. 4:30, taught by him, by him led into all truth, righteousness, and holiness, John 16:13, and consoled amidst all anguish and persecution. By these also they receive power to be children of God, whereby they cry Abba, Rom. 8:15; Gal. 4:6, beloved Father.

But those who on the contrary receive this grace in vain, do not keep it, never produce any fruit by it, walk according to the flesh, cannot enter into the heavenly Jerusalem, but shall have their part outside in the lake of fire, which is the second death, Rev. 21:8; 22:15. /211/

This will happen to all false Christians who have fallen away from the truth (which they have once known and received), Heb. 6:5[f.]; 10:26. In this occasion Jesus Christ has commanded his church and gave to her power to separate from herself all false brothers who break from it by disobedience, to testify that they shall have no part with Christ and all his saints, since they keep persevering in iniquity, Matt. 18:18. For he who wishes to reach life eternal with Christ must love him with true faith, John 3:16; 5:24; 11:26; 15:21, cleave to him, John 15:5, suffer and die with him, i.e., to be with him one spirit, 1 Cor. 6:17, and to be one body with his church, 1 Cor. 12:13, persevering therein perpetually.

We thus hold first that evangelical excommunication is a commandment of the Lord Jesus Christ, Matt. 18:18, and the teaching of the apostles, Rom. 16:[17], wherefore, it must be observed diligently by all Christians, as Word and commandment of the Lord, according to the instruction of the gospel in true faith and Christian discretion. For Jesus Christ, our Lord and Master, given us by God the Father, John 14:10; 15:15; 16:26; 17:23, said to his apostles that they should teach all who repent, who believe all that was commanded them and are baptized. Those are true friends of Christ, John 15:14, who do all that he has commanded them. Because the prophet also said: "Oh, Lord, You rebuke the arrogant, and those are cursed who do not keep your commandments," Ps. 119:21.

That which can be represented by Adam and Eve who were cast out of paradise by God, Gen. 3:23, because they ate, once, of the fruit that has been forbidden them, against the commandment of God. The wife of Lot was transformed into a statue of salt, Gen. 19:26, for having looked back, once, when God had expressly commanded the contrary. Nadab and Abihu, sons of Aaron, were consumed by heavenly fire because, just once, they had taken strange fire for sacrifice, Lev. 10:[1-]2. King Saul of Israel was rejected of God because, once, he spared the best animals of the Amalekites, thereby acting contrary to his Word, 1 Sam. 15:23. Uzziah fell dead in the presence of Israel for having touched the ark of God, once, against his will, 2 Sam. 6:6. Ananias and Sapphira fell dead at the feet of the apostle Peter for having lied a single time, Acts 5:5[-6]. The Scripture is full of such examples. As these demonstrate, none must despise the commandments of God, well imprinted in his heart. This is confirmed by the apostle, saying, "Who fails at one point is guilty of all," James 2:10.

From this it follows thus that excommunication with its effect comprised in the evangelical and apostolic doctrine, Matt. 18:18, must be observed as an express commandment of the Lord (as this was said above) in all diligence and Christian discretion, according to the pure understanding of the Holy Scripture and the gospel's intention: i.e., according to the nature /212/ of God, the affection of Jesus Christ, and the interpretation of Jesus Christ in true love, in such patience as is worthy in the gospel and conformed to the faith.

This evangelical excommunication is figured openly and in several manners in fleshly Israel, where all transgressions and disobediences received just and determined punishment, Heb. 2:2, without regard for any person. For which also Miriam, the sister of Moses, was separated from the army of Israel by the command of the Lord, because having murmured she was struck by God with leprosy, Num. 12:14. If then God wished to have such purity in this figurative Israel, how much more must it be in our spiritual Israel? All the more because the Spirit is more perfect than the letter and the truth more clear than the shadow.

Wherefore, there must be observed in the church of the Lord a true judgment on the false brothers without regard to any person, without inclining to one or the other party. Nevertheless, there is a difference between the excommunication of the law and that of the gospel: to wit, that by the excommunication of the law, several sins and transgressions were judged and punished by death. But by that of the gospel, the transgressors and sinners are segregated from the Christian church, 1 Cor. 5:13, in the name and power of our Lord Jesus Christ. For the church of God must be pure and the Lord's own and particular people. Wherefore, Jesus Christ commanded his church and [has] given it power to remove and separate from it the evil ones, Matt. 18:18, in order to be a holy people, sanctified to the Lord, and segregated from all other nations, as the Lord said by Moses: "I am the Lord your God, who separated you from the peoples, that you might also separate from among you between things pure and things impure. Thus you shall be holy for I your Lord am holy, who have separated you from the peoples to the end that you be my own, Lev. 20:24; Deut. 14:2. That which Balaam also testified when he spoke of Israel, prophesying, Num. [23:9-10], "The people shall remain apart and shall not be esteemed among the Gentiles. My love must suffer the death of the just, and my end must thus be like that." This therefore agrees with the words of Christ when he spoke to his apostles thus: "Thus you are no longer of the world, but I have chosen you from the world, therefore the world hates you," John 15:19. In his prayer to the Father, he confessed often that his disciples have been withdrawn from the world and given him by the Father, John 17:14.

From all this it follows that Christians are a peculiar people, separated from all nations which are under heaven, a people belonging to the Lord, 1 Pet. 2:9. Thus they can have no communion with the unfruitful works of darkness. What all true ministers and faithful servants of the Lord must teach in all diligence. For thus the Lord said by Moses, "Whoever from among the children of Israel, or of the strangers /213/ who sojourn in Israel, shall give of his offspring to Moloch, he shall die. The people of the land shall stone him with stones. I shall put my face against this man and shall exterminate him from the middle of his people; for he has given of his offspring to Moloch, for he has given of his offspring so as to profane my sanctuary and to contaminate my holy name. But if the people of the land are nonchalant on hearing the man who has given from his generation to Moloch, no longer putting him to death, I shall put my face against this man and against his family, to exterminate him from the midst of his people, with all those who have fornicated with Moloch," Lev. 20:2[-5].

These promises are the clear words of the Lord, by which we have testimony that God wishes just as well and equally to punish those who support and suffer the evil ones, by not separating them from themselves, as the same evil ones themselves. With this Esdras agrees: "Woe to you, Assyria, who hide the iniquities in your midst. Oh, perverse people! Remember what I did to Sodom and Gomorrah. This I will do to all those who do not listen to me, says the Lord almighty," 2 Esd. 2:8[-9]. Moreover, the church in Thyatira was reprimanded by the Son of God (although it was adorned with several virtues and gifts of the Spirit) because it permitted the prophetess Jezebel, (which means false doctrine) by whom the servants of God were seduced, Rev. 2:[18-23]. Likewise, the Lord spoke to the prophet

Jeremiah. Thus said the Lord, "If you are converted, I will restore you, that you may stand before me: and if you separate the precious thing from the vile, you shall be as my mouth. They will turn to you, but you will not return to them. I shall give you to this people here as a brazen and fortified wall. They will fight against you, but they will not conquer you, for I am with you in order to save you and in order to deliver you, said the Lord," Jer. 15:19[-20].

By this it is clearly demonstrated how necessary excommunication or separation from the church is, without which no church of God can subsist, that which all true ministers of the Word must teach and exhort so that the entire church not be polluted and guilty of the sins of others. Of which we have evident examples and assured witness in the book of Joshua: to wit, that Israel is become totally soiled by the sin and transgression of Achan so that the Lord would not combat for Israel, saying: "I will not be with you, for there is an interdict in the midst of you," Josh. 7:11.

In confirmation of this, Paul separated the lewd one from the church of Corinth, so that the church would not be totally soiled by his sin. For he said thus: "Do you not know well that a little leaven makes the whole dough rise?" 1 Cor. 5:6. By this is also established the difference between the excommunication of Moses and that of Christ. According to the law, this lewd one was worthy of death, but according to the gospel, he was punished by the sword of the Spirit toward the destruction of his flesh, in order that the spirit be saved in the day of the Lord Jesus.

/214/ Now the sins and transgressions for which excommunication was instituted by the Lord Jesus Christ, and which by the church must be punished, are specified expressly in the New Testament and are properly those which follow:

The first is when someone sins against his brother and does not want to be reconciled with him, thus despising and rejecting the reprimand of his brother, of witnesses, and of the church of God, in such a way that he remains persevering and obstinate in his iniquity. Of this Christ said to Peter: "If your brother has sinned against you, go and reprove him between you and him alone. If he listens to you, you have won your brother. But if he does not listen to you, take with you yet one or two, in order that in the mouth of two or three witnesses every word be confirmed. But if he does not listen to them, tell it to the church. And if he no longer listens to the church, then he must be as a pagan and tax collector," Matt. 18:[15-]17.

The second is false doctrine, as Paul says: "I pray you, brothers, that you watch out for those who cause dissension and scandal against the doctrine that you have learned, and turn away from them," Rom. 16:[17]. That which he has also taught Timothy and Titus, 2 Tim. 3:[15]; Titus 3:10. And John says: "If anyone comes to you, and does not bring this doctrine, no longer receive him in your house, and no longer greet him. For he who greets him, partakes in his evil works," 2 John 1:10[-11].

The third is a disordered and evil life, as the apostle Paul said: "If one who is called brother is lewd, or avaricious, or idolatrous, or a gossip, or drunkard, or ravisher, no longer eat with those who are such," 1 Cor. 5:[9-]10. Again, in another passage, "We command you in the name of our Lord Jesus Christ to separate you from every brother who walks disorderly and no longer according to the ordinance that he has received from us," 2 Thess. 3:[6].

The fourth is disobedience and despising the doctrine of the apostles, since Paul said: "If anyone does not obey our word, note him in writing, and no longer associate with him, so that he may be ashamed. In any case no longer hold him as an enemy, but admonish him as a brother," 2 Thess. 3:14[-15].

These above-mentioned things are not only pure words of the Scripture, in which are expressly comprised the sins which must be reproved by excommunication. Further, two reasons are weighty for which excommunication must be exercised in the Christian church. The first is in order that the church be not entirely polluted by the evil ones, 1 Cor. 5:5. That has been sufficiently enough recited and declared above.

The second is in order that the transgressor be ashamed and become able to recognize himself in genuine repentance, as Paul testified to the Corinthians and Thessalonians. According to which we may well trust that evangelical excommunication has been instituted by Jesus Christ in order that his name not be defamed by the misdeeds of some. For if the church tolerates the evil and unjust (which would however be against Scripture) without separating them from it, it shall give occasion to others to /215/ defame it and despise it. By such the name of God and the gospel would be detracted, which yet cannot be. For the Christians must endeavor that the holy name of the Lord be sanctified, and the heavenly Father magnified through them; to the end that they can be in this world a sweet fragrance of Christ, salt of the earth, light of the world, a city built on a mountain; the letter from Christ which is seen, read, and known by all, written by the finger of God in the tables of the heart, pure children of God without reproach, showing themselves before all to be such.

For when all this is well weighed and considered, it follows that evangelical excommunication is an ordinance of the Lord and a most profitable doctrine of the apostles. Thus it must be observed by the Christian church according to the above words with all discretion. For this is a certain thing, which one must not doubt, that Jesus Christ has not taught nor commanded anything vain or useless. Thus his Word and his commandments are spirit and life, John 6:63; 12:50. Thus he is the only Good Shepherd, whom God has called forth from Israel and given to his people, John 10:11, wherefore he cares for his sheep, keeping those who are healthy, searching for the strays, healing the sick, and restoring the wounded, Ezek. 34:4. For those who are mangy [*roigneuses*], and do not want to accept being remade by the oil of grace, these he does not wish to admit among his healthy sheep, since he rejects these in order that a mangy sheep (according to the common proverb) not contaminate the total flock.

Moreover, since he is the Savior of his body (which is his church), Eph. 5:23, he keeps it from all injury, keeping, fortifying, and confirming the healthy members by his Spirit and his Word. But the members who are weak and feeble, he lifts up with his salutary medicine. Those who are wounded, he restores with the oil and wine, in the example of the faithful Samaritan, desiring by this means to save his entire body. For if all this work, care, faithfulness, and love no longer helps certain ones of saved members; for they have been bitten by the old serpent or infected by a cancerous sickness (which is false doctrine) that there is no longer any hope of improvement; this he does and executes what he himself taught and said, to wit, that he purges the bad and corrupt member, in that by their malice and their venomous nature the whole body should not be brought to ruin and entirely lost.

This same he confirms also by calling his Father the vinedresser, himself the true vine, and the Christians the branches, John 15:1 [ff.], and that his Father cuts each branch which does not bear fruit, since they deform the vine and damage the good plant. The branches which bear fruit, he purges again in order that they bear fruit more abundantly.

Thus evangelical excommunication is principally a work of charity, because by it the church of Jesus Christ is preserved /216/ and maintained in healthy doctrine, in good order, in divine unity, in Christian peace, and in obedience of faith. And also by it transgressors are corrected, 1 Cor. 5:4[-5], if in any way they wish to be.

That is why no Christian church can consist without evangelical excommunication. For the Lord Jesus Christ did not give the keys of the kingdom of heaven to his church in vain, the power of binding and loosing, of pardoning sins and retaining them, Matt. 18:18; and with this his Spirit and his Word by which it must discern and remove the malignant ones. If thus the church does not judge otherwise than the Word and the Spirit of God testify and teach, it therein acts justly and its judgment is the judgment of God. But if the church does not judge and punish sins in conformity of the Word of the Lord and of his Spirit, it falls under the judgment of God, in that it is disobedient to the Word and makes itself a participant in the sin of the other. Thus by a little leaven, the whole dough is soured, 1 Cor. 5:[6].

In this cause the church of Christ must judge and punish all sins and transgressions (which are committed within the church and are worthy of punishment, Gal. 5:19[ff.] with a judgment conforming to the Scripture. This will be, or must be, done with such spirit, such divine nature, and such patience that Jesus Christ himself is our example, which the Holy Scripture testifies to us.

Now on this account there are some who formed some questions here. The first is: What does it mean that those who have fallen away from the truth must be shunned? To that we reply that Christ has made of this a rule and measure in the Gospel, Matt. 18:18. That rule and measure we must properly seek out in the words of Christ and the apostles. He instituted excommunication and wishes that those who are worthy of being excommunicated must be considered as a pagan and publican. Therein appears the effect of this excommunication both by the writings of the evangelists and apostles, which testify to us that the Jews did not wish to enter the house of the Gentiles nor eat anything with them. How the Gentiles were considered by the Jews, this is easy to understand by what Christ said to the Canaanite woman: "It is not good to take bread from the children, and throw it to the little dogs," Matt. 15:26. Again, the Samaritan woman, when Christ asked her to drink, said to him: "How do you, who are a Jew, ask drink of me who am a Samaritan woman? For the Jews have no relations with the Samaritans," John 4:9.

Thus the apostles clarify these aforesaid words of the Lord Jesus touching excommunication by expressed command to withdraw ourselves from those who fall away from the truth, not to eat with them, nor to have any acquaintance with them, Rom. 16:[17]; 1 Cor. 5:[11]; 2 Thess. 3:6; 2 John 1:10. In such manner, if anyone comes to you /217/ not bringing the doctrine of Jesus Christ, we must not (as St. John said) receive him in our house nor salute him.

Thus according to this doctrine of Jesus Christ and his apostles, they desire by the grace of the Lord that we judge ourselves. What is prohibited hereby, they hope not to do to anyone. That which is not forbidden or comprehended in this, no one can forbid it for us. For there is only one legislator, who is God the Lord, James 4:12. Wherefore, no one can judge anything or command more fully than the Word testifies and teaches.

But on the other hand, some say that one can converse, one can lovingly eat and drink with those who have fallen from the truth, until the time of their amendment. To which we reply thus: that we do not wish to contradict anything to those who maintain that one can speak to the fallen to admonish them with the Word of God, since the apostle, led by the Holy Spirit, has taught it thus, 2 Thess. 3:15. But we contradict those who wish to be allowed to treat with them more fully, to eat, to drink, or to have any acquaintance. There is not a single passage in the Scripture by which one can defend this. Paul says clearly that one must not eat or have any acquaintance with those fallen away from the evangelical doctrine, 1 Cor. 5:[9-]10; 2 Thess. 3:6.

Moreover, the kingdom of God is not meat nor drink, but justice, peace, and joy in the Holy Spirit, Rom. 14:17. And also, love does not consist properly in sharing meat and drink, since among the unfaithful that same love is demonstrated. But what is of God consists in truth and is clarified by observing the commandments of God, 1 Cor. 13:2; 1 John 3:18. Otherwise, correcting a delinquent does not come from eating and drinking, but by the grace of God and by exhortation of the divine Word. Thus the apostle said: Admonish the delinquent as a brother, and do not consider him an enemy, 2 Thess. 3:15. And not thus: Treat, eat, and drink with them.

Wherefrom we conclude that dealing with the fallen ones out of love to eat and drink with them until the time of their amendment, it is nothing other than apparent and contrived human wisdom. Such love is false and evil, since it does not agree with the truth; and it is nothing other than a hidden despising of the divine ordinance. Therefore, such love cannot amend, but rather destroy.

Thus if anyone wishes to claim the love of God and of the neighbor, it is necessary that before all things he keep the Word of God. For Christ said: "He who loves me, keeps my words," John 14:23. And John said: "This is the love of God, that we keep his commandments, which are not difficult," [1 John 5:3]. This is now a word and commandment of God, to remove from the church of the Lord the evil ones. Thus by this is the love of God rightly manifested, in that the said excommunication is a word /218/ and commandment of Christ.

Furthermore, the first thing that is required in fraternal love is that we search, with a benevolent heart and with all our power, the salvation of our neighbor by the means toward this ordained by God. If thus a brother has fallen away from the truth and cannot be helped by any instruction nor Christian exhortation, there is nothing more fitting for his soul than evangelical excommunication (which is a bitter medicine, but always very profitable for the members who are on the way to spoiling) by which he may be shamed, so that the exterior man be destroyed in order that the interior can be saved in the day of the Lord Jesus, 1 Cor. 5:[5]. After this separation from the church, nothing can serve him better than a fraternal exhortation.

The second question is: Is it permitted to give alms to such a fallen one being in necessity? To which we reply: Our understanding in the Word of God, with the testimony of our conscience, that excommunication is not instituted by the Lord for the destruction of the man, but for his amendment. Wherefore Christians in the usage of said excommunication must not follow the Pharisees who liked better to let a man be lost than to help him on the Sabbath day, Matt. 12:10. They did that, thinking that by that their Sabbath would be profaned and corrupted; always avoiding loss to themselves, they themselves corrupt the Sabbath.

Christians must not govern themselves thus unwisely, since love and compassion must hold first place among them, according to the discretion of the Scripture and where necessity requires it. By this excommunication is not refuted but confirmed, provided that there be a Christian and good intention for the love of God; and to the end that their light might shine, Matt. 5:14, to declare their divine nature, to restore the lost sheep to the right way, and to gain them for Christ; they desire to accomplish all this wholeheartedly, without frivolity, according to the doctrine of the Lord Jesus Christ, saying to his apostles: "Be merciful as your Father who is in heaven is merciful, Luke 6:36. For he makes the sun to rise on the good and on the evil, and sends the rain on the just and unjust," [Matt. 5:45]. Because also all Christians and children of God, who are participants in his nature, must be thus ruled and conformed, following their heavenly Father in all virtues, Eph. 5:1.

The third question is: If a Christian man and woman are conjoined by marriage, and one of them comes to fall away from God, being separated from the church, must he avoid and abstain from the company of the other who has fallen away? To which we respond thus: The excommunication of our Lord Jesus Christ is a general rule and must be observed simply and directly, without respect to any person, according to the prescribed manner. The father must avoid his son, judge him, and separate him from /219/ the church; the mother, her daughter; and the husband, his wife who fell away from the Lord. If the man and the woman are both faithful, and one of those defects from the truth, giving himself to all injustice, for which, judged by the Word of God, he must be separated from the Christian church, it is suitable that the other, not being guilty, abstains from the fallen away until the time of his amendment, and that in one act he is reconciled with the Lord, with the church, and with the husband or wife.

Against this some talk a great deal alleging that the married cannot be separated except because of fornication. For Christ said in the Gospel: "Whoever repudiates his wife (except because of fornication) and marries another, he commits adultery," Matt. 19:9.

Reply: By these words, Christ prohibited and totally rejected the manner of divorce which the Jews used for all occasions. For this was not properly commanded to them from God, being only permitted for the hardness of their hearts. On this subject, Jesus Christ (in whom are hidden all the treasures of wisdom and knowledge, Col. 2:3, and by whom God has restored all things revoked such divorce), arguing the ordinance of God which was from the beginning, Gen. 2:24, and named adultery as the only true ground for divorce. Considering this, from these words of Christ, it does not follow that the faithful partner, not being guilty, should not avoid and abstain from his spouse separated from the church. For Christ said: "Whosoever shall repudiate," etc., that is: Whosoever shall repudiate his wife. *Repudiate* and *avoid*, are certainly quite different one from the other. By reason of what has already been said, it [the prohibition of divorce] does not apply to any believer who would abstain from his wife for [the sake of] evangelical excommunication. A believer does not repudiate his wife after the example of the Jews (who without any necessity and reasonable occasion, hardened in their heart, repudiated their wives for carnal reasons) when abstaining from his spouse (who has fallen away from the Word of God) by his faith, for the sake of the gospel.

Afterward, in order to confirm what was said, Christ does not mention only repudiation and dissolution of marriage, but also being married to one another. This proposition is joined, the one to the other. Yet in this there is one other difference, to wit, that the Jews repudiated their wives and took to themselves others of their choice. On the other hand, Christians abstain from their married partner because of evangelical excommunication, not in order to take another, since they devote themselves to prayers and fasting, groaning and crying to God for the gift of chastity, waiting with patience on the spouse, fallen away from the truth, could once again be converted to the Lord by the grace of God and therewith be reconciled to him and to his church. When this is done, the /220/ brother or sister receives the spouse (that had been separated from the church) in joy, rendering thanks to God almighty for his profound mercy and unspeakable love shown to sinners.

Some will immediately object to us that a Christian can certainly adhere to his spouse who has fallen away from God, nevertheless be a real Christian. For evangelical excommunication (as they call it), would not be broken by this.

Reply: How is it possible that such a thing can happen? Since in so doing one contradicts openly the clear and express words of Christ and the apostles. For evangelical excommunication does not judge the apostate only according to the spirit, but also prohibits all exterior conversation and acquaintance, 2 Thess. 3:6, 15. How then can a Christian contradict such clear and open words of the Lord Jesus Christ and not observe excommunication in such form as the universal and total church does? Then they reply thus: That the spiritual separation suffices here, being that the marriage does not permit anyone to separate externally.

Reply: Natural marriage and mutual love cannot cause anyone to break with evangelical excommunication. For it is necessary that faith and the love of God have the first place; since all other love, to wit, paternal, maternal, fraternal, filial, marital, and common love must yield to them, since this is the first and greatest commandment: "You shall love the Lord your God from all your heart, all your soul, all your strength, and all your power," Deut. 6:5[f.]; Matt. 22:36[-37].

For this love of God must exceed all other love. That is sufficiently demonstrated to us by the Old and New Testaments. For Moses said: "Who has said to his father or mother, I have not seen them, and has no longer acknowledged his brother, and also has not recognized his children; these keep your words and observe your covenant. They shall teach your judgments to Jacob and your law to Israel," Deut. 33:9[-10].

From such an ardent love of God, Phinehas, the son of Aaron, pierced through and put to death Zimri, the Israelite, and Cozbi, the Midianite, Num. 25:8. This was so acceptable to God that he gave them the covenant of peace, saying that he and his seed shall forever be priests since, possessed by a zeal for God, he had thus reconciled the children of Israel: "When your brother, your mother's son, or your son or your daughter, or the wife who is in your breast, or your neighbor who is to you as your soul wishes to incite you, saying in secret, Let us go and serve /221/ other gods, etc. Do not consent to him and do not listen to him; let your eye not pardon him, do not have mercy on him, and do not hide him. But you shall kill him, your hand shall be the first on him in order to put him to death, and afterwards the hand of all the people," Deut. 13:6[-9].

It is manifested by these premises that all love must yield to faith and [the] love of God. The true Levites and Israelites could not have regard to their fathers, mothers, brothers, sisters, and to their wives, since they were to judge and punish according to the Word of God. If someone wishes to say that this was what should have been done in the time of the Old Testament, we reply to them in this manner: The faith of the ancient fathers of the Old Testament who lived in the fear of God, is that not a true faith? Since Paul said there is but one faith, Eph. 4:5. For the sake of their faith, the patriarchs are greatly praised, whereby it appears that they had the only true faith, Heb. 11 (all the chapter). That is in fact demonstrated by the patriarch Abraham, Gen. 15:6, inasmuch as he is the father of all believers, not only in the circumcision but also among Gentiles, Rom. 4:11; Gal. 3:7, not in Israel and Judah alone, but also in the church of Jesus Christ. Who was ready by faith beyond natural and paternal love to sacrifice his precious son, Gen. 22:10; demonstrating by this to all his posterity that the faith and love of God must surpass all things and have first place. Further, Christ said in the Gospel that Abraham had seen his coming, and rejoiced, John 8:56. For he knew, by faith in the spirit, the Messiah's coming as Redeemer and Savior, to wit, Jesus Christ our Lord: by whose grace and merit he hoped (with all believers in Christ) to be saved. That was his spiritual joy. To which Paul agrees, saying: We have a spirit of faith, 2 Cor. 4:13. That means, [one spirit] with the ancient fathers who lived in the faith and fear of God.

Finally, there is thus one God, one Lord, and one Spirit, Eph. 4:5, there is also one faith and one love. For faith is a firm confidence in God and his Word and a solid attachment of the soul and of the heart to the divine promise, Heb. 11:1. And saint John said: "God is love; who remains in love, he remains in God and God in him," 1 John 4:16. For since God is immutable, it follows that the love of God is also such and never changes, and that with the ancient believing fathers has been such as he is now among us. Who feels otherwise from this understanding about the faith and love is misled and does not know the efficacy of faith nor of love, since this faith addresses itself, lifts itself up properly to God, considering what alone is divine and not human. For the love which we must have toward God is the greatest and most excellent commandment, Matt. 22:36[-37], from which all other commandments touching our neighbor are derived. The love of God is that we keep his commandments, which are no longer difficult, as Saint John said.

/222/ Again: How much and with what obligation God commanded us to be obedient to father and mother, the second table of the commandments of the Lord have demonstrated expressly, Exod. 20:12. Nevertheless, this commandment must give way to another, which is that the husband leave father and mother and is joined to his wife, and these two shall be one flesh, Matt. 19:5. How much more thus must the institution of marriage yield to faith and the love of God, to the Word and commandment of the Lord, namely, to the spiritual marriage of Jesus Christ with faithful souls?

The sum of all we have said above is that evangelical separation is an ordinance of the Lord Jesus Christ, the doctrine and practice of the apostles, is a very necessary chastisement and a judgment of God and of his church, not biased toward any party: not for the destruction of the person, but rather for his correction: not to put to death according to the rigor of the Mosaic Law, but in order to vivify according to Christian nature and evangelical clemency. For this, such excommunication shall be diligently observed by all the faithful, with discretion and fairness according to the Scripture, just as Christ said to his apostles: "Teach them to observe all things which I have commanded you," Matt. 28:20.

See, my dear brothers, that which I have received according to my simple understanding from the Lord by grace, showing you briefly what I understand about evangelical excommunication. I give this to you, my precious brothers and companions in the faith, to consider and measure it with the true measure which is the Word of God. Wherein I have employed my only talent, which I have received from God, to the honor and profit of our Lord Jesus Christ, Matt. 25:15. I bring with me, after the example of the widow in the Gospel, all that I have, for the edification and conservation of the Christian temple, Luke 21:3. Whereby I have wished to demonstrate to all the faithful the love which I bear toward them and my ultimate intention in this matter of excommunication. Desiring heartily that another can correct this better and more perfectly, may almighty God give the same by his grace. AMEN.

Finally, my precious in the Lord, this is my conclusion: I have desired from the heart that this confession about excommunication could be added before my death to my *Enchiridion, Handbook*, in the form of a complement, as a memorial of my faith and of my last confession concerning said excommunication, hoping thereby to rest in God by his grace with a good and joyful conscience. Being well comforted by the consolation of the Holy Spirit against the defamatory words by which those who wish us ill, enemies of the truth, attack us unjustly. This happens to us according to the /223/ apostles of Christ, as he said to his apostles: "Blessed are you when persons have outraged you, persecuted you and said evil words, falsely, on account of me. Rejoice and be glad for your reward is great in heaven. Thus they persecuted the prophets who were before you," Matt. 5:11.

This is thus accomplished in us, for that we agree with the true apostolic and catholic church in the doctrine of the gospel, in faith in the truth, in the practice of baptism, of the Lord's Supper, and of excommunication. We are called heretics and Anabaptists by the world, corrupters of the sacraments, new Pharisees, too-strict observers of excommunication, merciless judges, and separators of marriage. Despite this, we commend all our concerns to almighty God who knows that in this we are unjustly defamed and detracted. And God, the Lord of heaven and earth, who has succored and delivered Susanna from false witnesses, [Sus. 60-61], and Daniel from evil accusers, Dan. 6:23, this same God and Lord who consoles and gives succor in the time of necessity to all innocents, shall also help and deliver us by his grace from all our adversaries and shall close their slandering mouths.

Now, however, we are seated under the shadow of the Almighty, and protected under his wings, saying with Jeremiah: "O Lord, you know that I have suffered reproach for you. Your words have been found and I have eaten them, and your word has been made the joy and mirth of my heart; for your name has been invoked over me, Lord God of hosts. I am no longer seated in the council of the scorned, and am no longer merry, but I am seated alone, because of your hand," etc., Jer. 15:15[-17].

Therefore, my very beloved, I commend you all together to Jesus Christ, the only Shepherd and Bishop of all faithful souls, 1 Pet. 2:25, which he has redeemed by his blood. May he deign to strengthen us all by his grace to the end that we all can persevere in the saving doctrine of the gospel, not falling from our steadfastness but increasing in the grace and knowledge of God and of the Savior Jesus Christ, 2 Pet. 3:17[f.], to whom be glory, praise, and thanksgiving for all his gifts and benefits forever. AMEN.

ENDNOTES

1. See Keyser, pp. 19ff.

2. This document does not appear in BRN X. It is taken from Koolman, pp. 207-223, where it appears in French as *Claire et Manifeste Remonstrance de L'Excommunication Evangelique. . . .* Par Theodore Philippe. Appreciation is expressed to John H. Yoder for his help in the preparation of this translation.

3. Keyser, pp. 19ff. The treatise may have been printed in Amsterdam. Koolman apparently found a copy in the Royal Library in Copenhagen, p. 230.

4. Ibid., p. 20. The use was made by Nicolai in his "Inlassingen," (insertions) in Bullinger, where a paragraph appears in BRN VII, p. 444. Cf: Koolman, p. 187, n. 19.

5. Koolman, p. 169. N. van der Zijpp adds that he was a native of Lyon, France, and probably a Protestant clergyman. ME III:296.

6. French translation of Dirk Philips. We note also that the French translator used the word doctrine in place of teaching and church in place of congregation.

7. Part A, pp. 49ff.

A CONFESSION ABOUT SEPARATION[1]

Introduction

Dirk Philips was involved in at least two major meetings of elders and ministers in 1547. The first was held at Emden with Menno Simons, Adam Pastor, Frans Reines Kuiper, Hendrick van Vreden, Antonius van Keulen and Gillis van Aken. At that meeting the question of shunning was a primary issue. Apparently avoidance was agreed upon as the more moderate practice, but it was not made a requirement. In any case Menno Simons seems to have taken a more moderate position according to a letter of November 12, 1556, to the congregation at Emden. He indicates that Dirk also agreed with that conclusion in 1547.[2]

A second point at the meeting was the issue of marriage outside of the Anabaptist-Mennonite faith, and a third issue was the incarnation of Christ. The latter question was raised by Adam Pastor and Frans Reines Kuiper who disagreed with the position held by Menno Simons and Dirk Philips.[3] No completely satisfactory answers to the questions raised were reached, but Menno appealed to Adam Pastor not to preach about his position openly in order to maintain the unity of the church.

The second meeting was held at Goch and dealt primarily with the issue of the true divinity of Jesus, including the doctrine of the heavenly flesh of Christ. Adam Pastor denied it and held to the pure humanity of Jesus from Mary. As a consequence of the debate, where Dirk seemed to be the leading opponent of Pastor, the ban was pronounced upon the latter. J. ten Doornkaat Koolman believes that Dirk was moderator of the meeting and formally pronounced the ban in the name of the others, because he was at that time elder of the congregation where they were meeting.[4]

This treatise about separation apparently grew out of the meetings at Emden and Goch. J. ten Doornkaat Koolman speculates that it was a report for a gathering of elders at some meeting of which we have no record.[5] The original copy of the treatise is found as No. 620

in the Mennonite collection at the archives of the University of Amsterdam.[6] It is reprinted in the J. ten Doornkaat volume as Appendix I.[7] It is written in the Oosters dialect with many Germanisms. The intended meaning was not always clear to J. ten Doornkaat Koolman when he transcribed it, nor to the present translators. That it was written before 1550 seems evident from the fact that the questions raised about the ban and avoidance are almost identical to the ones which Menno writes about in his treatise "A Clear Account of Excommunication."[8]

Since Dirk Philips' account where it is almost identical to Menno Simons' is briefer, it seems likely that he would have written before Menno wrote. It would not make much sense for him to have given a briefer report if Menno's account was already in circulation. Thus Dirk probably wrote his account between 1547 when the issue first became a controversial one and 1550 when Menno published his treatise.

A CONFESSION ABOUT SEPARATION BRIEFLY SUMMARIZED,

in how far we shall shun or avoid the apostate.

D. P.

/193/ First *with regard to eating*, the Scripture commands and teaches us not to eat with them. And after the Scripture has also forbidden a common meal, we cannot consent nor authorize that one may eat with the apostate, and if someone would direct us to the heathen and public sinners, we answer them that we cannot find in the Scripture that the Jews in the time of Christ ate and drank with the heathen and public sinners, neither in their houses, nor in the houses of the others, nor in an inn, nor by the way, nor in public locations or places.

Therefore we pray, advise, and admonish everyone through the love of Christ and on behalf of his holy words that everyone conform rightly in this matter, fear his God, and not eat with the apostate out of frivolity in any kind of places or areas of the land, so that he walks in certain security and cannot be accused on this account. For the kingdom of heaven does not lie in eating and drinking, but in righteousness, peace, and joy in the Holy Spirit. Thus he who serves Christ in this is acceptable to God and well pleasing to the people.

About buying and selling, we answer thus: After the Jewish commerce, to which Christ directed us, the common practice of buying and selling with the apostates is strictly forbidden, and a Christian may in no sense use a friend [as intermediary] for any such daily business. Thus it is also best that he abstain from such business, since to do so will make him to sin. And thus he may not aggravate or distress his brother and also not lose his own soul through ignorance. No one will regret walking the safest way, and we advise and encourage everyone to walk thus.

About the greeting, we answer thus: John says in his second letter that one shall not receive the apostate in his house /194/ nor greet him, for whoever greets him has fellowship with his evil works, [2 John 10f.]. We desire to remain right and correct with these words of John unchanged. For it does not say, "Do not receive him as a brother," nor "Do not greet him with peace as a brother," just as some do, but it states there, "Do not receive them, nor greet them," and John does not except any receiving or greeting.

Therefore, everyone may fear his God, since the ban is also ordained by God in order to shame the external person so that the internal person may be saved. And since the Holy Spirit has ordained to shame in order to improve the apostate and as a warning to the pious, thus according to our understanding it is dangerous to greet the apostate since shaming and honoring are two opposite things. Therefore, [let] each one watch for his own soul; that we advise from our heart. And if some cannot understand that John meant an ordinary receiving and greeting, that we let be, for we desire on our behalf to remain by what is most certain and secure. We can nevertheless remain without sin from the same if it is a certain freedom, as some understand it.

Therefore, we pray and admonish everyone through the love of Christ and his Holy Word that no one with such uncertain freedom aggravate or grieve his brother, and does not make his conscience restless, and remember where the pious Paul would rather leave his freedom (that was indeed a certain freedom) on account of his brother, and would rather not use such freedom than that he should aggravate his brother or give offence, on which account Christ Jesus poured out his red blood.

About the separation of husband and wife: Since the ban was given and left to us as a general command from the Lord, and God's Word is above all flesh without regard to persons, so the husband must also avoid his wife; the wife, her husband; the father, his child; and the child, his father; if one of the two were apostate and on that account judged by the congregation and separated according to God's Word and all Scripture—we say once again, /195/ avoid [shun]. And since the husband or wife must themselves also pass that judgment with the congregation, so they must also obey it with the congregation and also avoid for the necessary reason which was agreed therein. Separation happens because:

First, in order that pious Christians not be destroyed, not soured, [1 Cor. 5:6; Gal. 5:9], nor corrupted through the perverse apostate, as it generally happens and without any doubt must occur if the pious remains with the apostate.

Second, in order that the apostate will be ashamed, for there is in this matter no better medicine nor more beautiful means ordained by the Holy Spirit than to shame the external person if he will not let himself be instructed with God's Word in order to win his soul. Thus the pious Christian is in general commanded and obligated from the Lord to avoid the apostate, in order that he will be shamed thereby and that for his own improvement.

Third, that the pious Christian not be deceived, soured, or misled through the daily conduct of the apostate. Nevertheless, we desire to use all modesty in this matter as much as is possible for us with the Lord's Word and considering the present matter, the dimensions of the affair, the nature of the apostate, and the nature of the pious. In the meantime [let us] pray to the Lord that he give us wisdom and understanding in all such affairs according to his mercy and godly will and illuminate weak consciences, who do not have a clear comprehension in this article, with his Holy Spirit. Amen.

Whether one may also show mercy to the apostate in the time of need? Here we answer first that we do not desire to withhold or hold back mercy and welfare from anyone when they behave according to the right nature of godly truth and the Holy Scripture without frivolity; and we also hate false boasting of mercy; we consider it to be idle and useless if they have not seen it out of the true nature of Scripture and God's will. Therefore, we will briefly state our understanding of it:

First, we say that the questions of fools, [whether] to /196/ lie in fire or water, are not necessary to be answered, and since it does not happen to any person in his whole life and if [we] should now meet such a one, it may still happen without any fellowship.

Second, we say that it is imposed on us and seriously commanded in Holy Scripture that we should love the Lord our God out of our whole heart and all our power, out of all our soul and all of our ability. This love supercedes all other love and all other love must give way to this love, and this love, briefly, is found in obedience to his godly commandments which the entire Scripture reports.

Third, it is commanded us to love our neighbor in all decency as ourselves.

Fourth, it is taught us in the Scripture to practice a common love to the common heathen and people.

So we now advise, beg, pray, and admonish everyone that everyone seriously set as his purpose to act rightly in this earlier mentioned love; loving, honoring, fearing, thanking and obeying the Lord his God above all creatures.

Furthermore, that everyone deals with his neighbor in every way, with words, works, and thoughts as he would that it be done to him.

Third, that he have a [warm] compassionate heart for the ordinary poor and miserable of this world who daily need the [a] helping hand, and there are many before our eyes in great misery, and the poor are also still there and certainly will remain, so that no one is guiltless before the Lord.

So we think that it is very dangerous for those who complain about others that they withhold from showing mercy since they themselves often act so unfaithfully in the practice of ordinary love and are found to be unmerciful. Oh, we are concerned that many brothers themselves fall short, judge and perish in their business, since they do not help those who are trustworthy. They are already very corrupted, and [we] will watch if perchance over a year or ten an apostate corrupts himself; and they are already, yes, more needy than any apostate [i.e., the trustworthy ones], and the Scripture /197/ so earnestly admonishes them [the brothers] to help them according to all their abilities, and still they complain over others while they will withhold mercy from someone.[9]

All such boasting of love we consider to be useless chatter, yes, more a cause of controversy than of love, more a cause of slander than of mercy. For who has seen among us at anytime an apostate in such need, suffering, poverty, and misery as are the poor of this world before our eyes who are burdened with pox, sores, wounds, and indescribable illnesses? We [must] first advise, teach, and pray [that we may] help these sick and miserable people since they need help first, and already many are present who in their misery need help and assistance.

In sum, we admonish and pray all brothers that they do not offend anyone through blasphemy and carelessness to God or his [their] neighbor. He should act trustworthily in godly, brotherly, and ordinary love with words, works, and thoughts and show mercy according to their ability to the needy, poor, the miserable, and already ruined and sick of this world. Yes, according to his own will and good pleasure, he should act before the Lord trustworthily in all matters; and if still in addition, he deals with an apostate and his corruption, pray the Lord in the meantime for wisdom and understanding. Then do what the almighty God gives in his heart, freely, without anyone hindering. Yes, we say once again, without anyone hindering. And thus we also desire to do through the grace of God. For herein no one can be burdened through frivolity or his own wisdom. This is in short our understanding.

About that word holy, we say most briefly that we advise, teach, and praise everyone without any disputation that one call the names of the apostles and prophets and all servants of God simply the same as they name Christ Jesus himself and the Scripture calls and have a common manner. In which no one can be burdened, for in this matter we desire to quarrel with no one, etc.[10]

But the temples of idols and images, which are accursed, and to call such things more holy and to call them the guesthouse /198/ of the Holy Spirit, we consider to be an abomination and a great horror before the Lord.

About the naming of days, this is our meaning briefly summarized, that we see most certainly and securely that one not use and call the days according to the heathenish but according to the scriptural manner, so far as that is possible for each one. And when it should be disputed at length about this matter, still it cannot be supported with any Scripture that such can happen with a good conscience and be free before God, but much more is forbidden when one looks at the nature of the Scripture with understanding.

This every pious Christian and God-fearing heart may reflect upon in his own soul and conscience. We do not desire to have great disputations with anyone, but we pray, advise, and admonish everyone to walk with the Lord's Word through brotherly love the certain and narrow way, and to act toward his neighbor without a stumbling block in words and works as much as he is able and is possible for each one. Thus will the Lord, the God of peace, certainly be with him eternally without any doubt. Amen.

D. P. Your brother and fellow servant in the Lord.

ENDNOTES

1. This translation is prepared from "Bijlage I" in Koolman, pp. 193-199.
2. CWMS pp. 1050-1051, cf.: also pp. 644-645 of his *Opera Omnia Theologica* of 1681 and in BRN VII:448-450. Gerhard Nicolai's marginal commentaries in BRN VII about the Anabaptists need to be read with care. He was a rigorous Reformed opponent of them, particularly of Adam Pastor's incipient anti-trinitarianism.
3. See ME I:10 and bibliography, especially BRN V:317-381 which includes a record of the disputations.
4. Koolman, p. 37ff. Cf.: BRN V:319.
5. Koolman, p. 47.
6. J. G. de Hoop Scheffer, *Inventaris der Archiefstukken Berustende bij de Vereenigde Doopsgezinde Gemeente te Amsterdam*, Eerstse Stuk, p. 117, No. 620, dated 15 Dec. 1558, now located at the Gemeente Archief, Amsterdam.
7. Ibid., pp. 193-199.
8. CWMS pp. 455-485, especially 477ff.
9. This has been a particularly difficult paragraph to translate. Its meaning is not fully clear. Koolman believes the text has been spoiled. p. 199, n. 34.
10. Cf.: Klaassen, *Anabaptism.*, Chp. 2.

TWO ADDITIONAL LETTERS

Introduction

Several letters written by Dirk Philips are preserved either entirely or in part. Three general "Epistles to the Congregations of God" [Three Admonitions] are found at the end of the Enchiridion.[1] Six other letters are also spoken of in a discussion in 1622 between Jan Luies (? - d. 1637), a Flemish elder, and Pieter Jansz Twisck (1565-1636), the leading Frisian elder, at Hoorn, Twisck's hometown.[2] Three of them are printed above as "Related Letters." At least two of the letters have been lost. One letter follows as No. 1 below, and another was found by J. ten Doornkaat Koolman and published in 1959.[3] It appears as No. 2 below. We thus have a total of five letters, not counting the three "Epistles."

Letter No. 1 following here is the moving "Epistle to the Wife of I. the S. Who Lay Imprisoned at Antwerp."[4] She is soon to die a martyr's death. Dirk Philips urged this wife and mother to persist until the end and joyfully to sacrifice herself for the truth. Her husband, Joachim the Sugarbaker, is not referred to in the *Martyrs Mirror* because he later defected. He was an elder in the congregation at Antwerp. He had baptized many persons, according to a report from the inquisitor Pieter Titelman to the Countess of Parma (14 November 1561). The letter was probably not published prior to 1579 because Joachim had defected.

Adriaentgen apparently was arrested in May 1559, and escaped from Het Steen, the Antwerp prison, on November 10th with four other captive Anabaptists, but may have been recaptured again and executed.[5] The fact that she is not included in the *Martyrs Mirror*, however, except for the greeting reference of Laurens van der Leyen in 1559 as indicated, could mean that she was not recaptured and did not die a martyr's death; but a more cogent argument is the fact that the editor of the letter in 1579 states on the title page that she did die for her faith. There will have been other martyrs that were overlooked by van Braght, editor of the *Martyrs Mirror*.

No. 1 Epistle to the Wife of I. the S.

Who Lay Imprisoned at Antwerp

A very beautiful, comforting, and Christian epistle, written and sent to the wife of J. the S. who lay imprisoned at Antwerp and has left her life there after witnessing to the truth.

Written by Dierick Philips

Heb. 3:13 and 10:25, Admonish one another every day so long as it is called today and that so much more since you see that the day approaches. /675/

Psalm 125:1, Those who hope in the Lord shall not fall but remain eternally just as Mt. Zion.

Malachi 3:16, Those who fear God comfort one another.

Now first released in print Anno 1579

The Greeting /676/

The eternal, Exod. 6:10;8; Mark 10, almighty God and Lord, a God of all mercy, Isa. 54:7; 2 Cor. 1:3; Wisd. of Sol. 15:1, and a God of all grace, who alone can help and comfort, comfort you, my very dear sister, whom I love out of the depths of my heart on account of the truth, through Jesus Christ with the only comfort of his Holy Spirit, John 15:26; 16:8; Rev. 2:7, and helps you battle for righteousness and to overcome to his praise and to your salvation. Amen.

Heartfelt and chosen, yes, out of the innermost of my soul, dear sister in the Lord, Rom. 16:1, and in the fellowship of his gospel, and now a prisoner of Jesus Christ since I hear that the almighty God through his fatherly love [has allowed] this affliction and you have come into the hands of your enemies, [Wisd. of Sol. 4:4], so brotherly love compels me, and in part out of the duty of my ministry, and out of your own desire, as I understand, has caused me to write a little to you, although I have that trust for you that you are taught and comforted by God himself, Isa. 54:13; Jer. 31:34; Heb. 8:10, and do not especially have need of my writing.

Nevertheless, I cannot on account of the aforementioned reasons fail to greet you with a letter, whereby you might recognize and know how my spirit is inclined toward you, that we out of Christian compassion and sorrow remember your shackels, Heb. 13:3, and desire also with our weak prayer, Rom. 15:30; 2 Cor. 1:11, to come to your aid, as much as God gives us grace. Thus hear and take to heart my simple instruction out of Holy Scripture which I give to you to reflect upon.

First, it is a great unspeakable grace and gift of the most high God that he has called you out of darkness into his wonderful light, 1 Pet. 2:9, yes, to the knowledge and fellowship of his Son Jesus Christ, for to know Christ Jesus is complete wisdom, and to be united with him /677/ is a root of immortality, Wisd. of Sol. 15:3. Therefore, consider the great and overabundant love which God has shown to you, that you have come to such knowledge and fellowship of his Son Jesus Christ, that the eternal and merciful Father has chosen you as his child, 2 Cor. 6:18, that the Lord Jesus Christ accepted you as his dear sister and bride, Matt. 12:50, that the Holy Spirit has taught, endowed, and led you into the treasure house of godly wisdom, John 16:13, that he has opened to you the sealed book and given you to recognize the completeness of the heavenly kingdom, Rev. 5:5; Matt. 13:10[f.]. In sum, that the eternal, living, and only God has thus poured out over you the richness of his love that you may speak and boast in the Lord that you have been graciously created and recognized in a blessed time.

Therefore, my beloved sister, since you have become a participant in the grace of God with all the saints in that kingdom in the patience and glory of Jesus Christ, encourage this godly love with which you are provided and chosen by God's grace to the salvation and sanctification of the Spirit and in the belief of truth, on behalf of which truth you now suffer, to the praise of the gospel, Matt. 5:10, as an example to all believers and as a witness that you loved God in a special way, Matt. 10:16, even when he, in his eternal love, afflicts you, [Wisd. of Sol. 4:4]. [And that] you might always confess that you are his daughter and a sister of his Son Jesus Christ, 2 Cor. 6:18; Matt. 12:50. For the Scripture testifies plainly that God chastises, punishes, and tests his children in many ways, Prov. 3:11; Heb. 12:6, whom he loves and desires to receive into his arms.

In addition, it is the providential counsel of God that all pious Christians must suffer and enter into the kingdom of heaven through much pressure and suffering. For Jesus Christ was also handed over to the Jewish people out of providence and forethought, 2 Tim. 3:2; Acts

14:22. And Pilate and Herod, Annas and Caiphas with their co-helpers did as much to him as the hand and counsel of God had concluded must happen, Matt. 27; Mark 15; John 19, (read these all the way through).

The Lord also speaks to that in the Gospel, that not a sparrow or a little bird is forgotten by God, nor falls from heaven outside of the Father's will, Matt. 10:29; Luke 12:6. How much less then would a Christian be imprisoned without God permitting it. For God surely protects his people under the shadow of his wings. Yes, he keeps his children from all evil, just as the apple of his eye, Zech. 2:8. /678/ He thinks more about them than a mother [thinks about] her child, the fruit of her body, Isa. 49:15. He has mercy over them as a Father. For he is the El Shaddai (God almighty), Gen. 17:1, that is, the powerful and almighty, the overabundant fullness of all good, as he has spoken to our father Abraham.

Therefore I do not doubt [that] it is the good will and providence of God your heavenly Father and his counsel which he by himself has decided according to his eternal wisdom that you were surrendered to your enemies, the persecutors of truth, that they have now laid hands on you and met you in this affair, just as the Lord Jesus spoke to the Jews, you have come out to me as to a murderer with lanterns and torches and staffs, even though I have taught and been with you daily in the temple, Matt. 26:[55]; Mark 14:[48-49]; Luke 22:52, and you have not laid your hands on me or stuck me [as with a dagger], but this is your power and the hour of darkness.

Thus it proceeds with you also, for you have walked and stood in the midst of your enemies for a long time, and they had no power over you, for God did not permit it to them at the time. But now the power has been given to them from above, now is the hour of darkness with them, that they as the purposeless godless and those who have been struck by God with blindness of heart, Gen. 19:11; 2 Cor. 4:[4]; 2 Pet. 1:9, consulting against an innocent sheep how they might slay it as an acceptable sacrifice to the Lord, Rom. 12:[1], as a complete sacrifice, and as a sweet odor, but to themselves as a judgment and proof, Matt. 10:18, that they have shed innocent blood on earth, Jer. 26:[15], yes, that they are the true lovers, protectors, and members of the Babylonian whore, who is drunk with the blood of the saints, Rev. 17:6; 18:3, and of the witnesses of Jesus Christ, of which you are now one.

Therefore, my heartfelt dear beloved sister, commit yourself to patience, Luke 21:[19], and be content [in your] heart with the good will of God, your eternal and merciful Father, 2 Cor. 1:3, who on account of your salvation chastises [you] and portrays to you the yieldedness of all the saints, Heb. 12:6; Job 1:21, prophets, Matt. 23:[31], apostles, Acts 4:3; 12:3; 16:23, and witnesses to the truth, especially the yieldedness and patience of our Lord Jesus Christ who was led to the slaughtering bench as an innocent Lamb and was speechless before his shearer, Isa. 53:[7]; Acts 8:[32], as the prophet said.

And you also [are] a sheep from the flock of the only Good Shepherd, Jesus Christ; [you have been] led for a long time on his precious pasture and were given to drink the clear water out of the fountain of his grace and truth, Ezek. 34:18. Through that your soul is fattened well /679/ according to my undoubted hope, Mal. 4:3, through such spiritual food and drink. [Therefore], be still, patient, and courageous in your suffering, Rom. 12:12, so that you conquer for the sake of righteousness, Matt. 5:10; and if you will be led to the slaughter bench at any time, reflect on your only good, trustworthy Shepherd Jesus Christ, who has gone before you [and] left you an example that you should follow in his footsteps, 1 Pet. 2:21. For it happens with the Christians just as the prophet said, Oh, Lord, we are killed daily for your sake and are counted as sheep for the slaughter, Ps. 44:[22], but in all this we conquer, says the apostle, through the one who has loved us, Rom. 8:36.

Second, you have a free conscience before God that you are imprisoned on behalf of the truth of Jesus Christ, for there is, after all, no other gospel than you received, there is no other way to eternal life than you have accepted, Matt. 7:13, there is no other truth than God's Word, John 17:17, which you have believed, and there is no other congregation than that to which you are called, Heb. 12:22. Therefore, the world now hates you, that you separated from it, accepted the true gospel [and] have trodden on the right way, have become obedient to the truth, and have given yourself to the true congregation of the Lord, John 15:8.

When you were still of one mind with the world and liked unrighteousness and idolatry, 1 Pet. 4:3, then the world loved you, but now that you, through the grace of the Lord and through your faith in Jesus Christ, have departed out of the abominable Babel, out of the kingdom of antichrist, Gen. 19:15; Jer. 50:8; 2 Cor. 6:17; Rev. 18:4, now that you no longer want to drink out of the cup of whoredom and magic, therefore, the bloodthirsty whore of Babel hates you and seeks to kill you. Rejoice in the Lord then, that you are worthy to suffer in behalf of his name, Acts [5:41], and to fulfill the sum of the holy souls who lie under the altar, waiting that still more souls of the righteous will join them, and finally their blood will be avenged on those who have spilled it on earth, Rev. 5:9.[6]

You certainly know, my heartfelt dear sister, that you are one of this total if you are imprisoned on behalf of the truth of the gospel, and therewith you are, after all, assured that you are saved and that the Spirit of God rests upon you, which is a Spirit of grace. What is now more comforting for a Christian than such assurance of salvation in his conscience, 1 Pet. 4:14, accepted out of the Lord's Word with a true faith through the Holy Spirit, which is the guarantee /680/ of our inheritance, Eph. 1:14, and the sealing of the promises of God. The apostle Paul found that to be sufficient, and his boast was the witness of his conscience, 2 Cor. 1:12, that he with purity, that is, had walked in the world in the truth as a blessed and upright being.

Thus I hope also that in God's grace the Holy Spirit assures you in your heart, Rom. 8:[16f.], that you in your weakness have feared and loved the Lord your God from the time that God gave you to believe in Jesus Christ, on behalf of which faith you now suffer and are imprisoned. Whereas the world, because it is ruled by Satan who is a prince of the world, 2 Cor. 4:4, can do no other than to torment and torture true Christians, thereby proving that it is of the nature of Cain, Gen. 4:8, and of the seed of the accursed Ham, Gen. 9:22, and a remaining race of Pharisees that hates the truth and thirsts after innocent blood, Luke 21:29[ff.].

Blessed is the person who has departed from all such evil companionship and has come into the congregation of God, his holy angels, and all the God-fruitful ones, Heb. 12:22. Whether he lives or dies, he is thus saved eternally, Rom. 14:8, and therefore thanks God with all his heart and is happy in the Spirit, so that he also says with the prophet, even though I walk in the midst of the shadow of death, I am not afraid of any accident [evil] for the Lord is with me, his rod and staff comfort me, Ps. 23:4. And once more, the Lord is my light and my salvation, of whom shall I be afraid, the Lord is the strength of my life, whom should I fear, for the Lord is with me (in order to help me), what should a person do to me? Ps. 56:11; Heb. 13:6.

Again, God has become our refuge, a help in the great needs which have afflicted us, therefore we do not fear, even though the earth shake and the mountains sink into the middle of the sea, even though the sea rave and roll, so that the mountains collapse from its tempest, still the city of God shall remain fine and joyful with its fountains, Ps. 46:[1-]3.

Again, I am not afraid even if I were encircled by a hundred thousand, for the Lord helps me, he slays all my enemies on the cheeks, and breaks in two the teeth of the godless; with the Lord is help and his blessing is over his people, Ps. 3:7-8. Thus a Christian is comforted since God has given him such an eternal comfort and good hope through his grace, as the apostle said, 2 Cor. 1:4. Yes, a Christian is courageous unto death according to the sayings of Solomon, for he certainly believes that he shall not die although he is killed here.

Thus he is comforted with this that he /681/ shall live eternally, just as Christ has promised him, saying, truly I say to you, whoever hears my words and believes the one who has sent me shall not come into judgment, but he has passed from death into life, John 5:24. And in another place, I am the resurrection and the life. Whoever believes in me, that one shall live, although he also dies, and whoever lives and believes in me shall nevermore die, John 11:25. Therewith agrees what is written in the book of Wisdom, that the souls of the righteous are in God's hand and the pain of death shall no more touch them. Before the eyes of the unwise it appears as if they die, but they have the certain hope that they shall nevermore die; for a time they shall be troubled, but they will be rewarded in much, for the Lord has tested them and found that they are worthy of him. He has tested them as gold in the fire, and he shall receive them as an acceptable sacrifice; they shall sparkle as a spark in the reed, and rule over the people, and shall triumph eternally with the Lord, Wisd. of Sol. 3:[1-]8.

Third, consider how entirely brief and uncertain human life is here upon earth, yes, nothing compared to the time of eternity, as Jesus Sirach said, Ecclus. 18:[10]. Therefore, Jesus Christ our Lord has also taught us that we shall forsake this short, temporary, and perishable life, Matt. 19:28. Also, [that] we ourselves take upon us our cross and follow after him in the new birth. And once more, truly, truly, I tell you that if a little grain of wheat does not fall into the earth and die, it remains alone. But if it dies in the earth, it brings forth much fruit. Who will keep his life, that one shall lose it, but who loses his life on behalf of me, that one shall find it in eternity. Who wants to serve me [must] follow after me; and where I am, there shall my servant also be; and if anyone serves me, that one shall my Father glorify, John 12:24[-26]; Matt. 10:39[f.].

Out of such and similar sayings of Scripture, it is clear that we shall not pay attention to the temporary and natural life that is so short and uncertain, but will leave that willingly and surrender it. If we want to keep it, we must lose eternal life, and again, if we lose the temporary life on behalf of the Lord, we shall certainly find the eternal. How should a Christian not suffer willingly and die gladly, principally for the truth, in order that he may live eternally with God in his kingdom, Luke 17:33.

For in addition, it is very perilous for a Christian to live long in this world on account of the manifold temptations /682/ which meet him, Eccles. 2:[1], and we see that many who were led out of Sodom through the angel again looked back with Lot's wife, Gen. 19:26. Yes, love cools in many, just as Christ has said earlier, some follow after Balaam's teaching, Matt. 24:11, who there learned from Balak to set up an aggravation for the children of Israel, Num. 23:1; 2 Pet. 2:15; Rev. 2:14. Some let the woman Jezebel teach, who there said that she [was] a prophetess and thus misled the servants of God, Rev. 2:20.

Therefore, many do not remain firm in the truth which they have once confessed and accepted. So the merciful God who cares for his children now came and took some hastily out of the world, while they were still simple and in the first fire [of love], and protected them from evil, just as is written, Wisd. of Sol. 4:[14], the righteous were snatched away and no one paid attention to it, and the pious people were taken away, and no one took it to heart. For the pious were snatched away before evil, and those who have walked rightly, they come to peace and rest in their rooms. And in the book of Wisdom is [written], the righteous one, even though he die in time, is nevertheless in [eternal] rest, for old age is honorable, but not [simply] those who have lived long or many years.

Cleverness among people is truly gray hair and an unspotted life, that is the true old age. For he pleases God. Therefore, he will be snatched away out of the life of sinners; he is taken away in order that evil should not turn around his understanding and false teachings should not deceive his soul. For the wily examples mislead and destroy the good, and evil lusts pervert innocent hearts. The righteous has barely become perfect and has fulfilled many years, for his soul pleases God. Therefore he hastens with him out of [this] evil life, but the people who see that, those pay no attention and do not take it to heart, namely, that the saints of God are in grace and mercy and that he cares for his elect, Luke 18:7, for the dead righteous ones condemn the living godless ones, 1 Pet. 3:12, and a youth who is scarcely mature is the long life of the unrighteous. They see well the end of the wise, but they do not notice how the Lord considers them and why he keeps them. Behold, my dear sheep, thus God deals with his children whom he loves and delivers them out of many perils which the pious meet in this world.

Above all that, no Christian dies before the time which is determined for him by God. For the Scripture says plainly that God measures our days and has once established them, Ecclus. 37:[25], /683/ beyond which we may not go. Therefore, it is a special grace and gift of God that one surrenders that brief and perishable life that one must lose anyway, for the Lord's sake, and dies honorably for the truth. In the world it is a shame but with God it is a great honor, for it is written that the death of the saints is precious before God, Ps. 6:[4-]5; 9:13. The apostle Peter glorified Christ Jesus with his death, that is, to praise and make wonderful, John 21:18[f.]. So also all Christians do who are persecuted for righteousness sake and are killed. The Lord is honored in that his children suffer and die so perserveringly for his Word, Matt. 10:22.

It is that which Paul said, that Christians suffer for the gospel as an indication of the true judgment of God, that is, that God shall reward his pious, obedient children, but punish and condemn the world, 1 Cor. 11:31[f.], because they have killed his children unjustly and violently. Thus too a dying person shall comfort himself [in the knowledge of] the coming resurrection, that he shall not only live in God according to the spirit, but that his perishable body shall again become alive and shall arise again out of the dust of the earth to eternal salvation and glory, Job 17:16.

For just as we now bear the image of the first and earthly Adam, so also shall we bear the image of the other and heavenly Adam, Jesus Christ, in the resurrection, 1 Cor. 15:49, who shall change our mortal body and shall make [it] like his glorified body through his godly power, Phil. 3:21. Then the righteous shall shine like the sun in the kingdom of their Father, Matt. 13:43, then they shall sparkle as the stars like the brilliance of heaven eternally. Then they shall be completely blessed with body, soul, and spirit. Then we shall sit at the table with Abraham, Isaac, and Jacob in the kingdom of God and see that the unbelievers shall be excluded, Luke 13:27. Then shall happen what John wrote, see what love the Father has given us, that we are and are called his children.

Therefore, the world does not know us, for it does not know God. We have now all become children of God, but it is not yet revealed what we are, but that we shall know when the Lord Jesus shall reveal it. Then we shall be like him, for we shall see him as he is, 1 John 3:1[f.], that is, face-to-face in his godly glory. We shall be reflected in the eternal glory and rejoice in his great majesty. With what pleasure and joy of heart we shall look upon our Father and his Son Jesus

Christ there, John 16:22. How we then shall rejoice rightly in the Spirit with the angels, and fall down /684/ with them before the seat of God and before the throne of grace with great homage and reverence, and praise our God with spiritual hymns of praise, and sing the song with the heavenly host, holy, holy, holy is God, the Lord Sabbaoth. Heaven and earth are full of his honor, Rev. 4:1 (and all over); Rev. 14:1[ff.]. Oh, my heartfelt dear sister, thus we shall speak as Peter spoke on Mount Tabor in the transfiguration of Christ, it is good to be here, Matt. [17:4].

Fourth, comfort yourself with this, that the almighty God is with you in the prison, in every need and fear, John 14:18, and be aware of [his] manifold comfort, just as he said through Isaiah, Oh, Israel, my servant whom I have won; Oh, you seed of Abraham, my beloved, whom I have chosen from the ends of the earth and have spoken to you, you shall be my servant, I have chosen you and shall not reject you, fear not, for I will be with you and not cast you off. For I will be your God who strengthens you, who helps you, who upholds you with my right hand.

Behold, all who set themselves against you shall come to disdain and shame, and your adversaries shall disappear and be as nothing, so that whoever seeks them shall not find them. For I, your Lord and God, shall strengthen your right hand, who also says to you, fear not, I will help you, and be not afraid, you little worm of Jacob, for I will help you, Isa. 41:8[-14]. I have called you by your name, that you are mine. When you went into the water, then I would be with you, that the flood not drown you. If you walk into fire, that you not be burned and the flames not consume you, dear sister, according to the Spirit, for I, the Lord your God, the Holy One in Israel, am your deliverer, Isa. 43:1[-3].

Again, listen to me, you who know righteousness. Know, oh my people, who have my law in your heart. Be not defeated when people reproach you, do not be afraid when they slander you, for the moths shall eat them as a cloth and as worms devour a sheet. But my righteousness remains eternally and my salvation from now on until eternity, Isa. 51:7[-8]. Thus the righteous one must suffer much, just as the prophet David said, but the Lord helps him out of all, he keeps all his bones so that not one of them is broken, Ps. 34:[19-20].

Again, the righteous one shall call to me and I shall hear him. I am with him in sadness and deliver him out of it. I shall fulfill him with a long life. Yes, with an eternal life, and shall show him my salvation. Again, Christ said in the Gospel, fear not, little gathering, for it pleases the Father to give you his kingdom, Luke 12:32. /685/

Again, in the last day he shall speak to those also who will stand on his left hand, depart from me, you cursed, into that eternal fire that is prepared for the devil and his angels, for I was imprisoned, namely, in the members of my body, and you have not visited me, Matt. 25:[41, 43]. Where shall those then remain? Those who have imprisoned Jesus himself, woe then to all unrepentant and bloodthirsty tyrants, Matt. 26:46; Mal. 4:1. How then shall that innocent blood be avenged? Isa. 34:8.

Again, how blessed, wonderful, and happy shall then the believing and God-saved ones be who have come out of great sadness and have their clothes washed and made white in the blood of the Lamb. Therefore, they are before the seat of God and serve him day and night in his holy temple. They shall no more hunger or thirst, neither shall the sun fall upon them anymore, for the Lamb in the middle of the throne shall lead them to the living water fountain, and God shall wash away all the tears from their eyes, Rev. 7:15[-17].

Thus you then know, my heartfelt dear sister, who according to the providence of God on behalf of the truth have fallen into the hands of bloodthirsty persons, the Lord is with you. So be strong in the Lord, and consider what the old Simeon said when he held the child Jesus in his arm, Oh, Lord, now let your servant depart in peace, for my eyes have seen your salvation which you have prepared before the face of all the peoples, as a light to the heathen and as praise to your people Israel, Luke 2:28[-32]. Thus also, my dear sister, you have received Jesus Christ in the arms of your soul. Therefore, speak now with all your heart, Oh, Lord, let now your maidservant go in peace to [her] blessed rest. Let now my soul be brought with the soul of the poor Lazarus by the angels into Abraham's bosom, Luke 16:22. For with my eyes of faith I have seen my Deliverer and Savior Jesus Christ.

Your heartfelt dear husband and my dear [beloved] brother, whom I love out of the depths of my heart, commend him to the Lord Jesus Christ who is powerful to keep him from all evil and to place him before the face of his Father without offence, Acts 20:[18ff.], and to keep to his eternal kingdom your dear children whom God has given you, if they are still alive, commend them to the true Father and Creator of all creatures, who gave them body and soul, Gen. 2:[7]; 2 Macc. 7:[23], who is a true advocate of innocent beings. [He] shall also keep your body, prepared for the Lord as a living burnt offering of your spirit; commend it into the hands of Jesus Christ, John 14:18;

Rom. 12:1; Acts 7:59-60. Say now with Paul, /686/ Christ is my life and dying is my gain, Phil. 1:21.

Again, what may separate us from the love of God, pressure or fear, yes, I am certain that neither life, nor death, nor angels, nor principalities, nor powers, nor height, nor depth, nor present, nor future things, nor any other creature can separate us from the love of God, who is there in Christ Jesus, Rom. 8:35[-38] [conflated]. That the same prophet had also certainly considered when he said, Oh, Lord, when I only have you, then I do not ask for heaven or earth. Even though my body and soul should languish, you are still my heart's comfort and refuge, Ps. 73:25.

My heartily dear sister, be also thus minded and speak thus with the prophet and apostle. Let it be heard from you now and be seen and found with the truth, that you have love of your God above all that is on earth, Matt. 22:[37]. Show now that you have built your house on the true, only cornerstone, and not upon shifting sand, Matt. 7:[24]. Yes, that as a noble pearl, as pure gold and silver, one constructed on the only foundation, 1 Cor. 3:12. The day of testing is now here, that the work may be tested. Show now that you are a work in the Lord, a tilled field, and a building of God, and that they who have served you with the Word of the Lord have not labored nor run in vain on your behalf.

Let now your faith in Christ Jesus be revealed, that you are truly baptized into his death, in order to live and die with him, Rom. 6:3. Reflect now on your pioneer and king of your faith, Jesus Christ, what he has done and has suffered on our behalf, Heb. 12:2, how he has come out of heaven, yes, out of the bosom of his Father into this world John 16:[30], and after much pain and scorn which was done to him by the godless, Matt. 27:[34], at last came to the cross, and there was offered for us as our Passover Lamb; there he was through his fiery love on the wood of the cross, roasted as a spiritually sacrificed Lamb, becoming food to all believing souls who eat him spiritually, John 6:1-14, 50, through faith holding Passover with the unleavened bread of purity and truth.

Oh, what a spectacle the Lord Jesus Christ has been there for the world. The scribes and Pharisees have been his accusers before the worldly authorities, Matt. 26:[59]. Thus they still do today. All of their disciples, Caesar's officers, ridiculed him and finally condemned [him] to death. The heathen and warriors have cooled their lust on him. /687/ He is counted among the murderers, Isa. 53:[12]. He has become a curse for us, there is your beloved bridegroom, Jesus Christ, the spiritual Isaac slain on the altar of the cross, Gal. 3:13.

Now it has pleased God that you also, my dear sister, shall make your sacrifice. Thus prepare yourself willingly for it through the grace of the Lord, so that you might say with Paul, I will now be sacrificed, and the time of my departure is near. I have fought the good fight. I have finished my course. I have kept the faith, and now the crown of righteousness is prepared for me, which the Lord shall give to me on that day, on which the righteous shall stand on Mount Zion with Christ Jesus, the beautiful youth, the Son of God, whom they have confessed in the world, 2 Tim. 4:6[-8], and receive the crown on their head, 2 Esd. 2:[43], and palms in their hands as proof of the glorious victory, that they have conquered the world and everything that is in it, 1 John 5:4, yes, the dragon himself, through the blood of the lamb, through the Word of truth that they have witnessed, Rev. 12:10[-11]. And [they] have not sought to keep their soul, but have surrendered it with a happy conscience unto death and commended [it] to the heavenly Father as the trustworthy Creator, 1 Pet. 4:19, with a firm faith and with blessed yieldedness.

Oh, my chosen sister, the most high God help you also to such a victory, just as I commit [myself] to his grace and I have that confidence also in you. I should certainly write more to you here, but it is in my opinion not necessary since you have received the anointing from the one who alone is holy, true, and a God of all comfort, 1 John 2:20, which anointing can comfort, admonish, and teach you more sufficiently, 2 Cor. 1:3[f.]. than the little I have written out of brotherly love from a willing heart, according to your desire, as was related above. And now I commend you to the eternal and merciful heavenly Father and Lord Jesus Christ who strengthens and empowers you in the Word of truth and in true faith to the end, through the power of his Holy Spirit. Amen. Ecclus. 4:[28].

Oh, my heartfelt dear sister, fight for the truth until death. Thus shall the Lord fight for you. And [though] separated from one another here according to the flesh, we hope to see [each other] in the heavenly Jerusalem in the presence of eternal peace, in the imperishable kingdom of our God, which we all equally shall inherit with our Lord Jesus Christ /688/ and possess eternally, if we suffer with him here so that we may come to glory with him, Matt. 25:34; Rom. 8:17.

The almighty God keep you. The Lord Jesus Christ stand by you upon [your] right and [your] left hand. The Holy Spirit lead you into the eternal heavenly glory and splendor, John 4:[23]. Amen. Many good, fruitful ones in the Lord who are here greet you heartily, especially D. and his wife; D. Jansen and his wife; P. and his wife; Jan B. and his wife; Anthony and Arent Dad and their wives; and many others who love you in truth; greet your fellow prisoners with the kiss of peace. Amen. Rom. 16:16; 1 Pet. 5:4.

Your brother and servant in the Lord
Dierick P.

Finis

No. 2. An Unknown Letter of Dirk Philips

Introduction

This letter was found by J. ten Doornkaat Koolman on the first page of a book written by hand and bound in leather. It contained three other treatises by Dirk: 1) "The Book of Faith"; 2) "Concerning Spiritual Restitution"; and 3) "The Congregation of God." They are written in a beautiful seventeenth-century handwriting. The letter is in another handwriting, perhaps from the sixteenth century. The language of all four is in what is known as the Eastern dialect, but with a strong affinity to the Rhine-Westphalian dialect.[7] Frederik Pijper, editor of BRN X, cites this book but has not devoted attention to it.[8]

The contents also indicate the area of the Lower Rhine. "The brother Anthony" is no doubt Anthony of Cologne.[9] Govert has already died in the Lord but there are many others with the same name in the neighborhood of Maastricht and Antwerp.[10]

But the content leads one above all to suspect that one finds here traces of the dispute of Adam Pastor with the Anabaptists and the ban which was pronounced against him.[11] See the biography at the beginning of this volume for details about Adam Pastor and his relationship to Menno Simons and Dirk Philips in the 1540s and early 1550s. This is the context into which this letter from Dirk Philips needs to be placed.

Adam Pastor did not cease his work because of the ban. The disturbance created by him among the brothers is evidenced by the letter. The congregation in the area can be traced back to the visitation of 1533 held at the behest of Count John II of Julich, Cleve, etc. A large number of unchurched, Sacramentarians, and Anabaptists were established there.[12] The districts of Born, Heinsberg, Millen, and Wassenberg were "infected" above all others with Anabaptism. At Bracht (district of Bruggen) the alarm was sounded repeatedly when a preacher named Anthonius was noted.[13] He is no doubt the same as the brother Anthonius mentioned in the letter.

In 1550 a new visitation was commanded by the successor of Count John, Count Wilhelm V. Fewer Anabaptists were found than in 1533, but the investigation was done with great haste and rather superficially so that many could have escaped notice. Only one of the leaders was imprisoned. He was Theunis van Hastenaede who was burned at Linnich on the Roer on July 30, 1551.

Between 1547 and 1550, a dispute must have taken place about the deity and incarnation of Christ. On one side were the Sacramentarians (called Calvinists or Zwinglian in the letter), on the other the Christian brothers, accompanied by the teachers Anthonius and Govert. The Anabaptists were probably attacked by their adversaries because they were suspected of heresy about the trinity through the activities of Adam Pastor. This had the unusual result that Anthonius and Govert defected. In light of the whole situation, it is likely that they both inclined toward the teaching of Adam Pastor. For that reason the defense of the brothers was considerably weakened. Some time later the brothers directed a letter to Anthonius and in it made an appeal to Dirk Philips who through his opposition to Adam Pastor had received some notice. In order to satisfy the brothers, Anthonius sent the letter on to Dirk with the request that he answer it.

When was the letter written? It must certainly be later than 1547, the year of the dispute with Adam Pastor at Goch. The latest it would have been written is probably 1550 when, according to the report of the "Copia der Outsten" ("Report of the Elders"), Anthony of Cologne defected.[14]

On the ninth of September, 1550, Menno Simons completed "An Admonishing Confession About the Triune God."[15] In a postscript that is lacking in the manuscript at Hamburg,[16] Menno complains that "a great difficulty is found in the land southwards about the deity of Christ and the Holy Spirit."[17]

Menno was probably referring to Adam Pastor's movement and the dispute to which Dirk's letter was addressed. Menno speaks about the possibility that emissaries of Adam Pastor might come to the north to spread the propaganda for Pastor's concepts among the "Heijlingen" (saints).[18] On this account Menno first warns the believers to guard against disputes with these dangerous adversaries. Further he hopes through his writings to restore those who have become uncertain through Pastor's teaching.

An Unknown Letter of Dirk Philips

The grace of our Lord Jesus Christ and the peace of God be present with you in eternity! Dear brothers in the Lord! Our dearest brother Anthonius has given me a letter which you have written to him since you also remember me in it. In it you write of a dispute that you have had with the Calvinists about the deity and incarnation of our Lord Jesus Christ. The aforementioned Anthonius and our dear brother Govert, dead in the Lord, have spoken against it for you in your confession which you have done about Christ.

Thus Anthonius has asked me to answer a little to your letter and make a small confession about the deity and incarnation of the Lord Jesus Christ. And that is my confession about the deity and incarnation, that Jesus Christ is true God and human being, God born out of God the eternal Father and became a pure, unspotted human being in time, conceived by the Holy Ghost and born out of Mary, the virgin, a Son of the Most High.

Furthermore, his humanity has come out of the Word and not out of a human seed, after the birth out of God, which has happened from eternity. Thus he is God and God's Son, the only, unique, and firstborn Son of God. After his birth further, which happened in time, he is also a holy human being, Son of God and of human beings.

Therefore, one must speak differently about the deity and humanity of Jesus Christ so that one not confess and hold the deity for humanity nor the humanity for deity. For John writes that in the very beginning was the Word, and the Word was with God and God was that Word, [John 1:1]. And that Word has become flesh and has at the same time remained the Word of life, God and God's Word, wisdom, truth, and eternal life.

Since now Christ has become that flesh and had a beginning (certainly out of the Word) so may it not be held for God himself. For God has neither beginning nor end and the Scripture names Christ the first and last, that is to be understood as from his eternal deity.

Likewise, since Christ speaks to the Father, "You have prepared a body for me," [Heb. 10:5], so the body of Christ may actually not be held for [to be] God, but in the body dwells the entire fullness of deity bodily, and that God was in Christ and reconciled the world with himself, etc.

In this manner the Scripture teaches us to confess Christ Jesus and to distinguish in our speaking between the eternal deity and holy humanity of Jesus Christ. I desire to write more details about this to you out of Christian love if the Lord permits me, and ask you through the mercy of God that you will avoid unnecessary disputes with the Zwinglians and other adversaries, for they do not promote salvation but confuse the hearers. Let us thus confess Jesus Christ as we are confessed by him, and thus grasp [claim] him as we are grasped [claimed] by him. Then we shall be his true disciples and understand the truth correctly.

Herewith I commend you to almighty God and desire from you courteously that you accept for good this little writing of mine. For I have written this because of the desire of our brother Anthonius and out of love which we owe to one another. If I had the time, I would write more to you about this matter.

The merciful Father enlighten us all together always with the power of his Holy Spirit for the true confession of his son Jesus Christ, to his praise and to our salvation! Amen

D.P.J.B.J.H.
D.[irk] P.[hilips] Y.[our] B.[rother] I.[n the] L.[ord]

ENDNOTES

1. See *Admonitions* I, II, and III on pp. 383ff.

2. "Gespreck tusschen Jan Luies oudste bij de Vlamingen en Pieter Jansz. Twisck oudste bij de oude Friezen of het Jan Evertsvolk gehouden te Hoorn 13 April 1622 over de oorzaak der scheiding hunner beide gezindten en maatregelen tot hereeniging." Gemeente Archief, Amsterdam, *Inventaris der Archiefstukken* I (1883) manuscript No. 558, folios 26 and 28.

3. "An Unknown Letter of Dirk Philips," ("Een Onbekende Brief van Dirk Philips,") in *Nederlands Archief voor Kerkgeschiedenis, Nieuwe Serie*, Vol. XLIII (1959), pp. 15-21.

4. The translation below is based on the 1579 edition, the only one known to the editor of BRN X and the editors of this volume. The work is printed in a small volume deposited in the archives at Amsterdam. In BRN X it is located in pages 675-688, but the name of the wife is not given. We follow J. ten Doornkaat Koolman here, *Dirk Philips, 1504-1568*, pp. 103-104 who, in turn, is indebted to Karel Vos in assuming that the reference to "Adriaentgen Jochems wijf" in the *Martyrs Mirror* of 1685, p. 269, col. a, refers to her, p. 639 in the English edition. Other parallel references are ME III:111 by N. van der Zijpp and the Mellink and Verheyden citations in that bibliography.

5. Koolman, pp. 103-104. See also preceeding note.

6. This is the kind of thought John Calvin may have had in mind in writing his *Psychopannychia* (1544) against the "soul sleep" doctrine he accused the Anabaptists with. Neff may have been too hasty in defending them against it in ME 4:543. Further study is needed, but see also B. W. Farley, editor, *John Calvin: Treatises Against the Anabaptists and Against the Libertines*, Grand Rapids: Baker Book House, 1982, chp. 6, "On the State of Souls After Death" and Leland Harder, editor, *The Sources of Swiss Anabaptism*, Scottdale: Herald Press, 1985., pp. 295, 685, 759. Gerhard Westerberg (ca. 1498—1558) was, for a time, an Anabaptist leader in Cologne and wrote a pamphlet entitled *On the Sleep of the Soul*, which Zwingli also attacked. Westerberg later left Anabaptism; Harder, p. 571.

7. See Hendrik Rol, BRN V, p. 14f., 39; Adam Pastor, BRN V, p. 358. Language and content lead to questions about whether this letter was actually written by Dirk. The context would confirm this, but the content remains problematic. At points, for example paragraph 2, that Jesus is "God born out of God," clearly confirms Dirk's hand, as does the statement that Christ's humanity has come out of the Word and not out of human seed. But the appeal to the classical creeds, actually using the Latin phrasing "proprius, unigenitus et primo genitus filius dei," is unusual for Dirk, as is the implicit subordination of the Son to the Father, "so may the body of Christ actually not be held for [to be] God," (paragraph 6). Would this go counter to his heavenly flesh Christology which is implicit in the letter?

Even more problematic is the language and style. Could Dirk at will switch to this dialect and, if so, why only once as far as we know? The style is not Dirk. The sentences are shorter, more concise, and less repetitive than in his other writings. Perhaps he was not comfortable with the dialect, or maybe the publisher used a heavy hand. Or the letter just might have been written by the person who translated the three documents found with it.

8. BRN X, p. 53-54.

9. *Mennonitisches Lexikon*, Vol. I, ed. by Christian Hege and Christian Neff. Frankfurt am Main: Published by the editors, 1913, p. 76.

10. ME 2:557. Govert cannot be the same as the martyr who lived at Lier and was not burned until 1551.

11. About Adam Pastor and his antitrinitarian teachings, see F. Pijper, BRN X, pp. 20-26; Vos, *Menno Simons*. pp. 100-107; Vos, "Adam Pastor, de eerste Nederlandsche Vrijzinnig Doopsgezind," DB 1909. pp. 104-26; Kühler, *Geschiedenis* I, pp. 284-290;

Krahn, pp. 67 ff.; S. Cramer in BRN V, pp. 317-59.

12. O. R. Redlich, *Jülich-Bergische Kirchenpolitik*, Vol. I, II1 and II2, 1907-1915. The same writer gives a short summary in: *Staat und Kirche am Niederrhein zur Reformationszeit* .*Schriften des Vereins für Reformationsgeschichte*, no. 164. Leipzig, 1938.

13. Redlich, *Jülich-Bergische Kirchenpolitik*, Vol. II1, p. 146.

14. Vos, *Menno Simons*, p. 256

15. "Confession of the Triune God," CWMS pp. 489-498; *Opera Omnia*, fol. 385-391A.

16. Ibid, p. 1036; fol. 391B.

17. Ibid.

18. Ibid.

HYMNS

The following two hymns are the only ones known definitely to have been written by Dirk Philips. Both were originally published in early seventeenth-century hymnbooks from where they were reprinted by S. Blaupot ten Cate in 1839 and by the editor of the BRN X volume in 1914.[1] The first one was apparently composed to oppose the unitarian tendencies of Adam Pastor, who was banned by Dirk after 1547 but continued his work as an Anabaptist.

The second hymn is a Christmas and New Year's hymn. A large number of such hymns and chants had survived from the Middle Ages. Later the Protestants continued to write and sing them. This hymn is an example of such a practice also among the Anabaptists. The refrain at the end of each verse, "In this New Year," approximates the first line of a Christmas hymn of which Acquoy printed a part in 1897.[2]

With this new year
To us does appear
How a pregnant maiden
Made the world rejoice,

In his volume on the history of the Anabaptists in Friesland, Blaupot ten Cate comments that, while these hymns may have little poetic merit, they are important because they are all the hymns we have of Dirk.[3] They are included here to complete the collection of his known writings. They are also another example of the extensive hymnody of sixteenth-century Anabaptism.

Sixteenth-century Anabaptists wrote many hymns. The first hymns of the *Ausbund*, originating in Passau from 1535 to 1540 and first published in 1564, represented the Swiss tradition. Hutterite hymnody was more extensive and the Dutch even more so, beginning with the 1582 hymnal of Hans de Ries, followed by many other volumes. It is clear that hymns played an important part in their private and communal devotional life. We have no record of how much Dirk's hymns were used, but Keyser has identified eight hymnals in which they appeared, not including numerous reprints.[4]

As in the preceding material, these hymns are presented here in reasonably accurate translation but neither rhymed nor necessarily corresponding to the meter in which they were written because they were not translated to be sung. They could, of course, be adapted for singing, perhaps with new tunes. Since the first hymn addresses a specific theological issue, reworking it into a singable format might change the content, a problem found in many hymn and poetry translations.[5]

YOU CHRISTIAN BROTHERS TOGETHER

To the tune: God Help That I May Succeed[6]
(To be sung reverently)

1. You Christian brothers together,
Listen to a true hymn
Full of highly praised names
Told about the Son of God.
Behold the Scriptures in the Spirit,
That you may rightly confess
That he has been from the beginning.　　Mic. 5:[2]

2. First of all you will observe　　　　　　John 1:1
How Christ is the divine Word,
Through which the Father began to work　Eph. 3:9; Col. 1:16
In the beginning, as we have heard,　　　Gen. 1:1
When God founded a pure heaven and earth.
Thus was this Word exalted by him,
One with the Father together.　　　　　　John 10:30; 14:9

3. We acknowledge, as Scripture confesses,
Each one with ears should hear,
He has been from time eternal,　　　　　　Mic. 5:[2]
Who can relate his birth?　　　　　　　　　Isa. 53
He is the very image of God,　　　　　　　Wisd. of Sol. 7:25,26;
The appearance of his glory,　　　　　　　Col. 1:15; Heb. 1:3
A reflection of his pure being.

4. Exalted out of the mouth of the
　　Most High　　　　　　　　　　　　　Ecclus. 24:[3]
Is the Word from eternity,
And that Word was, in addition, God　　　John 1:1
And God was that Word, as John said.

He is alone the great wisdom of God,
Born of the Father
To deliver us from death.

5. When man[kind] had broken
    God's command   Gen. 3:[4-]6
Through the sly devil's advice,
Then God spoke to him,
And promised him a seed
That should deliver us from
    the enemy's envy,   Gen. 3:15
And break his head in pieces.
Because of this we are happy.

6. This seed full of all honor
Here became God's promised bride,[7]
To generate from the beginning,
Through the promises, hear this news,   Isa. 11:1
From generation to generation,
    as Matthew declared,
According to the promises in figures,   Matt. 1:1
The Son is revealed.

7. This seed, if rightly perceived,   Ezek. 37:24
Out of faith, free in the Spirit,
As a true Isaac full of trust,   Gen. 21:3
Was, nevertheless, before Abraham.   John 8:58
Of the wise category of Solomon,
Come from the true David,
Known according to the promise.   Ezek. 37:24

8. He is also called David,
As a root and true branch,   Rev. 5:5; 22:16
David called him a presumed Lord
Before he came to earth.   Ps. 110:1
All kings were a figure of him
That he should reign eternally   Ps. 2:8
With his scepter pure.

9. This rod was set in Zion,   Isa. 59:20
As a certain planting of the Lord,

Nobly high above all prophets
The righteous [true] Immanuel.   Isa. 7:14; 8:[8]
He is the Word of righteousness,
A true Prince of Peace   Isa. 9:6; Phil. 4:9
As Isaiah has said.

10. This Son full of all honor,   John 1:14
Who was in the form of God
Who went and humbled himself   Phil. 2:6[-8]
To conform to the Father's will,
He took on himself a servant's form
To be an example for us   1 Pet. 2:21
To follow in his footsteps.

11. A pure maiden was praised,   Isa. 7:[14]
Prepared by God and highly honored
When she consented to this,
She conceived through the Spirit's power,   Luke 1:[35]
She believed God's Word and to us   Matt. 1:25
A child was born out of her,   Isa. 9:[6]
Certainly given to us as a Son.

12. This Son high in worth
From heaven heavenly, as one finds,   John 3:13
The other Adam upon earth;
Yet he was not earthly minded,   1 Cor. 15:47
And he was not from the earth.   John 8:23
The Word has become flesh,   John 1:14
As John declares to us.

13. When he declared him to the world,
He was shown his divine authority,   Matt. 8; John 5:8
Revealed to him by his Father,
Honored as his beloved Son,   Matt. 3:17; Mark 1:11
This is the bread descended from heaven,   John 6:51
His flesh is food to us,
He has paid our debt.   Isa. 53:[5]

14. All that he heard from his Father,
And what he had earlier seen,   John 3:32
He responded to the same.

Never had one seen such wonder happen,	
No person had ever looked at God there	John 1:18
Except the only Son of the Father.	
Blessed is he who trusts in him.	

15. He gave life to the dead	
And sight to the blind.	Matt. 11:5; Luke 7:22
He could forgive sins.	Matt. 9:9[ff.]
These works fell lightly to him.	
He is the gate and the true way,	
No one comes to the Father	John 10:9
Except he enter through the Son.	John 14:6

16. This Son may teach us,	
For he himself is the fulness of truth.	John 14:6
He goes to inform his little sheep,	John 10
An only comforter through his Spirit,	
We will bear his yoke as he commands,	Matt. 11:29
He is a fountain of life,	
Freely he gives us his grace.	Isa. 55:1

17. Our sins he has borne,	Isa. 53:[12]
Much pain with great anguish,	
All from the beginning of days	Rev. 13:8
The lamb has been slain.	
For our sins he has suffered.	Isa. 53:[5]
When we were enemies of God	
He made peace [for us] with his Father.	Eph. 2:14; Col. 1:20

18. This is our true Savior	
A right arm of his Father	Isa. 52:10
In him thus lives bodily	
The full deity uniformly.	Col. 2:9
John calls him true God,	1 John 5:20
And in addition eternal life,	John [3:]16
Which is a mockery to some.	

19. Let us pray to the Father through Christ	
And assemble in his name,	Matt. 18:20
Thus he is in the midst of us,	
We who fittingly call on him in the Spirit,	John 4:[23]

Always as praise to his Father indeed,
Thus Thomas has confessed him,   John 20:28
And we confess Christ plainly.[8]

20. This Son so full of grace,
Gave power to his disciples.   Matt. 10:1; Mark 3:15
They did many wondrous deeds,   Luke 9:1
Honored through his name.
He commanded them to baptize in his name,
All those who believe in this,   Matt. 28:19; Mark 16:16
Who are also made able to do it.

21. All what further is written there
About this excellent Son,
We acknowledge already besides,
The Old and New Testaments.
He is God over all in eternity.
In the ninth chapter to the Romans   Rom. 9:5
Paul has explained it.

22. So I have not been discouraged,
Now to compose this song
In behalf of my companions true,
It has been done out of love.
And take this short hymn at its best,
Should one relate everything about Christ
My song would be much too long.

The 25th Hymn
To the tune: Rejoice You Christians All.[9]
By D. P.

1. Rejoice now and be glad,
Oh, friends, whoever you may be,
Who here serve God eagerly,
Behold God's love so pure,
Which he showers on everyone   1 John 2:2
In general on this earthly plain,
For we were all, through Adam's fall,   Rom. 3:24; Rom. 5:16, 18;
Completely lost: [2] Esd. 7:48
But God through his great grace,   Rom. 3:24

He has delivered us, out of pure love   John 1:9, 29
In this new year.

2. God has sent an angel   Luke 1:[26-27]
To Mary, the excellent maiden,   Matt. 1:18
And spoke, with known words:
Be greeted, full of fine grace,
You shall bear a child,
Whose name shall be Jesus:
Mary, one reads, "she was afraid
about this new tiding,"
And said: "How shall that happen,
For I know no man,"
In this new year.

3. God's Spirit from above, very fine,   Luke 1:[35]
Shall shine around you, hear mine,   Matt. 1:20
So that it may be born from you,
And shall be called God's Son, excellent,
He shall inherit David, his Father's throne,   Ps. 45:[6]
And rule Jacob's house without end: Heb. 1:8
Mary heard purely, she was satisfied
By the angel's declaration,
And said, "Here is your maidservant ready,
Let it happen to me as you have said,"
In this new year.

4. Observe still, friends everywhere,
At Bethlehem in the stall,   Matt. 2:1 [ff.]
She had her delivery   Luke 2:4[-15]
As the angels announced
To the shepherds in the field,
As the Scripture reports
They rejoiced "with happy gaity,
Praising God publicly,
And with joy hastened to Bethlehem,
There they found the mother with her little child,"
In this new year.

5. The wise ones from the East,   Matt. 2:[1-]2
Also received this understanding,

Through a star known to them,   Num. 24:17
They came, entering into Jerusalem,
And there sought more exactly
Where Christ's birth should take place.
Herod, hearing this, "was very disturbed   Matt. 2:3
About these new tidings,
He called his wise, knowledgeable ones
And sought very precisely from them,"
In this new year.

6. They spoke, at Bethlehem, listen to me,   Matt. 2:5
According to the prophet's prophecy.   Mic. 5:[2]
Herod called the wise ones very fine,
And spoke, Will you proceed there
And as you have worshiped him,
Will you also let me know it,
So that I, hear purely, "may come kneeling,"
He would oppress the child.
The wise ones departed from Jerusalem
To Bethlehem, as the Scripture admonished.
In this new year.

7. At Bethlehem the Scripture said,   Matt. 2:10
There they suddenly found the mother
With her child and were happy.
They opened their sweet treasures,   Ps. 72:10
And offered them with "happy mood,
Gold, incense, and myrrh very sweet,"   Isa. 60:6
They were gladdened "with great gladness,
Praising God publicly,
And worshiped the child with his mother pure,
Then they returned again with joy."
In this new year.

8. Praise Prince, honorable friends,
Let us this new year,
Rightly receive it and well,
That we do not receive God's grace,   2 Cor. 6:1
Observe it well, still in vain;   Heb. 12:15
For he has done so much for us,   Rom. 5:8
The bitter death "with great pain,"   2 Cor. 5:15

He clearly suffered out of love.　　　1 Thess. 5:10
Thus praise the Lord with grateful heart,　John 3:16
And practice no idolatry.　　　　　1 John 5:20
In this new year.

ENDNOTES

1. The first was published in *Sommighe Leerachtighe Gheestelijcke Liedekens*. . . . by P. G., Haerlem, 1628, pp. 168-173; the second in *Sommighe Stichtelijcke Liedekens, By diverse Persoonen gemaeckt*, published as an appendix to *Een geestelijck Liedtboecxken, Inhoudende veele stichtelijcke Liedekens*. . . . through a blind daughter, Soetjen Gerrits of Rotterdam, at Hoorn, 1618, pp. 82-85. Blaupot ten Cate published them in *Geschiedenis der Doopsgezinden in Friesland*, Leeuwarden, 1839, pp. 263-268, from where they were published by F. Pijper in BRN X, pp. 693-699. One of the hymns by Menno Simons [CWMS p. 1068-1070] is also found in the Soetjen Gerrits collection. See n. 4 below.

2. J. G. R. Acquoy, *Kerstliederen en Leisen* in *Archief voor Nederlandsche kerkgeschiedenis,* 's-Gravenhage, 1897, pp. 217-272.

3. *Friesland* (1839), p. 261.

4. Keyser, *Dirk Philips*, p. 156. D. F. Scheurleer, *Nederlandsche Liedboeken*. Utrecht: H & S Publishers, 1977., p. 31, list additional editions of the *Sommighe Leerachtighe Gheestelijcke Liedekens*, but we do not know whether these also included Dirk's hymn. Joe Springer of the Mennonite Historical Library, Goshen College, Goshen, Indiana has found the tune of Dirk's first hymn, presumably in a secular version, listed in Philipp Wackernagel, *Das deutsche Kirchenlied*. Leipzig: Verlag von B. G. Teubner, 1870., p. 84, where it is listed as "Mocht ich von Hertzen singen, mit Lust ein Tageweyss," written by a brother Heinrich [Muller] von Zutphen, a martyr. Variations of the melody are given in Johannes Zahn, *Die Melodien der deutschen evangelischen Kirchenlieder*. Hildesheim: Georg Olms Verlag, 1963., pp. 38-39, nrs. 4392a-32. We may assume that the first variation (4329a) is close to what was originally used with the 1556 text of Dirk's hymn.

5. On Anabaptism and hymnody, see Rosella Reimer Duerksen, *Anabaptist Hymnody of the Sixteenth Century*. Unpublished Ph. D. dissertation, Union Theological Seminary (New York), 1956. Idem. "Doctrinal implications in sixteenth century Anabaptist hymnody." MQR 35:38-49.

6. "Helpt Godt My Magh Ghelinghen." See n. 4 above.

7. Blaupot ten Cate, *Friesland*, p. 264 has servant [Knegt] instead of bride [Bruydt]. It has not been possible to verify this with the original source in *Sommighe Leerachtighe Gheestelijcke Liedekens* (1628), pp. 168-173. Neither of these readings correlate well with Psalm 89:5 indicated by Dirk for this line.

8. Blaupot ten Cate, *Friesland*, p. 266 has Christians [Christnen] which would then read "And we Christians [also] plainly confess."

9. "Verheucht u Christenen alle."

BIBLIOGRAPHY

Abbreviations
BRN   *Bibliotheca Reformatoria Neerlandica*, II, V, VII, X.
CWMS   *Complete Works of Menno Simons* (1956).
DB   *Doopsgezinde Bijdragen*, (1861-1919), (1975-).
IDC   Inter Documentation Center, Zug, Switzerland.
ME   *Mennonite Encyclopedia*, I-V, 1955-1959, 1990.
MQR   *Mennonite Quarterly Review*, 1927ff.

Bibliography
Bachmann, E. and Helmut T. Lehman, eds. *Luther's Works*. Philadelphia: Muhlenberg Press, 1960.
Bainton, Roland H. *Studies on the Reformation*. Boston: Beacon Press, 1963.
Beachy, Alvin J. "The Grace of God in Christ as Understood by Five Major Anabaptist Writers," MQR, 37 (1963).
_____. *The Concept of Grace in the Radical Reformation*. Nieuwkoop: B. De Graaf, 1977.
Bibliotheca Reformatoria Neerlandica. Vol. X, De geschriften van Dirk Philipsz. F. Pijper, ed., 's-Gravenhage: Martinus Nijhoff, 1914. Vols. II (1904), V (1909) and VII (1910) ed. by Samuel Cramer. All are Dutch Anabaptist-Mennonite sources.
Boekenoogen, J. G. *Catalogus der werken over de Doopsgezinden en hunne geschiedenis*. [Since 1968 in the University Library and in the Archives of Amsterdam.] Amsterdam, 1919.
Bornhäuser, Christoph. *Leben und Lehre Menno Simons'*. Neukirchener Verlag, 1973.
Braght, Thieleman J. van. *The Bloody Theater or Martyrs Mirror of the Defenseless Christians*. Tr. by Joseph Sohm. Scottdale: Herald Press, 1951.
Brons, Anna. *Ursprung, Entwickelung und Schicksale der altevangelischen Taufgesinnten oder Mennoniten in kurzen Zügen übersichtlich dargestellt*. Norden: Diedr. Soltau, 1891.
Cassander, Georg. *Opera Ovae reperiri potvernvt Omnia*. Paris: Apud Abr. Pacard, 1616.
Cate, Steven Blaupot ten. *Geschiedenis der Doopsgezinden in Friesland*. Leeuwarden: W. Eekhoff, 1839.
_____. *Geschiedenis der Doopsgezinden in Groningen, Overijssel en Oost-Friesland*. Leeuwarden: W. Eekhoff en J. B. Wolters, 1842.
_____. *Geschiedenis der Doopsgezinden in Holland, Zeeland, Utrecht en Gelderland*. Amsterdam: P. N. van Kampen, 1847.
Cornelius, C. A. *Geschichte des Münsterischen Aufruhrs*. I, 1855.
Cramer, Samuel. "De Doopsgezinde gemeente te Utrecht van 1560-1562 uit onuitgegeven bescheiden," DB (1903).
Dankbaar, W. F., ed. *Documenta Anabaptistica Neerlandica*. III. Leiden: E. J. Brill, 1981.

Deppermann, Klaus. *Melchior Hoffman.* Göttingen: Vandenhoeck u. Ruprecht, 1979.
de Vrie, O. H. *Leer en Praxis van de vroege dopers.* Leeuwarden: Uitgeverij Gerben Dykstra, 1982, pp. vii,+ 247.
Doopsgezinde Bijdragen, 1861-1919. Nieuwe reeks 1975-.
Dosker, H. E. *The Dutch Anabaptists.* Philadelphia: Judson Press, 1921.
Dyck, Cornelius J., ed. *A Legacy of Faith: The Heritage of Menno Simons.* Newton: Faith and Life Press, 1962.
_____. "The Christology of Dirk Philips," MQR, XXXI (1957).
_____. "The Place of Tradition in Dutch Anabaptism," *Church History,* 43 (1974).
Farley, B. W. *John Calvin: Treatises Against the Anabaptists and Against the Libertines.* Grand Rapids: Baker Book House, 1982.
Fast, Heinold. *Der Linke Flügel der Reformation.* Bremen, 1962.
Franck, Sebastian. *Chronica, Tijtboeck ende geschiet bibel....* Strasbourg, 1595 edition used. Original 1531.
Friesen, P. M. *Die Alt-Evangelische Mennonitische Bruderschaft in Russland (1789-1910).* Halbstadt: Raduga, 1911. Tr. as *The Mennonite Brotherhood in Russia* (1789-1910). Fresno: Bd of Christian Literature, Gen. Conf. MB Churches, 1978.
Grosheide, Greta. *Bijdrage tot de Geschiedenis der Anabaptisten in Amsterdam.* Hilversum: J. Schipper, Jr., 1938.
Harder, Leland. *The Sources of Swiss Anabaptism.* Scottdale: Herald Press, 1985.
Hazlitt, William. *The Table Talk of Martin Luther.* Philadelphia: The Lutheran Publication Society, n.d. Pp. 2-3. [Cf: *Weimar Ausgabe,* TR Vol. I, p. 486, No. 961]
Hegler, Alfred. *Geist und Schrift bei Sebastian Franck.* Freiburg in B., 1892.
Hegler-Köhler. *Beitrage zur Geschichte der Mystik.* Berlin, 1906.
Hillerbrand, Hans Joachim. *A Bibliography of Anabaptism, 1520-1630* Elkhart: Institute of Mennonite Studies, 1962. Nos: 1457, 2967, 3185, 3188-90, 3192, 3194, 3196-99, 3224-34, 3236, 3237 3242, 3243-46, 3251-55b, 3284, 3331, 3376, 3471, 3475.
Hullu, J. de. *Bescheiden betreffende de Hervorming in Overijssel.* I, Deventer 1522-45. Deventer: Boek en Steendrukkerij, 1899.
Kawerau, P. *Melchior Hoffman als religiöser Denker.* Haarlem:1954
Keeney, William E. "Dirk Philips." *Mennonite Life,* Vol. XIII, No. 2 (April 1958), 70-75.
_____. "Dirk Philips' Life." MQR, Vol. XXXII (1958).
_____. "The Writings of Dirk Philips." MQR, Vol. XXXII (1958).
_____. "Dirk Philips." *Mennonite Historical Bulletin,* Vol. XXII, No. 4 (Oct. 1961), 8.
_____. "Basic Beliefs of the Dutch Anabaptists" (pp. 13-25), and "Menno Simons on Faith and Reason" (pp. 27-33) in *No Other Foundation* (Commemorative essays on Menno Simons) by Walter Klaassen, William Keeney, et al. North Newton Kan.: Bethel College, 1962.
_____. "The Quiet Revolution: Menno Simons." *Mennonite Life,* Vol. XXV (1970).

_____. "Anabaptism Confronts Menno Simons," *Mennonite Life*, Vol. 30 (1975). Reprinted in two parts: "Anabaptism Confronts Menno Simons," and "Biblical Orientation Preserved Amid Severe Leadership Crises," *Mennonite Weekly Review*, May 22, l975, p. 8 and May 29, 1975, pp. 5, 6, 7 respectively.

_____. *The Development of Dutch Anabaptist Thought and Practice from 1539-1564*. Nieuwkoop: B. de Graaf, 1968.

_____. "The Incarnation, A Central Theological Concept" in *A Legacy of Faith*, Cornelius J. Dyck, ed. Newton Kan.: Faith and Life Press, 1962, pp. 55-68.

_____. Book Review: J. ten Doornkaat Koolman, *Dirk Philips 1504-1568*, in MQR, Vol. XL (1966).

_____. Book Review: H. W. Meihuizen, *Menno Simons, Ijveraar voor het Herstel van de Niuewtestamentische Gemeente, 1496-1561*. Haarlem: H.D. Tjeenk Willink en Zoon N.V., 1961. In MQR, Vol XLIV (1970).

_____. Book Review: Willem Balke, *Calvijn en de Doperse Radikalen*. Amsterdam: Uitgeverij ton Bolland, 1973, 387 pp. In MQR, Vol. XLIX (1971).

_____. Book Review: O.H. de Vrie, *Leer en Praxis van de vroege dopers*. Leeuwarden: Uitgeverij Gerben Dykstra, 1982, pp. vii,+ 247. In MQR, Vol. LIX (1985).

_____. Book Review: A. F. Mellink, *Documenta Anabaptistica Neerlandica, Part II*. In MQR, Vol. LVI (1982).

_____. Book Review: Meihuizen, H. W., *Het Begrip Restitutie in het Noordwestelijke Doperdom*. In MQR, Vol. XLI (1968).

_____. Book Review: *Theologie in de Universiteitsbibliotheek van Amsterdam*, Amsterdam: Universiteitsbibliotheek van Amsterdam. 1985, 200 pp. In MQR, Vol. LX (1986).

Keyser, Marja. *Dirk Philips, 1504-1568*. A Catalogue of His Printed Works in the University Library of Amsterdam. Nieuw koop: B. De Graaf, 1975.

Klaassen, Walter. *Anabaptism in Outline*. Scottdale: Herald Press, 1981.

_____. *Anabaptism: Neither Catholic Nor Protestant*. Waterloo, Ont.: Conrad Press, 1973.

Kolb. A. B. [trans., ed.] *Enchiridion* or *Hand Book*. By Dietrich Philip. First printing by John F. Funk, Elkhart, Indiana, 1910. Alymer, Ont. and La Grange, Ind.: Pathway Publishing Corporation, 1966.

Koolman, J. ten Doornkaat. *Dirk Philips, 1504-1568*. Haarlem: H. D. Tjeenk Willink en Zoon, 1964.

_____. "The First Edition of Dirk Philips 'Enchiridion,' " MQR, Vol. XXXVIII (1964).

Krahn, Cornelius, *Menno Simons*. Karlsruhe: Heinrich Schneider, 1936.

_____. *Dutch Anabaptism*. The Hague: Martinus Nijhoff, 1968.

Krebs, Manfred u. Hans Georg Rott. *Quellen zur Geschichte der Täufer*. I Teil, Bd. VII, 1959.

Kühler, W. J. *Geschiedenis der Nederlandsche Doopsgezinden in de zestiende eeuw*. Haarlem: H. D. Tjeenk Willink & Zoon, 1932.

_____. *Het Socinianisme in Nederland*. Leiden: A. W. Sijthoff's, 1912.

Latendorf, F. *Sebastian Franck's erste namenlose sprichwörtersammlung*. Paesnek, 1876.

Mannhardt, H. G. *Die Danziger Mennonitengemeinde*. (Ihre Entstehung und ihre Geschichte von 1569-1919). Danzig: Selbstverlag der Danziger Mennonitengemeinde, 1919.
Meihuizen, H. W. *Menno Simons, Ijveraar voor het Herstel van de Niuewtestamentische Gemeente, 1496-1561*. Haarlem: H.D. Tjeenk Willink en Zoon N.V., 1961.
_____. *Het Begrip Restitutie in het Noordwestelijke Doperdom*. Haarlem: H. D. Tjeenk Willink en Zoon, 1966.
_____. "The Concept of Restitution in the Anabaptism of Northwestern Europe," MQR, Vol. XLIV (1970).
_____. "Spiritualistic Tendencies and Movements Among the Dutch Mennonites of the Sixteenth and Seventeenth Centuries," MQR, Vol. XXVII (1953).
Mellink, A. F. ed. *Documenta Anabaptistica, Part I, Amsterdam*. Leiden: E. J. Brill, 1975.
_____. ed. *Documenta Anabaptistica Neerlandica, Part II, Amsterdam*. Leiden: E. J. Brill, 1980.
_____. *Amsterdam en de Wederdopers*. Nijmegen: SUN, 1978.
_____. *De Wederdopers in de Noordelijke Nederlanden, 1531-1544*. Groningen: J. B. Wolters, 1953.
Mennonitisches Lexikon. 4 vols. Frankfurt/Main, 1913ff.
Miller, E. W. *Wessel Gansfort (Life and Writings) Principal Works*. Tr. by Jared W. Scudder. New York: Putnam, 1917.
Müller, Lydia. *Glaubenszeugnisse oberdeutscher Taufgesinnter*. Leipzig: M. Heinsius Nachfolger, 1938.
Nederlands Archief voor Kerkgeschiedenis. Vol. 43 (1959).
Oyer, John S. "The Strasbourg Conferences of the Anabaptists, 1554-1607," MQR, Vol. LVIII (1984).
Packull, Werner O. *Mysticism and the Early South German-Austrian Anabaptist Movement, 1525-1531*. Scottdale: Herald Press, 1977.
Philips, Dirk. *Enchiridion oft Hantboecxken*. Emden 1564.
Philippe, Theodore. *Enchiridion ou Manuel de la Chrestienne*. Traduit du Bas-Aleman . . . par Virgile de Las Lionnais. Amsterdam? 1626.
Philip, Dietrich. *Enchiridon Oder Hand-Büchlein* . . . Harlem: Hans Paschiers von Weszbusch . . . 1627. Other German editions: 1765, 1802, 1851, 1863, 1872, 1917.
Poettcker, Henry. *The Hermeneutics of Menno Simons*. Unpublished Th.D. dissertation, Princeton Theological Seminary, 1961.
Redlich, O. R. *Jülich-Bergische Kirchenpolitik*, Vol. I, II (1907- 1915); *Staat u. Kirche am Niederrhein zur Reformationszeit. Schriften des Vereins für Reformationsgeschichte*. Leipzig: 1938.
Rempel, John D. *Christology and the Lord's Supper in Anabaptism*: A Study in the Theology of Balthasar Hubmaier, Pilgram Marpeck, and Dirk Philips. Scottdale: Herald Press, 1992.
Rupp, Gordon. *Patterns of Reformation*. Philadelphia: Fortress Press, 1969.
Scheffer, Jacob G. de Hoop. "De Bevestiger van Menno Simons," DB (1884).
_____. "Het Verbond der Vier Steden," DB (1893).
_____. *Inventaris der Archiefstukken Berustende bij de Vereenigde Doopsgezinde Gemeente te Amsterdam*. 2 vols. Amsterdam: Door den

Kerkeraad, 1883-1884. Now located at the Gemeente Archief, Amsterdam.
Schagen, Martin. *Naamlijst der Doopsgezinde schrijveren en schriften van 1539-1745*. Amsterdam, 1745.
Shantz, D. H. "The Ecclesiological Focus of Dirk Philips' Hermeneutical Thought in 1559: A Contextual Study." MQR, Vol. LX (1966).
Simons, Menno. *The Complete Writings of Menno Simons*. Tr. by Leonard Verduin and ed. by J. C. Wenger. Scottdale: Herald Press, 1956.
_____. *Opera Omnia Theologica*. Ed. by H. J. Herrison. Amsterdam: Joannes van Veen, 1681.
Schyn, Hermannus. *Historiae Mennonitarum Plenior Deductio*. Amsterdam: Apud Jansonio-Waesbergies, 1729.
_____. *Historia Christianorum Qui in Belgio Federato inter Protestantes Mennonitae Appellantur*. Amsterdam: Apud Waesbergies, 1723.
_____. *Uitvoeriger Verhandlung van de Geschiedenis der Mennoniten*. 2 vols. Tr. by Gerardus Maatschoen. Amsterdam: Kornelis de Wit, 1744.
Stupperich, Robert. *Die Schriften Bernhard Rothmanns*. Münster: Aschendorffsche Verlagsbuchhandlung, 1970.
Teufel, Eberhard. *"Landräumig," Sebastian Franck: ein Wanderer an Donau, Rhein und Neckar*. Neustadt a.d. Aisch, 1954.
Toews, John A. *Sebastian Franck: Friend and Critic of Early Anabaptism*. Unpublished Ph.D. dissertation, The University of Minnesota, 1964.
Troeltsch, Ernst. *The Social Teaching of the Christian Churches*. New York: Macmillan, 1931.
Verduin, Leonard, "An Ancient Version of Obbe Philips' 'Confession'," MQR, Vol. XXI (1947).
Verheyden, A. L. E. *Anabaptism in Flanders, 1530-1650*. Scottdale: Herald Press, 1961.
Vos, Karel. *Menno Simons, 1496-1561*. Leiden: E. J. Brill, 1914.
_____. "Kleine bijdragen Over de Doopersche bewegen in Nederland tot het optreden van Menno Simons," DB (1917).
Voolstra, S. *Het Woord Is Vlees Geworden*. Kampen: J. H. Kok, 1982.
Wessel, Jan H. *De Leerstellige Strijd tusschen Nederlandsche Gereformeerden en Doopsgezinden in de zestiende eeuw*. Assen: Van Gorcum, 1945.
Williams, G. H. *The Radical Reformation*. Philadelphia: Westminster Press, 1962.
_____. Dietrich Philips, "The Church of God," *Spiritual and Anabaptist Writers*. Vol. XXV, *Library of Christian Classics*. Philadelphia: Westminster Press, 1957.
_____. *A Confession: Obbe Philips*, in ibid.
Yoder, John H. *Täufertum und Reformation im Gespräch*. Zurich: EVZ-Verlag, 1968.
Zijpp, N. van der. *Geschiedenis der Doopsgezinden in Nederland*. Arnhem: Van Loghum Slaterus, 1952.
_____. "The Conception of Our Fathers Regarding the Church," MQR, Vol. XXVII (1953).
_____. "The Confessions of Faith of the Dutch Mennonites," MQR, Vol. XXIX (1955).

Scripture Index

Old Testament
Genesis
1:1 .... 62, 638
1:2 63
1:20-27.................... 139
1:26............................ 294
1:26-28..................... 571
1:27 ....68, 137, 140, 320
2:3 455
2:7 .....68, 137, 352, 455, 628
2:8 357
2:15............................ 595
2:16 161
2:18 ....557-558, 561
2:18ff. 560-561
2:18-25..................... 574
2:21-22..................... 320
2:23-24..................... 568
2:24 .... 320-321, 585-586, 605
2:25.............................77
3...................................257
3:1 .... 160, 191, 456
3:3 161
3:4-6 639
3:6 .... 294, 319, 353
3:7 76-77
3:15 ..... 68, 86, 141, 195, 320, 353-354, 418, 639
3:19 146
3:20 466
3:21 419
3:22 595
3:23 596
4:1 ....353, 374
4:4 310
4:8 .... 235, 321, 623
4:25 354
4:26 595
5:1 ... 294, 320, 352, 595

5:1-2 574
5:21 595
5:32 595
6 558
6:1-2 ....320-321, 558, 566-567
6:3 558
6:3-4 344
6:5 93
6:5-8 558
6:9 ....310, 595
6:14ff. 81
6:21 81
7................................. 309
7:23 ....344, 354
8 309
8:16 ....272, 322
8:19-20..................... 560
8:21 93
9:1 418
9:6 352
9:8 354
9:8-17 ....201, 237
9:9 ....195, 595
9:12 419
9:13 ....101, 322
9:22 623
9:22-25..................... 322
11:4-9...........................85
12:1 310
12:2 68
12:3 595
14:18 ...... 139, 156, 323, 355
15:2 355
15:5f. 261
15:5 356
15:6 ....221, 607
15:18 ....101, 366
16:15 105
17................................. 491
17:1 .... 257, 355, 418, 500, 621

17:1f. 261
17:1-2...................... 500
17:2..................417, 456
17:3-4....................... 105
17:5............................ 356
17:7............................ 366
17:8 142
17:9 419
17:9-14...................... 456
17:10 .... 101, 104, 108
17:10-11................... 105
17:12 105
17:16-17......................88
17:19 164
19................................ 324
19:2............................ 355
19:11 621
19:15 ....179, 622
19:16 352
19:24 257
19:26 ....87, 252, 596, 625
20:2............................ 355
21:1-21...................... 277
21:2 105
21:3 639
21:4 101
22................................ 221
22f. 261
22:2 156
22:2-6 192
22:7-8 192
22:9 454
22:9-10...................... 192
22:10 ....324, 607
22:15-17................... 195
22:16 355
22:16-17................... 164
22:17 366
22:17-18...........141, 356
22:18 .... 68, 142, 276, 305, 326, 328
24:1-61..................... 324

25:23 274-275	14:13-31 249	32:4 60
26:18 325	14:19 352	32:11-14 60
26:20 325	14:22-29 96	32:26-28 192
26:34f. 567	14:23 406	32:31-32 60
27:27-29 276	14:28-29 80	32:32 531
27:37-40 275	15:23 478	33:18-23 288
27:46 567	15:25 330	34:6-7 242
28:2 326	16:2-3 572	36 156
28:13 195	16:3 .... 169, 252, 330	
28:13-17 326	16:4-5 329	**Leviticus**
32:8 407	16:5 103	1-3 .... 156, 243
32:30 288	16:15 115	10:1-2 597
37:28 327	16:16 .... 156, 169	11 243
38:27-30 277	16:18 371	12 243
39 327	17:2-4 572	15:31 244
39:10 403	17:6 96-97	19:2 .... 312, 344, 595
41:1-45 327	17:11 478	19:17 219
42:18-25 156	17:12 330	20 243
48:13-20 278	19:6 .... 274, 595	20:2-5 598
49:10 275	19:16 ...... 224, 358, 360	20:7 244
	19:18 288	20:7-8 244
Exodus	20:1 358	20:24 598
2:13-15 495	20:2 .... 62, 288, 361	25:9 69
3-12 96	20:2-3 179	26:11 222
3:6 .... 288, 361	20:5 .... 261, 595	
3:7 328	20:6 242	**Numbers**
3:8 595	20:7 375	5:11-31 569
3:10 201	20:12 .... 585, 608	11:1ff. 572
3:14 .... 62, 413	20:19 359	11:6 252
3:18 97	22:18 375	11:21 98
4:24-26 108	23:1 512	12 .... 244, 334
6:8 619	23:2 548	12:1ff. 565
6:10 619	24:6 224	12:6-8 201
7:11-12 225	24:8 126	12:13-14 244
8 595	25:8-9 266	12:14 .... 586, 597
10 595	25:10 272	13:17-30 332
10:21 97	25:17 .... 272, 415	14:6-10 572
11 595	25:17-18 64	14:18 .... 242, 248-249
12 595	25:20 273	14:26-30 332
12:3 160	25:20-22 69	14:27-29 98
12:5 .... 64, 77, 130	25:22 103	14:35 96
12:7 .... 130, 329	25:30 271	15 243
12:8 .... 130, 329	29:20 364	16 .... 202, 480, 581
12:10 130	30:10 269	16:1ff. 572
12:11 130	30:17-18 270	16:11 369
12:27 123	31:18 291	16:26 179
12:37 98	32 502	16:28-35 202
13:1-2 276	32:1 330	16:31-32 331
13:21 .... 96, 329	32:2ff. 572	17:1-8 272

Scripture Index / 655

17:8 156	7:7-10 242	7:20-26 246
20:3 332	8:3 .. 107, 131, 167, 260,	24:23 179
20:10 .... 96, 156, 169	300, 309	
20:11 .... 115, 329	12:2-4 331	**Judges**
20:28 333	12:32 ...... 143, 147, 179,	1 .... 525, 587
21:8 .... 103, 505	260, 365, 504, 557	6:14 334
21:8-9 308-309	13 243	7:13 406
21:9 156	13:1-3 202	7:21-22 334
22 572	13:5 375	7:24-25 334
22:5 211	13:6-9 607	8:22 505
22:21-35 211	13:6-10 246	11 480
22:22-28 331	13:9 585	12:1-6 511
23 211	14:2 598	14:3 334
23:1 625	15 375	14:6 335
23:9-10 598	15:4 371	15:14-15 335
24 .... 211, 572	17 498	16:3 335
24:17 644	17:1-7 243	16:23-31 335
25 560	17:5 585	
25:1 478	17:7 246	**1 Samuel**
25:1ff. 572	17:8ff. 573	2:1-10 515
25:2 331	17:11 580	2:30 209
25:5 406	17:20 504	13:8 508
25:5-9 192	18:15 .... 61, 64, 172	13:8ff. 572
25:6-9 331	18:19 172	15:1ff. 572
25:8 606	18:20-22 201	15:9 179
31 572	19:15 580	15:11 508
	19:19 246	15:13 179
Deuteronomy	24:1ff. 586	15:22-23 179
1:39 ... 88-91, 93-94, 98-	27:15-26 68	15:23 .... 309, 597
100, 176, 297-299	27:16 375	16:7 178
2 193	28 527	16:11-13 336
4:1 179	30:6 500	17:50-51 336
4:2 .... 73, 83, 143, 147,	32:39-40 63	18:6-7 336
179, 260, 365, 504,	32:43 381	18:10 374
557	33 .... 500, 502	
4:12 461	33:9 .... 192, 261	**2 Samuel**
4:20 96	33:9-10 .... 204, 606	6:6 597
4:35 61-62	33:10 365	6:10 406
5:6 97	34:5 333	16:7-12 249
5:7 331	34:9 333	17:21-23 511
5:9 261		22:44 356
6:2 179	**Joshua**	
6:4 .... 62, 358	3:17 334	**1 Kings**
6:5 .... 192, 261, 453	5:2 217	1:34-40 339
6:5f. 606	5:3 334	2:12 143
6:13 179	7 .... 497, 581	2:45 339
7:2-3 344	7:1-26 368	3:1 340
7:3 560	7:11 599	3:12-13 339
7:3f. 559	7:20 396	6:19-20 156

6:22 156	4:3 344	9:13 626
8:20 337	4:16-18 345	12 .... 464, 493
8:46 .... 283, 307	4:24 23	12:4 215
12 518	9 560	12:6 339
12:8 498	9:2ff. 560	13:4 .... 326, 345
12:28 .... 185, 518	9:10ff. 565	15:1ff. 562
12:28-30 341	10:2 344	17:8 531
12:32-33 341	10:3 344	18:1 260
13:28 503	10:11 344	18:10 63
15 462		19 500
17:9 231	**Nehemiah**	19:1-6 318
17:10 509	4:2 346	19:4 216
18 462	4:2-5 345	19:8 287
18:1 229	4:8 346	19:9 271
18:13 186		19:9-10 168
18:17 229	**Esther**	19:10 .... 252, 287, 330
18:21 395	6:7 423	20:6 352
18:22 212		22 517
18:26 185	**Job**	22:6 387
18:30 229	1:1 355	22:6-7 162
19:1-2 229	1:6 322	22:16-18 163
19:3 229	1:21 622	22:18 163
19:4 508	4:16-21 352	23 .... 258, 517
19:18 186	4:17 137	23:1-2 265
22:5-23 212	4:17-18 308	23:4 .... 130, 334, 623
22:8 200	14:4 137	23:5 271
22:22 235	15:14-16 308	25:7 251
	17:16 626	25:21 307
2 Kings		26:2 551
5:10-14 309	**Psalms**	27:1 .... 262, 390, 532
9:22 209	1 .... 515, 539	31:11 389
10:28-29 209	1:1 217	32 258
17:5-7 341	1:2 168	32:1 .... 146, 243
17:22-23 342	1:3 340	32:1-2 ...... 285, 313, 565
18:4 505	1:5 245	32:1-5 576
22:8 224	1:5-6 265	32:3-5 247
23:21-23 224	2:6 .... 337, 341	32:5. 247, 283, 298, 313
	2:7 157	33:16-20 257
1 Chronicles	2:8 639	33:19 231
6:70 514	3:1-2 409	34:7 352
	3:1-8 514	34:9 62
2 Chronicles	3:7-8 624	34:9-10 231
11:13-16 186	3:8 424	34:19 .... 283, 386
12 518	6:4-5 626	34:19-20 627
13 518	7:9 483	35 530
13:9 405	7:10 551	36 509
	7:11-13 .... 566, 571	37:10 424
Ezra	7:12 .... 242, 257	37:12 .... 233, 389, 424
4:2 344	9:5 242	37:14 508

Reference	Page(s)
37:15	424
42:1-2	168
44:8	365
44:22	241, 334, 347, 376, 622
45:6	140-141, 159, 341, 643
45:6-7	159, 275, 323
45:7	64, 242, 246, 336-337, 566, 571
45:7-8	272, 340
45:10-11	155
45:12	340
46:1-3	623
46:1-5	263
47	478
48:9	380
50:16-18	211
50:21	369
51:1	247
51:3	247
51:4	110, 370
51:6	110
51:12	358
51:15	518
51:17	130, 283, 359
52	483
52:5	514
55	519
55:21	516
56:11	623
63:1	168
69:21	163
72:10	644
73	516
73:1	334
73:6	214
73:7-9	215
73:11	326
73:25	311, 629
73:25-26	263
73:26	390
78:14	329
78:15	156, 169
78:18	330
78:24	329
78:25	138
79:1	239, 404
82:6	145-146
84:11	148
87:3	350
91:1	454
91:1-10	517
91:5-6	341
91:7	546
92:12-13	424
94:15	234, 547
94:20	232, 237, 547
96:3	356
96:10	356
97:7	64
101:4	546
102:24	64
103:1	407
103:1-2	132
1©3:2	171
103:3	248
103:7	233
103:10	164
103:10-14	63
103:20	380
104:4	351
105:39	329
107	532
110:1	119, 143, 639
110:4	269, 323
111:2ff.	257
111:5	123
115	452
115:1	266
116:11	109, 164, 259-260, 413
116:12	171
118	461, 500, 515
118:14	329
119:21	596
119:89	115, 290
119:103	168, 252, 287, 330
119:105	271
119:114	260
120:2	177
120:4	514
122:3	377
122:6	406
124:1	390
125:1	423, 619
128:2	406
130:3	284
132:11-12	337
133	519
137:7	274
140:1-5	513
140:2-3	177
140:12	177, 513
143:1-2	308
143:2	283
147:13	478
147:19	233

Proverbs

Reference	Page(s)
1	516
1:7	453
3:11	388, 620
8:22	155, 159, 161
9:8	231
10:9	307, 576
11:5	536
11:6	528
14:12	576
15:8	270
16:18	459
17:12	528
17:28	538
18:1	570
20	505
21:16	252
21:27	270
24:11	508
25:11	533
25:18	527
26:12	306, 528
28	513
30:6	143, 147, 461, 557

Ecclesiastes

Reference	Page(s)
1:6	62
5:1	270
7:20	283

Song of Solomon

Reference	Page(s)
1	340
2	340
2:1	415
2:10-13	340
2:13	399

2:15 .... 379, 507	43:1-3 627	59:8 530
3:6 451	43:2 390	59:14 529
3:7-8 341	43:11 62	59:14-15 239
8:6 479	43:25 370	59:20 639
	44 500	60:1 357
Isaiah	44:3 .... 63, 399	60:6 644
1:16 339	44:6 .... 61-62, 157	64:4 289
1:22 109	44:14 63	66 562
2:3 356	45:21 62	
5:1 379	46:11 115	**Jeremiah**
5:20 259	48:12 157	1:5 .... 88, 90
5:21 .... 235, 306, 528	49:15 621	1:9 208
6:3 .... 62, 312, 403	51:7-8 627	1:10 463
6:7 208	52:7 216	1:18 540
6:13 340	52:10 641	2 500
7:14 .... 145, 640	52:11 179	2:13 .... 169, 452
8:8 640	52:13-14 200	3:23 62
9:6 ... 140-141, 159, 195,	53 .... 562, 638	4:14 339
300, 450, 640	53:1 216	5:30 531
9:6-7 .... 143, 154, 190	53:1ff. 205	5:30-31 213
9:7 360	53:1-2 63	6:14 459
11 518	53:2 155	7:4 351
11:1 .... 143, 336, 639	53:2-5 162	9:23-24 209
11:1-3 271	53:3 387	10:8 153
11:1-4 448	53:4-5 70	11:20 551
18 44	53:4-6 250	11:21 375
28:9 331	53:5 .... 82, 640-641	13:16 234
28:16 153	53:6 124	13:23 528
29:13 .... 180, 184	53:7 .... 324, 622	15:15-17 609
29:13-14 306	53:7-8 124	15:19 593
29:14 .... 153, 346	53:8 .... 162, 362	15:19-20 599
30:2 408	53:8-9 136	17 500
30:9-11 235	53:9 146	17:7-8 340
30:15 .... 44, 526	53:10 148	17:9 483
34:8 628	53:11 135	17:10 .... 59, 110
40 500	53:12 .... 629, 641	17:13 252
40:6 390	54:1 356	20 540
40:8 .... 73, 290	54:5 .... 154, 159	20:12 551
40:10 63	54:7 619	23:4 364
40:10-11 154	54:13 ...... 289-290, 619	23:5. 159, 318, 336, 341
40:11 265	55:1 .... 114, 170, 340,	23:5-6 .... 155, 205
40:25 159	641	23:6 .... 257, 360-361
40:28 363	55:10-11 .... 207, 218,	23:16 216-217
41:4 .... 62, 157	221	23:21 203
41:8 385	56:10-12 212	23:21-22 208
41:8-14 627	57 562	23:28-29 204
42:1 64	57:15 .... 191, 283	23:29 .... 208, 260
42:5 363	59:2 249	26:15 621
43:1 .... 385, 424	59:5 513	28:8-9 201

28:16 236	37:27 222	156, 257, 398, 414,
31:31-34 125	47:12 340	638, 644
31:33 .... 272, 290	**Daniel**	5:2-3 136
31:33-34 290	2:34-35 155	5:4 135
31:34 619	3:6 404	6:8 562
33:15 .... 155, 159	3:14 182	**Habakkuk**
50:2 348	3:16 186	2:4 .... 86, 309
50:8 .... 343, 622	3:17 403	
51:6 343-344	3:23 423	**Zephhaniah**
Lamentations	6:10 .... 186, 403	3:11-13 516
1:2 411	6:19 423	
2:13-14 236	6:23 609	**Zechariah**
4:1 109	7:14 190	2:8 .... 424, 621
	7:27 .... 347, 379	2:10 161
Ezekiel	9:27 188	11:9 541
9:4 250	11:24 322	11:10 241
13 459	11:33 354	11:17 .... 44, 541, 543
13-10 459	11:38 347	13:1 404
13 527	11:38-39 350	13:8-9 515
13:18 208	12:3 319	
13:18-19 211	12:13 340	**Malachi**
13:19 93		2:7 204
13:22 566	**Hosea**	3:1 380
14:9-10 235	2:3-4 246	3:16 619
14:14 87	2:19 378	4:1 628
16:4 246	2:19ff. 564	4:3 622
18:21-22 565	2:19-20 335	
18:23 232	2:23 276	**Apochrypha**
18:27 247	3:4 275	**1 Esdras**
18:31 541	4:6 531	4 587
20:7 179	6:9 .... 212, 369	8:93-94 344
20:18-19 179	13:14 336	9:10-13 344
22:18 109		
33:14 247	**Joel**	**2 Esdras**
33:15 247	2:28 .... 72, 357	1:24 275
33:16 247		2:8-9 598
34 265	**Amos**	2:36 324
34:2-3 325	2:12 375	2:42 297
34:3 399	8:11 232	2:43 .... 409, 630
34:3-4 241		6:54 68
34:4 601	**Obadiah**	7:7 82
34:15-16 205	Abdi 1 [Obadiah] 587	7:48 642
34:18 .... 169, 622	1:9-10 274	9:9 391
34:18-19 212		16:73 385
34:23 250	**Micah**	
35:15 275	3:5 211	**Tobit**
36:20 .... 246, 369	3:11-12 211	1:5-6 .... 186, 342
37:24 639	5:2 ..... 63, 140, 144, 148,	1:6 518

3:7ff. 561
3:8 400
13:11 379
13:18 478

Judith
12:13 423

Wisdom of Solomon
1 457
1:4 209
1:4-5 265
1:5 203
1:7 65
2:12-16 .... 182, 213
2:21-22 302
2:23 ... 77, 294-295, 320, 352
2:23-24 68
2:24 455
3:1-8 624
3:6 380
4:4 619
4:6 181
4:12 563
4:14 625
5:3 347
5:3-9 177
5:5 317
5:6 .... 318, 360
5:6-7 148
5:16 311
5:17 392
6:10 530
7:25 .... 157, 638
7:25-26 157
7:26 .... 163, 294, 319, 361, 379, 386, 638
9:13-16 289
9:17f. 259
15:1 619
15:3 .... 256, 376, 620
15:14 298
16:5-7 308
16:6 156
16:6-7 332
16:12 308
16:20 ...... 103, 138, 169, 407
16:20-21 168
16:26 309

Ecclesiasticus
1 463
1 516
1:1 140
1:4 141
1:14 530
1:16 359
1:29-30 177
1:30 .... 302, 307
2 516
2:1 625
2:5 380
2:7 409
2:12 395
2:18 304
4:1 179
4:28 .... 526, 537, 630
7 512
8:10 529
10:11 390
10:13 146
11:30 530
13:15-16 221
14:15 390
15:7-8 200
15:10 209
15:14 206
16:25 352
17:3 .... 294, 320
18:9 389
18:10 624
19:22-23 189
19:24 530
20 570
20:4 533
21:1-3 251
21:19 528
21:26 527
22:6 533
23:15 524
23:16 571
24:1-4 136
24:3 638
24:3-4 140
24:12 355
24:21 286-287

27:25 513
30 459
31 459
32 533
32:4 232
32:17 248
33:10 179
34:4 497
34:23 183
35:1ff. 565
35:3 247
35:3-4 576
37:25 626
42:15 197
51:29 382

Baruch
3:20-21 153
3:37 .... 161, 361
4:4 384
4:36-37 276

Susanna
1:44 423
1:60-61 609

Bel and the Dragon
1:3 185
1:9 176

1 Maccabees
1:50-53 182
1:60 182
2:15 182
2:19-22 186
6:24-26 347
7:5-7 347

2 Maccabees
3 587
3:38-39 588
6:1 182
6:18ff. 563
6:18-28 187
6:24 389
7 182
7:23 628

Scripture Index / 661

New Testament
Matthew
1:1 639
1:3 140
1:18 .... 361, 643
1:18ff. 569
1:18-19 63
1:20 .... 116, 136-138,
        143, 146, 160, 257,
        324, 414, 643
1:21 .... 195, 335,
        416-417
1:25 .... 143, 353, 640
2:1ff. 643
2:1-2 643
2:2 330
2:3 644
2:5 644
2:6 398
2:10 644
2:16 374
3 460
3:1-2 565
3:2 ... 257, 322, 351, 359
3:3 345
3:5 98
3:5-6 298
3:8 .. 207, 299, 303, 357,
        360, 376
3:8ff. 576
3:10 .... 247, 531
3:11 ..... 72, 76, 103, 300,
        304, 366
3:13-16 106
3:15 .... 176, 300
3:16 .... 166, 178, 260,
        361, 365, 406, 448
3:17 .... 108, 166, 373,
        457, 640
4:1 352
4:1-10 280
4:4 ... 107, 131, 167-168,
        260, 300, 309
4:10 179
4:17 .... 303, 322
4:18-19 214
4:19 205
5:3 372
5:3-11 372
5:4 130
5:6 ... 168, 287, 372, 556
5:9 .... 481, 525
5:10 .... 227, 376, 385,
        620, 622
5:11 .... 364, 375, 385,
        609
5:11-12 213
5:13 246
5:13-14 203
5:14 .... 189, 604
5:15 .... 189, 454
5:16 222
5:17 300
5:18 .... 87, 190, 290, 455
5:22 373
5:23-24 506
5:30 368
5:32 586
5:44 .... 60, 373
5:45 604
5:48 .... 312, 373
6:5 372
6:11 330
6:12 .... 283, 313
6:16 372
6:20 372
6:24 .... 71, 462
6:27 423
6:32f. 561
6:33 .... 261, 403
7:1 60
7:3 372
7:4 536
7:6 233
7:7 .... 86, 259
7:11 .... 334, 363
7:13 .... 82, 400, 622
7:13-14 207
7:14 334
7:15 .... 216, 263, 375,
        400, 463, 493
7:15-16 .... 199, 209
7:16-20 210
7:21 .... 178, 199
7:22-23 .... 70, 199
7:24 629
8 640
8:1-3 516
8:5 86
8:12 391
8:20 .... 214, 386
9:2 86
9:6 370
9:9ff. 641
9:13 .... 248, 407
9:15 154
10:1 .... 363, 642
10:5 205
10:5-6 277
10:6 .... 154, 228, 356
10:12-14 265
10:16 .... 213, 374, 385,
        620
10:16-17 227
10:18 621
10:20 .... 127, 215
10:22 .... 131, 213, 385,
        626
10:23 .... 234, 364
10:28 .... 62, 423
10:29 621
10:32 .... 189, 372
10:34-36 194
10:36 192
10:37 .... 261, 378
10:37-38 211
10:39 .... 388, 595
10:39f. 624
10:40 .... 127, 401
11:5 641
11:11 89
11:15 87
11:16ff. 259
11:16 529
11:16-17 227
11:20 322
11:23 322
11:25 .... 292, 450
11:25-26 .... 233, 346
11:27 157
11:28 .... 167, 170
11:28-30 359
11:29 .... 60, 405, 641
12 527
12:4 271
12:10 .... 583, 604
12:14 364

12:24 387	16:6 372	19:30 277
12:25 458	16:10 80	20:16 82
12:28-29 68	16:16 .... 135, 159	20:20-21 482
12:29 118	16:18 .... 53, 250, 329	20:24-27 482
12:30 .... 462, 504	16:19 .... 220-221, 369	21:39 327
12:33 504	16:23 .... 310, 378	21:43 .... 235, 275
12:38-39 223	16:24 ...... 192, 250, 453, 595	21:46 364
12:39 224		22:1 .... 464, 531
12:43-45 401	16:24-26 191	22:1-14 514-515
12:48-50 145	16:24-28 557	22:2-3 339
12:49 .... 312, 322	16:25 .... 240, 372	22:5 336
12:50 .... 150, 620	16:27 .... 119, 538	22:7 351
13 515	17:4 .... 326, 627	22:8 323
13:3 .... 123, 454	17:5 .... 108, 166, 361, 373, 413	22:13 391
13:3-9 207		22:14 555
13:8 .... 318, 340	18 518	22:29 298
13:9 .... 87, 96, 376	18:1 299	22:30 320
13:10 233	18:1-7 482	22:36 192
13:10f. 620	18:3 452	22:36-37 .... 606, 608
13:11 .... 232-233, 271	18:3-4 91	22:37 .... 62, 191-192, 261, 358, 453, 629
13:14 555	18:6 181	
13:16-49 348	18:6-7 563	22:40-45 144
13:28 214	18:7-9 559	23:3 181
13:29 375	18:10 352	23:8 221
13:31 454	18:12-14 250	23:8-10 265
13:43 ...... 291, 320, 386, 408, 626	18:15 .... 247, 369	23:8-11 214
	18:15ff. 580	23:10 64
13:44 .... 384, 454	18:15-17 .... 301, 599	23:12 351
13:45 .... 302, 384	18:17 .... 178, 368	23:23 372
13:47-50 464	18:18 .... 220-221, 345, 596-597, 602	23:24 536
13:52 .... 267, 365		23:30 375
14 527	18:19 176	23:31 622
14:3-4 568	18:20 .... 12, 131, 221, 641	23:34 336
14:13 229		23:34-35 354
15 .... 465, 492, 527	18:21-22 248	23:37 531
15:1 558	18:34-35 497	24 ..... 461, 500, 525, 557
15:1-9 .... 462, 557	18:35 373	24:4 152
15:2 331	19:3ff. 561, 586	24:9 .... 227, 373
15:3 .... 71, 109, 181, 306	19:3-6 571	24:11 ...... 198, 225, 412, 625
15:3-6 180	19:4 320-321	
15:4-7 503	19:4-5 568	24:12 492
15:7 180	19:5 .... 585, 608	24:13 .... 131, 555
15:8 306	19:6 .... 320, 568	24:15-16 188
15:9 .... 84, 184	19:9 605	24:20ff. 583
15:13 .... 84, 196, 463	19:13 86	24:23 351
15:14 .... 109, 209	19:14 .... 91-92, 94	24:24 555
15:24 228	19:17 413	24:31 66
15:26 .... 582, 602	19:27 .... 205, 214	24:32 372
15:28 86	19:28 624	24:35 ...... 115, 119, 190, 222, 290-291, 305

24:45-51 516	107, 126, 128, 135,	16:15-18 69
24:51 391	176-178, 218, 260,	16:16 .... 72-73, 78-79,
25 515	299-301, 303, 325,	82, 84, 87, 90, 99,
25:1 464	338, 357, 361-363,	104-107, 135, 176-
25:1-13 302	365, 460, 595, 642	177, 218, 222, 303,
25:9 87	28:19-20 .... 304, 339,	309, 365, 460, 642
25:13 372	464	16:17-18 225
25:14 .... 464, 526	28:20 ...... 120, 126, 190,	16:19 .... 126, 132
25:14-30 .... 302, 449	224, 226, 326, 330,	
25:15 608	372, 579, 608	**Luke**
25:30 353		1 453
25:31 .... 464, 538	**Mark**	1:17 90
25:32 425	1:4 ...... 77, 299, 351, 360	1:26-27 643
25:34 .... 236, 630	1:5 .... 98, 298	1:31 ... 63, 116, 137, 143,
25:40 123	1:8 72	161-162
25:41 .... 390-391, 628	1:9 365	1:32 .... 275, 374
25:43 628	1:11 640	1:32-33 154
25:45 123	1:15 .... 68, 303	1:35 .... 136, 143, 146,
26:3 374	3:15 642	160-161, 640, 643
26:11 119	4:3-9 207	1:41 .... 88, 90
26:23 366	4:10 233	1:46-55 69
26:25 219	4:11 233	1:69 ... 82, 141, 183, 190,
26:26 .... 112-113, 184,	8:34-35 192	256
301, 337, 366, 420	8:35 388	1:69-73 143
26:26-27 345	8:38 .... 119, 189	1:70 373
26:26-28 .... 116, 222	9:42 .... 181, 563	1:75 79
26:28 .... 112-113, 125	9:50 .... 194, 476	2 .... 479, 500, 515
26:28-29 103	11:30 72	2:4-15 643
26:46 628	14:1 374	2:5 .... 353, 569
26:55 621	14:22 ...... 116, 184, 219,	2:7 ... 257, 353, 361, 414
26:56 335	222, 366	2:9-10 326
26:59 .... 375, 629	14:22-24 345	2:14 476
27 .... 163, 621	14:22-25 103	2:21 .... 299, 324
27:22 163	14:23 366	2:27 456
27:34 629	14:23-24 112	2:28-32 .... 337, 628
27:35 163	14:24 .... 113, 125, 338	2:29 449
27:38 163	14:46 335	2:29-32 347
27:43 115	14:48-49 621	2:29-33 335
27:45 148	15 621	2:31 138
27:51 270	15:24 163	2:34 .... 153, 200
28:5-6 120	15:33 148	2:48 140
28:6-7 126	15:38 270	3 460
28:17-20 228	16:6-7 126	3:3 .... 299, 351
28:18 ...... 156, 222, 327,	16:15 .... 72, 74, 126,	3:8 .... 360, 376
341, 498	201, 217, 226, 228,	3:16 72
28:18-20 .... 228, 303	237, 325, 357, 595	3:22 166
28:19 .... 62, 64-65, 72-	16:15-16 ..... 73, 83, 299-	4:25-26 .... 232, 509
73, 77, 83-84, 87,	301, 338-339, 345,	4:29-30 337
90, 99, 104, 106-	464	4:30 228

5:11 205	17:26ff. 567	1:4 .... 140, 143, 300, 329, 348
6:22 385	17:26-27 566	1:5 325
6:26 213	17:27 567	1:9 .... 73, 106
6:29 60	17:32 .... 252, 324	1:11 327
6:36 604	17:33 .... 192, 372, 625	1:11-12 68
6:39 109	18:7 625	1:12 ...76, 103, 145, 298, 310, 322
7:6-8 223	18:8 567	1:12-13 .... 79, 296
7:9 86	18:14 306	1:13 .... 165, 221
7:22 641	18:18 .... 462, 555	1:14 .....63, 83, 114, 134-
7:30 85	18:28 205	135, 137-139, 143,
7:31-32 227	21:3 608	146-147, 157, 160-
8:5-7 207	21:16 374	161, 166, 258, 323,
8:15 372	21:19 621	336, 356, 409, 414,
8:21 310	21:29ff. 623	457, 640
9:1 .... 352, 642	21:31 372	1:16 ... 81, 102-103, 125,
9:23 372	22:2 374	166, 416, 494, 501
9:23-24 192	22:15-19 103	1:17 .... 94, 148, 159
9:26 .... 119, 189	22:17 .... 112, 125	1:18 .... 288, 641
9:48 127	22:17-19 345	1:19 376
9:58 .... 214, 386	22:19 ...... 113, 116, 184,	1:25 98
10:18 516	219, 222, 338, 366	1:28 79
10:21 233	22:20 .... 113, 366	1:29 .... 77, 91-92, 102,
10:22 156	22:24-27 482	163, 320, 332, 335,
10:30ff. 583	22:28 205	361, 364, 416, 643
10:42 528	22:52 .... 335, 621	1:31 460
11:28 .... 309, 339	23 327	1:32 166
12 465	23:4 148	1:33 300
12:4 .... 263, 388	23:9 233	1:36 .... 145, 148
12:6 621	23:44-45 270	2:1 131
12:8 460	24:14-15 221	2:3 451
12:32 .... 507, 628	24:25-26 338	2:24 479
12:35 130	24:26 214	2:24-25 228
13:24 .... 379, 556	24:44 .... 316, 517	3 558
13:27 626	24:46 .... 359, 365	3:1 456
13:30 277	24:47 .... 327, 595	3:2 .... 73, 416
13:34 531	24:48 595	3:3 ... 76, 78-79, 94, 145,
14:26 261	24:49 72	178, 293, 295, 310,
14:27 192		320-321, 357-358,
15:7 250	**John**	384, 515
15:11ff. 256	1 .... 455, 457-458, 465, 555	3:3-8 360
15:11-24 78	1:1 .... 63, 115, 135, 139-	3:5 .... 79, 94-95, 295,
15:22-23 250	141, 149, 159-160,	299, 366, 415
16:9 371	205, 257, 272, 348,	3:6 ...156, 280-281, 284,
16:13 71	413-415, 633, 638	312, 403, 415, 417
16:15 .... 71, 106, 307	1:1-2 .... 157, 240	3:7-8 95
16:22 628	1:1-3 .... 63, 136	3:11 300
16:23-26 391	1:1-14 69	3:13 .... 205, 416, 640
17:2 .... 181, 563	1:3 ... 139, 159, 166, 361	
17:21 317		

Scripture Index / 665

3:14 .... 332, 415, 418, 505	5:23 414	6:66 252
3:14-15 .... 295, 308	5:24 .... 190, 217, 255, 359, 384, 460, 596, 624	6:66-70 532
3:15 .... 60, 332, 361		6:68-69 252
3:16 .... 68, 70, 83, 99, 102, 135, 139, 146-147, 149, 163-165, 257-258, 360, 366, 384, 413, 417, 420, 464, 596, 641, 645	5:26 325	6:69 159
	5:26-27 327	7:3-5 226
	5:28-29 66	7:6-7 226
	5:30 273	7:7 .... 183, 213
	5:36 159	7:12 163
	5:38 322	7:16 .... 125, 166, 205, 273, 300
	5:39 156	
3:17 91	5:43 .... 226, 366	7:16-17 112
3:18 .... 149, 159	5:44 368	7:18 .... 205, 264
3:20-21 .... 230, 495	6 .... 41, 455, 465-466, 527	7:27 362
3:26 98		7:37-38 .... 96-97, 170
3:29 325	6:1-14 629	7:38 ... 90, 163, 167, 286, 329, 335
3:29-30 154	6:15 317	
3:31 .... 137-138, 140, 161	6:27 120	8:11 .... 248, 256
	6:29 120	8:12 .... 106, 300, 325, 329
3:31-32 64	6:32 .... 205, 415-416	
3:32 640	6:32-33 .... 103, 170	8:14 135
3:34 .... 198, 204, 218, 363	6:33 .... 97, 114, 362	8:17 580
	6:35 .... 114, 168, 170, 286, 338, 340	8:18 81
3:34-35 166		8:23 .... 138, 161, 640
3:36 ... 81, 160, 258, 322, 337, 351, 353, 363, 465	6:40 384	8:24 322
	6:45 .... 290, 556, 558	8:28 ... 64, 166, 205, 273, 300
	6:46 258	
4:2 80	6:47 .... 145, 322	8:30 220-221
4:9 .... 582, 602	6:50 .... 138, 629	8:31 .... 172, 240, 322, 392, 414
4:10 .... 97, 163, 399	6:51 ... 64, 114, 138, 143, 146-147, 161, 167, 171, 272, 286, 329, 407, 414, 640	
4:11 .... 297-299, 329, 335		8:32 .... 190, 209, 357
		8:33 .... 181, 303
4:13-14 .... 167, 286		8:39 .... 142, 303
4:14 .... 167, 170	6:52 252	8:40 415
4:23 .... 337, 630, 641	6:53 .... 120, 138, 271	8:41 303
4:24 .... 145, 280	6:53-57 170	8:42 .... 303, 323
4:32 120	6:54 .... 132, 149, 169-170	8:44 .... 141, 354, 481, 516
4:34 120		
4:48 223	6:55 .... 138, 145	8:47 .... 287, 372
4:51-53 90	6:55-56 114	8:48 387
4:53 89	6:55-57 147	8:51 .... 217, 309, 384
5:1 296	6:56 116	8:56 607
5:4 379	6:58 171	8:58 .... 157, 323, 639
5:8 .... 361, 640	6:60 252	8:59 337
5:18 135	6:60-61 252	9:4 135
5:19 .... 135, 205, 498	6:62 132	9:5 300
5:20 157	6:63 .... 107, 115, 147, 166, 171, 217, 252, 268, 309, 317, 601	9:7-8 309
5:22 374		9:48 127
5:22-23 158		10 .... 454, 500, 641
		10f. 613

10:1 .... 417, 507	13:3 135-136	15:6 .... 81, 252, 351, 368
10:1-18 486	13:4-5 178	15:8 .... 127, 209, 414, 622
10:3 556	13:4-10 301	
10:4 .... 265, 530	13:5 367	15:9 409
10:4-5 216	13:13 265	15:10 .... 261, 265, 366
10:5 .... 217, 375	13:14-17 368	15:12 ...... 261, 370, 479, 504
10:7 .... 118, 380	13:27 117	
10:7-9 300	13:34 .... 261, 370	15:14 596
10:8-10 216	14 .... 457, 465	15:15 .... 73, 83, 596
10:9 .... 325, 641	14:1 .... 159-160, 258	15:16 .... 205, 207, 463
10:10 .... 301, 463	14:2 .. 326-327, 338, 348	15:18 .... 227, 364
10:11 .... 64, 154, 250, 336, 399, 425, 601	14:3 .... 145, 328	15:18-21 214
	14:6 ..... 63, 81, 108, 119, 265, 300, 317, 324, 326, 329, 336, 348, 351, 361, 380, 413, 416-417, 641	15:19 .... 178, 598
10:12 372		15:21 596
10:14-15 205		15:22 138
10:16 274		15:26 .... 65, 102, 110, 127, 191, 199, 259, 381, 517, 619
10:16-17 148		
10:17 135-136	14:7 135	
10:20 387	14:8 464	
10:25 136	14:9 ... 64, 157, 257, 289, 294, 638	15:27 228
10:26-27 265		16 457
10:27 .... 217, 236	14:10 ...... 166, 273, 325, 416, 596	16:1 385
10:30 .... 148, 257, 638		16:2 373
10:31 337	14:10-11 300	16:5 .... 81, 138, 161, 327
10:34 145-146	14:12 .... 225, 555	16:7 ... 65, 102, 110, 127, 199, 259, 517
10:36 161	14:13 86	
10:38 351	14:15 .... 165, 193	16:8 .... 259, 374, 619
11:25 ...... 149, 166, 295, 359, 384, 624	14:16 ...... 102, 110, 127, 265	16:13 79, 259, 362, 381, 403, 596, 620
11:26 .... 322, 596	14:16-17 65	16:14 .... 157, 401
11:52 68	14:17 .... 79, 203, 362	16:14-15 304
12 .... 491, 527	14:18 627-628	16:15 .... 127, 156
12:2-8 528	14:21 .... 70, 165, 192, 261, 265, 322	16:22 ...... 327, 373, 385, 627
12:24 148		
12:24-26 624	14:21-22 233	16:25 104
12:25 ...... 189, 192, 388, 401	14:23 .... 70, 222, 603	16:26 596
	14:24 .... 70, 81, 165	16:27 323
12:26 348	14:26 .... 65, 127, 199, 259	16:28 .... 119, 325
12:28 382		16:30 .... 73, 629
12:32 308	14:27 ..... 194, 241, 378, 459, 476	16:33 ...... 190, 330, 334, 354, 459
12:42 458		
12:44 541	15 455	17 .... 458, 518
12:46 ...... 300, 327, 329, 357, 360	15:1 .... 114, 118, 141, 477	17:1-26 64
		17:3 ... 62, 135, 149, 165, 255-256, 298, 376
12:47 387	15:1ff. 601	
12:47-50 498	15:2 .... 252, 340	17:4 .... 304, 353
12:48 .... 172, 305	15:3 309	17:5 ... 63, 138, 140, 157, 161, 382
12:49 ...... 205, 273, 300	15:4 172	
12:50 .... 384, 601	15:5 .... 325, 407, 595-596	17:6 .... 205, 221, 465

Scripture Index / 667

17:8 .... 225, 323, 325	2:33 .... 327, 341	8:32 .... 155, 622
17:9-11 205	2:37 78	8:35-38 105
17:10 304	2:37-39 298	8:36 104
17:11 377	2:38 .... 72-74, 77, 83-84,	8:36-37 74
17:14 ...... 178, 205, 378,	87, 90, 95-97, 100,	8:36-38 176-177
598	299, 339, 365, 460,	8:38 104
17:17 .... 345, 413, 622	576	8:38-39 218
17:19 .... 313, 417	2:40 519	8:39 101
17:20-21 136	2:41 ... 72, 176-177, 218,	9:4-19 74
17:21 .... 146, 257-258,	322	9:5 .... 123, 405
481	2:42 .... 100, 129	9:15 .... 121, 348
17:22 .... 157, 360	2:44 262	9:25 229
17:23 596	2:46 .... 129, 230	10:30-33 298
17:24 .... 327-328, 348	2:47 366	10:34 305
17:25 .... 258, 323	3:15 327	10:42 334
18 465	3:19 73	10:44 ... 72, 97, 121, 322
18:6 228	3:20 347	10:44-45 335
18:36 317	3:21 316	10:47 176-177
19 .... 163, 621, 643	3:22 172	10:47-48 .... 74, 218, 304
19:11 423	3:25 143	10:48 .... 87, 365
19:29 163	4:3 622	12:3 622
19:34 .... 80, 103, 220	4:6 374	12:7 228
20:17 139	4:10 180	13:1-2 218
20:19 230	4:12 .... 60, 69, 81, 153,	13:1-3 486
20:21 .... 205, 363-364,	309, 413, 417	13:2 363
408, 477	4:19 195	13:2-3 .... 202, 485
20:22 .... 72, 79, 370	4:28 423	13:4 203
20:23 .... 220-221, 365	4:31 337	13:41 346
20:28 .... 158, 258, 642	4:32 .... 241, 262	13:46 .... 275, 278
21:15 203	4:33 .... 322, 339	13:50 374
21:15-18 211	5:5-6 597	14:14 359
21:17 212	5:18 228	14:16 334
21:18f. 626	5:31 327	14:22 .... 423, 621
	5:41 623	14:23 .... 202, 486
Acts	6:1-6 218	15:1-2 573
1:4 72	6:6 202	15:8-11 359
1:5 460	6:14 375	15:11 .... 93, 180, 190,
1:8 72	7:30-32 288	195, 307, 330
1:9 .... 126, 132	7:37 172	15:14 335
1:9-11 .... 119, 330	7:48 380	16:5 322
1:13 .... 230, 327	7:51 325	16:6-9 233
1:22 228	7:51-53 214	16:15 365
2:1 72	7:54 335	16:23 622
2:3-4 228	7:59-60 629	16:25-26 228
2:4 337	8:12 ... 72, 82-83, 87, 90,	16:30-31 298
2:14-21 341	104, 322, 365	16:31-33 250
2:17 357	8:14 486	16:32-34 99
2:30 337	8:19 460	16:33 .... 72, 74, 83, 87,
2:31 146	8:21 370	90, 176-177

17:9 234	2:26-29 356	5:6 ..... 82, 164, 190, 261, 337
17:18 346	2:28 419	
17:24 .... 60, 380	2:29 .... 105, 268	5:8 ... 164, 362, 457, 644
17:28 .... 145, 325	3 .... 69, 407, 478, 483, 502	5:9 328
17:30 384		5:10 .... 160, 194, 269
17:31 334	3:1-2 107	5:11 334
18:8 .... 176-177, 365	3:3 109	5:12 ..... 68, 77, 147, 163, 194, 308, 353
18:14-15 234	3:4 .... 110, 164, 259-260, 413	
19:1-6 98		5:15 .... 94, 162
19:2-4 74	3:5 131	5:16 642
19:4 98	3:9 284	5:18 ..... 91-93, 295, 320-321, 642
19:5 .... 74, 83, 90	3:10 137	
19:30 229	3:19 77	5:19 92
20 455	3:19-26 69	6:1-2 76
20:7 230	3:20 .... 68, 342, 359	6:1-4 565
20:18ff. 628	3:21 .... 275, 449	6:3 .... 81, 87, 97, 106, 219, 249, 328, 420, 629
20:18-21 298	3:21-24 190	
20:20 461	3:21-25 .... 69, 565	
20:27 .... 104, 373	3:21-26 .... 272, 356	6:3-4 98
20:28 .... 65, 147, 203, 226, 228, 272, 363, 485-486	3:22 .... 313, 367	6:3-7 75
	3:23-24 .... 320, 337	6:4 .... 328, 500
	3:24 ..... 70, 97, 105, 107, 125, 131, 366, 415, 419, 642	6:6-11 219
20:28-30 493		6:8 190
20:29-30 212		6:10 117
21:38 227	3:24-25 337	6:11 340
22:16 .... 176-177, 304, 365	3:25 ...98, 103, 171, 258, 272, 366, 384, 596	6:14 .... 108, 190, 393
		6:16 393
23:22 234	3:28 91	6:17 190
24:14 61	4 .... 69, 466, 502	6:18 190
24:25 207	4:3 .... 110, 142, 221	6:19 381
26:24 227	4:5 146	6:23 .... 243, 407
28:27 324	4:7 285	7:1ff. 562
	4:7-8 243	7:2-3 574
Romans	4:11 607	7:4 337
1:3 144	4:11-12 108	7:6 .... 108, 377
1:7 .... 403, 492, 524	4:12 .... 102, 105, 326-328, 355	7:7 .... 68, 359
1:8 .... 261, 338		7:14 268
1:16 .... 166, 265, 309	4:15 358	7:18 .... 145, 285
1:17 .... 87, 309	4:16 142	7:21 526
1:20 237	4:16f. 260	8 ...... 407, 460, 483, 517, 555
1:23 331	4:19 88	
1:28 324	4:25 .... 75, 362, 366	8:1 ..... 70, 107, 121, 131, 146, 243, 419
2:8 322	5 .... 69, 407, 466	
2:14 328	5:1 .... 68-69, 77, 105, 107, 125-127, 194, 265, 299, 313, 353, 378, 416, 419	8:1-2 285
2:14-16 355		8:2 .... 190, 328
2:16 334		8:3 .... 68, 93, 144, 146, 160, 162, 258, 269, 332, 362, 366
2:19-24 212		
2:24 .... 246, 369	5:2 .... 102, 360	
2:25 456	5:5 479	8:3-4 .... 320, 330

Scripture Index / 669

8:4 243	9:30-32 276	13:1 .... 110, 375
8:5 .... 243, 378	10:1 86	13:8 70
8:5ff. 562	10:3 .... 259, 276	13:12-13 230
8:6 .... 243, 317	10:4 .... 190, 224, 273,	13:12-14 563
8:9 .... 127, 203, 281	317, 356, 393	13:14 364
8:9-10 206	10:9 .... 83, 408	14:3-4 185
8:10 76	10:10 .... 189, 394	14:4 60
8:11 .... 181, 337	10:11 337	14:7 479
8:13 367	10:14 .... 88, 104, 218,	14:8 623
8:14 .... 145, 310, 359,	298	14:10 334
403	10:14-18 216	14:13 181
8:15 .... 65, 367, 596	10:15 .... 202, 325	14:15 181
8:16 ... 69, 102, 262-263,	10:16 370	14:17 .... 194, 340-341,
420	10:17 .... 87, 132, 191,	383, 556, 582, 603
8:16f. 623	260, 298	14:19 378
8:17 .... 240, 263, 325,	10:18 .... 318, 357	15:4 .... 61, 78, 84, 187,
374, 376, 384, 393,	11 480	192, 231, 248
405, 630	11:2 275	15:5 .... 478, 542
8:18 .... 392, 405	11:4 186	15:9 .... 266, 381
8:19-22 201	11:5 507	15:18 .... 127, 204
8:23 .... 282, 297	11:6 ... 60, 105, 109, 366,	15:27 371
8:24 294	413	15:30 620
8:26 259	11:17 76	16:1 619
8:29 ... 63, 106, 145, 152,	11:22 107	16:16 631
161, 266, 299, 311,	11:25 .... 323, 335, 356	16:17 .... 369, 374, 378,
314, 364, 373, 398	11:25-27 340	395, 580, 596, 600,
8:31 545	11:33 .... 289, 338	602
8:31-32 164	11:34 88	16:17-18 .... 322, 524
8:31-34 314	12 479	16:18 .... 206, 366
8:31-35 141	12:1 ... 83, 172, 250, 266,	16:26-27 314
8:32 ... 63, 125, 139, 147,	272, 345, 365, 413,	
258, 360, 413, 416,	483, 621, 629	**1 Corinthians**
420	12:1-2 453	1 .... 457, 479, 505
8:33 285	12:2 .... 189, 193, 401	1:1 226
8:33-34 285	12:3 .... 65, 408, 556, 574	1:2 .... 261, 323
8:35 390	12:4 .... 131, 153, 240,	1:3 ... 152, 240, 383, 555
8:35-38 629	246, 274, 518	1:4 555
8:36 .... 104, 241, 334,	12:4-5 285	1:9 250
622	12:4-6 219	1:10 .... 241, 377
9 .... 193, 491	12:6 59	1:12 241
9:3 .... 60, 531	12:9f. 261	1:16-17 265
9:4-5 158	12:10 367-368	1:18 .... 166-167, 290,
9:5 .... 61, 64, 139, 327,	12:12 .... 226, 346, 622	401, 556
642	12:13 371	1:18-20 153
9:6 .... 142, 144	12:16 .... 306, 377	1:19 .... 73, 368
9:6-7 275	12:17-18 193	1:19ff. 574
9:6-9 142	12:18 .... 110, 195, 266,	1:20 .... 106, 346, 448
9:7 .... 105, 355, 393	378	1:21 .... 159, 318
9:8 323	12:19 373	1:22 .... 387, 596

1:22-24 223
1:24 258-259
1:25 346
1:26-28 335
1:29-30 63
1:30 .... 163, 258, 313, 339, 360-361, 449
1:31 .... 209, 215
2:2 .... 152, 167, 214, 266, 574
2:6 362
2:9-10 ....: 289
2:10 .... 65, 362, 381
2:12 90
2:13 375
2:14 .... 106, 206, 516, 586
3 491
3:1-3 281
3:5 ....327, 379
3:10 81
3:10-11 345
3:11 .... 86, 167, 218, 402, 455, 465, 517
3:12 ....384, 629
3:16 .... 131, 185, 189, 246, 312, 319, 350, 352, 368, 380, 394, 403, 420, 564
3:16-17 576
3:17 ....337, 350
3:18-19 307
3:19 ....335, 368
3:22-23 360
3:23 ....366, 584
4 ....491, 532
4:1 81
4:5 533
4:9 376
4:9-13 214
4:20 .... 178, 209, 247, 303, 422, 556
5 .... 301, 581, 585
5:1-5 249
5:3 370
5:3-5 ....245, 369
5:4-5 ....249, 601
5:5 .... 246, 600, 604
5:6 .....84, 219, 246, 369,

396, 540, 581, 599, 602, 614
5:6-7 338
5:7 ...124, 130-131, 160, 329
5:7-8 130
5:9-10 ...... 246, 600, 603
5:9-13 178
5:10 ....368-369, 374, 580
5:10-11 246
5:11 .... 238, 249, 585, 602
5:13 597
5:21 162
5:22 464
6 458
6:9f. 584
6:9-10 245
6:11 .... 297, 363, 402
6:15 .... 189, 555, 564
6:15-16 575
6:15-20 576
6:17 .... 149, 281, 285, 415, 596
6:18 379
6:19 .... 127, 185, 246, 312, 352, 394, 403, 420
6:20 ....189, 394
7 562
7:4 564
7:10 568
7:12 554
7:12ff. 569
7:12-13 570
7:12-16 575-576
7:14 274
7:15 478
7:17-18 568
7:19 .... 306, 372, 402, 501
7:26-27 571
7:39 .... 321, 555, 563
8:2 ....290, 574
8:4 62
8:5 60
8:6 ....62, 84
8:9 214

9:14 211
9:19 394
9:27 209
10 ....518, 582
10:1 ....266, 477
10:3-5 .... 98, 170
10:4 ...97, 101, 118, 141, 169, 328-329
10:7 .... 84, 330
10:8 ....331, 583
10:10 ....332, 478
10:13 529
10:14 .... 71, 96, 174, 178, 263, 379
10:14-23 184
10:16 ...... 100, 113, 118, 121, 129, 184, 219, 301, 338
10:16-17 122
10:17 ....131, 366
10:18 122
10:20-21 174
10:21 ....117, 377
10:32 394
10:33 228
11:17-20 574
11:18-19 322
11:19 100
11:22 219
11:23-24 184
11:23-25 .... 103, 222
11:23-26 338
11:24 112-113
11:25 .... 113, 125, 366
11:26 113
11:27 116
11:28 129
11:29 117
11:31f. 626
12 518
12:3 ..... 65, 90, 100, 127, 203, 351
12:4 .... 65, 363, 413
12:4-7 219
12:4-11 229
12:6 62
12:8 203
12:11 ....100, 363
12:12 .... 103, 131, 153, 240, 407, 466

12:12-13 575
12:13 ...... 65, 78, 99-100,
    121, 123, 127, 219
12:13a 220
12:13 .... 266, 274, 595-
    596
12:27 .... 246, 274, 285
12:29 225
13 480
13:1-2 480
13:2 603
13:6 192
13:9-10 289
13:10 348
13:12 .... 263, 289, 382
13:13 .... 358, 371
14:20 .... 299, 452
14:33 .... 241, 378
15:3-4 82
15:4 .... 148, 324
15:4-5 ...... 126, 140-141,
    143
15:20 146
15:21 .... 258, 320, 353
15:21-22 161-162
15:24-27 329
15:25 362
15:25-26 320
15:28 .... 146, 169, 286
15:33 538
15:41 319
15:43 .... 146, 386, 415
15:45 321
15:45-47 143
15:47 .... 64, 137, 146,
    148, 161, 640
15:49 626
15:49-50 .... 333, 338
15:51 66
15:53 408
15:54 .... 320, 336
15:57 142
16:15 99

2 Corinthians
1:2 .... 383, 542
1:3 .... 196, 236, 252,
    398, 619, 622
1:3f. 630

1:4 624
1:11 620
1:12 623
1:21 102
1:21f. 263
1:22 .... 95, 195, 285
2:8 249
2:11 579
2:15-16 81
2:16 142
2:17 204
3:2-3 291
3:3 .... 125, 272
3:6 327
3:7 317
3:7-8 268
3:7-9 278
3:15-17 345
3:16 359
3:18 ..... 80, 163, 295, 393
4 518
4:2 204
4:3-4 200
4:4 .... 136, 157, 163,
    289, 294, 319, 358,
    361, 621, 623
4:6 169
4:11 241
4:13 .... 174, 268, 607
4:16 388
4:18 .... 239, 365
5:1 ..... 146, 327-328, 338
5:5 .... 102, 260
5:10 .... 66, 538, 557
5:15 .... 403, 644
5:15-19 139
5:16 .... 204, 310, 498
5:16-17 149
5:17 .... 293, 316, 318,
    351, 363, 378
5:19 .... 68, 163, 336
5:20 204
5:21 ..... 64, 144, 269, 362
6 478
6:1 .... 256, 644
6:2 380
6:4 373
6:8 346
6:14 178

6:14ff. 562
6:14-15 217
6:14-16 .... 342, 452
6:14-18 .... 185, 539
6:15 .... 71, 117
6:16 .... 82, 176, 185,
    189, 222, 246, 319,
    337, 350, 380
6:16-17 394
6:17 .... 175, 179, 189,
    343-344, 622
6:18 .... 420, 620
7:1 404
7:8-10 551
7:9-11 249
7:11 130
8:9 .... 161, 386
8:9-10 371
8:14 371
8:15 371
10 .... 493, 516
10:3 517
10:4 339
10:13 178
10:17 209
11:2 .... 154, 378
11:3 .... 395, 493
11:4-7 340
11:12-16 400
11:13 175
11:13-14 201
11:14 .... 199, 293, 400
11:14-15 226
11:29 483
12:2 .... 361, 421
12:7-9 279
13:1 580
13:14 .... 175, 252, 262

Galatians
1:3 524
1:4 .... 136, 140, 161,
    171, 178, 240, 359,
    362, 408
1:4f. 255
1:4-5 152
1:6 514
1:8 .... 73, 402, 416, 455
1:8-9 .... 167, 202, 234

1:9 .... 224, 379	4:26 .... 222, 262, 378	1:8-9 318
1:10 .... 71, 184, 194	4:26-27 323	1:10 .... 163, 194
2 479	4:27 356	1:11-12 325
2:8 .... 327, 335	5 458	1:11-13 189
2:11-12 183	5:4 180	1:13 .... 65, 102, 175
2:14 284	5:6 ... 70, 76, 80, 89, 306,	1:14 .... 363, 623
2:16 .... 342, 359	402, 417	1:19 298
2:20 530	5:9 .... 246, 614	1:20 .... 117, 323
3 .... 502, 537, 558	5:11 183	1:20-21 327
3:1 514	5:13 394	1:20-22 64
3:5 .... 69, 165, 338	5:16ff. 562	1:21 414
3:6 .... 221, 260, 466	5:17 279	1:22 .... 272, 341, 350,
3:6-7 142	5:19 243	352, 378
3:7 607	5:19ff. 602	1:22ff. 564
3:8 141-142	5:19-21 245	1:22-23 .... 129, 274
3:8-9 142	5:21 246	1:23 285
3:9 ... 195, 276, 326, 418	5:22 367	2 483
3:10 137	5:22-23 209	2:1 .... 252, 358
3:11 .... 87, 309	5:24 250	2:1-2 .... 68, 339
3:13 ..... 68, 93, 162, 272,	6:2 .... 123, 370-371	2:2 ..... 96, 182, 338, 352,
362, 366, 630	6:2ff. 262	456
3:14-15 501	6:3 243	2:3 68
3:15 128	6:4 365	2:3-9 164
3:16 .... 275-276, 305,	6:5ff. 80	2:4 .... 68, 70, 82, 258,
328, 356	6:7ff. 562	383
3:19 288	6:8 365	2:4-5 .... 69, 136, 180
3:20 224	6:8-10 371	2:4-6 195
3:22 .... 284, 413	6:13 327	2:4-7 .... 68, 298, 313
3:24 419	6:14 .... 310, 405	2:4-9 70
3:26 .... 76, 144, 296, 322	6:15 ..... 76, 79, 105, 189,	2:5 417
3:27 .... 78, 163, 364	293, 305, 310, 320,	2:6 .... 164, 258
3:28 .... 127, 274, 325,	363, 402	2:7 .... 77, 91, 135, 258,
377	6:16 .... 193, 306, 367,	338, 408
3:28-29 143	373	2:8 .... 89, 417
3:29 .... 91, 105, 355	6:18 421	2:8-10 70
4 491		2:11 .... 305, 355
4:4 .... 139, 353, 362	**Ephesians**	2:12 377
4:5 367	1 .... 458, 483	2:12-14 274
4:6 ... 140, 145, 322, 596	1:3 .... 146, 322, 383,	2:13 ..... 64, 69, 102, 171,
4:7 .... 325, 357	418, 423	250, 266, 328, 339,
4:8 514	1:3-4 240	359, 361, 419
4:19 327	1:3-5 69	2:13-14 194
4:21 .... 483, 574	1:3-6 312	2:13-16 278
4:22 .... 393, 408	1:4 .... 297, 314, 367,	2:14 .... 323, 641
4:22-26 142	398, 403, 419	2:15 334
4:23 105	1:5 .... 82, 359, 421	2:16 .... 160, 408
4:24-26 323	1:5-8 69	2:18 258
4:24-30 277	1:7 .... 105, 136, 180,	2:19 81
4:25 320	338, 342, 366	2:19-20 ...... 71, 195, 218,
		345

2:20 .... 109, 379, 423	5:1ff. 256	1:6 .... 252, 298, 412
3 525	5:1 604	1:21 629
3:5 319	5:2 .... 136, 140, 148,	1:27 .... 372, 421
3:6 352	269, 272, 324, 416	1:29 386
3:7 327	5:3ff. 584	2:1-5 483
3:8-10 318	5:4ff. 562	2:3 367
3:9 638	5:5 .... 243, 245-246,	2:4 556
3:14 387	364	2:5 310-311
3:14-15 62-63	5:5-6 562	2:5ff. 258
3:14-16 .... 293, 327	5:6 415	2:5-6 136
3:15 408	5:7-9 175	2:5-7 .... 63-64, 299
3:16 .... 169, 348	5:8 .... 256, 379	2:5-8 .... 139, 146, 335
3:17 417	5:11 .... 178, 183	2:6 ..... 63, 362, 386, 414
4 .... 480, 504, 525	5:12 231	2:6-7 147
4:1 .... 402, 421	5:14 82	2:6-8 640
4:1-3 .... 193, 421	5:14-16 338	2:7 161
4:1-6 481	5:15 452	2:8 324
4:1-16 486	5:16 226	2:9 .... 318, 327, 414
4:2 408	5:17-20 340	2:9-11 159
4:2-3 105	5:19 345	2:10 .... 64, 414
4:3 .... 195, 241, 263,	5:20 337	2:13 .... 298, 412
377-378, 421, 425,	5:21-33 574	2:14-16 222
530	5:22-23 141	2:15 379
4:4 .... 110, 195, 220,	5:23 .... 121, 378, 601	3:3 102
246, 274, 285	5:23ff. 564	3:7 402
4:4-5 518	5:25-26 220	3:7-9 311
4:5 .... 84, 110, 607	5:26 ... 78, 220, 246-247,	3:10 128
4:6 62-63	299, 373, 401	3:10-11 312
4:7 220	5:26-27 155	3:11 348
4:8 335	5:27 595	3:12-14 312
4:9-14 338	5:29-30 80	3:17 228
4:11-13 .... 220, 487	5:30 .... 118, 123, 149,	3:17-19 446
4:13-15 282	220, 246, 321, 325	3:18 206
4:15 .... 118, 272, 290,	5:31 320	3:18-19 422
361	6:6 459	3:20 .... 319, 365, 408
4:16 .... 153, 266	6:10 405	3:21 .... 146, 320, 382,
4:17-24 515	6:10-20 279	626
4:18 97	6:11 364	4 .... 482, 516
4:21 317	6:11-17 346	4:7 ... 195, 241, 378, 530
4:22-24 .... 295, 299	6:13 339	4:8 541
4:23 366	6:13-17 341	4:9 640
4:23-24 321	6:13-18 516	
4:24 ...... 78-80, 282, 402	6:14 130	**Colossians**
4:29-30 233	6:19 365	1 .... 458, 483
4:30 ... 95, 102, 195, 234,		1:3 .... 401, 407
259, 285, 360, 418,	**Philippians**	1:3-4 255
596	1 477	1:4-5 69
4:31 482	1:1 486	1:6 .... 217, 228, 396
5 .... 461, 504, 518	1:5 .... 152, 314	1:9 .... 367, 404

1:9-13 525
1:12 393
1:12-13 82
1:13 .... 140, 196, 295,
            334
1:13-14 342
1:14 .... 105, 220, 348,
            596
1:15 .... 63, 135-136,
      144, 157, 163, 289,
      294, 299, 319, 324,
      358, 361, 457, 638
1:15-16 155
1:16 .... 159, 327, 638
1:16-17 158
1:17 .... 119, 136, 140,
            159, 329, 352
1:18 272
1:19 .... 158, 166, 194,
            317, 356, 416, 457
1:20 .... 68, 102, 163,
      171, 194, 353-354,
            361, 641
1:21ff. 562
1:21-23 313
1:22 ..... 64, 247, 252, 255
1:23 237
1:27 .... 135, 233
1:28 357
2 .... 500, 503
2:2 .... 317, 416
2:3 ...... 83, 158-159, 266,
            318, 605
2:5 478
2:6 .... 250-251, 408, 479
2:8 .... 479, 494
2:9 .... 159, 166, 351,
            356, 416, 457, 641
2:10 .... 329, 501
2:10-13 75
2:11 .... 101-102, 105,
      246, 268, 328, 419
2:11-12 75
2:12 ...... 81, 87, 219, 298,
            328, 460
2:13 .... 68, 126
2:13-14 336
2:14 .... 64, 92, 190, 258
2:14-15 97

2:15 250
2:16 .... 183, 190, 268
2:18 400
3 480
3:1 ..... 88, 119, 126, 239,
      260, 330, 341, 378
3:2 .... 365, 403
3:3 407
3:5 .... 282, 366-367, 500
3:9 303
3:9-10 299
3:10 ..... 78-80, 295, 321,
            403
3:12 .... 373, 482
3:12-13 368
3:14 .... 261, 504
3:15 .... 195, 241, 377,
            425, 477, 530
3:16 .... 337, 340, 345

1 Thessalonians
1:1 555
1:3 135
1:5 479
1:9 399
1:9-10 250
1:10 ...... 60-61, 190, 338
2 541
2:1 386
2:3-4 204
2:5-8 206
4 503
4:3ff. 563
4:9 535
4:15 66
4:17 348
5:5-7 230
5:10 645
5:12-13 236
5:14 .... 368-370, 374
5:19 49
5:21-22 189
5:22 .... 181, 189-190,
            263
5:23 .... 400, 408

2 Thessalonians
1:3 .... 255, 412
1:4 238

1:5-8 239
1:7 526
1:8-10 348
1:11 .... 255, 370
2:3 .... 176, 321, 341-342
2:4 .... 188, 492, 499
2:8 448
2:9 .... 328, 350
2:9-10 225
2:9-11 252
2:13 .... 121, 135, 146,
      152, 220, 240, 314,
      384, 398, 492, 517,
            555
3 513
3:6 .... 238, 246, 249,
      301, 581-582, 600,
      602-603, 606
3:14 .... 246, 533, 581
3:14-15 600
3:15 .... 603, 606

1 Timothy
1 .... 466, 558
1:1 135
1:5 .... 44, 70, 82, 191,
            501
1:5-7 191
1:15 361
1:17 .... 62, 201, 266, 292
1:20 521
2f. 258
2:3 359
2:4 232
2:5 .... 62, 64, 102, 110,
      136, 148, 258, 353,
            359
2:6 .... 60, 93
2:8 .... 345, 364
3 .... 178, 507, 525
3:1-7 225
3:1-12 218
3:2 .... 363, 411
3:8 339
3:14 .... 350, 484
3:14-15 326
3:15 337
3:16 .... 134, 139, 147,
      158, 161, 362, 463

Scripture Index / 675

4:1 .... 152, 198, 341-342, 412, 461
4:14 .... 202, 486
4:16 210
5:20 534
6:3 532
6:3ff. 580
6:14 334
6:15-16 288
6:16 .... 314, 361
6:17-19 371

2 Timothy
1:12 .... 262, 526
1:15 514
2:1 370
2:2 409
2:12 .... 374, 376, 384
2:15 .... 236, 485
2:16-17 524
2:17 521
2:19 519
2:21 .... 69, 593
2:24-26 59
2:25 574
2:26 96
3 .... 461, 516, 527
3:1 .... 152, 198, 412
3:2 620
3:5 580
3:6 369
3:8 .... 225, 406
3:8-9 447
3:12 .... 374, 423
3:12-13 347
3:15 600
3:16 .... 61, 78
3:17 561
4:3 .... 213, 330, 532
4:5 409
4:6-8 630
4:8 .... 172, 262, 365
4:14 521
4:18 135

Titus
1 507
1:5 .... 202, 363, 486
1:5-9 225

1:9 204
1:10-13 322
1:12 538
1:15-16 70
1:16 322
2:11 .... 93, 270, 307, 384, 455
2:12 403
2:13 .... 172, 240, 357, 359
2:14 .... 140, 297, 373
3:2 580
3:4 525
3:4-5 .... 148, 270, 293
3:4-6 398
3:4-7 314
3:4-8 79
3:5 .... 79-80, 95, 164, 246, 296, 299, 303, 366, 456
3:5-6 97
3:5-7 296
3:6 363
3:6-8 407
3:7 247
3:9 370
3:10 .... 369, 374-375, 378, 512, 528, 600
3:10-11 .... 332, 524

Hebrews
1 .... 39, 147, 457
1:1-2 217
1:1-12 136
1:2 .... 135, 139, 147, 159, 166, 273
1:2-3 63
1:3 ..... 63, 119, 135-136, 157-158, 163, 166, 289, 294, 311, 319, 322-324, 358, 361-362, 379, 386, 414, 416, 457, 638
1:5 .... 157, 348
1:5-8 329
1:6 .... 64, 158-159, 414
1:7 351
1:8 ..... 64, 140-141, 275, 323, 336-337, 643

1:8-10 159
1:9 ... 272, 340, 365, 566
1:9-12 571
1:10 159
1:13 .... 119, 132
1:14 351
2:1 244
2:2 .... 595, 597
2:2-4 .... 171, 245
2:3 357
2:8 335-336
2:8-9 336
2:8-10 334
2:9 .... 97, 323
2:11 .... 144, 258
2:12 144
2:12-13 325
2:13 .... 81, 271
2:14 .... 119, 144-146, 190, 258, 320, 353, 392
2:15 .... 334, 354, 359, 361
2:17 .... 64, 131, 141, 364
3:1 ..... 64, 246, 337, 402, 420
3:1-15 515
3:5-6 .... 205, 218
3:6 185
3:7 421
3:12-14 251
3:13 619
3:14 .... 69, 76, 78, 251, 294, 303, 310-311, 378, 407
3:15 400
3:17-19 333
3:18 328
4 480
4:1-4 333
4:2-3 98
4:5 333
4:9 ... 326, 328, 334, 338
4:11 404
4:12 .... 102, 208, 339, 341, 346
4:12-13 231
4:13 350
4:15 350

5:1 ..... 68, 131, 141, 258, 272, 416
5:1-6 272
5:1-10 285
5:2 ..... 64, 119, 146, 160, 258, 299
5:3 .... 102, 360, 415
5:3-4 337
5:4 201-202
5:5 103
5:5-7 65
5:7 .... 364, 478
5:7-8 565
5:9-10 269
5:12 357
5:14 452
6:3 .... 345, 366
6:5f. 596
6:5-6 169
6:6 .... 117, 332
6:7 402
6:20 .... 64, 272, 285
7 333
7:1 355
7:1-3 .... 139, 323
7:3 .... 65, 140
7:11 .... 108, 224
7:14 .... 140, 144
7:16 140
7:17 269
7:18 .... 269, 272
7:22 416
7:26 269
8 333
8:1 .... 141, 258, 272, 364, 416
8:1-2 337
8:2 357
8:4ff. 561
8:5 .... 190, 264
8:6 .... 330, 333
8:7 323
8:8-12 125
8:9 333
8:10 .... 272, 619
9:1 273
9:4 272
9:5 .... 64, 156
9:6 .... 267, 269

9:6-7 275
9:7 269
9:9-10 330
9:11 .... 68-69, 416
9:11-12 131
9:12 .... 106, 118, 272, 384, 419
9:13 .... 122, 126, 224
9:13-14 224
9:14 .... 103, 269
9:24 119
10 39
10:1 .... 190, 266, 268, 330, 333
10:1ff. 561
10:1-10 337
10:5 .... 122, 137, 160, 633
10:9 323
10:10 .... 118, 162
10:11 ...... 364, 384, 416-417
10:12 323
10:12-14 119
10:14 .... 136, 416
10:16 290
10:19 ...... 270, 338, 357
10:22 .... 329, 364
10:25 619
10:26 .... 117, 596
10:27-28 169
10:29 .... 169, 332
10:31 .... 60, 390
10:36 405
10:38 .... 87, 309
11 .... 69, 191, 465, 607
11:1 .... 88, 102, 260, 298, 453, 607
11:1-3 89
11:6 ..... 62, 87, 160, 256, 258, 300, 453
11:8-10 261
11:9 310
11:10 .... 310, 327-328, 345, 365, 378
11:11 88
11:16 310
11:17 454
11:24-26 311

11:25 402
11:27 260
11:35 387
12 515
12:1 .... 263, 279, 328, 346, 367, 387
12:2 .... 97, 163, 222, 300, 333-334, 378, 419, 629
12:5 388
12:6 .... 423, 620, 622
12:7 388
12:11 388
12:12 364
12:14 .... 195, 378, 541
12:14-15 492
12:14-17 567
12:15 .... 476, 644
12:16 .... 401, 559
12:18 .... 358, 558
12:19 359
12:22 ...... 222, 338, 347, 499, 534, 622-623
12:22-24 .... 196, 270, 297, 352
12:23 352
12:24 .... 94, 97, 106, 110, 125, 224
12:25 .... 171, 245, 329
12:28 263
12:29 169
13:3 620
13:6 623
13:7 423
13:8 456
13:14 338
13:15 338
13:21 196

James
1 460
1:5 .... 63, 156
1:10 390
1:17 296, 363, 413, 452, 555
1:17-18 .... 95, 295
1:18 ..... 63, 99, 282, 296, 299, 314, 321, 338, 357-358, 360-361

Scripture Index / 677

1:21 .... 207, 224, 262, 309-310	1:18 419	3:9 322
1:27 .... 179, 193	1:18ff. 564	3:10 567
2:5 102	1:18-19 .... 136, 270, 297	3:12 625
2:10 597	1:19 ..... 68, 77, 106, 124, 145, 160, 246, 328-329, 364, 420	3:15 59
2:12 60		3:18 .... 136, 147-148, 162, 324
2:13 60	1:20 414	3:20 .... 81, 272, 322
2:15 193	1:21-22 310	3:21 ..... 79, 82, 101, 418, 420, 422
2:17 70	1:22 .... 193, 504	
2:19 149	1:23 ..... 79, 95, 137, 141-142, 145, 149, 221, 281, 295-296, 299, 310, 321, 325, 345, 357-358, 360-361, 454	3:21-22 80
2:23 221		3:22 .... 119, 126, 159
3:2 .... 284, 352		4:1 335
3:9 .... 294, 320		4:3 .... 384, 622
3:13 .... 209, 525		4:4 .... 182, 222
3:13-18 .... 422, 481		4:5 334
3:16 476	1:25 ..... 73, 95, 115, 290-291	4:8 261
3:17 352		4:10-11 220
4:1 .... 281, 480	2 525	4:11 .... 204, 485
4:4 ..... 71, 189, 243, 400, 459	2:1 477	4:13 405
	2:1-3 282	4:14 .... 376, 623
4:6 78	2:2 .... 170, 452	4:18 87
4:7 .... 352, 367	2:4-5 345	4:19 630
4:7-8 480	2:5 .... 272, 345, 365	5:1 379
4:10 367-368	2:6 329	5:1-4 210
4:12 .... 60, 603	2:6-8 153	5:2 .... 203, 212, 241
5:10 263	2:8 200	5:2-4 226
5:14 241	2:9 .... 141, 274, 297, 325, 344, 359, 373, 379, 384, 477, 525, 598, 620	5:4 ... 236, 247, 336, 631
5:14-15 86		5:5 .... 283, 367
5:19 370-371		5:6 ...... 78, 279, 359, 368
		5:8 352
1 Peter	2:10 407	5:8-9 335
1 .... 477, 527	2:11 .... 378, 492	5:10 .... 236, 240, 263, 293, 396, 466, 526, 542
1:1 378	2:11ff. 562	
1:2 ... 80, 94, 97-98, 190, 220, 297, 338, 492	2:11-12 338	
	2:12 372	12: 373, 402
1:3 .... 102, 263	2:13 110	12:32 365
1:3-5 492	2:15 393	
1:4 .... 69, 338	2:20-21 60	**2 Peter**
1:5 .... 347, 357	2:21 .... 64, 71, 82, 172, 240, 310, 324, 622, 640	1:1 255
1:9 381		1:2 135
1:10 517		1:4 .... 69, 79, 145-146, 161, 258, 280, 282, 285, 294, 310, 378, 384, 403, 408-409, 515
1:11 381	2:24 .... 124, 146, 162, 250, 256, 335-336, 362, 384	
1:12 163		
1:13 .... 60, 130, 307		
1:13-15 244	2:25 ... 64, 154, 236, 373, 417, 454, 531, 609	
1:13-16 422		1:7 .... 221, 261
1:14 453	3 479-480	1:9 .... 480, 499, 621
1:15 191	3:4 282	1:12 .... 383, 396
1:16 .... 312, 403	3:8 504	1:17 166

1:19 319	2:3 .... 165, 465	4:10 .... 164-165, 243, 257, 384
1:20 267	2:3-6 .... 166, 242	4:13 .... 127, 294, 418
1:20-21 135	2:4 504	4:14 501
1:21 .... 166, 201, 215, 259	2:6 209	4:16 ..... 63, 70, 191, 372, 607
2 .... 461, 587	2:11 .... 256, 372, 480	4:19 70
2:1 .... 152, 198, 412	2:14 .... 280, 452	4:21 .... 165, 504
2:4ff. 257	2:15 71	5 .... 465, 558
2:4 353	2:17 324	5:1 ..... 64, 139, 142, 145, 165, 221, 281, 298, 321, 413, 417, 465
2:4-6 256	2:18 .... 176, 331, 342, 461	
2:4-10 571	2:18-19 .... 322, 493	5:2 ... 193, 261, 409, 504
2:6 324	2:20 630	5:3 ... 165, 191, 265, 603
2:9 339	2:20-27 247	5:4 .... 190, 250, 275, 280, 303, 330, 341, 354, 367, 630
2:15 .... 211, 625	2:22 362	
2:16 331	2:24 252	
2:17 395	2:24-25 494	5:4-5 .... 296, 329
2:17-22 251	2:27 .... 340, 365	5:6ff. 260
2:18-19 459	2:29 .... 79, 191, 310, 363	5:6-8 .... 80, 328
2:20 .... 459, 537	3:1 .... 142, 145-146, 354, 384, 407	5:8 362
2:22 401	3:1f. 626	5:10 .... 258, 351
3 512	3:2 .... 289, 333	5:10-12 160
3:3 412	3:3 .... 69, 413	5:11 166
3:9 .... 232, 541	3:4 243	5:16 .... 86, 262, 371
3:10 291	3:4-10 242	5:18 312
3:13 319	3:5 .... 68, 161-162, 320	5:19 .... 195, 321
3:17f. 609	3:6 .... 209, 464	5:20 .... 140, 158, 641, 645
3:18 .... 290, 402	3:7 403	
	3:7-9 566	
1 John	3:8 564	**2 John**
1 .... 527, 585	3:9 .... 137, 149, 284, 296, 312-313, 454	:2 465
1:1 .... 135-136, 140, 143, 147, 149, 272, 323, 499	3:12 .... 235, 353	:3 350
	3:14 256	:7 246
1:1-2 .... 125, 134, 137, 157	3:15 480	:9 ... 206, 252, 301, 401, 493
1:1-3 415	3:16 .... 193, 420	
1:2 361	3:16-18 371	:10 .... 369-370, 602
1:3 246	3:18 .... 479, 582, 603	:10f. 580-582
1:5 .... 73, 413	3:20 256	:10-11 600
1:5-7 .... 242, 422	3:23 159	:11 .... 246, 368
1:6 243	4:1 .... 216, 456	
1:7 367	4:2 .... 139, 146	**3 John**
1:8-10 ...... 243, 284, 313	4:2-5 148	:9 .... 322, 521
1:12 413	4:5-6 217	:9-10 514
2 .... 465, 558	4:7 .... 409, 479	
2:1 .... 64, 258, 285, 327, 345, 361, 416	4:7-8 191	**Jude**
	4:8 .... 262, 372	:4 .... 152, 198
2:2 .... 101, 243, 332, 335, 416, 642	4:9 .... 102, 135, 137, 146, 164, 378	:11 331
		:12 413

Scripture Index / 679

:17-21 494	5:13-14 314	17:6 .... 239, 621
:18 412	6:11 239	18:3 .... 215, 239, 399, 621
Revelation	7:3 250	
1 492	7:3-8 239	18:4 .... 185, 343-344, 622
1:3 348	7:9-10 297	
1:5 ... 106, 246, 366-367, 384, 401, 564	7:9-17 240	18:4-5 188
	7:13 386	18:5 343-344
1:5-6 .... 136, 313	7:14 .... 354, 424	18:7-8 .... 188, 215
1:6 .... 141, 271	7:14-17 .... 168, 287	18:9 239
1:8 .... 300, 324, 348	7:15-17 628	18:24 239
1:9 .... 249, 424	9:2 456	19 .... 518, 527
1:17 .... 140, 157, 161, 363, 458	9:11 516	19:7 595
	11 280	19:7-8 220
1:18 148	11:8 .... 324, 328	19:8 .... 247, 364
2 .... 514, 527	12 527	19:9 343
2:3 .... 421, 486	12:1-2 319	19:13 .... 159, 414
2:7 .... 280, 321, 330, 376, 391, 619	12:4 319	19:16 155
	12:9-11 280	20:3 404
2:9 354	12:10 319	20:4 343
2:10-11 333	12:10-11 630	20:6 252
2:14 .... 406, 625	12:11 354	21 280
2:17 391	13:5 240	21:1 376
2:18-23 598	13:6-9 187	21:2 .... 220, 222, 246, 262, 377, 595
2:20 .... 215, 321, 395, 625	13:8 641	
	13:11-18 187	21:2-3 155
2:26 392	14:1 343	21:7 343
3 527	14:1-5 297	21:8 .... 185, 381, 391, 596
3:1-6 514	14:2-5 282	
3:4-5 333	14:4 334	21:9-11 155
3:5 392	14:4-5 338	21:21 404
3:6 376	14:9-12 188	21:22 .... 380, 398
3:11 425	14:13 334	21:23 290-291
3:12 .... 280, 392	14:19 391	21:26 381
3:14 .... 299, 323	15:2 343	21:27 595
3:14-22 514	16:8-9 324	22 527
3:15 421	17 280	22:1 .... 163, 357, 399, 404
3:17 .... 232, 302, 564	17:1 185	
3:18 .... 241, 302-303	17:1-4 321	22:5 .... 377, 425
3:20-21 159	17:2 239	22:9 351
3:21 392	17:3 343	22:10 541
4:1 627	17:3-6 188	22:11 ...... 287, 367, 403, 462
4:8 312	17:4 239	
5:5 .... 620, 639	17:5 239	22:13 .... 300, 363
5:6 145		22:14 382
5:8 393		22:15 .... 245, 582, 596
5:9 .... 297, 623		22:16 .... 317, 336, 357, 639

Name and Place Index

A

Aaron, 86, 122, 156, 184, 201-202, 244, 270-272, 331, 333, 337, 355, 364, 369, 405, 448, 478, 481, 489, 502, 519, 572, 596, 606
Abel, 41, 196, 235, 310, 321, 352-354, 374, 387, 436
Abimelech, 355
Abiram, 202, 331, 369, 435
Abraham, 91, 101-102, 104-105, 108, 139, 141-144, 157, 164, 191, 195, 197, 221, 223, 257, 260, 275-277, 288, 303, 305, 310, 319-320, 323-328, 345, 355-356, 378, 385, 391, 393, 418-419, 428, 434, 436, 453, 456, 461-462, 466, 491, 500, 595, 607, 621, 626-628, 639
Absalom, 249, 511, 546
Acquoy, J. G. R., 637, 646
Adam, 39, 41, 52, 75-77, 80, 92-93, 136-138, 140-141, 144, 146-148, 160-162, 164, 195, 257, 282, 284, 294, 299, 303, 308, 319-322, 352-354, 415-416, 418, 420, 436, 466, 553, 558, 560, 595-596, 626, 640, 642
Adriaentgen, Jochems wijf, 30, 618, 635
Agricola, Rudolf, 19
Ahab, 235
Aken, Gillis van, 26-28, 577, 611
Alenson, Hans Arentsz, 29, 520
Amalek (Amalakites), 179, 330, 478, 488, 508, 572, 597
Amish, 237
Amsterdam, 22-24, 30-31, 51, 57-58, 475, 610, 617, 635, 647-651
Ananias, 74, 304, 597
Anna, 355
Annas, 335, 374, 621

Anthonius, 632-634
Anthony Dad, 631
Anthony of Cologne, 631-632
Antioch, 485-486
Antiochus IV, Epiphanes, 182, 186, 234, 347, 404
Antwerp, 14, 618-619, 631
Apocrypha, 14, 38, 173-174, 197
Appingedam, 24-25, 32, 510, 522, 529, 543
Arent Dad, 631
Aristotle, 20

B

Babylon, 185, 188-189, 201, 215, 236, 239, 250, 256, 321, 342-344, 348, 350, 391, 399, 403-404, 423, 621
Bachmann, Theodore E., 111, 647
Bainton, Roland H., 37, 197, 647
Barentszn, van Zutphen, Otto, 30
Barnabas, 202-203, 284, 374, 485-486
Basel, 26, 445
Batenburg, Jan van, 25
Beachy, Alvin J., 12, 57, 647, 701
Benjamin, 186, 344-345
Bethlehem, 643-644
Biestkens, Nicolaes, 14, 174, 237
Blaupot ten Cate, S., 21, 27, 44-46, 51, 57, 637, 646-647
Blesdijk, Nikolaas Meyndertsz van, 26
Boeckbinder, Bartel de, 23
Boekenoogen, Jan Gerrit, 647
Boekholtzoon, Jan, 24
Bogaert, Pieter Willems, 36, 522
Bolsward, 24, 32, 469, 520, 522, 544, 551
Bontrager, Daniel S., 14
Born, 631

Bouwens, Leenaert, 26-29, 32-34, 36, 45, 56, 446, 468, 470-471, 473, 484, 488, 520, 534-535, 551
Bracht, 632
Braght, Thieleman J. van, 647
Brons, Anna, 46, 647
Bugenhagen, Johann, 14, 174

C

Cain, 41, 235, 321, 353-354, 374, 436, 623
Caiphas, 335, 374, 621
Caleb, 332, 572
Calvin(ism), 41-42, 553, 633, 635
Calvin, John, 38
Campanus, Johannes, 446, 463, 467
Campen, Jacob van, 24, 31
Cassander, Georgius, 44, 647
Claes, Weynken, 21
Clemmer, Lake S., 15
Cleve, 27, 631
Cologne, 29-30, 52, 631-632, 635
Constantinople, 147
Coornhert, Dirk Volkertsz, 237, 446
Cornelius, C. A., 20, 44-45, 647
Cramer, Samuel, 16, 44, 46, 520, 636, 647
Crete, 202, 486
Crous, Rose, 545
Cuijper, Egbert, 521, 547-548
Cuiper, William, 23
Cyril of Alexandria, 151
Cyrus of Alexandria, 344

D

Dagon, 335
Daniel, 87, 156
Dankbaar, W. F., 647
Danzig, 30-32, 46, 55, 411, 467-468, 470, 491, 521-522, 549
Dathan, 202, 331, 369, 435
David, 130, 141, 143-144, 154-156, 159, 162, 164, 168, 190, 248-249, 275, 283, 285, 290, 308, 313, 336-337, 342-343, 348, 355, 374, 404, 424, 428, 435, 511, 518, 587, 627, 639, 643
DeLeon, Sue, 15
Delft, 24, 467

Deppermann, Klaus, 57, 648
Devil, 31, 59, 68, 70, 77, 84, 97, 111, 117, 126, 141, 149, 160, 162, 174, 177, 182, 185, 188, 190-191, 213, 223, 225, 227, 242-243, 250-251, 256, 294, 302, 308, 320, 329, 332, 336, 353-354, 367, 387, 390, 392, 400, 403, 415, 418-419, 422, 436, 454-456, 458-459, 461, 480, 564, 566, 628, 639. *See also* Satan (serpent)
Dokkum, 28, 32, 468-469, 477, 484, 535
Dosker, Henry Elias, 648
Duerksen, Rosella Reimer, 646
Dyck, Cornelius J., 12, 151, 648-649, 699

E

Ebbink, Heinrich, 27
Eleazar, 186, 389, 437, 513, 563
Elijah, 90, 186, 212, 217, 229-232, 451, 460, 462, 491, 508-509
Elizabeth, 355
Emden, 22, 25-28, 30, 32-33, 35-37, 51, 55-56, 446, 470-473, 488-489, 494, 497, 510, 520-522, 534-535, 538, 549, 551, 554, 577, 611
Emkens, Anna Heinrick, 32
Enoch, 595
Erasmus, Desiderius, 14, 19, 38, 101, 111, 579
Esau, 54, 273-277, 279, 326, 401, 407, 433, 438, 483, 559, 567
Esther, 423
Eve, 41, 77, 140-141, 257, 320-321, 352-354, 418, 436, 466, 553, 558, 560, 596
Evertsvolk, Jan, 635

F

Farley, Benjamin W., 635, 648
Fast, Heinold, 467, 648
Flanders, 30, 33, 468-469, 651
Flemish, 14, 33-38, 55, 411, 468-471, 473-474, 489-491, 495, 520-524, 533, 539, 543-544, 551, 553, 578

Franciscans, 19
Franck, Sebastian, 38, 41, 52-53, 85, 111, 173, 445-447, 454-463, 465-467, 578, 648-649, 651
Franeker, 28-29, 32-34, 55, 411, 468-470, 472, 477, 484, 497, 535
Frankfurt am Main, 635
Freerks, Jacob, 538
Freerks, Sicke, 22, 45
Friesen, P. M., 473, 475, 648
Friesland, 19-20, 23, 31-33, 36, 44-46, 55, 411, 468, 470, 472, 476, 488, 491-492, 496-498, 503, 506, 508-510, 514-515, 520, 523-525, 544-545, 548, 551, 637, 646-647
Frisian, 14, 33-38, 55, 174, 411, 468, 470-473, 488-490, 495-496, 509-511, 520-524, 527, 539, 543-544, 551, 553
Froschauer, Christoph, 14, 16, 411

G

Gerrits, Lubbert, 30, 35-36, 471-473, 488-490, 505, 510, 520-522, 534, 544, 548, 550
Gerrits, Soetjen, 646
Ghendt, Carel van, 46, 475, 577
Gideon, 505
Goch, 27, 611, 632
Goliath, 336
Gomorrah, 257, 324, 598
Govert, Jaspersz, 631-633, 635
Gravenhage, 's, 16, 646-647
Groningen, 24, 36, 45-46, 510, 522, 529, 538, 650
Grosheide, Grete, 46, 648

H

Haarlem, 23-24, 446, 467, 473, 476, 551, 579, 648-650
Haerlem, P. G., 646
Hagar, 277, 323
Ham, 322, 354, 623
Haman, 423
Hamburg, 25, 545, 632
Harder, Leland, 111, 635, 648
Harlingen, 28-30, 32-35, 55, 410, 468-472, 477, 484, 489-490, 520-521, 535, 543, 551

Harms, Geert, 35, 522, 543, 549
Hartzel, Gerald, 15
Hastenaede, Theunis van, 632
Hazlitt, William, 648
Hege, Christian, 635
Hegler, A. - Kohler, W., 467, 648
Hegler, Alfred, 467, 648
Heinsberg, 631
Herod, 229, 233, 567, 621, 644
Heubuden, 544, 551
Heyns, Joriaen, 28-29
Hildesheim, 646
Hillerbrand, Hans J., 648
Hoffman, Melchior, 21-24, 39, 44, 52-54, 57, 445
Holstein, 22
Hoop Scheffer, J. G. de, 46, 543, 551, 617, 650
Hoorn, 30, 32, 35-36, 471, 473, 489-490, 497, 510, 521-522, 543, 549-551, 618, 635, 646
Horace (Quintus Horatius Flaccus), 44, 543
Houtsagher, Pieter, 23
Hullu, J. de, 648
Hut, Hans, 237, 254

I

Imbroich, Thomas von, 52
Inquisition, 173, 472
Irenaeus of Lyon, 39
Isaac, 88-89, 102, 105, 142, 156, 164, 191, 195, 197, 260-261, 273, 275-277, 279, 288, 310, 323-326, 328, 345, 355, 378, 393, 434, 436, 462, 483, 491, 567, 626, 630, 639
Isaiah, 292
Ishmael, 105, 277, 279, 323, 393, 483

J

Jacob, 54, 164, 190, 195, 204, 233, 273-279, 287-289, 310, 323, 326-328, 337, 345, 355, 365, 378, 385, 407, 411, 433-434, 436, 462, 483, 544, 567, 606, 626-627, 643
James, 184, 486
Jans, Beatris, 32

Janssen, Henrick, 30
Janszen, Willem, 32
Japheth, 354
Jeremiah, 89, 357, 462
Jeroboam, 185-186, 208, 341-342, 405-406, 435, 489-490, 502, 518
Jerome, 12, 174, 537, 543
Jesse, 271, 336, 448
Jezebel, 208, 215, 229-232, 301, 321, 395, 406, 491, 508, 598, 625
Joachim the Sugarbaker (J. den S.), 618
Job, 87, 423, 530
John, 88-90, 93, 98, 162, 168, 187, 195, 206, 227, 239, 242-243, 247, 312-313, 330, 371, 398, 401, 422, 452, 462, 479, 486, 493, 514, 529, 564, 566, 580-581, 608, 613
John II, Count, 631
John the Baptist, 72, 74, 88-89, 154, 229, 279, 324, 361, 456, 460, 529, 567
Jonah, 148, 223
Joris, David, 24-26, 38, 41, 54-55, 173, 445
Joseph (N.T.), 136, 140, 327, 355, 569
Joseph (O.T.), 156, 278, 327, 403
Joshua, 332-333, 369, 572
Judah, 125, 140, 144, 155, 186, 201, 277, 279, 342-345, 357, 398, 405, 463, 570, 607
Julich, 631

K

Karlstadt, Andreas Bodenstein von, 22
Kawerau, Peter, 44, 57, 648
Keeney, William E., 12, 44-45, 47, 57, 151, 577, 648, 700
Keller, John S., 15
Keulen, Antonius van, 26
Keyser, Marja, 16, 51, 53, 57-58, 577, 579, 588, 592, 610, 637, 646, 649
Klaassen, Walter, 15, 617, 648-649
Kolb, A. B., 11, 16, 649

Koolman, J. ten Doornkaat, 27, 29-30, 32, 44-46, 51-58, 411, 445-446, 467, 472, 474, 490, 520, 544-545, 551, 577-578, 588, 592, 610-612, 617-618, 631, 635, 649
Korah, 202, 331, 369, 572
Krahn, Cornelius, 636, 649
Krebs, Manfred, 467, 649
Krefeld, 545
Kühler, Wilhelmus Johannes, 21, 31, 33, 36, 44, 46, 411, 488, 520, 551, 649
Kukenbieter, Joachim, 25, 44
Kuyper, Egbert, 539. *See also* Cuijper

L

Laban, 326
Landis, Ernest, 15
Laodicea, 514
Las, Virgile de, 592, 650
Latendorf, Friedrich, 649
Lazarus, 223, 391, 628
Leeuwarden, 19, 23-24, 28, 32, 44-45, 468-469, 477, 484, 535, 646-649
Lehmann, Helmut T., 16, 111, 647
Leiden, 647, 649-651
Leipzig, 636
Lemke (Lambrecht Kremer), 29, 579, 588
Levi, 323
Leyen, Laurens van der, 618
Liesveldt, Jacob van, 14
Linnich, 632
Lot, 87, 248, 322, 324, 352, 596, 625
Lübeck, 26-28
Luies, Jan, 618
Luther, Martin, 12, 16, 21-22, 37-38, 52, 84-85, 111, 174, 197, 237, 648

M

Maastricht, 631
Maatschoen, Gerardus, 44
Mander, Carel van, 578-580
Mannhardt, H. G., 31, 46, 650
Martens, Harry E., 15

Name and Place Index / 685

Martha, 166
Mary, 39, 52, 63, 65, 116, 136-138, 140, 143-144, 146-147, 149, 151, 160-161, 200, 323, 353, 355, 361, 414, 428, 528, 569, 633, 643
Matthew, 113, 136, 207, 287, 639
Matthys, Jan, 23-24
Mecklenburg, 28
Meihuizen, Hendrik W., 649-650
Melchizedek, 65, 139, 141, 156, 269, 323, 355, 416, 428
Mellink, A. F., 44-46, 635, 649-650
Millen, 631
Miller, E. W., 44, 650
Miller, Kevin, 15
Miriam, 86, 244, 565, 597
Monnikendam, 21, 522
Moses, 60-61, 86, 93, 96-98, 107-108, 126, 156, 170-171, 178, 186, 193, 201, 204, 223, 225, 233, 244-245, 249, 264, 266-270, 272, 288, 291-292, 308, 310, 316-320, 326, 328-333, 342, 344, 355-356, 358-359, 361, 364, 369, 375, 393, 402, 406, 432, 447, 478, 495, 502, 505, 512, 527, 531, 557, 559-560, 567, 569, 572, 585, 597-599, 606
Mount Sinai, 288, 358, 360-361
Mount Tabor, 361, 627
Müller, Heinrich, 237, 646
Müller, Lydia, 650
Münster, 23-25, 42, 173, 350, 467, 651

N

Naeldeman, Henrik, 28-29
Neff, Christian, 635
Nestorius, Bishop of Constantinople, 147, 151
Nicodemus, 94-95, 295, 358, 433
Nicolai, Gerardus, 45, 588, 610, 617
Noah, 80-81, 87, 101, 195, 248, 272, 309-310, 322, 354, 418-419, 434, 436, 558, 566-567, 595

O

Onesimus, 36

Ottes, Aplonij (Apollonia), 29, 520
Outerman, Jacques, 472, 474, 520-521, 543, 551
Oyer, John S., 15, 650

P

Packull, Werner O., 237, 650
Paschal (Passover) Lamb, 123-124, 129-131, 160, 329, 338, 435, 629
Passau, 637
Pastor, Adam, 26-28, 38, 41, 52, 577, 611, 617, 631-632, 635, 637
Paul, 36, 60-61, 69-71, 74-76, 78-80, 86-87, 96, 98-100, 104, 113, 116-117, 119, 121, 123, 125, 127, 129-130, 137, 139, 142, 144-145, 147, 149, 154-155, 158, 162, 164, 166-167, 170, 175, 178, 180-181, 183-185, 189, 191, 193-194, 200, 202-206, 209-210, 212-213, 216, 219, 222-223, 225, 227-229, 233, 237, 243, 245, 248, 261-262, 266, 268, 276-277, 279, 281-282, 284-286, 288, 291, 293, 295-296, 299, 304-305, 307, 309, 311-313, 318, 321-322, 327, 346, 352, 355, 361-362, 371, 373-374, 378, 388, 390, 392-394, 396, 402, 407, 412, 415, 419, 421, 449, 455, 457, 460, 462, 481, 485-487, 493, 498, 503, 514, 516, 525, 528, 531, 533, 538-539, 554, 556, 562-564, 568-570, 574-576, 580-581, 595, 599-600, 603, 607, 613, 623, 626, 629-630, 642
Pelikan, Jaroslav, 197
Peter, 53, 72, 74, 80, 82, 87, 95, 119, 145, 147, 154, 172, 182-183, 195, 200, 204, 210-212, 215, 220, 222, 244, 247-249, 251-252, 280, 282, 284, 291, 295, 304-305, 307, 316, 347, 367, 393, 395, 402, 421, 452, 459-460, 485-486, 511, 527, 537, 597, 599, 626-627
Pharaoh, 80, 96-97, 160, 288, 311, 327-328, 338, 340, 406, 495

Philip, 74, 157, 294, 457, 567
Philips, Obbe, 19, 23-25, 37, 39, 44-45, 47, 53, 57, 173, 411, 445, 544, 651
Pieters, Ebbe, 33-34, 469-471, 535, 543
Pijper, Frederik, 11, 16, 53-54, 57, 173, 446, 521, 631, 635, 647
Pipkin, H. Wayne, 15
Poettcker, Henry, 16, 650
Prussia, 30-33, 35, 468, 471-472, 489, 494, 512, 520, 536, 544-545

R
Rebecca, 273-275, 324-326, 567
Redlich, O. R., 636, 650
Rempel, John D., 650
Renix, Hoyte, 32-36, 411, 469, 472-473, 488, 490, 496-497, 505, 508, 513, 520-522, 533-534, 536, 538, 544-545, 551
Ries, Hans de, 637
Rol, Hendrik, 635
Rostock, 25, 445
Rothmann, Bernhard, 23, 54-55, 58, 350, 651
Rotterdam, 101, 646
Rupp, Gordon, 237, 650
Rutgers, Swaen, 28, 33

S
Samson, 334-335, 435
Samuel, 179, 336, 489, 572
Sapphira, 597
Sarah, 88, 91, 102, 105, 142, 277, 323, 393, 408, 466, 491, 561
Sardis, 514
Satan, 41, 68, 71, 116-118, 124, 161, 175, 190, 196, 199-201, 217, 225, 252, 279-280, 293-294, 322, 328, 330, 334-336, 338, 341, 346, 353-354, 359, 393, 400, 404, 423, 438, 449, 530, 595, 623
Saul, 179, 374, 424, 462, 489, 508, 536, 572, 587, 597
Schagen, Martin, 51, 57, 651
Scheedemaker, Jacob Jan, 28-29
Scheerder, Hans, 23

Scheurleer, D. F., 646
Schyn, Hermannus, 44, 46, 651
Serpent, 601
Seth, 310, 354
Shantz, D. H., 651
Shem, 354-355, 595
Sikken, Hans, 31, 35, 522, 549
Silas, 74, 99
Simeon, 156, 355, 628
Simon, 200
Simons, Menno, 11, 14, 16, 22, 24-31, 37-38, 44-47, 51-53, 57, 151, 237, 254, 446, 468, 488, 511, 520, 544, 554, 577, 579, 588, 592, 611-612, 631-632, 646, 648-651
Sodom, 252, 257, 274, 324, 352, 598, 625
Solomon, 143, 156, 252, 283, 307, 337, 339, 341, 343, 435, 450-451, 459, 463, 479, 507, 527-528, 536, 540, 570, 624, 639
Souder, Elvin R., 15
South Germans, 29
Speyer, Diet of, 237
Springer, Joseph, 15, 646
Stephen, 172
Strasbourg, 22-23, 29
Stupperich, Robert, 651
Sweden, 22
Swiss, 29, 579, 587, 648
Sylis, 579, 588

T
Terence (Publius Terentius Afer), 543
Teufel, Eberhard, 651
Thomas, 158, 642
Timothy, 202, 210, 225, 371, 486, 580, 600
Tinnegieter, Jeroen, 33-34, 469, 471
Titus, 78, 202, 210, 295, 487
Tobias, 186, 561
Toews, John A., 651
Troeltsch, Ernst, 237, 651
Twisck, Pieter Jansz, 618, 635

U
Utrecht, 32, 646

Uzziah, 597

V
Verduin, Leonard, 651
Verheyden, A. L. E., 635, 651
Visscher, Alle, 520
Volkertszoon, Jan, 22-23
Voolstra, Sjouke, 47, 57, 151, 651
Voordt, Cornelius van, 32
Vos, Karel, 31, 45-46, 254, 411, 488, 577, 635-636, 651
Vreden, Hendrik van, 26
Vrie, de O. H., 648
Vulgate, 12, 14, 19, 174, 350, 411, 543

W
Wackernagel, Philipp, 646
Waldeck, Franz van, 24
Waldensian, 12, 85, 111
Wassenberg, 632
Waterlanders, 29, 553
Weierhof, 545
Wenger, J. C., 651
Wentz, Abdel Ross, 111
Wessel, J. H., 651
Westerberg, Gerhard von, 635

Wijer, Matthijs, 30, 54
Wilhelm V. Count, 632
Willems, Jan, 30, 35-36, 471-473, 488-490, 497, 505, 510, 520-522, 534, 544, 548, 550
Willems, Pieter, 522
Willemsz, Willems, 32
Williams, George H., 11, 45, 237, 467, 651
Wismar, 27-28, 577
Wittenberg, 22

Y
Yoder, John Howard, 15, 111, 610, 651

Z
Zacharias, 355
Zahn, Johannes, 646
Zeman, Jarold Knox, 15
Zerubbabel, 344-345
Zijpp, Nanne van der, 473, 610, 635, 651
Zurich, 14, 51, 411, 651
Zutphen, 30, 646
Zwingli, Huldreich, 22, 44, 111, 635
Zylis (and Lemke), 29, 588

Subject Index

A

Admonition, 29, 55, 128, 152, 218-219, 255-passim, 293ff., 383-426, 476-488, 514-515, 547, 549, 578-588, 591-630

Adultery, 28, 212, 245, 249, 331, 373, 403, 586, 593, 605

Allegorical, 22, 57

Angels, 64, 136, 147, 155, 158, 163, 167, 187, 192, 196, 199, 202, 215, 236, 238-240, 244, 250, 256-257, 280, 288-289, 293, 320, 326, 329, 331, 348, 351-352, 375, 377, 379-380, 389-391, 400, 402-403, 407, 414, 417, 424, 436, 455, 457, 493, 499, 517, 526-527, 535, 571, 623, 625, 628-629, 643

Antichrist, 84, 109, 148, 176, 188, 225, 252, 321-322, 325, 341-343, 375, 399, 412, 439, 455, 458, 461, 493, 504, 595, 622

Apocrypha, 14, 38, 173-174, 197, 350

Apostasy, 53, 117, 342-343, 352, 408, 435-436, 534, 570-572, 580, 592

Apostles, 72-75-passim, 125-126, 128-129, 136, 176-177, 195, 198-passim, 245, 259, 268, 282-284, 291-292, 296, 301, 318-319, 322ff., 359, 361-364, 366, 368-369, 371, 373-375, 378-380, 395, 413, 421-423, 458, 460-461, 463, 477, 480-481, 486-487, 512, 515, 517, 563, 575, 581-582, 584, 586, 594-596, 598, 600-604, 606, 608-609, 616, 622

Apostolic church, 71, 83, 173, 175, 195, 218, 337, 340, 455, 460-461, 573, 609

Arbitration, 35, 471

Atonement, 68-71, 293-315, 565

Authorities, 158, 409, 482, 537, 560

Authority, 13, 33, 174, 187, 205, 215, 303, 330, 339, 346, 375, 468, 470, 473, 484, 498, 516, 547, 549, 564, 584, 640

Avoidance, 26, 29, 54, 376, 429, 579-580, 582, 586-587, 592-593, 605, 611-617

B

Ban(ning), 26-30, 33-34, 36, 42, 53-54, 173, 219-220, 238-254, 301, 345, 369, 376, 385, 387, 395-396, 446, 469-470, 473-474, 497, 502, 508, 520, 522-523, 540, 543, 547, 550, 552-553, 565-566, 573, 576-588, 591-616, 631. *See also* Shunning

Baptism, 23, 25-26, 28-29, 32, 40, 52, 59, 71-111, 122, 128, 176, 184, 194, 196, 218-220, 224, 230, 237, 239-242, 246, 249-250, 258, 267, 269-270, 274, 276, 278-280, 285, 287, 298-301, 304, 306, 328, 337, 339, 342, 345, 354, 365-367, 376, 418-420, 427-428, 439, 445, 456, 460, 463, 466, 470, 474, 477, 481, 488, 500-501, 595, 609, 642

believers, 62, 65, 72-76, 78-80, 83-85, 87, 90, 95, 98-100, 104-106, 108, 121, 126, 163, 176, 218, 303-304, 365, 419-420, 422, 433, 460, 464, 575, 596, 629

infant/child, 22, 26, 40, 83-87, 90-94, 99-101, 103-104, 109, 111, 176, 427-428, 458, 575

Spirit, 72, 74, 76, 79-80, 98-100, 103, 105-106, 121, 123, 176, 220, 266, 274, 300, 420, 433, 457

water, 72, 79, 81-82, 304, 460
Beachy Amish, 14
Blasphemy, 401
Blood, 60, 66, 69, 77, 79-81, 92, 94, 97-98, 102-103, 106, 112-126, 128, 130, 132, 138, 144-147, 149, 162, 164, 170-171, 296-297, 301, 313, 328-329, 332, 336, 338, 342-343, 347, 352, 354, 357-358, 362, 364-367, 384, 386, 392-393, 401-402, 404, 415-416, 419-420, 422, 424, 458, 483, 485, 492-493, 519, 523, 532, 548, 558, 561, 564, 596, 609, 613, 621, 623, 628, 630
Born again/anew, 13, 76, 78-80, 95-96, 145, 165, 273, 281-283, 293, 295-296, 298-299, 310-311, 321, 325, 327, 353, 357-358, 360-361, 378, 384, 417

C
Calvinist, 35, 632
Canon, 174, 552
Celestial flesh, 39, 134-172. *See also* Heavenly flesh
Children, 21, 26, 36, 40, 76-77, 80, 83, 85-94, 96, 98-106, 111, 206, 227, 261, 273-275, 297-299, 354-355, 428, 433, 456, 460, 482, 501-502, 575, 628
Church, 26, 36, 38-42, 173, 175, 203, 237, 278, 307, 342, 350-351, 353, 368, 395, 436, 445, 468-469, 486, 592-597, 599-606, 608-611
Communion, 30, 32. *See also* Lord's Supper
Communism, 24
Compromise, 35, 471-472, 490-491, 498, 503-504, 506, 512-513, 515, 518, 520, 524, 528, 533-535, 538, 540, 549
Concubine, 19
Congregation, 22-23, 30, 32-37, 41-42, 51, 53-55, 65, 71, 78, 80-81, 83, 86, 99-101, 104, 106, 110, 123, 128-129, 141, 144, 147, 154-155, 173, 175, 177-178, 181, 184, 190, 195-196, 198, 202-203, 209, 218-222, 226, 228-230, 236-238, 240-242, 244-246, 248-250, 264-265, 272, 274, 277, 297, 301-302, 317, 319, 321-322, 325-326, 329, 331-335, 337, 339-346, 350-357, 363-370, 372, 374-383, 394-396, 398, 400, 404, 406, 409-410, 412-413, 415, 419-421, 424, 429-431, 435-439, 446, 451, 457, 461-464, 466-474, 476-479, 481-489, 491-494, 496-499, 503-504, 506-509, 511-512, 514-515, 518-519, 521-528, 532-536, 538-541, 543-545, 547-554, 556-560, 562-566, 569-578, 580-586, 594, 610-611, 614, 618, 622-623, 631
Conversion, 37, 256-passim. *See also* Born again, New birth
Councils, 32, 151, 208, 363, 468-469, 609
Covenant, 33-35, 55, 78, 80, 82, 101-102, 104-106, 130, 158, 195-196, 204, 211, 234, 237, 256, 259, 278, 322, 326, 328, 332, 337, 346, 354-355, 365, 406, 415, 417-422, 436, 439-440, 456, 468-470, 472, 479, 489-491, 496, 499-505, 512, 515, 518, 521, 524, 528, 540, 544-545, 549, 606
Creation, 52, 68, 138-139, 237, 293-294, 318-320, 348, 352, 362, 427, 434, 450, 455-457, 515, 557, 561, 568, 571, 631
Creator, 63, 68, 141, 145-146, 156, 159, 261, 310, 327-328, 331, 352, 361, 378, 516, 628, 630
Creature(s), 63-64, 99, 126, 155-156, 161, 191-192, 217, 228, 231, 237, 240, 257, 261, 282, 293-297, 299, 301, 303, 305, 310-311, 314-315, 320, 323, 331, 338-339, 351-353, 358, 361, 363, 390, 402, 414, 433, 450, 452, 457, 501, 615, 628-629

Subject Index / 691

D

Damnation, 59, 66, 68, 77, 126, 322, 353, 384, 400, 405, 447
Devil, 70, 84, 90, 97, 111, 117, 126, 149, 162. *See also* Satan
Disciples, 70, 73-74, 91, 98, 108, 112, 115, 118-120, 127, 129, 135, 160, 165, 178, 194, 205, 209, 213-215, 221-222, 226, 229, 233, 252, 265, 271, 283, 301, 303-304, 309, 312, 330, 360, 367, 370, 372-374, 384-387, 392, 413-414, 437, 452, 459, 463, 476, 482, 493, 532, 598, 629, 634, 642
Discipline, 33, 55, 115, 183, 193, 211, 218-219, 230-231, 246-248, 284-285, 331, 370, 395, 446, 450, 472, 488, 497, 563, 578-579, 588
Divinity, 26-27, 30, 64-65, 135-136, 139-140, 148, 153-157, 159-160, 165, 257-259, 271, 362, 416, 611
Divisions, 28-29, 32, 55, 173, 231, 237, 281, 322, 331, 395, 409, 468, 473, 476, 478, 480-484, 488, 502, 504, 506, 518, 523-524, 528, 532, 540, 544, 552-553, 573, 580
Divorce, 577, 593, 605
Docetism, 151
Drunkenness, 21, 245, 372

E

Elect(ion), 20, 91, 122, 135, 146, 178, 196, 202, 217, 225, 254, 272, 276, 285, 313, 338, 341, 363, 384, 471, 482, 485-487, 494, 535, 595, 625
Excommunication, 27, 29, 42, 218-219, 577, 591-594, 596-597, 599-602, 604-606, 608-609, 612

F

Fall, 31, 39, 41, 77, 138-139, 141, 146, 180-182, 217-218, 228, 238, 262, 284, 294-295, 320-321, 330-332, 341, 347, 353, 369, 371-372, 402, 406, 433, 455, 461-462, 477, 514, 516, 553, 571-572, 584, 594, 596, 602-606, 609, 615, 619, 642
Fire, 24, 72, 76, 103, 123-124, 130-131, 157-158, 169, 185, 188, 192, 204, 208, 210, 227-228, 238-239, 247, 250, 252, 257, 260, 272, 288, 300, 302, 304, 324, 328-329, 346, 351, 353, 373, 375, 380-381, 385-386, 390-391, 416, 419, 458, 508, 514-515, 526, 529, 562, 596-597, 614, 624-625, 627-628
Flood, 20, 80-82, 322, 354, 478, 568, 627
Foot washing, 54, 178, 301, 367, 376
Forgiveness, 35, 125, 136, 247-249, 256, 313, 337, 365-366, 370, 373, 407, 418, 458, 471, 482, 520, 531, 540, 565, 576, 641
Franciscans, 19
Free will, 182
Freedom, 39, 55, 173, 181, 183-184, 190, 248, 251, 392-395, 412, 422, 438, 458-459, 523, 548, 556, 562-563, 565, 573, 584, 613

G

Germanisms, 51, 446, 467, 612
Good works, 60, 70, 164, 222, 291, 373, 396, 402-403, 480, 525, 561, 593
Goodhearted, 210, 227, 351
Grace, 54, 57, 59-61, 66, 68-113, 121-127, 129, 131-137, 139, 141-142, 145-146, 152-172, 174, 176-177, 180-181, 186, 190, 194-195, 198-238, 240, 244-247, 249-251, 255-258, 260, 262-265, 269-270, 272-273, 277, 279, 283-286, 292-299, 301, 304, 307-309, 311-312, 314, 316-348, 350-426, 431, 433, 437, 447-448, 450-452, 455-458, 462, 464, 466, 476-479, 483-484, 486, 489-521, 524-526, 531-532, 537-539, 541-542, 545-546, 548,

552-577, 593-596, 601, 603,
606-609, 616, 619-620, 622-
627, 630, 633, 641-644
Guilt, 35-36, 40, 190, 219, 248, 283,
313, 336, 416, 473, 495-496,
507, 534-535, 544, 546, 565

H

Heaven, 41, 60, 62, 64, 69, 72-73, 87-
88, 97, 104, 114-115, 119, 126-
127, 132, 134-151, 153-156,
158-159, 161, 163, 166-171,
186, 188, 190, 192, 194-196,
198-237, 239, 245, 250, 252,
255-257, 260-261, 263, 269,
286, 288-291, 297, 300, 303,
305, 308-309, 311-312, 316-
348, 350-426, 428, 434, 436-
437, 449-450, 455, 458, 498-
500, 516, 525-526, 558-559,
571, 587-passim, 621, 626-627,
629, 638, 640
Heavenly flesh, 151. *See also*
Celestial flesh
Hell, 40, 64, 68, 97, 162, 190, 250,
329, 332, 334-336, 384, 388,
392-393, 400, 423, 449, 576
Heresy, 445
Heretic(s), 375
Heretics, 59, 135, 332, 375, 524, 609
History, 42
Holiness, 69, 75, 79, 121, 163, 183,
250, 256-258, 262, 274, 282,
287, 301, 303, 312, 318, 320,
339, 353, 355, 358, 360, 367,
373, 383, 407, 416, 453-454,
476, 479, 492, 500, 517
Humanity, 53, 64-65, 68, 76, 80, 93,
135-136, 138-141, 148, 151,
153-154, 162, 165, 210, 257-
258, 265, 271, 283, 289, 319-
320, 336, 362, 376, 416, 429,
456, 465, 493, 558, 566, 611,
633, 635
Humility, 78, 92, 124, 146, 190, 283,
299, 307, 367, 376, 399, 421,
434, 477, 481-483, 573
Hymn, 27, 627, 637-638, 642, 646

I

Idolatry(ous), 60, 84, 108-109, 175-
176, 179, 181-182, 184-186,
189, 193, 208, 212-213, 245,
250, 256, 263, 309, 317, 321,
331, 335, 342, 344, 366, 375,
379, 381-382, 384, 390-391,
394, 403, 405, 422, 429-430,
438, 449, 458-459, 461, 463,
500, 503, 505, 538-539, 543,
558, 586, 600, 622, 645
Idols, 60, 84, 111, 173-176, 179, 184-
186, 189, 192, 203, 212, 217,
238, 243, 245-247, 331, 335,
342, 347, 350, 375-376, 381,
394, 399, 452, 462, 502-505,
539, 559, 580, 616
Incarnation, 26-27, 29-30, 38-39, 42,
52-53, 134-136, 143-144, 148,
151, 153, 160, 428, 632-633, 649
Inflation, 20
Inquisition, 173

J

Judgment, 34, 59-61, 110, 124, 158,
171, 190, 200, 207, 209, 238,
245, 254, 257, 259, 265, 289-
290, 304, 308, 327, 334, 339,
348, 350-351, 353, 359, 370,
372, 374-375, 381, 391, 396,
464, 472, 489-491, 495-499,
503-508, 511-513, 516, 522-
524, 526-530, 532-536, 539-
541, 544, 546-548, 557, 579-
580, 584-588, 597, 602-603,
605-608, 614-615, 621, 624, 626
Justification, 40, 75, 82, 85, 162, 180-
181, 194, 213, 247, 259, 267,
285, 296, 314, 449, 490, 529,
539

K

Kidneys, 546, 551
Kingdom, 22-24, 42, 82, 93-95, 97,
102, 130, 150, 154-156, 159,
176, 178, 182, 190, 196, 201,
209, 232-233, 235-236, 245-
247, 249, 259, 261, 263, 271-
272, 275-276, 293-348, 350,

Subject Index / 693

357-358, 372-373, 379-380,
383-399, 401-426, 435, 448,
451, 457, 482, 491-492, 500,
503, 508, 525, 555-556, 582,
587, 603, 620, 625-626, 628, 630
Kingdom of heaven, 42, 85, 91-92,
94, 196, 199, 252, 263, 267, 270,
295, 310, 323, 326, 341, 360,
369, 374, 376, 382, 400, 410,
452, 464, 477, 482, 484, 532,
545, 602, 612, 620

L
Lamb, 76-77, 102, 145, 148, 155,
163, 168, 187-188, 192, 220,
222, 224, 240, 246, 280, 282,
287, 290, 297, 354, 364, 374,
377-378, 380-381, 386, 391,
393, 408, 416, 424, 449, 564,
595, 622, 628-630, 641
Law, 38, 61, 68, 72-111, 123, 125-
126, 158, 162, 168, 173-237,
243, 245, 248, 261, 266-273,
275-278, 282, 288-291, 299-
300, 311, 316-348, 350-382,
389, 393, 436, 456, 501, 531,
555, 561-562, 585, 597, 599,
606, 608, 627
Leaven, 84, 130, 134, 167, 169, 219,
246, 338, 369, 372, 396, 497,
540, 581, 599, 602, 629
Lord's Supper, 41, 44, 52, 59, 71,
100-103, 107, 110-113, 115-
124, 126-129, 131-132, 176,
184, 219, 300-301, 306, 329,
337, 345, 365-367, 376, 418-
420, 428, 439, 445, 456, 506,
609. *See also* Communion

M
Mandate, 237, 250, 346
Maozim, 347, 350
Marriage, 26, 28-29, 37, 321, 344,
378, 411, 434, 466, 552-558,
560-571, 573-578, 583-586,
593-594, 604-606, 608-609, 611
Martyrdom, 22, 41-45, 130, 387, 390,
420
Martyrs Mirror, 44-45, 254, 543, 618,
635, 647

Mediator, 64, 102, 136, 148, 196,
258, 300, 416, 428, 471
Mercy, 59-61, 63, 68-69, 72-111,
133, 139, 145, 152-153, 164-
165, 172, 193, 196, 208, 242,
247, 251-252, 255-257, 263,
266, 283, 292, 294, 314, 348,
350, 360, 362, 372-373, 382-
426, 437, 447, 480, 482-483,
492, 498, 501, 509, 517, 524-
525, 539, 542, 547-548, 555,
565, 576, 583, 593-595, 606-
607, 614-616, 619, 621, 625, 634
Mercy seat, 64, 69, 156, 272-273, 415
Millennium, 22
Minister, 33, 35, 53, 129, 198-237,
279, 293, 339, 341, 345, 351-
352, 363-365, 370-371, 373,
404, 409, 419, 431, 448, 467-
471, 473-474, 484-486, 488,
490, 492, 496-497, 506, 510,
523, 533-535, 549-550, 554,
573, 598-599. *See also*
Preachers/teachers
Ministry, 64, 494, 496, 508, 516, 526,
547, 556, 619
Miracle, 123, 169, 171, 201-202,
222-225, 237
Mission, 24, 277, 489
Mysticism, 237, 650

N
Nature
  divine, 39-40, 42, 52, 62-63, 69,
  76, 78-79, 108, 123, 135-136,
  145-146, 148-149, 156-157,
  193, 206, 208, 210, 221, 258,
  280, 282, 284-285, 289, 296,
  303, 310-311, 320, 357, 378,
  384, 403, 408-409, 453, 499,
  510, 516, 541, 597, 602, 604,
  608
  human, 39-40, 52, 63-65, 76, 78,
  105, 136-137, 146, 148, 151,
  284, 320, 334, 512, 527, 557,
  601, 623
  two, 63-64, 151, 284
New birth, 30, 54, 76, 79-80, 94-96,
  110, 122, 142, 145, 178, 191,

281, 293-300, 303, 310-311, 314, 320, 325, 345, 358-359, 363, 408-409, 414-415, 433, 436, 451, 456, 515, 525, 595, 624. *See also* Conversion

New creature, 30, 40, 79-80, 149, 293-294, 296-297, 299, 301, 303, 305, 310-311, 314, 358, 363, 402, 433, 501

New Jerusalem, 22-23, 42, 154-155, 220, 376-378, 382, 392, 403, 408, 437, 500, 562, 595

New Testament, 14, 21, 38-39, 45, 62, 64, 112-113, 118, 125-126, 142, 153-154, 156, 159, 192, 205, 214, 224, 245, 264, 267, 273, 277, 282, 299-300, 305, 317, 352, 365, 375, 431-432, 445, 460, 464, 501-502, 552, 561, 569, 571, 575, 599, 606, 642

Nonresistance, 22, 25. *See also* Sword

O

Old Cloister, 24

Old Testament, 21, 24, 38-39, 45, 62, 93-94, 102-105, 107-108, 126, 156, 192, 205, 214, 245, 264, 267, 270, 277, 282, 296, 299, 317, 364, 375, 450, 477, 552, 560-561, 592, 607

Ordinances, 40, 71, 73-74, 83, 87-88, 106-108, 110, 112, 129, 178, 196, 204, 208, 218, 300-302, 304-306, 343, 345, 351, 357, 365, 370, 372, 374, 376, 398, 401, 406, 412, 433, 436, 439, 455-456, 458, 460-461, 469, 472, 489, 502-503, 521, 523, 557-561, 565-566, 568, 570, 574, 600-601, 603, 605, 608. *See also* Sacrament

Ordination, 25, 27, 35, 53, 127, 202, 206, 219, 222, 269, 311-312, 324, 335, 363, 398, 411, 421, 486-487, 521, 604, 613

P

Patience, 59-60, 132, 177, 187, 231, 238, 240, 248-249, 258, 263, 346, 366-367, 371-372, 374, 383, 387-388, 391-392, 404, 407, 409, 412, 421, 424, 431, 453, 477, 481-482, 492, 499, 511, 525, 597, 602, 606, 620-622

Peace, 31, 65, 68-69, 102, 110, 118, 139, 141, 152, 154, 163, 173, 175, 178, 191, 193-195, 201, 208, 216, 236, 238-256, 264-266, 274-275, 292, 306, 316-348, 350, 367, 372-373, 375, 378, 383-426, 431, 439, 447, 450, 453, 458-459, 462, 470, 473, 476-478, 480-484, 486, 489-543, 545-547, 549, 552-577, 582, 593, 601, 603, 606, 612-613, 616, 625, 628, 630-631, 633, 640-641

Pentecost, 72, 228, 283-284, 337-338, 435

Perfect(ion), 38, 62, 67, 73, 156, 269, 286, 295, 312, 318, 333, 344, 348, 360, 373, 377, 382, 401, 408, 416, 461, 464, 482, 518, 561, 574, 608

Persecution, 33, 41-43, 53, 55, 107, 173, 175, 195, 213-214, 227, 234-235, 237-240, 249-250, 262, 306-307, 319, 327, 330, 336-337, 347, 363-364, 372-374, 376, 384-385, 387, 390, 404-405, 409, 412, 423-424, 434, 445, 543, 585, 596

Persecutors, 214, 227, 263, 274, 373-374, 386, 609, 621

Pilgrims, 338, 492

Pillows, 208, 459

Polygamy, 24

Pope, 101

Pray(er), 62, 131, 193, 202, 205, 242, 279, 307, 345, 360, 365, 370, 372, 384, 393, 399, 401, 404, 409, 413, 449, 471, 478-479, 485-486, 492, 499, 513, 518, 525-526, 531-532, 545, 549, 555-556, 560, 565, 569, 573, 580, 586, 598-599, 606, 612-613, 615-616, 620, 641

Preachers/teachers, 28, 30, 53-55, 59, 65, 81, 84, 198-200, 202-204, 206-222, 224-230, 232, 234-237, 244, 267, 282, 304, 322, 326-328, 331, 333, 335, 341, 345-346, 353, 360, 363, 394-395, 430, 460, 462-463, 470-471, 485, 487, 496-497, 501, 507, 517, 524, 528, 537, 554, 556, 558, 573, 595, 611, 632. *See also* Minister

Pride, 66, 169, 182, 185, 189-190, 194, 199, 214-215, 266, 292-293, 301-302, 345, 366, 372, 498, 506, 513, 517, 523, 549, 594

Prophet(s), 375, 409

Psychopannychia, 635. *See* Soul sleep

Q

Quiet(ness), 110, 227, 231, 234, 237, 526, 530, 535, 587

R

Reconciliation, 35-36, 118, 163-164, 194, 196, 243, 245, 337, 361, 370, 416, 420, 471, 506, 517, 544, 568, 599, 633

Redemption, 65, 69, 118, 194, 233, 313, 362, 366, 416, 427, 592, 596

Reformed Church, 26, 53, 55, 173, 445

Regenerate(ion), 79-80, 95

Register, 427

Repentance, 72, 74, 83, 98, 124, 169, 207, 245, 247-249, 303, 332, 351, 359-360, 365, 369-370, 372, 380, 431, 460, 466, 534, 553, 565, 568, 571-573, 575-576, 582, 585, 593, 595-596, 600

Restitution, 30, 32, 54-55, 58, 316-348, 350, 434, 631

Resurrection, 75-76, 82, 128, 166, 187, 219, 258, 312, 320, 324, 328, 348, 359, 386-387, 408, 421, 425, 454, 626

Righteousness, 65, 69, 72, 75-76, 78-79, 81-82, 104, 118, 121, 124, 159, 162-165, 167-168, 173-237, 239, 242-243, 245, 247, 250-252, 255-260, 262, 264-348, 350-426, 448-450, 452-453, 456-457, 476, 479, 481, 489-521, 529, 539-541, 555-557, 563-564, 566-567, 571, 582, 587, 596, 612, 619, 622-623

Roman Catholic Church, 13, 24, 26, 41, 53, 55, 173, 237, 350, 543

S

Sacrament, 21, 40, 61, 66, 71, 76, 85, 101, 103, 111, 116, 120, 123, 178, 183, 219-220, 222, 226, 230, 232, 300, 337, 342, 365-366, 455, 458, 460, 523, 609. *See also* Ordinances

Sacramentarian(ism), 21, 23-24, 31, 631-632

Sacrifice, 169, 260, 404

Saints, 12, 41-42, 65, 72, 99-100, 128-129, 131, 177-178, 184, 187-188, 190, 193, 195-196, 199, 215, 219-220, 231, 233, 238-239, 263, 279, 283-285, 310, 343, 345, 347-348, 352, 367-368, 371, 373, 376, 379, 387, 391-393, 403-404, 407, 412, 420, 423, 430-431, 477, 487, 493, 501, 515-516, 525-526, 559, 596, 620-622, 625-626, 632

Salvation, 39-40, 52, 54, 59-60, 62-63, 68-70, 78, 81, 86, 91-93, 95, 99, 101-107, 118-119, 121, 125-126, 128, 131, 133, 135, 141, 148, 152-153, 160, 163, 166, 169, 180, 189, 193, 204, 206, 212, 218, 238, 244, 247, 256-258, 260, 262-293, 301, 307-308, 313, 316-348, 350-351, 357, 359, 361, 365-366, 370, 380-381, 383-427, 434, 455, 457, 463, 465, 489-521, 532, 540, 542, 546, 548, 552-577, 583, 604, 619-620, 622-623, 627-628, 634

Sanctification, 88, 90, 121, 131, 144, 220, 240, 244, 259, 296-297, 310, 313-314, 332, 337, 363, 365, 384, 388, 401-402, 413, 416, 429, 449, 458, 476, 494, 501, 517, 567, 570-571, 597, 600, 620
Second Adam, 39-40, 141, 143
Separation, 27, 41, 173-197, 205, 218, 242, 244, 246, 249, 274, 278, 297, 320, 345, 368-370, 376, 390, 394-395, 447, 464, 470, 507, 512, 523-524, 528, 539-540, 547, 549-550, 552-577, 580-586, 593-594, 596-600, 604-606, 608-609, 611-612, 614, 622, 629-630
Serpent, 68, 77, 191, 225, 251
Shun(ning), 28-29, 42, 246, 375, 429, 438, 577, 602, 611-612. *See also* Ban
Sin(s), 39-40, 42, 52, 64, 66, 68-69, 72-111, 113, 117, 119, 124-126, 137, 144, 146-148, 160, 162-164, 169, 171, 179-182, 188, 190, 206, 219-221, 224, 230, 242-243, 245-251, 256-259, 264-292, 298, 307-308, 310, 312-313, 316-348, 350, 352-353, 358-362, 365-370, 374, 383-426, 432, 515, 530-531, 539-540, 552-577, 580, 582, 584, 595, 597, 599, 602, 613, 641
Socinianism, 27, 173
Soul sleep. *See* Psychopannychia, 635
Spiritual, 11, 20, 24, 30, 32, 39-40, 54, 58, 65, 69, 72-133, 142, 145, 170-171, 185, 198-200, 206, 249, 252, 256, 264-292, 294, 301, 305, 312, 316-348, 350, 354-356, 360-362, 365, 367, 371, 375, 379, 383, 396, 400-401, 408, 414, 418, 420, 434, 447-449, 451, 458, 460, 466-468, 477, 483, 490, 500, 515-516, 525, 552-577, 584, 586, 593, 597, 606-608, 622, 627, 630-631

Strasbourg meeting, 29
Subordination, 635
Suffer(ing), 60-63, 123-124, 126, 128, 148, 162, 187, 210, 231, 237, 241, 254, 256, 263, 285-286, 291, 301, 312, 334, 363, 366, 371, 373-374, 376, 383-388, 390-392, 405, 409, 420, 424, 457, 499, 507-508, 512-513, 526, 532, 547, 580, 582, 596, 598, 609, 615, 620, 622-623, 627, 629-630
Swiss brothers, 579, 586-587
Sword, 23, 41-42, 179, 194, 208, 227, 231, 239, 250-251, 280, 331, 336, 339, 341, 345-346, 374-375, 387, 390, 424, 451, 502, 508, 516, 518, 527, 541, 599. *See also* Nonresistance

T

Tabernacle, 30, 54, 57, 156, 264, 266-269, 271-273, 287, 292, 317, 319, 333, 338, 348, 369, 371, 377-378, 398, 404, 432, 435
Tetragram, 155
Thanksgiving, 43, 431, 437-439, 525
Thau, 254, 467
Theology, 20, 28, 38-39, 47, 199, 237, 445, 579
Tradition(s), 41, 173, 180, 183, 267, 306, 411, 468, 491-492, 494, 503-504, 637, 648
Trinity, 52, 99, 304, 632
Typology, 39, 237, 488

U

Unitarian(ism), 26-27, 52
Unity, 55, 112, 121-122, 128-129, 133, 160, 195, 219, 262, 264-266, 274, 292, 366, 377, 398, 408-409, 420-422, 431, 439, 464, 468, 471, 473, 476, 478, 481, 484, 501, 519, 539, 542, 545, 559, 601, 611

V

Vengeance, 238, 254, 336, 348, 373, 526

W

Whoredom, 21, 239, 256, 395, 399, 505, 622

Wilderness, 93, 96, 98, 103, 105, 107-109, 156, 169-170, 217, 229, 250, 280, 309, 328-330, 332-334, 337, 387, 399, 404, 451, 489-490, 505, 508-509

Wismar Conference, 27-28, 577

Worship, 60-61, 71, 84, 111, 155, 158, 173-175, 178-182, 184-189, 193, 195-196, 208-209, 217-218, 240, 247, 250, 278, 317, 327, 330-331, 335, 337, 341-343, 345, 347, 375-376, 391, 404, 406, 414, 418, 420, 422-424, 429, 435, 447, 453, 460-462, 502, 504-505, 518, 560, 565, 573, 576, 585, 644

THE EDITORS

Cornelius J. Dyck is a native of Saskatchewan. Four years of alternative service during World War II were followed by six years with Mennonite Central Committee in relief and refugee service in Europe and South America. Following his return he served as pastor of the Zion Mennonite Church, Elbing, Kansas, 1952-55.

He received his undergraduate degree from Bethel College, North Newton, Kansas, and an M.A. degree in history from Wichita State University. He earned B.D. and Ph.D. (1962) degrees from the Divinity School of the University of Chicago. His dissertation was entitled *Hans de Ries: Theologian and Churchman. A Study in Second Generation Dutch Anabaptism.*

Dyck's publications include numerous articles in *The Mennonite Quarterly Review* and other journals, encyclopedias, and papers, including *Doopsgezinde Bijdragen* and *Mennonitische Geschichtsblatter*. Young people may know him best through *Twelve Becoming* (Faith and Life Press, 1973), college and general readers through *Introduction to Mennonite History*, which he edited (Herald Press, 1967, 1981).

From 1958 until his retirement in 1989, Dyck taught historical theology/church history at the Associated Mennonite Biblical Seminaries, Elkhart, Indiana. He also served as director of the Institute of Mennonite Studies for twenty-one years. His role there involved him, among other things, him in facilitating and editing a variety of series: the present CRR series of which this book is Volume 6; the *Studies in Anabaptist and Mennonite History* (10 volumes); the *IMS Faith and Life Pamphlet Series* (4 volumes); *Mennonite Missionary Fellowship* (7 volumes); *The MCC Story* (5 volumes); three Mennonite World Conference volumes; and other single volumes. His most recent work involved editing Volume V of *The Mennonite Encyclopedia* (Herald Press, 1990).

Dyck has been active as a speaker and as a member of numerous conference committees and professional societies, especially as executive secretary of Mennonite World Conference for 12 years. He was an observer at Vatican Council II in 1965. He and Wilma Regier were married in 1952. They have three grown children.

William E. Keeney was born in a coal mining town, Thompson #1, in Fayette County, Pennsylvania. In the depression years, his family was accepted for an American Friends Service Committee (AFSC) project in which fifty families built homes with AFSC assistance. Carl Landis, a Mennonite minister, came with his family to assist the AFSC in the project. Through their influence William attended Bluffton (Ohio) College where he received his undergraduate degree.

At Bluffton he became a conscientious objector; he served three years in Civilian Public Service (CPS). He married Willadene Hartzler and joined the Mennonite church.

Together they spent over two years in Europe under Mennonite Central Committee (MCC), the latter part in the Netherlands. This sparked an interest in Dutch Mennonite history. After graduating from Mennonite Biblical Seminary and Bethany Theological Seminary, he served as assistant to the president and taught Bible at Bluffton College.

Keeney then earned a master's degree at Hartford Theological Seminary on a Hartzler Fellowship in 1957 and a Ph.D. in 1959. His thesis was on "Dirk Philips: A Study of His Life and Writings and of His Teaching Concerning the Church." His doctoral dissertation was published in 1968 as *The Development of Dutch Anabaptist Thought and Practice from 1539 to 1564*.

From 1961 to 1963 he and his family were in the Netherlands under MCC, where he served as a liaison to the Dutch Mennonites and chaired the MCC European Peace Committee. While there he edited a special issue of *Mennonite Life* on the Dutch Mennonites.

In 1968 Keeney became academic dean at Bethel College, North Newton, Kansas, and provost in 1972. From 1973 to 1974, he was education secretary for the MCC Peace Section and a fellow at the Institute of Mennonite Studies at Associated Mennonite Biblical Seminaries. During that time he prepared a series which was published as *Lordship as Servanthood, the Biblical Basis of Peacemaking*; it was translated into Spanish as *La estrategia social de Jesus*.

In 1974 he returned to Bethel College. From 1978 until 1984, he was executive director of the Consortium on Peace Research, Education, and Development (COPRED). In connection with that office, he moved to Kent (Ohio) State University where he taught peace and conflict studies in the Center for Peaceful Change from 1980 until his 1990 retirement. From 1978 to 1979 he served on the Governor's Commission on Peace and Conflict Management.

He has served as pastor or interim pastor at a variety of churches in Illinois, Connecticut, Kansas, and Ohio. He has published numerous articles and book reviews on Anabaptist, Mennonite, peace, and educational topics. He has served on the editorial boards of *Mennonite Quarterly Review* and *Mennonite Life*. He chaired the Peace Section of MCC from 1973 to 1983. He was elected chairperson of COPRED for the years 1989 to 1991. The Keeneys have four grown children.

Alvin J. Beachy was a native of Salisbury, Pennsylvania, where he lived as a member of the Amish community in that area. At age twenty-four he continued his elementary school education. Then he proceeded to Messiah Academy, Grantham, Pennsylvania and Bluffton (Ohio) College. He was not satisfied with his pursuit of knowledge until he had earned a Th.D. at Harvard University Divinity School in 1961.

Alvin loved the church. After he left the Amish for Mennonite church membership, he remained deeply committed to the pastoral ministry. He was a gifted pastor who benefited much from the example and influence of his Amish minister father, Moses Beachy, who shook his hand as he was leaving for a pastorate in Normal, Illinois, and said, "Alvin, be a man for Christ." Alvin also served several Congregational churches in Connecticut and Massachusetts, and from 1960 to 1968 he pastored the Zion Mennonite Church at Souderton, Pennsylvania.

Alvin taught at Bluffton College and later at Eastern Mennonite College, Harrisonburg, Virginia. From 1968 until his retirement in 1978, he taught at Bethel College, North Newton, Kansas. Among his writings are articles in *The Mennonite Quarterly Review, Mennonite Life*, and other journals; a pastoral handbook, *Worship as Celebration of Covenant and Incarnation* (1968); and particularly his revised doctoral dissertation, *The Concept of Grace in the Radical Reformation* (1977).

He was married to Vera Clouse in 1942. They are the parents of two children. Alvin died in 1986 at the age of 72, after an extended illness. His contribution to this volume is noted in the editors' introduction.

www.ingramcontent.com/pod-product-compliance
Lightning Source LLC
Chambersburg PA
CBHW050300010526
44108CB00040B/1899